3rd Edition
Version **CS6/5.5/5**

AFTER EFFECTS

Real-World Skills for the
Aspiring Motion Graphics Artist

TRISH & CHRIS MEYER

Focal Press
Taylor & Francis Group

NEW YORK AND LONDON

DEDICATED to the After Effects team, past and present: from those hearty pioneers at the Company of Science and Art (CoSA) who revolutionized our industry, to the current innovators at Adobe who keep this vital program fresh.

First published 2013
by Focal Press
70 Blanchard Road, Suite 402, Burlington, MA 01803

Simultaneously published in the UK
by Focal Press
2 Park Square, Milton Park, Abingdon, Oxon OX14 4RN

Focal Press is an imprint of the Taylor & Francis Group, an informa business.

Library of Congress Cataloging in Publication Data
Application submitted.

ISBN: 978-0-240-81736-1

Printed in the United States of America by Courier, Kendallville, Indiana

Table of Contents

x   **Introduction**

xi   **Getting Started**

▽ Pre-Roll 1

Exploring the After Effects landscape.

1	project structure	6	Timeline panel
2	main application window	7	Layer panel
3	Tools panel	8	Info, Preview, Audio panels
3	Project panel	9	Effects & Presets; Effect Controls
4	importing footage	10	Workspaces
5	Composition panel	12	Adobe Bridge

▽ Lesson 1 – Basic Animation 14

Building your first animation while you learn a typical After Effects workflow.

16	creating folders in the Project panel	23	dragging footage to the Timeline panel
17	creating a new composition	24	editing a keyframe's Bezier handles
17	importing media	25	editing spatial keyframes; motion paths
18	interpreting alpha channels	26	animating Opacity, Scale, and Rotation
19	adding layers to the Comp panel	28	arranging and replacing layers
20	changing the Background Color	30	adding solid layers
20	scrubbing parameter values	30	applying, copying, and pasting effects
20	interactively transforming layers	32	rendering
21	animating Position; RAM Preview	33	RAM Preview options; the Work Area
22	navigating between keyframes	34	caches and memory
22	adding a background layer	36	importing layered Photoshop and Illustrator files

▽ Lesson 2 – Advanced Animation 38

Manipulating keyframes to create more refined animations.

38 keyframe basics
40 Anchor Point overview
41 Anchor Point tool
42 motion control moves
44 the Graph Editor
45 speed versus value graphs
46 panning and zooming time
47 editing graph curves
48 easing animations
49 editing multiple keyframes
49 Graph Editor Sets
50 Separate Dimensions

54 Motion Sketch
55 smoothing keyframes
56 Auto-Orient
57 Motion Blur
58 Roving keyframes
59 Time-Reverse Keyframes
60 Hold keyframes
62 time display and timecode

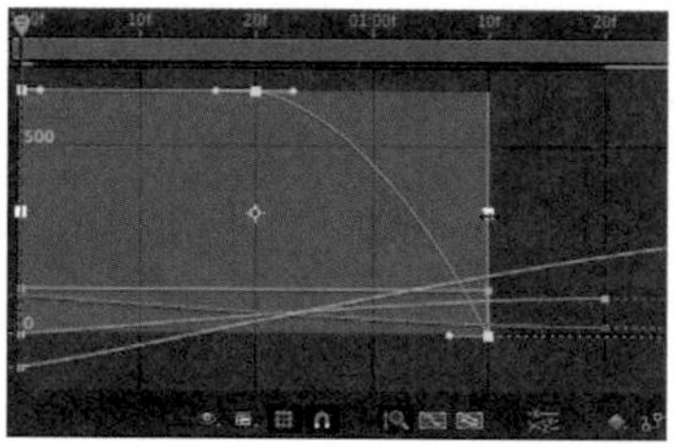

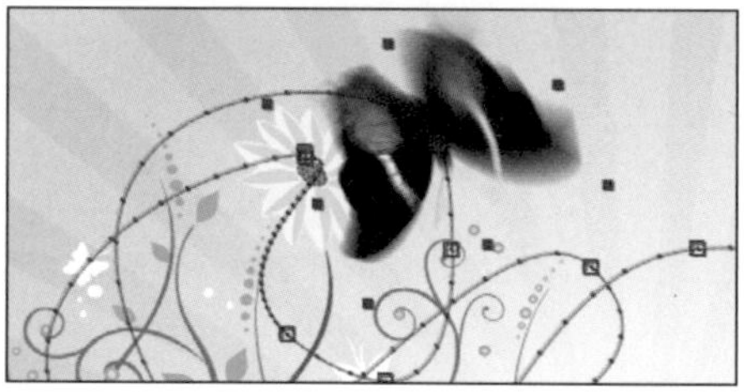

▽ Lesson 3 – Layer Control 64

Learning how to trim layers and enhance them using blending modes and effects.

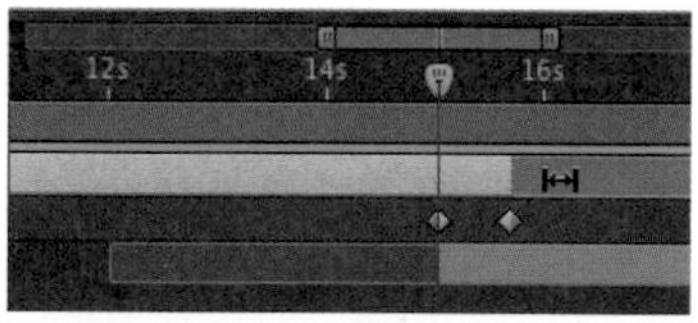

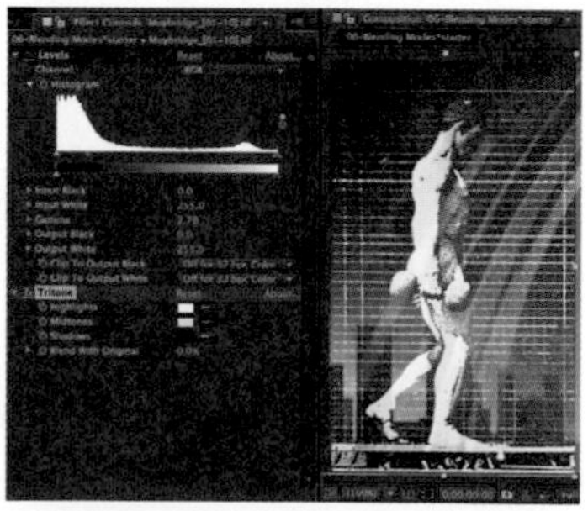

64 layers and stacking order
65 moving layers in time
66 trimming layers
67 trimming in the Layer and Footage panels
68 slip editing
69 Sequence Layers keyframe assistant
71 looping footage
72 image sequences
73 changing the frame rate; Time Stretch
74 blending modes
76 effects and solids
77 effect motion path
79 Effects & Presets panel
79 searching for effects

80 animation presets
83 Behavior presets
84 Layer Styles
86 adjustment layers
87 filmic glow trick
88 Brainstorm; the Cartoon effect
90 non-square pixels

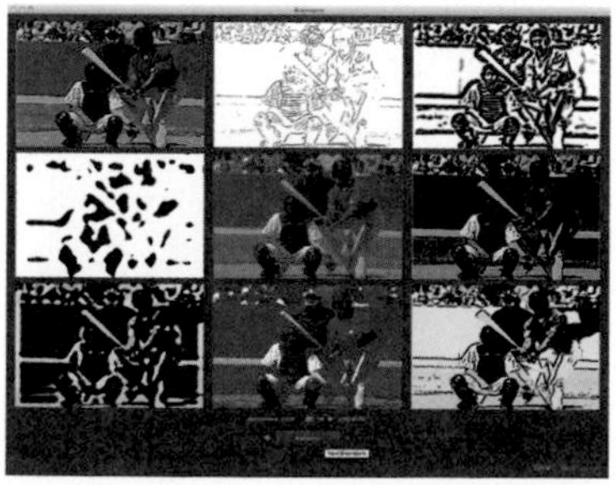

Lesson 4 – Creating Transparency 92

Using masks, mattes, and stencils to cut out portions of a layer.

94 masking tools; creating mask shapes
95 Rounded Rectangle tool
96 Free Transform Points
96 masking in the Layer panel; Ellipse tool
97 Mask Feather
98 animating a mask path
99 creating a vignette; Mask Expansion
100 masking with the Pen tool (Bezier masks)
101 applying an effect to a masked area
102 controlling mask path interpolation
103 using effects with the mask path
104 Mask Modes and multiple masks
105 Mask Opacity

106 creating and editing RotoBezier masks
107 Audio Spectrum effect
108 variable mask feathering (*new in CS6*)
112 Alpha Track Matte
114 nesting a track matte composite
116 Luma Track Matte
117 animating matte layers
118 Stencil Luma and Stencil Alpha
121 effects with track mattes and stencils

Lesson 5 – Type and Music 122

Animating text and working with music are essential to motion graphics design.

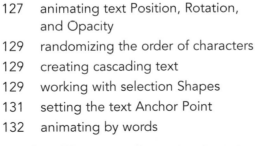

123 creating basic text
125 creating text animators; Range Selectors
127 animating text Position, Rotation, and Opacity
129 randomizing the order of characters
129 creating cascading text
129 working with selection Shapes
131 setting the text Anchor Point
132 animating by words

133 title safe areas
134 animating text Blur and Tracking
135 text on a path
136 Per-character 3D
140 separating fields
141 adding the Wiggly Selector
142 rendering with an alpha channel
143 field rendering
144 adding audio to a comp
145 spotting audio; using layer and comp markers
146 mixing and enhancing audio
148 using text animation presets
150 saving text animations as presets
151 editing Photoshop Text layers

▽ Lesson 6 – Parenting and Nesting 152

Grouping layers to make them easier to coordinate.

152   parenting, nesting, and expressions defined
154   assigning a parent
155   parenting, opacity, and effects
156   parenting with null objects
158   nesting to group layers; using guides
160   editing precomps
162   navigating composition hierarchies
163   nesting a common source

165   sizing precomps
167   ETLAT (edit this, look at that)
168   precomposing a group of layers
170   precomposing a single layer
172   render order explained
173   splitting work between comps
174   precompose options compared
174   using precomposing to reorder
176   continuous rasterization
178   collapsing transformations
179   compound effects

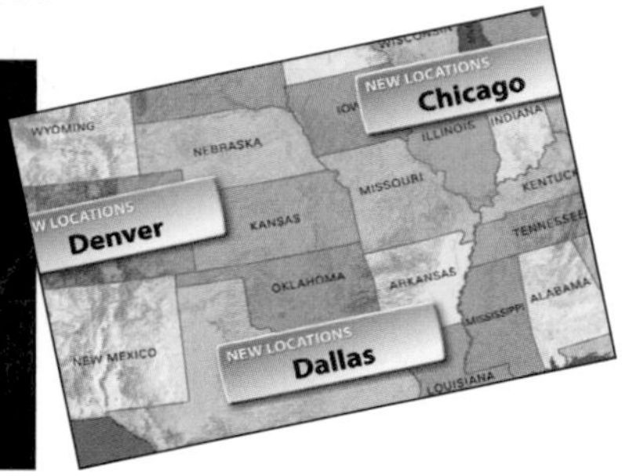

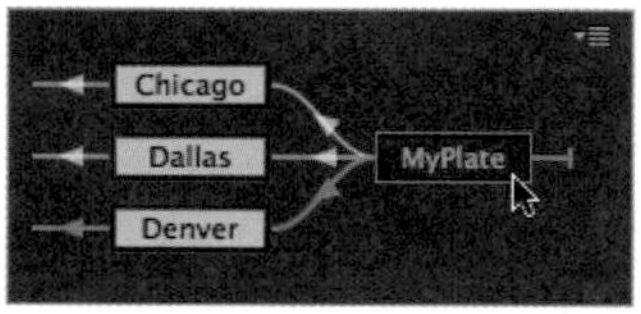

▽ Lesson 7 – Expressions and Time Games 182

Using expressions and playing with time.

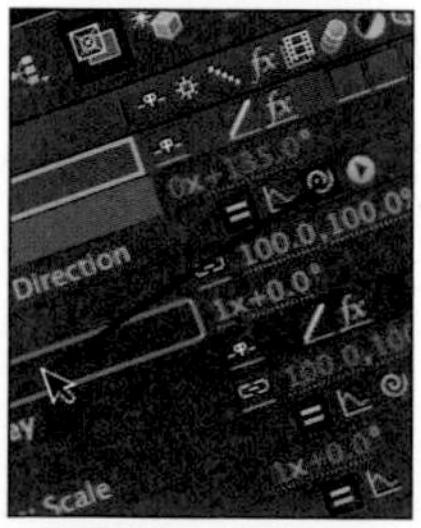

184   using the pick whip to create expressions
185   altering expressions
186   stabilizing shadows
188   matching value ranges (the linear expression)
190   looping keyframes
191   expression tips
192   the wiggle expression
193   expression controllers
193   keyframing the wiggle expression
194   creating a master controller with a null object
195   converting sound to keyframes
196   frame blending
197   Pixel Motion

198   stop motion tricks
199   preserve frame rate
200   creating freeze frames
201   time remapping
205   resources for learning more
      about expressions

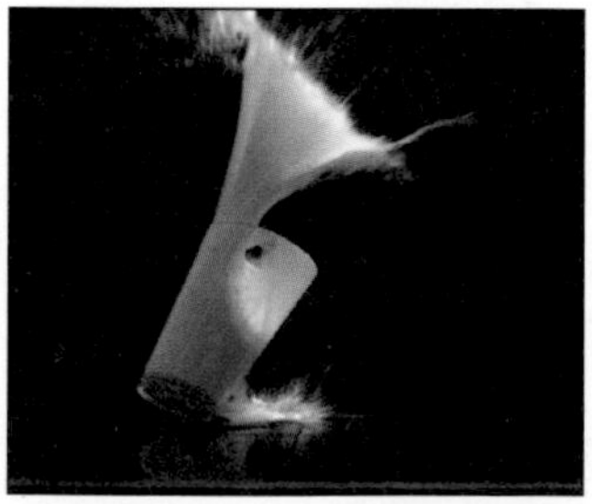

▽ Lesson 8 – 3D Space 206

Adding a new dimension to your animations.

207 enabling layers for 3D
208 moving and rotating layers in 3D space
210 multiplaning effects
212 3D motion paths
213 multiple views
214 adding a camera; camera settings
215 using the camera tools; 3D views
216 moving and animating cameras

218 building a camera rig
220 layer and camera auto-orientation
222 camera depth of field blur
224 3D lights
226 casting shadows
228 Light Falloff; Material Options
230 Ray-traced 3D Renderer (*new in CS6*)
231 extrusion and beveling
233 bending footage layers
234 transparency; index of refraction
236 reflections
238 environment layers
239 ray-tracer image quality
240 Fast Previews

▽ Lesson 9 – Track and Key 244

Tackling several essential skills for creating special effects.

244 tracking overview
246 Warp Stabilizer (*new in CS5.5*)
249 point-based tracking and stabilization
250 creating track points
252 applying stabilization
253 fixing bad tracks
254 2D motion tracking
255 applying a motion track
256 tracking interlaced footage
256 Radio Waves effect
257 applying tracks to effect points
259 planar tracking with mocha AE
262 pasting the mocha track into After Effects
263 Bezier Warp effect
264 3D Camera Tracker (*new in CS6*)

265 defining the plane; moving the target
266 creating a track null; parenting
268 adding 3D text and a shadow catcher
270 stabilizing position, rotation, and scale
273 keying using the Keylight effect
275 creating garbage mattes
276 Rolling Shutter Repair (*new in CS6*)

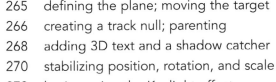

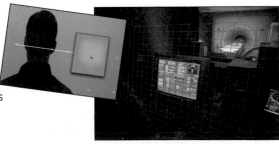

▽ Lesson 10 – Paint, Roto, and Puppet 278

Exploring Paint, Roto Brush, and the Puppet tools.

279 basic painting
281 erasing strokes
281 Paint Channels
282 Paint blending modes
282 brush duration bar
283 animating strokes
284 revealing a layer

285 creating organic textures
286 tablet settings
287 cloning
288 transforming strokes
289 basic Roto Brush
292 Roto Brush workflow; the base frame
294 propagating strokes
296 corrective strokes
298 refining the matte
300 Puppet Pin tool
301 animating Puppet pins
302 Puppet Overlap tool
303 recording puppet animation
303 Puppet Starch tool
304 multiple shapes

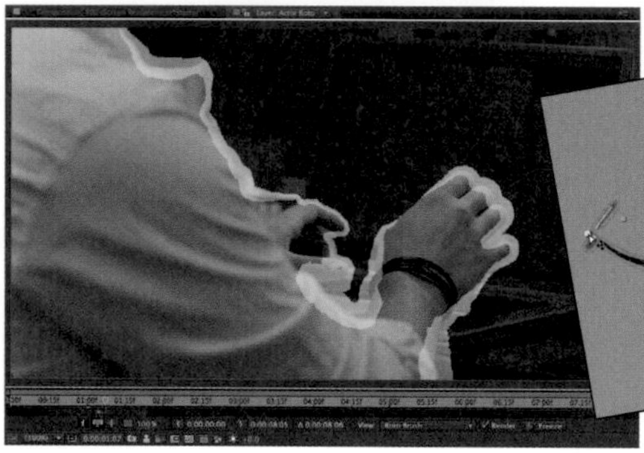

▽ Lesson 11 – Shape Layers 306

Creating, animating, and extruding vector-based shapes.

306 creating a shape layer
307 Stroke and Fill settings, editing shapes
308 multiple shapes
309 Even-Odd Fill
310 shape effects
311 creating buttons
312 Shape Repeater
314 compound shapes; Merge Paths
316 gradients
317 shape pen paths
318 Wiggle Transforms

320 advanced strokes
321 dashes and gaps
322 animating a stroke
323 create shapes from vector layers (new in CS6)
324 extruding shape layers (new in CS6)

▽ Lesson 12 – Final Project 326

Creating a show opening, from draft to completion.

326   delivery specifications
327   music considerations; creating the main comp
328   spotting music
329   mocking up the 3D world; Label colors
330   3D view layouts
331   initial camera move; Separate Dimensions
334   placing the 3D background
335   3D Camera Tracker
336   time stretch; frame blending
337   typesetting the title
338   applying text animation presets

339   timing animation to music
340   using shapes to create a video frame
342   creating a reusable element
343   crafting an efficient composition hierarchy
344   replacing placeholders; ETLAT
345   filling out the background
346   creating animated lines
348   using expressions to animate to music
350   enabling Motion Blur; rendering a proof
351   delivering a broadcast package
352   ideas for enhancing the final project

▽ Appendix – Rendering 354

Unleashing your creations on the world.

354   The Render Queue (movie)
354   rendering: under the hood
355   Render Settings Templates
355   Output Module Templates
356   rendering movies

356   rendering sequences
357   issues that affect image quality
359   field flicker (movie)
361   3:2 Pulldown

▽ Back Matter

362   Resources, Production Credits
363   Index

Introduction

A moving picture can be worth a thousand career choices.

It must have something to do with mankind's primeval fascination with fire: We're attracted to interesting imagery that moves. Adobe After Effects excels at creating that imagery, be it an opening title for a television program, special effects for a commercial or film, an animated banner in a sports stadium or at a trade show, or informational displays in elevators, at airports, on websites, or even on phones.

After Effects is a deep, mature tool that allows you to combine video, film, 3D and Flash animations, photographs, scans, illustrations, PDFs, text, and music in myriad ways, plus create elements of your own. You can arrange, animate, and treat these components, and render the result to a wide variety of formats for print, the web, video, film, and more. In short, master After Effects, and you will be able to craft compelling moving imagery for a wide variety of clients and tasks.

Our goal in *After Effects Apprentice* is to teach you the most important core features through a series of practical, hands-on exercises. Every lesson is grounded in our own real-world experiences, showing you the right way to use the right feature for a given task. We start out with simple animations to help you over that first step in learning the program, eventually working up to animating text, creating 3D worlds, motion tracking and stabilization, and keying greenscreen shots. The final project combines multiple skills you'll learn in the previous lessons, taking you through a typical project workflow from testing your ideas to creating a complete package for a television program.

This book has been designed for a variety of users. Our primary target is a beginner or student new to motion graphics or visual effects. Or, perhaps you are a video editor or web designer who wants to learn "just enough" After Effects to help raise the quality of your productions. On the other hand, you may be a longtime or former user returning for a refresher course; in this edition we've put special emphasis on the new features and other changes introduced in After Effects CS6, 5.5, and 5.

We realize different people learn differently: Some prefer to read; some prefer to watch. That's why in addition to this book, we've created a companion *After Effects Apprentice* video series. We've tried to make this book as concise as possible while still conveying the information we think you need; the videos allow us to expound a bit more and explain what we're thinking when we make certain design or technical decisions. The videos are available through multiple outlets, listed on *onlinetraining.crishdesign.com*; we've included some of them on this book's DVD as bonus material to go beyond what we had room to explain inside these pages. Whether you choose one or use both, we hope *After Effects Apprentice* helps you on your path to a fulfilling career.

Trish & Chris Meyer
Crish Design

Getting Started

How to use this book, terminology, version numbers, and tech support.

Learning any new piece of software can be as frustrating as it is rewarding – especially if you are unfamiliar with how it works or what a book is trying to tell you to do. Although we know you're probably anxious to jump right in, please take a few moments to read these introductions – we promise they will help reduce your stress level:

• This *Getting Started* section explains how to use this book and its associated files.

• The following *Pre-Roll* section will help familiarize you with the "lay of the land" inside After Effects including the user interface, plus explain how projects are structured.

In a program as broad as After Effects, there are features you will use almost every day, and those you may use only once a year or less. The exercises in this book are designed to familiarize you with the core tools and features in After Effects (plus a few important "gotchas"), preparing you for many of the real-world tasks you will encounter. In Lesson 12's *Final Project*, we take the training wheels off and give you less-detailed instructions (as well as more design latitude) to make sure you're now able to work and create on your own inside (or using) After Effects.

We have tried to make this book visually rich, but we understand that some people learn better watching others work. Therefore, we created a companion video training series that walks you through all of these lessons. It's a way to look over our shoulder and hear us think out loud as we deal with various technical or design challenges; it also gave

us the opportunity to expound on additional topics. We include links to these videos – including free passes – on our web page *onlinetraining.crishdesign.com*. Several of those movies (as well as content from some of our other video training courses) are included as bonus material on the DVD-ROM that comes with this book.

Loading Up

To use this book, you need to install Adobe After Effects CS6, CS5.5, or CS5 on either your Macintosh or Windows computer. If you do not have a licensed copy, Adobe makes fully functional time-limited trial versions available on its website at *www.adobe.com/downloads/*.

Everything else you need to re-create the exercises in this book is contained on the DVD-ROM found in the back of this book. Each lesson has its own self-contained folder; copy the entire folder intact onto your computer's hard drive. You may delete the folder when you're done with a lesson.

This book, including all of the screen shots, was created using After Effects CS6. However, most of the lessons can be executed in CS5.5 or CS5. We will note where this is not true because of a feature or user interface change between versions. Inside each lesson's folder you will find project files for versions CS6, CS5.5, and CS5; open the version that matches the software you have installed. *(Note that older versions of After Effects usually cannot open projects created in later versions.)*

After opening any lesson's project for the first time, you should use Edit > Save As and give it a new name. This will ensure you can keep the original version intact for future reference. Indeed, the original project file may be locked – especially if you are accessing it directly off the DVD-ROM.

If After Effects is unable to find a project's source files, it will report them as missing and their names will appear in italics in the Project panel. Simply double-click the first missing item: This will bring up a standard file navigation dialog where you can locate that item. Select the missing file from its corresponding **Sources** subfolder and click OK. Provided the folder relationship between the project and the source files it uses has not changed, After Effects will search for the other missing items and link them in as well.

Virtually all of the material inside this book and on the DVD-ROM are copyright protected and are included only for your own learning and experimentation. (The United States map in Lesson 6 and the Indian Territories map in Lesson 9 are in the public domain.) Respect copyrights: Some day, it could be *you* who made that cool graphic…

By the way: Just because we provide you with all of the materials you need, this does not mean you can't use your own images and video instead! Indeed, we encourage you to use your own sources and to try your own variations on our ideas instead of just typing in the numbers we give you. There are gazillions of motion graphics styles out there. Although we can demonstrate only a few of them here, you will learn what you need to re-create a lot of what you see on TV – or in your own imagination.

Shortcuts and Phrases

After Effects runs on both Mac OS X and Windows and is nearly identical on both platforms. That said, there are numerous elements in an After Effects project to keep straight, such as files, compositions, effects, and expres-sions. To help indicate what we're talking about, we have a handful of particular type conventions and shorthand phrases that we will be using throughout this book:

• **Words in bold** refer to the names of files, folders, layers, or compositions you are using. These words refer both to files on disk and to items inside your project file.

• "**Words in bold and in quotes**" are text you should enter – such as the name for a new composition or solid.

• Words in this typewriter font indicate code inside an expression.

• Menu items, effects, and parameter names do not get a special font.

• When there is a chain of submenus or subfolders you have to navigate, we separate links in the chain with a > symbol: For example, Effect > Color Correction > Levels.

• To help make you a faster user, we mention keyboard shortcuts throughout this book. They are indicated by a special keyboard font. The Macintosh shortcut – such as ⌘ S to save a project – is presented first and is colored red (followed by the Windows shortcut – such as Ctrl S – in parentheses, colored blue). Keyboard shortcuts that are the same on both platforms are in gray, such as typing S to reveal a layer's Scale parameter.

The modifier key icons we use mean:

⌘ Command (Mac)

⌥ Option (Mac)

Ctrl Control (Windows)

Alt Alt (Windows)

• After Effects makes extensive use of "context-clicking" on items to reveal additional menus or options. To context-click, use the right mouse button; we will often say "right-click" in the instructions. If you are using a Macintosh single-button mouse, hold down the **Ctrl** key while clicking.

• After Effects makes a distinction between the normal section of the keyboard and the numeric keypad, especially when it comes to the **Enter** or **Return** key. When you see **Enter**, we mean the key on the keypad; **Return** indicates the carriage return key that is part of the normal keyboard.

• The Preferences are located under the After Effects menu on the Mac (and under the Edit menu on Windows). We'll just say "Preferences" and assume you can find them.

Speaking of preferences, we will assume you are starting out using the default preferences. Where they are saved depends on the operating system. If you have modified your current preferences, created custom templates, and so on, and want to save those preferences, search for "Adobe After Effects 11.0-x64 Prefs" for After Effects CS6 (CS5.5 is version 10.5; CS5 is version 10.0), make a note of where you found them, and copy that file to a safe place. Then, to restore the default preference settings, hold down **⌘** **⌥** **Shift** on Mac (**Ctrl** **Alt** **Shift** on Windows) while launching the program. You can always later copy your saved preferences file back to where you found it to return to your custom prefs. *(Note that if you have only added Render Settings and Output Module templates, and have not changed the program's Preferences, you should be okay using your current Preferences file.)*

Finally: Relax! Have fun! It's only software; you can't break it. And remember there is often more than one solution to any problem – especially when artistic expression is involved. Rather than give you a set of rigid recipes that must be followed exactly, our hope instead is to give you a set of skills that you can draw on to realize your own ideas while using this wonderful program.

System Requirements

Adobe lists the system requirements for After Effects on its packaging as well as on the associated web page: *www.adobe.com/products/aftereffects/systemreqs*.

In addition to Adobe's processor and operating system restrictions, we personally suggest that you use an extended keyboard (or that you learn how to access the function and numeric keypad equivalent keys on your laptop), and a three-button mouse; one with a scroll wheel is a nice bonus. Adobe also has created a document on optimizing your hardware configuration for After Effects CS6 as well as its other video programs; it may be found at *www.adobe.com/go/dv_hw_performance*.

If you are using After Effects CS6, there are two specific areas of hardware to pay attention to:

• If you plan to take advantage of the Ray-traced 3D Renderer (introduced in Lesson 8 and optionally used in portions of Lessons 9 and 11), you really want to have a compatible NVIDIA CUDA-enabled GPU (Graphics Processing Unit) in your video card or on the motherboard of your laptop. This greatly accelerates ray-traced rendering. You can still use the ray tracer without it, but performance will be so poor that you will quickly become discouraged. Compatible GPUs are listed on the System Requirements web page mentioned above.

• After Effects CS6 introduced a greatly enhanced caching scheme that can recall your previous RAM Previews – even after you've quit After Effects. The disk used for this cache is set in Preferences > Media & Disk Cache. Assign it to your fastest hard drive; an SSD (Solid State Drive) is ideal.

One of the best features of After Effects is its ability to create compositions at virtually any size and aspect ratio, and we take advantage of that in this book. Most of the exercises have been created at the North American/Japanese DV video size of 720×480 pixels, which uses non-square pixels (explained at the end of Lesson 3). The first two lessons use a 640×480 square pixel format to ease you into working with non-square pixels. Many of the lessons also include compositions created at the "half HD" (High Definition) size of 960×540 pixels; Lesson 9 contains a full-HD exercise at its end. The bigger display you have, the more pixels you can see, while more RAM allows you to create longer previews to check your results as you work.

DVD Tech Support

If your DVD becomes damaged, please contact Focal Press' parent company Taylor & Francis at: *www.taylorandfrancis.com/info/contact/*

Choose Customer Service from the Category menu, and make sure you state that you have the 3rd Edition of *After Effects Apprentice*.

As this contact page is subject to change, we will keep Focal Press contact information updated on our website at: *crishdesign.com/contact.html*

For Instructors

Each lesson in *After Effects Apprentice* demonstrates essential features through a series of hands-on exercises. They are supplemented with sidebars and numerous tips that cover technical issues and other features of interest. Additionally, many of the lessons end with a series of challenges you can give your students to have them build on what they've learned. We hope that you will find this format useful and can adapt it to your specific needs.

Lesson 12 has been structured as a potential "final exam" for you to give your students, as our instructions are looser here than throughout the rest of the book (so you can see if they can now use the program on their own, rather than just follow instructions), while also leaving more room for creative interpretation by each individual student. We've also included a lot of real-world tips, including how to work with clients, suggestions on ordering music for a job, and potential delivery requirements.

We have created a companion *After Effects Apprentice* video training series which you may find useful to watch. In addition to getting to see and hear us actually walk through the steps, we share a lot of our thought process as we make design and technical decisions. This background may aid your own understanding, as well as provide additional ideas for how to explain individual concepts to your students. Excerpts from these and other courses are included as bonus material in many of the individual lessons. Check our web page *www.crishdesign.com/online_training.html* for distributors of these video courses.

The contents of this book and its accompanying disc are copyrighted. Each student must own his or her own copy of this book. You may not duplicate this book's text, project files, and associated materials for your students if they do not own a copy of this book. If your school has the available disk space, students may copy contents from the DVD to their computers, or you may place the files on a classroom server, but again only as long as each student owns his or her own copy of this book. Provided each student owns the book, you are free to then modify the tutorials and adapt them to your specific teaching situation without infringing copyright.

Thank you for helping protect our copyrights, as well as those who contributed sources – your cooperation enables us to write new books and obtain great source materials for your students to learn from. We hope you and your students enjoy the results.

Qualified teaching professionals can acquire evaluation copies of our books directly from Taylor & Francis, parent of Focal Press. Please email orders@taylorandfrancis.com.

Exploring the After Effects landscape.

In this section, we want to give you the "lay of the land" inside After Effects and show you how to move around inside it. You will learn what each of the major sections of the user interface are called and what they are for, as well as how to rearrange the interface to best suit the task at hand.

The After Effects Project

Before we explain the pieces of the puzzle, we should first explain the puzzle they are part of: namely, an After Effects project. A project file points at the *footage* – sources or pieces of media – you want to use to build one or more *compositions*. After Effects does not store a copy of the footage inside the project file; just a pointer to it. When you move a project to a different folder or computer, you need to move the footage it uses as well. You can use movies, FLVs, still images, sequences of stills, or audio files – all in a variety of formats – as footage items.

When you add a piece of footage to a composition (or "comp" for short), it becomes a *layer* inside that comp. Once a footage item is a layer in a comp, you can arrange it in relation to other layers, animate it, and add effects to it. Another way of thinking of a comp is as the place where your sources get composited together into the final image.

You can create virtually unlimited compositions in a project, as well as virtually unlimited layers in each comp. The same footage item can be used in more than one comp, as well as more than once in the same comp. You can even use comps as layers inside of other comps (this is called *nesting*, which we'll cover in Lesson 6).

▽ In This Lesson

1   project structure
2   main application window
3   Tools panel
3   Project panel
4   importing footage
5   Composition panel
6   Timeline panel
7   Layer panel
8   Info, Preview, Audio panels
9   Effects & Presets; Effect Controls; other panels
10 Workspaces
12 Adobe Bridge

▽ tip

Help!

Pressing **F1** opens the After Effects Help in your web browser. This landing page contains a number of helpful links to specific topics. It also includes a Search box to find specific information.

User Interface Videos

We have included a pair of movies from our *After Effects Apprentice* video series that give a quick tour of the user interface, including how to use Workspaces. They can be found in the **00-Pre-Roll > 00-Video Bonus** folder on the DVD-ROM that came with this book.

The Application Window

The box all of these puzzle pieces fit into is the After Effects *application window*. By default, this window is designed to fill your entire display, although you are able to resize it by dragging on its lower right corner, and reposition it by grabbing it along its top.

This window is split into several different sections known as *frames*. Each frame can hold one or more tabbed *panels*; a full list of available panels is included under the After Effects Window menu.

Each panel type holds a different kind of information, such as what footage items you have already imported into your project, or which effects you have applied to a layer.

Different types of panels – or in some cases, multiple copies of the same type of panel – can share the same frame, appearing as tabs along the top of the frame. An orange outline around a panel indicates it is currently "forward" or selected.

An arrangement of panels and frames is called a *workspace*. After Effects comes with a number of prearranged workspace layouts; you can also save your own custom arrangements. You will learn how to do this later in this Pre-Roll. But first, let's become familiar with the panels you will encounter most often, what information they hold, and how you will use them while working on a project in After Effects. You won't be putting them to use quite yet; that will be your task in the following lessons!

The Tools Panel

The After Effects main window features a toolbar along its top. This provides an easy way to switch between different tools until you learn the keyboard shortcuts. The keyboard shortcuts are worth learning; they'll make you a much faster After Effects user. If a tool you want is grayed out, make sure you select a comp or a layer – it should then become active. Selecting some tools (such as Type or Paint) may also open one or more panels that go along with it.

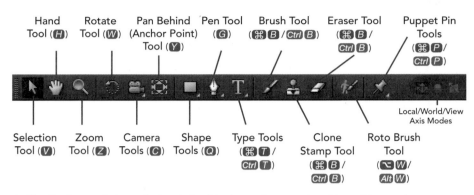

△ **The Tools panel.** A small triangle beside the tool means that this tool has options, in which case its shortcut key will cycle between them. The Tools panel is the only one that cannot be docked into a different frame. However, you can hide and reveal it using the Window menu.

The Project Panel

The Project panel is the central hub of an After Effects project. Whenever you import a footage item or create a new composition, it appears in the Project panel.

The Project panel displays information such as file type, size, and location in a series of columns. You can drag the horizontal scroll bar at the bottom of this panel to view the different columns. Selecting a column header causes After Effects to sort the Project panel based on this column's information; look for the arrow along its top to tell which one's selected. To add or subtract a column, right-click on any column header and select or deselect it from the list that appears.

When you select a footage item in the Project panel, a thumbnail of it will appear at the top of this panel, along with its vital statistics. If you are already using it in a composition,

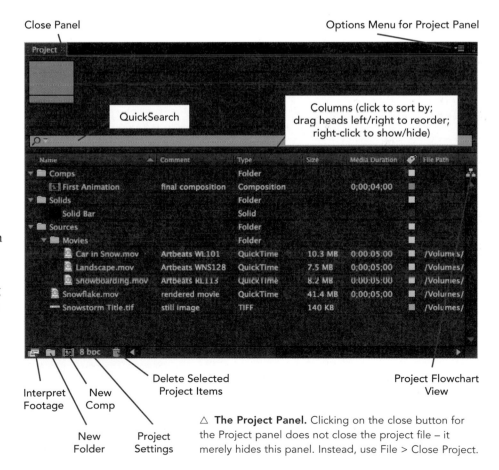

△ **The Project Panel.** Clicking on the close button for the Project panel does not close the project file – it merely hides this panel. Instead, use File > Close Project.

the name of the comps it appears in will be added to a popup menu to the right of its name (see figure, right). If you need to change some settings for a footage item – such as its frame rate, or alpha channel type – select it in the Project panel, then click the Interpret Footage button at the bottom of this panel.

As projects become more complex, the Project panel can quickly become messy. Fortunately, you can create folders inside this panel to keep things organized. To do this, click on the Create a New Folder icon along the bottom of this panel or use the menu command File > New > New Folder. You can double-click a folder or use the arrow to its left to open and close it; to rename a folder, select its name, press (Return), type in your name, and press (Return) again. (You'll be creating folders in Lesson 1.)

▼ Importing Footage

There are two main ways to add or "import" sources (known as *footage*) into an After Effects project. If you know where the source is, and generally what it looks like, use the File > Import menu item. This will open a dialog where you can browse to the file you want. Pay attention to the area under the file browser, as it contains important options such as whether you want to import the file as a single footage item or as a self-contained composition (handy for layered Photoshop and Illustrator files), whether you want to import a single still image or whole sequence of stills as a movie, and whether to import an entire folder in one go. You will learn how to import footage and layered files in Lesson 1.

The other approach is to use File > Browse in Bridge, which launches Adobe Bridge: a handy utility standardized across Adobe applications. Using Bridge, you can sort and preview files, then double-click items to import them into After Effects. Bridge is covered in more detail later in this lesson.

Toggle
Viewer Lock

Viewer
Dropdown Menu

Close Panel

▽ **The Composition Panel.**

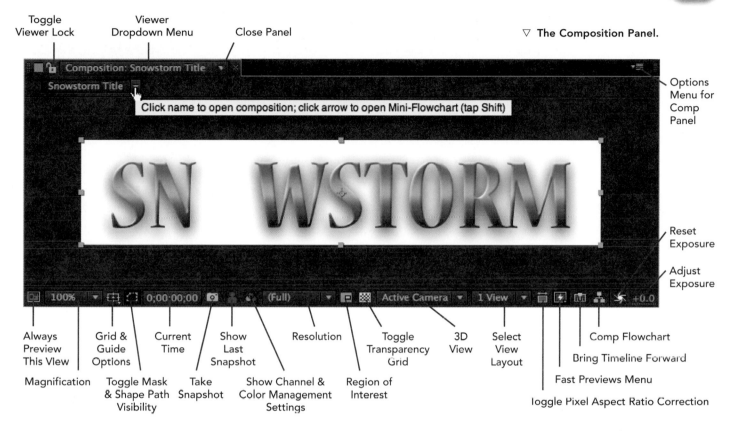

Options
Menu for
Comp
Panel

Composition: Snowstorm Title

Snowstorm Title

Click name to open composition; click arrow to open Mini-Flowchart (tap Shift)

SN WSTORM

Reset
Exposure

Adjust
Exposure

100%   0;00;00;00   (Full)   Active Camera   1 View   +0.0

Always
Preview
This View

Grid &
Guide
Options

Current
Time

Show
Last
Snapshot

Resolution

Toggle
Transparency
Grid

3D
View

Select
View
Layout

Comp Flowchart

Bring Timeline Forward

Magnification

Toggle Mask
& Shape Path
Visibility

Take
Snapshot

Show Channel &
Color Management
Settings

Region of
Interest

Fast Previews Menu

Toggle Pixel Aspect Ratio Correction

The Composition Panel

The Composition panel – or Comp, for short – is where you see your creations. It displays the current frame of your composition. You can also directly click on and drag the objects (layers) that make up your comp. After Effects renders only the pixels that fall inside the comp's image area (which we'll refer to sometimes as the Comp viewer), but you also have a pasteboard beyond this area to work with.

The buttons along the bottom of the Comp panel affect how you view the composite of your layers, such as magnification, resolution, color channels, and mask and shape path outlines. The tab along the top includes a popup menu that allows you to select which open comp to view.

Whenever you set Magnification to something other than 100%, After Effects will merely grab the nearest pixel when choosing which ones to display. This can result in the image looking very crunchy as pixels are

skipped – especially if you choose the "Fit" option in the Magnification popup. Don't panic; your final image will look smooth when you render.

Note that Magnification is the zoom level, while Resolution decides how many pixels After Effects is going to process (Full means every pixel, Half is every second pixel in the width and height, and so on). Setting the Resolution popup to Auto will keep these two in sync – such as Full Resolution when at 100% Magnification, or Half Resolution when at 50% Magnification. This gives the fastest playback speeds and avoids the common mistake of processing at Full Resolution when viewing at less than 50% magnification – why spend time rendering more pixels than your monitor is set to display?

The Comp panel's companion is the Timeline panel, which we'll show next.

The Timeline Panel

The Timeline panel gives you details on how the current composition is built: what layers it includes, what order they are stacked in, where they start and end, how they are animating, and what effects have been applied to them. It is the left brain to the Comp panel's right brain.

The Timeline panel is broken down into two sections: the timeline section to the right, which shows how the layers have been trimmed and any keyframes applied to them, and a series of columns to the left that display different switches, information, and options. The timeline section is also where the Graph Editor (introduced in Lesson 2) is displayed.

Like the Project panel, you may select which columns to view by right-clicking on any column header and selecting or deselecting it from the list that appears. These columns may also be dragged left and right to reorder them – for example, we prefer placing the A/V Features column to the right near the timeline, rather than its default position of far left. Once you reorder these columns, all new compositions you create will have the same arrangement.

The Timeline panel features a tab for each currently open comp, which makes it easy to see which ones are open and to quickly jump between them. Note that the Render Queue docks into the same frame as the Timeline panel.

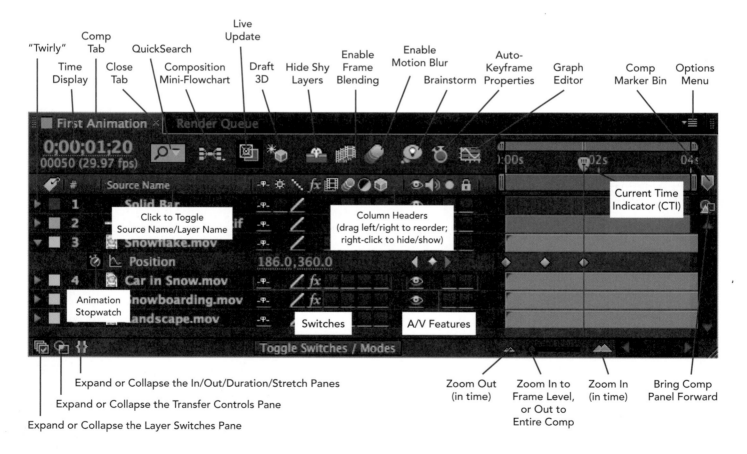

△ **The Timeline panel.** Click on a tab to bring that particular Composition and Timeline pair forward. Note that we have moved the A/V Features column (the column with the eyeball) to the right, so that the keyframe navigator arrows in this column are closer to the keyframes.

The Layer Panel

When you add a footage item to a comp, it becomes a layer in that comp, where it is combined with the other layers you've added. But there are times when it is hard to view what is going on with a particular layer in the Comp panel because it's fading out, has been effected or scaled down really small, has been dragged out of the visible area of the comp, or the view is otherwise confused by other layers. This is where the Layer panel comes in.

Double-click a layer in either the Comp or Timeline panels to open it in its own Layer panel. By default, it docks into the same frame as the Comp panel. The most interesting feature here is the View popup along the bottom right side. This gives you the option of viewing a layer before or after a *mask* (cut-out shape) has been applied, as well as after it has been processed by any effects you have added to the layer. If you have added more than one effect, you can view it at any point in the effect chain. The Render checkbox to the right of the View popup is a quick and easy way to view the layer with or without the modifications selected in the View menu.

A layer may be slid in time in a comp's overall timeline. That means the local time in a layer – how far you are from its start – often will not match the master time in the comp. A second timeline and time marker in the Layer panel shows you where you are in the layer.

If the layer is a precomp (Lesson 6), double-clicking will open that comp. To open the Layer panel for a precomp, press ⌥ on Mac (*Alt* on Windows) when you double-click.

▽ **The Layer panel.** Some functions can be performed only in the Layer panel.

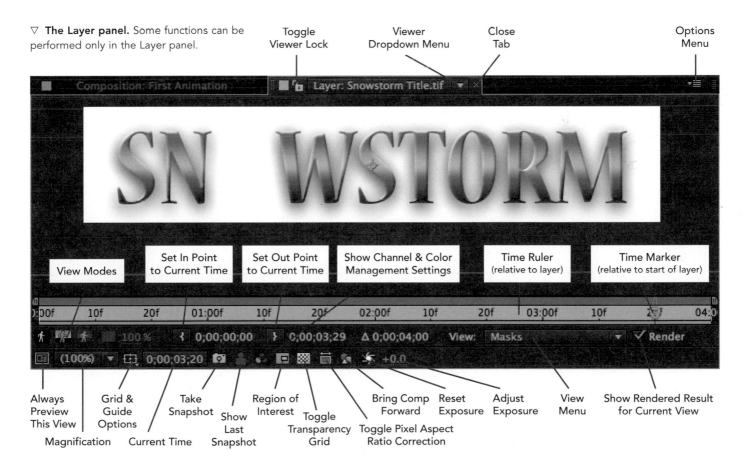

Other Panels

There are numerous other types of panels that we will be putting to work throughout this book; we will explain them in more detail as we need them. However, so they won't seem so foreign when you first encounter them, here's a quick overview of some you will use most often:

Info

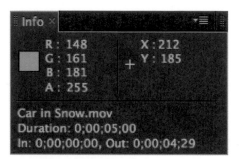

△ **The Info panel** displays information such as the color currently under the cursor.

The top portion of this panel gives a numeric readout of the color value underneath the cursor in a comp, layer, or footage panel, as well as the cursor's current X/Y coordinates in those panels. Additional useful information – such as the in and out points of a selected layer – are displayed in the lower portion of this panel.

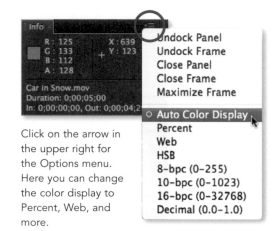

Click on the arrow in the upper right for the Options menu. Here you can change the color display to Percent, Web, and more.

Preview

Previous Frame   Next Frame   Mute Audio

First Frame   Play/Pause   Last Frame   Loop Options   RAM Preview

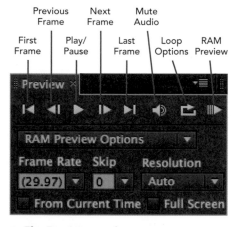

△ **The Preview panel.**

△ Hide the RAM Preview Options to allow more room for other panels. Move your cursor over the area below Preview until the icon changes, then drag up.

Your transport controls in After Effects. The Preview panel also contains options for RAM Previews (discussed in Lesson 1). Once you learn some basic keyboard shortcuts – such as the spacebar for Play – you will find you rarely, if ever, use this panel.

Audio

The Audio panel features volume controls for the selected layer, plus a level meter that is active while previewing a comp or layer.

When working with audio, you can also view the audio waveform in the Timeline panel; this is covered in Lesson 5.

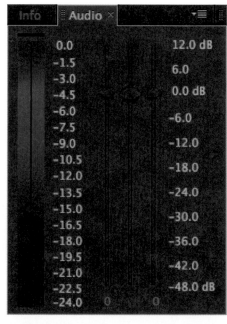

△ **The Audio panel.**

Effects & Presets

This very handy panel provides a quick and easy way to select and apply effects and animation presets. The QuickSearch box along the top provides a search function for your Effects and Presets, which is usually faster than searching through a menu or file dialog. This panel is demonstrated in Lesson 3.

Effect Controls

When you add an effect to a layer, the effect's settings and user interface appear in this panel. The shortcut to open this panel is to select a layer and press **F3**.

You can also reveal effects applied to a layer by selecting it and typing **E**, which will twirl them open in the Timeline panel. From there, you can click on the "twirly" arrow next to the effect's name to reveal its parameters.

◁ **The Effects & Presets panel.** In Lesson 3, a QuickTime movie will explain the different options available for searching and organizing effects and animation presets.

▽ tip

Maximize Frame

To temporarily view a panel full screen, select it and press the tilde (~) key. Press ~ again to switch back to the normal multiframe view.

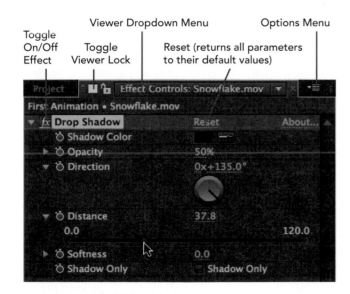

△ **The Effect Controls panel.**

Character & Paragraph Panels

Covered in detail in Lesson 5, these are the controls you need to help typeset text. Selecting Workspace > Text will open both panels.

Paint & Brush Panels

After Effects contains a pretty nifty paint and clone engine, which will get a workout in Lesson 10. Selecting Workspace > Paint will open both panels.

More Panels

Additional miscellaneous panels (such as Smoother, Align, and more) will be covered as they are needed in various lessons.

△ Select Standard from the Workspace menu. If you make a mess moving around panels, select Reset Standard. To save your new layout, select New Workspace.

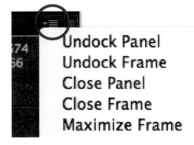

△ Every frame has an arrow in its upper right corner; click on it to see its Options menu. The options at the top are universal to all panels and frames.

▽ tip

Quick Undocking

There are three ways to undock a panel and turn it into a floating window: using its Options menu (upper right corner), dragging it somewhere that a drop zone does not appear, or holding down the ⌘ key on Mac (Ctrl on Windows) and dragging it out of its current frame.

Managing Workspaces

After Effects comes with a number of preset workspaces which open sets of panels that come in handy for doing specific tasks. You can select them by using the menu item Window > Workspace, or by clicking on the Workspace popup menu in the top right corner of the application window. Try out a few and notice how the panels and frames change. Then select the Standard workspace.

If you want to give a frame more or less room, move your cursor over the area between frames until it changes to an icon of two arrows connected to two parallel lines (see figure to the right). When you see this icon, click and drag to balance the size of adjacent frames, such as those that hold the Project and Composition panels.

Every frame has an options arrow in its upper right corner. Click on it, and a menu will appear. The options near the top are universal to all panels and frames, such as undocking or closing panels. The options near the bottom are specific to the panel currently being shown in that frame (see page 8 for an example of the Info panel's Options menu).

△ Here we show the Effect Controls panel after it has been undocked (in the Standard workspace it shares the same frame as the Project panel). Once a panel is undocked, you can then dock more panels into this window, or drag this panel back into another frame.

With the Standard workspace still selected, turn your attention to the column of frames along the right side of the application window. The top frame has two panels docked into it: Info and Audio. The default in the Standard workspace is for Info to be forward; click on the tab that says Audio to bring it forward instead.

The Audio panel could benefit from being in a taller frame, but rather than extend its height, you can also change where it is docked: Click on the Audio tab, then drag it until you are hovering over the center of the Effects & Presets panel (see figure to the right). The center of the Effects & Presets panel will turn blue, indicating that if you were to release your mouse now, Audio would be docked into this frame instead. Keep the mouse depressed for now.

In addition to this central "drop zone" you will see four smaller zones around it. Drag to these and watch them highlight. If you release the mouse over one of these, you will create a brand-new frame for the Audio panel on that side of Effects & Presets. Finally, drag your cursor to the tab that says Effects & Presets until it highlights in blue: This option also means "add me to the same frame as this panel." Go ahead and release your mouse, and Audio will be tabbed into the same frame as Effects & Presets.

Now click on the Window menu, and select Smoother. It defaults into opening a new frame to the right of the Timeline panel and frame. Because this layout reduces the width of the timeline, feel free to move it too. Drag the Smoother tab and dock it into the same frame as Effects & Presets and Audio. Notice that a gray bar appears above their tabs; this allows you to scroll between the tabs for the panels docked into the same frame.

Have some fun practicing rearranging the workspace. If you make a big mess, you can always select the Reset option from the bottom of the Workspace popup. If you have an arrangement you like, select New Workspace from the Workspace popup or Window > Workspace menu, and give it a name.

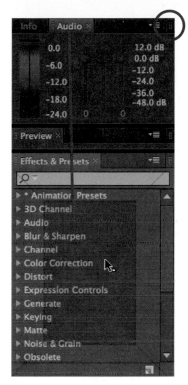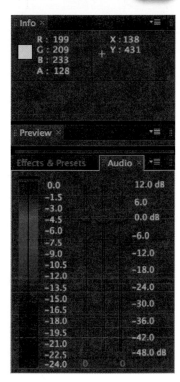

△ Click on the Audio panel tab and drag it to the center of the Effects & Presets panel (left). Once you release the mouse, the Audio panel will be docked into the same frame (right). Note that the dots near the Options arrow (circled in red) moves the entire frame, not just the panel.

◁ A gray bar appears above a frame when there is not enough space to display all the panels within. This allows you to scroll left and right to view all panels.

▽ gotcha

Finding Your Way Home

After Effects remembers changes you make to a workspace, including the presets. You can't undo individual changes to a workspace. To get back to the current workspace's original layout, select the "Reset" option at the bottom of the Workspace menu, then click Yes in the dialog box that pops up.

Adobe Bridge

Adobe Bridge provides several useful functions, including previewing the animation presets that come with After Effects and acting as an advanced file browser to select your own content. If you're not familiar with Bridge, the following is a quick overview to get you up to speed so you can preview sources and import them into After Effects.

1 Adobe Bridge is a central file organization and preview program that works across many Adobe products. Bridge's Preview panel has the ability to show still images as well as play movies.

1 Open After Effects (if not already open). Then select the menu item File > Browse in Bridge, which will launch Adobe Bridge. You will notice that it is similar to After Effects in that it has a single application window, divided into several frames that contain tabbed panels. You can resize the frames by dragging the bars between them; you can also re-dock some of the panels.

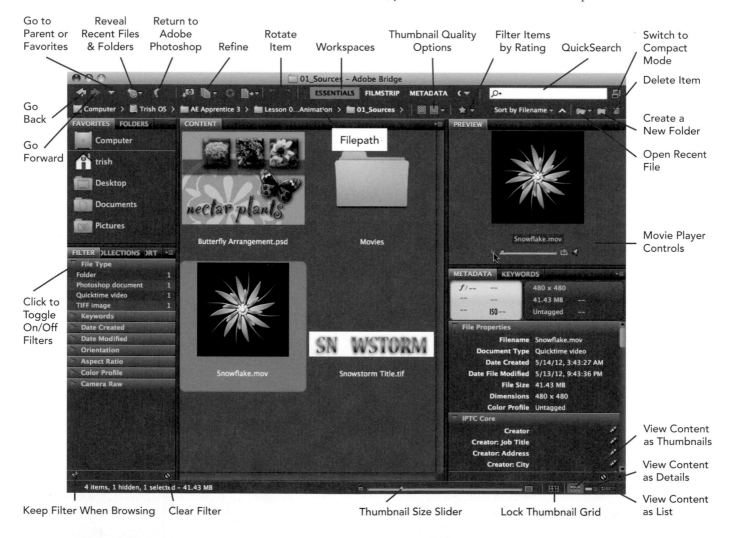

Go to Parent or Favorites

Reveal Recent Files & Folders

Return to Adobe Photoshop

Refine

Rotate Item

Workspaces

Thumbnail Quality Options

Filter Items by Rating

QuickSearch

Switch to Compact Mode

Delete Item

Go Back

Go Forward

Create a New Folder

Open Recent File

Click to Toggle On/Off Filters

Movie Player Controls

View Content as Thumbnails

View Content as Details

View Content as List

Keep Filter When Browsing

Clear Filter

Thumbnail Size Slider

Lock Thumbnail Grid

2 Bridge also comes with a number of workspaces; for now, choose Window > Workspace > Essentials. One of the first things you will notice is a tab in the upper left corner called Favorites which includes several preset locations, including your computer's desktop and its default folders for documents and images.

3 Click on the tab in the upper left named Folders. Use this to navigate your mounted drives. As you click on a drive or folder, its contents will appear in the large area to the right. Double-clicking on a folder in either place will open it.

Use these to navigate to the **Lesson 01** folder from this book's disc, then open the **01_Sources** folder inside (or feel free to use a folder of your own sources).

4 Click on the still image file **Snowstorm title.tif**. Notice how its image appears in the Preview panel, and its file info appears in the Metadata panel.

Then open the **Movies** folder, and click on one of the QuickTime movies. A set of transport controls will appear along the bottom of the Preview panel. Click Play to start playback; the Play arrow will change to a Pause icon. Click on Pause to stop. Experiment with the location scrubber and Loop button along the bottom.

5 Along the bottom right of the main Bridge window are tools for deciding how your files are displayed. For example, drag the slider to change the thumbnail size. Then click on the View icons to the right of this slider.

6 Pick one of the files in the **Movies** folder, then click on the Label menu: This allows you add a Rating for each file, as well as give it a Label. Go ahead and give star ratings and colored labels to a few of the files.

7 Along the top right of the Bridge window, you will see a star icon with a menu arrow next to it – click and hold either one of these. This gives you a way to quickly sort through your labeled files. For example, say you gave 4 or 5 stars to at least one file in this folder: Select Show 3 or More Stars, and only those files will shown. You can also click on the "Sort by" header to order the main window based on a number of different criteria.

To import a file from Bridge into After Effects CS6, you can double-click it, type ⌘ O (Ctrl O), or use the menu command File > Open With. To import multiple files at once, simply preselect them first. Bridge will return you to After Effects, with these files imported into your project.

As you can see, Bridge can be very helpful when you have to sort through and select a large number of files, or files you are not familiar with. When we prompt you to import a source in the lessons in this book, feel free to select File > Browse in Bridge instead of using File > Import.

▽ tip

Bridge Help

Adobe Bridge is used by all the applications in Adobe's Creative Suite. It has far more features than we have room to discuss here. Open Bridge, then press **F1** to open Adobe Bridge Help to learn more about what Bridge has to offer.

▽ tip

My Favorite Place

If you have a folder you expect to return to often – such as where you keep your photos – select the folder in Bridge, and use File > Add to Favorites. You can also right-click on a folder and get this option.

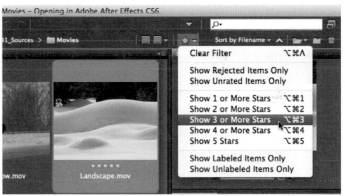

7 Bridge allows you to rate and color-code your files, and then filter which ones you see based on these tags. Note the shortcut keys in the Label menu: These are well worth learning so you can do "selects" on a large number of files quickly. Holding ⌘ (Ctrl) while typing a number directly corresponds to the star rating a selected file or files receive. Also check out the "Sort by…" popup next to the Filter popup for additional display options. Movie footage courtesy Artbeats.

Basic Animation

Building your first animation while you learn a typical After Effects workflow.

▽ In This Lesson

16 creating folders in the Project panel
17 creating a new composition; importing media
18 interpreting alpha channels
19 adding layers to the Comp panel
20 changing the Background Color
20 scrubbing parameter values
20 interactively transforming layers
21 animating Position; RAM Preview
22 navigating between keyframes
22 adding a background layer
23 dragging footage to the Timeline panel
24 editing a keyframe's Bezier handles
25 editing spatial keyframes; motion paths
26 animating Opacity, Scale, and Rotation
28 arranging and replacing layers
30 adding solid layers
30 applying, copying, and pasting effects
32 rendering
33 RAM Preview options; the Work Area
34 caches and memory
36 importing layered Photoshop and Illustrator files

▽ Getting Started

Make sure you have copied the **Lesson 01-Basic Animation** folder from this book's disc onto your hard drive, and make note of where it is; it contains the sources you need to execute this lesson. Our versions of these exercises are in the project file **Lesson_01_Finished.aep**.

In this lesson, you will learn how to build a typical After Effects project. Although the design itself is simple, you will learn principles you can use over and over again in the future. For example, you will see how to import sources while keeping your project file organized. As you add layers to a composition, you will learn how to manipulate their transform properties, as well as how to keyframe them to create animations. Along the way, you'll learn important tricks and keyboard shortcuts. We'll also discuss how to handle alpha channels as well as layered Photoshop and Illustrator files.

Composition Basics

In the Pre-Roll section, we discussed the basic hierarchy of an After Effects project: Sources are called *footage* items; when you add a footage item to a *composition* ("comp" for short), it is then known as a *layer*. Potential sources can include captured video, Flash or 3D animations, photographs or scans, images created in programs such as Photoshop or Illustrator, music, dialog…even film footage that has been scanned into the computer.

Layers are flat objects that can be arranged in a comp's space and animated around that space. We'll work in 2D space (the X and Y axis) at first, adding the Z axis in Lesson 8, *3D Space*. The order they are stacked in the Timeline panel determine the order in which they are drawn (unless they are in 3D space). Layers can start and end at different points in time (more on this in Lesson 3).

All properties in After Effects start out constant: You set them, and this is the value they have for the entire comp.

However, it is very easy to enable *keyframing* for virtually any property, which means you can set what their values will be at different points in time. After Effects will then automatically interpolate or "tween" between these values over time. Once you enable keyframing, changing a property's value automatically creates a new keyframe – you don't have to explicitly say "make new keyframe."

You have considerable control over how After Effects moves between keyframes. In this lesson, we'll demonstrate editing the *motion path* for position keyframes, and in the next lesson we'll dive into further refining the speed at which After Effects interpolates between values.

A layer can be smaller or larger than the composition and its "resolution" (pixels per inch) is ignored by After Effects. In addition to fading a layer in and out using its opacity, a footage item may also have an *alpha channel* that determines where the image is transparent and where it is opaque.

But before you start arranging and animating, you need to know how to make a new project and comp, as well as how to import sources – so let's get started!

After Effects compositions combine multiple layers together. Movies courtesy Artbeats, from the Recreation & Leisure, Winter Lifestyles, and Winter Scenes collections.

▽ factoid

File Format Support

For a full list of file formats that may be imported in After Effects, open the program, press **F1** to open the After Effects Help, and search for "**supported import formats**."

Individual layer properties may be keyframed in the Timeline panel to create an animation.

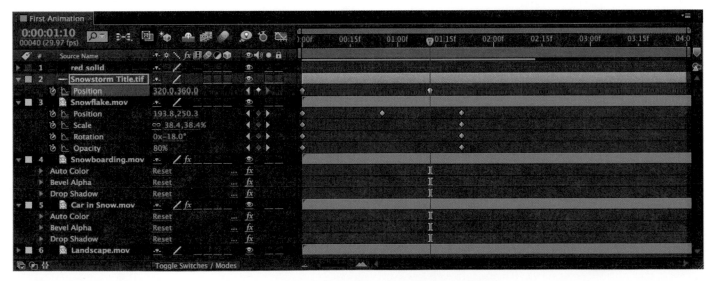

1 Set the Workspace to Standard and then reset it to make sure you are starting with the same arrangement of frames and panels as we are. That way, our instructions will make a lot more sense.

2 To create a new folder, click on the folder icon along the bottom of the Project panel. To rename it, type your new name while "Untitled 1" is highlighted, then press *Return*.

Starting a Project

In this first lesson, you'll create a simple animation of a winter scene. To see where you'll end up, locate the movie **First Animation_final.mov** in this lesson's folder, and play it a few times in QuickTime Player. (To keep things simple, we "pre-baked" the title and snowflake designs; the original sources are included in our finished project. You'll learn how to create text in Lesson 5, and how to animate Shape Layers in Lesson 11.) Bring After Effects forward when you're done, and we'll guide you through building this animation from scratch.

1 When After Effects is launched, click Close in the Welcome screen, and it will create a new, blank project for you. In the upper right corner of the application window, locate the Workspace popup, and select Standard. To make sure you are using the original arrangement of this workspace, from the same popup select Reset "Standard" (it's at the bottom). A Reset Workspace dialog will appear; click Discard Changes.

2 The Project panel can quickly become a confusing mess of sources and comps. To avoid this, let's create a couple of folders to help keep it organized. Click on the New Folder icon along the bottom of the Project panel. A folder called **Untitled 1** will be created. It defaults to its name being highlighted; to rename it, type "**Sources**" and press *Return* (on a Windows keyboard, this is the main *Enter* key – not the one on the extended keypad). You can rename it at any time; just select the folder and press *Return* to highlight the name.

3 Click in a blank area of the Project panel to deselect your **Sources** folder; the shortcut to Deselect All is *F2*. Now create a second folder; rename it "**Comps**" and press *Return*.

(If the **Sources** folder was selected when you created the **Comps** folder, **Comps** will be nested inside **Sources**. Place it on the same level by dragging the **Comps** folder outside of the **Sources** folder.)

Saving a Project

4 Select File > Save to save your project. The shortcut is ⌘ S on Mac (*Ctrl* S on Windows). A file browser window will open; save your project file in this lesson's folder (**Lesson 01-Basic Animation**), and give it a name that makes sense, such as "**Basic Animation v1**".

It is a good idea to give projects version numbers so you can keep track of revisions; it also allows you to take advantage of the nifty File > Increment and Save function. Instead of just saving your project, Increment and Save will save your project under a new version number, leaving a trail of previous versions in case you ever need to go back. After Effects also has an Auto Save function; it's under Preferences > Auto-Save.

Creating a New Composition

5 Select the **Comps** folder you created in step 3. That way, the new comp you are about to create will automatically be sorted into it. Then either select the menu item Composition > New Composition, or use the keyboard shortcut ⌘ N (Ctrl N). A Composition Settings dialog will open in which you can determine the size, duration, and frame rate of your new comp. A good habit to get into with After Effects is naming your compositions as you create them. Enter "**First Animation**" in the Composition Name dialog.

At the top of this dialog is the Preset popup menu, which includes a number of common comp sizes and frame rates. You can also enter your own settings. For this starting composition, uncheck the Lock Aspect Ratio box, then type in a Width of 640 and Height of 480. Click on the menu next to Pixel Aspect Ratio and select Square Pixels (we'll discuss pixels that are not square in the *Tech Corner* at the end of Lesson 3).

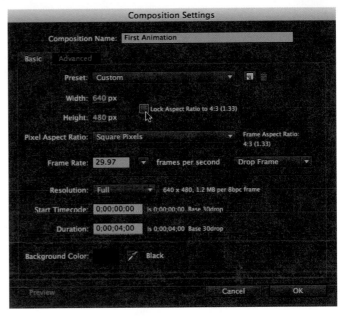

Highlight the value currently in the Duration field, and enter "**4.00**" for four seconds. Then make sure the remaining settings are at their defaults: Frame Rate of 29.97, Resolution of Full, and Start Timecode of 0;00;00;00. The Background Color defaults to Black, but we can change that later if we need to.

Finally, click on the Advanced tab and check that the Renderer popup is set to use the Classic 3D Renderer (we'll use the Ray-traced 3D Renderer in Lesson 8). Click OK. Your new comp will open into the Comp and Timeline panels.

6 Your comp will also appear in the Project panel, inside your **Comps** folder (if it's not in there, drag it in). If you cannot read the entire name in the Project panel, just place your cursor along the right edge of the Name column (a double-sided arrow will appear) and drag the column wider. Finally, save your project.

Importing Footage

There are two main ways to import footage into After Effects: using the normal Import dialog, and using Adobe Bridge (covered in Pre-Roll). We'll explore the Import dialog here, but feel free to use Bridge if you prefer. (You can also drag and drop from the Finder or Windows Explorer, but that can be awkward as the After Effects application window tends to take up the entire screen.)

7 It's time to import some sources into your project. First, select the **Sources** folder you created in step 2. Then use the menu item File > Import > File. Navigate to the **Lesson 01-Basic Animation** folder you copied from this book's disc, and open the folder **01_Sources**. Select **Snowstorm Title.tif** and click Open.

5 These are the settings we will use for our first composition (above). Remember to uncheck the Lock Aspect Ratio box before typing in new dimensions. In the Advanced tab, check that the Renderer popup is set to use the Classic 3D Renderer (below).

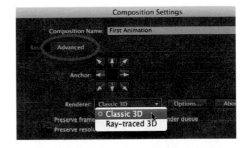

6 At this point, the Project panel will have two folders and one composition. Drag this Name column wider if the comp's name is bring truncated.

▼ Managing the Comp View

You learned in the Pre-Roll how to resize the user interface's frames. You can resize the frame that holds the Comp panel to decide how much screen real estate you can devote to it. There are several ways to control how this space is used to display the comp's image area:

• In the lower left corner of the Comp panel is a Magnification popup. A popular setting for this is Fit up to 100%, which uses as much of the Comp panel's frame as it can up to full size; that's the setting we used when creating most of these lessons and comps. A downside of the Fit option is that your image can look a bit crunchy if the result is an unusual size, such as 78%. Therefore, some users prefer picking a set size such as 100% or 50% that gets close to using the space available, then resizing the frame again as needed.

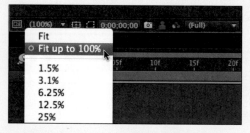

• When the Comp panel is selected (surrounded by a yellow outline), you can hold down ⌘ (Ctrl) and press the ➕ key to zoom in larger, or the ➖ key to zoom out smaller.

• If you have a mouse with a scroll wheel, hover its cursor over the Comp panel, and use the wheel to zoom in and out.

• For more targeted zooming, select the Zoom tool (shortcut: Z), and click to zoom in and center around where you click, or ⌥+click (Alt+click) to zoom out. Don't forget to press V when done to return to the Selection tool!

• Even better, press and hold down the Z key to *temporarily* switch to the Zoom tool; add ⌥ (Alt) to zoom out. When you release the Z key, the Selection tool will still be active.

• To pan around your composition, hold down the spacebar to temporarily bring up the Hand tool, then click and drag in the Comp panel to reposition it. (Tapping the spacebar previews the timeline.)

8 The Import dialog will be replaced with an Interpret Footage dialog. This file has an *alpha channel*: a grayscale channel that sets the transparency of the RGB color channels. There are two main types of alpha channels: *Straight*, which means the color has been "painted beyond" the edges of the alpha channel, and *Premultiplied*, which means the color is mixed ("matted") with the background color around the edges.

If you knew what type of alpha your file has, you could select it here. Since you don't, click Guess. In this file's case, After Effects will choose the Premultiplied – Matted With Color White option, which is correct. Click OK, and it will appear in your **Sources** folder.

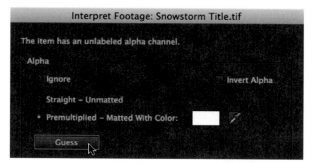

8 To get the best results out of sources with alpha channels, you want to select the correct alpha channel type. You can do this while importing a file, or any time later using the Interpret Footage dialog. After Effects has a Guess function to help.

9 Now it's time to import some more sources. Make sure the **Sources** folder (or a file inside it) is still selected, and use the shortcut ⌘ I (Ctrl I) to open the Import dialog. Select **Snowflake.mov**, and click Open. This is an animation created using Shape Layers in After Effects (these are the subject of Lesson 11). We then rendered it as a QuickTime movie with an alpha channel.

10 Finally, double-click on an empty area of the Project panel – this will also open the Import dialog. Select the folder named **Movies**, and click the Open button. This will import all the contents of the folder for you with a single click; it will also create a folder with the same name in the Project panel. Drag the **Movies** folder inside your **Sources** folder, and save your project.

Building a Comp

Now that you have your sources, you can add them to your comp, arrange them, and have some fun animating them. First, make sure the Timeline and Composition panels have the name of your comp (**First Animation**) in a tab along their tops. If not, double-click this comp in the Project panel to open it.

Transform Fun

11 Select the footage item **Snowstorm Title.tif** in your **Sources** folder in the Project panel, and drag it over to the image area of the Composition panel. While keeping the mouse button down, drag it near the center of the comp: You will notice After Effects tries to snap it into the center for you. With the mouse button still down, drag near the four corners of the comp: After Effects will try to snap the outline of the source against these corners.

Place it in the center, and release the mouse. It will be drawn in the comp's image area, and appear as a layer in the Timeline panel as well. (To get this snapping behavior when you try to drag an already-added layer in the future, press the ⌘ Shift (Ctrl Shift) keys after you start dragging a layer.)

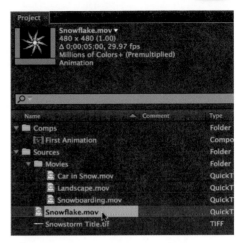

After importing your sources, select a source to see its thumbnail and details above. You can expand the Project panel wider to see details about each source, such as Type, Size, Media Duration, and File Path.

11 When you first drag a footage source into the Comp panel, it will helpfully try to snap to the center or corner of the comp's image area. (From then on, the layer will behave normally, with no snapping behavior.) The layer will appear in the Comp and Timeline panels.

By the way, we have dragged the Timeline panel's A/V Features column (circled in red) from its default position over to the right, to be near the timeline. You can do the same by dragging the column header to the right until it drops into place.

12 Pick white for this composition's background color.

13 To "scrub" a value in the Timeline panel, place the cursor over the value until a two-headed arrow appears, click, and drag. Scale has its X and Y dimensions locked together, so scrubbing one value also changes the other.

14 Highlight a layer, then use the Selection tool to interactively scale a layer by dragging its corners in the Comp panel. The values in the Timeline panel will update while you drag. It is easy to accidentally distort the "aspect ratio" of a layer while doing so (as we are here); add **Shift** while dragging to constrain a layer's proportions.

12 The Comp's Background Color defaulted to black. Let's change that so you can see the drop shadow effect that is applied to the title:

Select the menu item Composition > Composition Settings, then click on the Background Color swatch; the standard Adobe Color Picker will appear. Drag inside the color field to select white. Click OK, and OK again in the Composition Settings dialog to accept your changes. The text and its shadow should now be easily readable against the white background color.

13 In the Timeline panel, click on the arrow to the left of **Snowstorm Title.tif**: This will reveal the word Transform. Click on the arrow to the left of Transform; this will reveal all of the Transform properties for this layer. In the future, we will refer to clicking these arrows as "twirl down" (and "twirl up" when closing a section).

Notice the numeric values next to each property: Place your cursor over one, then click and drag while watching the Comp panel to see the effect of editing these properties. This technique is referred to as *scrubbing* a value, and is a skill you'll use over and over in After Effects.

You can also type an exact value by clicking a value, which makes that field active. Press **Tab** to advance to the next value, and press **Return** when done.

Some properties – such as Scale and Position – have separate X (horizontal, or left-right) and Y (vertical, or up-down) dimensions to their values. By default, Scale's X and Y dimensions are locked together to prevent distorting the layer; you can unlock them by clicking on the chain link icon next to their value.

14 After you've experimented with scrubbing, click on the word Reset to the right of the Transform header to return these values to their defaults. Next you're going to play with directly manipulating the layer in the Comp panel to edit its Transform properties. While doing so, keep an eye on the values in the Timeline panel to get a better feel for what's going on.

• To edit Position, directly click on and drag a layer in the Composition panel. To constrain movement to one dimension, start to drag the layer, *then* hold down the **Shift** key and drag some more.

• With the layer still selected, edit Scale by clicking and dragging one of the eight square dots ("handles") around the outline of the layer in the Comp panel. To avoid distorting the layer and keep its original aspect ratio, start to drag the layer, *then* hold down the **Shift** key and drag some more.

• To edit Rotation, press **W** to select the Rotate tool (known affectionately to some as "Wotate"), click on the layer, and drag around in circles. Add the **Shift** key to constrain movement to 45° increments. When you're done, press **V** to return to the Selection tool (↖).

As before, click on the word Reset next to Transform to return these values to their defaults.

Animating Position

Now you know how to transform a layer manually; next comes making After Effects transform a layer for you over time. This involves a process known as keyframing.

15 There are keyboard shortcuts to reveal select Transform properties. With **Snowstorm Title.tif** still selected, type **P** to reveal just its Position property.

You're going to make this layer move onto the screen from below and settle into place. Drag the title totally out of sight and onto the pasteboard just below the Comp panel. Then make sure the current time indicator is at the start of the timeline (the numeric time display in the Timeline panel should read 0;00;00;00). If it isn't, grab the yellow head of the current time indicator and drag it there, or press **Home** to quickly make it jump to the start.

To the left of the word Position is a small stop-watch icon. Click on it, and it will now be outlined and highlighted. You have now enabled Position for keyframing and animation. [The

shortcut to toggle on and off the Position stopwatch for a selected layer(s) is **⌥ Shift P** (**Alt Shift P**).] Enabling keyframing also places a keyframe – indicated by a yellow diamond to the right in the timeline portion of the display – at the current time, using Position's current value.

16 Drag the current time indicator to 01:10 in the timeline. Pick up and drag the **Snowstorm Title.tif** layer where you want it to end up. (We used a Position value of X = 320, Y = 360.) A new keyframe will automatically be created for you with this value, at the current time.

You may have noticed that a line appeared in the Comp panel, tracing the path from where your layer started to where it is ending up. This is known as the *motion path*. It is made up of a series of dots. Each dot indicates where that layer will be at each frame in your timeline. The motion path is visible only when the layer is selected.

Drag the current time indicator back and forth along the top of the timeline, and notice how your layer moves along its motion path. To see what it would look like playing back in real time, press **0** on the numeric keypad to initiate a RAM Preview, or press the RAM Preview button at the right side of the Preview panel. After Effects will work its way through the frames once as fast as it can, then play back the animation in real time. Press any key to stop the preview.

▼ Transform Shortcuts

The following shortcut keys reveal specific Transform properties for the selected layer(s):

A Anchor Point

P Position

S Scale

R Rotation

T OpaciTy

To add a property to those already being displayed, hold down **Shift** when you press these shortcuts.

15 In the Timeline panel, click on the stopwatch icon next to the word Position to enable keyframing for it; this also creates the first keyframe (the yellow diamond).

16 Move to a different time, and drag the layer to a new position; a motion path will appear in the Comp panel illustrating its travels (above). Click RAM Preview (below).

17 It is easy to change the timing of keyframes: In the Timeline panel, drag the second diamond keyframe to the left or right to make it occur earlier or later in time. RAM Preview to see the new timing, then return the keyframe to 01:10.

18 Under the A/V Features column are a pair of keyframe navigation arrows, which make it easy to jump to the previous or next keyframe for a given property. If the diamond between them is yellow, the current time indicator is parked on top of a keyframe.

18 You can also easily edit the value of a keyframe after you've created it. In the A/V Features column of the Timeline panel are a pair of gray arrows surrounding a small diamond. These are known as the *keyframe navigation* arrows. Clicking on them will jump to the next keyframe in line for that property, confirmed by the diamond changing from hollow to yellow. Once you're "parked" on a keyframe, to edit that keyframe either scrub the layer's Position values, or drag the layer around in the Comp panel.

If you don't jump to the exact time of a previously existing keyframe, you will instead create a new keyframe. If you create one by accident, you can delete it by selecting it in the timeline and pressing **Delete**. Or, use the keyframe navigation arrows to jump to it, then click on the yellow diamond between the arrows to remove it.

Save your project. Indeed, now would be a good time to use the File > Increment and Save option, so your work to date will be saved under a new version number.

▽ tip

Multiple Undos

By default, you have 32 levels of Undo in After Effects. If that's not enough, you can set it as high as 99 in Preferences > General.

Adding a Background Layer

19 To add interest, let's bring in our background layer. In the Project panel, open the **Sources > Movies** folder, select **Landscape.mov**, and drag it to the left side of the Timeline panel so it sits below the title layer. It should fill the Comp panel. RAM Preview to see how it looks.

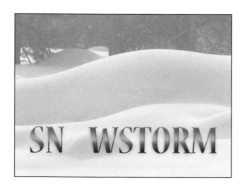

19–20 Add **Landscape.mov** as a background and reduce its Opacity (right) so that it appears "ghosted" (above).

20 Note that because the background color is white, if you make the background movie semitransparent, it will appear more pale and "ghosted." With **Landscape.mov** selected, press **T** to twirl down Opacity property, and scrub its value to taste.

Adding a Middle Layer

The Snowstorm title has a missing "o" that will be filled in by adding an animated snowflake icon (yes, we desperately needed something for you to animate along a curve…). First, let's learn a few more tricks for adding footage to a comp:

21 In your **Sources** folder in the Project panel, select the footage item **Snowflake.mov**:

• Drag **Snowflake.mov** down to the *left side* of the Timeline panel, near the names of your other layers. Hover your cursor above your existing layers, and you will see a thick black horizontal line, which indicates you're about to place it above these layers. Drag it downward until this line appears *between* both layers and release the mouse. The new layer will appear as Layer 2, behind the title and in front of the background movie. Note that no matter where the current time indicator was parked, the new layer starts at the beginning of the comp (00:00).

• Press ⌘ Z (Ctrl Z) to Undo this addition, and try another method. This time, drag **Snowflake.mov** to the *right side* of the Timeline panel until your cursor is hovering over the timeline area. You should see a second yellow time indicator head appear. This indicates where it would start *in time* if you were to release your mouse now, and provides an interactive way to decide your initial starting time. You can also move it up and down in the layer stack with this method. Pick some location in the middle of the timeline, and in the middle of the two layers, and release the mouse. The new layer will be added at the time you've picked. (If the snowflake is not visible, check if it ended up below the background movie; if so, drag it up one layer so it is Layer 2.)

22 Drag the current time indicator back and forth, and notice how the snowflake symbol does not appear in the Comp viewer until after the current time indicator crosses the start of the layer in the timeline. You can click and drag the middle of the layer bar for **Snowflake.mov** to make it start sooner or later in time; for now, avoid dragging the ends of the layer bar, which trims the layer. (Moving and trimming layers is covered in more detail in Lesson 3.)

Finally, with **Snowflake.mov** still selected, press ⌥ Home (Alt Home) to make it start at the beginning of the comp and let's animate it into position.

▽ factoid

Comp versus Timeline

When you add a layer to a comp by dragging it to the Timeline panel, the layer will be automatically centered in the Comp panel. When you add a layer to the Comp panel, the default is to start the layer at 00:00 (set by Preferences > General > Create Layers at Composition Start Time). Toggle this off to add layers starting at the current time.

21 When you drag a new source from the Project panel to the Timeline panel, you can decide when and where to drop it in the layer stack. Notice the ghosted outline and second current time indicator before we let go of the mouse (top), and how it corresponds to the layer's placement after we let go (above).

▽ tip

Quick Location

To make a layer start where the current time indicator is, select it and press [(left square bracket).

▽ future vision

Drawing a Path

In the next lesson, we will demonstrate the Motion Sketch Keyframe Assistant, which gives you a fun, interactive way to create a motion path.

23 Place **Snowflake.mov** where the missing "O" should be in **Snowstorm Title.tif**, then scale it down to fit.

Crafting a Motion Path

Right now, the snowflake movie is dominating the center of your composition. The plan is to have it fly across across the screen and land in place of the missing "O" in the Snowstorm title.

23 Let's allow the title to settle into place at 01:10 and then have the snowflake drop into position 10 frames later at 1:20. To move to an exact point in time, you can click the timecode readout in the Comp or Timeline panels, enter "120" and press Return.

• Next, click on the snowflake in the Composition panel, and drag it into place where the missing "O" should be. You can use the cursor keys to nudge it into place.

• Then drag one of the layer handles (the eight boxes around its edges) for **Snowflake.mov** to scale it down to a good size that will fit in with the rest of the title. Hold down the Shift key *after* you start dragging one of these handles to force the layer to keep its original aspect ratio; otherwise, the snowflake will be distorted. We used a Scale value of 23% but feel free to size it to taste.

24 With **Snowflake.mov** still selected, press P to reveal its Position, then click on its animation stopwatch to enable keyframing (just as you did for the **Snowstorm Title.tif** layer back in step 15). This will create a Position keyframe at 01:20 with the current value.

Move the current time indicator to the start of the composition (00:00 in time); the shortcut is to press Home. Drag the snowflake to the upper right corner of the comp. A new Position keyframe will be created at this time, and you will see a straight motion path line join the two keyframes in the Comp panel. Again, the dots along this line indicate the layer's position at each frame in time; the spacing between these dots indicates how fast it is moving. RAM Preview to get a feel for the straight motion path.

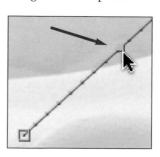

24 After creating two Position keyframes, tug on the Auto Bezier handles (right) to create a motion path that arcs across the comp (left). If you can't find these dots, you can also hold down ⌘ ⌥ (Ctrl Alt) and drag in the Comp panel from the (square) keyframe icon outward to create visible handles.

If you look closely, you will see two slightly larger dots along the motion path line, close to each keyframe icon. Motion path keyframes default to an interpolation type known as Auto Bezier, which automatically tries to smooth the path. These dots are the interpolation handles for those keyframes. Pull them toward the upper left corner of the comp to cause the snowflake's path to arc across the screen. If you cannot see these handles, hold down ⌘ ⌥ (*Ctrl* *Alt*) and drag in the Comp panel from the (square) keyframe icon outward to create visible handles. If you accidentally drag the background layer instead, Edit > Undo, reselect **Snowflake.mov**, and try again. RAM Preview again.

25 To make the flight path even more interesting, move the current time indicator to 00:25 (between both keyframes), and drag the snowflake to a new position. A new Position keyframe will be created automatically, and the motion path will bend to connect your three spatial keyframes. Tug on the Bezier handles protruding from the keyframes to create a more interesting motion path. RAM Preview, and save your project.

25 Add a third keyframe and play with the motion path's Bezier handles to create a more involved flight path.

If you noticed a speed shift in the snowflake's flight, this is because it is traveling farther between one pair of keyframes than between the other pair. You can confirm this by looking at the spacing of the dots along its motion path: Different spacing means different speeds. Slide the middle Position keyframe in the timeline until the dot spacing is more balanced. (In the next lesson you'll learn how to precisely edit a layer's speed.)

▼ Spatial Keyframe Types

The Position keyframes in the Comp viewer are referred to as spatial keyframes, as they define where the layer is supposed to be in space at a given time. How the motion path flows into and out of a spatial keyframe is also important, and can be deciphered both by looking at the path itself, and by looking at a selected spatial keyframe:

• The default spatial keyframe type is Auto Bezier. It is indicated by two dots in a straight line on either side of the keyframe (A). This means After Effects will automatically create a smooth bend through this keyframe.

• Dragging one of these dots results in the keyframe being converted into a Continuous Bezier type, indicated by the straight line ("handle") that connects the dots (B). Drag these handles to explicitly control the motion path.

• If you want to create a sudden change in direction at the keyframe, hold down **G** (to temporarily toggle to the Pen tool) and drag one of the handles to "break" their continuous nature. You can then drag the handles of this Bezier keyframe independently (C).

• To create a hard corner without a curve or handles, hold down **G** and click the keyframe's vertex itself to convert it to a Linear keyframe (D).

• To return a Linear keyframe to an Auto Bezier keyframe, hold down **G** and click on the keyframe again.

Press **V** if you need to return to the Selection tool.

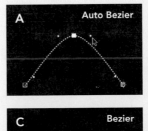

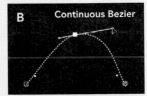

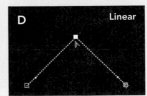

Animating Opacity, Scale, and Rotation

Having a layer "fly into position" rarely involves just Position keyframes; you can also animate its Scale parameter to make it appear to fly toward or away from you, and its Opacity parameter to have it fade up or down.

26 You have already created a good ending pose for the snowflake that works nicely in relation to the rest of the Snowstorm title. Therefore, first you will want to create keyframes to remember this pose:

• Move the current time indicator to 01:20 to align with the final Position keyframe for **Snowflake.mov**. You can press the **Shift** key as you drag to "snap" to existing keyframes, or use the keyframe navigator arrows to jump to the next or previous keyframes.

26 To remember your ending pose, create keyframes for Scale and Opacity aligned in time with your final Position keyframe.

• Select **Snowflake.mov**. Its Position parameter should already be revealed. To reveal additional properties, hold down the **Shift** key, then press **S** for Scale and **T** for Opacity.

• Click on the animation stopwatch for Scale and Opacity to enable keyframing for these parameters. This creates keyframes with their current values at the current time (01:20).

27 Move the current time indicator to 00:00 (shortcut: **Home**), when the snowflake's flight begins. Scrub **Snowflake.mov**'s Scale parameter in the Timeline panel while watching the result in the Comp panel and pick a nice starting size. It can be larger or smaller than its final Scale value, depending on the visual effect you want. One thing to keep in mind is that with most layers,

▽ tip

Slow Scrubbing

To scrub a value by smaller increments for precise control, hold down the ⌘ (**Ctrl**) key while scrubbing. To jump by larger increments, hold down **Shift** while scrubbing.

> **▼ Nudging Position, Rotation, and Scale**
>
> Sometimes it's easier to use the keyboard to nudge the transform values for a layer. Here are the magic keys:
>
> Position: cursor keys ⬆ ➡ ⬅ ⬇
>
> Rotation: numeric keypad's ➕ and ➖
>
> Scale: ⌥ (**Ctrl**) plus numeric keypad's ➕ and ➖
>
> If you hold down the **Shift** key while doing any of these, the transform values will jump in increments of 10 rather than 1.

27–28 Animate the snowflake's Scale and Opacity values to cause it to fade up and fly down as it moves into position. Note that you can edit values numerically in the Timeline panel (top).

it is a bad idea to increase Scale past 100%, as this may result in softening of the image plus other visual artifacts.

You may also enter keyframe values numerically. Click on the Scale value in the timeline, which will highlight it. Type in your new value and press **Enter** or **Return**. You can also double-click a keyframe, which will open a dialog where you can enter your desired value. The advantage of double-clicking a keyframe is that you can edit it without having to first align the current time indicator with the desired keyframe.

28 To have the snowflake fade on, you need to reduce its initial Opacity value. With the time indicator still at 00:00, scrub **Snowflake.mov**'s Opacity value to the left to reduce its opacity. A value of 0% means fully transparent. You can also directly enter a number such as 0. RAM Preview to test your animation.

29 If you want to add more complexity to your animation, you can animate its Rotation property as well:

• Place the time indicator at 01:20.

• To work faster, hold **⌥** (**Alt**) and press **R**: This will reveal the Rotation parameter, plus enable keyframing for Rotation.

• Press **Home** to move the time indicator to 00:00.

• Enter a new initial Rotation value, such as –90°.

RAM Preview to test your new animation, and tweak the parameters to taste. When satisfied, File > Increment and Save to save a new project file.

▽ try it

Smooth Moves

By default, After Effects creates linear keyframes in the timeline. These result in sudden starts and stops. Keyframe interpolation and velocity are covered in the next lesson. But until then, to add a more elegant touch, you can select a starting or ending keyframe and press **F9** to apply the Easy Ease Keyframe Assistant, which will create smooth starts and stops.

(Mac users will have to change Exposé in System Preferences to free up the shortcuts **F9** – **F12**.)

31 Drag the Snowboarding movie to the top left side of the comp and scale it so that it makes a nice inset movie.

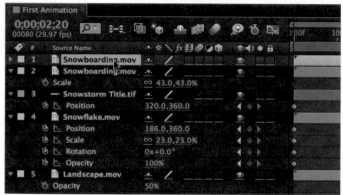

32–33 Duplicate the video layer you added (above), then move the copy to the right to create a balanced arrangement (below).

Arranging and Replacing Layers

In the next few steps, you will learn a few strategies for working with multiple layers in a composition.

30 Move the time indicator to a point after the title and snowflake have settled into position so you can use their placement for reference.

31 Return to the Project panel, and make sure the folder **Sources > Movies** is twirled open. Select **Snowboarding.mov** and drag it into the Composition panel to a position between the title and the top of the comp, offset to the left (you will eventually be placing another video to the right). Release the mouse, and this layer will be added to your timeline starting at 00:00.

Press **S** to reveal the layer's Scale parameter and reduce it in size until it acts as a nice inset above the title. Feel free to tweak its placement, but leave some space along the top of the comp for another graphical element you will be adding later.

32 With **Snowboarding.mov** selected, choose Edit > Duplicate. This will create a copy of the original layer with the exact same transform parameter values (including Position and Scale). The duplicate layer will be selected.

33 Move the duplicated layer to the right to create a second video inset. You can drag it in the Composition panel, adding **Shift** after you start to drag to constrain your movements to a straight line. Or, scrub its X Position value in the Timeline panel to constrain movement to a straight line left and right. You can also use the left and right cursor keys (**←** and **→**) to nudge its position one pixel at a time (add the **Shift** key to nudge in 10-pixel increments).

34 It is easy to replace a selected layer with a new footage source while maintaining any changes you've made to its position, scale, and so on. So let's replace the duplicated layer with a new source. With the target layer selected in the composition (in this case, the rightmost movie), return to the Project panel and select **Sources > Movies > Car in Snow.mov**. Hold down **⌥** (**Alt**) and drag this new movie over either the Comp or Timeline panel; the exact place-

34–35 Swap in a new footage source for the duplicated layer, and scale them together in the Timeline panel. We settled on a size of 40% for both movies.

ment does not matter. Release the mouse, and the target layer's source will be replaced with this new source.

35 Once both movies are side by side, you might decide that they are too big or too small. With **Car in Snow.mov** selected, *Shift*+click on **Snowboarding.mov** to select it as well. Scrub the already-exposed Scale value for **Snowboarding.mov**, and **Car in Snow.mov** will be rescaled in tandem. Add the ⌘ (*Ctrl*) key to scrub in finer increments. Feel free to also tweak the position of both layers to get a nice arrangement, but keep them aligned vertically.

▼ More Precise Placement

If you want to move beyond "eyeballing it" to arrange your layers, After Effects has a few tools you might find useful:

- Right-click on the Position value for a layer, and select Edit Value. In the Position dialog that opens, you can set the Units popup to % of Composition. This simplifies the math when insetting layers a certain distance from the comp's top left-hand corner, rather than calculating it in pixels.

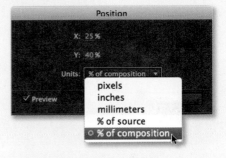

- Select the layer(s) you wish to align, then open Window > Align. You can align selected layers to each other or to the sides of the comp, or distribute layers evenly across the comp.

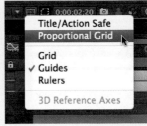

- Click on the Choose Grid and Guide Options button along the bottom of the Comp panel (above) and enable Proportional Grid for a handy visual reference. The spacing of the grid may be modified in Preferences > Grids & Guides.

- There are also rulers and user-definable guides. Rulers display the X and Y coordinates of a comp in pixels. They can be toggled on by selecting Rulers from the Choose Grid menu (above) or by selecting View > Show Rulers. To create a guide, click in the ruler area and drag into the Comp panel. The Info panel will tell you its exact coordinates. Layers will snap to guides if View > Snap to Guides is on. Hide or show guides using View > Show Guides. Drag guides back to the ruler to delete them.

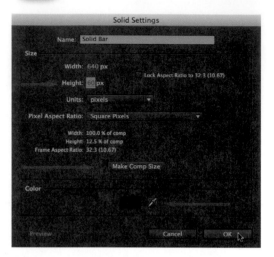

36 Create a solid bar that is the width of the comp and 60 px high, and choose a red color to complement the red in the inset videos.

38 Reduce the Opacity for **Solid Bar** to create a tint across the top of your comp.

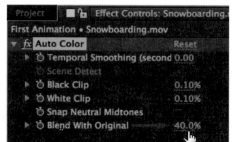

39 Applying the Auto Color effect immediately removes the bluish cast (left).
For a less drastic result, adjust Blend With Original in the Effect Controls Panel (right).

Solid Design

Footage items are not the only objects that can be layers in a comp. For example, After Effects can create *solids*, which are simple graphical elements of a solid color. Let's use a solid to add a colored bar across the top of our composition:

36 Choose the menu item Layer > New > Solid. To create a full-width bar, click on the Make Comp Size button; this will create a solid that fills the entire comp. Then enter a smaller value for Height, such as "**60**".

Next, click on the eyedropper next to the color swatch along the bottom of the dialog, then click on the red color from the car's taillights or the snowboarder's jacket to visually relate the bar to the video. Give this solid a name that makes sense – such as "**Solid Bar**" – and click OK.

37 In the Comp panel, drag the bar upward. When you get close to the top of the composition, hold down ⌘ Shift (Ctrl Shift) and the layer will "snap" to the top of the comp. After placing **Solid Bar**, you may want to tweak the position of the inset videos to get a better overall balance. To further edit the solid's color or size, select it and go Layer > Solid Settings.

38 Press **T** to reveal **Solid Bar**'s Opacity. Reduce it until it just provides a nice tint across the top of the composition, allowing part of the background video to peek through.

Quick Effects

Time for a little instant gratification: Add some polish to your composition using *effects*. We'll focus on some quick improvements to the look of the video inset layers (effects will be covered in more detail in Lesson 3):

39 The snowboarding video has a pronounced bluish cast. To make it more neutral, select **Snowboarding.mov** and apply Effect > Color Correction > Auto Color. The clouds and snow will now be a more natural white color.

When you apply an effect, the Effect Controls panel immediately opens. Here is where you can edit the effect's parameters. In this example, increase Blend With Original to bring back a touch of the bluish cast.

40 Now add some dimension. With **Snowboarding.mov** still selected, apply Effect > Perspective > Bevel Alpha. In the Effect Controls panel, scrub Edge Thickness for Bevel Alpha until you get a nice frame around the video.

41 Apply Effect > Perspective > Drop Shadow. In the Effect Controls panel, increase Distance and Softness for the Drop Shadow effect to achieve a pleasing result.

42 Now that you have a treatment you like for one video inset, it is easy to apply the same treatment to the other video. Click inside the Effect Controls panel to bring it forward, and choose Edit > Select All followed by Edit > Copy.

40–41 Add Auto Color, Bevel Alpha, and Drop Shadow effects to **Snowboarding.mov**.

Then select **Car in Snow.mov**, and choose Edit > Paste. This second video will now have the same effects and settings as you applied to the first. After you have copied and pasted effects, you can continue to tweak them individually. For example, select **Car in Snow.mov** to ensure that its Effect Controls panel is forward, and increase Auto Color > Blend With Original until both videos have approximately the same overall tint.

43 RAM Preview your composition: We've been focusing so much on treating the inset videos, we ignored the fact that they now obscure the snowflake for part of its flight path! That's easy to fix; you just have to reorder some of the layers in the Timeline panel. Select **Car in Snow.mov**, then Shift+click on **Snowboarding.mov** so that both are selected. Drag them downward in the Timeline panel's layer stack until they appear between **Snowflake.mov** and **Landscape.mov**.

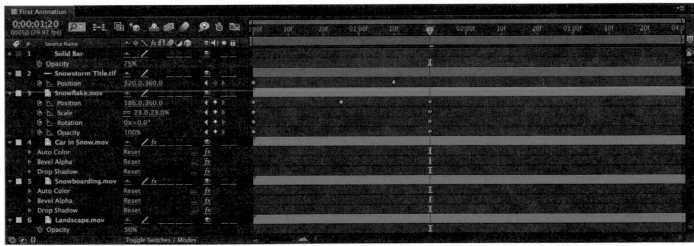

43 The final project, with effects duplicated for the two inset videos.

Rendering

Time for the final payoff: rendering your animation to a movie file. Save your project first; it's always a good idea to save your file before you render, just in case the render crashes or your computer loses power.

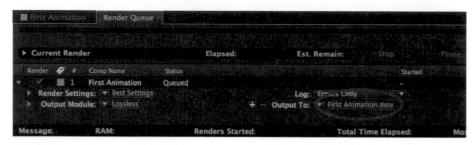

44 Make sure the **First Animation** Composition or Timeline panel is selected (not the Project panel). Select Composition > Add to Render Queue. This will open the Render Queue panel. By default, it will appear in the same frame as the Timeline panel. If you have a cramped screen, you may need to drag this frame larger to see your comp's full entry in the queue.

45 To choose where to save and what to name your render, in the Render Queue panel click on the name to the right of Output To. (The default filename will be the same as the comp's name thanks to the Preferences > Output > Use Default File Name and Folder option.)

45 The default Render Settings and Output Module are fine for our first effort (we'll show how to modify them in the Appendix).

Click on the name to the right of Output To. This will open up a standard file dialog. Pick a place on your drive where it will be easy to retrieve the movie later. The default movie name is the same as the comp's name; you can change it at this stage if you like. Click Save.

46 The Render Queue keeps you apprised of what frame it is working on, and how much longer it thinks the render will take. If the composition being rendered is open and the Comp panel is visible, you can watch the frames while they're rendering.

46 Click on the Render button, or press [Return]. Your composition will start to render. The Render Queue panel will tell you what frame it is currently working on, and when it thinks it will finish. If the Comp panel is visible, you will get visual feedback of what each frame looks like after it is rendered.

47 When the render is done, twirl down the Output Module section in the Render Queue and click on the file path to reveal the movie on your hard drive. Double-click it to open it in QuickTime Player and play back your work. Nice job! If you'd like to compare your results, our project **Lesson_01_Finished.aep** is included inside the **Comps_Finished** folder.

You may think you're done at this point…but in reality, motion graphics jobs are rarely done at the first render. This is the stage where you will analyze your work, decide how to improve it, make changes, and render another version. Indeed, we will end this lesson by giving you a series of ideas to try out.

▼ RAM Preview Options

You will become used to regularly pressing
0 on the numeric keypad to initiate a RAM
Preview (Mac laptop users can also press
Ctrl + **0**). By default, this calculates every
frame of your work area (detailed to the
right), stores it in a RAM cache (designated
by the green bar over your timeline), then
plays back your work area in real time.

To render your current RAM Preview
to disk, select Composition > Save RAM
Preview. (To edit the settings for the RAM
Preview output module, select Edit >
Template > Output Module.)

There are also a few variations on RAM
Previews that you may want to explore:

Shift+RAM Preview

When you have a particularly slow-to-calculate
("render intensive") composition, you can
reduce the time you have to wait for a RAM
Preview to calculate by holding **Shift** when
you press **0**. By default, this calculates and
plays back every other frame.

If you want to play back fewer frames, open
the Preview panel, select Shift+RAM Preview
Options (shown below), and change the
Skip value. This determines how many frames
are skipped in-between the ones that are
calculated. You can change Skip for normal
previews as well, but we recommend against
it; it's good to have one option that plays
every frame.

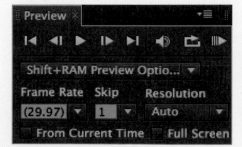

▼ The Work Area

The gray bar just above the layer bars in the timeline defines the length of the current
work area. RAM Previews – and in some cases, renders and Keyframe Assistants
(introduced in Lesson 2) – are restricted to the duration of this bar. You can grab and
move the start and end of the work area, as well as slide the bar along the timeline.
Right-click on the bar itself for more options, including Trim Comp to Work Area.
The keyboard shortcuts are worth learning too:

- **B** sets the beginning of the work area to the current time.
- **N** sets the end of the work area to the current time.
- Double-clicking the bar returns the work area to the full length of the comp.

Option (Alt) + RAM Preview

There may be occasions when you need
to preview only a small number of frames
before the current time – perhaps to check
the details when masking (Lesson 4), keying
(Lesson 9), or painting (Lesson 10). Rather
than having to set and move a small work
area, as of version CS5 you may press **⌥**
(**Alt**) before pressing **0** to preview just a
handful of frames leading up to and including
the current time. The number of frames is
set in Preferences > Alternate RAM Preview
(see figure below); it defaults to 5.

Cache Work Area in Background

Waiting for a render-intensive composition
to RAM Preview can be akin to watching
paint dry. After Effects CS6 added the menu
command Composition > Cache Work Area
in Background. You can use this command
to start calculating frames, then switch to
a different composition inside the same
project and continue work. The Info panel
will update you periodically with its progress.
The keyboard shortcut to initiate this
preview is **⌘** + **Return** (**Ctrl** + **Return**).
As with the regular RAM Preview function,
only the work area is calculated.

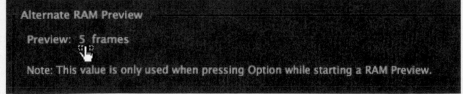

Caches and Memory

When you RAM Preview a composition, After Effects is saving to RAM far more than just the final composited image – it is also storing the contributions of individual layers. Changing one of these layers will make the green RAM cache bar disappear – as the final composite needs to be re-created – but the next RAM Preview will often go faster as the other layers have already been rendered.

Green bars are cached in RAM; blue bars are cached on the disk. Disk cached frames are copied back into RAM as needed for playback. (Note that this comp is from Lesson 8; 3D layers are slower to render and therefore more likely to be cached to disk.)

Previous to After Effects CS6, whenever you made a change that caused the RAM cache to no longer be accurate, those frames were lost forever. Now After Effects will keep those discarded frames in available memory. If a composition returns to a previously cached condition – for example, if you performed a RAM Preview, edited a parameter, didn't like your edit, then used Undo to return to that previous condition – the green cache bar will reappear as well, and you can RAM Preview again without delay.

When After Effects has to discard frames from its RAM cache, it calculates whether it would take longer to rerender them or to retrieve them from disk. If the render time is significant, After Effects will copy those frames from RAM to a disk cache. This cache is set up in Preferences > Media & Disk Cache. A blue bar in the timeline represents frames that exist on disk; when you initiate a RAM Preview for a composition in this state, the disk-cached frames are copied back into the RAM cache before playback (unlike nonlinear editing systems, After Effects does not play back from disk).

Previous to After Effects CS6, when you closed a project, both the RAM and disk caches were erased. Now After Effects makes the same determination of how long it took to render RAM cache frames and

The Disk Cache is set up in Preferences > Media & Disk Cache. Assign it to the fastest drive you have connected.

copies the slower frames to disk. The disk cache is also now preserved between sessions. When you reopen the same project later, any saved frames corresponding to this project will appear as blue bars in the timeline, meaning RAM Previews of previously previewed material are much faster.

▼ Backgrounds, Solids, and Transparency

The Background Color is not really a layer in your composition. You can see it in the image area, and if you render to a file format that does not have an alpha channel (such as a DV movie or sequence of JPEG stills), it will appear – but inside After Effects, it's actually transparent. This means if you placed (or *nested*) this comp into another comp, or if you rendered to a file format that also included an alpha channel, the background color would disappear. If you want to fill in the background of your comp with a color that will always be there, use a solid (Layer > New > Solid) instead.

When you view the RGB channels of your comp, the Background Color is evident; we used a white background in this project to blend with the layer **Landscape.mov**. However, if you were to view the alpha channel of the comp (right), you would see that it is actually transparent, represented by the gray areas in the image (black = transparent, white = fully opaque, and gray means the underlying RGB pixels are partially transparent). You can use the Show Channel popup along the bottom of the Comp panel to switch between these views.

The Toggle Transparency Grid button (the checkerboard icon) is another way to check transparency in a comp.

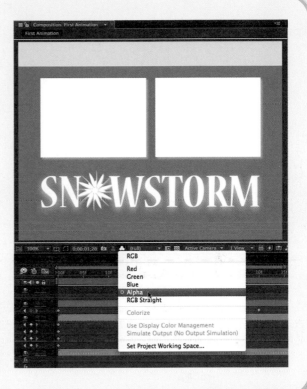

Idea Corner

In addition to teaching you After Effects, the goal of this book is also to teach you the art of motion graphics – which includes creative thinking and being able to craft variations on a theme. We even include some "Try This" tips sprinkled throughout the lessons. Below are some ideas to try for this lesson:

• Make the snowflake land at the same time as the title reaches its final position. You can do this by sliding its second keyframe later in time. Or keep the same tempo by sliding the snowstorm layer 10 frames later in time instead. (Timing of layers and keyframes is discussed in more detail in the following two lessons.)

• Animate the solid bar onto (or off!) the screen.

• Animate the video insets to appear in a more interesting fashion, such as by fading or scaling up. Stagger their timing by sliding their layer bars in time.

You've learned quite a bit in this lesson – skills you will use in virtually every After Effects project you tackle. In the next lesson, we'll show you several ways to fine-tune your animations.

▽ tip

Solid Tips

When you create a solid, After Effects automatically creates a **Solids** folder in the Project panel. Solids may be reused in a project, just like other footage items. When you duplicate a solid in a comp, it will use the same source. If you edit one of these layers, a switch at the bottom of the Solid Settings dialog will ask if you want to update all solids that use this source or create a new solid.

▼ Importing Layered Photoshop and Illustrator Files

In this lesson, you learned how to build a composition from scratch in After Effects by importing sources, dragging them into a comp, arranging them to taste, and animating them. Indeed, this is our preferred way of working.

However, some of you may be more familiar working in Photoshop or Illustrator, and may want to start your project there. Perhaps you work for a company with a separate print department where they want to hand you their Photoshop or Illustrator files to animate. After Effects also accommodates this type of workflow.

After Effects can import Photoshop and Illustrator files several different ways: flattened into a single image, selecting just a single layer to bring in, or as a composition where all of the layers exist as their own footage items which you can then animate. Let's try all three options in that order:

1 Create a File > New > New Project. Double-click the Project panel or type ⌘ *I* (*Ctrl* *I*) to import a file. Navigate to the **Lesson 01** folder you copied from this book's disc, open it, then open the **01_Sources** folder inside that. Locate the file named **Butterfly Arrangement.psd** and select it.

Turn your attention to the bottom of this dialog, and click on the Import As popup. Here you see options of whether to treat this file as a single source or as a composition. These options are presented again later, so the best choice here is to just accept the default (Footage) and click Open.

2 A second import dialog will open. The top popup – Import Kind – is similar to the Import As dialog; for this first exercise, make sure it says Footage as well. Then look under Layer Options: You have a choice of whether to bring

in the entire layered file merged into a final image, or to choose just a single layer. For now, choose Merged Layers, and click OK.

3 A single footage item will be added to your project. Select it, and choose File > New Comp From Selection (you can also drag it to the Create a New Composition button at the bottom of the Project panel). After Effects will create and open a comp that is the same size

2–3 You can import a layered file as a single footage item (and either merge all the layers, or select a single layer), or a composition (includes all layers). If you choose to import as Footage (left), you will get a single layer in After Effects (above).

as your file, flattened to a full-frame single layer without access to the individual elements.

4 Repeat step 1, but this time in step 2 select Choose Layer under the Layer Options in the second dialog. Pick a layer from this popup, such as **Butterfly**. Underneath it, the Footage Dimensions popup will become active. If you select Document Size, After Effects will create a footage item the size of the entire layered file, with this one layer placed where it was in the original file.

We prefer the option Layer Size, which auto-trims the layer to just the pixels needed. Select it, and click OK.

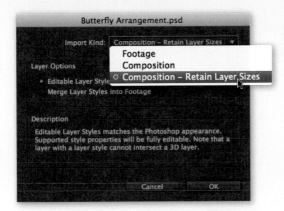

6 For maximum flexibility, set Import Kind to Composition – Retain Layer Sizes. For Photoshop files, enable the options for Editable Layer Styles. (*Note: Versions CS5 and CS5.5 include an additional checkbox for importing Live Photoshop 3D; this feature is not included in CS6.*)

5 Notice that just the butterfly appeared as a footage item in the Project panel. Drag it into the comp you created in the previous step. You can move this single element freely around your comp.

6 Delete what you've imported so far in this exercise. Repeat step 1 again, but this time in step 2 select Composition – Retain Layer Sizes from the Import Kind dialog. To extract the most from a layered Photoshop file, select Editable Layer Styles under Layer Options. Click OK. Note that Illustrator files have similar choices with the exception of Layer Styles. (We will explore Layer Styles in Lesson 3.)

7 You will now have two new items in the Project panel: a comp and a folder, both named **Butterfly Arrangement**. Double-click the comp to open it; you will see a stack of layers representing the individual layers in the Photoshop file. Back in the Project panel, double-click the **Butterfly Arrangement Layers** folder to twirl it open; each layer will be there as a footage item.

If your Photoshop file includes text layers, you can make them editable in After Effects (see Lesson 5); note that Illustrator text is *not* editable. While this feature is very flexible, there are some limitations: The individual layers have already been scaled down, and in some cases treated by effects. We find it more flexible to build things from scratch in After Effects so that layers are fully editable.

7 If you import a layered file as a composition, all of the layers in the original Photoshop file (left) will appear in After Effects as individual elements in the Project panel and arranged in a composition (right). A number of Photoshop features are translated into equivalent features in After Effects, such as Opacity, Blending Modes, Vector Shapes, Layer Styles, Layer Groups, and Editable Text (more on this in Lesson 5).

Advanced Animation

Manipulating keyframes to create more refined animations.

▽ In This Lesson

38 keyframe basics
40 Anchor Point overview
41 Anchor Point tool
42 motion control moves
44 the Graph Editor
45 speed versus value graphs
46 panning and zooming time
47 editing graph curves
48 easing animations
49 editing multiple keyframes
49 Graph Editor Sets
50 Separate Dimensions
54 Motion Sketch
55 smoothing keyframes
56 Auto-Orient
57 Motion Blur
58 Roving keyframes
59 Time-Reverse Keyframes
60 Hold keyframes
62 time display and timecode

▽ Getting Started

Make sure you have copied the **Lesson 02-Advanced Animation** folder from this book's disc onto your hard drive, and make note of where it is; it contains the project file and sources you need to execute this lesson.

In this lesson, you will work through a number of easy exercises to help build your animation skills. Along the way, you will become familiar with managing a layer's Anchor Point for "motion control" and other style movements, taking advantage of Keyframe Assistants, and using the Graph Editor for the utmost in animation control. We'll also show you advanced tricks such as using Motion Sketch to hand-draw your animation path, using roving keyframes to maintain smooth speed changes over complex paths, and the crucial component needed to create "slam down" animations.

Keyframe Basics

When animating in After Effects, the center of your universe is the *keyframe*. Keyframes provide two main functions: They define what a parameter's value is at a specific point in time, and they contain information about how those values behave before and after that point in time.

This behavior is referred to as a keyframe's *interpolation*. It consists of two components: the *velocity*, or how fast a value is changing over time, and the keyframe's *influence*, which defines how abruptly speed changes occur around the keyframe. A keyframe may have both incoming and outgoing velocity and influence. For example, if you are animating position, and a keyframe has an incoming velocity of zero (which means it will come to a stop) with a very high influence, the object would seem to slowly glide into its new position. If its velocity was zero but the influence was very low, the object would instead seem to abruptly stop when it reached that keyframe.

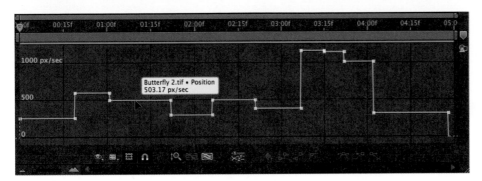

Most keyframes are *temporal*, meaning they describe how values change over time, and these changes can be viewed and edited in the normal Timeline panel or in the Graph Editor (pictured above). However, keyframes that describe changes in position also have a *spatial* component. Remember the motion paths with Bezier handles that you played with in the previous lesson? Those were spatial keyframes. The length and direction of their Bezier handles define the path the layer travels along in space.

After Effects is unusual in that it gives you separate temporal and spatial control over keyframes by default. This is good, because you can split your work into first deciding how an object moves through space, then concentrating on how quickly it moves. Many other programs change the path as you change the speed, which can be more difficult to control (although you can recreate this behavior inside After Effects by using the Separate Dimensions command).

We're going to start this lesson by focusing on the pivot around which all of this animation takes place: the Anchor Point. Most beginning users ignore the Anchor Point, but it's an important piece of the animation puzzle. For example, there are occasions where it is better to animate the Anchor Point than the more familiar Position parameter.

We will then move on to the Graph Editor, where you have very precise control over keyframe interpolation. The Graph editor may seem daunting initially, but you will come to find it's the best way to visualize what is happening with an animation. The skills you learned while editing spatial paths will also come in handy in editing temporal keyframes, as the Graph Editor gives you Bezier handles to edit velocity and influence.

After bending your brain inside the Graph Editor, you can relax a bit as you get the chance to play with a pair of fun Keyframe Assistants, including the ability to hand-sketch a motion path. You'll also learn how to have a layer auto-orient itself to point along its motion path, enable Motion Blur to create smoother movement, and apply Hold keyframes to create abrupt animations. Later lessons also touch on the subject of advanced animation, including Behaviors in Lesson 3, text animation in Lesson 5, and Expressions in Lesson 7.

Spatial keyframes define where a layer is in the composition's space at a given time (right). *Temporal* keyframes (left) numerically define a parameter's value at a given time (the red and green curves), and also show how fast that value changes (the white curve plus the text). Butterfly courtesy Dover. Background courtesy iStockphoto, Goldmund, image #6002397.

▽ tip

Do U See What I See?

A great keyboard shortcut is **U**: It reveals all of the animated properties for the selected layer(s). If you type **U** twice quickly (**U U**), you will see all of the edited properties whether they are animating or not. This is a great way to quickly get an idea of who's doing what.

▽ tip

Reset Property Value

Clicking Reset in the Transform section of the Timeline panel will reset *all* of the Transform properties for a layer to their default values. To reset an individual property, right-click on the name of the property and select Reset.

Anchor Point 101

The Anchor Point is the center of a layer's universe around which it scales, rotates, and moves. Although it defaults to the center of a layer, it may be moved anywhere, including outside the layer's boundaries.

2 Double-click **Flower.ai** to open its Layer panel. Dock the Layer panel with the Project panel so that you can see it, the Comp panel, and the Transform properties in the Timeline panel all at the same time.

3 In the Layer panel, set the View popup to Anchor Point Path. (If View is set to Masks, you can move the Anchor Point but you won't see its motion path if it is animated.)

1 Open **Lesson_02.aep**. In the Project panel, make sure the **Comps** folder is open. Then locate and double-click on the empty comp **01-Anchor Point*starter**.

Back in the Project panel, open the folder **Sources**, and select **Flower.ai**. Use the handy keyboard shortcut ⌘ **/** on Mac (**Ctrl** **/** on Windows) to add it to the center of the current comp. In the Timeline panel, twirl open all of its parameters by pressing ⌘ (**Ctrl**) and clicking on the arrow to the left of the layer's name.

2 Scrub the layer's Rotation parameter: Notice the flower symbol rotates from its center, not its base. Scrub its Scale; again, that's not the behavior we would want, say, to simulate the flower growing. Click Reset in the Timeline panel.

Whenever you add a layer to a comp, think: What should this layer logically rotate or scale around? Here, the answer would be the base of the flower stem.

Double-click **Flower.ai**: It will open in a viewer known as the Layer panel. This allows you to see a layer without distraction from the rest of the layers in your comp. (If you have trouble keeping these two panels straight, look at the top of the panel for the word "Composition:" or "Layer:" before its name. The Layer panel also has its own timeline and a different set of switches.)

Click on the top left corner of the Layer panel and drag the panel to the center of the Project panel to dock it into the same frame. This will place the Layer and Comp panels side by side. Resize the panels so that you can see them both clearly, as well as the Transform properties in the Timeline panel.

3 In the Layer panel, click on the View popup, and select Anchor Point Path. The small crosshair in the middle of the panel is the layer's Anchor Point.

• Drag the Anchor Point while carefully watching the Comp and Timeline panels. You will notice that as you drag down, the flower moves up in the Comp panel. As you drag left, the flower moves right. Does this mean you're editing the layer's Position?

• Drag the Anchor Point again in the Layer panel, but this time watch what happens to the Anchor Point in the Comp panel. The position of the Anchor Point in the Comp panel stays the same, as does the Position value in the Timeline panel. So why does the layer appear to change position? Because you are changing where the Anchor Point is in relation to the layer. This in turn changes where the layer's pixels are drawn in relation to this position coordinate – a subtle but important difference.

• When you're done playing, drag the Anchor Point in the Layer panel to the base of the flower's stem. Any rotation or scale will now occur around this point.

4 In the Comp panel, drag the flower down so that its stem rests on the bottom of the comp's image area.

Scrub the values for Rotation and Scale: The flower animates more naturally now.

Anchor Point Tool

This is a great tool for moving the Anchor Point without using the Layer panel:

5 In the Timeline panel, click Transform > Reset to reset the layer to how it was when you first added it to the center of the comp.

• Type **Y** to select the Pan Behind (Anchor Point) tool. *In the Comp panel only*, drag the Anchor Point while carefully watching the Layer panel and the Transform values: The Position and Anchor Point values change in opposite directions, resulting in the layer remaining stationary!

Close the Layer panel, and press **V** to return to the Selection tool.

6 Here's how to move the layer to the bottom of the comp more precisely: Right-click on the Position value and select Edit Value. In the Position dialog that opens, set the Units popup to % of Composition, then set X = 50, Y = 100. Click OK and the layer's position will be centered at the bottom of the comp.

3–4 In the Layer panel, move the Anchor Point to the base of the stem of the flower. Then in the Comp panel, move the flower so its stem touches the bottom of the comp.

4 When the Anchor Point is relocated to the bottom of the flower, animating Scale and Rotation will look more natural. (See **Comps_Finished > 01-Anchor Point_final**.)

Pan Behind (Anchor Point) Tool (Y)

5 Select the Anchor Point tool (top), and *in the Comp panel* move the Anchor Point to the bottom of the stem (above). The Anchor Point will also move in the Layer panel.

6 The Position dialog allows you to place a layer based on a percentage of the composition.

3 The problem with Position: After you've moved the layer into place (A), when you edit its Scale, it will appear to slide out of place (or even out of frame!) (B), requiring you to reposition it (C). This is because layers scale around their Anchor Point, not the center of the comp. Photo courtesy Chris Meyer.

▽ tip

Nudging Scale

To edit the Scale value in 1% increments, press ⌥ (*Ctrl*) and use the **+** and **−** keys on the numeric keypad. To nudge in 10% increments, add *Shift*.

Faux Motion Control

You can add a layer larger than your comp size to a composition, then pan and zoom around that image. However, if you animate using Position and Scale, it can quickly become an exercise in frustration, because scaling happens around the anchor. The secret is to animate the Anchor Point instead of Position. To compare both approaches, try these exercises:

1 In the Project panel, locate and double-click on the comp **02a-Motion Control*starter1**.

This comp already has a layer in it – **Auto Race.jpg** – that is considerably larger than the comp's size. Drag it around in the Comp panel to get a feel for how it looks (you can view the entire image in the Footage panel by double-clicking **Auto Race.jpg** in the **Sources** folder in the Project panel).

2 With the Selection tool active (shortcut: **V**), select this layer in the Timeline panel and type **P** to reveal its Position, followed by **Shift S** to also reveal its Scale. Press **Home**, and enable keyframing for Position and Scale at 00;00.

3 Drag the layer to focus on some cars you like. Then reduce the Scale to get more of them in the picture. Notice that as you alter Scale, the image is no longer framed the same. This happens because the layer is scaling around its Anchor Point – not the portion of it you were viewing in the comp. Drag the layer back to where you like it.

4 Press **End**, and drag the layer to focus on a different set of cars, then set a different "zoom" level (Scale value). Again, you'll have to retweak the position as the scale edit made them move. Hmm…there's got to be an easier way…

5 Select Close All from the Composition dropdown menu.

• Back in the Project panel, double-click **02b-Motion Control*starter2**. This is a blank composition. In the **Sources** folder in the Project panel, select **Auto Race.jpg** and press ⌘ **/** (*Ctrl* **/**) to add this to the center of your comp, starting at 00;00. Resist the urge to reposition the layer; you want the Anchor Point to stay centered in the comp.

• Type **S** to reveal Scale, but this time type **Shift A** to also reveal the Anchor Point. Press **Home**, and enable keyframing for these two properties. *Throughout the remainder of this exercise, do not reposition the layer in the Comp panel.*

6 Now double-click **Auto Race.jpg** to open its Layer panel. This panel should open to the left of the Comp panel from an earlier exercise (if it does not, dock it with the Project panel). With the Layer and Comp panels side by side, arrange your workspace so that you can see the entire image in both panels, as well as the Timeline panel. Setting Magnification > Fit to Comp Size can be useful here.

In the Layer panel, set the View popup to Anchor Point Path. Drag the crosshairs *in the Layer panel* to the center of the car or cars you want to see. Then edit the layer's Scale to get the zoom amount you want. Notice how you smoothly zoom in and out of the center of your framed image – it doesn't slide off the screen.

7 Press **End**. In the Layer panel, drag the Anchor Point to a different car or cars to focus on. *Again, resist the temptation to drag the layer in the Comp panel!* Then edit Scale to change your zoom amount. Notice how the layer stays "centered" as you scale – that's because Position (where the Anchor Point is in relation to the comp) is always in the center of the comp.

8 If you remembered to enable keyframing in step 5, you will now see a motion path in the Layer panel (not the Comp panel). It has Bezier handles, just like a position motion path. Tug on those handles and create a nice arc for your motion control camera move.

(If you can't see the handles clearly, press **⌘** (**Ctrl**) and drag out a handle from the keyframe icon.)

To preview, bring the Comp panel forward (otherwise, you'll preview the Layer panel) and either press the RAM Preview button or press **0** on the numeric keypad.

In a real job you would enable Motion Blur and add ease controls to taste (both covered later). To compare, our version is **Comps_Finished > 02-Motion Control_final**.

6 By moving the Anchor Point in the Layer panel (top left), you can easily set the center of what your virtual camera is looking at in the Comp panel (top right).

8 You can tweak the Bezier curve for the Anchor Point path in the Layer panel (above) to create a "motion control" move that sweeps around your photo (below).

In this exercise, you will be using the Graph Editor to refine the animation you created in Lesson 1. Footage courtesy Artbeats' Recreation & Leisure, Winter Lifestyles, and Winter Scenes.

The Graph Editor

The next step in mastering animation is refining your keyframes and the way values interpolate between them by using the Graph Editor. You can switch between the Graph Editor and normal layer bar view at any time; the Graph Editor merely provides a more precise tool for manipulating keyframes.

1 Select Close All from the Comp panel's dropdown menu to close all previous comps. In the Project panel, double-click **Comps > 03-Graph Editor*starter** to open it. It includes a version of the animation you created in Lesson 1.

2 Type ⌘ **A** (**Ctrl** **A**) to select all the layers in your composition. Then type **U**: This reveals the animating properties of the selected layers.

Slowly drag the current time indicator back and forth in the timeline to get an idea of how the **Snowstorm Title.tif** and **Snowflake.mov** layers are animating. Then click the RAM Preview button (or press **0** on the numeric keypad), which buffers up the animation so that you can see it at normal speed. All of the movements have sudden speed changes, which correspond to the default linear keyframe interpolation each keyframe has. You can also tell they are linear because all the keyframe icons in the timeline are diamond shaped. Experienced animators can spot linear keyframes a mile away; they are a telltale sign of less-experienced animators. Assuming you weren't going for an edgy, herky-jerky feel, the goal is to refine these movements.

3 Press any key to stop the RAM Preview. With all of the layers still selected, click on the Graph Editor icon along the top of the Timeline panel. The layer bars and keyframes will be replaced with a graph, and a new set of icons will appear along the bottom of the Timeline panel.

Click on the eyeball icon along the bottom of the timeline, and select

Show Animated Properties from the popup menu. You will now see a series of colored lines, which correspond to how each animated property in this project is changing over time. The color of these lines corresponds to the colored boxes around their values to the left of the Timeline panel. (Since the Scale's X and Y dimensions are currently locked together, the red X Scale value and green Y Scale are drawn on top of each other, resulting in just a red line in the Graph Editor.)

4 Press **F2** to deselect all of the layers, and select **Snowflake.mov**: just its animating properties will be visible. Open the Choose Graph Type and Options

▽ tip

Show Reference Graph

When Show Reference Graph is enabled under Choose Graph Type and Options, both the value and speed graphs are displayed at the same time. Choose Edit Value Graph or Edit Speed Graph to determine which type of curve you wish to edit; the other type will be displayed with reduced brightness. Having all of these lines on screen at once can be confusing, so we usually disable this option unless we explicitly want to see the impact on one graph type while we edit the other.

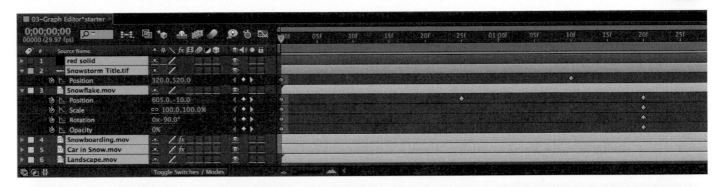

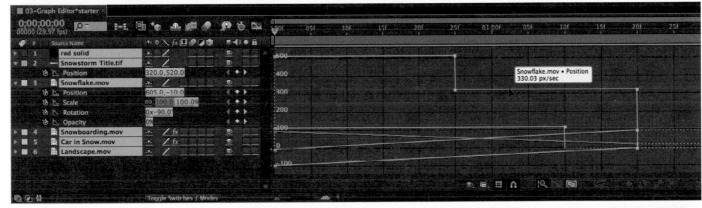

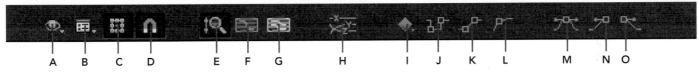

2–3 The normal keyframe view displays keyframes for each property underneath each layer's bar in the timeline (top). The Graph Editor allows you to see multiple layers and properties overlaid in a single display (middle). The Graph Editor icons explained (right).

menu (the button to the right of the eyeball); it is currently set to Auto-Select Graph Type. While in this mode, After Effects is choosing to show you the value graph for Scale, Rotation, and Opacity (the red, cyan, and blue lines), and the speed graph for Position (the pink line).

5 In the Choose Graph Type and Options menu, choose Edit Value Graph. The pink Position speed graph will be replaced with separate red and green graphs showing how those individual dimensions are varying over time as the snowflake animates across the screen.

Scrub the time indicator, watching how the numeric values along the left correspond to the lines and curves to the right. You can also press the **J** and **K** keys to jump back and forth between visible keyframes. Hover the cursor over

Legend Key

A Choose which Properties are shown in Graph Editor

B Choose Graph Type and Options

C Show Transform Box when Multiple Keys Are Selected

D Toggle Snap On/Off

E Auto-zoom Graph Height

F Fit Selection to View

G Fit All Graphs to View

H Separate Dimensions

I Edit Selected Keyframes

J Convert Selected Keyframes to Hold

K Convert Selected Keyframes to Linear

L Convert Selected Keyframes to Auto Bezier

M Easy Ease

N Easy Ease In

O Easy Ease Out

▼ Panning and Zooming Time

You can zoom in and out in the Graph Editor and the normal timeline keyframe display in a variety of ways:

- Drag the end handles of the Time Navigator bar that runs along the top of the timeline area.
- Drag the Zoom slider along the bottom of the timeline area.
- Use the normal magnification shortcut keys − and +.
- You can also use the normal Zoom tool: Press Z to engage, then drag a region to auto-fit it to the Graph Editor display.

Once zoomed in, you can slide the Time Navigator bar or hold down the spacebar and drag to pan earlier or later in time.

The Graph Editor has an Auto-zoom Graph Height button; this defaults to On and is handy for making sure you see the full value range of your graphs. When the Auto-zoom button is disabled (not highlighted), you can use a mouse scroll wheel: The normal wheel movement is up and down; Shift +scroll moves horizontally.

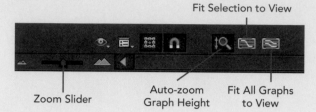

Fit Selection to View

Zoom Slider

Auto-zoom Graph Height

Fit All Graphs to View

If you have zoomed in on a graph and want to quickly get back to viewing your entire curves, click the Fit All Graphs to View button along the bottom of the Graph Editor. To zoom in on selected keyframes, first select the keyframes you want to focus on, then click on the adjacent Fit Selection to View button.

Remember that the eyeball icon offers a Show Animated Properties option. When enabled, simply selecting a layer will show a graph for every animated property. To view just one property at a time, disable this option and select individual properties, or Shift +click to view multiple properties.

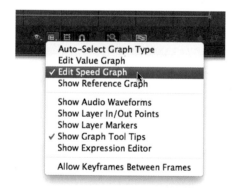

6 When Choose Graph Type and Options is set to Edit Speed Graph (above), the lines in the Graph Editor show the amount of change in each parameter from frame to frame. Hover the cursor over one of these graphs to see its speed at this particular point in time (right).

Note: Normally, you cannot edit the value graphs for Position. Later in this lesson we will show you a special mode – Separate Dimensions – where you can.

the graph lines, and a popup will appear that provides the name of the layer, the name of the property, and that property's value at that given moment in time.

6 Now open the Graph Type and Options menu and choose Edit Speed Graph. When viewing speed graphs, the height of the lines indicate their rate of change in units per second. Note that all of the lines are perfectly flat. This indicates that all of the displayed properties are maintaining a constant speed between keyframes – a natural result of the linear keyframe interpolation type. Flat speed graphs often imply less-sophisticated motion.

7 Click the Choose Graph Type and Options button again, and reset it to Auto-Select Graph Type.

Editing Graphs

In the following steps, you will be using the Graph Editor to edit your animation keyframes. RAM Preview after each change to verify the results.

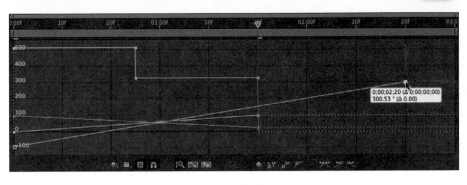

8 Make sure **Snowflake.mov** is still selected. The cyan-colored line along the bottom of the Graph Editor represents its Rotation, animating from –90° to 0°. To increase the amount of rotation, click on its second keyframe and drag it upward. As you do so, a tooltip will appear, displaying the keyframe's new value. This information will also be echoed in the Info panel. In comparison, on the left side of the timeline, the Rotation value shown is the value *at the current point in time* – not necessarily the keyframe's value.

If you accidentally wander left or right as you drag this keyframe upward, add the **Shift** key as you drag; this will help constrain your movements. If you cannot get the exact value you desire, double-click the keyframe to numerically edit its value. You will also notice that the keyframe attempts to snap to the values of other keyframes as you drag; this is because Snap (the magnet button at the bottom of the Graph Editor) is enabled.

9 To have the snowflake continue to rotate later in time, drag its second keyframe to the right. If you want it to rotate for the entire duration of the composition, drag it until it snaps along the right edge of the Timeline panel.

10 Rather than have the snowflake spin at a constant speed, it may be more interesting to have it "settle down" as it reaches the end of the composition. A quick way to do this is to employ the Easy Ease Keyframe Assistant. With the second Rotation keyframe selected, do one of the following:

• Select Animation > Keyframe Assistant > Easy Ease or > Easy Ease In.

• Click on one of the Easy Ease buttons along the bottom of the Graph Editor.

• Press **F9** for Easy Ease, or **Shift** **F9** for Easy Ease In.

11 After you apply Easy Ease, the cyan-colored line will gently bend into its second keyframe, and a yellow Bezier handle will appear. Easy Ease applies a default interpolation to a keyframe so that its value changes more slowly as it approaches the keyframe. This is reflected in the changing slope of the value's line in the Graph Editor. To make this slowdown more or less gradual, drag the yellow handle to the left or right.

8–9 To increase the amount of rotation, drag the keyframe upward; to make the animation extend later in time, drag it to the right. Add Shift as you drag to constrain your movements.

▽ tip

Easier Shortcut

You can use the Easy Ease shortcut **F9** on the first or last keyframes, even if they have only incoming or outgoing handles – not both.

10 To have the snowflake slow down at the second Rotation keyframe, select it and then press the Easy Ease or the Easy Ease In button at the bottom of the Graph Editor.

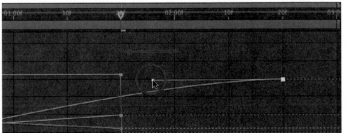

11 Pressing **Shift** as you drag the Bezier handles will constrain the movement to the horizontal axis.

12 Now let's smooth out the snowflake's animation. Currently, it just "plonks" into place; we desire a softer landing. Select the last keyframe for Position, then **Shift**+click the last keyframes for Scale and Opacity (you can also drag a marquee around all three to select them). Then click the Easy Ease In button along the bottom of the Graph Editor.

Remember that its pink line was showing us the speed graph for Position. After applying Easy Ease In, this line will be lowered to a value of 0 speed at its final keyframe. The arc in this line shows its speed easing to a halt.

13 There is a discontinuity in the middle of Position's speed graph. This indicates that its speed is changing suddenly at the middle keyframe, caused by an imbalance between how far the snowflake has to travel between keyframes versus the spacing between those keyframes in time. The linear keyframe interpolation does nothing to help smooth the transition. Let's fix these problems:

• Place the cursor over one of the yellow keyframe boxes for Position at 00:25 in time. Hold down the ⌥ (**Alt**) key to change the cursor to a Convert Vertex tool. Click on one of the yellow boxes, and the keyframe interpolation will change to Auto Bezier which joins the discontinuous keyframe handles and helps smooth the motion through this keyframe.

 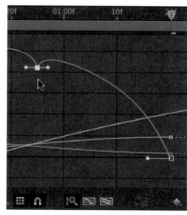 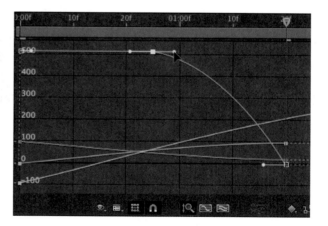

13 Kinks in the speed graph for Position (left) indicates that there will be a "hitch" in the motion through that keyframe. Hold down ⌥ (**Alt**) then click on the keyframe to convert to Auto Bezier (middle), and then reposition it to smooth out the graph (right).

• There is still a slight kink in Position's speed graph. To cure it, drag the middle keyframe up or down (changing its velocity at this point) as well as left or right (changing its timing) until you have a smooth graph. You can tug on its Bezier handles to further shape its curve; this converts it to Continuous Bezier interpolation. (Later in this lesson you'll learn about *roving keyframes*, which would be another good solution for smoothing out this particular graph.)

RAM Preview: You should notice that your animation is now a lot smoother and more refined than when you started. (If you can't remember, compare your animation to the comp **03-Graph Editor2_reference**.)

Coordinating Keyframes

An additional feature of the Graph Editor is that it allows you to see keyframes from several different layers overlaid in the same view. This makes it easier to coordinate the values and timing of multiple layers and properties. For this to happen, you need to add properties to a Graph Editor Set so that they will be displayed regardless of which layer is selected.

In this composition, we've initially animated the title to arrive at its final position before the snowflake does. What if you (or more important, your client) want them to arrive at the same time?

14 Select the layer **Snowstorm Title.tif**. The graphs for **Snowflake.mov** will disappear, replaced by the single graph for **Snowstorm Title.tif**'s Position. To see them all at once, create a Graph Editor Set:

• Between the word Position and the animation stopwatch to its left is a Graph Editor Set button. Enable it for **Snowstorm Title.tif**'s Position.

• Enable this switch for **Snowflake.mov**'s Position, Scale, Rotation, and Opacity properties. You can click on one switch and drag the mouse across the others to enable them all in one movement.

• Click on the eyeball icon along the bottom of the Graph Editor to open its properties menu. Make sure Show Graph Editor Set is enabled.

• Click anywhere in the Timeline panel, deselecting your layers. The graphs for your Graph Editor Set properties remain visible in the Graph Editor.

15 Double-click on the word Position for **Snowflake.mov**. This will select all of its Position keyframes, and a white box in the Graph Editor will enclose them. Place your cursor over the right edge of this box; a double arrow will appear, indicating you are about to resize it and all of its selected contents. Drag this edge to the left until it aligns with the final Position keyframe for **Snowstorm Title.tif**.

Have fun further refining this composition. For example, smooth out how the **Snowstorm Title.tif** stops by easing into its second Position keyframe. Drag the final keyframes for **Snowflake.mov**'s Scale and Opacity to also align with the Position keyframes you've been working with. Animate the **red solid** layer to move into position at the same time as **Snowstorm Title.tif**, or stagger the timing of all your animating layers. You have the tools; now it's just a matter of taste.

▽ tip

Quick Keyframe Assistance

You can right-click on any keyframe to get quick access to the Keyframe Assistants, as well as several other handy keyframe interpolation and selection options.

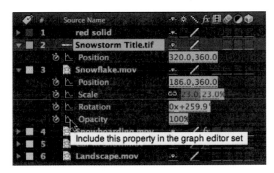

14 To view selected graphs regardless of whether or not a layer is selected, enable the Graph Editor Set button for the desired property. Also verify that Show Graph Editor Set is enabled in the Graph Editor properties menu.

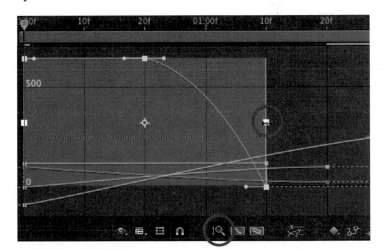

15 To alter the timing (or values) of several keyframes at once, select them, and then resize the bounding box that surrounds them. (Note that as you drag, keyframes may move out of view until you release the mouse; if they don't reappear, check that Auto-zoom is enabled.)

Separate Dimensions

After Effects bundles X and Y position data (and when employing 3D space, Z position) into one "temporal" keyframe to manipulate in the Timeline panel as well as one "spatial" keyframe in the Composition panel. This is a good system for many jobs, and makes it easier to manipulate position data. However, some movements require separate control over each dimension. Next we'll work through an exercise where this comes in handy: animating a bouncing ball, where the object's speed as it moves from left to right (the X dimension) is different from its speed as it bounces up and down (the Y dimension). Note this is an advanced technique; you can skip ahead to *Float like a Butterfly* if you wish.

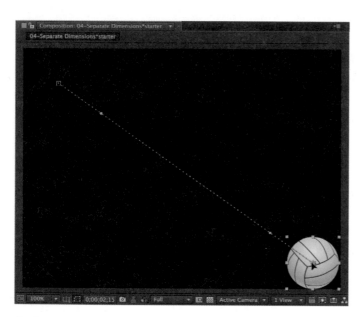

2–3 Enter two Position keyframes for the volleyball so it starts in the upper left and comes to rest in the lower right. Ball courtesy iStockphoto, boris64, image #5752295.

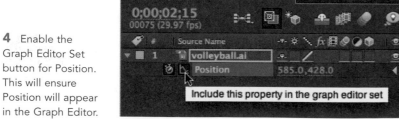

4 Enable the Graph Editor Set button for Position. This will ensure Position will appear in the Graph Editor.

Include this property in the graph editor set

1 Close your previous comps by selecting Close All from the Composition panel's dropdown menu. Return to the Project panel and double-click the comp **04-Separate Dimensions*starter** to open it. It contains a yellow volleyball in the upper left corner. The plan is to have you animate it to bounce off the "floor" of the comp while moving from left to right at a steady speed.

2 Select the layer **volleyball.ai** and press ⌥ P (Alt P) to toggle on the animation stopwatch for Position and also reveal it in the Timeline panel. (Alternatively, press P to twirl down Position and then toggle on the stopwatch.)

3 Move the current time indicator to the end of the composition (the shortcut is to press End). Drag the volleyball to the lower right corner of the comp, as if it were resting on the floor. You will notice a straight motion path in the Comp panel connecting these two Position keyframes.

4 When you enabled keyframing for Position, a second switch appeared to its right of the animation stopwatch in the Timeline panel. Click on this Graph Editor Set button to enable it: This will ensure that Position will always appear in the Graph Editor. Then reveal the Graph Editor in the Timeline panel by clicking its button along the top of the panel. You will see a single horizontal white line, representing the constant speed of the ball as it travels between these two keyframes.

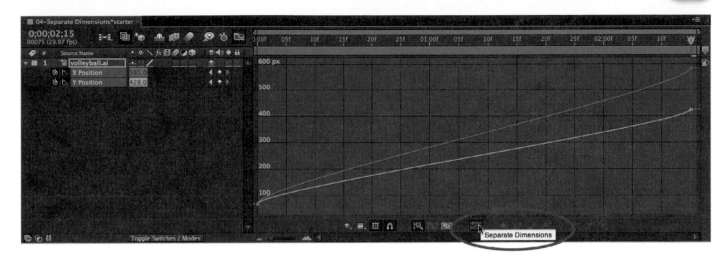

5 Make sure the Position parameter is selected in the Timeline panel. Then click on the Separate Dimensions button underneath the Graph Editor. Along the left, the former unified Position value will now be replaced by separate X Position and Y Position parameters, color-coded red for X and green for Y. In the Graph Editor, the single white velocity graph will be replaced with separate sloping red and green X and Y Position value graphs. (If you see flat horizontal lines instead, make sure the Choose Graph Type and Options popup has been set to Auto-Select Graph Type.)

6 We're happy with the left-to-right movement, so we can leave X Position alone for now. Let's work on the bounces, which means editing the Y Position (up and down) graph. First we're going to set the keyframes for where the ball hits the floor, then in the next step edit the Y Position graph to create the flight path between those hits:

• Move the current time indicator to 00:15.

• Scrub the Y Position value until the ball just touches the bottom of the comp. (You don't want to drag the ball in the Comp panel, because that would add both X and Y keyframes!)

• Make sure just the new Y Position keyframe is selected; it will have a solid yellow box in the Graph Editor, rather than a hollow yellow box. Edit > Copy this keyframe.

• Move the current time indicator to 01:15.

• With Y Position still highlighted along the left of the Timeline panel, Edit > Paste to create a keyframe at this new time with the same value as the previous keyframe.

5 After enabling Separate Dimensions, separate X and Y Position values will appear. You will also see color-coded lines for the X and Y values and velocities.

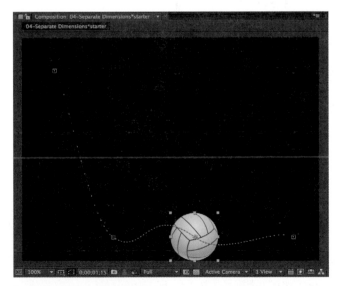

6 After pasting the second keyframe for Y Position at 01:15, the ball lurches more than bounces across the floor.

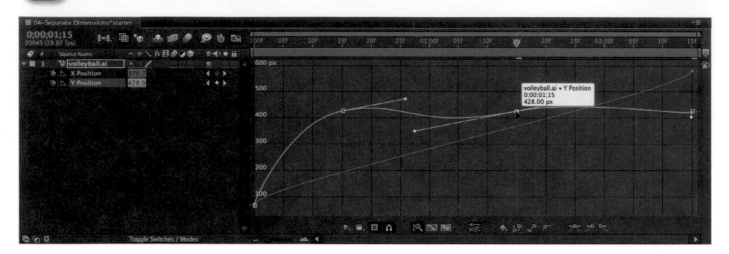

7 *start* The red line in the Graph Editor indicates the ball is moving left to right at a fairly constant speed. The green line is the Y Position, and looks similar to the motion path on the previous page. You will tweak this curve to fix the path.

7 RAM Preview: At this point, the volleyball just hits the ground and slowly lurches across it. Time to add a bigger bounce to its step:

• A bouncing motion is not continuous; the ball reverses direction when it hits the floor. This means you need to create discontinuous motion at the keyframes. Currently, Bezier handles appear in the Graph Editor around each keyframe indicating Auto Bezier keyframes (the default). Press the ⌥ (*Alt*) key and drag one of the Bezier handles for the keyframe at 00:15 to "break" them.

• Now that the handles are broken for that keyframe, release the ⌥ (*Alt*) key and drag both handles down until you get a nice arc coming into and leaving this keyframe – you will see this arc in both the Graph Editor and in the resulting motion path in the Comp panel.

• Repeat to also break the handles and create a steep arc at the keyframe at 01:15.

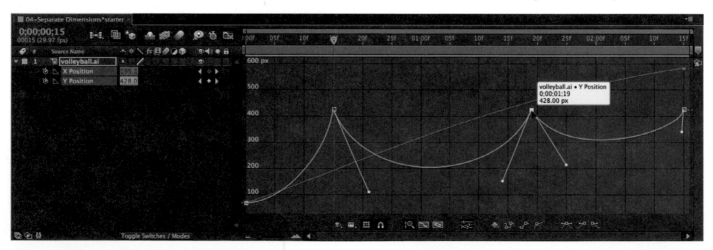

7 *end* The final X and Y Position value graphs.

• Also edit the curves for the first and last keyframes to help trace out a nice bounce motion path.

• RAM Preview, and continue to tweak until you like your motion. You can also move the Y Position keyframes in time by dragging them left and right in the Graph Editor. For example, move the third keyframe later to shorten the "flight time" during the last bounce. Note that this does not alter the ball's speed in the X dimension, just when it bounces in the Y dimension.

8 Remember that the X Position graph is separate! You can ⌥+click (*Alt*+click) on the Auto Bezier keyframes in the Graph Editor to revert them to Linear.

Experiment some more:

• Select the second (last) X Position keyframe and add Easy Ease (*F9*) to it. RAM Preview, and notice how the ball slows toward the end of the animation while the bounces remain the same.

• Press *End* and decrease the X Position value. RAM Preview, and note how the ball doesn't travel as far across the comp, but the up and down bounce motion remains the same. Our version is in the **Comps_Finished** folder.

This animation would have been very difficult to pull off with normal, joined-together Position values – you would be fighting to keep a constant speed in X while you created your bounces in Y. However, using Separate Dimensions does come with a price: You can no longer directly edit the motion path in the Comp panel (note that the Bezier handles disappeared); you have to craft your path in the Graph Editor. The good news is that you can select Position and disable Separate Dimensions by clicking the same switch along the bottom of the Graph Editor – After Effects will then approximate your final animation using traditional joined Position keyframes.

Quick Quizzler

How would you make the ball "squash" each time it hits the floor? Remember: Layers scale around their Anchor Point... The answer is in the **Quizzler Solutions** folder.

8 The final motion path. Remember that the dots along the motion path indicate the distance the ball travels between frames in time. Note the lack of Bezier handles on the motion path; this is a side effect of using Separate Dimensions in the Graph Editor.

▽ tip

Motion Blur

Enabling Motion Blur for the ball really helps this animation. The faster the ball moves or changes direction, the more it will be blurred – automatically! (Motion Blur is covered on page 57.)

Float like a Butterfly

In this next exercise, we're going to take an object with an alpha channel – a butterfly – and fly it around a composition by literally drawing its flight path. Then we'll employ some Keyframe Assistants and a few other tricks to refine its animation, while also working with the Graph Editor.

3 Selecting and resetting the Animation workspace opens a variety of Keyframe Assistant panels down the right side of the application window.

4 In the Motion Sketch panel, enable the Background checkbox so you can see the other layers while you sketch.

1 Close all previous comps by selecting Close All from the Comp panel's dropdown menu. Return to the Project panel and open **Comps > 05a-Butterfly Flight*starter**.

2 The butterfly is a bit large. Select **Butterfly 2.tif**, type **S** to reveal its Scale parameter, and reduce it to around 65%.

3 Click on the Workspace popup above the Comp panel, and select Animation, which will open a few new panels. Then select Reset "Animation" from the same menu, and click Yes to recall the default arrangement. If necessary, resize the Comp panel to see its entire image area, and press **—** (minus key) to zoom out the timeline to view the full duration again.

4 Turn your attention to the Motion Sketch panel along the right. This captures your mouse movements in the comp's image area and converts them into Position keyframes. Its Start and Duration are determined by the work area (page 33).

To see a box indicating the size of your layer while you're sketching, keep the Wireframe checkbox enabled; to see the other layers (which we want to do here, to determine the butterfly's path), enable the Background checkbox.

5 The plan is to draw a path of the butterfly starting on the largest flower head, have it fly about the screen, then settle back on the same flower, all during the duration of this comp (five seconds). Practice this by dragging the butterfly around while counting to five to get a feel for what you would like to do, and how fast.

• Make sure that Background is checked, then click the Start Capture button in the Motion Sketch panel. After Effects will wait until you click and start dragging the mouse in the Comp panel. Click on the flower head to start, then draw your

path, keeping the mouse key pressed. It's okay if you finish early; just release the mouse. Your new motion path will be drawn in the Comp panel.

• Press **P** to reveal your new Position keyframes in the timeline.

• RAM Preview your movement. If you're not happy with it, or if time ran out before you were finished, type **⌘ Z** (**Ctrl Z**) to undo until your new path and keyframes disappear, then try again! You can also toggle off the stopwatch for Position to delete all keyframes. When you're happy, save your project.

The Smoother

After you use Motion Sketch, you'll probably have a large number of Position keyframes. This makes it really difficult to edit your path. So let's simplify things.

6 Click on the word Position for **Butterfly 2.tif** to select all of its keyframes; they will turn yellow. Then turn your attention to the Smoother panel (if its text and buttons are grayed out, deselect then reselect your keyframes).

This assistant plots what would be a theoretically perfectly smooth curve for the selected keyframes, then looks at the actual keyframes to see how far they deviate from the ideal case. How much deviation you allow is set by the Tolerance parameter. You can scrub the Tolerance value or click it and type an absolute value. Try a value of, say, 10 for Tolerance and click Apply (its Apply To popup is set automatically depending on the keyframes selected).

Press **F2** to Deselect All. Notice how you have fewer keyframes, and your path has been simplified. RAM Preview; the movement should be an idealized version of your original sketch. You can always undo and try another Tolerance value. The goal is to avoid leftover clusters of keyframes that are too close to one another. Feel free to also remove keyframes manually if they are unnecessary. It should be relatively easy to tweak your motion path now that you have fewer keyframes.

Motion Sketch includes its own Smoothing parameter which it applies after you draw a path. We prefer to keep this value low, and use the Smoother afterward to get our desired result as it's easier to try different smoothing values without having to redo the entire motion sketch.

5 Select the butterfly, click Start Capture in Motion Sketch, and trace a flight path for the butterfly by moving your mouse. After you are done, you will see the motion path in the Comp panel (above); press **P** to reveal the Position keyframes in the Timeline panel (top).

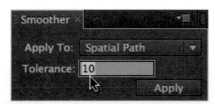

6 After applying the Smoother (left), you will have considerably fewer keyframes to deal with in the Comp (above) and Timeline (below) panels, even though the path is very similar to your original sketch.

Auto-Orient and Motion Blur

Let's clean up a few details before further refining our motion.

7 Currently, the butterfly stays pointed toward the top of the frame, regardless of how it's flying. To fix that, select **Butterfly 2.tif**, and choose Layer > Transform > Auto-Orient to open the Auto-Orientation dialog (the shortcut is ⌘ ⌥ O, *Ctrl* *Alt* *O*). Select Orient Along Path, and click OK.

  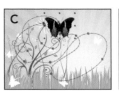   

7 Normally, layers keep the same orientation as they move around a comp (A–C). By setting Layer > Transform > Auto-Orient to Orient Along Path (top) and adjusting its initial rotation, it will now appear to automatically rotate to follow its path (D–F).

8 When you enable the Motion Blur switch for the butterfly layer and the comp (below), you will notice the butterfly's wings get blurry as it moves – especially as it turns a corner (above).

• At this point, your butterfly will automatically rotate to follow its path…but it's skidding sideways! No problem: Type *Shift* *R* to reveal its Rotation parameter in addition to Position, and scrub the degrees value (the rightmost value with the ° symbol) to point it the right way.

When using auto-orientation, pay close attention to the handles for the beginning and ending spatial keyframes in the Comp panel. Zoom in, and you'll often find that the default dots (the Auto Bezier handles) are pointing a little off to the side, causing the layer to do a little twist as it exits the first keyframe and enters the last keyframe. To fix this, drag the dots to create Bezier handles and edit them so that they are exactly in line with the motion path.

8 In the sidebar on the following page, we discuss Motion Blur. Let's enable it for our butterfly:

• In the switches panel for **Butterfly 2.tif**, toggle on the Motion Blur switch (the hollow box underneath the switch that looks like a circle with an echo).

• To see the effect in the Comp panel, also toggle on the large Enable Motion Blur button along the top of the Timeline panel. RAM Preview and enjoy the blurred result.

• To render more or less blur, open Composition > Composition Settings, click on the Advanced tab, and change the Shutter Angle. Try various values between 90 and 720 and compare the effect.

▼ Motion Blur

When moving objects are captured by a normal camera, they might appear blurry, depending on how far they have moved while the camera's shutter was open during the course of capturing a frame. After Effects can mimic this through the use of Motion Blur.

To add this to a layer, the layer's Motion Blur switch must be enabled (see figure on previous page). To preview what the blur looks like in the Comp panel, you also need to turn on the master Enable Motion Blur switch along the top of the Timeline panel. There is a separate Motion Blur popup in the Render Settings to determine whether this blur is rendered for "checked layers" (layers with their Motion Blur switch on).

When enabled, After Effects will automatically add blur to layers where the Transform properties are animating; some effects also can calculate motion blur.

To control the amount of blur, open Composition > Composition Settings and click on the Advanced tab. The Shutter Angle controls how much blur is calculated. There are 360° of possible blur per frame. Real cameras typically have 180° of blur; the maximum in After Effects is 720°. The length of the blur is also affected by the frame rate: The slower the rate, the longer the shutter is open, and therefore the longer the blur streaks. It is preferred to set the Shutter Phase to negative half of the value of the Shutter Angle – this way, an equal amount of blur is happening before and after the current frame in time.

Motion blur helps prevent fast-moving objects from appearing to strobe or stutter across the frame. If you notice strobbing or stuttering, increase the Samples Per Frame and Adaptive Sample Limit values. We typically increase these to their upper limit (64

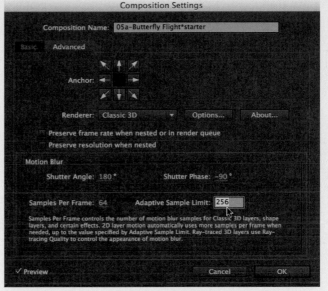

△ The amount of motion blur is adjusted under the Advanced tab in the Composition Settings dialog. Shutter Angle controls how long the blur streaks are, Shutter Phase controls the timing of the streaks, and Samples Per Frame plus the Adaptive Sample Limit control how smooth the blur is.

and 256 respectively), and then reduce them only if we notice the composition seems to be taking too long to render.

If Motion Blur is taking too long to render previews, simply turn off the master Enable Motion Blur switch in the Timeline panel to temporarily disable motion blur. Don't turn off the Enable Motion Blur switch for the layers themselves!

• When you've settled on a shutter angle you like, RAM Preview again. Notice how the outside of the wings are more blurred whenever the butterfly turns a corner quickly because the pixels are traveling faster than the butterfly's body.

Save your project. In the next exercise, you will learn how to smooth out the butterfly's speed across this complex motion path, and add eases onto the ends of the path. When you're done, enable Motion Blur, and take note of how the blur amount automatically ramps up and down as the speed of the layer changes. Our version so far is in **Comps_Finished > 05a-Butterfly Flight_final**.

▽ try it

Keyframe Strrrreettcchh

To stretch or compress the amount of time that a group of keyframes is spread across, select them, hold down ⌥ (**Alt**), and then drag the first or last keyframe (not the middle ones).

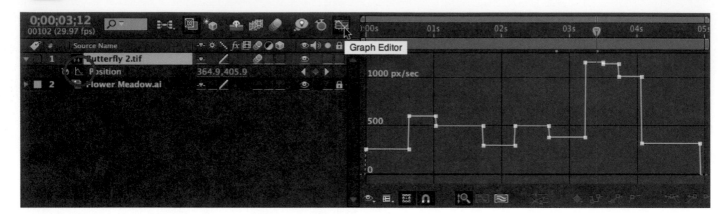

9 The butterfly's initial speed graph. The flat lines between keyframes reflect the constant speeds that result from the default linear temporal keyframes. (Enable the Graph Editor Set button for Position – circled above – to ensure you always see this property.)

▽ tip

Right-Click to Rove

You can right-click a keyframe in the Graph Editor or timeline view to toggle on and off Rove Across Time. If this option is grayed out, make sure the first or last keyframe is not also selected.

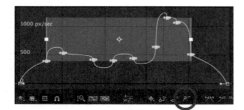

10 Before trying to smooth out the speed graph by hand, apply Easy Ease to the first and last keyframes, and then ⌥+click (*Alt*+click) on the keyframes in-between to convert them to Auto Bezier. You can also click the Auto Bezier button (circled in red). Even though your overall speed is still inconsistent, the changes will be smoother.

Roving Keyframes

Next, we want to show you how to create smooth speed changes over time even when you have a bunch of Position keyframes in space. Make some room for the timeline by selecting Workspace > Standard, and resize the Comp panel if needed. Our starting point can be found in **Comps > 05b-Butterfly Flight*starter**.

9 Click on the Graph Editor button along the top of the Timeline panel to open this display. Make sure Position is exposed for **Butterfly 2.tif** (press **P** if it isn't), then enable the Graph Editor Set button to the left of the word Position.

You should see a squared-off white graph. If not, click on the Choose Graph Type popup underneath the Graph Editor, and select Edit Speed Graph. In this graph, higher values mean faster motion. You can "read" this graph to tell that speed changes at keyframes are sudden, not smooth, because the butterfly enters the keyframes at one speed and exits at a different speed. It is also cruising at a speed higher than 0 at the start and end, which makes for sudden starts and stops. Remember that the dots in the motion path also indicate speed – the closer the dots are together, the more slowly the butterfly is traveling.

10 The sudden changes in speed are the result of using linear interpolation. Take a stab at trying to smooth out this speed graph by hand:

• Drag the first keyframe all of the way down to the horizontal line at zero, or select it and press the Easy Ease Out button.

• Do the same for the last keyframe, or select it and press the Easy Ease In button.

• Marquee around all the keyframes in the middle (excluding the first and last); the selected keyframes will have a bounding box around them. Change these linear keyframes to smooth keyframes by pressing ⌥ (*Alt*) to temporarily switch to the Convert Vertex tool, then click on any one of the selected keyframes: All the keyframes will convert to Auto Bezier (smooth) keyframes with short Bezier influence handles. Click outside the selection box to deselect the keyframes.

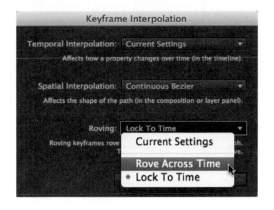

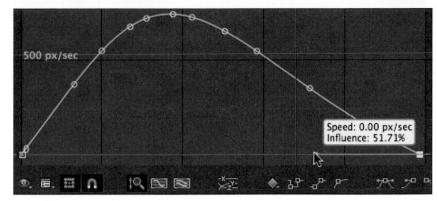

• Now try dragging individual keyframes up and down and left and right to smooth out bumps in the curve; dragging the handles longer will also help.

RAM Preview; even though the butterfly's flight should have smoother speed changes, there is an easier way to achieve this goal using one of the best-kept secrets in After Effects: *roving keyframes*. This trick leaves your motion path alone (in other words, it doesn't touch the spatial keyframes in the Comp panel), but simplifies your temporal keyframes (where they are in time in the Timeline panel) so that you have to edit only the starting and ending keyframes. After Effects will then automatically move ("rove") all of the keyframes in-between to work out the required timing.

11 Still in the Graph Editor, double-click Position to make sure all of the Position keyframes are selected. Then open Animation > Keyframe Interpolation. Click on the Roving popup, and select Rove Across Time. Click OK. All of the keyframes between the first and last automatically adjust to maintain a smooth speed curve between these two keyframes; RAM Preview to verify this.

The first and last keyframes cannot Rove Across Time. Select them individually and drag their handles to alter their influence; namely, how the butterfly speeds up out of the first keyframe, and slows down to the last. Notice how the ease controls now apply across the entire animation as if the keyframes in the middle didn't exist in the timeline.

12 Last trick, and then you can break for tea:

• Double-click Position again to make sure all keyframes are selected, then select the menu item Animation > Keyframe Assistant. These are a series of utilities that automatically edit keyframe values for you.

• Select Time-Reverse Keyframes. It does just what it says: It reverses all of your keyframes in time. RAM Preview, and now you'll see your butterfly travel in the opposite direction along your path. For comparison, our version is in **Comps_Finished > 05b-Butterfly Flight_final**.

11 Select all the Position keyframes, then select Animation > Keyframe Interpolation and set Roving to Rove Across Time (left). Afterwards, you only need to adjust the interpolation of the first and last keyframes (right), and the ones in the middle will slide ("rove") in time to ensure smooth speed changes in-between.

▽ tip

Rove in Either View

The Keyframe Interpolation dialog may be opened while in either the Graph Editor or the normal keyframe view.

12 Select all of the keyframes, and choose Animation > Keyframe Assistant. You can also right-click on one of the keyframes to bring up a version of the Animation menu. (Note that you can also apply Rove Across Time to selected keyframes from this menu.)

▽ insider knowledge

Supersize Me

Normally, it's a bad idea to increase Scale beyond 100%, because you will lose image quality. However, if the layer is created using vectors – such as Illustrator artwork – you can enable its Continuously Rasterize switch so that it remains sharp. We've done that for you in this comp. We'll explain this more in Lesson 6.

Hold Keyframes

Sometimes an animation requires sudden, jerky movements. The perfect tool for this job is the Hold keyframe. Hold is another type of interpolation – like linear – except this one says "hold my value until you encounter another keyframe." Let's put it to work on a common animation style known as the "slam down." If you'd like to see where you're going with this exercise, take a peek at our finished version in comp **06-Slam Down_final** and RAM Preview it.

1 In the Project panel, locate and double-click the comp **06-Slam Down*starter**. This comp already has two layers in it: **REJECT**, which is the word in the middle of the comp, and **frame**, which is the rounded rectangle bordering it. The goal here is to have the word stagger and slam into position by 02;00 in the timeline, then to slowly drift as the frame around it blinks.

2 Click on a time display in the Timeline or Comp panels, type "1." (don't forget the period) and press **Return** to jump to 1;00. Select the **REJECT** layer, type **P** to reveal Position, **Shift S** to reveal Scale and **Shift R** to reveal Rotation. Press the stopwatch for Position and drag down across the stopwatches for Scale and Rotation to enable keyframing for all three parameters in one smooth move; After Effects will remember the current values at this point in time.

3 Keyframe the **REJECT** layer to strike a few poses as it falls into position, then to drift away.

3 Move the current time indicator 10 frames earlier in time to 00;20. The shortcut is **Shift Page Up**. Choose a new pose for your word: Try something larger (increase Scale), offset a bit (edit Position), and perhaps rotated (Rotation). After Effects will automatically create the new keyframes for you.

• Press **Shift Page Up** again, and create a new pose at 00;10 in the same fashion. Then press **Home** to jump to 00;00 and create your beginning pose.

• Finally, press **End** and set up a final pose that's slightly smaller and perhaps slightly rotated from the main pose you set up at 01;00.

4 Preview your animation: The word REJECT slides around between keyframes then drifts away as After Effects interpolates between your keyframes. Hmm… we had something harder-edged in mind.

Click on the word Position in the Timeline panel, then **Shift** +click on Scale and Rotation – this will select all of their keyframes. Now, select the menu item Animation > Toggle Hold Keyframe. Notice how the shapes of the keyframes

▽tip

Toggle Hold Shortcut

To change a selected keyframe to Hold, type **⌘ ⌥ H** (**Ctrl Alt H**), or press **⌘ ⌥** (**Ctrl Alt**) and click on the keyframe you wish to change.

changed to have squares on the outgoing side. Also, in the Comp panel, all the handles retracted so that the motion path moves only in straight lines.

RAM Preview again: Now we have sudden movements...but we lost our drift! That's because we also converted the keyframes at 01;00 to Hold, which means they can't change their value until the next keyframe.

5 Select just the three keyframes at 01;00 by dragging a marquee selection around them. Press the ⌘ (Ctrl) key, and click on one of them: All selected keyframes will change back to linear keyframes (diamond shape). RAM Preview; now you have your desired animation.

6 If you know you want a parameter to use Hold keyframes, you just have to set up the first one; subsequent keyframes will then get the same interpolation.

Let's say we want the border around the title to blink on and off, starting when the word lands:

• First, move to 01;00, select **frame** (layer 2) and press [(left square bracket) to make it start at this point in time.

• Press ⌥ Shift T (Alt Shift T) to enable keyframing for Opacity; it defaults to 100% and a linear keyframe. Toggle it to a Hold keyframe using this shortcut: Press ⌘ ⌥ (Ctrl Alt) and click on it.

• Press Shift Page Down to jump 10 frames to 01;10 in the timeline, and set **frame**'s Opacity to 0%. It automatically gets the squared-off keyframe shape on the right side, indicating it also will "hold" its value and not interpolate.

Finish off this animation using copy and paste to save time. Select the Opacity keyframes at 01;00 and 01;10 and copy. Press Shift Page Down to move to 01;20 and paste: Both keyframes, with the copied values and spacing, will be created for you. Move to 02;10 and Paste again. RAM Preview; the **frame** layer will blink on and off. Our finished version is shown in comp **06-Slam Down_final**.

4 Select all of the keyframes, and either right-click on them or use the Animation menu to select Toggle Hold Keyframes. The square shape on the right (outgoing) sides of the keyframes indicates "hold."

5 Select just the keyframes at 01;00, and ⌘+click (Ctrl+click) on them to convert them to normal linear keyframes. You need this interpolation to get the drifting motion at the end.

6 Our final timeline, including Hold keyframes for **frame**'s Opacity so that it blinks on and off. (If the keyframes are not visible, select both layers and press U to reveal animated properties.)

▼ Tech Corner: Time Display and Timecode

After Effects features three different ways to count time: SMPTE Timecode, Frames, and Feet + Frames. The counting method used can be changed in File > Project Settings. You can also ⌘+click (*Ctrl*+click) on the frame number in the top left of the Timeline panel to toggle between the choices. Regardless of the counting system chosen, the starting number can be set for each comp inside its Composition > Composition Settings dialog. Additionally, the starting number for each movie source can be set in its File > Interpret Footage dialog.

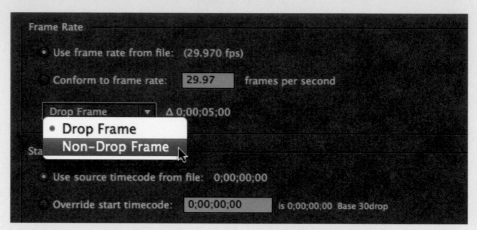

△ The File > Interpret Footage dialog for each source movie allows you to set its frame rate, start timecode, and whether to use the Non-Drop or Drop Frame counting method.

SMPTE

This is the most common frame counting format – and the most confusing. SMPTE displays the number of hours (HR), minutes (MN), seconds (SC), and frames (FR) in the format HR:MN:SC:FR.

△ SMPTE Timecode

△ Frames

△ Feet + Frames

After Effects supports three different ways to represent time: SMPTE Timecode, Frames, and Feet + Frames.

There are three standard frame rates: 24 frames per second (fps) for film, 25 fps for PAL video, and 29.97 fps for NTSC video. It's harder to count to 29.97 instead of a simple number like 30. Therefore, SMPTE has two different ways of counting this rate: *Drop Frame* and *Non-Drop Frame*.

Non-Drop Frame assumes the frame rate is 30 fps, *just for the sake of counting*. It counts neatly from 00 to 29, then rolls over to 01:00. Most people in NTSC-land working on shorter programs (say, under a half hour) use Non-Drop. After this lesson, we will use Non-Drop Frame counting as our project default for the rest of this book.

If the actual frame rate is 29.97 fps (the NTSC standard) instead of 30, the Non-Drop frame number displayed will eventually drift compared with real time. Therefore, Drop Frame counting was created. To even things back up, Drop Frame skips the frame numbers 00 and 01 (just the numbers, *not* the actual frames) every minute, except for 10s of minutes. You can tell Drop Frame counting is being used by the semicolons between the numbers.

After Effects attempts to determine if a 29.97 fps source uses Non-Drop or Drop Frame. This may be overriden in the Interpret Footage dialog. Preferences > Import sets the default to use if a source movie is not tagged. Non-Drop or Drop Frame counting may also be set per composition.

Frames

This simple format just displays the frame number, starting from the beginning of the timeline. It is preferred by some animators and visual effects artists.

Feet + Frames

This is the way film editors used to count time – they actually measured the amount of film that had gone past. Different film sizes have different numbers of frames per foot; 35mm film has 16 frames per foot. Therefore, time in this format is displayed as FEET + FR.

Idea Corner

The following will help you build on the animation skills learned in this lesson:

• Create an animation in **02b-Motion Control** that explores multiple areas of the image. You could pause at some areas by using Hold keyframes, or "whip pan" quickly from one area to another, using Motion Blur for added effect. Our version is **Idea1 – Motion Control**. Also feel free to use your own image!

Use Hold keyframes whenever you "pause" Position or Anchor Point paths to ensure that Bezier handles are retracted (this avoids odd behavior in the motion path). If you have trouble moving the Anchor Point when keyframes are stacked on top of each other, scrub the Anchor Point value in the timeline to move them apart, and drag from there.

In **Idea1 – Motion Control**, we used a combination of different keyframe types and motion blur.

• At the end of Lesson 1, we showed you how to import a layered Photoshop or Illustrator file as a composition. Import the file **Reject_split.ai** from this lesson's **02_Sources** folder as a comp – it contains each character on a separate layer. Animate a slam down (as you did in **06-Slam Down**) for each character, this time using more steps and animating faster. Our version is **Idea2 – REJECT on 3s**, where we animated the slam down every 3 frames (known as "animating on 3s").

Idea2: By giving each character its own layer, you can create even more interesting slam-down effects, with drop shadows falling from one character to another.

Quizzler

A large part of becoming a motion graphics artist is looking at another animation, and "reverse engineering" it. Play the movies inside the **Quizzler Movies** folder, and try to figure out how they were done:

• The animation in **Quiz_Butterfly Orbit.mov** can be done a couple of different ways. Try it using Position keyframes; it's hard to get that perfectly circular path. What other two Transform properties could you combine to get a perfect rotation like this?

• Overshooting animations are a staple of character-style animation. You can do it using three keyframes, including one for the peak of the overshoot, or with just two keyframes: start and end. Play **Quiz_Overshoot.mov** and see if you can re-create this. (Hint: This will require a trip into the Graph Editor...)

▽ solutions

No Peeking!

Our versions of the Idea Corner and Quizzler animations are contained in folders with the same name in the **Lesson 02.aep** project file. Don't peek at the **Quizzler Solution** comps until you've tried them yourself first! There is no "right" answer to the Idea Corner challenges, so feel free to take a different path and use your own sources instead.

Layer Control

Learning how to trim layers and enhance them using blending modes and effects.

▽ In This Lesson

64 layers and stacking order
65 moving layers in time
66 trimming layers
67 trimming in the Layer and Footage panels
68 slip editing
69 Sequence Layers keyframe assistant
71 looping footage
72 image sequences
73 changing the frame rate; Time Stretch
74 blending modes
76 effects and solids
77 effect motion path
79 Effects & Presets panel
79 searching for effects
80 animation presets
83 Behavior presets
84 layer styles
86 adjustment layers
87 filmic glow trick
88 Brainstorm; the Cartoon effect
90 non-square pixels

▽ Getting Started

Make sure you have copied the **Lesson 03-Layer Control** folder from this book's disc onto your hard drive, and make note of where it is; it contains the project file and sources you need for this lesson. Open the file **Lesson_03.aep** to work through the exercises in this lesson.

In the first two lessons, we focused on animating the properties of layers. However, your sources may have built-in "animation" of their own – namely, the frame-to-frame movement inside a video clip. Therefore, we're going to spend a good portion of this lesson showing how to move a clip in time, edit its in and out points, and work with its frame rate and ability to loop. From there, we'll move onto combining clips using blending modes – the secret sauce that creates rich, deeply layered looks. We'll end with ways to apply and take advantage of effects, including using animation presets, adjustment layers and Brainstorm.

Working with Layers

Before we get into trimming and editing, first let's take a refresher course on the significance of how layers are stacked in the Timeline panel.

1 Open this lesson's project file **Lesson_03.aep** – you will be using it for the exercises in this lesson. In the Project panel, twirl open the **Comps** folder if it isn't already, then double-click the comp **01-Layer Practice*starter** to open it.

2 In a typical two-dimensional comp such as this one, layers closer to the top in the timeline stack also appear closer to the top in the comp viewer. This is particularly an issue with full-frame footage, as a layer can completely obscure the layer behind it.

Note that this timeline has three layers, none of which are as long as the comp – their colored layer bars are "ghosted" before and after them.

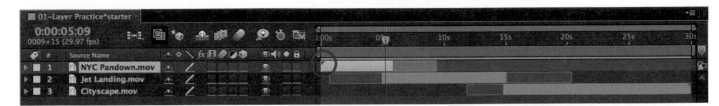

2 Studying the timeline (above) allows you to "read" which layer will play when. Higher layers are drawn on top of layers they overlap underneath, such as here where the NYC clip overlaps the jet landing. Selected layers are drawn lighter and with a texture. "Ghosted" areas of layer bars indicate there are additional frames of footage that are currently trimmed away. The triangle indicates a layer has been trimmed to the very first or last frame of its source.

With an eye on the Comp panel, scrub the current time indicator between 00:00 and 10:00, and notice how the image switches as the first layer bar ends.

3 In the Timeline panel, grab the first layer (**NYC Pandown.mov**) and drag it just below the second layer (**Jet Landing.mov**). Now scrub the current time indicator, and note the change: **Jet Landing.mov** starts playback earlier in time, as it is now above **NYC Pandown.mov** where they overlap.

Practice swapping layers while scrubbing the current time indicator until you have a solid grasp on the interaction between layer stacking order, and when they start and stop in the comp.

Moving Layers in Time

With layers, there are two sets of times we are interested in: the layer's internal in and out points which determine what portion of the clip we use, and its external in and out points which determine when a trimmed layer starts and stops in the comp. You can edit these separately or together. We'll continue working in **01-Layer Practice** to demonstrate this; **Jet Landing.mov** should be the top layer at this point.

4 Along the bottom left of the Timeline panel is an icon of a pair of brackets. Click on this icon to expose the In, Out, Duration, and Stretch columns in the Timeline panel. Then right-click on the top of the Stretch column and select Hide This: You won't need it for this exercise, and we could use the space.

3 Dragging **NYC Pandown** below the **Jet Landing** layer in the timeline (above) results in the jet being drawn on top in the Comp panel (below). Footage courtesy Artbeats/Transportation.

4 Click on the Expand or Collapse In/Out/Stretch/Duration button in the lower left corner of the Timeline panel to reveal these parameters. Then right-click on the Stretch column header to hide it.

After Effects defaults to using Best Quality when rendering layers. This means animated layers are positioned with 16 bits of precision within each pixel of a comp to create exceptionally smooth movement, and transformations and effects are anti-aliased to produce smooth rather than jaggy edges. Draft Quality renders pixels with just "nearest neighbor" resolution, which is faster, but looks a bit rough. Click the Quality switch to toggle a layer to Draft Quality (dotted line); click again to toggle back to Best Quality (solid line). See the Appendix for more on image quality considerations.

▽ tip

Ins and Outs

To quickly locate the current time indicator to a layer's in point, select it and type **I**. To locate to its out point, type **O**.

▽ tip

Splitting Layers

To split (divide) a layer into two at the current time, select Edit > Split Layer. This will duplicate the layer and automatically trim both copies so that they meet up at the split. Any keyframes and effects will appear on both layers after splitting.

5 Place the current time indicator where it overlaps the first layer. In the timeline, click in the middle (not the ends) of the layer bar and drag it left and right along the timeline while watching the Comp panel; note that the frame being displayed changes. As a result, the layer will play earlier or later in the comp. Notice how the in and out times in the Timeline panel change, but the duration doesn't – this is confirmation that you're not trimming the layer, just sliding it.

• A good shortcut to slide a layer is to place the time indicator where you want a layer to start, make sure the layer is selected, and press **[** (the left square bracket) – the layer will move so that its in point matches the current time.

• To move a selected layer so that it ends at the current time indicator, press **]** (the right square bracket). Note that these shortcuts also work when multiple layers are selected. When you're done experimenting, drag layer 1 so that you can see both its in and out points in the timeline.

Trimming Layers

Oftentimes you don't want to use all the frames in a movie clip. There are several ways to nondestructively trim a layer:

6 Place the current time indicator where it overlaps the first layer. Click and drag the start of the layer bar: Its In and Duration times change, but the frame being dis-

played in the comp does not change (unless you trim it so much that you reveal the layer underneath). You can do the same to its out point. This is referred to as trimming a layer "in place" because you are *not* sliding which frame of the footage will play at a given point in time. Note the "ghosted" area of the layer bar that shows how much you have trimmed off the front.

7 Time for more shortcuts, this time for trimming layers:

• Place your current time indicator where you want the layer to start, such as when the plane's tires first touch the runway. Select this layer, and type **⌥[** on Mac (**Alt [** on Windows) – the layer will be trimmed in place to start at this time. The out point stays the same, and the duration changes.

• To trim the out point to the current time without moving the layer, select it and type **⌥]** (**Alt]**). The in point stays the same, and the duration changes. Note that these shortcuts also work when multiple layers are selected.

▼ Trimming in Other Panels

Those with an editing background might be used to trimming sources in a separate clip window. You can work like this in After Effects as well:

• In the timeline, double-click any layer to open its Layer panel. To see the original layer before any masks or effects are applied, set the View popup to None or turn off the Render button. Trim the clip's in and out points by dragging the ends of the layer bar in this panel's timeline, or press the In button (the { icon below the ruler) to set the in point to the current frame. Either way, when you change the in point in the Layer panel, *the layer will slide in time to maintain the same start point in the composition.* Trimming in the Timeline panel doesn't offer this feature.

• You can trim a clip before you even add it to your comp. In the Project panel, select one of the movies in the **Sources** folder and double click it to open its Footage panel. The trimming controls are identical to the Layer panel.

To add the trimmed clip to your comp, make sure the comp you want it to appear in is the forward comp; the Footage panel will verify this with its "Edit Target" in its lower right corner. Click on the Overlay Edit button to add this clip into a new top track in the comp beginning at the current time without disturbing the other layers. The Ripple Edit button to its left has the added function of splitting any underlying clips at the insertion point and moving all of the later clips after the new clip is done.

△ Opening a source from the Project panel into its own Footage panel allows you to trim the source before overlaying or ripple-inserting it into the currently forward composition. Footage courtesy Artbeats/Timelapse Cityscapes.

△ Double-click a layer to open it in its Layer panel, where you can focus on its internal in and out points – how it has been trimmed, regardless of how it is being used in a comp.

△ Trimming in the Layer panel affects the in and out points relative to the source clip, but does not change its in point in the comp's timeline (notice the two "In" times are different here). You can also click the { button (circled in red) to set the in point to the current frame.

8 Place the cursor over the ghosted area of a layer bar, and the Slip Edit tool will appear. This allows you to edit the frames of the source that will be played back without moving its in and out points in the comp's overall timeline.

9 By selecting the Pan Behind tool (above), you can slip edit a layer by dragging its layer bar (below). This is especially handy if you can't see the start or end of the layer in the Timeline panel. When you're done, type **V** to return to the Selection tool.

10 If you slip edit with keyframes deselected, the keyframes will not move relative to the comp, meaning they keep their same relationship to other layers.

If keyframes are related to specific frames in the layer (such as with masking and "rotoscoping" keyframes) then they should be preselected before you slip edit so that they keep the same relationship to the layer.

Slip Edit

We'll finish our editing tour with the Slip Edit tool. This is a great way to change the portion of a clip that plays without disturbing its overall timing in a comp.

8 Trim the in and out points of the layer you've been working with so that you see some "ghost" layer bar at its head and tail. Place the current time indicator around the middle of the layer, and hover the cursor over the ghost areas until you see a two-headed arrow bracketed by two lines: This is the Slip Edit tool. Click and drag while this tool is visible; note that the In, Out, and Duration values do not change, but the frame visible in the Comp panel does. How far you can slip a layer is determined by how much trimmed space exists at its head or tail. This is a lot faster than sliding a layer, then retrimming its ends!

9 Sometimes, you will not be able to see the ghosted portions of the layer bar – maybe you are zoomed into the middle of the clip in the timeline, or it extends beyond the end of the comp. You can still use the Slip Edit tool.

Type **Y** to switch to the Pan Behind (Anchor Point) tool we introduced in the previous lesson. Now you will get the Slip Edit tool when you hover over the layer bar itself; drag the layer and try it out! Don't forget to type **V** to return to the normal Selection tool when you're done.

10 Life gets more interesting when the layers you are sliding or trimming have keyframes as well. For example, open comp **02-Layers & Keyframes*starter**. Type **⌘ A** (**Ctrl A**) to Select All, then **T** to reveal their Opacity keyframes. These perform crossfades between the layers. Press **F2** to Deselect all layers.

Note that because we were working with full-frame sources, we animated Opacity only for the topmost layer; if we also animated the lower layer, both layers would be semitransparent and the background color would show through.

• Keyframes are attached to the layer, and therefore frames in the source, not a specific time in a composition. As a result, moving a layer in time also slides its keyframes by default. Move layer 2 by dragging its layer bar, and notice that its keyframes go along for the ride. Undo to return layer 2 to its original location.

• Place the current time indicator at around 10:00 so it's over layer 2, and use the Slip Edit tool to slide the layer. Because the keyframes were not selected, they remain in the same place in the comp. This is useful for occasions when the keyframes need to keep the same timing relationship to the rest of the composition.

• Now select the Opacity keyframes near the out point of layer 2, and perform a slip edit. As you drag, selected keyframes should remain selected and move along with the movie; keyframes that are not selected won't move. If keyframes are timed to the overall composition – such as fades – deselect them to leave them in place. If keyframes are timed to a clip – such as a rotoscoping mask – select them to have them move with the clip.

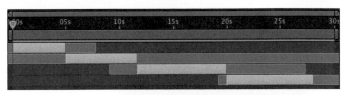

Sequence Layers

After Effects can automate some common editing tasks. Let's start with a group of layers that are supposed to play back end to end:

1 Open the comp **03a-Sequence – Full Frame*start**. It contains four already trimmed layers that are placed at the start of the comp.

2 Type ⌘ *A* (*Ctrl A*) to Select All, then choose the menu item Animation > Keyframe Assistant > Sequence Layers. For now, turn the Overlap option off, and click OK. The layers are automatically placed end to end.

2 Selecting layers and applying Sequence Layers with Overlap disabled (above) results in the layers being placed end to end (top).

3 Undo to get back to your initial timing. With the layers still selected, type *T* to reveal their Opacity parameter, and let's talk about that Overlap option.

• Right-click on one of the layer bars and select Keyframe Assistant > Sequence Layers again. When the dialog opens, enable the Overlap button. This automatically creates crossfades determined by the Duration value. For now, use the default Duration of 01:00, and set Transition to Dissolve Front Layer.

• Click OK, and preview. The layers have been arranged to have one second of overlap, and the layer on top fades out to reveal the layer underneath.

4 When you have layers that cover the entire frame – or otherwise perfectly line up and cover each other – you want to use the Dissolve Front Layer option. To verify why, undo and try step 3 again using the Cross Dissolve option instead, then scrub the time indicator around where layers overlap: There will be a dip in opacity as the layer on top fades out while the layer underneath is fading up.

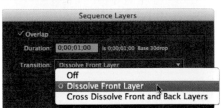

3 Enabling the Overlap option in Sequence Layers (above) both overlaps the layers by the specified duration, and creates Opacity keyframes so that they will crossfade (top).

5 The Cross Dissolve option comes in handy if you have layers of different sizes, or layers with interesting alpha channels:

• Open the comp **03b-Sequence – Alpha*starter** that contains a number of 3D wireframe renders.

• Select All, and press *T* to reveal Opacity.

• Apply Sequence Layers using the Dissolve Front Layer option. Notice how the layer underneath "pops" on through the transparent areas of the layer on top?

• Undo, and try again using the Cross Dissolve Front and Back Layers option. Opacity keyframes are created for both the outgoing and incoming layer. Much nicer, yes?

▽ tip

Sequence and Slip

After performing Sequence Layers, you can then slip edit moving footage to adjust the frames you see without disrupting the overall timing.

▼ Solo Switches

When layers are stacked on top of each other, it can be difficult to see what each one looks like. Use the Solo switches (the hollow circle to the left of the padlock) to preview them individually:

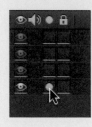

• For instance, turn on the Solo switch for layer 4 to see it in isolation; layers 1–3 will temporarily be disabled and their eyeballs will be grayed out.

• Then turn on the Solo switch for layer 3 to preview it; notice that layer 4 remains soloed.

• ⌥ +click (*Alt* +click) on the Solo switch for layer 2. Only layer 2 will be soloed. All other layers are disabled.

When you're done, and you want to see all the layers again, *turn off the Solo switch for all layers*. If you turn them all on, any layers you add to the comp in the future won't be displayed unless you solo them also!

6 Time to put a few tricks together. Open the comp **03c-Sequence – trim*starter**. Say you want to crossfade between its photographs at a nice, orderly pace:

• Select layer 4, then **Shift**+click to select layer 1. This will select all layers, but from the bottom up (layer 4 will then be sequenced first in time).

• Type ⌥ **Home** (**Alt Home**) to make them all begin at the start of the comp.

• If you want a layer to play for four seconds and then crossfade for one, each layer needs to have a total duration of five seconds. Since After Effects starts counting at 0, move the time indicator to 04:29 for a five-second duration, and type ⌥ **]** (**Alt]**) to trim their out points.

• Right-click on one of the layer bars and select Keyframe Assistant > Sequence Layers. Set the Overlap > Duration to 01:00 crossfade time. (Which Transition option should you use for full-frame sources?) Click OK.

• Press **T** to show the Opacity keyframes, and RAM Preview. Our version is in the **Comps_Finished** folder. Save your project at this point.

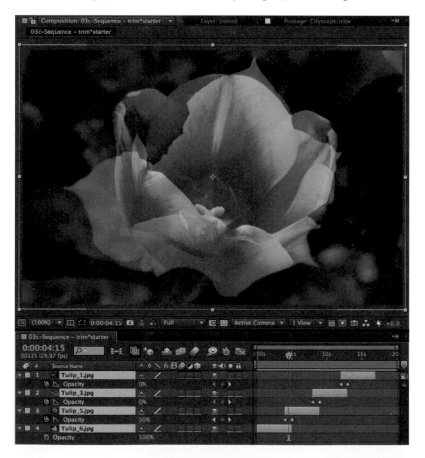

6 To quickly trim layers to have the same duration, line them up to start together, and trim their ends as a group (above). Then use Sequence Layers to automatically spread them across time, with crossfades (right). Photos courtesy Wildscaping.com.

Looping Footage

You now know how to shorten footage by trimming; how can you make it longer? You could increase the Time Stretch value, but that also slows down the playback speed. Fortunately, some clips have been designed to be seamlessly "looped" or repeated. After Effects can make them look like one long clip:

1 Select Close All from the Comp panel's dropdown menu to close all previous comps. In this lesson's Project panel, locate and open **Comps > 04-Looping Footage*starter**. It should be empty.

2 Back in the Project panel, select the folder **My Sources** so that the file you're about to import will automatically sort into it. Type ⌘ I (Ctrl I) to open the Import File dialog.

Navigate to where you copied this lesson's files onto your computer and open the **Lesson 03 > 03_Sources > Movies** folder. Select the file **Clock+Skyline.mov**, and click Open.

Double-click this movie in the Project panel to open it in the Footage panel. Play it, and watch what happens when the movie reaches the end: It looks the same as it did at its beginning, indicating this footage file is a candidate for looping.

3 Select the Project panel, and type ⌘ / (Ctrl /) to add this footage item to the already open comp **04_Looping Footage**. The clip is 10 seconds long, but the comp is 30 seconds long, so it doesn't reach the end.

Select **Clock+Skyline.mov** in the Project panel (not the Timeline panel), and click the Interpret Footage button at the bottom of the Project panel to open its Interpret Footage dialog. Near the bottom is a parameter called Loop. Enter 3 (3 × 10 = 30), and click OK.

4 Back in the comp, you will now see the "ghost" layer bar after the layer's out point, indicating it can be longer. Press End to jump to the end of the comp, select **Clock+Skyline.mov**, and type ⌥] (Alt]) to retrim its out point to this time.

Practice importing, looping, and extending the other files you find in the **Lesson 03 > 03_Sources > Movies** or **> Wireframes** folders on your drive. Most real-world footage does not loop cleanly, but other items – such as the wireframe 3D renders – do.

1 Play the **Clock+Skyline.mov** in the QuickTime Player and it will seamlessly loop. However, it won't automatically loop when After Effects uses it as footage. Footage courtesy Artbeats/Digital Biz.

3 The movie is initially not long enough to play for the entire comp (above). However, it was designed to be looped.

3 *continued* Select the movie in the Project panel, open the Interpret Footage dialog (left) and Loop it 3 times (above).

4 After you loop the movie, you will see that the ghosted (trimmed) duration of its layer bar now reaches to the end of the comp (above). Retrim its out point (below) by dragging or by using keyboard shortcuts.

Image Sequences

Sometimes, you will receive a set of still image files that are intended to be played back as if they were a continuous movie. You don't need to use the Sequence Layers assistant to make this happen; you can do it during import, setting the spacing between frames by "conforming" the resulting file's frame rate.

1 Open Preferences > Import. Because sequences of images have no inherent frame rate, After Effects defaults to setting them to 30 fps. In the Sequence Footage field, enter the correct NTSC frame rate of 29.97 (or 25 fps for PAL). Click OK. This preference will be retained for future projects on this computer.

• In the Project panel, select the folder **My Sources** so that the file you're about to import will automatically sort into it. Type ⌘ I (Ctrl I) to open the Import File dialog.

• Navigate to this lesson's files on your computer, and open the **Lesson 03 > 03_Sources > Muybridge Sequence** folder. It contains 10 similarly named TIFF format files. Select the first one. Along the bottom of the Import File dialog will be a checkbox for TIFF Sequence; make sure it is checked, then click Open.

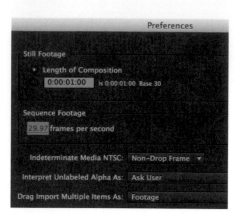

1 Set Preferences > Import > Sequence Footage to the frame rate you expect to be working at, such as 29.97 fps for NTSC video.

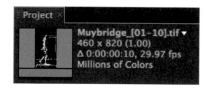

2 After importing, a footage item named **Muybridge_[1-10].tif** will be selected in the **My Sources** folder in the Project panel. Along the top it says it is 10 frames long at 29.97 fps (or 25 fps for PAL).

Ten frames is rather short for a movie; fortunately, this sequence was designed as a seamless loop – so let's loop it. With this file selected, click the Interpret Footage button at the bottom of the Project panel. Enter a large number such as 100 for its Loop Times value, and click OK. The duration should now read 33:10 at the top of the Project panel.

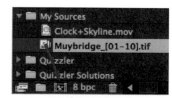

3 Back in the Project panel, drag the image sequence (**Muybridge_[1-10].tif**) to the Create a New Composition icon at the bottom of the Project panel. A new comp will be created with the same width and height, frame rate, and duration as the footage. Press ⌘ K (Ctrl K) to open Composition Settings, and change the duration to something shorter, such as 05:00.

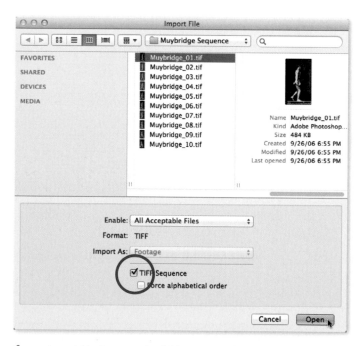

1 *continued* Navigate to the folder that holds your file sequence, select the first frame, and make sure the Sequence option is checked before clicking Open. Footage courtesy Dover.

The new comp – **Muybridge 2** – will be created in the same folder as the footage; move it to the **My Comps** folder.

RAM Preview and check out the speed this sequence plays at (remember that the preview speed is not accurate while it's caching, only when it plays back). Does it seem a bit too fast to be realistic? Let's conform just this layer's frame rate without affecting the global Import Preference.

4 Bring the Project panel forward, select **Muybridge_[1-10]** in your **My Sources** folder, and open its Interpret Footage dialog again. Look for the section named Frame Rate; enter a new number for Assume This Frame Rate (such as 10), and click OK. Bring your comp forward, and RAM Preview again. The footage will play back at this rate in your comp, independent of the comp's frame rate, skipping or repeating frames as needed. Try out different rates until you find one you like the feel of.

4 You can conform your sequence to an alternate frame rate in the Interpret Footage dialog to slow it down (or speed it up!).

Frame Rate versus Time Stretch

There is another way to change the playback speed of a source: Time Stretch. But it has an important difference compared with "conforming" the frame rate…

5 Add a fade-up to your Muybridge sequence: Select the layer, type **T** to reveal Opacity, enable keyframing and set Opacity to 0%. Then move to 01:00 in the timeline and set Opacity back to 100%.

• Change Interpret Footage > Assume This Frame Rate again as you did in step 4; the timing of the keyframes stays the same. This is because settings in the Interpret Footage dialog affect source files *before* they are processed in a comp.

• Reveal the Stretch column in the timeline by right-clicking on any column head and selecting Columns > Stretch. Enter a value of 200%, which means the layer will take twice as long to play back. RAM Preview, and note that not only does the layer slow down, the timing of its Opacity keyframes is stretched as well: Your second keyframe now appears at 02:00. Scrub the value for Stretch and watch this keyframe move. Time stretching affects the speed of a layer *after* the keyframes are applied.

▽ insider knowledge

Stretching Keyframes

Time Stretch is a good way to give multiple copies of the same footage item different playback speeds. However, unlike adjusting a source's Frame Rate, Time Stretch also changes the spacing of any keyframes already applied to the layer.

5 If you place keyframes (top), then use Stretch to retime your footage, the timing of the keyframes will change as well (above).

1 At 100% opacity with its blending mode set to Normal (the default), the Muybridge sequence completely blocks out the background behind it.

Blending Modes

We're going to move on from ways to edit layers in time to ways of stacking layers to make them look cool. The secret to this is *blending modes*.

When you place one layer on top of another, its pixels normally replace the pixels of any image underneath. As you fade the top layer, its pixels are mixed with those underneath. Blending modes provide alternate ways to mix (blend) these pixels together, such as adding together their color values. Let's try out a few to get a feel for them.

1 Open comp **06_Blending Modes*starter**. Select layer 1, **Muybridge_[1-10].tif**, and type **T** to reveal Opacity. Scrub its Opacity value and note the result of fading it in and out over the layer behind it. Set it back to 100% for now.

2 Open the Mode column. You can press **F4** to toggle between it and the normal Switches column. If you have a fairly wide monitor, right-click on any column header in the Timeline panel and select Columns > Modes from the popup: Now you can see both Switches and Modes at the same time (reorder them to taste by dragging the column heads left and right).

Expand or Collapse the Transfer Controls pane

In the Modes column, note that each layer has a Mode popup, which decides how it blends with the layer below. It defaults to Normal. Different types of modes are roughly grouped in this popup – for example, the second group tends to make the results darker; the third group tends to make the results brighter; and the fourth group creates interesting, colorful blends of layers.

△ **2** Press **F4** to toggle the Switches/Modes columns. If you forget the shortcut, two buttons in the bottom left corner of the Timeline panel (above) open and close the Modes (also known as Transfer Controls) and Layer Switches columns. You can also open and close columns by right-clicking on any column header and selecting them; reorder them by dragging the column heads left and right.

▷ *continued* The Mode popup has a long list of choices. They tend to be grouped: Modes that brighten the result, for example, are in the same section.

To move up and down the Mode menu without using the popup, select a layer and press **Shift** **+** (the plus key on the regular keyboard) to move down, and **Shift** **−** (the minus key) to move up.

3 Click on the Mode popup for the **Muybridge** layer, and pick Multiply. This says "take my brightness, and multiply it by the brightness of the pixels underneath." You can think of black pixels as having a value of 0, meaning the result will be 0 (black); think of white pixels having the value of 1 or 100%, which means the result will keep the color of the underlying pixel.

Try other modes in this first group, and notice they have similar but different results.

4 Now select Add mode – this adds the color values of pixels together. If the pixel on top is black (0), it will have no effect on the pixel underneath. If it is white, it will cause the result to be white. Try other modes in this group such as Screen, which is a less intense version of Add.

Normal
Dissolve
Dancing Dissolve

Darken
Multiply
Color Burn
Classic Color Burn
Linear Burn
Darker Color

Add
Lighten
Screen
Color Dodge
Classic Color Dodge
Linear Dodge
Lighter Color

Overlay
Soft Light
Hard Light
Linear Light
Vivid Light
Pin Light
Hard Mix

Difference
Classic Difference
Exclusion
Subtract
Divide

Hue
Saturation
Color
Luminosity

Stencil Alpha
Stencil Luma
Silhouette Alpha
Silhouette Luma

Alpha Add
Luminescent Premul

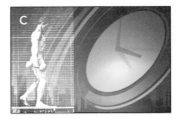

5 Staying with the **Muybridge** layer, select Overlay from the third group. This is a more complex mode, providing colorful, richly saturated results. Black pixels on top darken underlying pixels, but do not cause them to go completely black; white pixels lighten and tint rather than go to white. Again, try other modes in this group.

The next level is applying effects to the layer that is being "moded" onto the layers underneath:

6 Select the **Muybridge** layer, and apply Effect > Color Correction > Levels; it will appear in the Effect Controls panel. The Levels effect is the preferred way to alter the brightness and contrast of a layer. Take a look at the Histogram in the Effect Controls: This gives you a visual representation of the darks and brights that exist in the image.

Try scrubbing the Gamma value, which sets the gray midpoint of a layer; you can also drag its pointer under the middle of the Histogram. Note how it changes the contrast of the image sequence. Try this with the different modes. Remember that you can temporarily solo the layer to see the results of the effect without the blending mode.

7 Turn off Levels by clicking on the stylized "fx" switch next to its name in the Effect Controls panel. Then, with the **Muybridge** layer still selected, apply Effect > Color Correction > Tritone. Click on the Midtones color swatch, and pick a color such as yellow. Or to more closely match the **Muybridge** layer to the background, use the eyedropper to pick a color from the background layer. Notice how the result is richer again and more colorful. Try different colors and modes, and reduce Opacity to tone down intensity.

Save your project, and close all previous comps by selecting Close All from the Comp panel's menu.

3–5 Choosing different modes for **Muybridge_[1-10].tif** creates different "looks" in the way it blends with the underlying layer. Here we compare Normal (A), Multiply (B), Add (C), and Overlay (D).

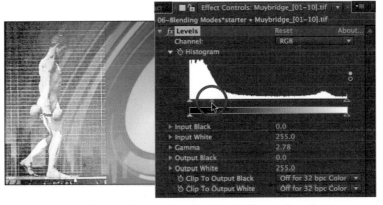

6 You can use effects to further alter the blend. Here we're using Levels to adjust the image's Gamma (right) to alter the midpoint values in the composite using Overlay mode (left).

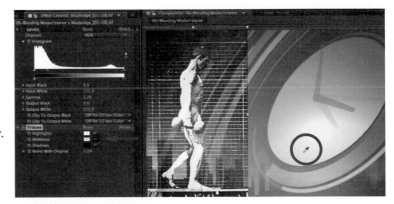

7 We disabled Levels, added Tritone, and used its Midtones eyedropper to select a color from the background to tint the Muybridge image. The result (with Overlay mode) is an even richer composite compared with using the original grayscale source.

2 If the Lens Flare effect is selected (top), you can see and drag around its Flare Center in the Comp panel (above) to interactively place the flare.

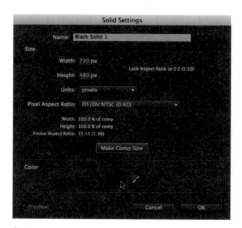

3 Many effects – such as flares – work best if applied to a black comp-size solid.

Effects, Solids, and Modes

Now that you have a working knowledge of modes, let's employ them to give us more control over how we apply effects. While we're here, we'll also show you how to edit the motion path for an effect point.

1 Click on the Project panel tab to bring it forward; if you can't see it, drag the scroll bar along the top of its frame to the left or press ⌘ O (Ctrl O). Then double-click the comp **Comps > 07_Effects Solids Modes*starter** to open it.

2 This comp has a single layer in it: **Cityscape.mov**. Select this layer and apply Effect > Generate > Lens Flare.

While Lens Flare is selected in the Effect Controls panel, you will see a crosshair at the center of the flare's brightest point in the Comp panel – this is its *effect point*. Drag it around the comp and note how the flare changes.

Let's say you generally like this flare, but want to tweak it a bit. You can explore its parameters in the Effect Controls panel, but unfortunately this effect has no way to directly change its color. You could try applying Effect > Color Correction > Hue/Saturation, but this will change the color of the underlying footage as well as the flare. So let's explore a better approach:

3 To gain more control over an effect, we need to give it its own layer.

• Start by removing the effect from the movie, but rather than deleting it, select it in the Effect Controls panel and Edit > Cut.

• Select Layer > New > Solid; the shortcut is ⌘ Y (Ctrl Y). Click on the Make Comp Size button. Then click on the Color swatch and set it to pure black. Click OK in the Color Picker, then OK in the Solid Settings.

• With your new **Black Solid 1** layer selected, select Edit > Paste. The Lens Flare should now appear on the solid layer, using exactly the same settings.

4 If the Mode column is not visible, type F4 to reveal it. Set the Mode for **Black Solid 1** to Add – the black solid will disappear, leaving just the bright flare.

4 Apply the Lens Flare to the solid, and place it above the layer to be treated (left). Try different modes such as Add (A), Lighten (B), and Color Dodge (C) to get different looks.

Now press **Shift +** (the plus symbol on the regular keyboard) to move down the Modes list without using the popup. Screen will give you the same look as when you applied it directly to your footage layer. Linear Dodge looks identical to Add in this mix, while Color Dodge creates a tight single flare. Use whichever mode you like best.

Note that pressing **Shift −** (the minus key) moves back up the modes list.

5 Apply Effect > Color Correction/Hue Saturation to your **Black Solid 1** layer; it will be added to the Effect Controls panel below Lens Flare. Scrub the Master Hue value to change the color of the flare; notice that your underlying footage remains unaffected – this is why you used a solid!

Effect Motion Path

Remember in step 2 where you played with the location of the flare's center? This gives us a good excuse to take a brief detour and show you another important skill: animating the motion path for an effect point path.

6 Make sure the current time indicator is at 00:00. In the Effect Controls panel, click on the stopwatch to the left of the Flare Center parameter to enable keyframing. This should also select the Lens Flare effect, which will cause its Flare Center crosshair to be visible in the Comp panel.

• Drag it to a good starting location, such as near the upper left corner. (If you can't see its crosshair, click on the crosshair in the Effect Controls panel, then click where you want it to be in the Comp viewer.)

• Press **End**, then drag the Flare Center to a good ending location. RAM Preview, and your flare will trek in a straight line across the sky.

The effect point creates *spatial* keyframes (they have an X and Y value), but these values are in relation to the layer, not the comp. That's why you won't see its motion path in the Comp viewer. But all is not lost…

• Double-click the **Black Solid 1** layer to open its Layer panel. In the bottom right corner, check that the View popup is set to Lens Flare and that the Render button is on.

You should now see the Flare Center's motion path.

5 Apply other effects such as Hue/Saturation to the solid layer to alter the lens flare without affecting the underlying footage.

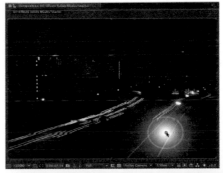

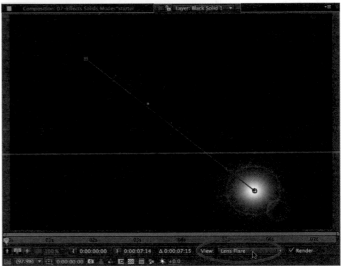

6 Effect Point paths are not visible in the Comp panel (top). Double-click the layer to open its Layer panel (above) where you can edit the effect point path. (If the motion path is not visible, select Lens Flare from the View popup.)

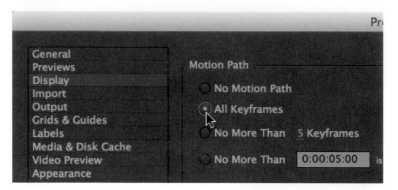

7 We are assuming that you are using the default After Effects preferences. If this is the case, you will see only the keyframe icons for 15:00 worth of time (07:15 seconds on each side of the current time indicator). So at the end of the comp (07:29) you won't see the first keyframe's icon. To fix this, open Preferences > Display, set the Motion Path option to All Keyframes, and click OK. This preference will be retained for future projects on this computer.

△ **7** We suggest you set Preferences > Display > Motion Path to All Keyframes so that you see the entire motion path. (This preference will be retained for all future projects on this computer.)

▷ *continued* To edit the motion path, press **G** to temporarily switch to the Pen tool, then pull out a Bezier handle from the keyframe itself.

Go ahead and edit the Flare Center's motion path, perhaps making a nice arc going across the frame. If you have trouble spotting the two dots that you pull to create Bezier handles (they are in line with the motion path), hold down **G** and drag handles out from the keyframes. Preview the comp to try out your new path, and close the Layer panel when you're done. Our version in the **Comps_Finished** folder is **07-Effects Solids Modes_final1**, where we also animated Flare Brightness and the color.

Lens Flare pivots around the center of the layer it is applied to. By applying it to a solid larger than the comp (as we did in **07-Effects Solids Modes_final2**), you can reposition it as desired.

Big Solids

You may have noticed that a lens flare always pivots around the center of the layer it is applied to. Another reason to apply effects to a solid is that you can increase the size of the solid, then reposition or otherwise transform the solid in the comp to change how the effect appears.

In this exercise, select **Black Solid 1**, type ⌘ *Shift* **Y** (*Ctrl* *Shift* **Y**) to open its Solid Settings, enter a larger number such as 1000 for its Width and Height, and click OK. The flare is no longer required to pivot around the center of the comp, giving you more flexibility in deciding its path. Have fun scaling, rotating, and moving this layer. We provide one alternative idea in **Comps_Finished > 07-Effects Solids Modes_final2**. Save your project when you're done playing.

Deeper into Effects

Next we're going to show you a few more ways to work with effects, including finding them in a hurry, and alternate ways to animate them. Then we'll reveal how to save and use animation presets, which can recall not only what effects you have applied to a layer but any keyframes you have applied as well.

Finding and Animating Effects

It can be a challenge to remember which Effect submenu a particular effect resides in (for example, is Invert in Color Correction or Channel?). Fortunately, After Effects has a panel that makes it much easier to find effects: Effects & Presets.

2 Click on the Options arrow in the upper right corner of the Effects & Presets panel, and temporarily disable Show Animation Presets so only actual effects are searched (left). Then type "**radial**" into the QuickSearch box to search for these characters in any effect name (below).

Effects & Presets is one of the default panels that appear in the Standard workspace. However, it's a bit cramped along the bottom of the right side. To make more room for it, you can close the Preview panel; its frame will close too, making more room for Effects & Presets. (Don't worry; you can always get Preview back by selecting it in the Window menu, or by using Workspace > Reset "Standard".)

1 If the Comp or Timeline panel is forward, close all previous comps by selecting Close All from the Comp panel's dropdown menu. Next, click on the Project panel tab to bring it forward; if you can't see it, type ⌘ **O** (Ctrl **O**) to reveal the Project panel. Then double-click **Comps > 08_Save Preset*starter** to open it. It has one layer in it; select it.

2 Turn your attention to the Effects & Presets panel. Click on its options arrow in its upper right corner: This is where you determine what this panel will show you, and how it will show it. For now, disable the option Show Animation Presets so that you see only the names of actual effects.

Along the top of the Effects & Presets panel is a QuickSearch box, akin to the ones that appear along the tops of the Project and Timeline panels. Type "**radial**" into this box. As you type, the area underneath will sort through all of the effects that contain the characters you are typing. Double-click the effect named Radial Blur, and it will be applied to the layer you had selected. If you forgot to select a layer, you can also drag and drop it onto the desired layer.

3 The Effect Controls panel will open, showing the effect you applied. In addition to some of the normal user interface elements you have seen so far, Radial Blur contains a custom element in the form of the blur graphic. To change the

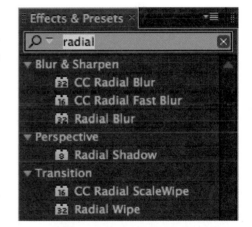

Effects & Presets Guided Tour

The Effects & Presets panel offers many different options for searching through effects and animation presets. There is a QuickTime movie in the **03-Video Bonus** folder that walks you through these options, as well as advice on searching and organizing animation presets.

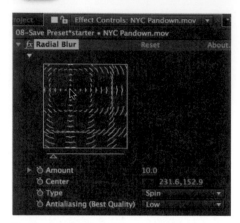

3 The Radial Blur effect has a custom user interface to adjust the center and amount of blur. Drag inside the graph to change the center of the blur.

center of the blur, either drag around inside the graph in the Effect Controls, or drag the effect point directly in the Comp panel. The slider directly below the graphic changes the Amount of blur. Change the Type popup from Spin to Zoom for a different effect.

• Come up with a look you like, and at 00:00 enable keyframing for the Amount property by clicking on the stopwatch to the left of its name in the Effect Controls panel. Type **U**, and this animated property will be revealed in the Timeline panel as well.

• Move the current time indicator a few seconds later to around 04:00, and set the Amount to 0. Type **N** to end the work area here, and press **O** on the numeric keypad to RAM Preview. Your blur effect will animate from your initial setting to unprocessed video over this time.

4 Let's apply another effect to help create a sort of flashback look. In the Effect & Presets panel, delete "radial" and instead type "**tint**" in the QuickSearch box to reveal the Tint effect. (Note that recent and saved searches appear above where you are typing.) Double-click Tint, and it too will be applied to your layer.

3–5 Animate Radial Blur and Tint (top) to resolve from a blurry black-and-white image to a sharp, full-color one (above). Footage courtesy Artbeats/New York Scenes.

5 Press **Home** to return to the start of the comp (and where you placed your first Radial Blur keyframe).

• In the Effect Controls panel, enable keyframing for the Amount to Tint parameter at its default value of 100%, which creates a nice black and white treatment. Press **U** until both this and the Radial Blur keyframes are revealed in the Timeline panel.

• Press **Shift** **End** to jump to the end of the work area around 04:00. In the Effect Controls panel, set the Amount to Tint value to 0%, restoring the original color in the image.

Save your project, and RAM Preview. If you'd like to compare results, we saved our version as **Comps_Finished > 08-Save Preset_final**.

Saving Animation Presets

Let's say you like that treatment, and decide you'd like to apply it to other layers. You could copy and paste the effects and their keyframes, but that's cumbersome – especially if that layer was in a new project, started sometime in the future!

You should know by now that whenever we present you with a problem, we're about to show you a better way:

6 In your **08-Save Preset*starter** comp, select the **NYC Pandown** layer and press **F3** to bring the Effect Controls panel forward (if it isn't already). Click on the effect name Radial Blur to select it, then **Shift**+click on Tint to select it as well.

There are various ways to save your effects as an animation preset:

• Choose the menu item Animation > Save Animation Preset.

• Click on the Create New Animation Preset icon at the bottom right of the Effects & Presets panel.

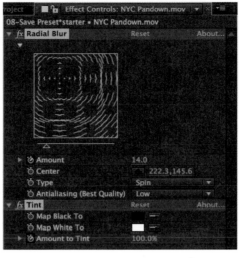

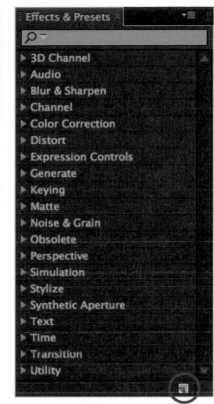

A file browser dialog will open. It should default to the folder **Adobe > After Effects CS6 > User Presets** inside your operating system's user documents folder. Save your presets in either this or the **Adobe After Effects CS6 > Presets** folder, and it will automatically appear in the Effects & Presets panel later. It's a good idea to create your own subfolders inside **Presets** to keep track of the presets you save. So create a New Folder, give it your name, then give your new preset a name you'll remember it by – say, "**radial flashback.ffx**" (keep the .ffx suffix). Then click Save. After a slight pause, the Effects & Presets panel will refresh.

6 Select both effects (above left), then use either the Animation menu item or the button in the lower right corner of the Effect & Presets panel (above) to Save Preset.

7 To see how easy it is to apply your new preset to a different layer, bring the Project panel forward and open a different comp: **09_Apply Preset*starter**. Preview; it currently has an untreated video layer in it called **City Rush.mov**. Select that layer (if you don't select a layer first, After Effects will create a solid and apply the preset to that).

Animation presets apply their keyframes starting at the location of the current time indicator. If you want to make sure that your keyframes start when the layer starts, select the layer, and type **I** to jump to its in point *before* applying a preset.

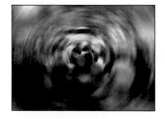

7 There are several ways to search for saved animation presets; if you've just saved it or used it, it will appear in the Animation > Recent Animation Presets menu (above). You can then apply the preset to any other layer (left). Footage courtesy Artbeats/City Rush.

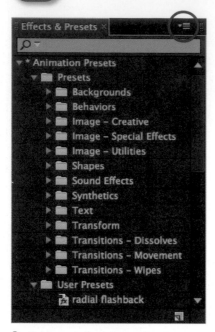

2 Twirl open the *** Animation Presets** folder. It contains hundreds of presets supplied by Adobe, broken down by category into folders; it also contains any folders you created (such as the one you made in the previous exercise).

Remember that you won't see animation presets unless the Show Animation Presets option is selected from the Effects & Presets options menu (click arrow in top right).

3 The **Image – Creative** presets include treatments ranging from **Colorize – gold dip** (below left) to **Bloom – crystallize 2** (below right). Footage: Artbeats/Aerial Clouds.

Just like you have options on how to save a preset, you have options for applying presets. With the layer selected, either:

• Open the Animation menu. If you hover over the Recent Animation Presets submenu, your new preset will appear there.

• You could use the handy Effects & Presets panel and its search function! For this to work though, you will need to include presets in the search. Click on the Effects & Presets options arrow, and reselect the choice Show Animation Presets. Then start typing "**flashback**", or whatever name you gave your preset, until it appears. Double-click it or drag it onto your layer.

• If it exists outside your After Effects application folder, you can use Animation > Apply Animation Preset and navigate to the preset on disk.

Whichever method you use, the Effect Controls panel will come forward to show which effects are part of the preset. Type **U** to reveal animated properties in the Timeline panel; you should see your two effects as well as your keyframes. Preview, and you will see your entire treatment has been re-created on this new layer in this new comp.

Adobe's Animation Presets

In addition to creating and saving your own animation presets, After Effects ships with hundreds of presets that Adobe has developed for you to use. Let's take a quick trip through applying them. While we're at it, we'll explore a few of our favorite categories:

1 Save your project, and open the comp **10_Adobe's Presets*starter**. It has two layers in it; currently, the first layer (**Kite.ai**) has its Video switch turned off. Select the second layer: **Aerial Clouds.mov**.

2 Delete any text left over in the Contains box of the Effects & Presets panel. Twirl open the top folder – *** Animation Presets**. (If you can't see it, enable Show Animation Presets from Effects & Presets Options menu.) This contains Adobe's presets, and if you saved your own presets as we instructed above, your own folder will show up here as well.

3 Twirl open the **Image – Creative** subfolder (resize the panel wider if the names are truncated). It contains a number of interesting image treatments. For example, double-click **Colorize – gold dip**; the footage will take on deep red and gold tones (press **End** to see it on a mixture of clouds and sky). Undo to remove this preset, then try another, such as **Bloom – crystallize 2**. Now the clouds will take on a more painterly, impressionistic appearance.

4 In the Timeline panel, turn on the Video switch (the eyeball icon) for the layer **Kite.ai** and select it.

Twirl up the **Image – Creative** folder, and instead twirl down the subfolder **Behaviors**. These use a combination of effects and "expressions" (a user programming language for After Effects) that creates animation moves without the need for keyframes.

For example, double-click the preset **Rotate Over Time**, then preview: The kite will slowly rotate clockwise over the course of the comp. Look at the Effect Controls panel, and scrub the Rotation parameter in the top effect – this controls how fast the layer rotates, and in what direction.

Undo until the Rotate Over Time preset is removed, and apply the **Wiggle – position** preset. Preview; the kite will now wander about the comp – without you having to keyframe a motion path! Edit the two values in the Wiggle parameters at the top of the Effect Controls panel to change how turbulent the wind is.

Note that there are separate Behavior presets for wiggling position, rotation, scale, and skew, but the most fun to play with has to be **Wigglerama**, which throws them all into one mondo preset! Try it on some of your own footage items, or a text or logo layer.

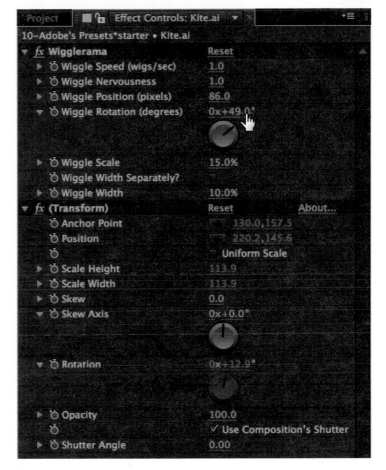

4 Some presets – such as **Wigglerama** – add a specialized "controller" effect, followed by one or more effects that it actually controls.

4 *continued:* The Behaviors presets create automated animation, such as **Wigglerama**'s random movement. Kite courtesy iStockphoto, ggodby, image #229044.

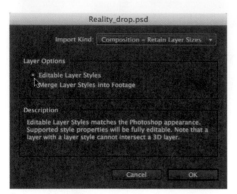

2 When importing a layered Photoshop file (format = PSD), set Import Kind to Composition – Retain Layer Sizes and enable Editable Layer Styles. This will give you maximum flexibility in using the file.

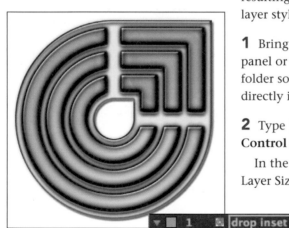

3 This stylized waterdrop-like badge (above) was created by Andrew Heimbold of Reality Check using layer styles in Photoshop. Unlike normal effects, Layer styles may be edited only in the Timeline panel (right). You can toggle each style on and off individually, as well as twirl them down to edit their parameters.

Layer Styles

In addition to plug-in effects, After Effects also features *layer styles*, which originated in Adobe Photoshop. They offer a different way to add bevels, shadows, gradients, and other treatments to layers. Layer styles usually offer more sophisticated options than their counterparts such as Effect > Perspective > Drop Shadow or > Bevel Alpha.

You can import a Photoshop file that has layer styles embedded in it, or apply them to virtually any layer inside After Effects. They are applied from the Layer menu (rather than the Effect menu), and their parameters are edited directly in the Timeline panel rather than in the Effect Controls panel.

Importing a Photoshop File with Layer Styles

There are two ways to treat a Photoshop file that has layer styles embedded: You can "flatten" the file on import, which will render layer styles into the resulting image, or you can import the file as a composition with editable layer styles. We'll take the latter path, as it provides maximum flexibility:

1 Bring the Project panel forward by clicking on its tab; if you can't see this panel or tab, use Window > Project to reveal it. Then select the **My Comps** folder so you can import a Photoshop file and its accompanying composition directly into the correct folder.

2 Type ⌘ *I* (*Ctrl* *I*) to open the import dialog. Navigate to **Lesson 03-Layer Control > 03_Sources** and select **Reality_drop.psd**. Click Open.

In the dialog that opens, set the Import Kind popup to Composition – Retain Layer Sizes. Under Layer Options, enable Editable Layer Styles. Then click OK.

A composition and folder – both named **Reality_drop** – will be created in the **My Comps** folder in the Project panel. If you like, drag the **Reality_drop Layers** folder into your **My Sources** folder.

3 Double-click the comp **Reality_drop** to open it. Two layers will appear: **drop inset** and **drop frame**. Toggle their Video switches (the eyeball icons) on and off to confirm which piece is which in the final image.

In the Timeline panel, twirl down **drop inset**, then twirl down Layer Styles. You will see a list of all possible layer styles. In the A/V Features column, you will see a Video switch for each of the styles. Toggle them on and off to get a feel for what each style is contributing to the final render.

4 Sometimes, a Layer Style has a visual contribution that is different from its name. For example, when you toggle Outer Glow on and off, a dark shadow around the raised inset appears and disappears. Twirl down Outer Glow and scrub its Opacity value: This affects how dark the "shadow" is. Look a little farther down the list, and you will notice that Outer Glow's Color is black; this is what is creating the shadow effect. Click on the Color swatch to change its color, and now you will see its true effect.

Have fun experimenting with the other parameters for Outer Glow, then move onto the other layer styles. Note that each parameter also has an animation stopwatch next to it, meaning it can be animated!

Applying Layer Styles

As mentioned on the previous page, you can also apply layer styles to other layers inside After Effects. They work best on layers that have interesting alpha channels, such as icons or text.

1 In the Project panel, double-click **Comps > 11-Layer Styles*starter** to open it. This composition features the beginnings of a DVD menu. Your goal is to make the buttons look more interesting.

4 Layer Styles > Bevel and Emboss can convert flat buttons (above left) to ones with dimension (above). Experiment with Bevel and Emboss's parameters (below). Background courtesy Wildscaping.com.

2 Select layer 2 – **Button 1** – and apply Layer > Layer Styles > Bevel and Emboss. The buttons will suddenly have more dimension, appearing to be raised off the surface of the background.

3 In the Timeline panel, twirl down **Button 1** > Layer Styles > Bevel and Emboss. Change the Technique popup from Smooth to Chisel Hard, noting the change in the bevel profile. Set Technique back to Smooth, and increase the Size parameter to get a larger rounding.

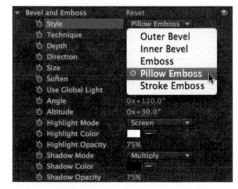

4 Change the Style popup to Outer Bevel or Emboss; now the buttons appear to be pushing up from the background surface. Change Style to Pillow Emboss, and now the buttons appear to be cut into the background image.

5 Change the Style popup back to Inner Bevel. Now add Layer > Layer Styles > Outer Glow or > Drop Shadow to **Button 1**. Experiment with the parameters of these layer styles to create different looks – for example, increase the Size to get more dimension. For practice, give the other two buttons similar or different looks: There is a lot you can do with layer styles.

▽ future vision

Adjustment Ideas

Anything you do to effect the shape or opacity of an adjustment layer is fair game; see *Idea Corner* at the end of this lesson for one suggestion. In later lessons you'll learn about masks and track mattes; you can also apply these techniques to adjustment layers to create interesting shapes for the effected area.

2 The half-moon icon in the Timeline panel indicates that a layer is an adjustment layer.

5–6 Scaling down the adjustment layer (below) results in just an inset portion of the composite being affected by the effects applied to the adjustment layer (above).

Adjustment Layers

Another great tool to use with effects is an *adjustment layer*. These allow you to apply effects to just one layer, and have them affect all of the layers underneath. Then we'll wrap this lesson by showing you one of our favorite tricks.

1 Bring the Project panel forward by clicking on its tab; if you can't see it, type ⌘ 0 (*Ctrl* 0). Then open **Comps > 12_Adjustment Layers*starter**. How would you go about blurring all three layers in it? Happily, you don't have to apply a blur effect three times!

2 Select Layer > New > Adjustment Layer. This creates a solid that is the same size as the comp and places it at the top of the layer stack, with one difference: Its Adjustment Layer switch (the half-moon icon in the Timeline panel's Switches column) is on. You can't "see" adjustment layers; you need to apply effects to them and observe their results.

3 With your **Adjustment Layer** selected, add Effect > Blur & Sharpen > Fast Blur. The Effect Controls panel will come forward. Enable Repeat Edge Pixels, then increase the Blurriness value; the entire composite image gets blurrier.

4 Adjustment layers treat only those layers underneath them in the layer stack. In the Timeline panel, grab **Adjustment Layer** and drag it down a level, just above the **Muybridge_[1-10].tif** layer: The title is no longer blurred, but the layers underneath still are.

Drag **Adjustment Layer** down one more level, to just above the layer **Clock+Skyline.mov**. Now just the background image of the clock and skyline are blurred, and the other two layers above it are sharp.

5 If adjustment layers don't cover the entire comp image area, then only the area underneath them will get treated.

Select **Adjustment Layer**, and type **S** to reveal its Scale. Reduce the Scale to around 80% while keeping an eye on the comp: You will see that only the areas below the adjustment layer are blurred. Drag it to reside just below **Why We Work.ai** so the text remains sharp, while part of the background is blurred.

6 Try out some other effects: Add Effect > Color Correction > Hue/Saturation, and scrub its Master Hue and Saturation values to colorize the underlying layers.

7 With **Adjustment Layer** still selected, type **Shift T** to reveal its Opacity. Scrub this value, and note how much of the adjustment layer's effect is blended into the final composite.

Applying a Filmic Glow

Adjustment layers are handy for adding effects to a number of layers that have been stacked to create a composite image. They are equally useful for quickly treating a number of layers that have been arranged in time, such as a video montage.

1–4 The original image is sharp and literal (A). Adding an adjustment layer with some blur results in the entire image becoming blurry (B). Choosing a mode such as Overlay (left) results in a much more interesting treatment (C).

1 Reopen one of the comps from this lesson's earlier exercises where you were playing with editing layers, such as **03a_Sequence Layers – Full Frame**.

2 Add a Layer > New > Adjustment Layer to this comp – a new layer will appear above your edit.

3 Apply Effect > Blur & Sharpen > Fast Blur to your new adjustment layer, increase its Blurriness parameter, and toggle on the Repeat Edge Pixels option. Drag the current time indicator through the timeline, and note how all of your layers – including any crossfades between them – get the same amount of blur.

4 Type **F4** to reveal the Modes panel, and select a blending mode such as Screen or Overlay for the adjustment layer. The result will be that a blurred composite of your layers will be blended back on top, creating an intense, dreamy, sort of filmic look that is very popular. You can alter this layer's Opacity, or add Color Correction > Levels and alter the Gamma of the adjustment layer to balance the grayscale values in the final composite. You can even duplicate your adjustment layer and use a different mode for each.

This general technique is often referred to as "Instant Sex." One version of it is saved in **Comps_Finished > 03a-Sequence – Full Frame_final**. In our version, we duplicated the adjustment layer then set one to Overlay and the other to Screen. You don't have to blur both layers, but you must apply an effect in order for the mode to actually work.

▽ tip

Universal Tint

A great way to help unify a group of disparate clips is to give them all the same color treatment. For example, apply Tritone (or even Colorama) to an adjustment layer above an edited group of clips, and tweak its Opacity to get the amount of tint you want.

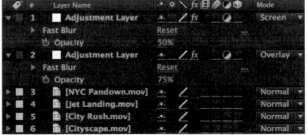

We often apply two adjustment layers to create the Instant Sex look. See example: **Comps_Finished > 03a-Sequence – Full Frame_final**.

▽ tip

Preset Variations

Brainstorm works particularly well with Snimation Presets to generate variations on their themes. In particular, try Brainstorm on presets in the Backgrounds, Behaviors, and Synthetics folders by selecting the effects they apply to a layer. In the case of Behaviors, select only the first "controller" effect; don't select the effects whose names are in parentheses.

1–2 To add an illustrated feel to video (above), apply the Cartoon effect and tweak its Fill and Edge parameters to taste (right). Footage courtesy Artbeats/ Sports Metaphors.

3 Select the Cartoon effect and click Brainstorm in the Timeline panel.

Brainstorm

A large portion of graphic design is playing "What if?" The game can be as simple as deciding how far or how fast to animate a layer, or as complex as trying to learn an effect that has a seemingly endless list of sliders and values. As much fun as this game is, it can take a while to play.

This is where Brainstorm comes in. You select as many or as few parameters, keyframes, or effects as you like on a single layer and let Brainstorm create different combinations of values for you. It presents nine variations at a time; you can toss them all away and start over, or select ones that are close and have Brainstorm generate new ideas based on those. You can apply one of Brainstorm's results to the layer you are working on, or have it save intermediate variations into new compositions. Here we'll use it to discover the wide range of "looks" you can get with the Cartoon effect.

1 Close any previous compositions and double-click **Comps > 13-Cartoon Brain*starter** to open it. It contains a clip from a baseball game. Say you want to give this clip a hand-drawn appearance akin to a cartoon.

2 Select **Baseball.mov** and apply Effect > Stylize > Cartoon. You will see the colors take on a flat "posterized" look with edges between colors outlined in black. In the Effect Controls panel, experiment with Cartoon's parameters.

We personally start with the Fill section; you can get some really interesting looks by lowering Shading Steps and Shading Smoothness. We also tend to lower Edge > Width and Edge > Threshold.

3 With **Baseball.mov** still selected, press **E** to reveal the Cartoon effect in the Timeline and select Cartoon (or a desired subset of its parameters). Then click the Brainstorm icon along the top of the Timeline panel. A dialog box with nine copies of your comp will appear, each showing a variation on your original layer.

4 Brainstorm defaults to creating relatively mild variations of your original idea. If you want to see the full range of what is possible with the Cartoon effect, increase the Randomness value to 100% and click on the Brainstorm button at the bottom of this dialog box. You will get nine more choices, with more variations. Keep clicking the Brainstorm button until you see one or more variations you like. If you feel you went past a good screen of variations, click the Back button to the left of the main Brainstorm button. There is also a Play button to see these variations in motion.

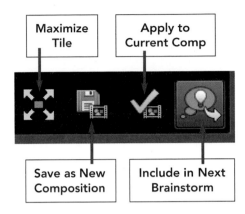

Maximize Tile

Apply to Current Comp

Save as New Composition

Include in Next Brainstorm

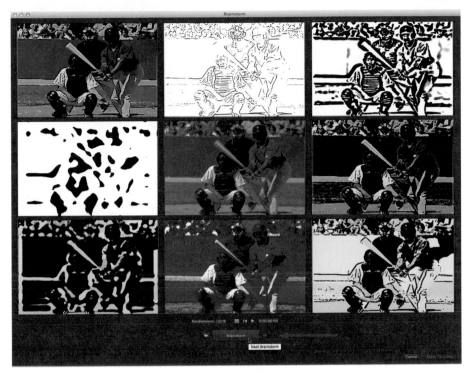

5 Hover your cursor over a preferred variation, and a series of four buttons will appear floating on top of it. Click on the Include in Next Brainstorm button to tell After Effects "more like these." You can include more than one variation if you like. Reduce Randomness to 25% or less and click Brainstorm again to get more tightly focused variations.

6 If you see a variation that you like but are not quite sure if it is "The One," click the Save as New Composition button. It will be saved in the same folder as the comp you are currently working on, with its ending number incremented automatically. You can reverse-engineer these later to learn how to get those particular looks.

7 Keep going, clicking Brainstorm and checking different variations you like, until you find one you'd like to continue with. Move your cursor over your chosen variation so that its buttons appear and click Apply to Current Composition. The Brainstorm dialog obx will close, and these parameters will be applied to your selected effect.

Feel free to keep tweaking Brainstorm's results to get the precise look you want. You can also modify the results effects like Cartoon gives you by adding colorization effects, as we did in **Comps_finished > 13-Cartoon Brain_final**. Of course, you can also Brainstorm these effects or just select specific parameters to Brainstorm. Brainstorm isn't a replacement for creativity, but it can help you get over creative blocks.

4–5 Brainstorm presents you with nine variations of the selected parameters. Click the large Brainstorm button to generate new variations (above). When you see a variation you like, hover your cursor over this image to see what your options are (above, left).

7 Our final, after using Brainstorm to generate new ideas with Cartoon, plus pre- and post-processing with other effects.

▼ Tech Corner: Non-Square Pixels

Most of the exercises in this lesson use compositions that have a size of 720×480 pixels. This is the size of a standard definition DV NTSC (North American Television Standards Committee) video frame. Another common standard definition format is the NTSC D1 (professional digital video) size of 720×486 pixels; in Europe and some other parts of the world, the common size is 720×576 pixels.

All of these sizes describe an image area that has an aspect ratio of 4:3 – four units wide for every three units tall. But if you dragged out a calculator, you would find that none of these frame dimensions work out to a 4:3 ratio. What's going on?

Computers assume that every pixel (picture element) will be drawn as wide as it is tall – in other words, as a square. However, many digital video standards are designed using *non-square pixels*. This means they expect to be "projected" during playback in a slightly distorted manner. The amount of this distortion is referred to as the *pixel aspect ratio* (PAR for short).

In the case of NTSC DV, images will be drawn wider on the computer screen compared with how they will look when corrected for the television screen; in the case of PAL, they will be drawn narrower on the computer than they'll appear on television. As a result, if a D1/DV composition looks correct on the computer screen, it'll probably look wrong on a television screen where the pixels are rectangular.

Some widescreen formats (such as HDV) have a more extreme distortion. If looking at this distortion drives you crazy, the Footage, Composition, and Layer panels have Toggle Pixel Aspect Ratio Correction buttons to compensate for this in the way they are

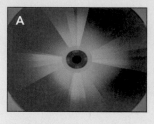  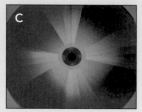

△ Objects that are supposed to appear perfectly round (A) may appear on the computer to be too fat (B) or skinny (C). This is the natural result of non-square pixels. Footage courtesy Artbeats/Digidelic.

△ Along the bottom of the Comp panel is a Pixel Aspect Ratio Correction switch that will rescale the Comp view to make non-square pixels appear correct on a square pixel computer screen.

displayed on your computer screen. This is for preview purposes only; it does not affect the Make Movie or Export functions.

After Effects does an excellent job of managing PARs, automatically stretching and squashing layers as needed to line things up – as long as everything is tagged correctly! For footage items, this is done in the Interpret Footage dialog: Video should have the Pixel Aspect Ratio popup set to match its format (this happens automatically in most cases); photographs and the like should be set for square pixels.

In Composition > Composition Settings, all comps should also have their Pixel Aspect Ratio popup set to match their video format. Selecting from the Preset popup will also set the PAR popup appropriately.

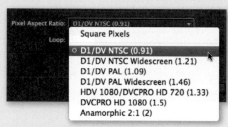

△ For After Effects to properly manage pixel aspect ratios, it is absolutely essential that you set this ratio correctly and truthfully for all footage in the Interpret Footage dialog (above), and when creating compositions (below).

Idea Corner

• Do you have access to a still-image camera and a tripod? Use it to create a time-lapse or stop motion "video" of a scene. Import the stills as an image sequence, or import them individually and use Sequence Layers to add crossfades.

Idea-Adjustment Layer Alpha: We used the butterfly layer as an adjustment layer and animated it with Motion Sketch. Butterfly courtesy Dover.

• In the **Idea Corner** folder in the Project panel, open the **Idea-Adjustment Layer Alpha** comp. Layer 1 is an animated butterfly created with Motion Sketch (Lesson 2). It has the Hue/Saturation effect applied. Turn on the Adjustment Layer switch (the black/white split circle) for this layer. The butterfly becomes an adjustment layer, and any effects are now applied to the layer below using the butterfly's alpha channel! Try this with your own sources; text or logo layers work well, too.

• Also in the **Idea Corner** folder, open the **Idea-Animated Bars** comp. Layer 1 (**bar 1**) is a full frame adjustment layer. Select it and open Layer > Solid Settings, and change the width to 100 pixels. Press **F3** to open the Effect Controls, and edit the effects to taste. Animate this bar moving left or right across the frame (extra points for using Behaviors > Drift Over Time). Create additional bars for a more complex look. (*Note: We used the Transform effect to scale the layers below, as the regular Scale property scales only the size of the adjustment layer solid.*)

Idea-Animated Bars: Animated adjustment layers can create interesting looks.

• The Muybridge frames in our image sequence were originally part of a "film-strip" that contained five images in a row – see the **Idea Corner > Muybridge > Sources** folder. We used Hold keyframes to line up and pose these individual images inside the **barbell walk sequence** comp and then rendered them out as a sequence that we could then import and loop. If you have one of the Muybridge books* (from Dover Publications), scan a different image and create another sequence using the same technique.

Quizzler

• Inside this lesson's **Quizzler** folder is a movie called **Quiz_pyro.mov**; play it. The explosion was originally shot against black, with no alpha channel. Open **Quiz-Pyro*starter** – how would you composite it on top of the drumming shot?

• In the Quizzler folder, play the movie **Quiz-Build on Layers.mov**; four objects build on over time, two seconds apart, each one fading up for one second. We used Sequence Layers to help create this effect. Open the **Quiz-Build*starter** comp and see if you can re-create this look. It's a brain teaser! (The answer is in the **Quizzler Solutions** folder.)

Our versions of some of the Idea Corner and Quizzler animations are contained in a folder of the same name inside this project file. Don't peek!

Quiz-Pyro: Composite of an explosion shot on black on top of the **Musical Instruments** footage. Footage courtesy Artbeats' Reel Explosions 3 and Musical Instruments.

* Muybridge was a photographer who in the 1870–'80s devised ways of taking timelapse photographs of humans and animals in motion. Muybridge released two books of his plates – *Animals in Motion* and *The Human Figure in Motion* – which Dover publishes to this day.

Creating Transparency

Using masks, mattes, and stencils to cut out portions of a layer.

▽ In This Lesson

94   masking tools; creating mask shapes
95   Rounded Rectangle tool
96   Free Transform Points
96   masking in the Layer panel; Ellipse tool
97   Mask Feather
98   animating a mask path
99   creating a vignette; Mask Expansion
100 masking with the Pen tool (Bezier masks)
101 applying an effect to a masked area
102 controlling mask path interpolation
103 using effects with the mask path
104 Mask Modes and multiple masks
105 Mask Opacity
106 creating and editing RotoBezier masks
107 Audio Spectrum effect
108 variable mask feathering *(new in CS6)*
112 Alpha Track Matte
114 nesting a track matte composite
116 Luma Track Matte
117 animating matte layers
118 Stencil Luma and Stencil Alpha
121 effects with track mattes and stencils

▽ Getting Started

Copy the **Lesson 04-Transparency** folder from this book's disc onto your hard drive, and make note of where it is; it contains the project file and sources you need to execute this lesson.

In this lesson, we will be focusing on different ways to create transparency. One of the keys to creating an interesting composite of multiple images is to make portions of those images transparent, so that you can see other images behind or through them. This is one of the main techniques that sets motion graphic design and visual effects compositing apart from video editing.

Masks, Mattes, and Stencils

In previous lessons, we introduced two basic forms of managing transparency: altering the Opacity property of a layer, and taking advantage of a layer's built-in alpha channel that defines which parts of it are supposed to be transparent. In this lesson, you will go beyond these by adding your own transparent areas to an image using *masks*, *track mattes*, and *stencils*.

Masking is a way to cut out sections of a specific layer. At its default, a mask path says "I want to see only the area inside this shape; make the area outside transparent." You can draw your own shapes and paths directly on the layer, or copy paths from the Adobe companion programs Photoshop and Illustrator and paste them onto an After Effects layer to create a mask path. You may have multiple masks per layer, and combine them in a variety of ways such as adding together their shapes or using only the area where they overlap. You can also control the opacity of a mask (making its cutout semitransparent), define its feather (how soft its edges are), and invert it so areas inside of its shape – rather than outside – are transparent. As an added bonus, some effects can use mask paths, and you can also have

Masks take a layer (A), and allow you to cut out portions to make them transparent or opaque (B). Mattes use either the alpha channel or luminance of one layer (C) to define the transparency of a second layer (D) to create a final composite image (E). Video fill courtesy Artbeats/Virtual Insanity.

text follow a mask (which we'll show in the next lesson). You can even create a mask path that is just a line or path rather than an enclosed area; these are particularly handy when used in conjunction with effects or text.

Note that the same shape tools are used to create mask paths and shape layers (Lesson 11). For this lesson, be sure to select a layer first so you only create masks.

Track mattes, by contrast, involve the combination of two layers. One layer – the matte – is used just to define transparency; you don't directly see the image it contains. This matte is then used to decide what portions of the layer immediately below it are visible. There are two types of mattes: *alpha mattes*, which use the matte's alpha channel to define the transparency of the second layer, and *luminance* (or *luma*) *mattes*, which use the luminance – grayscale values, or brightness – of the matte layer to define the transparency of the second layer.

Stencils take the concept of track mattes further: Rather than define the transparency of the next layer below, a stencil layer defines the transparency of *all* the layers below, cutting a hole through the entire layer stack. Just like mattes, stencils can also be based around alpha channels or luminance.

It's easy to confuse these methods of creating transparency, so just remember: Masks involve one layer, mattes involve two layers (the fill and the matte), and stencils are basically mattes that can affect multiple layers below them. In this lesson, you'll learn how to put all three to work.

▽ future vision

Keying

Keying – the art of making certain colors in a layer transparent – is another way of creating transparency. Unlike the techniques demonstrated in this lesson, keying relies on an effect to create transparency. Keying is covered in Lesson 9.

▽ tip

Help with Shortcuts

For a full list of Pen tool and mask editing shortcuts, see Help > Keyboard Shortcuts and click on Shortcuts: Masks.

Shape tools (**Q**)   Pen tool (**G**)

The Shape tools menu includes five basic shapes (press **Q** to select this tool and toggle between the choices, shown below). Both this and the Pen tool are used to draw *both mask paths and shape layers*. You'll be creating mask paths only in this lesson so be sure to *preselect the layer first* before drawing a path (when no layer is selected you may inadvertently draw a Shape Layer!)

☐	Rectangle Tool	Q
☐	Rounded Rectangle Tool	Q
●	Ellipse Tool	Q
⬟	Polygon Tool	Q
★	Star Tool	Q

You can use modifier keys (see table) to alter shapes as you drag them, as we did here with the Star shape. Note that you can add the spacebar while dragging to reposition the mask shape before you release the mouse. Footage courtesy Artbeats/Timelapse Landscapes 2.

Masking

There are several ways to create masks, and several ways to use them. Before we get started, spend a few minutes getting used to how the masking tools work.

1 We assume you've already opened the project **Lesson_04.aep**. In the Project panel, open the **Comps** folder and double-click the comp **00-Masking*practice**.

• Select the layer **Wildflowers.mov**. If no layer is selected, you will create a Shape Layer instead of a mask path (just Undo if that happens in this lesson).

• Select the basic Rectangle tool from the Tools panel along the top of the application window. Click and drag in the Comp panel to create a rectangular shape. As you draw this mask shape, the areas beyond the mask will disappear, revealing the background color. That was easy, so try out a few more shapes for size!

• Undo to remove your first mask. Click on the Shape tools popup menu. It contains five choices: the Rectangle and Ellipse tools are fairly straightforward; note you can add the **Shift** key to draw perfect squares and circles.

• To start over, either Undo or select Layer > Mask > Remove All Masks.

• To create a full-frame mask, select the layer and double-click the shape tool.

• The Rounded Rectangle, Polygon, and Star shapes have additional parameters: how rounded the corners are, how many sides there are to the polygon, and how many points there are on the star. You can interactively change these shapes if you add the following keys *after* you start drawing the shape but *before* you release the mouse:

Shape Type	Up/Down Cursor Keys (or scroll wheel)	Left/Right Cursor
Rounded Rectangle	corner roundness	toggle rectangle/ellipse
Polygon	number of sides	corner roundness
Star	number of points	point roundness

In addition, pressing **⌘** on Mac (**Ctrl** on Windows) while dragging out a Star shape alters just the outer radius, while pressing **Page Up** and **Page Down** alters the inner roundness.

The Rectangle, Rounded Rectangle, and Ellipse are drawn from corner to corner as you drag; add **⌘** (**Ctrl**) while dragging to draw them from their centers. The Polygon and Star are always drawn from their centers outward; add the **Shift** key to stop them from rotating.

Once you are done dragging out the mask, it will immediately be converted into a Bezier path. Unlike with Shape Layers (Lesson 11), there is no easy way to edit the roundness or number of points in a mask after the fact.

▼ Masks versus Shapes

Both Masks Paths (this lesson) and Shape Layers (Lesson 11) are created using the same Shape and Pen tools. So, how do you know which you are creating?

- If no layer is selected, you will create a new Shape Layer.
- If any layer other than a Shape Layer is selected, you will draw a Mask.
- If a Shape Layer is selected, a pair of buttons to the right in the Tools panel determine whether you are creating a new Shape Path or a Mask for the Shape Layer.

▽ gotcha

Reset Shape Tools

If you use a modifier key while drawing a shape, this will become the new default for that tool from then on, even if you quit After Effects. To reset the tool to its basic shape again, double-click the Shape tool (then immediately Undo to remove the mask or shape created if you don't need it).

▽ tip

Shapes by Numbers

Clicking the word Shape in the switches column of the Timeline panel opens the Mask Shape dialog, where you can enter values numerically.

2 Now that you have some idea of how masking works, in this first exercise, we will focus on using the basic mask shapes to create windows on footage, to reveal a title, and to create a vignette. (Subsequent lessons will cover using the Pen tool to create more intricate mask paths, using mask modes, and more.)

If you'd like to preview what you'll be creating in this exercise, open the **Comps_Finished** folder and RAM Preview the comp **01-Masking_final**.

- Return to the Project panel, and double-click **Comps > 01-Masking*starter** to open it.

- Select the foreground layer **Cityscape.mov**. Then select the Rounded Rectangle tool from the Shape tools menu in the Tools panel. Click and drag in the Comp panel to surround a few of the major buildings on the right, plus some of the freeway. As you draw this outline, the areas of **Cityscape.mov** beyond the outline will disappear, revealing the background.

- After you release the mouse, Mask 1 will be revealed in the Timeline panel. With **Cityscape.mov** selected, press **M** to reveal its Mask Path parameter as well. **M** is the shortcut to reveal Mask and Mask Path for any selected layer.

2 Select the Rounded Rectangle tool (top right). Select the layer to mask, then select the Rounded Rectangle tool. Click and drag in the Comp panel to define the mask path you want (right). Press **M** to view the Mask Path in the Timeline panel (above). Foreground courtesy Artbeats/Timelapse Cityscapes; background 12 Inch Design/ProductionBlox Unit 02.

In the Comp panel, you should see a colored outline around the mask shape. If you don't, click the Toggle Visibility button along the bottom of the Comp panel to turn it on.

3 Double-click the mask outline to enable its Free Transform Points; the shortcut is `⌘ T` on Mac (`Ctrl T` on Windows). Here we are grabbing the top point to change the height of the shape.

3 Press `V` for the Selection tool. Then double-click on the yellow mask outline; this will enable its Free Transform Points, which means you can edit its shape. Note the eight small boxes ("handles") around its shape: As you hover your cursor over these, the cursor will change to icons that indicate you can click and drag to resize or rotate the shape. Dragging anywhere else moves the entire shape.

Tweak the size and position of the mask to taste, then press `Enter` to accept your edits and turn Free Transform off.

4 Double-click a layer to open its Layer panel. Set the View popup to Masks and turn off the Render switch. You can then draw and edit masks undistracted by other layers or the results of previous mask paths.

4 Next, you want to reveal a different section of **Cityscape.mov** – but you can't see the rest of the image as it's already been masked out. No problem: You can also create masks in the Layer panel where you can view the entire image.

• Double-click **Cityscape.mov** to open its Layer panel. It opens docked into the same frame as the Comp panel, but feel free to rearrange your workspace so the Comp and Layer panels are side by side.

• Along the bottom of the Layer panel is a View popup; check that it is set to Masks. Uncheck the Render button (to the right of View): This will reveal the entire layer without the effect of masking.

• Select the Ellipse mask shape tool. This time, hold down the `Shift` key while dragging out a new mask shape in the left half of the layer; this will constrain it to draw a circle. (It will look slightly wide, as this layer has non-square pixels – refer to the *Tech Corner* at the end of the previous lesson.) Release the mouse before releasing `Shift`. When you're done, Mask 2 will appear in the Timeline panel below Mask 1.

5 Press **V** to return to the Selection tool. After you are done drawing a mask shape in the Layer panel, you will see the individual mask points or "vertices" that define it; by default, all vertices are selected. While all points are selected, you can drag any one point to move the entire mask, or use the arrow keys to nudge it by one screen pixel. You can **Shift**+click or drag a marquee around individual vertices to select or deselect them, and edit the position of these directly. You can also double-click the mask to use the Free Transform Points as you did in the Comp panel.

Tweak your second mask shape to taste, and bring the Comp panel forward again when you're done. Note that in the Comp panel, selecting a mask's name selects the entire mask shape, making it easier to move as a unit. Click on Mask 1 in the Timeline panel to select it, then try using the arrow keys to reposition it by one screen pixel; add the **Shift** key to nudge by ten pixels.

6 By default, masks have sharp, crisp edges. However, it is possible to soften these. With **Cityscape.mov** still selected, type **Shift F** to reveal the Mask Feather parameter in addition to Mask Path. Turn the Toggle Visibility button (at the bottom of the Comp panel) off to more clearly see the outlines, and scrub Mask Feather to soften the masks. Set Feather for both masks to taste. (After Effects CS6 added the ability to vary the amount of feather around a mask shape; we'll explore that trick later on page 108.)

7 After Effects calculates effects for a layer *after* masks have been taken into account. Apply Effect > Perspective > Drop Shadow to **Cityscape.mov**; notice that both masks get the same shadow. Slightly increase the Distance and Softness of the shadow to taste, and save your project.

6 We increased the Mask Feather value (below) to soften the edges of Mask 2 (above).

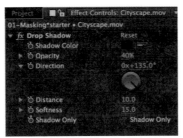

7 Effects are applied after masks have been calculated. That means the single Drop Shadow effect (above) applied to this layer affects both masks. (Return Mask Feather back to 0 if the shadow is not obvious.) Remember that you can toggle off the colored outline around masks to better see the effect.

9–10 Add a title, use the Fill effect to color it white, and add the Drop Shadow effect. Then double-click the Rectangle mask tool to apply a full frame mask.

11 To wipe on the title (above), animate the mask to reveal it by setting two keyframes for Mask Path. To soften the leading edge, press *Shift* *F* to also show Mask Feather, toggle off the Mask Feather lock, and increase the horizontal feather amount (below).

Animating a Mask Path

Masks do not need to be fixed windows onto a layer – their shapes can also animate. This is particularly useful for revealing the content of layers.

8 Press *Home* to make sure you are at the start of the composition. Bring the Project panel forward, and open the **Sources > stills** folder. Select **Bring on the Night.ai** and type *⌘* */* (*Ctrl* */*) to add it to your comp.

9 This black title is hard to read against your video. With it selected, add Effect > Generate > Fill. Click on its Color swatch, and change it to white.

That's better, but it still looks a bit flat on top of your composite. Add Effect > Perspective > Drop Shadow, and adjust the Distance and Softness to taste.

10 As we mentioned in a previous lesson, sometimes it's easier to start where you want to end up, and work backward. With **Bring on the Night.ai** selected, select the Rectangle mask tool, then double-click it. This will add a mask to it that is the same size as the layer – a perfect ending point for a reveal. Enable the Toggle Visibility switch to see its outline in the Comp panel.

11 Type *M* to reveal the Mask Path parameter in the Timeline panel. Move the current time indicator to 01:00, and click on the stopwatch next to Mask Path to enable keyframing and create the first keyframe.

Press *Home* to return to 00:00. Then double-click on the mask outline in the Comp panel to bring up the Free Transform Points; the shortcut is *⌘* *T* (*Ctrl* *T*). Drag the handle on the right edge all the way to the left until the title is completely hidden. A new Mask Path keyframe will be created automatically at 00:00.

To soften the leading edge of your wipe, increase the Mask Feather for the title's mask. You need to increase only the first value, which is in the X (horizontal) direction.

12 Press *0* on the numeric keypad to RAM Preview your animation. Add a dramatic pause by moving **Bring on the Night.ai**'s layer bar to start later in the timeline, such as at 01:00 – its keyframes will move with it. Save your project!

Creating a Vignette

Masks can also be used to create a "vignette" where the edges of an image are darkened, focusing the viewer more toward the center of the screen.

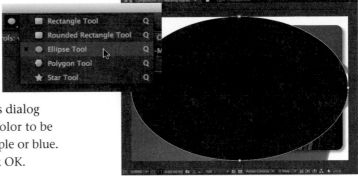

13 Press **Home** to return to 00:00. Create a Layer > New > Solid; the shortcut is **⌘ Y** (**Ctrl Y**). In the Solid Settings dialog that opens, click the Make Comp Size button, and set the Color to be something complementary to your scene such as a dark purple or blue. Give it a name that makes sense such as "**vignette**" and click OK.

14 Click and hold on the Mask tool; a popup will appear. You want a rounded mask for this task, so select the Ellipse tool option, and release the mouse. (You can also cycle through the options by pressing **Q**.) Then, with the **vignette** layer selected, double-click this tool in the Tools panel to create a full-size oval mask.

14 Select the Ellipse tool (inset), then double-click it in the Tools panel to create a full-size oval mask on your new solid (above).

15 Now you have a big dark oval obscuring the center of your image – probably not what you had in mind. But that's easy to change. With **vignette** still selected, type **M** once to hide the Mask, then type **M M** (two **M**s in quick succession) to reveal all of the mask's properties. Make the following edits:

• Click on the checkbox next to Inverted: Now the mask solid will be transparent inside and opaque outside.

• Scrub the Mask Feather until you get a nice, soft falloff around the edges.

• Scrub the Mask Expansion property: This offsets a mask to draw inside or outside of the original mask path. (To better see its effect, temporarily turn Mask Feather down to zero.) Increase Mask Expansion to push the vignette off into the corners.

• If the corners are too dark, reduce the Mask Opacity value (or use the regular Transform > Opacity property). Then feel free to balance the Mask Feather, Opacity, and Expansions values off of each other to get the look you want.

▽ tip

All Keyframes

When you add or delete a point on an animated mask, points are added or deleted for each keyframe.

Congratulations – you've created a tasteful little animation, plus now have a handle on creating simple masks. Go ahead and tweak your animation to taste. If you like, compare your results with ours – see comp **01-Masking_final** in the Project panel's **Comps_Finished** folder.

15 To finish off the vignette, invert the mask (A), increase its feather (B), increase its expansion (C), and reduce its opacity (D). Our version is in **Comps_Finished > 01-Masking_final**.

2 Select the Pen tool, and turn off the RotoBezier option for now.

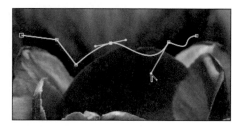

3 The Convert Vertex Point tool is used to toggle between smooth and hard corners, and to break or unbreak the continuity of the Bezier handles.

Masking with the Pen Tool

Next up is practicing using the Pen tool to create more detailed mask paths. It has two basic modes: One that creates common Bezier curves with handles (which we'll do first), and a RotoBezier mode which automatically determines the curve of the path. As with the Mask tool, you can create shapes in either the Comp or Layer panels, plus keyframe their shapes.

Drawing a Path

1 In the Project panel for this lesson's file, locate **02a-Bezier*starter** in the **Comps** folder and double-click it to open it. Select **PinkTulips.psd**.

2 Select the Pen tool (the shortcut is **G**). When you do, a RotoBezier option will appear on the right end of the Tools panel; turn it off for now.

3 Drawing with the Pen tool is similar to drawing paths in programs such as Photoshop and Illustrator, although the shortcuts can differ slightly. To practice, start by just making a random shape:

- To create straight line segments, click with the mouse to create a series of points.
- To create curved segments, click and drag to pull out Bezier handles for the point you are creating.

While drawing with the Pen tool, you can edit the points you've just placed:

- To reposition any point or handle before you're finished drawing a mask, click and drag that point (in previous versions, you had to press the ⌘ [*Ctrl*] key).

- To toggle between a sharp corner point and a smooth point, press ⌥ (*Alt*) and click on a point. The cursor will automatically change to the Convert Vertex Point cursor, which looks like an upside-down V. To toggle the last point you drew, just click on it without holding down these extra keys.

- To break the continuous handles of a smooth point, press ⌥ (*Alt*) and then click and drag one handle. To switch back to a smooth point, hold ⌥ (*Alt*), click on the vertex, and then drag to make them continuous again.

- To delete a point, press ⌘ (*Ctrl*) to get the Delete Vertex tool and click on it (previously, you did not need to press a special key). To delete the most recent point, Undo.

- To add a new point between points you've already drawn, click on the line joining them – the cursor will automatically change to the Add Vertex tool while doing so.

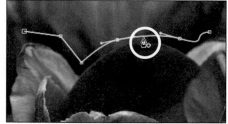

3 *continued* To delete a vertex, place the cursor over a point and press ⌘ (*Ctrl*); it will change to the Delete Vertex tool (left). To add a vertex, place the cursor between points (right).

- To pick up drawing a mask path where you left off, make sure only the last point is selected, then continue creating points with the Pen tool.

- To close a mask path, click back on the first point. Only closed masks create transparency. If you want to create an open path, simply change to the Selection tool (shortcut: **V**) when you're done creating the path.

Editing the Path

You can switch back to the Selection tool for editing a mask. However, some of the shortcuts will then change. Because closing the mask creates transparency, if you need to see the entire image, we suggest you edit the mask path in the Layer panel with the Render switch off. Feel free to zoom in as well.

4 Press **V** to change to the Selection tool, and practice the following:

- To add a point, hold down **G** (to temporarily switch to the Pen tool) and click between vertices. To delete a point, hold **⌘ G** (**Ctrl G**) and click on that point. (In versions prior to CS6, just hold **G**; the tool will change automatically.)

- To toggle a point between a smooth and sharp corner point, press **⌘ ⌥** (**Ctrl Alt**) and click on the point.

- To break Bezier handles, press **⌘ G** (**Ctrl G**) and drag on one of the handles. (In versions prior to CS6, just press **G**.) To rejoin the handles, start dragging one of them, then press **⌥** (**Alt**) and continue dragging to recreate a smooth point.

5 After you've had some fun, delete your experimental mask, and practice drawing a mask around the foreground tulip. It will require a combination of smooth shapes and sudden direction changes where some of the petals overlap or meet the stem. It's fairly challenging, but a good example of a task you will often need to perform in the real world. Our version is in the **Comps_Finished** folder (**02a-Bezier_final**), pictured to the right.

▼ Applying an Effect to a Masked Area

To apply an effect to an area of a layer in Photoshop, you would create a selection first. In After Effects, you need to duplicate the layer, create a mask path on the top layer, then apply the effect to the top or bottom layer depending on whether you want the area inside or outside the mask to be effected.

For instance, let's say you wanted the foreground flower in the **PinkTulips.psd** layer to be in color, and the rest of the image to be in black and white. Open the comp **02b-Masked Effects*starter**, and follow these steps:

- Select the **PinkTulips.psd** layer, and select Edit > Duplicate – the shortcut is **⌘ D** (**Ctrl D**).

- Select the bottom layer, and select Layer > Masks > Remove All Masks.

- With the bottom layer still selected, apply Effect > Color Correction > Tint to make it black and white. Our version is in **Comps_Finished > 02b-Masked Effects_final**.

You could also have started by duplicating your original layer and masking just the top one. The end result is the same: Two layers, the top one has the mask, and effects are applied as needed to one or both layers.

Which Point Is First?

The First Vertex Point (FVP) is the point where you started drawing a shape with the Pen tool; it is the top right if you used the Rectangle mask tool, and it is the top point if you used the other mask tools. It appears slightly larger than the other points.

2 The maple leaf (left) and oak leaf (right) mask paths unfortunately do not interpolate smoothly (center).

2 *continued* The maple leaf's First Vertex Point (FVP) is at its bottom (left); the oak's FVP it at its top (right). This misalignment is what causes the funky interpolation.

Smarter Mask Interpolation

Lesson 04-Transparency > 04-Video Bonus on this book's DVD contains a movie from our *After Effects Apprentice* video series that demonstrates the Mask Interpolation panel, which gives you more control over how mask shapes animate.

How Mask Paths Interpolate

In the first exercise, you animated a simple mask shape to wipe on a layer. You can also animate more complex shapes made with the Pen tool. However, the more complex the mask, the harder it is to get smooth interpolation from one shape to another. Here are some ways to make it smoother.

1 Open the comp **03-Interpolation*starter**. It contains a solid that has an animated mask. If the Mask Path property and its keyframes are not visible, select the layer **leaf shapes** and press **U**.

2 RAM Preview; the maple leaf shape interpolates to an oak leaf shape. Unfortunately, it twists inside-out on its way.

When you see mask interpolation problems such as this, the most likely culprit is the little-known First Vertex Point (FVP). The FVP of one mask path always interpolates to the FVP of the next mask path, and the rest of the points do what's necessary to follow.

Click on the words Mask 1 in the Timeline panel to select the mask path, and make sure Toggle Mask Path Visibility is on. Move the current time indicator to the first keyframe at 00:00, and carefully look around the shape until you see one mask point that is larger than the others (hint: it is at the bottom left of the maple leaf stem). This larger point is its FVP. Type **K** to jump to the second keyframe, and look for the FVP; it is at the top of the oak leaf.

Changing the First Vertex

Interpolation works best if all of the FVPs are at the same relative point of a shape, such as the top or bottom.

3 Type **J** (or press **Home**) to jump to the earlier maple leaf shape keyframe. Drag a marquee around the top mask point so just this one keyframe is selected. Then select Layer > Mask and Shape Path > Set First Vertex; you can also right-click on the point and choose the same option. (If it's grayed out, you have more than one point selected.) RAM Preview, and note how the interpolation is much smoother – not perfect, but a lot better!

Another reason mask paths don't interpolate smoothly is if there are different numbers of points in each shape. Watch the mask points move as you scrub the time indicator; they will "crawl" around the leaf stems, causing the shape to twist. You can often fix this by adding extra points to one side of one shape to balance them out. We added extra points to the bottom left of the maple leaf; our results are in **Comps_Finished > 03-Interpolation_final**.

Mask Paths and Effects

You now know how to create and animate interesting mask shapes. You can make them even more interesting by employing effects that can use their paths.

1 Open the comp **04-Effects*starter**. It contains the leaf shape animation from the previous exercise, this time cutting out a more interesting source image.

2 Select the **Sunprints_A** layer, and apply Effect > Generate > Scribble. The leaf's outline will be filled with a scribbled white line. Preview, and note how the scribble automatically animates while staying inside the changing outline of the leaf.

In the Effect Controls panel, you will see that Scribble has a Mask popup. This allows you to select the mask it uses, in the event you have multiple masks on the same layer. It defaults to the first mask path it finds. If there are no masks, the scribble will not be drawn.

2 Scribble fills the area defined by a mask.

3 Scrub the Start and End values; they control how much of the leaf is filled. Set Angle to 90° so that the scribble will fill in from top to bottom.

• Press **Home**, and set both Start and End to 0%; the scribble will disappear. Click on the stopwatch to enable keyframing for End, which will set a keyframe at this value.

• Move the current time indicator to 02:00, and set End to 100%, which fills the mask shape. A keyframe will be created for you. Preview, and enjoy the scribble animation.

3 By animating Scribble's End value from 0% to 100%, it will fill in the outline over time.

4 The whole point of this lesson is to create transparency – so let's place something behind this masked-out solid.

Bring the Project panel forward, and open the **Sources > movies** folder. Select **Wildflowers.mov**, and drag it to the left side of the Timeline panel below **Sunprints_A**. It will appear where the leaf shape is transparent, starting at 00:00.

What if you want to see both the masked shape and the effect? Select **leaf shapes** and press **F3** to bring the Effect Controls panel forward. Change the Composite popup from On Transparent to Reveal Original Image. Now the Scribble effect will act as a matte for the original image (more on mattes later).

Feel free to play with the other Scribble parameters, including Fill Type and the parameters inside Stroke Options. Our version (with some additional enhancements) is in **Comps_Finished > 04-Effects_Final**.

Our final **04-Effects_Final** comp, which includes rendering just the Stroke effect as well as adding a Drop Shadow.

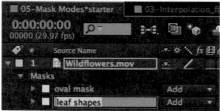

1 For your first mask path, add a full-frame elliptical mask to **Wildflowers.mov**.

3 For your second mask path, paste in the animated mask from an earlier exercise. Rename the masks to keep track of them.

▽ insider knowledge

Advanced Modes

The Lighten and Darken modes are useful when Mask Opacity is set to less than 100%: Lighten affects how the alpha channel value is calculated when Add mode is used for overlapping mask paths; Darken affects the alpha value when Intersect is used.

Multiple Mask Madness

You've probably noticed that every mask has a popup next to it in the Timeline panel, which defaults to Add. This is the Mask Mode, which determines how multiple masks on the same layer interact. By default, they add together – but great fun can be had with the other possible combinations.

1 Open **Comps > 05-Mask Modes*starter**, and select the **Wildflowers.mov** layer. Type **Q** until you see the Ellipse mask tool appear in the Tools panel. Then double-click this tool to add a full-frame oval mask. The wildflowers will appear inside an oval; the color around the outside is the comp's Background Color.

Type **M** to reveal Mask 1; its Mask Modes popup is set to Add. Rename Mask 1 by selecting it, pressing **Return**, typing "**oval mask**", and pressing **Return** again.

2 Open **Comps_Finished > 03-Interpolation_final**. It contains the finished version of the earlier leaf shape animation. Select the layer, reveal Mask 1, click on the words Mask Path to select its keyframes, and type **⌘ C** (**Ctrl C**) to copy.

3 Bring the comp **05-Mask Modes*starter** forward again by clicking on its tab along the top of the Timeline panel. Make sure **Wildflowers.mov** is still selected, then type **Shift F2** to deselect your first mask path but leave the layer selected – otherwise, you may paste over the first mask by accident!

Press **Home** to position the current time indicator at 00:00, and type **⌘ V** (**Ctrl V**) to paste the leaf mask and its keyframes. It will default to Add mode, which was its setting in its original comp. Make sure Toggle Mask Path Visibility is enabled; you should now see the leaf mask inset inside the oval mask. Rename this new mask "**leaf shapes**" to help remember which mask is which.

4 Change the Mask Mode popup for leaf shapes to Subtract: You will now see the wildflowers inside the oval, but not inside the leaf shapes. Continue to experiment with the Mask Modes to get a better feel for them – for example, set the oval mask to Subtract and leaf shapes to Add. Your result should then look the same as our version in **Comps_Finished > 05-Mask Modes_final**.

4 You can get different results from the same masks by changing their Mask Mode settings.

There's no need to stop with just two! Experiment with drawing a third mask path that overlaps both existing masks (we drew a simple rectangular mask along the bottom), then playing with the Intersect and Difference modes. Keep in mind that masks are rendered from the top down (similar to how effects are rendered), so the third mask would be combined with the result of the first two.

To make a mask inactive while experimenting without having to delete it, set its mode to None. We also suggest you avoid Inverting a mask unless you cannot achieve the result you are looking for with the Mask Modes popup – inverting masks makes the logic doubly confusing!

Our "going further" comp is **Comps_Finished > 05-Mask Modes_final2**, where we resized the first leaf shape, added a third mask, and applied a Drop Shadow effect with Distance set to 0. Just for fun, we also placed a blurred version of the original movie in the background, offset in time.

You can create some interesting looks by combining multiple masks, placing the masked layer on top of an unmasked copy, and giving each different effects such as drop shadows and blurs.

▼ Mask Opacity

Another fun way to work with multiple masks is to use their Mask Opacity to fade individual shapes on and off. Open **Comps_Finished > 06-Transition_final**, select **Cityscape.mov**, and make sure Toggle Mask Path Visibility is enabled to see the mask paths. If the Mask Opacity keyframes are not visible, type **U** to reveal them.

Scrub the current time indicator through the timeline, and note how the mask shapes inside the Comp panel are filled in as you go between Mask Opacity keyframes. This is a very useful transition, as it gives precise control over what part of the image comes on in what order.

Once you feel you understand how we created this look, try it yourself! Open **Comps > 06-Transition*starter**, and follow these general steps to create your own version:

• To view the entire, unmasked video while creating your mask paths, double-click **Cityscape.mov** to open its Layer panel. Set the View popup to Masks, and uncheck Render.

• Draw a series of masks, focusing on different parts of the video. If your shapes do not add together to cover the entire video, draw one more mask shape that includes the entire video image.

• Close the Layer panel, and type **T T** (two **T**s in quick succession) to reveal the Mask Opacity properties for your masks. Keyframe them fading up from 0 to 100% to bring on the masks. Offset the timing of the keyframes to create a staggered fade.

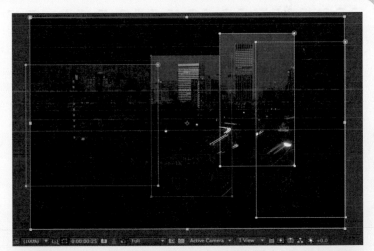

The combination of multiple masks and animating their Mask Opacity creates interesting transitions.

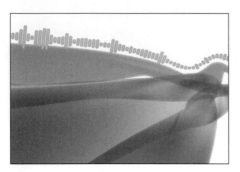

In this exercise, you will animate a path above the purple ribbons and add an Audio Spectrum effect that will draw along it.

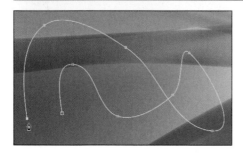

2 Select the Pen tool, and enable the RotoBezier option (top). Practice clicking around the comp; RotoBezier automatically creates curves between your points, with no visible Bezier handles (above).

▽ tip

To Mask or Not to Mask

To create a closed mask but not have it create transparency, or to temporarily turn off a mask, change its Mask Mode popup to None. You can still apply effects to it.

RotoBezier Mask Paths

The final step in your path to mask enlightenment is working with RotoBezier mask paths. You just click where you feel mask points should be, and After Effects will automatically create a curve to smoothly join them. You can tweak the "tension" at each point to influence this curve. RotoBezier is great for organic shapes; they also generally animate more smoothly.

To get an idea of where you are headed with this exercise, close all previously opened comps, and open **Comps_Finished > 07-RotoBezier_final2**. Press **0** on the numeric keypad to RAM Preview. Notice how the audio spectrum line along the top bops along with the music – that's what you're going to create.

1 Open **Comps > 07-RotoBezier*starter**. Select **PurpleFlow.mov**; that's the layer you're going to draw on.

2 Select the Pen tool; the shortcut is **G** (and verify the Pen is selected). Along the right side of the Tools panel, a checkbox for RotoBezier will appear. Check it.

Get a feel for RotoBezier masks by clicking around in the Comp panel. You don't need to drag any handles to create a Bezier curve; After Effects will create curves automatically.

To form a hard corner at a RotoBezier point, with the Pen tool still active hold down the **⌥** (**Alt**) key and click on an existing point. To change its tension, hold down **⌥** (**Alt**) and click-and-drag left and right to select from a range between a sharp corner to a generous curve.

Once you feel you've got the hang of this behavior, select Layer > Mask > Remove All Masks.

Trace the Flow

3 Press **Home**, and using the same technique, create an open path that runs just above the flowing purple shape. This will be your first mask path. Press **M** to reveal its Mask Path in the Timeline panel, and enable keyframing by clicking on its stopwatch.

The yellow mask path can be hard to see against the white background, so click on the yellow swatch for Mask 1 and choose a more visible color, such as red.

4 Next, you will edit this starting mask path to animate along with the undulations of the flowing purple ribbon.

Move the current time indicator forward 15 frames, and press **V** to return to the Selection tool. By default, all of the mask points are selected. Drag a marquee around just one mask point to select that point, and move it into a new position that better follows the purple shape. Tweak the rest of the points to follow the purple shape as needed, remembering these tips:

- If you want to add a point, hold **G** and click along the mask shape; to delete a point, hold **⌘ G** (**Ctrl G**) and click on it. Note that adding or deleting a point will affect existing and future keyframes as well.

- If you want to tweak tension of a point when the Selection tool is active, press **⌘ ⌥** (**Ctrl Alt**), click on a point, and drag left and right through that point.

Continue this for the duration of the comp. You can scrub the current time indicator back and forth to check your progress. Press **J** or **K** to jump between exisiting keyframes. If you lack patience, open our comp **07-RotoBezier_final** where we've animated the mask path and changed the temporal keyframes to Auto Bezier. Continue with the rest of this exercise using our comp.

Audio Spectrum Effect

Audio Waveform and Audio Spectrum are two examples of effects that draw along a mask path. Although they must be driven by an audio layer in the comp, you don't apply them to the audio layer – you apply them to a layer with pixels!

5 Select **PurpleFlow.mov**, and apply Effect > Generate > Audio Spectrum effect. The Effect Controls panel will open. Make the following changes to the default settings:

- Set the Audio Layer popup to **CoolGroove.mov** (the audio track in this comp).

- Set the Path popup to Mask 1; otherwise, Audio Spectrum will draw along a straight line defined by its Start and End Point.

- Enable the Composite On Original option at the bottom of its settings.

RAM Preview, and feel the groove. Disable the Toggle Mask Path Visibility option to see the effect more clearly in the Comp panel. You can tweak the other Audio Spectrum settings to taste. For our version, we eyedroppered colors from the **PurpleFlow.mov** for Audio Spectrum's Inside and Outside Colors. We also increased the Thickness, reduced the Softness, and set Hue Interpolation to 90°. Play with increasing the Maximum Height, and check out the different styles in the Display Options popup. Save your project when you're done.

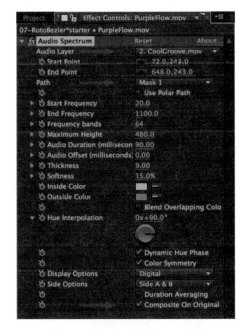

▽ try it

Smoother Interpolation

All temporal keyframes – Mask Path included – default to Linear interpolation, which can result in a jerky animation. For a quick improvement, click Mask Path in the Timeline panel to select all of your keyframes, and **⌘**+click (**Ctrl**+click) on any one to change them all to Auto Bezier. We've already done this with our final versions.

5 By default, Audio Spectrum just draws a straight line. You need to edit a few of its Effect Controls (left) to get it to render your audio along your mask path (above). Tweak the effect controls to taste (below).

▽ tip

Effects and Masks

Examples of effects which can use mask paths include Audio Spectrum, Audio Waveform, Fill, Scribble, Stroke, and Vegas.

2–4 The client likes the graphical clock (A) but wishes to have a real instead of synthetic cityscape behind it. Mask out the clock face (B), and for your first attempt softly blend it into your new background (C) using a combination of Mask Feather and Mask Expansion (right). Clock render courtesy Artbeats/Digital Biz.

Variable Mask Feathering

So far we've used the Mask Feather parameter when we've wanted to soften the edges of a mask. This creates an even amount of feathering all around the resulting shape. However, there are some applications for which you would prefer to vary the amount of feather around the mask path – either to create a more balanced composite or to match where the edge of an object is sharp and in focus or blurred and out of focus. After Effects CS6 added the ability to create a second mask path around a shape, softening the edge between these two paths. Let's look at a pair of examples where this is useful.

Soft Composite

1 Click on the Comp Viewer dropdown menu (along the top of the Comp panel) and select Close All to close any compositions left open from the previous exercises. Bring the Project panel forward and open **Comps > VMF_1-Soft Composite*starter**.

2 This composition contains a graphical rendering of a clock over a city skyline. Say you're working for a client who says she likes the clock but wishes it was over a real skyline rather than a synthetic one. To keep her happy, go into the **Sources > movies** folder and drag **Cityscape.mov** into the Timeline panel below the layer **Clock+Skyline.mov**.

3 You need to mask out the clock face so that the new skyline will be visible behind the clock. Select **Clock+Skyline.mov**, then choose the Pen tool. (It is your call whether to use RotoBezier masks; we disabled this option.) Create a mask path around the clock face. Feel free to change the mask color to make it more visible against the yellow and orange face.

4 First, let's try to solve this the old way: Press **M** **M** (two **M**s in quick succession) to reveal all of the mask parameters. Increase Mask Feather to create a soft edge around the clock face. Since ordinary feather softens both inside and outside of the mask shape, increase Mask Expansion until the entire face is opaque again.

It's not a bad look, but pretty soon you'll find yourself having to compromise. We personally like the look of a broad feather along the left edge of the clock to blend it more softly into the underlying buildings, but we also prefer a tighter feather along the bottom and lower right so the lights in the freeway are not obscured. It also gets fiddly to constantly balance Mask Feather and Mask Expansion off each other to keep the entire clock face opaque.

5 Reset Mask Feather and Mask Expansion to 0 and click on the Pen tool until its dropdown menu appears. After Effects CS6 added a new Mask Feather tool at the bottom of the list. Choose it and make sure Mask 1 is still selected.

• Hover the cursor over the mask path in the Comp panel: The Feather cursor will gain a + symbol at its base. Click and drag outward from the mask; you will create a feathered edge that starts at the original mask path and ends at the feather path (as opposed to straddling the mask path).

• With the Feather tool still active, click and drag another section of either the mask or feather path. The amount of feather will interpolate between these two feather points.

6 There are two different algorithms for the way the feather "falls off" between the mask and feather paths. The default Smooth algorithm follows an S-curve where the opacity tapers slowly away from the mask path, changes somewhat quickly between the two paths, then tapers very gradually to fully transparent at the feather path. Aesthetically this looks very nice, but it can require you to drag the feather path out farther than you may expect.

With Mask 1 still selected, choose Layer > Mask > Feather Falloff > Linear. The result is a more mathematically even transition between the mask and feather path, at the expense of creating the illusion of a harder transition away from the mask path.

5 Select the Mask Feather tool (top left), click on the mask path in the Comp panel, and drag out a feather path (above). After creating this first point, click on either the mask or feather path and drag out additional feather points (below).

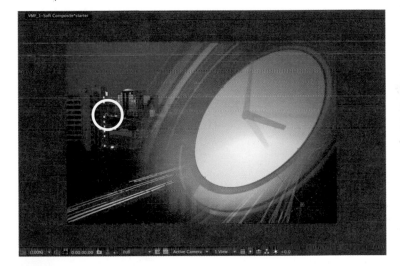

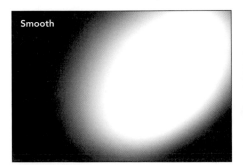

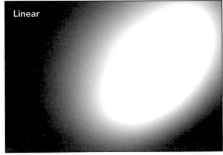

6 The default Mask Feather Falloff of Smooth creates a visually pleasing transition (far left). The alternative Linear is more mathematically even, but can create a noticeable transition away from the mask path (left). For clarity, we soloed layer 1 and used the Show Channel popup at the bottom of the Comp panel to view just the alpha channel.

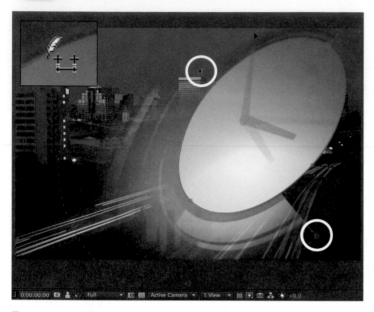

7 Hold the **Shift** key while hovering the cursor over the mask path to feather a segment between two vertices (inset). The result creates hold feather points (circled above), identified by their teardrop pointer shape.

7 *continued* Hold **⬚** (**Alt**) and scrub to change the tension of a feather point (circled above); right-click a feather point to get more options (inset).

7 Before we wrap this up for the client, let's play a bit more with the options available with variable mask feathering. Save your project so you can use File > Revert to retrieve it later (often easier than hitting Undo a bunch of times) and try out these tricks:

• Hold the **Shift** key and hover the cursor between two vertices along the mask (not feather) path: The cursor will change to show two + symbols joined by a bar. This means you can feather just a specific span of the original path. Click and drag while this cursor is visible; you will see sudden feather transitions before and after these mask vertices. These transitions are referred to as "hold" points around the feather path; you can manually insert a hold point by right-clicking on a feather point.

• Hold **⬚** (**Alt**) and hover over a feather point: You will see the familiar "change direction" cursor with a two-headed arrow at its base, which indicates it can be scrubbed. Doing so will change the "tension" through a feather point, just as with a RotoBezier mask point. (This effect is more obvious when the angle at the point is more pronounced.)

• With the Feather tool still selected, right-click on a feather point; a popup menu will appear with additional parameters that can be edited on a per-point basis. Picking an "edit" choice will open a dialog where you can enter a numeric value.

Our final composite, using variable mask feathering, effects, and blending modes.

• You can feather to both the inside and outside of the original mask path: Just click on the mask path and drag inward to create a second set of Variable Mask Feather points.

Undo or File > Revert to clear the results of your playing. Now create a nicely feathered mask to blend these two clips together. You can also apply a color correction effect such as Hue/Saturation to match their colors and optionally use blending modes (Lesson 3) to create a final composite that really looks like one image. Our version is saved in **Comps_Finished > VMF_1-Soft Composite_final.**

Feathering to Match Focus

1 For a challenge that relates to a real-world issue you might encounter on a visual effects project, open **Comps > VMF_2-Depth of Field*starter**. The foreground clip **Clock.mov** was shot with a very shallow depth of field. As a result, only a small portion of the clock face is in focus, while sections that are closer or farther away fall progressively out of focus.

2 Select the Pen tool and create a curved mask path that follows the bright edge along the top of the clock face. Create the remainder of the mask path outside of the image frame so you won't have to worry about accidentally making any of the other edges transparent. Again, you may use RotoBezier or normal Bezier masks; we used the latter.

3 Press **G** to switch to the Mask Feather tool. Click in the upper left corner of the mask path and drag downward a short distance, corresponding to the width of the blur along that edge (observe how much wider the edge trim appears compared with the center of the shot). Do the same for the corner on the right side.

4 Add one or two feather points near the center top of the mask path where the clock face is in focus. You can either drag these points close to the original mask path to create a slender feathered edge or drag them directly against the mask path and later use the Mask Feather parameter to antialias this edge. Tweak the mask and feather points to create a visually appealing, realistic composite. When you're done, the left and right edges should appear to "melt" into the blurry background. For reference, our version is in **Comps_Finished > VMF2_2-Depth of Field_final.**

▼ Masking Changes in CS6

Aside from the introduction of variable mask feathering in After Effects CS6, a few details of how normal masking works also changed in CS6:

• Previously, pressing the **G** key toggled through all the Pen tools, including Add, Delete, and Convert Vertex. As of CS6, pressing **G** defaults to alternating between just the Pen (drawing) and Feather tools. You may restore the previous behavior by disabling Preferences > General > Pen Tool Shortcut Toggles between Pen and Mask Feather Tools.

• In earlier versions, hovering over an existing mask vertex with the Pen tool resulted in it automatically changing to the Delete Vertex tool – which resulted in numerous accidentally deleted mask points. Now it changes to the Selection (move) tool. To delete a point in CS6, add ⌘ (*Ctrl*).

This clock was originally shot on 35mm film with a shallow depth of field (inset, left). A mask with variable feathering that matches the focus across the edge of the clock face (above) creates a more realistic composite. Footage courtesy Artbeats/Time & Money.

Using Track Mattes

Masks create transparency directly on the layer they are applied to. But what if you want to borrow transparency from another layer? That's where Track Mattes come in.

The most common use of Track Mattes is to play video from one layer inside a window defined by either the transparency (alpha) or grayscale values (luminance) of a second layer. In this exercise, you will learn how to set up an Alpha Track Matte.

1 Still in **Lesson_04.aep**, click on the Comp Viewer dropdown menu (along the top of the Comp panel) and select Close All to close all open comps.

Bring the Project panel forward, and open **Comps > 08a-Alpha Matte*starter**. It is currently empty, with its Background Color set to white.

2 Track mattes require two layers, and the stacking order of these layers in the Timeline panel is important: The matte layer must be on top of the "fill" layer.

• Open the **Sources > movies** folder and select **VirtualInsanity.mov** – this will be the fill. Type ⌘ / (Ctrl /) to add it to your comp.

• Then select **Sources > stills > Night Vision.ai**, and either drag it into the Comp panel and position it, or type ⌘ / (Ctrl /) to add it centered in your comp. This text will be your matte. Remember that the matte *must* be on top of the image that will fill the matte, so reorder the layers if that's not the case.

3 Make sure the Modes column is visible in the Timeline panel – if not, press **F4** to reveal it.

For the **VirtualInsanity.mov** layer, click on the popup menu under the "TrkMat" heading: It will give you four choices for the type of matte, all of which should mention **Night Vision.ai** (the name of the layer above). Select Alpha Matte, which says use the alpha channel of the layer above for the matte.

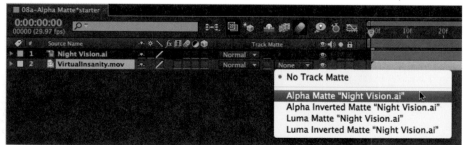

3 Start with the matte layer – the text – on top of the fill layer (A). Set the Track Matte popup for the fill layer to Alpha Matte (above). When you release the mouse, the fill will be seen only inside the matte (B).

Once you release the mouse, the movie will now appear only inside the text, and you will see the white background color outside the text.

If you want to verify that these areas are transparent, click on the Toggle Transparency Grid button along the bottom of the Comp panel (it's the one with the checkerboard pattern); the checkerboard indicates transparency.

You will also notice a few changes in the Timeline panel. For one, the Video switch (eyeball icon) for **Night Vision.ai** will be turned off. This is because you no longer want to directly see the content of the matte layer; you just want to borrow its alpha channel. You will also notice that some additional icons appear to the left of the layer names, representing the matte (top layer) and fill (bottom layer).

If your results don't match the figures, compare your comp with our version: **Comps_Finished > 08a-Alpha Matte_final**.

3 *continued* Toggle the Transparency Grid on to verify the resulting alpha channel.

3 *continued* After setting the Track Matte popup, the matte layer on top will have its Video switch (the eyeball) turned off, and new icons will appear to the left of the layer names indicating that one is being used as a matte for the other. Notice there is no track matte popup for layer 1 because there is no layer above it. If there were additional layers above **Night Vision.ai**, the track matte popup would appear for the matte layer as well, which can be a source of confusion.

4 To understand the difference between Alpha and Alpha Inverted, go ahead and set the Track Matte (TrkMat) popup to Alpha Inverted Matte: Now the area inside the text will be transparent, and the area outside will be filled with the **VirtualInsanity.mov** layer.

Set the popup back to Alpha Matte before performing the next step.

4 The result of using Alpha Inverted Matte. The white areas are the background color, showing through where the result is transparent.

Nesting with Track Mattes

The two-layer combination required to create a track matte gives you a lot of flexibility in combining layers, plus the freedom to animate them independently from each other. However, there are a couple of downsides to this combination:

• You can't directly add an effect to the composite (the result of the track matte). This can be a problem when adding normal drop shadow or glow effects; layer styles help work around this (see the sidebar on the last page of this lesson).

• It is trickier to move the pair as a group and keep them in sync.

The best way to work around this is to leave the track matte layers in their own composition, then "nest" this comp into a second comp where it will appear as a single layer. We'll discuss nesting in greater detail in Lesson 6, but for now all you need to know is that you can treat a nested comp just like a normal layer (with the added perk that you can go back and edit the contents of the first comp, and have the results automatically show up in the second comp).

5 Open **Comps > 08b-NightVision*starter**. This is a background we've built for you, using elements you've already worked with in the earlier exercises.

6 To nest your track matte pair into this new comp, locate **08a-Alpha Matte*starter** in the Project panel, and either drag it on top of **08b-Night-Vision*starter** in the Project panel, or press ⌘ **/** (*Ctrl* **/**) to add it to

08b-NightVision*starter. Using either of these techniques will ensure it is the top layer in the Timeline panel, and centered in the Comp.

After you've "nested" the comp, you will see the name of your first composition **08a-Alpha Matte*starter** appear as a layer in the second comp, with a special "comp" icon to reinforce this.

6 Nest the comp with your track matte pair into a new comp that already includes two video layers and one audio layer. Note the icon for **08a-Alpha Matte*starter** layer: It looks like the comp icons you see in the Project panel, which helps you identify it as a nested comp.

7 RAM Preview your composite: Fun, but a bit too much may be happening all at once. In the timeline, slide the **08a-AlphaMatte*starter** layer bar to the right to start around 00:28, which happens to line up with a good beat in the music. (Hold down **Shift** after you start dragging to snap it to the marker we've already placed for you.) This allows the masks in **Cityscape.mov** to build on and be the hero before the title comes up. Preview and see if you like that better.

8 The fill movie in **08a-AlphaMatte*starter** contains flashy red-orange colors against black. Go to 03:16 in time; the black doesn't read very well against the dark city footage. To quickly fix that, apply Effect > Channel > Invert to this nested comp layer. Now the black areas become white, and the red-orange areas become blue (the opposite color on the RGB color wheel).

8–9 To increase the readability of the text (A), add an Invert effect to make the black areas white (B), use Hue/Saturation to alter its color (C), and add Bevel Alpha plus Drop Shadow to give it some perspective (D).

That cured the problem with the black text, but what about the colors? Go to 01:13 in time; the turquoise text needs some color coordination help! With the layer still selected, apply Effect > Color Correction > Hue/Saturation, and dial the Master Hue to somewhere between 50° and 90°. This will shift the cool blue color to the warmer purple range.

9 The masked city footage has drop shadows to set it off from the purple background; you can do the same to your title here. Experiment with different layer styles: Layer > Layer Styles > Drop Shadow will make the title appear to float above the city footage; Layer Styles > Inner Shadow will make the title appear to be cut out from the city footage. If you chose Drop Shadow, add Layer Styles > Bevel and Emboss to add more dimension; if you chose Inner Shadow, add Layer Styles > Inner Glow to add contrast to the cut-out title. In either case, experiment with their parameters to go beyond the default look.

9 Experiment with different layer styles to create different looks, such as the title floating above (left) or being cut into (right) the city footage behind.

10 As we mentioned, an advantage of nesting a composition is that you can treat its results as one layer, making animation easier. Go ahead and animate the **08a-Alpha Matte*starter** layer to come on in an interesting fashion.

If the layer is moving quickly, turning on the Motion Blur switch for the layer plus the Timeline panel's Enable Motion Blur switch will give a nice look.

If you're curious, our version of these steps is in **Comps_Finished > 10b-Night Vision_final**. Compare it to make sure you followed the steps correctly, but feel free to deviate from its precise settings to create your own look.

10 The final animation. Since the track matte is created in a precomp, you needed to animate only one layer.

Luma Track Matte

In the previous exercise, you used an Illustrator layer – which inherently has an alpha channel around its shapes – as an Alpha Track Matte. This time, you will use a high-contrast grayscale layer as a Luma Track Matte.

1 Bring the Project panel forward, and open **Comps > 09-Luma Matte*starter**. It is currently empty, with its Background Color set to black.

2 As you learned in the previous exercise, track mattes require two layers, with the matte on top and the "fill" underneath:

• In the Project panel's **Sources > movies** folder, select **Firestorm.mov** and add this to your comp. This will be your fill layer.

• In the same folder is **Cloud matte.mov**; this will be your matte. Add it to your comp on top of **Firestorm.mov**. Scrub the current time indicator; you will see the **Cloud matte.mov** spew out a white cloudy stream over a black background.

2 The fire (top) will be your fill; the clouds (above) will be your matte. Footage courtesy Artbeats/Reel Fire 2 and Cloud Chamber.

3 When you set **Firestorm.mov** to Luma Matte (above), it plays through the bright areas of **Cloud matte.mov** (below).

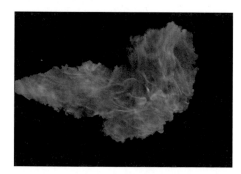

3 If the Modes column is not visible, press **F4** to reveal it. Set the TrkMat popup for **Firestorm.mov** (remember – always the bottom layer of the two!) to Luma Matte. The matte layer will turn off, track matte icons will appear in the Timeline panel next to the layer names, and the fire will now play inside the cloudy stream. If you like, click on the Toggle Transparency Grid button to confirm that the black area outside the clouds is transparent.

As we noted earlier, you can edit the two components of a track matte independently from each other. For example, press **Home**: You won't see the fire, because the luma matte layer is all black at its first frame. Slide the luma matte layer **Cloud matte.mov** to start earlier in time (before 00:00), and you will see some of the fire from the first frame of your comp. This is what we did in our version **Comps_Finished > 09-Luma Matte_final**.

4 To help confirm what the different matte modes do, select Luma Inverted Matte; now the fire plays outside the clouds.

Then select Alpha Matte: The fire plays full frame, ignoring the clouds. This is because **Firestorm.mov** is using the alpha channel of the full-frame movie **Cloud matte.mov** above it, and its alpha channel is all white.

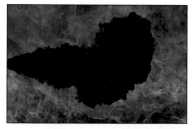

4 Using Luma Inverted Matte.

▽ tip

Hicon

Layers that have high contrast between white and black levels make good luma mattes. Indeed, you will often hear them referred to as "hicons" or as a hicon matte.

Animated Track Matte

You're not stuck with the original content of a still image or movie to use as a track matte. You can also animate and add effects to it to create more interesting matte shapes.

1 Open **Comps > 10-Animated Matte*starter**. It is currently empty, with its Background Color set to black. In the Project panel's **Sources > stills** folder, locate the image **inkblot matte.psd** and add it to the comp. (To create this, we dropped some India ink on a piece of paper, squished another one on top, pulled them apart, scanned it once it had dried, and inverted it. Very high tech.)

2 We created **inkblot matte.psd** larger than the comp so you would have some room to animate it:

- Type **P** to reveal Position, and click on its stopwatch to enable keyframing.
- Slide it downward until the top of **inkblot matte.psd** just reaches the top of the comp. Remember you can hold **Shift** while dragging to constrain your movement in the Comp view, or scrub just the Y Position value (the second one) in the Timeline panel.
- Press **End**, and slide the blot upward until its bottom just touches the bottom of the comp view.

  Press **0** to RAM Preview. Hmm…not all that exciting. But all is not lost; we know of an effect that can add some interesting movement…

3 With **inkblot matte.psd** selected, apply Effect > Distort > Turbulent Displace. In the Effect Controls panel that opens, scrub its value for Evolution: The blot will now undulate in an organic manner.

  This effect does not self-animate, but it's easy enough to keyframe:

- Press **Home** to return to 00:00. Reset Evolution to 0x +0.0° and click on the stopwatch for Evolution to enable keyframing.
- Press **End**, and set Evolution to a different value, such as 1x +0.0° (one full revolution). Feel free to experiment with the other parameters too, if you like.

  RAM Preview again. Now that's more interesting!

4 Bring the Project panel back forward, locate **Firestorm.mov** (your fill layer) in the Sources folder, and add it to the Timeline panel *below* **inkblot matte.psd**. Check that **Firestorm.mov** starts at the beginning of your comp; if not, press **⌥ Home** (**Alt Home**).

5 Make sure the Modes column is visible, and set the TrkMat popup for **Firestorm.mov** to Luma Matte. The fire will now play inside the animated track matte. Note that just the shape of the matte – not the fire footage – is distorted by Turbulent Displace, which reminds us of the flexibility of mattes.

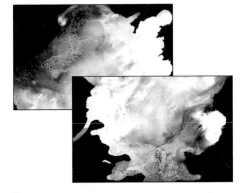

2 The file **inkblot matte.psd** is larger than the comp, so you have room to animate it moving up over time.

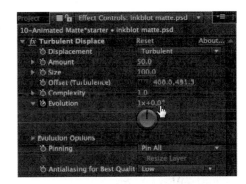

3 Effect > Distort > Turbulent Displace is handy for adding organic movement to layers. You need to animate the Evolution parameter to have the distortion change over time.

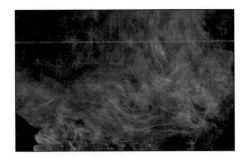

5 The displaced ink blot is used as a matte for **Firestorm.mov**. The black areas are where the image is transparent; you could put another image behind this if you wished.

Stencils

The third and final method of creating transparency that we'll explore in this lesson is stencils. Stencils can be thought of as mattes that overachieve: Rather than define transparency for just one layer, they define the transparency of the composite of all the layers underneath (remember that After Effects renders from the bottom up). In other words, stencils cut all the way through to the bottom of the layer stack in the Timeline panel, but they don't affect layers that sit above them. Like mattes, they come in two flavors – alpha and luma.

Stencil Luma

1 Bring the Project panel forward, and open **Comps > 11-Stencil Luma*starter**. It contains a pair of movies we've used earlier in this lesson, with a twist: **Cityscape.mov** has been inverted to make it look more graphical, and **VirtualInsanity.mov** has been applied on top of it in Overlay mode (you played with blending modes in the previous lesson).

2 In the Project panel's **Sources > movies** folder, select **Cloud matte.mov** and add it to the top of the layer stack. Move the current time indicator a bit later to where the cloud stream emerges, or drag **Cloud matte.mov** to start a second or two earlier so you see some action at the beginning of the comp.

3 In the Modes column (press **F4**), set the Mode popup for **Cloud matte.mov** to Stencil Luma – it's near the bottom of the list. Just as in a previous exercise, the image will appear only inside the clouds. (If your version doesn't look like our figures here, compare it with **Comps_Finished > 11-Stencil Luma_final**.) Note that unlike mattes, the Video switch for the stencil layer must stay on.

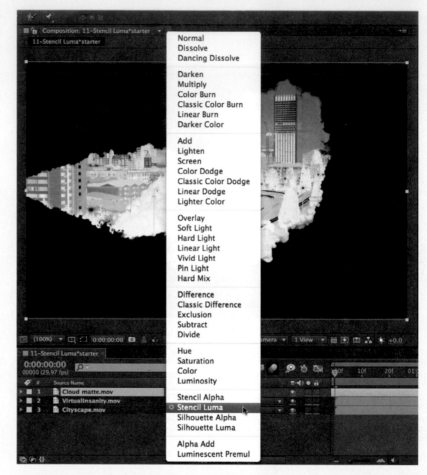

Just for fun, also try the Silhouette Luma option; the area outside the cloud stream will now be visible. Continuing the matte analogies, you can think of Silhouette as being "stencil inverted."

4 Remember that stencils affect only the layers below them; not above. Drag **Cloud matte.mov** down one space in the layer stack so that it sits between **VirtualInsanity.mov** and **Cityscape.mov**. The layer below – **Cityscape** – will be cut out by the cloud stream, but the layer above – **VirtualInsanity** – will now play full frame.

3 Placing **Cloud matte.mov** on top of the other two layers and setting its Mode to Stencil Luma causes it to cut out both layers below (above). Silhouette Luma gives the inverted result (below).

Stencil Alpha

As with track mattes, stencils can also be based on a layer's alpha channel. Effects can be used on the stencil layer, just as we treated the matte layer earlier in this lesson.

1 Open **Comps > 12-Stencil Alpha*starter.** The background layers are the same as in the previous exercise. Layer 1 – **Night Lites.ai** – is an Illustrator layer that you will use as a stencil. Because it is black, it won't work as a Stencil Luma (black pixels = zero opacity), but it will work as a Stencil Alpha.

2 Set the Mode popup for **Night Lites.ai** to Stencil Alpha. The composite image of all layers below will now be contained inside the stencil's alpha channel. (Silhouette Alpha is akin to "inverted stencil alpha" and will yield the opposite result; stick with Stencil Alpha.)

3 Make sure **Night Lites.ai** is selected, and apply Effect > Distort > Turbulent Displace. Animate the Evolution property from 0 at time 00:00 to a value of 1 revolution at the end of the comp. RAM Preview. If the title isn't "oozing," verify that you animated one whole revolution and not just one degree!

Just to make life more interesting, make the amount of ooze change over time: Animate Turbulent Displace's Amount to increase from 0 to, say, 25. While you're at it, have fun experimenting with the options under the Displacement popup too.

4 Finish off your animation by animating the stencil to make it come on in a more interesting fashion. When you're done, check out our version in **Comps_Finished > 12-Stencil Alpha_final.** You applied Turbulent Displace to the stencil layer, but we applied it to an adjustment layer (Lesson 3) so it would affect layers below. Move it below the stencil layer and it will distort the movies only, and not the stencil. Choices, choices!

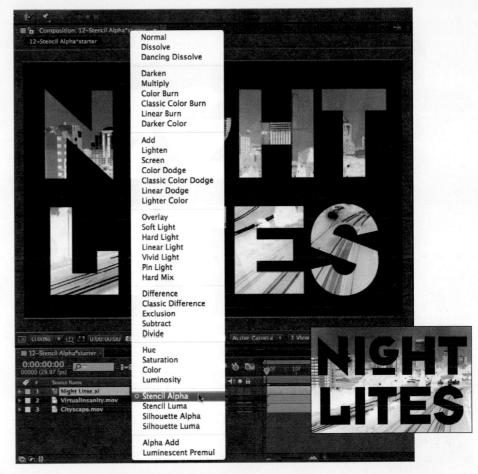

1–2 The comp **12-Stencil Alpha*starter** initially has black type on top of a composite of two background layers (inset). Setting the type to Stencil Alpha results in it cutting out the underlying layers (above).

4 Add and animate Turbulent Displace to the type to make it ooze over time. You can also animate the scale and rotation of the type to create additional movement. The disadvantage of using stencils is that you can't put a background layer in the same comp, as the stencil will cut through that as well. To add a background, nest the stencil comp into a second comp (as you did earlier with the Alpha Matte exercise).

Idea Corner

If you want to practice the techniques you've learned in this lesson, try out the following variations on the exercises you've already performed. Some of our versions are included in the Project panel's **Idea Corner** folder.

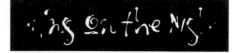

The Transition effects provide an alternative to using masks to wipe layers on and off. The effects shown here include Venetian Blinds, CC Grid Wipe, and CC Twister.

There is a big difference between applying an effect such as Turbulent Displace to a matte (left), and using an adjustment layer to apply the same effect to the result of a track matte (right). The latter is demonstrated in **Idea Corner > Adjustment Layer**.

We rotated the **inkblot matte.psd** layer 90° (left), and used it as a Stencil Luma layer in **12-Stencil Alpha_final** comp to erode the edges of the title (right).

• Animating a mask shape is one way to wipe on a title; another approach is to use a transition-style effect. For example, in **01-Masking** delete the mask used to wipe on **Bring on the Night.ai**, and instead apply Effect > Transition > Linear Wipe. Re-create the same animation using this effect. Also experiment with the other effects in this category; the CC effects installed with the Cycore FX plug-in set can create a lot of interesting looks. (CC effects are installed automatically with After Effects; the more capable Cycore FX HD is bundled with CS6.)

• Effects applied to mattes or stencils treat only the shape of the matte or stencil – they don't affect the image being cut out. For example, in the comps **10-Animated Matte** or **12-Stencil Alpha** where we used Turbulent Displace to alter the matte and stencil, you might have noticed that the background cut out by the matte or stencil didn't ooze as well. If you want to ooze the entire composite, delete the effect from the matte or stencil, and instead apply it to an adjustment layer (introduced in the previous lesson) sitting above all the other layers. Our version is shown in **Idea Corner > Adjustment Layer**. You could also nest your track matte or stencil comp into a second comp where you can apply effects to the nested layer. (Nesting is covered in detail in Lesson 6.)

• You can stack stencils on top of stencils. In **12-Stencil Alpha**, try adding **Cloud matte.mov** or **inkblot matte.psd** as a Stencil Luma layer to the top of this comp!

• Create a series of high-contrast grayscale images using whatever means take your fancy (digital images, India ink, Photoshop). Number them sequentially and import the series as a sequence, then loop and set the frame rate in Interpret Footage. Use this sequence as a luma matte or stencil for another layer.

▼ Effects with Track Mattes and Stencils

Track Mattes involve the combination of two layers. Effects are applied to a single layer. So in the comp where you applied the track matte, you can apply effects to the fill layer or the matte layer, but this applies them to the layer *before* the track matte is composited together. Edge effects (such as drop shadow, glow, and bevel alpha) need to be applied to the track matte *result*.

If you need to see this problem for yourself, in the Project panel, select **Comps_Finished > 08a-Alpha Matte_final**, duplicate it (Edit > Duplicate), and then open the duplicate comp.

• Try adding Effect > Perspective > Drop Shadow to **VirtualInsanity.mov**: You won't see any change. This is because the effect is being applied to the rectangular movie layer *before* the track matte is composited.

• Now try adding Drop Shadow to the **Night Vision.ai** layer and increase the Distance parameter. You may think you're seeing a normal shadow, but RAM Preview and you will realize that the fill movie is playing inside the shadow. This is because a black drop shadow at 50% opacity is being applied to the matte layer *before* the track matte is composited. Since the fill layer is using the alpha channel of the layer above as a matte, it plays at 50% opacity inside the shadow.

There are a few potential solutions to this problem:

• If all you need is a drop shadow applied to the result of a track matte, select the second layer in your track matte pair (the fill), and apply Layer > Layer Styles > Drop Shadow. Layer Styles render after the matte has been calculated.

• Composite the track matte or stencil in one comp, then nest this comp into another comp. The resulting layer will look like any other source with an alpha channel, meaning you can apply any effect or layer style you want, including Drop Shadow, Roughen Edges, and the like. (After you complete Lesson 6, you will also know how to use precomposing to achieve the same result.)

• Composite the track matte or stencil in its own comp, and then apply an Adjustment Layer on top of these layers. You can now apply any effect you like to the Adjustment Layer, and it will affect the result of the track matte or stencil composite below. The one catch is, if you apply Layer Styles to the Adjustment Layer, they will be ignored because they are not "effects."

If you add a drop shadow to individual layers of a track matte pair, you either won't see the result, or the shadow will become part of the matte that the fill plays inside of (above). However, if you apply Layer > Layer Styles > Drop Shadow, the shadow will be calculated after the matte, giving the desired result (below).

Quizzler

And finally, a few mask-related challenges to make you think:

• Inside the Project panel's **Quizzler** folder, play back the movie **Pop on by word.mov**. Note that the title pops on a word at a time, rather than wipes on. How did we do that using an animated mask? To test your theory, try re-creating it yourself using **Pop on*starter** as a starting point.

• In **Quizzler > Stroke play**, we made a Stroke effect animate clockwise around the leaf shape mask. How would you make it animate in the opposite direction?

Once you figure that out, how would you make it start at the top of the leaf shapes and go all the way around, instead of start at the bottom?

The solutions to all of these are in the **Quizzler Solutions** folder. No peeking!

▽ tip

Take Any Matte

You can take almost any layer and use its luminance as a luma matte. To better "see" a layer's luminance, apply the Color Correction > Tint effect to make it grayscale. Use other effects such as Levels to increase the contrast between the black and white values.

Type and Music

Animating text and working with music are essential to motion graphics design.

▽ In This Lesson

123 creating basic text
125 creating text animators; Range Selectors
127 animating text Position, Rotation, and Opacity
129 randomizing the order of characters
129 creating cascading text
129 working with selection Shapes
131 setting the text Anchor Point
132 animating by words
133 title safe areas
134 animating text Blur and Tracking
135 text on a path
136 Per-character 3D animators
140 separating fields
141 adding the Wiggly Selector
142 rendering with an alpha channel
143 field rendering
144 adding audio to a comp
145 spotting audio; using layer and comp markers
146 mixing and enhancing audio
148 using text animation presets
150 saving text animations as presets
151 editing Photoshop Text layers

▽ Getting Started

Copy the **Lesson 05-Type and Music** folder from this book's disc onto your hard drive, and make note of where it is; it contains the project file and sources you need to execute this lesson.

From opening titles to closing credits, bullet points to lower thirds, and conveying information to creating abstract backgrounds, one of the most common elements in motion graphics is the use of text. Fortunately, After Effects has a very powerful text engine – but it's hardly the most intuitive tool in the world. In this lesson, we'll show you how to professionally typeset text, then animate it in interesting ways.

Another important – but often overlooked – element in motion graphics is the use of sound. By tying your animations to music and dialog, you can greatly increase the impact of your designs. Later in this lesson, we will show you how to add audio layers to compositions, mix audio, view the audio waveform, and place layer markers that will help you time your animation to events in the audio.

Type Tools

The Type tool in After Effects borrows heavily from other Adobe applications such as Photoshop and Illustrator. If you are familiar with creating text in those applications, you already have a good head start. You can still create type in these programs and import them into After Effects, but whenever we have the choice, we prefer to start from scratch in After Effects. (At the end of this lesson we'll show you how to convert Photoshop Text layers to After Effects editable text, but be aware that this option still does not exist for text created in Illustrator.)

Beyond creating text is animating it. In After Effects, the most important concept is that of the *selection*. Typically, selected characters are treated or offset in some way (such

as by position, scale, rotation, color, opacity, and so forth), while characters outside the selection retain their normal appearance. The selected characters also show a transition from the ordinary appearance of the text to their treated appearance – for example, gradually growing in size. The fun comes in animating this selection zone so that characters will appear to fly in, zoom down, and do all sorts of other tricks as they move between their treated and ordinary states. And if that's not enough, don't forget that many effects and layer styles also enhance the look of text.

Text Basics

After Effects allows you to create individual characters, words, or lines of text (sometimes referred to as *point text*), or paragraphs that are auto-wrapped to fit inside a box that you define (referred to as *paragraph text*). Text can be created horizontally or vertically as well as set along a curve. Paragraphs can be left justified, right justified, or centered, with additional control over how the first and last lines are treated. You have a lot of control over *tracking* (the space between characters over an entire block of text), *kerning* (the space between individual pairs of characters), *leading* (space between lines), and *baseline shift* (the upward or downward offset of characters in superscripts and ordinals such as the "st" in 1st). You can also freely mix and match fonts, styles (bold, italic, et cetera), sizes, and colors in each word, line, or sentence – not that you necessarily should! Quite often, less is more when it comes to elegant text design.

To get you quickly up to speed, we've included a movie from our companion *After Effects Apprentice* video training series that provides a quick start on creating and typesetting text. We suggest you watch it before going any farther so you'll know how to create and edit basic text. The rest of the exercises in this lesson will assume you've been through this and know how to create starting text on your own. If this is all new to you, go ahead and try your hand at creating some text: Open this lesson's project file **Lesson_05.aep**. Select Window > Workspace > Text and then Workspace > Reset "Text", or create your own custom workspace where the Character and Paragraph panels are both visible.

After Effects can create animated text by manipulating properties such as position, scale, rotation, opacity, and more. Here, text is blurred per character and animates along a mask path. Footage courtesy Artbeats/Light Alchemy.

▽ factoid

Size Doesn't Matter

Normally, increasing the scale of a layer above 100% will make the image appear soft. But no matter what size you make your text layer, it will always render with sharp edges because it is vector-based. This is technically known as *continuous rasterization*, meaning After Effects creates pixels for the text layer only after it knows what size they should be. The only word you have to remember is "cool!"

Text Basics Guided Tour

As part of our *After Effects Apprentice* video series, we created a movie walking you through the basics of creating and editing type with After Effects' Type tool. It's located in the **05-Video Bonus** folder.

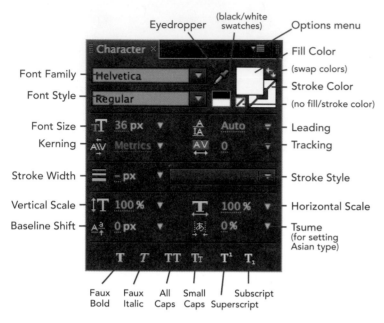

Font Family — Helvetica

Eyedropper

(black/white swatches)

Options menu

Fill Color

(swap colors)

Stroke Color

(no fill/stroke color)

Font Style — Regular

Font Size — 36 px

Leading — Auto

Kerning — Metrics

Tracking — 0

Stroke Width — – px

Stroke Style

Vertical Scale — 100 %

Horizontal Scale — 100 %

Baseline Shift — 0 px

Tsume — 0% (for setting Asian type)

Faux Bold | Faux Italic | All Caps | Small Caps | Superscript | Subscript

△ **The Character panel**

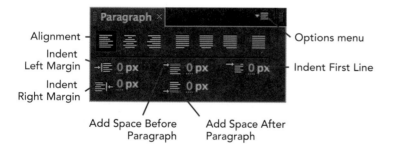

Alignment

Options menu

Indent Left Margin — 0 px

Indent First Line — 0 px

Indent Right Margin — 0 px

0 px

Add Space Before Paragraph

Add Space After Paragraph

△ **The Paragraph panel**

When the cursor is visible, you are in *editing mode* (left). After you press the **Enter** key, handles will appear around the text block; this is *layer mode*, where changes you make in the Character and Paragraph panels apply to the entire title. Double-click an existing text layer in the Timeline to enter layer mode.

In the Project panel, open the folder **Comps**, then double-click the composition **01-Basic Text*starter** to open it – it will initially be blank. Then select the Type tool in the Tools panel; the shortcut is **⌘ T** on Mac (**Ctrl T** on Windows).

01-Basic Text*starter ▾
720 x 480 (0.91)
△ 0:00:03:00, 29.97 fps

Select the Type tool from the application window's toolbar to create some text. To switch between the Horizontal and Vertical Type tools, click and press this icon. The shortcut to select the Type tool and toggle between Horizontal and Vertical modes is **⌘ T** on Mac (**Ctrl T** on Windows).

Here are some key points to remember when creating basic text:

• Click anywhere in the Comp panel with the Type tool to start a Text layer, or double-click the Type tool to start with the cursor in the center of the Comp panel.

• When the cursor is visible, you are in *editing mode*, and the style of the title you type will be determined by the Character and Paragraph panels. To change how existing text looks, you must select the text first before you change the settings in these panels.

• When you are done typing, press the **Enter** key to exit editing mode. The layer's name will update to reflect what you typed. The cursor will disappear and handles will appear around the text block to indicate that you are in *layer mode*. Any changes you make in the Character and Paragraph panels will now apply to the entire title.

Once you've created a text layer, you can animate its regular Transform properties and apply effects to it, just like any other layer. In Lesson 8 on 3D Space, we'll explore the ability to extrude and bevel text, which was introduced in CS6.

Text Animators

Many effective titles consist of just good typesetting and simple transform animations. However, the real fun begins when you add *text animators*. These enable you to animate individual characters, words, or lines, virtually telling the viewer a story (or at least grabbing their attention) in the way that you bring words on and off the screen! But before you get animating, we need to cover a few basic concepts:

• Nothing in the Character and Paragraph panels can be animated directly – there are no stopwatches to turn on for font size, color, tracking, and so on. All animation is created by applying *text animators*.

• When animating on a title, start by creating the title the way it should look normally. For example, if you want the title to "resolve" to a certain color or size, or be in a certain position when the animation is over, use the Character panel and Transform properties to create the text looking that way, *then* add a text animator to transition the text on.

Setting the Text

In this exercise, you will create a title and use a text animator to make it drop down into position one character at a time while fading up.

1 If you haven't already, open this lesson's project file **Lesson_05.aep**. In the Project panel, locate and open **Comp > 02-Dropping In*starter** – it will be blank to start with. Make sure the Character and Paragraph panels are visible; if they aren't, you can select Window > Workspace > Text to pick a preset arrangement that has them open.

2 To start with a clean slate, click on the arrow in the upper right corner of the Paragraph panel to open its Options menu, and select Reset Paragraph to clear previous settings. Then select the Center text option.

Likewise, click on the arrow in the upper right corner of the Character panel, and select Reset Character. Assuming your Composition > Background Color is black or some other dark color, click on the small white swatch underneath the eyedropper to set the character Fill Color to white.

3 Bring the Composition panel forward, and double-click the Type tool. The cursor will be centered in the comp. Type your title – something that fits on one line, like "**Just Dropping In**" – and press *Enter* on the numeric keypad. The layer will be named automatically to match what you typed.

The default character style on Mac is Helvetica 36 px ("px" = pixels), but feel free to change the font style and color to taste – for example, we changed the font style to Bold and increased the size to 60 px. For this exercise, we suggest you stick with one style for the entire text layer to make things more clear.

Typesetting Tips

In the **Lesson 05** folder is a PDF file named **Typesetting Tips.pdf** that includes information on using smart quotes and dashes for creating professional-looking titles.

2–3 Reset the Character and Paragraph panels using their Options menu, accessed via the arrows in their upper right corners (circled). Select the Center text option in the Paragraph panel, and set the Fill Color in the Character panel to white. We set the font style to Helvetica Bold at a size of 60 px (above) and created a single line of text to animate (below).

Just Dropping In

4 Clicking the Animate button to the right of the word Text reveals the properties you can animate on a per-character basis. Selecting Position creates Animator 1.

6 The characters "selected" by the Start and End values in Range Selector 1 are bracketed by the vertical lines with the arrows in their middle (above). As you scrub the values for Animator 1's Position, the selected characters will be offset by this amount (below).

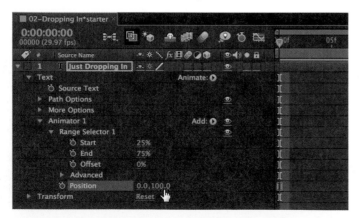

Range Selectors

To animate text, you need to apply a text animator:

4 In the Timeline panel, click on the arrow next to the text layer to twirl it down, revealing its Text and Transform sections. Then twirl down the Text section.

To the right of the word Text will be the word Animate, followed by an arrow. Click on this arrow, and select Position from the popup menu that appears. Animator 1 will be created; nested inside will be Range Selector 1, and inside that, a Position value.

5 Deselect All (**F2**) and twirl down Range Selector 1. Select only Range Selector 1 and you will see vertical lines with triangles at the start and end of the title in the Comp panel. These indicate where the Start and End values of the Range Selector are: 0% means the beginning, and 100% means the end. Scrub the Start and End values, and note how these indicators move along the text. (Note that you can also drag these triangles directly in the Comp panel.)

• When you're done, set Start to 25% and End to 75%.

6 Animator 1's Position value indicates how much the selected text should be *offset* from its original position. It starts at 0, 0, which means no offset.

• Scrub the X Position value (the first of the pair); the selected characters will move left and right.

• Scrub the Y Position value, and the selected characters will move up and down.

Important concept: By default, only the selected characters – those inside the Start and End bars – are affected by the text animator properties. Any characters outside the selection are unaffected, and appear in their original style as created. You can toggle Animator 1's eyeball off and on if you ever need to check what effect it is having.

To reinforce what is going on, leave Position at a value such as X = 0, Y = 100 and scrub the values for Start and End to change the characters that are included in the selection. This will result in characters switching between their original and offset position.

Just Dropping In

By scrubbing the Start and End values, light bulbs should be going off about how you might create an animation: By keyframing the Start and End values to animate the characters that are selected, you can make the title, say, fall down from the top of the frame:

7 Start over with a clean slate: Select Animator 1, and press `Delete`. The text should return to being centered in the comp.

Then select Animate > Position again from the text layer's popup menu to create a fresh text animator, just as you did in step 4.

8 Press `Home` to ensure you are at the start of the comp.

Twirl down Range Selector 1, and click on the stopwatch icon next to Start to enable keyframing for it. The first keyframe will be created for you, using Start's default value of 0%.

Then scrub the Y Position value to around –200 so that the text is hanging from the top of the comp (keep it visible for now).

9 Go to time 01:00, and set the Start value to 100%. This will create a second keyframe at this value.

Press `0` on the numeric keypad to RAM Preview your animation, and watch the text drop into place. Save your project at this point.

Adding More Properties

Once you have created this basic "dropping in" move, it is easy to add more properties to your animation.

10 Press `Home` to return to the start of the comp where the text is at the top of your frame. In the Timeline panel, look along the line that Animator 1 sits on: You will see the word Add followed by an arrow. Like Animate, this will reveal a list of properties, but in this case a new animator will *not* be created – the selected property will just be added to the existing animator.

Motion Blur

Animating text often looks great with motion blur (Lesson 2). Enable the Motion Blur switch for your text layer, then turn on the master Enable Motion Blur switch along the top of the Timeline panel. Remember that motion blur takes longer to calculate, so your previews may be slower.

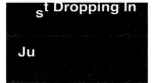
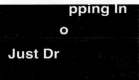

8–9 Set Animator 1's Y Position to –200 and animate the Start value from 0% to 100% (top). The result will be the text dropping from its offset position to its original position, a character at a time.

Text Animator Guided Tour

We freely admit that text animators are not particularly intuitive the first time you use them! If you have trouble following this exercise, we've included a movie introducing text animators from our *After Effects Apprentice* video series – it's also in this lesson's **Video Bonus** folder .

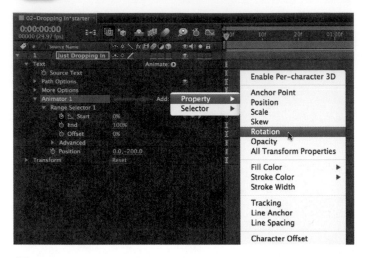

10 Once you have created the initial Animator, you can animate additional properties by clicking on its Add arrow. (You can also click on the Animate arrow provided Animator 1 is selected.)

12 Adding Opacity (above) will cause the characters to also fade in as they fall into place (below). (And if you return Animator 1's Position and Rotation values to zero, your characters will appear to type on in place!)

Click the Add arrow, and select Property > Rotation. The Rotation property will be added to the existing Animator 1. (If you created Animator 2 instead, you may have clicked on the Animate button by mistake! Undo and try again.)

11 Scrub the Rotation value to about 45°. Now all characters included in the Start/End selection will be affected by the rotation offset.

RAM Preview again. As the title drops into place, the characters will fall outside the selection and are no longer rotated. You did not need to animate the Rotation value itself; the animation happens automatically as characters are transferred from inside the selection (where they get the position and rotation offset) to outside the selection.

11 By adding Rotation as a property included in Text Animator 1, and setting Rotation to 45°, the characters will drop in and rotate back to 0° while doing so.

12 So far, so good. But at the start of the animation, you have a row of silly-looking characters sitting along the top of your comp. How can you make them invisible before they drop in? You could offset their position further so they started above the frame, but there's an even better way: Make them invisible!

Return to 00:00. Click the Add button arrow again, and select Property > Opacity. Scrub the Opacity down to 0%; the selected text will disappear. RAM Preview again: The characters return to their normal opacity value as they fall outside the selection.

If you want to make sure you followed the steps correctly, compare your result with our version: It's in the Project panel's **Comps_Finished** folder, and is named **02-Dropping In_final**. And don't forget to save your project.

Now that you have the basic idea, feel free to experiment by adding other properties to Animator 1. Try Scale (the characters will appear to zoom up or slam down), or Fill Color > RGB (their color will change as they fall into place). Obviously, thousands of variations are possible! Just remember that you don't have to animate these properties individually; you need to animate only the Range Selector, then let these properties decide how different the characters will look when they're inside the selection.

▼ Randomize Order

To have the characters fall down in a random order, twirl down the Advanced section of Range Selector 1, and set Randomize Order to On (click the Off value to toggle). The characters will now drop down in a random order rather than from left to right. The Random Seed value allows you to jiggle the order and find a more pleasing pattern.

To see this result, check out our version in **Comps_Finished > 02-Dropping In_final2**.

Creating Cascading Text

In the previous exercise, you learned how to make text animate in one character at a time. Sometimes it is nice to spread this movement across several adjacent characters. This creates what we refer to as a "cascading" animation, and is the subject of this next exercise. To get a peek at where you are heading, preview **Comps_Finished > 03-Cascade_final**.

1 Select Close All from the menu at the top of the Comp panel. In the Project panel, locate and open **Comps > 03-Cascade*starter**. We've already created a title for you to start with, but feel free to change the text or font style to taste.

2 In the Timeline panel, twirl down the text layer, and select Animate > Scale. This will create Animator 1 and Range Selector 1, with a Scale property. Change Scale to 400% (for now, don't worry about how the letters overlap).

3 Click on the Add arrow on the same line as Animator 1, and select Property > Fill Color > RGB. Fill Color will be added below Scale, using a default color of red. Change the Fill Color to taste by clicking on its swatch in the Timeline panel.

4 Twirl down the Range Selector, then twirl down the Advanced section inside Range Selector 1. Try the different Shape options by selecting them from its popup, while also experimenting with the Range Selector's Start and End values. Here's a quick rundown of how they behave:

• The default Shape is Square, which means that characters inside the range selection are fully affected by the Scale and Fill Color properties. Scrub the Start value, and note how characters outside the selector are immediately returned to their original settings, with little to no transition to speak of.

A "cascading" animation is when multiple characters slide into place, like a wave. This requires a slightly different technique, which you will learn in this exercise.

2 Select Animate > Scale, and set the Scale value to 400%. The characters will swell to a size where they overlap; don't worry about that right now, as they will eventually fade up as they cascade in from this size.

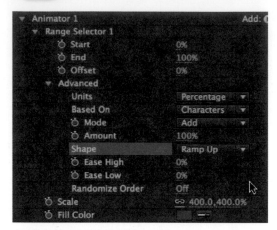

4 Twirl down Range Selector's Advanced section and explore the different Shape options. Then select the Ramp Up shape.

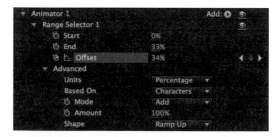

4 *continued* The Ramp Up shape allows cascading animations by creating a smooth transition from the unselected (white, normal size) to the selected (red, 400% scale) states.

6–7 Using the Ramp Up shape in combination with animating Offset from left to right (above) results in our characters transitioning from being large and red to their original appearance (below).

• Try the Triangle, Round, and Smooth Shapes. You will notice that they have a wider transition zone. Also note that the characters in the center of the selection are fully affected, but the effect of your Scale and Fill Color offsets fall off the closer the selected characters are to the Start and End points. Characters outside the range selection are not affected, just as is the case with the Square shape.

• Next, select Ramp Up, which behaves differently: It uses the Start and End values to create a *transition* from the original text (white color, normal size) at the Start of the selection, to the fully affected text (red, 400% size) at the End of the selection. Any characters after End are also fully affected (red, 400%), as if they were inside the selection; any characters before the Start are not affected, as if they are outside the selection. Ramp Down does the same, but in reverse.

In short, the Ramp Up and Ramp Down Shapes transition between selected and not selected, and the size of this transition is determined by the number of characters between the Start and End points. These are the Shapes that you need to create cascading text animations.

When you're done experimenting, select Ramp Up from the Shape popup, and twirl up the Advanced section.

5 In Range Selector 1, set the Start to 0%, and scrub the End parameter to about 33%. All the characters after the End parameters will be fully affected (red, 400%).

Take note of the Offset value in Range Selector 1. Offset is added to the values for Start and End. As a result, Offset is a handy way to animate both Start and End at the same time, keeping the same relationship between them so that the width of the selection remains the same.

Scrub the Offset parameter while watching the Comp viewer, and note how the transition area moves back and forth along the line of text.

6 To create the cascading effect, make sure the current time indicator is at 00:00, and enable the stopwatch for Offset. Set its value to –33%. This will move the transition completely to the left of the title. Why did we pick this particular number? It's simply the negative of the End value, which ensures the selection has been offset to just before the Start.

7 Move to 02:00, and set Offset to 100%. This adds 100% to both Start and End, resulting in Start and End both being 100% (the maximum); the transition will be pushed off to the right. Scrub the current time indicator back and forth along the timeline to get a feel for this animation.

Leave the current time indicator around 01:00 to better see what is about to happen in the next step.

8 The finishing touch is to make the characters fade up as they cascade on. To do this, click on Animator 1's Add arrow, and select Property > Opacity. Then set Opacity to 0%. Because you're using the Ramp Up shape, the characters will transition from 100% opacity at the Range Selector's Start, to 0% opacity at its End. Characters after the End will be fully transparent. RAM Preview to see this in motion – a nice cascading effect! You can compare your results with our version in **Comps_Finished > 03-Cascade_final**.

Again, remember: You didn't need to animate Opacity! It is merely another property that is being used to treat the text as you transition from being inside the selection (in Ramp Up's case, after the End point) to outside the selection (before the Start point).

Adjusting the Anchor Point

If you watch closely, you'll notice that the scaling occurs around the *baseline* (bottom) of the text. What if you want the characters to scale from their centers?

9 Move to 01:00 to catch the animation mid-cascade, and temporarily increase the Animator's Opacity value to 50% to better see what's about to happen:

• Click the Add (not Animate) arrow and select Property > Anchor Point. This will add the Anchor Point property to Animator 1.

• Scrub the Anchor Point's Y value slowly to the left while watching the Comp panel; add the ⌘ (*Ctrl*) key to scrub in finer increments. A small negative Y value should center the characters vertically. Experiment with different X and Y values of Anchor Point and RAM Preview to see the results.

• Change Opacity back to 0% when you're done.

Our experiments with Anchor Point are demonstrated in **Comps_Finished > 03-Cascade_final2**. Layer 1's Anchor Point is offset in X and Y. Layer 2 serves as a reminder: Randomize Order and motion blur are two enhancements that you can add too!

8 Adding Opacity to Animator 1 and setting it to 0% will make characters fade from 100% to 0% within the transition zone.

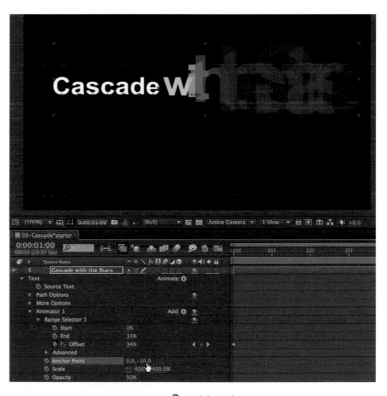

9 Add Anchor Point to your Animator and offset its Anchor Point Y value slightly negative to center the expanded text vertically.

◁ We created a pair of alternate versions in **Comps_Finished > 03-Cascade_final2** that include both X and Y Anchor Point offset (both lines), as well as Randomize Order plus motion blur (bottom line).

2 Reveal the Text property for layer 1, click on the Animate button, and select Opacity. An Animator and Range Selector will be created. Set this Opacity value to 0%.

4 By default, when you set the Range Selector's Opacity to 0% and animate its Start, the text will type on one character at a time. Footage courtesy Artbeats/Digidelic.

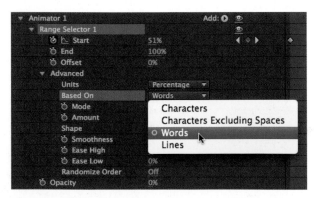

5 In Range Selector 1's Advanced section, set Based On to Words to have entire words be selected or unselected. To cause the words to "pop" rather than fade on, set Smoothness to 0%.

One Word at a Time

So far, you've been animating text a character at a time. However, After Effects also makes it easy to animate entire words as units.

1 Close your previous comps and open the composition **04-RockinText*starter**. It includes some basic text that we've already created for you, with a drop shadow applied. We chose the font Adobe Birch, which is installed with After Effects. (If you don't have this font, pick another condensed font and adjust it so that it fits nicely inside the comp.)

2 Twirl down the text layer (layer 1), and select Animate > Opacity. Animator 1 and Range Selector 1 will be created, with the Opacity property already added. Set Animator 1's Opacity value to 0%. Because all of the text is selected by default, the entire line will become transparent.

3 Twirl down Range Selector 1. At 00:00, turn on the animation stopwatch for Start. This will create a keyframe with a value of 0% at the beginning of the animation.

4 Move to 03:00, and set the Start value to 100%. Preview your animation. Because the text is using the default Square shape, it will type on from left to right, one character at a time.

5 Here's the trick to make the text appear one *word* at a time: Twirl down the Range Selector's Advanced section, and set the Based On popup to Words. Preview again; the title now fades on one word at a time.

Below the Shape popup is the Smoothness parameter. For now, set Smoothness to 0% so the letters pop on with no fade up.

6 Let's add some rotation to the mix, while also learning an important gotcha. Click Animator 1's Add button, and select Property > Rotation.

Set Animator 1's Rotation value to –1 revolution (meaning it should read –1x 0.0°). As the title types on, you might expect the characters to rotate into position. But nothing happens!

Remember the Smoothness parameter? The combination of the Square shape and no Smoothness results in no transition time, meaning no chance to see the Rotation. Set Smoothness back to 100%, and now you will see your Rotation animation (as well as the Opacity fade).

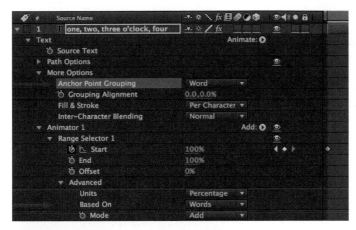

7 To have each word rotate as a unit as well (left), set More Options > Anchor Point Grouping popup to Word (above).

7 Although the Range Selector is set to animate word by word, the characters themselves are rotating around their own individual anchor points. To have them rotate word by word as well, twirl down the Text > More Options section and set the Anchor Point Group popup to Word also. RAM Preview to see the difference this makes.

8 The text is rotating around its baseline. To have it spin from a different location, play with the More Options > Grouping Alignment parameter. For example, change the Y value to –200%, and the text will rotate in from above.

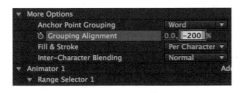

8 More Options > Grouping Alignment allows text to travel in interesting ways. You can also animate this parameter.

Our version is in **Comps_Finished > 04-RockinText_final**. We had a bit of fun by also adding Scale to Animator 1 and setting it to 200%, so that the text scales down as it rotates. And remember: Save your project.

▼ Safe Areas

If you are creating video to be played back on a television set, you need to know about *safe areas*. While you are working, After Effects shows you the entire video frame. However, the viewer doesn't get to see part of this frame – it gets cut off by the bezel around a TV's screen. Also, part of the frame might be too distorted to allow text to be read clearly.

To avoid the bezel problem, you need to keep any imagery you expect the viewer to see inside the *action safe* area. This margin is 10%, cutting 5% off the top, bottom, left, and right. As bezels vary from TV to TV, you need to put some imagery out there to prevent the viewer from seeing only black; just don't put anything important out there. To avoid the distortion problem, you need to keep text inside the *title safe* area. This margin is 20%, or 10% on each of the four sides.

To check your work, you can toggle a Title/Action Safe grid on and off in After Effects. The shortcut is ❓ (the apostrophe key); you can also select it from the Grid and Guide button along the bottom of the Comp, Layer, and Footage panels. ⌥+click (*Alt*+click) this button to toggle it directly.

Yes, many break these rules by putting news, sports, and stock price tickers between the action and title safe areas. And there are far fewer problems with today's flat-panel TVs. But regardless, if you are creating commercial video, you will be expected to respect these safe areas.

1 Open **05-Path*starter**, which contains a basic title over a cool background.

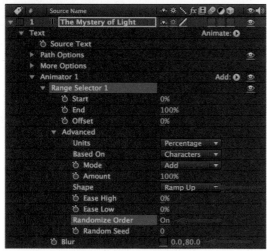

3–4 Turn off the Constrain Proportions switch for Blur, and set the Blur Y value to around 80. This turns the characters into vertical rays of light. Then change the Shape to Ramp Up to get a transition from sharp to blurry characters. Toggling Randomize Order to On scrambles the order of which characters are sharp and which are blurry.

Flowing Text

In this exercise, you'll create some elegant, cool-looking type by animating character spacing and blur, plus flow text along a mask path.

Animating Blur

1 Close your previous comps and open **05-Path*starter**. We've already created the basic title using the font Trajan Pro (another font that comes free with After Effects; pick another if you like) and placed it over a cool background. Indeed, we're going to use this background to inspire our animation…

2 In the Timeline panel, twirl down the text layer (layer 1) to reveal the Text properties and the Animate button. Select Animate > Blur. This creates Animator 1 and Range Selector 1, with the Blur property added.

3 We want our characters to start out as vertical rays. To do this, click on the Constrain Proportions button (it's the chain link icon) next to Blur to disable this lock, and set the Blur Y value to around 80.

4 We would also like some variation in how blurry each character is. Variation usually means randomization, so we need to seek out a parameter that lets us introduce this.

• Twirl down Range Selector 1, then twirl down its Advanced section. Change the Shape popup from Square to Ramp Up. Note that now the characters transition from being sharp near the Start of the range to being blurry near the End.

• Then toggle Randomize Order to On. This will scramble which characters appear sharp and which appear blurry.

5 Now create a cascading-type animation:

• At 00:00, enable keyframing for Offset, and set its initial value to –100% (the negative of the End value). All the characters will be blurred.

• At 02:00, set Offset to 100%. Now all of the characters will be sharp, as Offset has moved through the entire range. Preview to see the effect.

Animated Tracking

Characters coming together is a popular look. This requires animating the tracking of the text:

6 Select Add > Property > Tracking; this will add Tracking Type and Tracking Amount parameters to Animator 1. Return to 00:00 where the text is fully selected. Scrub the Tracking Amount, and observe how the blurred characters spread out. Set it to about 6.

RAM Preview: The text will come together as the animation resolves (see right). This is because the amount of tracking applied is controlled by Range Selector 1's animating Offset.

Text on a Curve

The text looks cool, but it's a bit rigid compared with the flowing background – so let's create a curved path for the text to follow, using the masking skills you learned in Lesson 4.

7 Make sure the text layer is selected, then choose the Pen tool, and enable the RotoBezier option in the Tools panel.

Create an open curved path by clicking a few points from left to right across the Comp panel, using the curves in the background layer for inspiration. When done, press **V** to return to the Selection tool.

8 In the Timeline panel twirl down the Text > Path Options section, and set the Path popup to Mask 1. (If you don't see Mask 1, make sure the mask was applied to the text layer!) The text will now sit on top of your mask path.

Press **Home** to return to 00:00 and study your text; you might want to increase the Tracking Amount value to spread your text out more along its path.

9 The Path options exist outside the Animator and Range Selector. To make the text slide along your path, keyframe one of its Margin parameters:

• Return to 00:00, and scrub Text > Path Options > First Margin until you are happy with where it starts. Enable the animation stopwatch for First Margin.

• Press **End** to jump to the end of the comp, and scrub First Margin to make the text travel. RAM Preview; ease into the second Offset keyframe to create a smoother move.

Our version is in **Comps_Finished > 05-Path_final**. We also added Effect > Blur & Sharpen > Radial Shadow, and animated the mask path over time.

7 Select the Pen tool, and enable the RotoBezier option (above). Then create an open curved path in the Comp panel.

8–9 To have the text sit on your newly drawn mask path (above), set the Text > Path Options > Path popup to Mask 1 (below). Then animate the Path Options > First Margin parameter to slide the text along your path. Feel free to animate the mask path as well.

Real 3D

After Effects CS6 added the ability to extrude and bevel type and shape layers. We'll demonstrate extruded type in Lesson 8. There are also plug-in alternatives available from Zaxwerks, Boris, Mettle and Video Copilot. They allow you to extrude, bevel, and texture them in ways more powerful than After Effects CS6.

Per-Character 3D

Up to now you've been animating characters in two dimensions: X (left and right) and Y (up and down). Per-character 3D allows text animators to be manipulated in three dimensions: X, Y and Z. With this third dimension, individual characters or words can be rendered at different distances from the viewer. In this lesson, we'll focus on using the simpler, faster Classic 3D Renderer which treats each character as a flat postcard in space; in Lesson 8 we'll show you how to extrude and bevel these characters using the Ray-traced 3D Renderer introduced in After Effects CS6.

Anything you can do to a regular 2D text layer – such as text on a path, as well as adding the Wiggly Selector (page 141) – you can also apply to Per-character 3D text. To get the most out of Per-character 3D animation, you need to be working in a composition that also has a 3D camera (and optionally, lights). If you've been following these lessons in order, you haven't encountered 3D cameras and lights yet, as they are introduced in Lesson 8. In the meantime, for simplicity's sake, the following exercises take advantage of Custom Views which already have dummy cameras set up for you.

Text Position in Z

To get started, close all previous comps (select Close All from the menu at the top of the Comp panel). In the Project panel, open **Comps > 06-3D Position*starter**; a few words have already been typeset for you (feel free to change the words or restyle them).

1 In the Timeline panel, twirl down the text layer, click on the Animate button, and select Position. This will create Animator 1 with a Position property. Position will have two values: X and Y.

2 Here is the magic feature to enable 3D text: Click either the Animate or Add button and select Property > Enable Per-character 3D from the top of the list. In the Timeline panel, the text's 3D Layer switch will sport two small cubes to show that Per-character 3D is enabled. Study the Comp viewer: The text layer now has a set of red, green, and blue 3D axis arrows that indicate how the layer is oriented in X, Y, and Z respectively. Their origin is where the layer's Anchor Point is located.

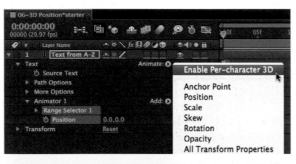

2 When you Add > Enable Per-character 3D for a text layer (top), you will see two small boxes appear in its 3D Layer switch (above). The text's XYZ axis arrows will help show how it is oriented in the Comp view (right).

You will also notice that Position has three values: X, Y, and Z. Scrub the Z Position value (the third one) while watching the Comp viewer. Negative values bring the text forward in space (or closer to the front of an imaginary "stage"), while positive values send it farther back in space.

Selecting Custom View 1 will give you a perspective view of your comp.

3 To better visualize what you are about to do, change the 3D View popup at the bottom of the Comp panel from Active Camera to Custom View 1. You should now see the text from above and at an angle. (If not, use the menu option View > Reset 3D View.)

4 You can animate these characters in a fashion similar to the methods you learned earlier. For example:

• Set Position to 0, –75, –350 to position the characters inside the Range Selector higher and forward in Z space compared with where the axis arrows are.

• Twirl down Range Selector 1. At 00:00, enable the stopwatch for Start with a value of 0%.

• Move to 02:00 and change the Start value to 100%. RAM Preview and the characters will animate back to their original position.

• Return the 3D View popup to Active Camera and press Home to return to 00:00. Notice how characters that are closer to the camera appear to be larger, even though you haven't changed their Scale value. And no matter how close they get to the camera, they will always remain sharp because they are being continuously rasterized (explained near the end of Lesson 6).

• Click the Add button and select Property > Opacity. Set Opacity to 0% so that the characters will be invisible when they are outside the selector's range.

4 As the Range Selector's Start animates from 0% to 100%, the characters will move from their offset position in 3D space back to their original plane. (Note that the layer bounding box is a new feature in CS6.)

Our version is shown in **Comps_finished > 06-3D Position_final**.

Note that not all text properties are affected by Per-character 3D. For instance, Opacity, Skew, Fill Color, and Tracking appear the same whether or not it's enabled. However, Anchor Point, Position, Scale, and Rotation all will gain a third parameter: Z. In the case of Rotation, its X, Y, and Z values appear as separately keyframeable parameters for even more control – which we'll play with next.

3D Text Rotation

Open **Comps > 07-3D Rotation*starter** and RAM Preview it. To save time, we've already created a basic cascading type-on effect using the same technique you learned earlier in this lesson. Select layer 1 and press **U U** to see the relevant properties; namely, Opacity is set to 0%, the Shape is Ramp Up, and Range Selector 1's Offset is animated.

As a starting point, the composition **07-3D Rotation*starter** has a basic cascading animation already set up.

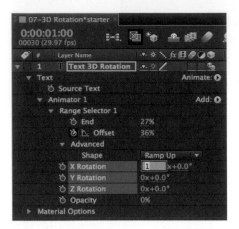

2 After enabling Per-character 3D, adding Rotation will yield three separate parameters (above). Below: X Rotation swings characters around their baseline; Y Rotation twirls characters around their vertical axis; and Z Rotation behaves the same as rotation in 2D.

1 In the Timeline panel, click the Add button for Animator 1 and select Property > Enable Per-character 3D. Set the 3D View popup in the Comp panel to Custom View 1. You should now see the text from above and at an angle.

2 Click on the Add button for Animator 1 and select Property > Rotation. Parameters for X, Y, and Z Rotation should appear (if not, check that you correctly enabled Per-character 3D in step 1). Let's explore what happens when you rotate on each axis individually:

• Set X Rotation to 1 revolution and RAM Preview. The characters swing around their baseline as they fade up.

• Undo your X Rotation and set Y Rotation to 1 revolution. Now each character swivels around to face the viewer as it fades up. Try other values, such as 60° or –100° for a more subtle effect. Return Y Rotation to 0° when done.

• Set Z Rotation to 1 revolution: This parameter is equivalent to the rotation property when text is animating in 2D.

Explore combinations of X, Y, and Z Rotation. It doesn't take much before your characters are performing complex gymnastics – all with just two Range Selector keyframes!

X Rotation

Y Rotation

Z Rotation

Setting the Anchor Point in 3D

By default, characters rotate around their baseline. A lot of fun can be had rotating them around a different point. To do this, manipulate their Anchor Point:

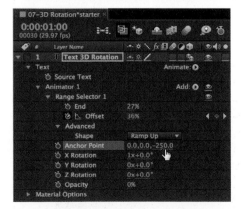

4 Add > Property > Anchor Point and edit the Z value to offset the pivot point.

3 Continue with comp **07-3D Rotation*starter**. Set X Rotation to 1 revolution, and zero out Y and Z Rotation. Move to a time in the middle of the animation.

4 Click on the Add button and select Property > Anchor Point. You will see three values, again corresponding to X, Y, and Z. These offset the pivot point for the characters. Scrub the third value (Z) and note how the characters move away from their baseline. RAM Preview to observe how they spiral into place.

5 For more fun, try offsetting the X or Y Anchor Point and preview the result.

Note that you don't have to view the text animation from a perspective view: Change the 3D View popup back to Active Camera, and you will still get a sense of dimension.

Per-character 3D can give you interesting results even while working in 2D! Our version is shown in **Comps_finished > 07-3D Rotation_final**.

4 *continued* Offsetting the Z Anchor Point causes the characters to spiral into place.

3D Text in a 3D World

After you work through Lesson 8, you will have a much better understanding of 3D space in After Effects. To whet your appetite for what you'll be able to create with Per-character 3D text layers, open **Comps_finished > 07xtra-3D World** (which uses the Classic 3D Renderer) and RAM Preview:

• The wall is a 3D layer so it can accept shadows from the animated text.

• The text layer uses an animation preset that ships with After Effects called 3D Flutter In Random Order (see page 148 for more on text presets).

• A camera plus a shadow-casting light were added to the scene, and the text had its Cast Shadows parameter turned On. (All of these are explained in more detail in Lesson 8.)

The real power comes when you set your 3D text into a 3D world and enable it to cast shadows on other objects in that world.

▼ 3D Text Animation Presets

After Effects ships with 30 text animation presets that take advantage of Per-character 3D. They can be found in the Effects & Presets panel under Animation Presets > Text > 3D Text. You can apply these to any Text layer (not just in compositions that have cameras and lights) and use them as is, or as a starting point for your own animation.

For your convenience, we've created a sample comp in this Lesson's project for each of these presets: They are inside the **Comps_finished > Adobe Animation Presets** folder. Open each one and RAM Preview, then select the layer and press **U U** to delve into understanding how they were done. Edit them to taste and save your variations as your own animation presets! (See page 150 for details on saving text animators as presets.)

Additional 3D text animation presets can be found on Adobe Exchange: *http://tinyurl.com/ShapeTextPresets*

1 To start, we've created a title to suit our penguin footage in the background. Your mission will be to make the title's movement even cuter than the penguins. Footage courtesy Artbeats/Penguins.

▽ tip

What's My Line?

You can set strokes to use Miter, Round, or Bevel styles. This is set via the Line Join submenu of the Character panel.

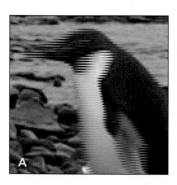 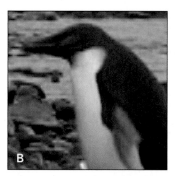

2 Initially, you will see a "comb teeth" pattern in penguins that are moving – this is known as interlacing (A). When you see this, it is best to separate the fields in the Interpret Footage dialog (below), which will remove the artifacts and process it properly (B).

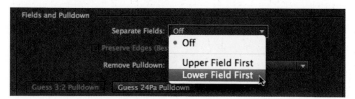

Wiggling Text

Most of your text animations so far have included simple, two-keyframe, "from here to there" movements. For those times when you want to get a little wacky, such as having text jiggle and dance, just add the Wiggly Selector:

1 Close all comps and open comp **08-Wiggly*starter**, where we've created some basic text using the font Adobe Poplar (installed free with After Effects; again, feel free to pick your own). We made the text a pale blue, with a 1-pixel Stroke, and added the Drop Shadow effect.

Separating Fields

Before you start wiggling, we need to deal with another issue specific to video. If you are viewing this composition at 100% magnification, you may notice that some of the penguins have a "comb teeth" artifact, where alternating pairs of horizontal lines appear to be drawn offset from each other. This is caused by a video phenomenon known as *interlacing*.

Although it is becoming less common, a good deal of video is shot where one set of horizontal lines is captured at one point in time, and every other line is captured at a slightly later time. Video uses this trick to capture and play back smoother motion, as well as to get around a problem with the imperfections in the phosphors that lit up early CRT-style TV sets.

These two different points in time are called *fields*. Two fields are combined (interlaced) together to make a frame. It is best if we work on one field at a time in After Effects, to make sure we don't accidentally scramble together pixels that originally came from two different points in time. Therefore, when you see interlacing in your composition, you should separate the fields of the source in question.

2 Right-click on the **Penguins.mov** source in this comp, and select the menu item Reveal Layer Source in Project. The Sources folder in the Project panel will twirl down to reveal this footage file.

At the bottom-left of the Project panel, click on the first button to open the Interpret Footage dialog. In the Fields and Pulldown section, set the Separate Fields popup to Lower Field First, and click OK. The comb teeth will now disappear from the penguin footage in your comp.

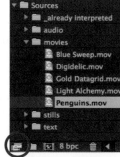

The Wiggly Selector

To wiggle text, you need to add at least one parameter to wiggle. Let's wiggle color, then add transform properties:

3 Twirl down the text layer, and select Animate > Fill Color > Hue. Scrub the Fill Hue value to 300°, and the blue text will now appear green.

4 Click Animator 1's Add button, and choose Selector > Wiggly. RAM Preview: Each character now has a random color that varies over time automatically!

5 Select Add > Property > Position. Scrub the Y Position value to around 50 or so. RAM Preview; the characters wiggle a *maximum* of 50 pixels up *or* down.

6 Select Add > Property > Rotation, and set Rotation to around 15°. As with Position, the Wiggly Selector treats this value as a maximum offset; notice that characters rotate clockwise and counterclockwise (ranging from +15° to –15°).

7 Twirl down the Wiggly Selector and experiment:

• To make the title easier to read as it animates, increase the Correlation value to around 80%. Now adjacent characters behave more alike.

• Try setting Wiggly's Based On popup to Words; now "Penguin" and "Playhouse" will jiggle as words instead of individual characters. Adjust Correlation to 0% to have them be as different as possible, or set to taste.

• To randomize the color and location of the characters without having them animate, set Wiggles/Second to 0.

• To fade out the entire wiggle effect, animate both the Max Amount and Min Amount from their default value down to 0%. Or, fade up or down a single property (say, Position or Rotation) by setting keyframes for that property only.

   Our version can be found in **Comps_Finished > 06-Wiggly_final**. We added a couple of touches, such as animating the Amount parameters in the Wiggly Selector. We also faded out the Position and Rotation offsets, leaving just the color variation at the end.

4 Adding a Selector > Wiggly causes the property we are animating – Fill Hue – to automatically randomize per character over time.

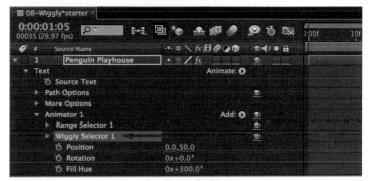

6 By default, the Wiggly Selector randomizes each character by a maximum of the animation properties you set, in either direction (positive or negative).

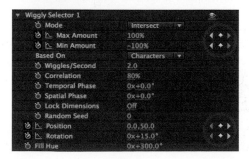

7 In our final version, we animated the Wiggly Selector's amount and faded down the Position and Rotation leaving just Fill Hue.

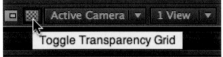

3 Turn off the background layer, and use Toggle Transparency Grid to verify that there are no other layers present (such as a black solid) that are not supposed to render.

5 In the Render Queue, select the Lossless template from the Output Module popup, then click on the underlined "Lossless" to open the Output Module Settings.

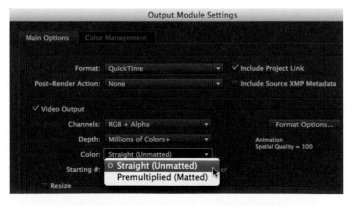

Rendering with an Alpha Channel

Say that after you've finished your penguin title animation in the previous exercise, the editor says he might still change the video behind it – so can he have the title by itself? To do that, you need to render it with an alpha channel.

1 Open or select the **08_Wiggly** comp you created in the previous exercise. If you didn't finish it, open ours: **Comps_Finished > 08-Wiggle_final**.

2 Turn *off* the Video switch (the eyeball icon) for the background layer, **Penguins.mov** – the editor is planning on replacing that.

3 To confirm that you have nothing else behind your type, click the Toggle Transparency Grid button along the bottom of the Comp panel. You should see a checkerboard pattern everywhere the type isn't.

4 Select Composition > Add to Render Queue. The Render Queue panel will open, with an entry for your composition. Inside this entry are two lines: Render Settings and Output Module. To the far right of the Output Module header is a line of text that says Output To, followed by a file name (it may say *Not yet specified* initially). Click that name, and a file dialog will open. Name your movie, and choose a place to save it. Include the word "alpha" in the name to remind you that this movie will have an alpha channel in it.

5 To the immediate right of the Output Module header, it should say Lossless; this is the default template, and it uses the QuickTime Animation codec which is well suited for our needs. If it doesn't, click on the arrow and select Lossless from the popup menu that appears (or select the Lossless with Alpha template).

Click on the underlined "Lossless" text to the right of this arrow to open the Output Module Settings dialog and change these settings:

• In the Video Output section, set the Channels popup to RGB+Alpha. The Depth popup should change to Millions of Colors+ (the "+" stands for alpha).

• Click on the Color popup and change it to Straight (Unmatted): This is the preferred format for most editing systems in order to obtain the highest quality. (The Lossless with Alpha template outputs a Premultiplied alpha.)

• Set the Post-Render Action popup to Import. This will bring the finished movie back into After Effects.

Click OK to close the Output Module Settings dialog. You can also save this as a template (see the *Appendix*, page 355).

5 *continued* In the Output Module, set Channels to RGB+Alpha, Depth to Millions of Colors+, and Color to Straight (Unmatted).

6 Click the Render button. When After Effects is done, the file will appear in the Project panel.

Select your rendered movie and choose Edit > Edit Original to open it in QuickTime Player. See that coarse black fringe around your type? That's the result of a Straight Alpha render, where After Effects "oversprays" the color pixels beyond the edges of an alpha, just as you would do when painting through a stencil. You actually *want* to see this; it verifies that you rendered a Straight Alpha. If your editors panic when they see it, tell them it will look fine when it's composited in their editing system, after the alpha channel does its job.

To see what your render really looks like, close the QuickTime Player, return to After Effects and double-click the movie to display it in its Footage panel. This After Effects viewer factors in the alpha channel. Turn on the Transparency Grid, and you will see clean edges around your type, including any drop shadow effects. Likewise, it will look great if you add this movie to an After Effects composition. Save your project when done.

6 If you view your straight-alpha render in a QuickTime viewer, you will see just the RGB color channels, which includes pixels that extend beyond the alpha (above). View it in the After Effects Footage panel which factors in the alpha channel, and you will see that it is actually clean (below).

▼ Rendering with Fields

When you started working on the **08_Wiggly** comp, we had you separate the fields in the **Penguins.mov** source footage. If your sources have fields, and you are rendering content to be played back on a normal television or monitor (not a computer), you will want to reintroduce fields on output. This will give you the smoothest possible motion, retain all of the resolution in your sources, and match the feel of the motion between your sources and any elements you added in After Effects.

After you've added a comp to the Render Queue, you should see the words Best Settings (the default template) next to Render Settings – if you don't, select Best Settings from the popup menu to its right. Then click on the words Best Settings to open the Render Settings dialog.

In the Time Sampling section, set the Field Render popup. This will cause After Effects to render each frame twice using slightly different times, creating two fields. It will then *interlace* these fields together to create the final frame. Which field order

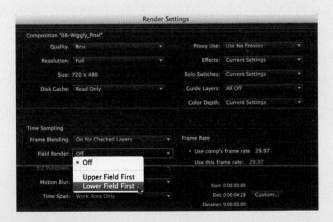

you choose in this popup depends on the format you are rendering to: Use Lower Field First for NTSC or PAL DV; NTSC D1 could be either Lower or Upper Field First depending on hardware. Use Upper Field First for HD or PAL D1. Note that if you pick the DV Settings template instead of Lossless, After Effects will set Field Render to Lower Field First for you.

Animating to Sound

One of the best things you can do to improve the look of your motion graphics is coordinate them with audio, such as dialog and music. To do this, you need to "spot" where the important "hit points" are in your soundtrack and place layer markers at these times. These serve as signposts for placing keyframes and edit points.

Adding Audio to a Comp

1 Open the finished version of **08-Wiggly** from the previous pages (you can use your version or our comp **08-Wiggly_final**) and press the (Home) key to return to 00:00.

2 In the Project panel, twirl down **Sources > audio** and select the file **Playhouse.wav**. Its sample rate and bit depth will appear at the top of the Project panel. Add this file to your comp just as you would any other footage layer: by dragging it to the Composition or Timeline panels or by pressing ⌘+*/* (*Ctrl*+*/*).

3 RAM Preview your composition; the audio will play back with the video. (If you can't hear any sound, aside from the obvious checking of cables, open Preferences > Audio Hardware and > Audio Output Mapping to make sure After Effects is sending audio to the connections you expect.) To preview audio by itself, press the decimal point key [.] on the numeric keypad; MacBook users can press ⌘+. (period). Just tapping the spacebar to preview will *not* play audio.

4 In the Timeline panel, you will notice that **Playhouse.wav** has a speaker icon under the A/V Features column. You can toggle this on and off to mute or unmute an audio layer. Layers that have both audio and video will have both speaker and eyeball icons, which can be toggled independently. Audio must be turned on to see the audio waveform, which we'll play with next.

2 Footage items that contain audio are identified with a generic waveform graphic at the top of the Project panel; their sample rate and bit depth are also displayed.

▼ Audio Basics

Audio is often embedded alongside video in the same file. However, you can also import audio-only files just as you would a video-only movie. There are many valid formats for audio, such as AIFF, WAV, and MP3 files; you can also create a QuickTime or AVI file that contains just audio.

Like pictures and video, audio's resolution is defined by its bit depth, with higher being better. The most common format is 16 bits (the same as CDs); 24 bits is a high-end format. Audio is also defined by its sample rate, which is akin to frame rate. Again, higher is better. Consumer DV has an audio rate of 32 kHz (thousands of samples per second); audio CDs have a rate of 44.1 kHz; professional video uses 48 kHz.

4 Layers with audio display a speaker icon in the A/V Features column of the Timeline panel (above). Click the speaker icon to mute the track. Audio for all layers may be muted in the Preview panel (right).

Spotting an Audio Waveform

The audio *waveform* illustrates how loud the audio is at any given instant. The taller the waveform, the louder the sound is at that particular time. Spikes in the waveform indicate percussive events such as drum hits or "plosive" consonants such as "P." Those spikes are often great spots to place keyframes or to trim a layer to.

5 Twirl down Audio > Waveform for **Playhouse.wav**. The shortcut is to select the layer and press **L L** (two **L**s in quick succession). Feel free to change the height of the waveform (see figure).

6 Press the decimal key on the numeric keypad to preview the audio, studying how the moving time indicator relates to spikes in the waveform. Tap your fingers along with the beats in the music to get a feel for its rhythm.

Using Markers

One of the more useful features in After Effects is the ability to place markers on each layer or in the overall composition. You can use these to note special events in the layer or comp, making it easy to synchronize keyframes and other layers to these times.

7 Select **Playhouse.wav** to make sure it is the layer that receives your markers. There are two ways to add a marker:

- Start a preview and tap the ✳ key on the numeric keypad at the instant you want a marker to be placed.

- Move the current time indicator to a spike you think you might want to animate to later, and press the ✳ key on the numeric keypad (MacBook users can press ⌘+**8**).

To name a layer marker as you create it or to give it a duration, press ⌥+✳ (*Alt*+✳) to open the Marker dialog. You can also double-click an existing marker. To delete a marker, ⌘+click (*Ctrl*+click) it. Right-click on a marker for additional options.

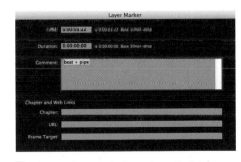

5 Press **L L** to reveal a layer's audio waveform. To make the waveform taller, position the cursor under the waveform until it changes to a two-headed arrow. Click and drag up or down to change the height of the waveform display.

7 Use markers to indicate important moments of time in a layer (below). Double-click a marker to add a text comment and optionally give it a duration (above). The same dialog can be used for chapter markers, web links, and Flash cue points.

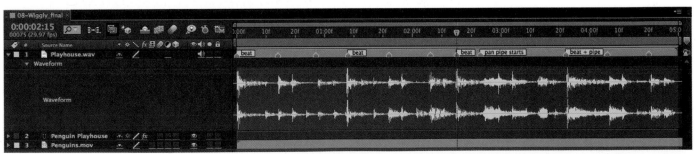

▽ tip

Comp Markers

Layer markers are attached to their layer:
As you slide the layer in time, its markers
will move with it. When you need to mark a
time in the composition that doesn't move
with the layers, add a comp marker. Move the
current time indicator to the desired place,
hold **Shift**, and press **0**–**9** from along
the top of the keyboard (not the numeric
keypad). A numbered pointer will appear.
To jump to that marker, just type its number.
You can also drag out comp markers from
the "bin" at the right side of the Timeline
panel. Comp markers become layer markers
when you nest the comp into another comp.

9 We use markers to note important
times in both audio and video layers,
as well as to leave ourselves notes
about what we did and why.

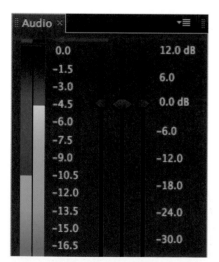

2 Keep the Audio panel visible to make
sure you're not distorting (indicated by
the red segment on top of the "meters")
as well as to quickly adjust the Levels
parameter for a selected layer.

8 After spotting and marking the musical events in **Playhouse.wav**, twirl up
the waveform display. This saves space and speeds up redraws.

9 Practice moving the keyframes for the **Penguin Playhouse** text layer to
line up your markers; RAM Preview and note how the music and visuals work
together. You can also mark and slide the **Penguins.mov** video layer so the
antics of the penguins better synchronize with what's happening in the soundtrack. Our version is in **Comps_Finished > 08-Wiggly_final2**.

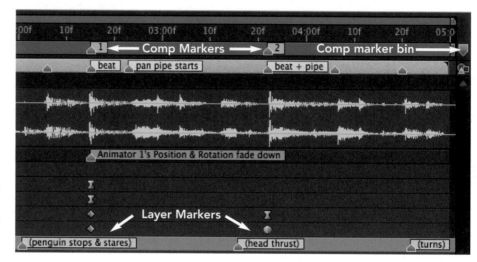

Mixing Audio

After Effects provides two ways to change the loudness of a layer with audio:
the Levels parameter and the Stereo Mixer effect. Levels animates too abruptly,
so we use it just to balance the relative loudness of the audio tracks, then
keyframe Stereo Mixer to perform fade ins and outs.

1 Open **Comps > 11_Audio Mixing*starter**. It contains a music soundtrack,
plus a voiceover from the Apollo 15 moon mission. We've already spotted the
waveforms for both of the layers, trimmed the voiceover to include just a few
select phrases, and slid it in time so the voice starts when the drums come in.
RAM Preview; the music drowns out some of the words.

2 Select **Musical Messages.wav** and press **L** to reveals its Levels parameter
in the Timeline panel. Then open Window > Audio to reveal a set of level meters
and controls: The meters reflect the combined loudness of all audio layers in the
comp; the Levels controller in this panel applies only to the selected layer.

Preview the comp's audio and decrease Levels for the music layer **Musical
Messages.wav** to make it easier to hear the words over the music. (You can also
increase Levels slightly for **Lunar Rover audio.wav** to +3 dB, but mind those

red "peak" indicators in the Audio panel!) That helps, but what you really want is the music to be loud when there is no voice, and to be quieter when the astronaut is talking. So set the **Musical Messages.wav** layer back to 0 dB and let us show you a better way.

3 Start dragging the current time indicator toward the marker labeled "hit" for **Musical Messages.wav**. Add the ⬚Shift⬚ key as you get close; the indicator will snap to that marker. Select **Musical Messages.wav** and apply Effect > Audio > Stereo Mixer. In the Effect Controls panel, enable keyframing for Left Level and Right Level, then press ⬚U⬚ to reveal your keyframes in the timeline.

4 Locate to the "rhythm starts" marker and set both Left and Right Level to 50%. RAM Preview the entire comp; the audio will "duck" down out of the way when the voiceover starts.

▽ gotcha

Avoiding Distortion

Levels work akin to Scale, in that lower values reduce the volume and higher levels increase it. As with Scale, going over "100%" (0 dB in audio-speak) is generally a bad idea – especially if the red bars along the top of the Audio panel light up during previews, indicating the audio is being distorted.

5 Move the current time indicator to 11:09, where the voiceover ends for **Lunar Rover audio.wav**. Add a keyframe for both the Left and Right Level parameters (the values will be 50%, based on the previous keyframes).

6 Locate to the "last bar" marker and set both Left and Right Level back to 100%. Preview the entire comp; now each audio layer is loud when it should be, not fighting the other. Tweak their Levels to balance their relative loudness while maximizing the comp's volume without distorting.

7 You can improve the tone quality of the scratchy Apollo 15 voiceover by applying frequency "equalization" to it. The simplest way to accomplish this is to select **Lunar Rover audio.wav** and apply Effect > Audio > Bass & Treble.

• Increase the Bass parameter to fill in the low frequencies; this is a common technique to add gravitas to a voiceover. Conversely, reducing Bass makes audio sound cheaper or farther away; it can also reduce hum and rumble in a poorly recorded audio track.

• Decrease Treble to reduce the scratchy, crackly, hissy nature of the voiceover. Conversely, increasing Treble can improve the intelligibility of muffled audio.

 Comps_Finished > 11_Audio Mixing_final contains our version, with video edited in time with the music. We also keyframed the Apollo soundtrack so the background noise fades in and out rather than cuts abruptly.

3–6 Keyframe the Stereo Mixer effect for the music layer to "duck" its loudness while the astronaut is talking. (You can use the expression pick whip – introduced in Lesson 7 – to make the Right Level to follow the Left Level, cutting down on keyframing.)

 Advanced Audio

After Effects has only the most rudimentary of audio manipulation tools. For more advanced audio processing, we suggest using a standalone audio application such as Adobe Audition. This lesson's **05-Video Bonus** folder contains a pair of movies we created using After Effects and Audition together.

3 Selecting Browse Presets from the Effects & Presets Options menu (above) opens Adobe Bridge (below), which makes it easy to preview the Adobe-supplied presets. Double-click one to apply it to a selected layer in After Effects. If you don't need to see an animated preview, you can apply presets directly from the Effects & Presets panel.

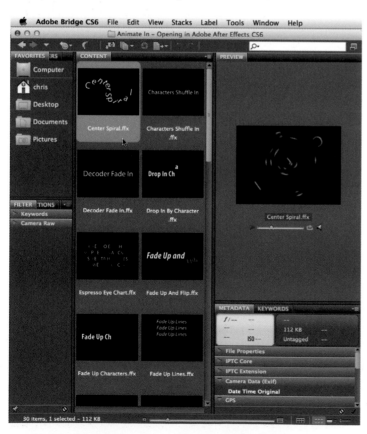

Text Animation Presets

In Lesson 3, we introduced animation presets, which are a great way to save favorite arrangements of effects as well as keyframed animations. In addition to providing a way to save your own creations, Adobe ships After Effects with literally hundreds of prebuilt animation presets that you can explore and use. One of the richest areas to mine is that of Text Presets.

Applying a Text Preset

1 Open **Comps > 09-Apply Preset**. It contains a text layer and an audio layer. With the current time set to 00:00, select the text layer **Jazz It Up!**.

2 Click on the Options arrow in the upper right corner of the Effects & Presets panel, and select Browse Presets. (If this panel isn't open, select it from the Window menu.) Selecting Browse Presets will open Adobe Bridge (introduced in *Pre-Roll*, page 12) and navigate to the Presets folder for you.

3 Double-click the folder **Text**. Inside it will be several subfolders that represent categories of presets such as Animate In, Blurs, and Rotation. Double-click the **Animate In** folder to open it. You will see a number of thumbnails, representing each preset. Select one by single-clicking it; an animation of it will start playing in the Preview panel. Go ahead and preview a few. If you like, click on the Go Back button (top left corner), and explore some of the other text preset categories.

4 Once you've found a preset you like, double-click it. Bridge will return you to After Effects and apply that preset to your text. (If your text layer was not selected when you applied a preset, you will get a new layer named Adobe After Effects instead. If you see this, Undo, select **Jazz It Up!**, return to Bridge, and try again.) Press **U** to reveal the keyframed properties this preset is using to create its animation.

RAM Preview the comp to see how the animation looks full-size with your text. If you're less than thrilled, no problem; Undo to remove the preset, press **Home** to jump back to 00:00, return to Bridge, and select another preset. After you've had some fun, undo and apply the preset **Curves and Spins > Counter Rotate.ffx**, as we'll be using it in the next section.

Editing a Preset

Applying an animation preset is not the end of the road; you can freely edit the layer afterward. Let's make a couple of customizations to the **Counter Rotate** preset we applied in step 4.

5 While watching the Comp viewer, drag the current time indicator until you observe several characters overlapping.

Twirl down the parameters for **Jazz It Up!** until you open the Text > More Options section. Inside there is a popup for Inter-Character Blending. This uses blending modes to affect how overlapping characters interact. Try a few, and pick one you like; we thought both Multiply and Add were interesting.

6 Now, tie the text's animation more closely to the music. Select layer 2, **CoolGroove.wav**, and type **L L** to reveal its waveform. RAM Preview this comp, noting how the spikes in the waveform relate to the drum hits, and when the saxophone wail starts and stops. You can add layer markers to remind yourself where these events are.

7 Select **Jazz It Up!** again, and press **U** until you see just its keyframes. Slide them in time to line up with some event in the music. Since these keyframes have had Easy Ease applied to them, they will not seem to "hit" your beats as tightly as they slide out of and back into position again. Feel free to tweak their timing to compensate for this, or to change them to Linear keyframes by ⌘+clicking (*Ctrl*+clicking) on them. Save your project when you're done. Our final version can be found in **Comps_Finished > 09-Apply Preset_final**.

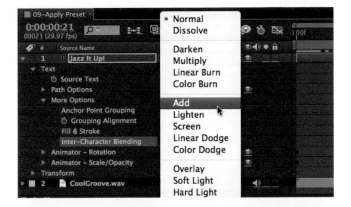

5 Play with More Options > Inter-Character Blending (top) to create some different looks when characters overlap. Here, we show their normal interaction (A), using Multiply (B), and using Add (C).

7 In our version (below), we keyframed the animation to follow the rise and fall of the saxophone's wail.

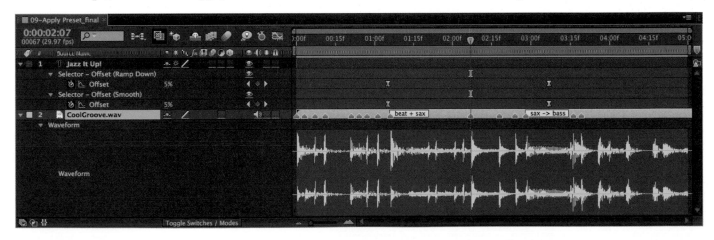

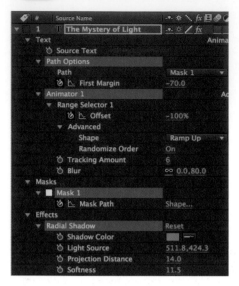

2 Carefully select just the parameters and parameter groups that you want to remember in your animation preset. Any keyframes are included automatically for selected items. Note that we did *not* select Source Text.

▽ gotcha

Unaltered Effects

If you apply an effect to a layer, but don't change any of its parameters, After Effects might not reveal this effect when you select a layer and type **U U**. Press **Shift E** to also reveal Effects in the timeline.

Saving Text Animations

As we've mentioned, you can save your own animation presets, including presets you've modified. However, text layers can require a bit of additional thought. If you save everything about a text layer, you will save its Source Text as well – which means that every time you applied it, it would replace any text in the target layer with your old text! So let's get some practice being selective in how we save properties in a preset:

1 Open **Comps > 10-Save Preset**. It contains the Mystery of Light animation you built earlier in this lesson.

2 A great way to remind yourself of what you've done to a layer is select it and type **U U** (two **U**s in quick succession) to reveal all of its parameters that have been changed from their defaults. Do this to **The Mystery of Light**. You will see you've made changes to Source Text, parameters inside Path Options and Animator 1, and applied a mask as well as an effect.

• In this case, you don't want to save your Source Text, so don't click on that.

• Click on Path Options to remember its settings for Path and First Margin.

• **⌘**+click (**Ctrl**+click) on Animator 1; this will by default remember all of the settings indented inside of it, such as Range Selector 1 and the properties you added to the animator.

• **⌘**+click (**Ctrl**+click) Mask 1 (which includes Mask Path) to remember the path the text is supposed to follow.

• Finally, **⌘**+click (**Ctrl**+click) on Radial Shadow to select the entire effect.

3 Select Animation > Save Animation Preset to save your preset. Remember, it is preferred to place it somewhere inside the **Presets** folder, which exists alongside the After Effects application on your computer's drive. You can make your own subfolders inside here if you wish. (Saving and applying animation presets was covered in more detail in Lesson 3.)

▼ **Source Text**

The Source Text parameter bundles together a bunch of information into one keyframe: your actual text, plus the settings in the Character and Paragraph panels for that text. If you wish, you can keyframe Source Text to change over time, although only Hold keyframes (covered in Lesson 2) are allowed.

   Because you can't save the actual text separately from its style, think carefully whether you want to include Source Text when saving an animation preset. If the essence of the preset is the animation, regardless of the actual text, then don't select Source Text when saving the preset.

   On the other hand, if the styling of the text – its size, its color, and the like – are important, then you will need to include it. Just be prepared to replace the underlying text after you apply the preset to your new text layer.

▼ Editing Photoshop Text Layers

Although we have focused on creating and animating text inside After Effects, you may end up working with a Photoshop file with text already in it. That's okay; you can import the layered Photoshop file as a composition, then convert the Photoshop text to After Effects editable text.

For this final exercise, you'll need the Myriad Pro Condensed and Bold Condensed fonts that are installed free with After Effects. (If you don't have these fonts currently installed, open this lesson's **RightWrongPoll.psd** file in Photoshop and replace the fonts to taste.)

1 In the Project panel, select the **PSD Text_starter** folder so that the PSD file will be imported into this folder.

2 Use File > Import and select **RightWrongPoll.psd** from the **05_Sources > text** folder on your drive. Click Open.

In the options dialog that appears, set the Import Kind popup to Composition – Retain Layer Sizes (so that layers are only as big as the content). Click OK, and the folder will now contain a composition and a folder of the individual layers.

2 Import the layered Photoshop file as a composition, using the Retain Layer Sizes option to automatically trim the layers.

3 Open the **RightWrongPoll** comp that appears inside the **PSD Text_starter** folder. Say that the network graphics department has set up this template with the name of the poll and created dummy text for the date and percentages. It's your job to edit the text and animate the text and bars. Problem is, you can't edit the Photoshop-created text the way it is. Time for a little magic:

3 Select any Photoshop Text layer inside After Effects, and under the Layer menu select Convert to Editable Text (above). The result will be an After Effects text layer, noted by the "T" icon next to it (below).

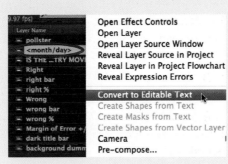

To change the date, select **<month/day>** (layer 2), and choose the menu item Layer > Convert to Editable Text. The layer will now appear with a "T" icon to indicate it's an After Effects text layer. Double-click and type today's date; press **Enter** when done.

To force edited text layers to have the same name as the new text you've typed, select the layer in the Timeline panel, press **Return**, **Delete**, **Return**.

From here on, think of this as an Idea Corner for you to explore your own design impulses. Convert any other layers you wish to edit or apply an animation preset to. For instance, convert the poll's title (layer 3) to editable text, then try out some of the text presets you played with earlier in this lesson.

4 The graphic designer created the **dark title bar**, **right bar**, and **wrong bar** in Photoshop using its Shape layers feature. When they were imported into After Effects, they were automatically converted into solid layers with masks. Select **right bar** and **wrong bar**, and type **M** to reveal their masks. Animate their mask paths to make the bars grow out to their final values. You could also use Effect > Transition > Linear Wipe to achieve the same result, as we did in our version **PSD Text_finished > RightWrong-Poll_finished**. (Feel free to explore our final composition for some other ideas you can apply or modify for your own comp.)

4 In our final version, we converted some text layers and changed the content to suit our needs, then animated some layers to build on the graphic. Background images courtesy 12 Inch Design/ProductionBlox Units 3 and 8.

Parenting and Nesting

Grouping layers to make them easier to coordinate.

▽ In This Lesson

152 parenting, nesting, and expressions defined
154 assigning a parent
155 parenting, opacity, and effects
156 parenting with null objects
158 nesting to group layers; using guides
160 editing precomps
162 navigating composition hierarchies
163 nesting a common source
165 sizing precomps
167 ETLAT (edit this, look at that)
168 precomposing a group of layers
170 precomposing a single layer
172 render order explained
173 splitting work between comps
174 precompose options compared
174 using precomposing to reorder
176 continuous rasterization
178 collapsing transformations
179 compound effects

▽ Getting Started

Copy the **Lesson 06-Parent and Nest** folder from this book's disc onto your hard drive, and make note of where it is; it contains the project files and sources you need for this lesson.

Rather than use a single project file, for this lesson we have provided several different project files to make it easier to keep track of all the compositions you will be creating and using.

No layer or composition is an island – at least, not in complex animations. In this lesson, you will learn how to group layers and build composition hierarchies, making it easier to create and manage complex animations. First up will be parenting, where one layer's animation can influence that of others. After that we'll work with nesting and precomposing compositions: ways to bundle together layers, keyframes, and effects into one comp and treat the result as a single layer in another comp.

Approaches to Grouping

There are three general approaches to grouping inside After Effects: *parenting* layers together, *nesting* and *precomposing* compositions, and applying *expressions* to individual parameters. Here is an overview of their relative strengths, weaknesses, and uses:

Parenting: With this technique, you "parent" (attach) as many *child* layers as you want to a *parent* layer. The children remember their relationships to the parent at the time you attach them. Any changes in the parent's position, scale, or rotation results in the children being dragged along for the ride. The children may have their own animation as well, but these are not passed back to the parent. To better visualize this, image a person walking several dogs. The dogs may be running around their minder, but as their minder walks down the street, all of the dogs move down the street as well.

The advantage of parenting is that all of the layers involved are in the same composition, which makes them easy to keep track of. A disadvantage is that changes in opacity are not passed along from parent to child, so you can't use parenting to fade out a group of layers together. Effects are also not passed from parent to child.

Nesting: The process of adding a composition to another composition is referred to as *nesting* comps. The nested comp (often referred to as a *precomp*) appears as just another layer in the second comp. You can animate, fade, and apply effects to the nested comp layer as if it were a normal movie file. The primary difference is that it is "live": You can still go back to the first (nested) comp and change it, and those changes will appear immediately in the second (master, or main) comp without the need to first render the precomp.

Another use for nesting is that a single source comp can be nested into more than one master composition. The same source comp may also be nested several times into the same master comp. By doing this, you can easily change the original nested comp, and the change will ripple through to any comp it is nested into. This is ideal for creating (and updating) repetitive elements such as animated logos that may be used multiple times throughout a project; some animators may refer to this process as creating an "instance."

Precomposing: When building a chain of nested compositions, ideally you're thinking ahead: You use several layers to build an element in one comp, then use the result nested into a second comp. However, the creative process is rarely that orderly and logical. You might build a complex composition, only to later think, "You know, life would be easier if I could just group these layers into their own nested comp…"

Well, you can: The process is known as *precomposing*. You can select one or more layers in the current comp and "send them back" into their own comp – called a "precomp"– that automatically becomes a nested layer in the current comp. It's almost as if you planned it that way ahead of time (you're so smart…). Once you do this, as far as After Effects is concerned, there is no difference between the resulting precomp and a normal nested comp.

Expressions: After Effects also allows you to connect virtually any parameter to another parameter. This involves creating small pieces of JavaScript code referred to as *expressions*. We cover expressions in the next lesson, but in short, basic expressions could be considered a highly targeted form of parenting, where only individual parameters are connected rather than all transform properties at once. The big advantage is that you can connect any parameter you can keyframe – not just position, scale, and rotation.

In this lesson, you will learn several ways to group together layers to make complex animations easier and to reuse elements multiple times in the same composition.

▽ tip

Effects and Children

Effects applied to a parent are not passed along to its children. To apply the same effect to a group created by parenting, use an adjustment layer (Lesson 3), or precompose the parent and its children into a precomp and apply the effect to the resulting layer.

▽ factoid

Family Trees

You can create parenting chains where one layer is parented to a second, the second layer is parented to a third, and so on. This makes parenting an essential tool in character animation: For example, you can attach a hand to a forearm, a forearm to an upper arm, and the upper arm to a body.

Use Parenting to make the text and planet scale up as a group, with the text rotating around the planet. Background courtesy Artbeats/Line Elements.

▼ Choosing a Responsible Parent

When grouping together layers using parenting, it is important to think about who should be the parent and who should be the child.

A parent's animation gets passed along to its children. Therefore, the layer that is going to be doing the least animating often (but not always) makes the best parent. That way, the children are free to run around the parent without their animation being passed onto the parent.

If you can't find a suitable parent, use a null object (see page 156).

Parenting

In this first parenting exercise, you will be grouping together two layers to make it easier to animate them as a unit. In it, the "child" will keep its animation, which will also be affected by its parent.

1 For these first two exercises, open project **Lesson 06 > 06a-Parenting.aep**. In the Project panel, twirl open the **Comps** folder, then double-click the comp **Parenting1*starter** to open it.

Press **O** on the numeric keypad to RAM Preview this comp. It consists of a movie of a globe rotating, and a Photoshop still image of text on a circular path.

For this animation, let's make the text and planet scale up as a group, with the text rotating around the planet. We'll then try to fade them out as a unit.

2 Select the first two layers, then press **S** to reveal their Scale followed by **Shift R** to reveal Rotation and **Shift T** to reveal Opacity. If you scrub these values for each layer, they will act independently of the other layer. Undo to get back to their original state.

3 To set up a parenting group, you need to reveal the Parent column in the Timeline panel. If it is not already visible, you can either right-click on any column header in the Timeline panel and choose Column > Parent, or use the keyboard shortcut **Shift F4**. We tend to drag the Parent column to reside alongside the layer names, making it easier to read who is connected to whom.

The next step is deciding who the child should be, and "parenting" it to the layer you want it to follow. In our case, we know we want to rotate the text independent of the planet. Therefore, it would be best if the text was the child, so that its rotation will not get passed onto the planet.

4 There are two ways to assign a parent:

• Click on the Parent popup for the prospective child **Text on a circle.psd** and pick its new parent – **planet.mov** – from the list that appears.

• Alternatively, click on the spiral icon (the pick whip tool) in the Parent column for the child and drag it to the name of the layer you wish to be the parent.

4 There are two ways to attach a child to a parent: Use its Parent popup (left), or its pick whip tool to point to its parent (right).

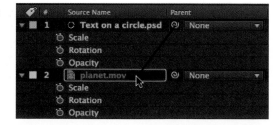

5 Scrub the Scale for **Text on a circle.psd**; only that layer scales. Return it to 100%, then scrub Scale for **planet.mov**: When you scale the parent, both layers scale as a group. Note that the Scale value for **Text on a circle.psd** does not change; its Scale value is now shown relative to its parent.

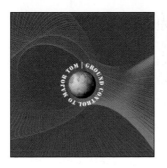

• Press **Home** to make sure the current time indicator is at 00:00, then click on the stopwatch for **planet.mov**'s Scale to enable keyframing. Enter a value of 0%; both layers will disappear.

5 As the parent (the planet) scales up, the child (the text) scales up as well, by the same proportional amount.

• Move the time indicator to 02:00 and set Scale back to 100%, returning both parent and child to full size. Press **F9** to make this an Easy Ease keyframe.

6 Now let's rotate the child layer:

• Scrub Rotation for **Text on a circle.psd**; it rotates, but its parent does not.

• Press **Home** again, and enable keyframing for **Text on a circle.psd**'s Rotation. Return its value to 0°.

• Press **End**, and enter 2 for Revolutions (Rotation's first value). The second keyframe should read 2x+0.0°.

RAM Preview: The text rotates as both scale up together, then continues to rotate without affecting the parent.

6 Nothing applied to the child – for example, rotation, or the color fill effect we applied to the text in this figure – are passed along to the parent.

7 Parenting passes scale, position, and rotation from parent to child, but nothing else:

• Move to 10:00, select **planet.mov**, and press **⌥ T** on Mac (**Alt T** on Windows) to reveal Opacity and enable keyframing.

• Press **End**, and set **planet.mov**'s Opacity to 0%: The text will still be visible. You will have to fade out the Text layer separately.

In addition to opacity, effects are also not passed from parent to child. Go ahead and try adding an effect such as a blur to **planet.mov**; the text will not be affected. This can be a blessing or a curse, depending on what you are trying to accomplish.

7 For better or worse, neither effects (left) nor opacity (right) are passed from the parent to the child. The latter means fading just the parent will not fade out both layers as a group.

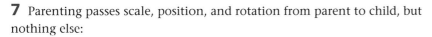

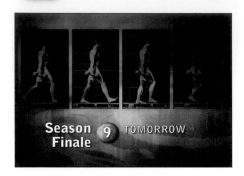

1 Play the finished movie. You will use parenting to animate the title layers and the Planet 9 logo together as a group. (You will build the background animation in the next exercise.)

3 The number 9 and the planet form a logo (left), so use parenting to parent the **Nine** layer to the **planet.mov** layer and make a sub-group (right).

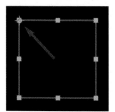

4 Null objects appear in the Comp viewer as an outline of a square, with the Anchor Point in its upper left-hand corner. You can use the Solid Settings dialog to change the size of the null without affecting the children.

Parenting with Nulls

Sometimes it is not clear which layer would make the best parent. The solution is to hire a nanny: a *null object*. Nulls are layers that do not render, but otherwise have normal transform properties such as position, scale, and rotation.

1 Bring the Project panel forward, open the **Finished Movies** folder, and play **Parenting2.mov** to see what you will be building. Close the movie when done.

2 Double-click **Comps > Parenting2*starter** to open it. If the Parent column is not already visible in the Timeline panel, press **Shift F4** to reveal it.

Parenting Chain

3 When you start parenting, first build any sub-groups that make sense to handle as one element. In this case, the number 9 and the planet form a logo.

Click on the Parent popup for **Nine**, and select **planet.mov** to be its parent. Now when you move the planet, the number will stay with it.

4 Let's employ a null object to move the rest of the title layers as a group. Still at time 00:00, select Layer > New > Null Object; it will be added to the timeline.

To rename the null, select it, choose Layer > Solid Settings, enter a name such as "**Title Parent Null**", and click OK. In the Comp viewer, the null will appear as a square outline. The null may be hard to see, so temporarily turn off the Video switch for **Muybridge_textless.mov**; you can also change its Label color in the timeline. Note that a null's anchor point defaults to its upper left corner.

5 Since scaling and rotation happen around the parent's anchor point, it is important to first move the parent into the desired position *before* attaching the children to it. The center of the planet would make a good center for scaling this group, so let's borrow its Position value:

• Select **planet.mov**, type **P** to reveal its Position, click on the word Position to select it, and use Edit > Copy.

• Then select **Title Parent Null** and Edit > Paste. The top left corner of the null will now appear centered over the planet.

5–6 Copy the planet's position value to the null's position (left). Then select and parent the remaining children to the null (right).

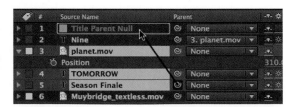

6 Time to parent the other layers. Click **planet.mov** to select it. Then Shift+click on **Season Finale** to select layers 3 through 5. (Don't select layer 2, as it is already parented to layer 3.) Then drag the pick whip tool for any of the selected layers to **Title Parent Null**, and they will all become attached to it.

Animating the Null

Now that we have everything set up, we can animate the group. The plan is to have them move forward to make the "9" logo and "Tomorrow" the heroes.

7 Select **Title Parent Null**. Type P to reveal its Position, then Shift S to also reveal Scale. Move to 02:00, then click on the stopwatches for Position and Scale to enable keyframing for these parameters, as well as set their first keyframes.

8 Press ' (apostrophe) to turn on the Action and Title Safe grids. These help you position the text in a legal area of the screen.

9 Move the time indicator to 02:15. Increase the scale of **Title Parent Null** to 150%; the entire group grows larger and a second Scale keyframe is created.

Then click inside the null's outline and drag it to the left until the planet is positioned just inside the Title Safe lines. The group will move together, and a second Position keyframe will be created. (If only one layer moves, you accidentally grabbed a layer other than the parent null; undo and try again.)

10 To clean up the title, fade out the words to the left: Keyframe the opacity for **Season Finale** from 100% at 02:00 to 0% at 02:15.

Now that the major structural work is done, you can work with the children without worrying about affecting the parent and the overall move. Animate the **planet**, **Tomorrow**, and **Season Finale** child layers to your personal taste. Turn the Video switch for **Muybridge_textless.mov** back on to see the title in context.

Our version is in **Comps_Finished > Parenting2_final**. We scaled up the planet subgroup, slid in **Season Finale**, and applied a Text Animation Preset to **Tomorrow**, all with staggered timing so that each would get their turn at being the center of attention.

▼ Parenting and Scaling

Scaling a layer past 100% normally reduces its quality. However, the Scale values for a parent and its children are combined before After Effects calculates how to draw the pixels for each layer. Therefore, if a child has already been scaled down, you can get away with scaling up its null object parent without any loss of image quality for the child – as long as the combined Scale values amount to 100% or less.

7–9 Keyframe the null object to grow from 100% to 150% (left), and place the planet logo at the edge of the Title Safe area (below) at the second keyframe.

In **Parenting2_final**, we animated each of the children independently, and added a text animation preset to the Tomorrow title. Muybridge images courtesy Dover; background footage courtesy Artbeats.

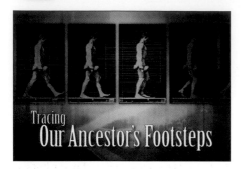

The final composite includes multiple copies of the Muybridge "walking man" animation in a nested composition.

Nesting a Group of Layers

One of the more powerful features in After Effects is the ability to treat a composition as a layer in another comp. This process is referred to as nesting, and is a great way to group layers together.

Creating the Wide Comp

1 Open the project **Lesson 06 > 06-Nesting1.aep**. Look inside the Project panel's **Finished Movie** folder and play **Human Figure in Motion.mov**: This is what you are going to make. You'll start by building a wide comp that holds multiple copies of the Muybridge human figure sequence. This wide comp will be nested into a second comp that includes all the other layers.

2 In the **Sources** folder, single-click the sequence **Muybridge_[00-09].tif** to select it. The top of the Project panel informs you that its size is 270×500, with a rate of 10 frames per second (fps). The sequence consists of only 10 unique images, so it was looped 10 times in its Interpret Footage dialog. Your first task will be creating a large composition to hold copies of this sequence.

Select the **Comps** folder so that your new comp will automatically sort into it, and type ⌘ N (Ctrl N) to create a new composition. Enter the following parameters in the Composition Settings dialog:

- Disable Lock Aspect Ratio. Set Width to 2300 pixels (more than eight times the width of the sequence), and Height to 500 pixels (the sequence's height).

- Set the Pixel Aspect Ratio popup to Square Pixels.

2 Create a large composition to hold several copies of the Muybridge sequence.

- Set the Frame Rate to 10, Start Timecode to 0, and the duration to 10:00.

- Enter a name of "**Figures_group**", and press OK.

Resize your user interface frames to give the Comp panel as much room as you can, and set its Magnification popup to Fit up to 100%.

3 Drag **Muybridge_[00-09].tif** from the Project panel to the left edge of the Comp viewer – it should snap into place.

4 We want eight copies of the Muybridge animation spread across this comp. With **Muybridge_[00-09].tif** still selected, type ⌘ D (Ctrl D) seven times to duplicate it. Verify that you have eight layers in the Timeline panel; delete or duplicate layers as needed to achieve that goal.

5 In the Comp panel, click and drag one of the duplicates to the right. As you get near the right edge of the Comp panel, add ⌘ Shift (Ctrl Shift) so it will snap to the right side of the comp.

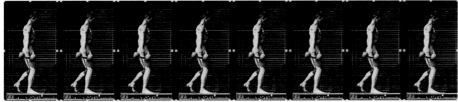

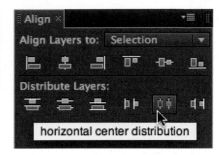

4–6 Create eight copies of the Muybridge layer, with the first and last ones justified to the edges of the comp (top left). With all layers selected, click on the Horizontal Center Distribution button in Align (above), and they will be evenly spaced (left).

6 Type ⌘ A (*Ctrl* A) to select all the layers. Open Window > Align, and click the Horizontal Center Distribution button (bottom row, second from the right). The layers will now be spread out evenly across the composition.

Nesting the Wide Comp

Next, let's create a main comp to nest this group of Muybridge sequences into:

7 In the Project panel, select the **Comps** folder and click the New Comp button. Set the Preset popup to NTSC DV. Change the duration to 06:00, rename it "**Figures Main**", and click OK. (You can hide the Parent panel if it appears.)

8 To nest a comp, you have two choices: You can drag your first comp into your new comp, same as adding any footage item to a comp. Alternatively, in the Project panel you can drag the comp **Figures_group** on top of the icon for the comp **Figures Main** and release the mouse to nest it. After either move, **Figures_group** will appear as a single layer in **Figures Main**.

9 The next step is animating the nested comp to slide from left to right:

• Select the **Figures_group** layer; press S to reveal Scale and *Shift* P to reveal Position. Set the initial Scale value to 50%.

• Type ⌘ R (*Ctrl* R) to reveal the Rulers in the Comp panel, and make sure Window > Info is open for reference. Click along the top ruler and drag down a guide, placing it around Position Y = 50 (the Info panel will display the coordinates). Drag the layer upward until its top snaps to the guide. Then press ⌘ R (*Ctrl* R) to hide the rulers.

• Change the Align panel's Align Layers To popup to Composition, then click the Horizontal Right Alignment button. Enable the stopwatch for Position to create the first keyframe.

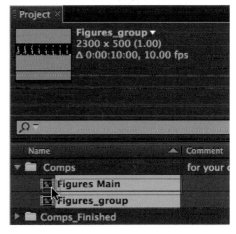

8 To nest one comp into another, you can just drag it onto the target comp in the Project panel. It will then appear as a layer with a comp icon in the target comp.

9 The **Figures_group** comp appears as a single layer when nested, so one set of Position keyframes can be used to move the eight layers as a group.

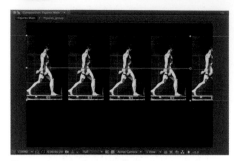

9 *continued* Animate the nested comp to pan across its new comp. (We changed its label color to yellow to make it easier to see its motion path in this figure.)

▽ **tip**

Opening Precomps

Double-clicking a precomp's layer in the main comp opens the precomp. Pressing ⌥ (*Alt*) and double-clicking opens its Layer panel.

11–12 In the precomp, offset the In time of each layer (below) so that they will appear staggered in time (bottom). This edit will automatically show up in the main comp (below right).

• Press *End* to go to the end of the comp (at 05:29). Then with **Figures_group** still selected and the Align panel's popup still set to Composition, click its Horizontal Alignment Left button. The second keyframe will be created automatically.

RAM Preview. The figures should be marching to the right (if not, check you didn't pan the layer in the other direction!). The problem is, they're all marching in lock step, which is kind of boring…

Editing the Precomp

It is common to call a nested comp a precomp, as it renders first, with its result included in the master or main comp. Although the main comp appears to get a "flattened" layer to work with, the precomp is still live: Any changes you make to the precomp will ripple through into the main comp.

10 Double-click on the layer **Figures_group** to open this nested comp, or select the **Figures_group** tab in the Timeline panel.

11 Let's stagger the timing of the Muybridge sequences so that the layers are not all in sync:

• In the Timeline panel, right-click on any column header, and select Columns > In.

• For layer 7, click on the In value, enter –1 in the Layer In Time dialog, and click OK. The In time will change to –0:00:00:01.

• Set the In time for layer 6 to –2. Continue to set each layer one frame earlier in time, ending at –7 for layer 1.

Each copy of the sequence will now look different. After sliding the layers earlier, they run out before the end of the comp. In this instance, that's okay because the main comp is much shorter than this precomp.

12 Bring the **Figures Main** comp forward, and RAM Preview. Your staggered timing for the sequence has been automatically rippled up to this main comp.

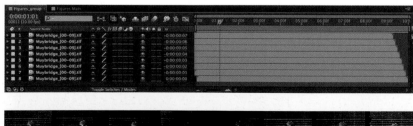

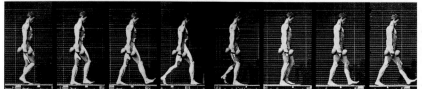

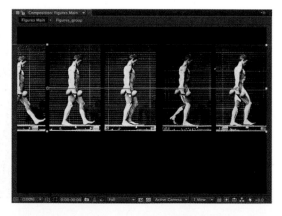

Finishing the Project

Congratulations – you've completed the major steps (save your project…). Here are some ideas for dressing up the final composite; please take artistic liberties and use your own sources to create your own design!

13 Locate **Sources > Digital Web.mov** and **> Code Rage.mov** in the Project panel, and add them as background layers in **Figures Main**. Blend to taste.

14 To better match the background, let's warm up the gray **Figures_group** layer plus give it some dimension:

• Select **Figures_group** and apply Effect > Color Correction > Channel Mixer. Set to taste; we increased Red-Red to 140 and reduced Blue-Blue to 80.

• Add Effect > Perspective > Drop Shadow and set to taste. Effects applied to nested comp layers affect all of the elements in that comp, with the benefit of having only one set of effects to edit.

15 Now let's add a lighting treatment: Select **Sources > Alien Atmospheres.mov**, and this time add it on top of the other layers in **Figures Main**. Press **F4** to toggle to the Modes panel, and set its mode to Vivid Light. This creates a richer look, with a tinge of the new layer's blue color. If you don't like the blue tinge, apply Color Correction > Tint to **Alien Atmospheres.mov**: Its default settings will convert the layer to grayscale. Feel free to try out different modes for each of the layers until you get a blend you like.

16 If you completed Lesson 5, here's a chance to put your new-found skills to work! Add your own title to this composition. Choose whatever font you think works best (we used a condensed font so that it would fit on one line but still be fairly tall), and add Effect > Perspective > Drop Shadow to lift it off the back-ground. Then apply a Text Animation Preset, or create your own design using Text Animators.

Save your project when you're done. If you're curious, our alternate version is saved in **Comps_Finished > Human Main_final**.

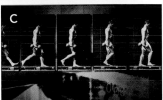

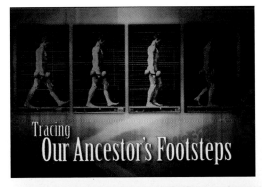

13–15 Add a background to your main comp (A), then tint and add a shadow to the nested precomp (B). Add **Alien Atmospheres** on top using Vivid Light blending mode (C); optionally, convert it to grayscale to remove the blue tint (D).

16 For a final touch, add a text animation to your composition (left). Our version is shown in **Comps_Finished > Human Main_final** (below)

▼ Navigating Composition Hierarchies

As you build more complex hierarchies, your new challenge is to visualize how compositions flow into each other, and how you'll navigate between them. After Effects offers several tools to facilitate this.

Composition Navigator

Along the top of the Composition panel is a series of buttons that represent the currently open composition plus the chain of any compositions linked to it, if any. (If these buttons are not visible, click on the Options menu in the upper right corner for the Comp panel and enable Show Composition Navigator.) Clicking on any of these buttons

△ The Composition Navigator resides at the top of the Composition panel, and gives you quick access to nested compositions. You will use this to navigate between compositions in the next exercise.

will open the corresponding comp. If more than one comp is linked to the current comp, only one is shown in the Navigator; After Effects automatically chooses which to display (usually the nested comp that you've opened most recently).

△ The Mini-Flowchart shows three steps in a hierarchy of compositions.

Mini-Flowchart

The Mini-Flowchart is a floating window that provides more detail than the Composition Navigator – for example, it shows all of the nested comps that flow into a composition, rather than just one. There are several ways to open it, including:

• Click on the Composition Mini-Flowchart button along the top of the Timeline panel.

• Tap the **Shift** key when either the Comp or Timeline panels are forward.

• Click on the arrow to the right of a comp's name in the Composition Navigator.

• Select Composition > Composition Mini-Flowchart

△ The Mini-Flowchart may be opened several ways, including clicking its icon in the Timeline panel.

In all cases, the Mini-Flowchart will open near where your cursor is. It shows three stages of the composition hierarchy; to move up and down longer hierarchies, click on the arrows between comps. Clicking on a comp's name opens that comp.

▼ Full Flowchart

The full flowchart (below) shows all interconnected compositions, plus optionally layers and effects inside these comps. It may be opened from the Options menu for either the Comp or Timeline panels, or by selecting Composition > Composition Flowchart. It has its own Options menu with several choices on how information is displayed. Additionally, there is a Flowchart button at the top of the vertical scroll bar in the Project panel (inset) that shows you all comps in a project. The full flowchart is a good tool to use to help sort out a project you are unfamiliar with. However, unlike other compositing programs that offer a "nodes" flowchart, you cannot actually rearrange a composition from this flowchart view.

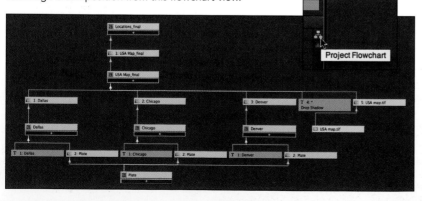

Nesting a Common Source

In this exercise, you will build a more complex hierarchy of compositions. As part of it, you will see how a single change can update several elements in a project at once – a real time-saver!

The Common Element

1 The idea in this exercise is that your client has three new locations opening in the United States, and they want to highlight this in a five-second animation.

Open the project file **Lesson 06 > 06c-Nesting2.aep**. Twirl open the **Finished Movie** folder in its Project panel and play **Locations.mov**. Notice that the colored backplate and the words "New Location" are common to all three cities. When you have a repetitive element like this, plan your composition hierarchies so that this element can be isolated in a separate precomp, then nest it multiple times. Close the movie when done.

2 In the **Comps** folder, double-click the composition named **MyPlate** to open it. It's only 300×100 pixels, and is twice as long as the client requested. In general, it's a good idea to create precomps that are longer than necessary, as it's a hassle to have to go back through multiple precomps and make each one longer at a later date.

The **MyPlate** comp consists of two layers: the text layer **New Location** and the shape layer **Rectangular Shape** (shape layers are covered in Lesson 11). Because you will be nesting the **MyPlate** comp into three **City** comps, you will be able to edit the text or characteristics of the rectangular plate in this one precomp, and the changes will ripple through to all the **City** comps.

Creating the First City Comp

Now let's create the first of the three **City** comps and add the individual city names on top of this common plate:

3 In the Project panel, drag **MyPlate** to the New Comp icon at the bottom of the Project panel. A new comp will open, with **MyPlate** nested into it. Type ⌘ K (*Ctrl* K) to open the Composition Settings, rename this new comp "City1" and click OK. Then in the Timeline, click on the Lock switch for the nested **MyPlate** layer so you don't accidentally move it while creating your text.

Nested comps are helpful when you have repeated elements, such as the "plate" behind the name of each new city. Map courtesy National Atlas of the United States (*www.nationalatlas.gov*).

2 The backing badge in the **MyPlate** comp will be reused in each of the **City** comps.

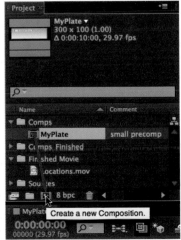

3 Nest **MyPlate** into a new composition with exactly the same vital statistics by dragging it to the New Comp icon (above). Lock this nested layer (left) so you don't accidentally move it.

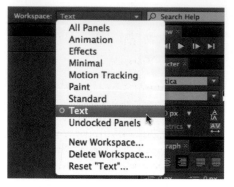

4 Change the Workspace to Text (above), type in the name of a city centered in the backing plate, and then style the text to taste (right).

6–7 Enter your desired city names for the **City2** and **City3** comps. The text will be styled the same as in the original **City1** composition.

9 Create a new comp for the map graphic and nest the three city comps into it, positioning them over their respective states.

4 Click on the Workspace popup near the upper right corner of the application window and select Text to open the relevant tools. The Character and Paragraph panels should appear; if not, select Workspace > Reset "Text" and click OK.

Set the Paragraph panel to the Center Text option. Double-click the Type tool to create a blank text layer centered in the comp. Type the name of the city

you'd like to use. Press **Enter** when done, move the layer down as needed, and spend a few moments using what you learned in Lesson 5 to select a font, size, and color; the other cities will be based on this style.

Duplicating Comps

5 Once you're happy with how your text in the **City1** comp looks, select **City1** in the Project panel and press **⌘ D** (**Ctrl D**) to duplicate it. After Effects will automatically increment the number at the end of its name, labeling it **City2**. Duplicate again to create **City3**.

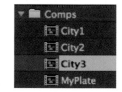

6 Open the **City2** comp. Double-click the text layer to select the text and type the name for your second city. Press **Enter** when done.

7 Open the **City3** comp and edit the text layer to your third city. When you're done, press **V** to return to the Selection tool, and save your project.

If you like, rename the individual city comps so that you can better keep track of who is who. You can do this directly in the Project panel: Select a comp, press **Return** (not **Enter**) to highlight its name, type in the city's name, and press **Return** again.

Creating the USA Map Comp

Now it's time to place your individual city comps around a map:

8 In the Project panel, locate **Sources > USA map.tif** and drag it to the New Comp icon. A comp called **USA Map** is created that is the same size as the still image map (if needed, set the Comp panel's Magnification to Fit up to 100%). It will be created inside the **Sources** folder; drag it up to the **Comps** folder.

With **USA Map** selected, open the Composition Settings: Verify that its duration is 10 seconds and that the frame rate is 29.97 fps. Click OK when done.

9 Drag one of your city comps from the Project panel into the **USA map** Comp panel, and position it over the state where it belongs (yes, this is a geography test). Do the same with the other two cities. Don't worry about animating them right now; let's finish building the comp hierarchy first.

Creating the Main Comp

Now that the cities are placed in position on the map, you can treat the **USA Map** comp as a group. So let's nest it into the final composition and animate it as a group:

10 Select the **Comps** folder, and type ⌘ N (Ctrl N) to make a new comp. In the Composition Settings dialog that opens, select NTSC DV from the Preset popup. Enter a duration of 05:00 (shorter than your precomps), change the default name to "**Locations Main**", and click OK.

11 Nest the **USA Map** comp into **Locations Main** by dragging it from the Project panel to the left side of **Locations Main**'s Timeline panel. This will center the map in the composition (see figure to the right). If needed, set the Magnification popup in the Comp panel to Fit up to 100%.

Let's take a moment to contemplate the composition hierarchy you've created. Study the Composition Navigator along the top of the Comp panel (above) for **Locations Main**, and you will see that the nested comps flow from **MyPlate** to one of your city comps to **USA Map** to **Locations Main**. Click on any one of these navigation buttons, and After Effects will bring that comp forward.

Select **MyPlate**, and tap the *Shift* key to open the Mini-Flowchart (right). This flowchart will show you that **MyPlate** flows into each of your city comps, meaning that changes made to **MyPlate** will affect all of those comps downstream.

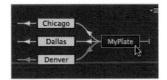

Switch to **USA Map**, and tap *Shift* again: The Mini-Flowchart (right) will show you that all of the city comps flow into **USA Map**, which then flows into

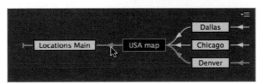

Locations Main. Note that you can click on the arrows between comps in the Mini-Flowchart to navigate along the chain.

Click on **Locations Main** to bring it forward again.

▼ What Size Should Precomps Be?

Precomps do not need to be the same size as the compositions they are nested into. But what size *should* they be? The answer is based more on experience, intuition, and compromise than a simple formula.

Rule number one is that you do not want to have to zoom a nested precomp to be larger than 100%, or you will likely lose image quality. Having some extra size will also give you freedom later to decide how much you want to zoom in or pan around a nested comp (as is the case with nesting **USA Map** into **Locations Main** in this exercise).

Rule number two is that you don't want to make a precomp much larger than it has to be. Larger precomps take more RAM and time to render. If it's just going to be a small button (such as the **Plate** comp in this exercise), there's no need for it to be as large as the final comp.

In general, when you have a complex chain of comps, try to create a test of the comp hierarchy before you spend time finessing the animation in each potentially wrong-sized precomp.

12 Now animate the big map inside this smaller comp:

• With **USA Map** layer selected, press **P** to reveal Position, then **Shift** **S** to add Scale.

• Press **Shift** **Page Down** to jump to 00:10, and enable the keyframing stopwatches for Position and Scale.

• Change Scale to 50% or a little larger, and position the map to what looks like a good starting point.

• Move to 04:20, increase Scale to around 70%, and reposition the map as needed to frame all three of your cities. If your cities are fairly tightly grouped, this simple "push in" animation will suffice. If your cities are more spread out, you might want to do a "pull out" instead (animate from zoomed in on one title to pulling back to include the entire map). In the real world, an animation like this may be driven by a voiceover (narration), in which case you might end up needing to do a more complex "motion control" move (as covered in Lesson 3).

12 Pan and zoom **USA Map** inside **Locations Main** to start with a zoomed-out overview (above), and end up zoomed in on your three cities (below).

▽ future vision

3D Polish

After you have completed Lesson 8 on 3D Space, come back to this exercise and think about how you might use 3D to make it more interesting. For example, rather than animate the scale of the city plates to zoom them up, move them forward in Z space, perhaps with 3D shadows or transparency and refraction. Or rather than panning and scaling in the final comp, use a 3D camera to move around your world.

13 Through the power of nesting, any changes to **MyPlate** (right) are automatically rippled through to the final comp (above).

13 This is about the point during a real project that the client calls and says "We changed our mind – it can't say New Locations; it has to say New Cities!" Fortunately, those words are in a single precomp that feeds all of your city comps:

• Click on **MyPlate** in the Comp Navigator to bring it forward. Double-click the layer **New Location**, type "**NEW CITIES**", and press **Enter**.

• Click on **Locations Main** in the Comp Navigator: all of the city precomps have been updated to say NEW CITIES.

And that, my friends, is the power of nested comps and building intelligent hierarchies!

Final Polish

Preview your animation. Once you have the basic move down, bring the **USA Map** comp forward and experiment with animating the three city layers so they appear at different times.

In **Comps Finished > Locations_final** we scaled each city layer up from 0% to 100% over 20 frames, and staggered them to start at 01:00, 02:00, and 03:00 as we moved from west to east across the country. Of course, you could also have them spin in and slam down with a huge lens flare! (Just kidding…)

On a more serious note though, this project has revealed another common trick advanced motion graphics artists employ: They create a complex world in one oversized composition that is full of detailed animations, and then nest this world into a final comp that moves around their world. This is much easier than trying to animate all of the individual component layers in a single composition.

In our final version, we zoomed up each city, and staggered when they came on.

Extended ETLAT

Edit This/Look At That (ETLAT) is a technique to edit in one After Effects panel while viewing another. The **06-Video Bonus** folder contains a movie from our *After Effects Apprentice* video series that demonstrates a trio of approaches to ETLAT.

▼ Edit This, Look at That

Let's say you need to alter the color of the backing rectangles in the **MyPlate** comp and observe what this color looks like against the map layer in **Locations Main**. How can you see both at once?

Open **MyPlate** comp, select the **Rectangular Shape** layer, and press F3 to open its Effect Controls panel. Lock this panel by clicking the padlock icon at the top left. Then bring the **Locations Main** comp forward. The Effect Controls panel for **Rectangular Shape** in **MyPlate** should still be visible. Now you can edit the Hue/Saturation effect already applied to **Rectangular Shape** while viewing the results "in context" in **Locations Main**.

If you lock an Effect Controls panel for a layer in a precomp, it will stay forward even if you display a different comp in the Comp panel.

After you've created a basic design (top), you decide it would be better if the text and logo – but not the background – had a crazy warp effect at the start (above).

Precomposing a Group

So far, we've demonstrated using nested comps when you can plan ahead and decide what your composition hierarchy should be. As if life always worked out so neatly… More often, you'll be in the middle of a design and discover that you would be better off if some layers already in the main composition were actually in a nested comp of their own. That's where precomposing comes in.

1 Save your current project, and open the project file **Lesson 06 > 06d-Precompose-Move.aep**. In the **Comps** folder is **wiredfruit*starter**; open it by double-clicking.

This comp contains five layers: three that make up the title and logo, plus two for the background. After building it, you have the sudden brainwave that it would be cool to warp the title and logo as a unit. However, if you applied a warp effect with an adjustment layer, or nested this comp into another and then applied a warp, everything – including the background – would get warped.

The solution is simple: Go back in time. Or more practically, select the three layers to be warped and send them back into their own nested comp. Then you can warp the resulting single layer in the current comp. And it's easier than it sounds:

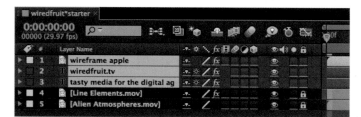

2 Select the layers you want to be in their own nested comp (above left). Use Layer > Pre-compose (below), and they will be replaced with a single layer which is a comp that contains those three layers (above right).

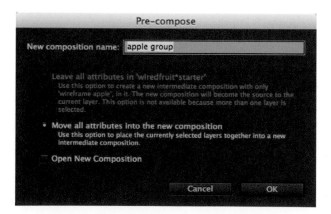

2 In the Timeline panel, click on layer 1, then **Shift**+click on layer 3. The first three layers will be selected. Then choose the menu item Layer > Pre-compose.

The Pre-compose dialog will open. When you select multiple layers, the only option available is "Move all attributes into the new composition." This means a new composition will be created (with the same size and duration as the current comp), and the selected layers – including their current transformation, effects, and any animation – will be moved intact into that new comp.

Disable the Open New Composition checkbox, enter a name that makes sense such as "**apple group**", and click OK. Nothing will appear to change in the Comp panel, but in the Timeline panel, those three layers will now be replaced by a single layer that points to the new nested comp – or precomp, as we like to call it.

3 You can treat this new precomp layer just as you would any other layer: transform it, animate, or apply effects to it.

Select the single nested layer **apple group**, and apply Effect > Distort > Warp. The Effect Controls panel will open. Set the Warp Style popup to Squeeze, and Bend to −100 to get a squished distortion. To animate the effect, press (Home) and click on the stopwatch for Bend to enable keyframing. Move a second or two later in the comp, then set Bend to 0 to "come out of" the effect.

And that's the basic technique for precomposing. Bring the Project panel forward and note that your **apple group** precomp appears in the Comps folder. Precomps are still live, like any other nested comp. You can double-click it at any time to open it and any changes you make will ripple up to the top comp where it's nested.

Twirl down the **Comps_finished** folder and take a moment to explore some enhancements we put into our version:

• We removed the Drop Shadow from the three individual layers in the precomp **apple group_finished** and applied it instead to the nested layer in the main comp **wiredfruit_finished**. Now we have only one effect to tweak (and render), rather than three.

• We timed the second keyframe in the warp to align with a point in one of the background layers where lines wipe past the viewer (look for the layer marker).

• In the comp **wiredfruit_finished**, select the Bend value for the layer **apple group_finished** and click on the Graph Editor button along the top of the Timeline panel. You'll see how we played with its value graph to overshoot the second keyframe's final value, adding a little bounce when it lands. RAM Preview to see this, then see if you can re-create a similar overshooting in your version.

3 After precomposing, the Warp effect (below) is applied to the precomp group without affecting the background (above).

▽ **tip**

Anchor Point and Precomps

After you precompose a group of layers, the anchor point defaults to the center of the resulting layer. If you want to scale or rotate this precomp around a different location, use the Anchor Point (Pan Behind) tool (Lesson 2) to move the anchor point.

In our finished version, we added an overshoot to Bend's value graph to add a little bounce to the end of its animation.

The goal in this exercise is to take this near-finished composition and add a track matte to the apple that animates along with it without having to re-create any of the existing keyframes.

Precomposing a Single Layer

Precomposing is a great way to group together layers. However, it also comes in handy for individual layers. Sometimes, you need to perform a series of treatments on a layer that must happen in a specific order. Precomposing allows you to divide up the chores across more than one comp, making it easier for you to determine what happens when.

1 Open the project file **Lesson 06 > 06e-Precompose-Leave.aep**. In the **Comps** folder is **Red Apple*starter**; open it by double-clicking, then press **O** on the numeric keypad to RAM Preview it.

In this comp, the apple is scaling up and gently bouncing around (thanks to Animation Presets > Presets > Behaviors > Wigglerama). The gray color in the apple is a little boring though, so the idea struck us to use the apple as an alpha matte (Lesson 4) and fill it with a colorful movie.

The problem with this brilliant idea is trying to match the fill layer to the apple's animation. We would need to also scale up the fill, and possibly wobble it to match. Even if we could do that, we would have another problem with the Drop Shadow effect needing to render after the track matte has been composited.

What you really want is for the track matte effect to be composited in a separate precomp. This precomp would be used as a source in the current comp, where its existing attributes – effects and keyframes – would continue to be applied. Pre-compose to the rescue:

2 Select layer 1 (**wireframe apple**), and choose Layer > Pre-compose. In the Pre-compose dialog, choose the option Leave All Attributes. This will move just the underlying source layer back into a new comp and keep all of the transforms and effects in the current comp. Enable Open New Composition (since you want to work in it), give your new precomp a clear name such as "**apple+matte**", and click OK. The precomp will open in the Comp and Timeline panels.

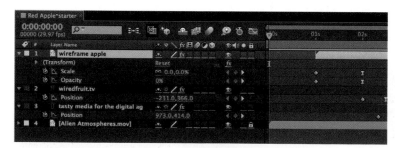

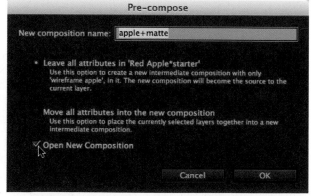

2 Select the apple layer (above) and precompose, using the Leave All Attributes and Open New Composition options (right).

2 *continued* After you precompose, the result is a new precomp (above left) the same size and duration as the apple layer (above right).

If you open Composition > Composition Settings for **apple+matte**, you will see that the precomp is the same width, height, frame rate, and duration as the **Apple_loop** layer's source. (Before CS6, the Leave All option would incorrectly pick up the original comp's frame rate.) Close this dialog when done.

3 Bring the Project panel forward, and twirl down the **Sources** folder. Select the **Light Illusions A.mov** footage and drag it into the **apple+matte** comp *below* the **Apple_loop.mov** layer.

4 This colorful new layer is considerably larger than the comp. There's nothing wrong with leaving it as is. But to create a more intricate pattern for the fill, let's shrink it down to just fit this precomp. With **Light Illusions A.mov** selected, use the menu item Layer > Transform > Fit to Comp.

5 Time to fill the apple's alpha channel with this colorful movie. Press **F4** to reveal the Modes column. Then set the TrkMat popup for **Light Illusions A.mov** to Alpha. Rather than gray, the apple will be filled with the background image.

6 Click on the tab for **Red Apple*starter** and RAM Preview: The colorful apple you created in the precomp appears in this main comp, with its zoom, fade, and wobble intact. Mission accomplished; save your project.

As usual, our version of this exercise is in the Project panel's **Comps_Finished** folder. It includes a few extra touches: We applied Effect > Color Correction > Hue/Saturation to the apple and rotated its Hue 50° to make the apple more red than pink, and enabled motion blur for our animating layers.

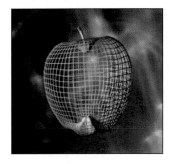

3–4 In the precomp, add a background movie behind the apple, and use Transform > Fit to Comp to shrink it down. Background courtesy Artbeats/Light Illusions.

5 Set the background to use the apple above as an Alpha matte (left), resulting in the apple's wireframe being filled with the Light Illusions movie (above).

wiredfruit.tv
tasty media for the digital age

6 Our final version includes a hue shift.

The Basic Render Order

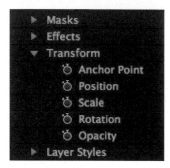

When you twirl down a layer's properties in the Timeline panel, After Effects informs you of its internal rendering order: Masks, followed by Effects, followed by Transform, followed by Layer Styles.

2–4 Take the original movie (A) and apply the Wave Warp effect (B). Then draw a rectangular mask: The mask gets waved (C) even though you applied it "after" the warp effect! Edit the layer's Rotation value, and both the mask and effect are rotated (D). Footage courtesy Artbeats/Digidelic.

Render Order

Sometimes, After Effects will appear to have a mind of its own: You try to treat an image a certain way, but you get an unexpected result. This occurs because After Effects has a very particular order in which it performs operations, which you need to know and understand. Gaining this understanding is the purpose behind the next few exercises in this lesson.

The Order Things Render

Frustration often precedes enlightenment. To help make it clear what's really going on, let's first work through an example in frustration:

1 Open the project file **Lesson 06 > 06f-Render Order.aep**. The **Comps** folder should be twirled down; focus first on the nested folder **Render Example 1**. Inside it is the comp **Basic Order**; double-click it to open it. It contains a single layer: **Digidelic.mov**.

2 Select **Digidelic.mov** and apply Effect > Distort > Wave Warp. The default settings are fine; press the spacebar to play, and notice that this effect even self-animates.

3 With **Digidelic.mov** still selected, choose the Rectangle mask tool and draw a mask around the center of the layer. Rather than cutting a clean rectangular mask, the mask's edges are warped as well!

From the result, you can deduce that the Wave Warp (and for that matter, any effect you apply) is being rendered after the mask – even though you applied the effect before creating the mask.

4 To see how Transform factors into the mix, press **R** to reveal Rotation and scrub its value. The movie, mask, and wavy pattern are all affected. This proves that transformations are calculated after masks and effects have already been calculated.

If this is the look you wanted, fine. But perhaps you wanted a straight-edged mask and to have the image wave inside. Or you might want to rotate the underlying image and not have the mask rotate. Who will win this war of wills: the artist or the software?

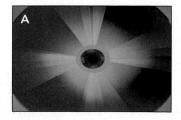

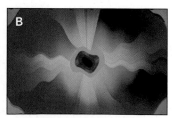

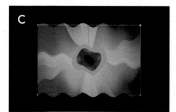

First, it is important to grasp that the order in which you *apply* transformations, masks, and effects doesn't matter – After Effects will calculate them in the set order of Masks, Effects, and Transform. And there is very little you can do inside one composition to change this basic rendering order – for example, you can't drag Effects before Masks, or move Masks after Transform.

Two Comps Are Better Than One

There are hundreds of similar render order issues you might encounter, and there's almost always more than one way to solve them. However, the simplest solution is often to use two comps.

Take our **Basic Order** comp as an example. If you were to spread the **Digidelic** layer across two comps, you could then pick and choose the attributes that are rendered in the first comp, and those that are rendered in the second.

5 In the Project panel, drag the **Basic Order** comp down to the Create New Composition button at the bottom of this panel. This will nest **Basic Order** into a second comp called **Basic Order 2**. This new comp will open automatically. The chain now goes as follows: The **Digidelic.mov** source is in **Basic Order**, and **Basic Order** is nested in **Basic Order 2** (you can see it in the timeline of the comp that just opened).

6 The tabs for both comps should be visible. Remember that the **Basic Order 2** comp renders *second*, so if you want the mask to render after Wave Warp and Rotation, you need to move the mask into the second comp:

• Click on the **Basic Order** tab in the Timeline panel to bring this comp forward, and if necessary twirl down Masks. Select Mask 1 and Edit > Cut. The mask will be removed.

• Bring the **Basic Order 2** comp forward, select the nested layer, and Edit > Paste. The mask will be applied, but will have straight edges because the effects and transformations rendered in the first comp and are not affecting it

5 Drag **Basic Order** to the Project panel's Create New Composition button (top), and **Basic Order** will be nested as a layer in the new comp **Basic Order 2** (above).

6 Select the first comp **Basic Order** (A) and cut the mask from **Digidelic.mov** (B). Then select the second comp **Basic Order 2** and paste the mask onto the nested layer (C). Now the source will be rotated and waved inside a clean rectangular mask.

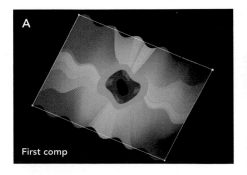

First comp

Second comp

▼ Precompose Options Compared

The Pre-compose dialog offers two options, and the results differ depending on which one you choose. The term *attributes* refers to masks, effects, transformations, blending modes, in and out points, and so on.

Leave All Attributes

- This option is available for single layers only.

- After you precompose, the precomp will have one layer in it, and the size and duration of the precomp will be the same *as the original layer*. In CS6, the frame rate will also match the source.

- Any attributes applied to the layer before you precompose will remain in the *original comp*.

- The precomp will have a fresh render order, and any attributes applied to the layer in the new precomp will render *before* the attributes in the original comp.

Move All Attributes

- This option is available for single layers and multiple layers.

- The precomp created will be the same size and duration *as the original comp*.

- Any attributes applied to the layer(s) before precomposing will be moved to the *precomp*.

- The nested layer in the original comp will have a fresh render order, and any attributes applied to this layer will render *after* the attributes in the precomp.

Open New Composition

Selecting the Open New Composition option has no effect other than if it is selected, the precomp will come forward after you click OK so you can more easily edit it. If it's not selected, the current comp will remain forward.

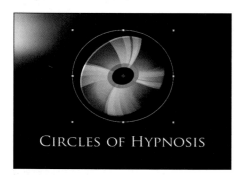

CIRCLES OF HYPNOSIS

Nice design – too bad the circular logo isn't actually a circle.

Using Precomposing to Reorder

In our first example, you fixed the visual problem with the wavy mask by nesting the comp into a second comp, then moving the mask. If the comp you're working in has only one layer, that method works fine.

In the real world, you'll likely come across a rendering order problem in the middle of a project, when there are already multiple layers in the comp. If you were to nest this complex comp, you would be grouping *all* of its layers into the second comp – perhaps not what you had in mind. You need a scalpel not a hatchet, as it were – and this is where precomposing becomes your friend.

1 Still in **06f-Render Order.aep**, select Close All from the Comp panel's dropdown menu to close all previous comps. Bring the Project panel forward, and open **Comps > Render Example 2 > Circle**.

This comp has three layers: **Digidelic.mov** with a circular mask and effects applied, a title, and a background. The client likes the idea, but insists that the result be a clean circle, not a wavy circle.

2 Select layer 1. If the mask and effects aren't visible in the Timeline panel, press **M** to reveal masks, then **Shift E** to reveal the effects. Now let's sit for a second and think this through.

• Currently, Mask 1 renders first followed by all the effects. But the Warp effect needs to be applied *before* the mask so that the mask doesn't get warped.

• The Bevel Alpha and Drop Shadow effects need to be applied *after* the mask is calculated (if beforehand, they will apply to the rectangular movie).

• The three color correction effects treat the entire layer, so we don't need to worry about whether they are applied before or after the mask.

So – how to accomplish this? If you precompose this layer, you will spread the layer across two comps and can then pick and choose which attributes should render in the first comp (the new precomp) and which should render in the second comp (the current main comp):

3 Select layer 1, **Digidelic.mov**, then Layer > Pre-compose. Select the Leave All Attributes option (you want the attributes to remain in the main comp for now), and enable Open New Composition. Name your new precomp "**Digi_precomp**" and click OK. The precomp will be forward, displaying the source movie in its original form.

4 Click on the tab for **Circle** comp in the Timeline panel to bring the main comp forward again. The movie in layer 1 has now been replaced with the output of the **Digi_precomp**. (Note that after you precompose, the layer always twirls up.)

• Select layer 1, press **M**, then **Shift E** again. Because you precomposed with the Leave All Attributes option, the mask and effects remained in the **Circle** comp. Let's move the Warp effect back to the precomp, where it will render first:

• Select just the Warp effect and Edit > Cut. The distortion will be removed.

• Click the **Digi_precomp** tab to bring the precomp forward. Select **Digidelic.mov** and Edit > Paste. The image should twist. Press **E** to twirl down effects and confirm that the Warp effect is now in this comp.

• Click the **Circle** tab again and look at the Comp viewer: The warped movie is now cut out by the mask as a perfect circle.

The precomp (which renders first) is used only to distort the movie; the original comp (which renders second) applies all other effects and the mask.

Quick Quizzler: If you were to rotate this layer over time, would it matter which composition you applied the Rotation keyframes in? (Think…what would the consequences be to the light direction in the Bevel Alpha and Drop Shadow effects? Would using layer styles instead of effects allow for a different result?)

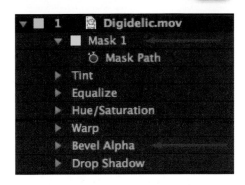

2 The mask currently renders before all of the effects. What we *need* is for the mask to render after the Warp, but before the Bevel Alpha and Drop Shadow.

4 Cut the Warp effect from the main comp and paste it into the precomp (left), causing the movie to become warped (above).

4 *continued* Back in the main comp, the mask will be applied to the precomp, followed by the other effects (above), giving us the desired result (above left).

CIRCLES OF HYPNOSIS

Continuous Rasterization

In the last few exercises, we put a lot of emphasis on the order in which After Effects processes layers: Masks are calculated first, followed by Effects, followed by Transforms such as Rotation, and then Layer Styles.

However, there are exceptions to every rule. The biggest exception is layers that are *continuously rasterized*: For these special layers, the pixels you see are calculated on the fly by After Effects, rather than ahead of time when the footage item was created. Text and shape layers fall into this category automatically; so do Illustrator, PDF and SWF files, as well as Solids when an optional switch is set.

If a layer is being continuously rasterized, the render order changes: Transforms are calculated first instead, followed by Masks and Effects. Unfortunately, these sections are not re-ordered in the Timeline panel to provide a clue as to what's going on underneath the hood. To tell if a layer is being continuously rasterized, look for the sunburst icon under the Timeline panel's Switches column (shown at left). This switch is always on for text and shape layers. It is permanently disabled for movies and most other layers, as their pixels have already been calculated. For Illustrator and PDF layers as well as solids, you will see a hollow box, which means it defaults to off (layer renders normally) but can be switched on (layer behaves like text and shape layers). The status of this switch can have a large impact on how the final image appears:

The sunburst icon indicates if a layer's Continuously Rasterize switch has been enabled. It defaults to off for Illustrator files (layer 1); it is unavailable for pixel-based layers such as movies (layer 2).

1 Still in **06f-Render Order.aep**, close any previously opened comps and open **Comps > Render Example 3 > Rasterization**.

2 The first layer in this comp was created in Adobe Illustrator. Select it and press **U** to reveal its Scale and Rotation transform keyframes, followed by **Shift** + **E** to reveal its effects. Its Continuously Rasterize switch defaults to off, which means After Effects will treat it as a normal pixel-based layer such as a photo or a movie.

Scrub through the timeline and pay attention to the direction of the shadow: Unfortunately, it rotates with the text. This is because effects are normally

2 With continuous rasterization disabled for the Illustrator layer, effects are calculated before transforms, so the bevel and shadow rotate.

calculated before transforms such as rotation. On the other hand, look at the size of the shadow and the beveled edges relative to the text: As the text scales up, so does the shadow and bevel, which is what you would expect. In this case, transforms occurring after effects is a good thing.

3 Press **End** and look at the quality of the text: Here it is being scaled 150%, where it looks quite fuzzy and aliased as After Effects "blows up" its pixels.

4 Enable the Continuously Rasterize switch for **Illustrator Vectors.ai**. After Effects will now treat it as a vector-based layer, such as a text or shape layer. It will use the Transform values to scale, rotate, and position the vectors, convert the result to pixels, and *then* apply any masks or effects.

4 With continuous rasterization enabled (above), the rotation and scale are calculated before the bevel and shadow (left).

In this case, at time 04:29 the size of the bevel and drop shadow will appear smaller, as they are being applied at "100%" size rather than 150% scale (as the scaling has already been calculated). The layer will also appear to be much sharper – continuously rasterized layers look sharp at all levels of scale.

Scrub through the timeline, and you will also observe that the drop shadow continues to fall in the correct direction even as the text rotates, which is a useful result of effects happening *after* transforms. On the other hand, as this text scales up, the shadow distance and bevel amount stay the same size regardless of the size of the text, with quite unrealistic results – a down-side of this rewired rendering order.

You can solve some (but not necessarily all) of these short-comings using nested compositions to rewire the rendering order, or by using the Distort > Transform effect, which allows you to insert transformations at any point in the Effects stage of the render order. The **Comps_Finished > Ex.3_finished** folder contains two versions of the above composition, employing the Transform effect to perform select transformations. (Remember that when a layer is continuously rasterized, all regular transformations are rendered before effects, despite what the order in the timeline might suggest!)

Just to make things more confusing, the Continuously Rasterize switch is also used for nested compositions. In this case, it changes function and becomes the Collapse Transformations switch – which we'll discuss next.

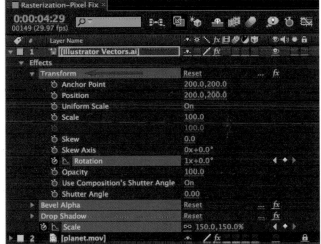

In **Comps_Finished > Ex.3_finished > Rasterization-Pixel Fix**, the Transform effect rotates the layer before the shadow and bevel are calculated, so the direction of these effects remains stationary. Then the normal Transform > Scale parameter resizes the entire effected layer. Unfortunately, the layer still goes soft as it is scaled beyond 100%; to really fix this, create a larger source image either in Illustrator or in a precomp (with continuous rasterization enabled).

Beware of Flattening

To apply a mask or an effect to a collapsed nested comp, After Effects first flattens the layer(s) internally to a simple RGBA image. This is why you lose some of the features of collapse transformations.

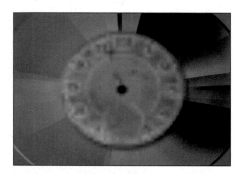

4 A layer that is scaled down in a precomp and then scaled back up in a later comp can look ugly, as scaled-down pixels are being blow up.

5 Enabling the Collapse Transformations switch for this precomp (below) can restore its original quality, as well as other settings such as blending modes applied in the precomp (above).

Collapsing Transformations

There is one other render order exception you should be aware of: the ability to "collapse" the transformations of layers in a nested composition so they are calculated together with any additional transformations applied to the nested precomp layer. This can result in a considerable increase in image quality, but it comes with a few caveats.

1 Still in the **06f-Render Order** project, close any previous comps and open **Comps > Collapse Transformations > Collapse*starter**. It contains a watch face with a drop shadow, composited on top of a background layer using a blending mode.

2 Select **watch_face.tif** and press **S** to reveal its Scale. Set this value to 10%.

3 Right-click on **watch_face.tif** and select Pre-compose. Enable the Move All Attributes option, which means the Scale value, effect, and mode will all be moved to the precomp. Disable Open New Composition, give it a good name such as "**watch face precomp**" and click OK.

4 Your new nested precomp layer should be selected in your original comp. Press **S** to reveal its Scale and increase this value to 1000%. Its image quality will look very poor, as you are taking what is now a small image and blowing up its pixels. Also notice that the watch face itself is opaque, as the contribution of the blending mode has been lost.

5 Make sure the Switches column is visible (press **F4** if it isn't) and enable the Collapse Transformations switch for your nested precomp – it's in exactly the same place as the continuously rasterize switch was for the previous exercise. Now the watch face will be sharp again, and its mode will be employed.

When you enable the Collapse Transformations switch for a precomp, After Effects looks at the Transform values for the layer(s) in the precomp and factors them together with the Transform values for the nested layer in the current comp. These transformations are then applied once at the precomp level, after masks and effects. Since 10% times 1000% = 100%, the image appears at its original resolution.

In addition, the layers in the precomp behave as if they resided in the main comp. That means the settings under Modes (including Stencil or Silhouette) will cause a precomped layer to interact with other layers in the main comp. The comp boundaries of the precomp are also ignored, so if you were counting on the size of the precomp to crop its layers, you will be surprised to see this previously cropped material reappear in the main comp. Strange things can also happen with collapsed Opacity values, as each layer will render with their own individual opacity values.

6 Interactions become more complex if you apply masks and effects to the precomped layer. Press **F4** to reveal the Modes column in your main comp. Its options will be disabled for your precomp layer. Then apply Effect > Blur & Sharpen > Box Blur to your precomp layer: The Overlay mode applied in the precomp will be ignored, and the Mode popup in the main comp reappears.

The moral of this story is: Don't just blindly enable Collapse Transformations for nested comps; although it may indeed improve image quality by only transforming (and antialiasing) the layer(s) once, it might also have other unintended consequences. For example, if the precomp includes a 3D camera and/or lights, you'll see the effect of these camera and lights in the final image when you nest it. However, if you collapse the nested comp layer, the layers will be rendered by the camera and lights in the second comp (if there is no camera, then the default camera is used).

6 Normally, the Modes popup for a collapsed nested layer is disabled (above), and the mode applied to each layer in a collapsed precomp is honored. But when you apply an effect to the collapsed precomp layer, the modes set in the precomp are ignored (right) and now you can only choose a single mode for the entire collapsed precomp (below).

Compound Effects

Another situation that requires you to pay attention to the internal render order is when you apply a *compound effect*. These are effects that refer to the color or alpha channel values of a second layer to decide how to process the layer they are applied to. Popular examples of compound effects include Compound Blur and Displacement Map, although any effect with a Layer popup follows the same rules. The "gotcha" with compound effects is that they look at the source of that second layer *before* Mask, Effects, and Transforms have been applied.

▽ tip

Troubleshooting Tip

You apply a compound effect to Movie A and tell it to use Movie B, but the result is unexpected. Open the Layer panel for Movie B and set the View popup to None: This is the source that the compound effect is using.

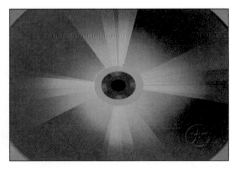

1 Open project **Lesson 06 > 06g-Compound Effects.aep**. In the Project panel, twirl open the **Comps** folder, then double-click the comp **Compound Effects*starter** to open it. It contains a piece of background footage, plus a pulley object that your boss thinks would make a great embossed bug for the video.

1 Your goal is to convert the large pulley object (left) into a discrete embossed bug in the lower right corner (above).

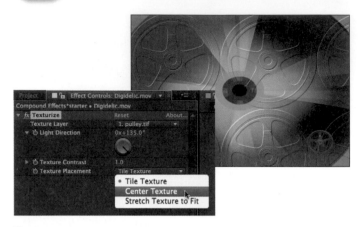

3 Compound effects usually have options on how to deal with size mismatches between the references and underlying layer. The best solution is to make sure there is no mismatch.

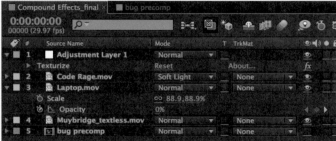

5 By applying a compound effect to a comp-sized adjustment layer and making sure the reference layer is the same size, you can do what you want with the layers underneath without worrying about alignment.

2 Select **pulley.tif**, press **S** to reveal its Scale, and reduce it to 25% of its original size. Press **'** (the apostrophe key) to toggle on the Title/Action Safe areas and position the pulley in the lower right corner of the inner Action Safe area. Press **'** again to hide the safe areas overlay.

3 Select **Digidelic.mov** and apply Effect > Stylize > Texturize. The Effect Controls panel will open; change the Texture Layer popup to **pulley.tif**. Initially, you will see a grid of embossed pulleys. Try the different Texture Placement options; none give the desired result. The problem is that the effect has no idea that the Texture Layer has been scaled and moved inside this comp as it's looking only at layer 1 at its source. The solution is to perform those transformations in a precomp. Set Texture Placement back to Center; this is the best option for the comp chain you're about to build.

4 Right-click on **pulley.tif** and select Pre-compose. Be sure to choose the Move All Attributes option; this will create a precomp the same size as the current comp with the pulley in its current position. Disable Open New Composition, name it "**bug precomp**" and click OK. Turn off the Video switch for **bug precomp** so it doesn't obscure the background layer. Ta-da! The embossed bug now appears just as you intended.

5 Note that this worked only because the footage you applied the compound effect to was the exact same size as the precomp you created. If the background layer was a different size, you could precompose it into a comp the same size as your main comp (making sure you applied the compound effect to its precomp layer in the final comp), or take advantage of Adjustment Layers as we have in **Comps_Finished > Compound Effects_final**. Applying compound effects to an adjustment layer that is the same size as the comp ensures it will be aligned properly, regardless of what you've done with the layers underneath. (Under the hood, adjustment layers apply their effects to a copy of the composite of all layers below, cropped to the comp size.) This also makes it easy to swap out the footage underneath the bug, or even build an edit underneath the adjustment layer.

Quizzler

If you learn how to manipulate the render order, you won't be tempted to compromise the design or change your ideas. That alone will help you realize your full potential as an After Effects designer!

So here are a couple of brainteasers to practice your newfound knowledge of the rendering order. Both may be found in the project **06q-Quizzler.aep**:

Alien Puzzle

Look inside the **Quizzler 1** folder in the Project panel. There are two comps in it: **Alien-1** consists of two layers and is nested into **Alien-2** where it is masked. All in all, not much different from the chain of comps you explored earlier in the Render Order section, except that the first comp has two layers instead of one.

Your mission – should you decide to accept it – is to apply a distortion to the layers in **Alien 1** using Effect > Distort > Warp without affecting the shape of the mask in **Alien 2**. You can apply only one instance of the Warp effect (use any settings you think look good), and you cannot create additional precomps. There are two possible solutions, using features covered in earlier lessons.

Picture in Picture Effect

Now turn your attention to the **Quizzler 2** folder in the Project panel.

⬧+double-click (**Alt**+double-click) the **Quiz 2.mov** to open its Footage panel and play the movie. Focus on the now-familiar **Digidelic.mov** layer panning inside a small "picture in picture" hard-edged shape, floating over the background. A Fast Blur effect animates from very blurry to zero, while a Drop Shadow effect sets this layer off from the background. Looks simple enough?

Leave the Footage panel open for reference, then open the **Quiz 2*starter** comp, which just has the background layer. Create the same result; you'll find the **Digidelic.mov** in the **Sources** folder. There are no restrictions on what you can do, provided the result is essentially the same.

After you've taken a crack at it, check out **Quizzler Solutions > Quiz 2_solution** – we think this is a fairly elegant solution to the problem.

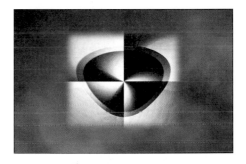

In **Quizzler 1**, your goal is to warp the inset movie (above) without disturbing the square box it resides in (below). Give it your best shot, then look in our **Quizzler Solutions > Quiz 1** folder for the answers.

▽ tip

Transform Cheat

The Effect > Distort > Transform effect has all of the features of the Transformation section and more. Because you can drag the Transform effect before other effects, you can use it to manipulate the render order or even have two sets of, say, Position or Rotation keyframes on one layer.

In **Quizzler 2**, the plan is to blur and pan the inset movie while keeping things as simple as possible.

Expressions and Time Games

Using expressions and playing with time.

▽ In This Lesson

184   using the pick whip to create expressions

185   altering expressions

186   stabilizing shadows

188   matching value ranges (the linear expression)

190   looping keyframes

191   expression tips

192   the wiggle expression

193   expression controllers

193   keyframing the wiggle expression

194   creating a master controller with a null object

195   converting sound to keyframes

196   frame blending

197   Pixel Motion

198   stop motion tricks

199   preserve frame rate

200   creating freeze frames

201   time remapping

205   resources for learning more about expressions

▽ Getting Started

Make sure you have copied the **Lesson 07 – Expressions and Time** folder from this book's disc onto your hard drive, and make note of where it is; it contains the project file and sources you need for this lesson.

I n this lesson, you will become acquainted with two admittedly mind-stretching areas of After Effects. First we will cover expressions: Little bits of code that can help save you large amounts of time while animating. After you master those, we will show you how to make time literally stand still – as well as speed up, slow down, and go by more smoothly.

Expressions 101

The geek explanation of expressions is that it's a JavaScript-based programming language that allows you to manipulate time-based streams in After Effects. The artist explanation is that it's an easy way to make any keyframeable parameter react to what another parameter is doing – such as having two layers rotate or scale together without having to copy and paste keyframes between them.

Although expressions can be very deep and powerful, in reality the majority of expressions are very simple and therefore easy to create. Indeed, After Effects does most of the work for you: In many cases, all you have to do is literally point one parameter to another using the *pick whip* tool. Beyond that, the most common task you will need to do is add little bits of math such as "times two" or "minus 180." We will also show you three simple *functions* (basic pieces of code) that will come in handy time and again. Not only will expressions save you a lot of time and tedium, they often inspire new animation ideas – something both geeks and artists can get enthused about.

The Problem

1 Open this lesson's project file: **Lesson_07.aep**. In the Project panel, the **Comps** folder should be twirled open (if not, click on its twirly arrow). In this folder, locate and double-click **01-Pick Whip*starter** to open it.

Press **0** on the numeric keypad to RAM Preview this comp. The blue pulley on the left scales and spins; the red pulley on the right just sits there. The client says he wants them both to do the same thing. That's easy enough to do the old-fashioned way:

2 The Scale and Rotation keyframes for **Blue Pulley** should be visible in the Timeline panel; if they aren't, select this layer and type **U** to reveal its animating properties.

• Click on the word Scale for **Blue Pulley**; all of the Scale keyframes will be selected. Hold down **Shift** and click on Rotation: Its keyframes will be selected as well. Then type **⌘ C** on Mac (**Ctrl C** on Windows) to copy the selected keyframes.

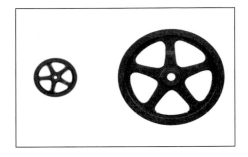

Your goal is to make these two pulleys perform the same animation. You can copy, paste, and hand-edit keyframes...or let expressions do a lot of the work for you.

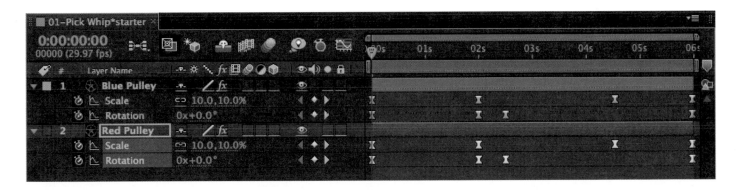

• Press **Home** to make sure the current time indicator is at 00:00 before pasting, as pasted keyframes always start at the current time. Select **Red Pulley** and type **⌘ V** (**Ctrl V**) to paste. Press **U** to reveal its new keyframes.

• RAM Preview; both pulleys scale and rotate the same.

3 Now that the client sees both pulleys together, he decides he wants the rotation to finish before the pulleys scale back down. Okay – move the last Rotation keyframe for both layers back to 04:15.

4 RAM Preview. Now the client thinks the pulleys are spinning too fast, so edit the last Rotation keyframe for both pulleys to be –1 rotation, not –2.

You can quickly see how tedious client changes can become, just with two layers. Now imagine if you had 10 or 100 layers! This is a perfect example of how expressions could make your life easier.

2 Select the keyframes for **Blue Pulley**, copy, select **Red Pulley**, and paste. Their animations will be identical – for now...

The Pick Whip

The main tool you will use to create expressions is the pick whip. This tool makes it easy to link one parameter to another.

5 Turn off the stopwatch for **Red Pulley**'s Scale and Rotation to delete their keyframes. Press **F2** to deselect these parameters.

• Hold down the ⌥ (**Alt**) key, and click on the stopwatch for **Red Pulley**'s Scale. This enables expressions for the associated property. Scale will twirl down, revealing a line that says Expression: Scale, with a set of new icons next to it. **Red Pulley**'s Scale value will change from gold to red, indicating it is now controlled by an expression. You will also see some text appear: `transform.scale`. This says **Red Pulley**'s Scale is currently "expressed" to its own Transform property, Scale.

• Click on the spiral icon next to Expression: Scale – this is the pick whip tool. Drag it up to the word Scale for **Blue Pulley**; this word will highlight when you're close. A line will connect the two properties as you drag.

Release the mouse, and the text for **Red Pulley**'s scale will change to say `thisComp.layer("Blue Pulley").transform.scale`. Expression code can look like an alien language, but it's not hard to read: In this comp is a layer called **Blue Pulley**; use its Transform property Scale.

• To accept this new expression, press **Enter** on the numeric keypad (not on the regular keyboard), or click elsewhere in the panel.

RAM Preview: **Red Pulley** will now have the exact same scaling as **Blue Pulley** – but not its rotation. Expressions are applied to individual properties,

5 ⌥+click (**Alt**+click) on an animation stopwatch to enable expressions. Click on the spiral icon and drag it to the parameter you want to copy (above). Release the mouse and press **Enter**; After Effects will write the expression and the value will be copied (below).

not entire layers. If you want **Red Pulley**'s Rotation to follow **Blue Pulley**, you will need to create an expression for that property as well:

6 Just as you did for Scale, ⌥+click (**Alt**+click) on the stopwatch for **Red Pulley**'s Rotation, and it will twirl down to reveal its expression. Drag its pick whip to **Blue Pulley**'s Rotation property. When it highlights, release the mouse and press **Enter**. RAM Preview; both pulleys will now scale and rotate together.

7 Edit the Scale and Rotation keyframes for **Blue Pulley**, then preview: **Red Pulley** will faithfully follow along. No matter how many changes you make to their values, or whether you move the keyframes earlier or later in time, **Red Pulley** will follow its leader. Compared with copying and pasting, there will be a lot less work when the client wants additional changes.

Simple Math

We know that many may consider the phrase "simple math" to be an oxymoron, but adding or dividing a number here and there will greatly multiply (ahem) what you can do with expressions.

Continue with the composition you were working with in the previous step, or open **Comps > 02-Simple Math*starter**.

8 Move the current time indicator to 02:00. Select **Blue Pulley**, and apply Effect > Perspective > Drop Shadow. Increase Drop Shadow's Distance parameter to make it more obvious.

Preview, and you will notice that the shadow rotates with the pulley. To cancel out the layer's rotation, you need to animate the shadow's Direction to spin the opposite way. Expressions to the rescue:

9 Make sure that **Blue Pulley**'s Rotation property is exposed in the Timeline panel (press **R** if it isn't) and that you have some spare room in this panel to see more lines of properties.

• In the Effect Controls panel, ⌥+click (**Alt**+click) on the stopwatch for Drop Shadow's Direction parameter. The Direction parameter will be exposed in the Timeline panel, enabled for expressions.

8 Effects (such as Drop Shadow) are calculated before transforms (such as Rotation), resulting in the shadow spinning with the pulley.

9 ⌥+click (**Alt**+click) on the stopwatch for Drop Shadow's Direction parameter.

9 Enable expressions for Shadow's Direction, and use the pick whip to connect it to the layer's Rotation (right/top). Then add the text * –1 to the end to make Direction spin in the opposite direction as Rotation (right/bottom).

After applying the initial expression, the shadow points straight up at 0° (below).

▽ try it

Inherent Value

If you want to add a parameter's original value to an expression, type "+ value" at the end. Try it yourself: In Step 10, replace + 135 with + value. A benefit of this approach is that you can scrub the Direction property to change the angle of the shadow without having to edit the expression.

• In the Timeline panel, drag the pick whip for Direction to the word Rotation. Release the mouse, but don't press *Enter* yet!

• To have the shadow rotate in the opposite direction, place the cursor at the end of the expression `transform.rotation`, and type " * –1" (multiply by negative one).

Press *Enter* and preview. The shadow now stays in the same place – but it's in the wrong place, pointing straight up. A little math can fix that, as well:

10 Click on the expression text for Direction to activate it for editing.

• To be safe, surround the current expression with parentheses so it looks like (`transform.rotation * –1`). Everything inside parentheses is calculated as a self-contained unit, so this is a good way to keep things separated.

• Press ⬇ (the down cursor arrow) to move to the end of the expression. Then type " + 135" to add the original Direction value of 135° to the current calculation. Press *Enter* and preview – now the shadow is where it belongs!

If you got lost, our version is in **Comps_Finished > 02-Simple Math_final**, where we also applied the same correction to **Red Pulley**'s shadow. Save your project before moving on.

10 Add an offset to the end of the expression (right), and now it will point at the desired angle (above).

Clockwork

In this next exercise, we'll expand on the skills you've just learned to build a clock. You'll use the pick whip and some simple math, then augment these with the *linear* function, which will make it easier to translate between different parameters.

1 Select Close All from the Comp panel's dropdown menu to close all previous comps. Bring the Project panel forward, locate **Comps > 03-Clockwork*starter**, and open it.

This composition contains the pieces needed to make a clock: the face, plus the hour, minute, and second hands. There are also a couple of background layers. We've already arranged the layers and set their anchor points so that everything lines up and spins properly. We've also animated the minute hand's rotation.

Your task is to make the hour and second hands follow the minute hand. You will then create a transition between the two background layers which follows the minute hand as well.

We've already animated the minute hand; now you have to animate the hour and second hands to follow, using expressions instead of keyframes. Background courtesy Artbeats/Alien Atmospheres.

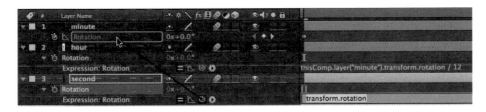

2 Select the **minute**, **hour**, and **second** layers, and press **R** to reveal their Rotation properties. Again, only layer 1 – the minute hand – is keyframed.

Think for a moment about what you need to do: The second hand needs to rotate 60 times as fast as the minute hand, while the hour hand needs to rotate at only one-twelfth the speed.

- ⌥+click (*Alt*+click) on the stopwatch for **hour**'s Rotation to enable expressions for it. Drag its pick whip up to the word Rotation for the **minute** layer. Release the mouse, and type " / 12" to divide the minute hand's rotation by 12. Press *Enter*.

- ⌥+click (*Alt*+click) on the stopwatch for **second**'s Rotation to enable expressions for it. Drag its pick whip up to the word Rotation for the **minute** layer. Release the mouse, and type " * 60" to multiply the minute hand's rotation by 60. Press *Enter*.

Press *Page Down* to step through the timeline a frame at a time, watching the Rotation values for these three layers to verify your math. For example, when you move the current time indicator to 01:15 where the minute hand has rotated 90° (15 minutes), the second hand should have rotated 15 times, while the hour hand should have rotated only 7.5°.

2 Use the pick whip to tie the Rotation values for **hour** and **second** to **minute**'s Rotation. Then modify the expressions as needed with simple math such as / 12 and * 60.

2 *continued* After you have created these expressions, the hour and second hands should now keep their correct relationships to the minute hand.

4 If you simply use the pick whip to express Radial Wipe's Transition Completion to follow **minute**'s Rotation (above), the transition will race ahead of the minute hand (top). Second background courtesy Artbeats/Digidelic.

 tip

Preset Shadow

We use the trick of having the Drop Shadow effect react to the layer's Rotation quite a bit. Rather than create an expression for its Direction parameter every time you want to use it, set it up once, select Drop Shadow in the Effect Controls panel, then select Animation > Save Animation Preset. You can now apply this preset – with the expression intact – whenever you want.

Translation Services

Now let's have some fun and tie what's happening in the background to the minute hand's animation.

3 Select **Alien Atmospheres.mov** and apply Effect > Transition > Radial Wipe. The Effect Controls panel will open; scrub the Transition Completion to get a feel for how it sweeps away this layer, revealing the layer underneath.

4 ⎇+click (*Alt*+click) Transition Completion to enable expressions for it. In the Timeline panel, drag the pick whip from Transition Completion to the word Rotation for the **minute** layer. Release the mouse, and press *Enter*.

RAM Preview, and you'll see a problem: The transition races ahead of the minute hand. Why? Well, there are 360° in one rotation, but Transition Completion goes from 0 to 100. As a result, it reaches 100% completion after only 100° of rotation.

The math to translate between these two isn't so bad (the answer is to divide the Rotation value by 3.6), but there will be numerous other cases where the translation isn't so straightforward. Therefore, we think it's worth the effort to learn an expression function called *linear* that will translate for you:

5 To remember how to use the linear function, memorize this mantra: "As a parameter goes from A to B, I want to go from Y to Z." After Effects will even help us write most of this code:

• Click on the arrow to the right of Transition Completion's pick whip to bring up the expression language menu. Select `Interpolation > linear(t, tMin, tMax, value1, value2)`. Release the mouse, and this text will replace the code created by the pick whip.

• Select `t` (being careful not to select the parenthesis before or the comma after). This is the parameter you want to follow – namely, **minute**'s Rotation. Use the pick whip tool and drag it to the parameter as you did before.

• Select `tMin` (you can double-click it to select it) and type the beginning Rotation value: 0.

• Select `tMax` and type the ending Rotation value: 360.

• Select `value1` and type the desired beginning Transition Completion value: 0.

• Select `value2` and type the ending Transition Completion value you need: 100.

Press *Enter*, and the Radial Wipe will now snap to line up with the minute hand. RAM Preview to verify this, and save your project.

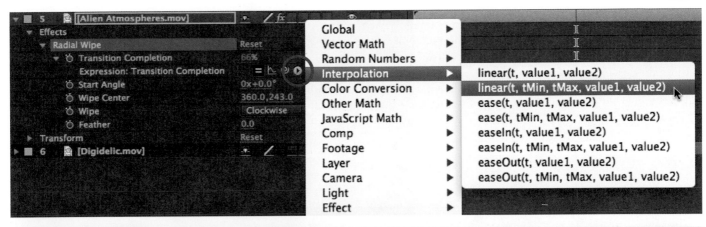

5 You can use the expression language menu (top) to remind you of the format of common expression functions. Replace each of its generic values with the values you need (above). After you're done, the wipe transition will follow the minute hand correctly (below). Once you're familiar with the structure of the linear expression, you can type it directly (we'll use this approach in an exercise on page 195).

If you like, edit the second keyframe value for **minute**'s Rotation, perhaps entering a lower value such as 120°. The hour hand, second hand, and transition will all update to stay in sync with the minute hand's rotation. Hopefully, the beauty of expressions has now become more apparent: Once you set them up, you need to edit only one set of keyframes to update a complex animation.

In the Project panel, locate and open our version: **Comps_Finished > 03-Clockwork_final**. We added a few tricks, such as animating a hue shift of the **Alien Atmospheres.mov** layer using the linear function. We also added drop shadows to the clock pieces, and used expressions to stabilize their positions so that they didn't spin around with the hands.

Our version (**03-Clockwork_final**) includes additional tricks, such as enabling motion blur, varying the hue of the fog during the transition, and adding drop shadows to the clock pieces. Everything that animates is driven by one pair of keyframes: those for the minute hand's rotation.

Going for a Loop

Time to introduce another expression into your repertoire: the ability to repeat a keyframed animation for the duration of a layer.

1 Open **Comps > 04-LoopOut*starter**. Select **watch_widget.tif**, and press **U** to reveal its keyframes: There are two for Rotation, at 00:00 and 01:00. RAM Preview; it rocks in one direction, then stops.

Your task is to make this widget rock back and forth for the duration of the layer. You could create a bunch of additional Rotation keyframes, but that would be a pain to edit later. Or, we could introduce you to the *loopOut* function.

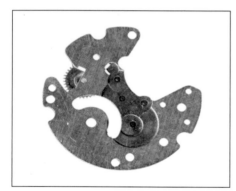

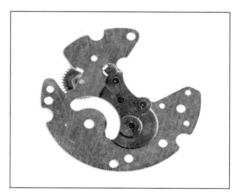

2 The combination of just a few keyframes and the loopOut expression (top) can create an animation that repeats from the first frame to the layer's out point (above).

2 ⌥+click (**Alt**+click) on the stopwatch for Rotation to enable expressions for this property. Carefully type (paying attention to capitalization):

```
loopOut("pingpong")
```

and press **Enter**. This will tell After Effects to follow the animation from the first keyframe to the last keyframe, then animate in reverse back to the first keyframe. It will then repeat this until the out point of the layer. RAM Preview: The widget now rocks back and forth continually.

3 There are other options available for the loopOut expression:

• Click on the expression text to select it, and replace the word **pingpong** with the word **cycle** (don't accidentally delete the parenthesis!). Press **Enter** and RAM Preview; the animation will go from the first to the last keyframe, then jump suddenly back to the first.

▽ gotcha

Return versus Enter

When you are finished working on an expression, remember to press the **Enter** key on the numeric keypad, not the normal **Return** (or **Enter**) key – the latter will add a carriage return to the expression, as if you wanted to write another line.

▽ gotcha

Copying and Pasting Expressions

If you right-click on a parameter name in the Timeline or Effect Controls panel, and if there is an expression applied to that parameter, you will see an option to Copy Expression Only. This makes it easier to copy and paste expressions between layers.

• Replace the word `cycle` with the word `offset`, press **Enter**, and RAM Preview: The animation will proceed from the first to the last keyframe, and remember the value of the last keyframe. It will then proceed from the first to last keyframe again, but the rotation will be offset by the value of the last keyframe, creating a continuous motion.

4 Slide the last keyframe earlier or later in the timeline, and RAM Preview again: The speed of the animation will change to match and continue for the duration of the layer.

Our version is in **Comps_Finished > LoopOut_final**. We had fun creating several copies of **watch_widget.tif**, then moved their last keyframe to vary their speeds.

▼ Alternate Loops

There are several variations on the loop function:

• `loopOut()` repeats the animation from the last keyframe to the end of the layer; `loopIn()` repeats the animation backward from the first keyframe to the start of the layer.

• If you don't want to loop all of the keyframes, you can say how many to loop. For example, `loopOut("cycle", 3)` repeats just the last three keyframes in an animation.

• You can also define how much time is looped, rather than the number of keyframes. `loopOutDuration("cycle", 1.5)` would repeat just the last 1.5 seconds of the keyframed animation.

▼ Expression Tips

Here are a few shortcuts and pieces of advice that you will find helpful as you use expressions:

• To delete an expression, **⌥**+click (**Alt**+click) on the stopwatch again. You can also select the expression text and delete it.

• To temporarily disable an expression without deleting it, click on its = icon; it will change to ≠. To re-enable it, click on the ≠.

• Selecting a layer and typing **U** will reveal the properties that have keyframes or expressions. To reveal just the properties with expressions, select the layer and type **E** **E**.

• Expressions use the same characters as your computer's numeric keypad for math functions: * means multiply (don't type an 'x'); / means divide.

• After Effects can convert an expression into normal keyframes: Select the property you want to convert and use the menu item Animation > Keyframe Assistant > Convert Expression to Keyframes.

• Expressions can be applied across multiple comps in the same project. To do this, you need to arrange their Effect Controls or Timeline panels – one panel for each comp – to see both at the same time, then use the pick whip to reach across them.

If you accidentally click in the wrong place in the middle of creating an expression, After Effects may think you're done when actually you're not. One of two things will then happen:

• If the expression fragment you wrote makes sense, After Effects will assume that's what you meant and enable the expression.

• If the expression fragment creates an invalid piece of code, After Effects will give you an error message and turn off the expression.

In either case, it is easy to correct the expression. Click in the area where you see the code, and either delete it and start again, or add the missing piece you intended. When you press **Enter**, After Effects will re-enable the updated expression.

tip

Behaviors

If you want to wiggle the position, rotation, or other transformations of a layer, we suggest you apply an animation preset (introduced in Lesson 3). Look inside the **Behaviors** folder for the presets that start with the word "Wiggle." These handy presets are based on the wiggle expression.

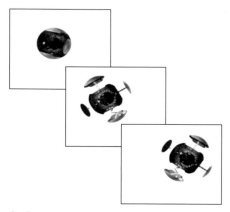

2–3 By adding the wiggle expression to Position and Rotation (right), you can make the gizmo fly drunkenly around the screen without adding keyframes (above). Gizmo courtesy Quiet Earth Design.

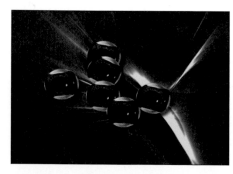

4 Duplicate the gizmo several times. Each copy will wiggle differently, automatically. Background courtesy Artbeats/Light Alchemy.

The Wiggle Expression

The third expression function we really feel you should learn is *wiggle*. This simple expression can add random variation to virtually any parameter. To use wiggle, you only need to think about two things: How fast do I want to wiggle, and how much?

1 Select Close All from the Comp panel's dropdown menu to close all previous comps. In the Project panel, locate and open **Comps > 05-Wiggle*starter**. It contains two layers: a background and a yellow gizmo that opens and closes.

2 Select **Gizmo.mov** and press **P** to reveal its Position. ⌥+click (**Alt**+click) on the stopwatch for Position to enable expressions. In the expression text area, type the following:

• Type "**wiggle(**" (without the quotes) to start the expression.

• How fast do you want the object to wander, in wiggles per second? Type that number, followed by a comma – for example, "**1,**" for one wiggle/second.

• How much do you want this value to wiggle by? Enter that number, followed by a closing parenthesis – for example, type "**200)**" for up to 200 pixels of wanderlust.

Your final expression should be

```
wiggle(1,200)
```

Press **Enter**, then RAM Preview – the gizmo will wander about the comp.

3 Let's have the gizmo rotate as it wanders, as if it's having trouble stabilizing. Say we want it to wiggle only half as fast (0.5 wiggles/second) and rotate by as much as 45°:

• With **Gizmo.mov** still selected, press **Shift R** to also reveal the Rotation parameter.

• Enable expressions for Rotation.

• Type "**wiggle(0.5,45)**" – the values we decided on – and press **Enter**. RAM Preview, and enjoy the flight of the drunken gizmo!

4 As if that isn't cool enough…wiggle also randomizes its actions based on the layer it is applied to. Select **Gizmo.mov** and duplicate it several times. You will now have a flock of out-of-control gizmos. Our version is saved in **Comps_Finished > 05-Wiggle_final**.

Expressions and Effects

Expressions such as wiggle are great, but it can be a bit of a pain to have to edit the expression text every time you want to tweak their values. The solution is a special set of effects known as Expression Controls. These effects don't change how an image looks; instead, they provide user interface elements that allow you to control expressions.

Expression controls will make it easier to tweak and keyframe the amount of wiggle applied to this text's distortion. Footage courtesy Artbeats/Under the Sea 1.

1 Open **Comps > 06-Effects*starter**. RAM Preview, then select **underwater** and press **E E** to reveal the expressions applied to it. We've added the wiggle expression to the Angle parameter of a Twirl effect to animate this text layer.

2 You may find our initial wiggle values a bit manic. What if you wanted to tweak it, or keyframe the amount and speed of the wiggle? The solution is to create your own user interface for the expression:

• With **underwater** selected, apply Effect > Expression Controls > Slider Control. The Effect Controls panel will open. Select the effect name Slider Control, press **Return** to highlight it, type in a useful name such as "**Wiggle Speed**" and press **Return** again.

• Then apply Effect > Expression Controls > Angle Control. Rename this effect "**Wiggle Amount**".

• Twirl these controls open in the Timeline panel. You need to expose their parameters to drag the pick whip to them. You can also drag the pick whip to the parameters in the Expression Controls panel.

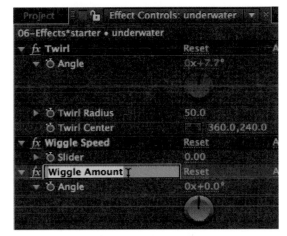

2 Add a Slider and Angle Control, and rename them to reflect the expression parameters you want them to control.

3 Back in the Timeline panel, click on the expression text to make it active.

• Carefully select just the 3 inside the parentheses; you want to replace it. Drag Angle's pick whip to the word Slider (not the effect's name) for Wiggle Speed. The expression code `effect("Wiggle Speed")("Slider")` will now appear in the timeline.

• Select the 60 after the comma, being careful not to select the comma or closing parenthesis. Drag Angle's pick whip to the word Angle for Wiggle Amount to replace it as well. Press **Enter** to accept this new expression.

4 Try keyframing the values for Wiggle Speed and Wiggle Amount, RAM Previewing to check your results. Our version is **Comps_finished > 06-Effects_final**.

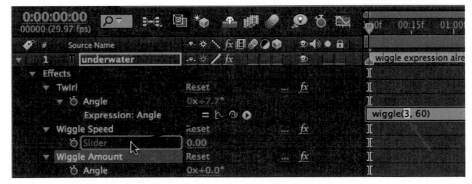

3 Select the first value in the expression, then drag the pick whip to the Wiggle Speed > Slider parameter (not the name of the effect). You can drag either to the Slider parameter in the Timeline panel or the same parameter in the Effect Controls panel.

Master Controller

Another great use for Expression Controls is to have one master controller for multiple layers – such as to pick colors.

1 Open **Comps > 07-MasterControl*starter**. It contains several lines of text, plus a shape layer (these layers are demonstrated in Lesson 11; they're a good replacement for solid layers). We created all of these in white. However, the client has requested they be something more colorful. Rather than change the color for each layer individually – every time the client changes her mind – let's set up a master color that controls all of the layers.

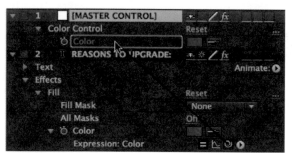

2 Choose Layer > New > Null Object, then select Layer > Solid Settings to open the Solid Settings dialog. Change its name to "**MASTER CONTROL**" to make it easy to find. Click OK, then turn off its Video switch (the eyeball icon).

3 Apply Effect > Expression Controls > Color Control to this new layer. Press **E** to reveal it in the Timeline panel, and twirl it down to reveal its Color swatch.

4 Select the first text layer: **REASONS TO UPGRADE**.

4 Use the pick whip to attach the text layer's Fill effect's Color parameter to the Color parameter of your **MASTER CONTROL** layer.

• To colorize it, apply Effect > Generate > Fill. The text will change to Fill's default color of red.

• **⌥**+click (**Alt**+click) on the stopwatch next to Fill's Color in the Effect Controls panel; this will reveal it in the timeline and enable it for expressions.

• Drag its pick whip to the word Color for the Color Control effect applied to **MASTER CONTROL**. Then press **Enter** to accept the expression.

5 Click on the Color swatch for **MASTER CONTROL** and change it (you can also click and "scrub" it directly in the timeline). Pick a color complementary to the background, such as a golden yellow. The text will change too.

6 After you've "wired" the other layers to be controlled by your master layer, you need to change only the master swatch (top) to change the color of all the layers wired to it (above). Background composite: Artbeats' Digital Aire and Digital Biz.

6 Time to make the other layers follow: In the Timeline, click on the word Fill for **REASONS TO UPGRADE** and type **⌘ C** (**Ctrl C**) to copy the effect. Twirl up the Fill effect to gain more space in the Timeline panel.

• Click on **dividing line** to select that Shape layer, then **Shift**+click on **24/7 e-commerce** to select all of the remaining text items below it.

• Type **⌘ V** (**Ctrl V**) to paste the Fill effect – with the expression that points to **MASTER COLOR** – to all of the selected layers. They will all change to yellow to match. (If not, it may be just a temporary caching issue.)

• Alter the Color for **MASTER CONTROL**, and all of the text and shape layers will update as well.

▼ Driven By Sound

Motion graphic designs are often more powerful if the visuals are tied to the audio. The combination of expressions plus a special keyframe assistant make this easier to accomplish.

1 Open **Comps > 08-Audio*starter**. It contains a soundtrack, background movie, and still image of a speaker. Our goal is to make the speaker's woofer bounce in and out in time with the music.

2 Expressions cannot directly access sound. However, After Effects has a keyframe assistant that can convert the comp's audio into keyframes applied to an Expression Controller.

Select Animation > Keyframe Assistant > Convert Audio to Keyframes. A null object named **Audio Amplitude** will be created at the top of the layer stack. Select it and press **U** to reveal its keyframes.

Drag the current time indicator along the timeline while watching the values for Both Channels (an average of the left and right channel amplitude). Some peaks go over 50, although it seems most values are under 30. (You can also use the Graph Editor to more clearly see how the keyframe values change over time; select the Both Channels > Slider parameter in the timeline to see its graph. Toggle off the Graph Editor when done.)

3 Select **speaker.jpg** and press **F3** to open its Effect Controls panel. We've already applied a Bulge effect to it and centered the bulge on the woofer. Scrub the Bulge Height parameter and watch the speaker flex. Get a feel for what would be a good range of values – maybe –1.0 to +1.0.

4 A few exercises ago, we showed you how to use the linear expression to convert between different value ranges. Remember

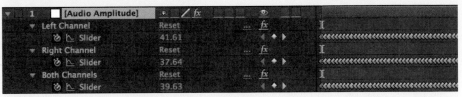

2 Convert Audio to Keyframes creates a null object with three Slider Control effects. Their keyframes match the amplitude of the comp's audio.

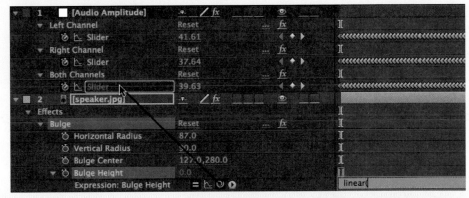

3 Use the pick whip to help connect Bulge Height to one of the Slider parameters.

3 *complete* Check our version **Comps_finished > 08-Audio_final** if you have trouble.

the mantra: As a parameter goes from A to B, I want to go from Y to Z.

• **⌥**+click (**Alt**+click) on the stopwatch next to Bulge Height to enable expressions.

• Type "**linear(**" to start the expression.

• Drag the pick whip to the parameter you want to follow: Both Channels > Slider. Then type a comma to separate it from the numbers that follow.

• As the audio amplitude goes from 0 to 40, you want Bulge Height to go from –1 to +1. So type "**0, 40, –1, 1**" followed by a closing parenthesis, "**)**".

Press **Enter** and preview – the woofer will now bop along with the music! If you want to have some more fun, duplicate the speaker, and instead of hooking the expression up to Both Channels, hook one speaker up to Left Channel and the other to Right Channel.

This same basic technique can be used to drive virtually any parameter with audio. If you got lost, our version is in **Comps_finished > 08-Audio_final**.

If you find you like this technique, check out the more powerful third-party plug-ins Trapcode Sound Keys or Boris Beat Reactor.

Soft objects – such as clouds and blurry backgrounds – are excellent candidates to frame blend. Footage courtesy Artbeats/Aerial Cloud Backgrounds.

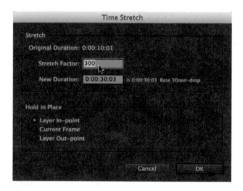

2 In the Time Stretch dialog, change the Stretch Factor to 300% to make the duration three times longer.

Time Games

We're going to change subjects. Now we'll deal with time: How to make it go by more smoothly, or to chop it up. We'll also look at how to change its speed.

Frame Blending

There will be occasions when you wish the action in footage you receive was happening faster or slower. It's relatively easy to "stretch" the footage, but this can result in staggered motion as frames are repeated or skipped. To help counter this, After Effects offers *frame blending* to smooth out the final motion.

1 Project file **Lesson_07.aep** should still be open. Select Close All from the Comp panel's dropdown menu to close all previous comps. In the Project panel, locate and open **Comps > 09-Frame Blending*starter**, and RAM Preview it. The comp contains one layer, which is footage of flying over clouds.

2 Say you wanted to slow down this clip to one-third of its original speed. In the Timeline panel, right-click on one of the column headers. Select Columns > Stretch to open this additional parameter column. Click on the current value (100%); the Time Stretch dialog will open. Change the Stretch Factor to 300% and notice how the duration is now three times longer. Click OK.

RAM Preview: You'll notice that the clouds move more slowly (each frame now plays for three frames), but are also jerky in their motion. Smoothing this out is something frame blending excels at.

3 In the middle of the Switches column header is an icon that looks like a film strip. This is the Frame Blend switch. Click once in the hollow area underneath this icon for **Aerial Clouds.mov** to enable basic frame blending. A pixelated backslash will appear in this hollow, saying this layer will have frame blending calculated when it renders.

If you want to see the effects of frame blending in the Comp panel's viewer before you render, you also need to enable the master Frame Blending switch along the top of the Timeline panel. To do this, click on the large filmstrip icon. RAM Preview again, and the cloud motion will be much smoother!

Ah, if only every clip worked that well… Unfortunately, you will find many clips that don't blend nearly as smoothly.

3 Enable Frame Blending for both the layer and for the entire composition to view the results in the Comp viewer.

4 Open **Comps > 10-Pixel Motion*starter**. This comp contains footage of a man walking past a car. Its Stretch column should be visible; you'll see that it has already been slowed down 300%. RAM Preview it; you will notice considerable staggering in the motion as frames are duplicated.

5 Click on the Frame Blend switch once for **Business on the Go.mov** to get the pixelated backslash. Then enable the large Enable Frame Blending switch.

RAM Preview. The result no longer looks like a stop motion animation, but it is still a bit rough. Stop the preview and press **Page Down** to step through the frames, and you will see echoes around sharp edges such as his jacket. Frame blending just mixes together adjacent frames; you can obviously see this crossfading effect on sharp footage.

Pixel Motion

6 Move to 00:08 where you can see ghosting. Click on the Frame Blend switch one more time, to where it becomes a solid forward-leaning slash. This enhanced frame blending mode is known as Pixel Motion. The ghosts will disappear. Pixel Motion studies the movement of every pixel between frames and calculates where each pixel should be to create a new in-between frame at the requested time.

RAM Preview; it takes longer because Pixel Motion requires a lot of computing power. The movement – particularly at the start and end of the shot – is much smoother now. However, it doesn't always work…

7 Move the current time indicator to 01:20, where the man's arm starts to swing away from his body and across the hood of the car. Pixel Motion – and other similar time interpolation algorithms – has more difficulty deciding what to do when one set of pixels crosses another. Press **Page Down** to slowly step through the next 30 or so frames, watching what happens around the man's arm: there's a lot of distortion. Pixel Motion is certainly not perfect; you should carefully study every shot you use it on. But when it works, it's great!

5 Normal frame blending creates visible ghosting along sharp edges as it crossfades between layers (right). Footage courtesy Artbeats/Business on the Go.

6 Clicking a layer's Frame Blend switch a second time changes it to a slash, which engages Pixel Motion. This creates brand new in-between frames, resulting in cleaner images (right).

▽ tip

After Effects comes with the Time > Timewarp effect, which performs a similar task as Pixel Motion but with more user control. There are also third-party solutions available; we like RE:Vision Effects' Twixtor (*www.revisionfx.com*).

7 Pixel Motion can cause strange distortion when objects are moving across each other. Notice what's happening to the windshield as the man swings his arm (below).

subject:

subject: Mark

subject: Mark Evans

The goal is to make the video look like a series of stills, while keeping the smooth type animation.

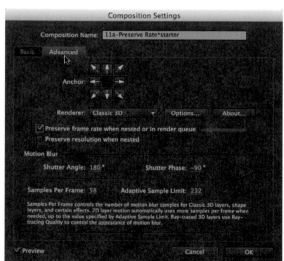

4 If you want a lower frame rate in a precomp to be honored throughout a project, enable its Preserve Frame Rate option in Composition Settings > Advanced.

Stop Motion Tricks

There are occasions when you don't want your animations to play back smoothly – for example, if you are trying to simulate a low frame rate "stop motion" look, or if you are trying to slow down an overly nervous effect that randomizes every frame.

Preserve Frame Rate

First, we need to show you how After Effects may try to thwart your attempts to create a stop motion look. Then we'll show you how to thwart After Effects.

1 In the Project panel, locate and open **Comps > 11a-Preserve Rate*starter** and RAM Preview it. It contains the footage of the executive walking to his plane that you saw in the previous exercise. Our plan is to make this footage look like it was a series of still photographs, shot as part of an undercover surveillance.

2 Type ⌘ K (Ctrl K) to open its Composition Settings. You will notice that it (and the footage) is at a film-like rate of 23.976 fps. Change the Frame Rate to 1 fps, and click OK. RAM Preview, and you will see After Effects "holds" on some frames and skips others to create that stop-motion look.

3 Open **Comps > 11b-Output Rate*starter**. This has the previous comp nested into it. Its frame rate is also set at 23.976 fps, to simulate how your final render might look in the final composite. RAM Preview: Hey, the motion's smooth again! What happened?!

The frame rate in each composition is actually a preview rate that takes effect just while working in that comp. If you nest it into another comp that has a different frame rate, After Effects will honor this second comp's rate and process any nested sources at this new rate. When you render, After Effects honors the rate in the Render Settings and calculates all the animation at *this* final speed. But there's a way around that…

4 In the Timeline panel, click on the tab for the comp **11a-Preserve Rate*starter** to bring it forward again. Type ⌘ K (Ctrl K) to open its Composition Settings again. Then click on the Advanced tab in this dialog. Check the box next to the text "Preserve frame rate when nested or in render queue" and click OK. This will lock in this comp's frame rate regardless of what you do with it later.

Bring **11b-Output Rate*starter** forward again, and RAM Preview: Now you have your surveillance look again. Notice that the text animation proceeds at the same pace as before; it is obeying the frame rate of the comp it's in – not that of the nested comp.

Calming Down Effects

Now let's use that Preserve Frame Rate trick to alter the behavior of effects:

1 Open **Comps > 12a-Numbers*starter**, and RAM Preview it. This small composition contains a solid with Effect > Text > Numbers applied to it: a very handy effect for creating data readouts and similar graphics.

2 Select the **numbers** layer and press **F3** to open its Effect Controls panel; you will notice that we've checked its Randomize option. RAM Preview: The numbers change every frame, making the result virtually unreadable.

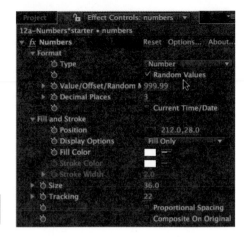

Some effects such as Numbers randomize on every frame. To slow them down, you need to place them in their own precomp with a lower frame rate and enable Composition Settings > Advanced > Preserve Frame Rate.

3 Type **⌘ K** (**Ctrl K**) to open this comp's settings, enter a lower frame rate such as 5 fps, and click OK. RAM Preview, and now you can take in each number before it changes.

4 Open **Comps > 12b-Nested*starter**. Its frame rate is 29.97 fps. The **12a-Numbers*starter** comp is nested into it. RAM Preview, and you'll see the numbers randomize on every frame again. This is the exact same issue as you observed with the footage in the previous exercise.

5 Bring **12a-Numbers*starter** forward again, open its Composition Settings, click on the Advanced tab, enable the Preserve Frame Rate option, and click OK. Now when you RAM Preview **12b-Nested*starter**, your lower frame rate will "stick" for the numbers.

Open our final versions of these two in the **Comps_Finished** folder – there's a neat trick in there. In **12a-Numbers_final**, we kept the full frame rate of 29.97 fps, but enabled the Preserve Frame Rate option to lock it in. In **12b-Nested_final**, we duplicated this precomp several times, then gave each one a different Stretch value to slow them down while maintaining the stop motion look.

▽ tip

Blended Motion

To create an interesting, dream-like look, combine stop motion and frame blending. Render out an intermediate movie of your stop motion animation, import this render, add it to a composition, and enable frame blending for this new movie.

In our final version (left), we duplicated the nested numbers precomp several times, and used Stretch to vary their resulting frame rates (right). This trick works because the precomp's frame rate is locked at 29.97 fps thanks to the Preserve Frame Rate option.

#	Source Name	Stretch
1	12a-Numbers_final	500.0%
2	12a-Numbers_final	700.0%
3	12a-Numbers_final	600.0%
4	12a-Numbers_final	900.0%
5	12a-Numbers_final	450.0%
6	12a-Numbers_final	1000.0%
7	12a-Numbers_final	667.0%
8	12a-Numbers_final	875.0%
9	12a-Numbers_final	525.0%
10	12a-Numbers_final	750.0%

Time Remapping

In After Effects, you can keyframe almost anything – including time itself. The door to this world is *time remapping*. This parameter allows you to define which frame of a source should be playing at a specific frame of your comp. After Effects will then speed up or slow down the footage as needed between keyframes to make this happen.

Adding Handle

Before getting too insane, let's start with a common task: extending the duration of a shot with a freeze frame.

1 Continue with **Lesson_07.aep**. If you've been following earlier exercises, close the old compositions by selecting Close All from the Comp panel's dropdown menu.

In the Project panel, locate and open **Comps > 13-Freeze Frame*starter**, and RAM Preview it. It contains a pan across the facade of the Supreme Court. The problem is, the news editor wants the shot to be longer so he can build and hold a title animation over it.

2 Select **Supreme Court.mov**. Then select the menu item Layer > Time > Enable Time Remapping. The Time Remap property will appear in the Timeline panel, with keyframes set at the beginning and end of the original duration of the layer.

▽ tip

Freeze Frame

If you want to freeze a clip on a single frame for its entire duration, make sure Time Remapping is disabled, move the current time indicator to the desired source frame, select the layer, and choose Layer > Time > Freeze Frame. This will create a single Time Remap keyframe at the chosen time. You can scrub its value in the Timeline panel to change it.

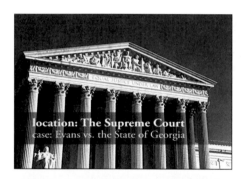

location: The Supreme Court
case: Evans vs. the State of Georgia

2 Select Layer > Time > Enable Time Remapping, and Time Remap keyframes will appear for the layer. As seen above, you can then drag the layer's out point later to extend the clip. The top image is from the final version in the **Comps_Finished** folder. Footage courtesy Artbeats/Washington DC.

3 You might also notice that the area past the end of the layer in the timeline has changed from being empty to being a gray bar that indicates there is more of the clip to reveal. Drag the clip's out point (the end of its layer bar) to the end of the comp. Scrub the current time indicator around the end of the timeline; the clip will be frozen on the last frame.

4 What if you need additional handle at the head of the clip as well? Click on Time Remap in the Timeline to select its keyframes and drag them later in time (be sure to move them together, keeping the same number of frames between both keyframes). Alternatively, you can slide the layer bar later in time, and then extend the in point of the layer earlier in time. In either case, the clip will freeze on the first frame and start playing when it crosses the first Time Remap keyframe.

Time Remap Fun

You're almost done with this lesson, so let's get crazy: We're going to use time remapping to make a glass of milk dance.

1 Open **Comps > 14-Time Remap*starter**, which contains a super-slo-mo shot of a glass of milk being dropped. RAM Preview it or scrub back and forth through the shot to get a feel for it.

Your task will be to alter the way this clip plays back to make it start playing in real time, slow down to a stop after it hits the table, then dance back and forth from there.

2 Select **Milk Drop.mov**, then select Layer > Time > Enable Time Remapping. Time Remap keyframes will appear in the Timeline panel at the beginning and end of the clip. Let's set some additional Time Remap keyframes to mark important frames in the original clip:

• Scrub the time indicator while watching the Comp viewer, looking for the frame just before the glass appears (around 02:07). In the Timeline panel, click on the hollow diamond between the keyframe navigator arrows to set a keyframe here. The diamond will turn gold. Note the time readout under the Switches column; this keyframe is remembering the frame number of the source.

• Scrub until the glass hits the table, around 04:13. Add another Time Remap keyframe here.

• Scrub until the splashing milk strikes a nice pose, such as when the lower splash rebounds off the table around 05:16. Set another keyframe.

• Pick one more good pose – such as around 07:16 – and set one more keyframe. These should be enough to have some fun with.

2 Scrub to find interesting points in time in the footage (top) and place Time Remap keyframes at these points (above). The time readout under the Switches column indicates the frame of the source footage. Footage courtesy Artbeats/Ultra Motion.

3 Move the current time indicator to around 05:00, and press **N** to end the work area here. Then press **Home**, and zoom in a bit on the timeline. Make sure the Info panel is visible; press **⌘ 2** (**Ctrl 2**) if it isn't.

4 The time before the glass appears is boring, so delete the first Time Remap keyframe at 00:00. Click on Time Remap to select the remaining keyframes, and drag them back until the first keyframe you created is now at 00:00. (Add the **Shift** key after you start dragging and the keyframe will snap to the time indicator.)

4 Delete the first Time Remap keyframe, and drag the remaining ones back so that the first keyframe you created (around 02:06 in the original clip) is now at 00:00 in the comp.

5 Deselect the first keyframe, and drag the others so that they start at 00:10 in the comp (right). The Info panel will confirm the time as you drag (below). Note that the value of this keyframe is 04:13 – that's the frame of the source footage that will play at this time.

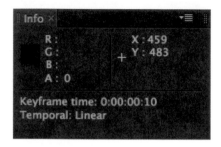

5 Our next idea is to make this drop appear as if it was happening at normal speed – even though the original footage was shot in slo-mo. To speed up playback, you need to reduce the amount of time between Time Remap keyframes.

Make sure all of the remaining Time Remap keyframes are still selected, then **Shift**+click on the first one to deselect just it. Drag your second keyframe to 00:10 in time. The Info panel will confirm where you are dragging it.

RAM Preview; the glass will drop fast, then slow down as soon as it hits the table – in other words, as soon as it crosses your second keyframe. Since you have not changed the spacing between the second keyframe and those after it, the clip will continue to play from here at its unaltered speed.

6 Now we want to slow down the milk splash until it stops, frozen at its first pose:

• **Shift**+click on the second keyframe to deselect it; the other Time Remap keyframes should remain selected.

• Increasing the time between Time Remap keyframes will slow down playback. Drag the remaining keyframes later in time, until the third keyframe is around 02:00 in the overall timeline.

• Deselect the third keyframe, and slide the fourth keyframe later to 05:00. Playback will now be slowed down from the second keyframe onwards.

• Select the third keyframe only, and press **F9** to apply Easy Ease to it. This will cause the playback speed to slow down as it approaches this keyframe, stop while on it, then speed up again as it moves past it.

▽ tip

Speed Shift

Although time remapping plus frame blending can create that play fast/play slow trick you see in commercials and music videos, bear in mind that big-budget productions shoot on high-speed film for better quality slow motion.

6 Your timeline should look like this after Step 6. By applying Easy Ease to the third keyframe, playback will slow to a stop at this keyframe, then pick up speed again.

RAM Preview to check your progress so far. The milk splash will slow down until it encounters the third keyframe, then resume playing again. (We've already enabled frame blending for you, so playback shouldn't look *too* rough…)

7 Time to make the milk dance by playing backward. To do that, we need to create a Time Remap keyframe that stores an earlier time than that stored by a previous keyframe.

- Select the second keyframe, which stores a source time of 04:13 when the glass first hit the table. Copy it.

- Move the current time indicator to 03:00 (past the keyframe where the milk was splashing), and Paste.

7 By pasting an earlier Time Remap keyframe after a later one, you can reorder time so that playback backs up, then goes forward again.

RAM Preview, and absorb for a moment what is going on: Playback is initially fast, slows down to a stop, plays backward (retracing its steps to an earlier Time Remap keyframe), then resumes in the forward direction as playback progresses to the last Time Remap keyframe you created in step 2.

8 To see what's going on in a graphical manner, select Time Remap, and type **Shift F3** to open the Graph Editor. Click on the eyeball icon along the bottom and make sure Show Selected Properties is enabled. Then click on the icon to its right (Choose Graph Type) and make sure either Auto Select Graph Type or Edit Value Graph is selected.

The white graph line indicates how time is progressing during this composition. It starts at just past 2 seconds into the clip (the first keyframe you created in step 2), moves very quickly to just past 4 seconds into the clip, moves more slowly to 05:15 (where it encounters the keyframe with Easy Ease applied), then plays in reverse (arcs downward) to just past 4 seconds. The upward slope after this keyframe indicates playback is going forward again.

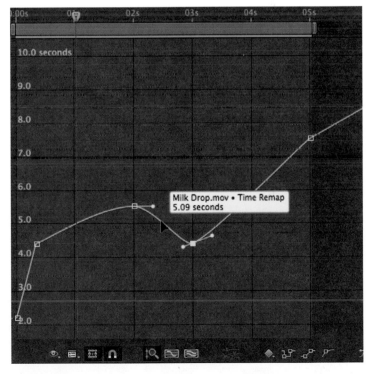

Then click on the Choose Graph Type button again and select Show Speed Graph. Move your cursor along the graph and you'll get a reading for the velocity of the layer at that point in time. When viewing either graph type, you can toggle on Graph Type > Show Reference Graph; the gray line that appears will show you the other graph type for comparison.

This composition, up to this point in time, is saved in **Comps_Finished > 14-Time Remap_so far**. Feel free to continue from here by turning off the Graph Editor and further manipulating the Time Remap keyframes, or have fun applying time remapping to your own footage.

8 The Graph Editor gives a more pictorial view of what is happening to the clip's playback over time. A steep slope means fast playback; a downward slope means playing in reverse. We've also converted the fourth keyframe to Auto Bezier to smooth out the reversal in playback.

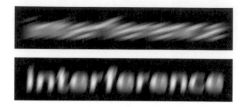

In **Idea1–Nervous Text**, Directional Blur's Blur Length and Direction are both controlled by wiggle expressions.

▽ factoid

Expressing Paths

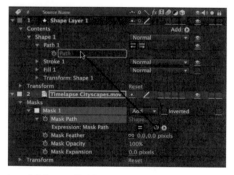

In addition to linking parameters, you can link mask paths, paint paths (Lesson 10), and shape paths created with the Pen tool (Lesson 11). Make sure you enable expressions for them and drag the pick whip tool between parameters named "Path."

Idea Corner

The single most useful thing you learned in this lesson (aside from the pick whip tool) may well be the wiggle expression. It's something we use all of the time, creating everything from wild automated animations to slight "human" imperfections to our movements.

One of the richest areas to explore is using wiggle to control effect parameters. In the **Idea Corner** folder in this lesson's project file are a few simple examples of combining wiggle with effects:

Idea1–Nervous Text: We applied a Directional Blur effect to a text layer, then used wiggle to randomize both the blur's Direction and Blur Length parameters, creating a "vibrating with energy" look. We added expression controllers for the wiggle speed as well as the maximum blur length and angle; experiment with them to see the different looks they create.

When you preview this comp, you may notice that about half the time, you see no blur. This is because when you set the wiggle amount for blur length to, say, 100, wiggle is generating numbers between –100 and +100. However, Directional Blur doesn't understand the concept of a negative blur length, so it just calculates no blur when this value is less than 0. You will notice a similar result if you apply wiggle to a layer's Opacity: Since Opacity can't go below 0 or above 100, it will "clip" at these values.

Idea2–Lens Flare: We used a wiggle expression on the Flare Brightness parameter to cause the flare to flicker.

Wiggle's random values are always added to a parameter's underlying value. We keyframed this value – Flare Brightness – to decrease as the timelapse footage behind faded into night.

We then added one more trick by basing wiggle's "how much" parameter (the second number inside the parentheses) on this underlying value, so the number that wiggle adds also fades down over time.

In **Idea2–Lens Flare**, wiggle causes the lens flare to flicker. Footage courtesy Artbeats/Timelapse Cityscapes.

Idea3–Electric Arcs: We employed the Advanced Lightning effect applied to a solid layer. With this effect, you can define where the bolts start and what direction they move in. We set the start to be the middle of the comp, then let wiggle decide where they should end, resulting in a wandering arc that searches around the frame.

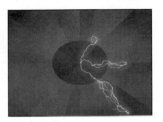

In **Idea3–Electric Arcs**, wiggle is used to randomize the end points of a trio of Lightning effects.

We added Expression Controls for the speed and amount, applied to a null object. We could then duplicate the solid layer that had the lightning effect, and all of the duplicates would point at the same master controller layer. Also remember that wiggle behaves differently for every layer it is applied to – so the result was three independently wandering arcs of electricity.

Quizzler

• Play the movie **Quizzler > Quiz_Gears.mov**. There are three wheels, scaled 100%, 50%, and 25%. Only the largest one has keyframes, but they all stay in perfect sync. How would you make this happen using expressions? Use the comp **Quizzler > Quiz_Gears*starter**; two different solutions are saved in the **Quizzler Solutions** folder.

When wheels touch, they rotate in opposite directions. And their speeds are based on their relative sizes. Can you create the expressions needed to make this work?

• In Lesson 3, you learned how to loop footage. In this lesson, you learned how to loop keyframes. Can you loop an entire composition? Yes, you could nest it and then duplicate it end to end; you could also render it out, import the resulting movie, and loop that in Interpret Footage. But in this lesson you've also learned a pair of techniques that can be combined to loop a nested composition as a single layer without having to render it first. See if you can figure it out using the **Quiz_Looped Comp*starter** comp. The answer is in **Quizzler Solutions > Looped Comp**.

▼ **More on Expressions**

There are a number of references available on expressions and JavaScript. Our favorites include:

www.motionscript.com
This website teaching expressions and scripting was created by expert Dan Ebberts, who actively participates in a number of online forums.

www.aenhancers.com
This community web forum includes discussions, tutorials, and a library of After Effects expressions, scripts, and animation presets.

After Effects Expressions
by Marcus Geduld (Focal Press)
The only book currently available dedicated to expressions in After Effects, starting with basic concepts and ending with creating physical simulations.

JavaScript: A Beginner's Guide
by John Pollock (Osbourne)
Of the many books available on the subject, this one contains some of the simplest, clearest, mose useful explanations we've seen of the JavaScript language.

3D Space

Add a new dimension to your animations.

In This Lesson

207 enabling layers for 3D

208 moving and rotating layers in 3D space

210 multiplaning effects

212 3D motion paths

213 multiple views

214 adding a camera; camera settings

215 using the camera tools; customizing 3D views

216 moving and animating cameras

218 building a camera rig

220 layer and camera auto-orientation

222 camera depth of field blur

224 3D lights

226 casting shadows

228 Light Falloff *(new in CS5.5)*; Material Options

230 Ray-traced 3D Renderer *(new in CS6)*

231 extrusion and beveling

233 bending footage layers

234 transparency; index of refraction

236 reflections

238 environment layers

239 ray-tracer image quality

240 Fast Previews

Getting Started

Make sure you have copied the **Lesson 08-3D Space** folder from this book's disc onto your hard drive, and make note of where it is; it contains the project files and sources you need to execute this lesson.

3D Space is one of the most rewarding areas to explore in After Effects. A simple switch allows each layer to move in the Z dimension – closer to and farther away from the viewer – in addition to left and right. Layers may also be rotated in 3D, which gives the ability to view them from new angles. You can selectively add cameras and lights to a composition, allowing you to cast shadows and move around your imaginary 3D world. And as of After Effects CS6, certain layer types may be extruded or bent, providing depth.

The beauty of 3D in After Effects is that you don't *have* to build an entire world to use it – you can be quite selective, adding a little perspective here, a little lighting there. If you're new to 3D, don't worry – we'll go slowly, adding to your skill set a step at a time.

Basic 3D

Any After Effects layer can be placed into 3D space. Even without adding lights or cameras, this allows some neat perspective tricks, plus it permits objects to move more naturally as they animate about your composition.

As soon as you enable the magical 3D Layer switch, some of the rules change with regard to how you move and arrange layers in the Comp and Timeline panels. We'll use this first exercise to get you up to speed on this new reality.

1 Open this lesson's project file **Lesson_08.aep**. In the Project panel, locate and double-click **Comp > 01-Basic 3D*starter** to open it. It contains two overlapping text layers. First, let's reinforce the way you would normally interact with these layers:

- With 2D layers, the stacking order in the timeline determines who renders on top. Swap the order of **Enter a New** and **Dimension** in this comp; the higher one in the Timeline panel is the one drawn the most forward in the Comp viewer.

- With 2D layers, you can move them only in the X (left and right) and Y (up and down) dimensions. To make a layer appear to move closer or farther away, you need to play with its Scale value.

- 2D layers rotate like a pinwheel around their Anchor Point. (We've already centered the Anchor in these text layers to get a nice rotation.)

2 Undo any of your experimenting in Step 1 to return to **Enter a New** on top of **Dimension**, both set to 100% scale. Make sure the Switches column is visible in the Timeline panel (press **F4** if it isn't).

Select both layers, then click in the hollow box underneath the three-dimensional cube icon: This is the 3D Layer switch. The layers will not change size or place in the Comp viewer. However, you *will* see red, green, and blue axis arrows sticking out of the Anchor Points of layers that are selected. Press **P** to reveal their Position values: There is now a third value, known as Z. It defaults to 0.0.

Mastering 3D space opens the door to natural multiplaning, bringing illustrations to life, and creating 3D logos or other objects with depth and dimension.

2 When you enable their 3D Layer switch, layers gain a third Position value: Z (below). In the Comp panel, selected 3D layers will have a set of red, green, and blue axis arrows sticking out of their Anchor Points (above).

▼ Scale, Quality, and 3D

Scaling up layers beyond 100% usually reduces image quality. But with 3D layers, you can't just look at their Scale value; their size also depends on how close the layers are to the virtual camera.

To tell if a layer is being scaled larger than 100%, duplicate it, turn off the 3D Layer switch for the duplicate, and set its Scale to 100%. If the duplicate is still the same size or larger than the 3D version, you're okay. If the duplicate is smaller, you are "blowing up" the 3D version: Get a higher resolution source, or move the layer farther away from the camera.

Layers that continuously rasterize (covered in Lesson 6, page 176) are your friend in 3D space, as After Effects can rerender them as needed so that they stay sharp. This includes text and shape layers (Lesson 11). You can also enable the Continuous Rasterization switch (the sunburst icon) for Illustrator layers; we've already done that for you as required throughout this lesson.

3 As you reduce the Z Position value for a 3D layer (left), it will move toward you, including moving in front of other layers with a higher Z Position value (right), regardless of the stacking order in the Timeline panel.

▽ factoid

Two Renderers

As of After Effects CS6, you have two 3D rendering engines to choose from: Classic 3D (formerly Advanced 3D) and Ray-traced 3D. This is set in Composition Settings > Advanced and is displayed in the upper right corner of the Comp panel. Use Classic 3D for these initial exercises; it's faster.

4 If you see an X, Y, or Z next to the cursor, your dragging will be constrained to this dimension. (X is red, Y is green, and Z is blue.)

5 3D layers have four rotation parameters: Orientation, plus Rotation for X, Y, and Z.

3 Press **F2** to deselect the layers. While closely watching the Comp viewer, scrub the third Position value (Z) for **Dimension**. As you scrub to the left to reduce the Z Position value, **Dimension** will appear to grow larger as it comes toward you. As you scrub to the right (increasing Z Position), it will appear to grow smaller as it moves away from you.

Key Concept #1: *The size a 3D layer is drawn is determined by a combination of its Scale value and how close it is to the camera. (If you have not explicitly created a camera, After Effects uses an invisible default 50mm camera.)*

There is a second phenomenon you might have noticed: If the Z Position value for **Dimension** is less than the Z Position for **Enter a New**, **Dimension** will appear to pop in front of **Enter a New**, even though **Dimension** is below it in the timeline.

Key Concept #2: *With 3D layers, stacking order in the timeline no longer determines which one draws on top in the Comp viewer. What matters now is how far they are from the camera. (If they are the same distance, then stacking order matters.)*

4 In addition to scrubbing the Position values for 3D layers, you can also drag the layers around in the Comp panel. However, pay attention to the cursor as you try this:

• If you place the cursor near the layer's Anchor Point and do not see an additional letter at the cursor's tail, you can freely drag a layer in any direction.

• If you see an X, Y, or Z next to the cursor, your dragging will be constrained to that dimension. To ensure you get this special cursor, place it near the desired axis' arrow.

5 Set **Dimension**'s Z Position back to 0. With **Dimension** selected, press **R**: Instead of getting just Rotation, you will see *four* parameters! Here's what they do:

• Orientation is used to "pose" a layer in 3D space – for example, to face up or to the right. This parameter won't animate as you might expect, so don't use it for keyframing.

• Z Rotation is the same as the normal 2D Rotation you're used to.

• Y Rotation spins the layer around its vertical (up/down) axis. Go ahead and scrub it!

• X Rotation spins a layer around its horizontal axis.

You can scrub these Rotation values, or press **W** to select the "Wotate" (Rotate) tool and manipulate them directly in the Comp panel. (Keep an eye out for the axis letters replacing the circular cursor – like Position, they indicate your dragging will be constrained to that one dimension.)

As you play with X and Y Rotation, notice that **Dimension** will intersect **Enter a New** as portions of them cross – another cool bonus of 3D space. (If layers ever don't intersect as you expect, check if there is a 2D layer in-between.)

6 Scrub **Dimension**'s X or Y Rotation values to 90° while watching the Comp viewer: They will disappear when viewed on-edge.

Key Concept #3: By default, 3D Layers in After Effects do not have any thickness. A major new feature in After Effects CS6 is the ability to extrude text and shape layers; we'll explore that later in this lesson.

Press **V** to return to the Selection tool. Continue to experiment with Position and Rotation values for **Enter a New** and **Dimension**, including enabling keyframing for them and trying an animation or two.

If you feel more like watching than doing right now, twirl down the **Comps Finished** folder in the Project panel and double-click **01-Basic 3D_final** to open it. Press **0** on the numeric keypad to RAM Preview. We've animated Z Position and Y Rotation for the two text layers to make them fly and swivel into position.

Once you've digested this, open **01-Basic 3D_final2** and RAM Preview. In this comp, we removed the Position animation and instead applied a 3D Text Animation Preset to each text layer. (As discussed back in Lesson 5, individual characters in text layers may also exist in 3D space.)

5–6 You can rotate 3D layers in each of their three dimensions using the Rotation tool. Note how **Dimension** intersects **Enter a New** as they cross.

▽ gotcha

Avoiding the Rotation Flip Flop

When the Rotation tool is selected, a popup menu appears on the right side of the Tools panel. Here you can toggle the tool's behavior between editing Orientation and editing Rotation values for a 3D layer. However, if you use the Rotate tool to alter Y Rotation or Orientation and go beyond ±90°, the X and Z values flip by 180° (try it!). That's why we prefer scrubbing values directly in the Timeline panel.

In **Comps_Finished > 01-Basic 3D_final2** we applied 3D Text Animation Presets to our swiveling text.

▽ factoid

Disney and Multiplaning

Disney is often credited with inventing the multiplane animation camera to create more realistic cartoon animation. This device placed animation plates at different distances from a real camera.

1 In 2D, the relationships between layers do not change when they move as a group. Illustration courtesy iStockphoto, RUSSELLTATEdotCOM, Image #1858615.

▽ tip

3D View Shortcuts

You can use **F10**, **F11**, and **F12** to quickly switch between alternate 3D Views. To change which view is assigned to which key, select your desired view, hold down the **Shift** key, then press **F10**, **F11**, and **F12**.

4 The 3D View menu offers six orthographic views and three custom views in addition to the Active Camera view. Only the Active Camera view can be rendered.

Multiplaning

Perspective in 3D is not just placing things closer, farther away, or at an angle to the camera. Another important 3D trick is known as *multiplaning* where objects close to you whiz by quickly, while those farther away appear to move more slowly. This phenomenon can be faked in 2D by animating each object by hand. In 3D space, it happens naturally. While demonstrating this trick, we'll also show you some highly useful alternate ways to view your work.

1 In the Project panel's **Comps** folder, double-click **02-Multiplaning*starter** to open it. This composition contains a set of 10 layers all parented to a Null Object (Lesson 6) – which is a great way to group layers. RAM Preview this comp: All of the buildings drift from right to left, as if locked together.

2 The plan is for you to arrange each of the buildings and trees at different distances from the imaginary camera. Type **⌘ A** on Mac (**Ctrl A** on Windows) to select all of the layers. Enable the 3D Layer switch for any one of them, and it will be enabled for all selected layers. Type **P** until Position is revealed for all of the layers. Then press **F2** to deselect them – otherwise, you might accidentally edit all of the layers at the same time!

When viewing only the result, it is easy to get lost in space. Therefore, After Effects provides a number of alternate 3D views. You can also see more than one view at the same time, making it easier to understand what is going on.

3 Along the bottom of the Comp panel is the Select View Layout popup menu; it currently says 1 View. Click on it and choose 2 Views – Vertical. The Comp panel will split into two. (If you have a wide monitor, you might prefer 2 Views – Horizontal; if you do, click the right half of the Comp panel when we say top.)

4 With the Selection tool active, click in the top half of the Comp panel – there will be yellow triangles in the corners of its Comp panel to confirm its selection. Now look at the 3D View popup to the left of Select View Layout: It should say Active Camera (if it doesn't, set it to this). The Active Camera is what your 3D camera sees and is the view that will ultimately render.

Click in the bottom half of the Comp panel, then on the 3D View popup. The first six choices below Active Camera are called *orthographic* views. These are the standard "drafting" views that observe your 3D scene from a specific side, with no perspective distortion. Select Top for now; think of this as looking down on your "stage."

Click on a layer in the Comp view; it will be highlighted in the Timeline panel. Scrub the Z Position (the third value) for this layer to a negative value: You will see it move down in the Top view (toward the camera), while the same object comes forward in the Active Camera view.

Select the lower view and click on the 3D View popup again. The last three choices are temporary camera angles you can use while rearranging layers. Select Custom View 3. Now as you scrub the Z Position for a layer, you get a much better idea of what's going on on your "stage."

5 Move the buildings, trees, and clouds (but not the null!) back and forth in Z to create an arrangement you like. Press **Home** and **End** as needed to see all the layers in the Active Camera view.

6 When you think you're getting close to a good arrangement, RAM Preview: The Active Camera view (the top) will calculate and play back your animation. Now as the buildings drift past, the objects closer to your imaginary camera (lower Z Position values) move faster, and those farther away (higher Z Position values) move more slowly, causing their relationships to change over the course of the animation. Note that you didn't have to create any additional Position keyframes to make this happen!

Continue to tweak. When you want to see your final animation at full size, set Select View Layout to 1 View and 3D View to Active Camera, and preview again. For comparison, our version is saved in **Comps_Finished > 02-Multiplaning_final**. Save your project before moving on.

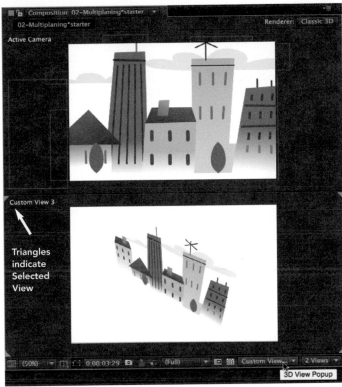

Triangles indicate Selected View

3–5 To better visualize the position of objects in 3D space, it is helpful to set the View Layout to 2 or 4 Views, then pick different 3D Views for each. Here we have set the top view to Active Camera and the bottom to Custom View 3.

6 In 3D, the relationships between layers arranged at different positions in "Z space" drift automatically as they move.

3D Animation

We often tell clients "it's called 3D because it takes three times as long." This is particularly true when it comes to editing motion paths for a 3D layer, as you need to look at the path from multiple angles to fully understand what's happening.

1 Select Close All from the Composition panel's dropdown menu to close all of your previous comps. Return to the Project panel and open **Comps > 03-3D Animation*starter**.

This comp contains four small layers with their 3D Layer switches already enabled, and are slightly separated in Z. Your goal is to make the layers **Under** and **Pressure** fly down into their current locations.

2 Since **Under** and **Pressure** are already in their "at rest" positions, this is a good place to set keyframes:

• Move the current time indicator to around 01:00.

• Select **Under** and **Pressure**, and press ⌥ P (*Alt* P) to turn on the stopwatches for Position and reveal this property in the Timeline panel.

3 Think about where you want these layers to fly in from. For example, it may be fun to have **Under** fly in from the upper left, and **Pressure** from the lower right, both starting out closer to the viewer.

• Press *Home* to return to 00:00.

• Press *F2* to deselect the layers.

• Hover your cursor over **Under**'s blue axis arrow until you see a Z appear next to it. Click and drag downward, and you will pull **Under** forward in Z (confirm this by watching its Position Z value in the Timeline panel).

• Drag **Under** to the upper left of the frame; this moves it in X and Y.

• The dotted line in the Comp panel is **Under**'s motion path. Look for the slightly larger dots; these are the handles for the keyframes. Click and drag these dots to create an arcing motion path. If you can't see them, press ⌘ (*Ctrl*), click on the keyframe icon in the Comp viewer and drag out the handles (you may need to move in time so you can see the icon clearly).

• Repeat the same for **Pressure**, making it arc in from a different location at 00:00, and changing its Position Z value.

The goal in this exercise is to have the two words arc in and slam down in 3D space. Editing their motion paths will be trickier than working in 2D.

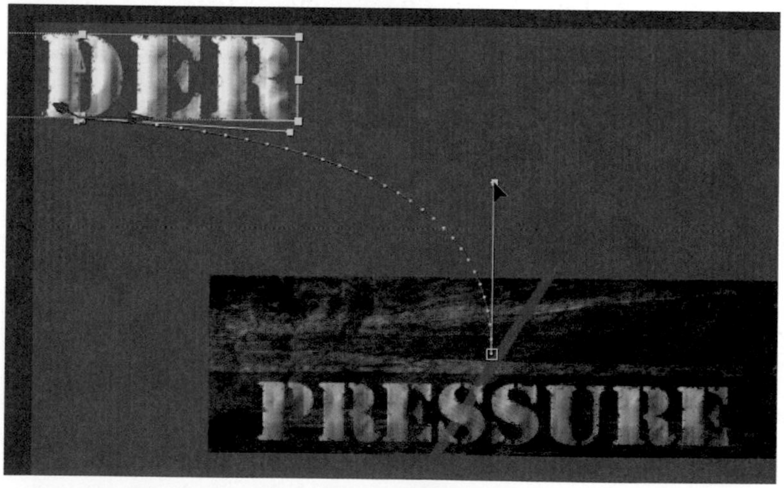

3 Pull **Under** forward in Z (top), and drag it to the upper left corner. Then drag its keyframe handles to create an arcing motion path (above).

Editing in Multiple Views

By working just in the Active Camera view, you've seen only part of the picture of what's really going on with your motion paths.

4 Set the 3D View popup to Left to view the layers edge-on from the side. Select **Under** to see its motion path. Scrub the time indicator and you might see that this layer is actually sliding in from above, rather than slamming straight down.

To edit more interactively, set the Select View Layout popup to 4 Views. Click on the upper left view, and set its 3D View popup to Top. Set the upper right view to Front, the lower left view to Left, and the lower right view to Active Camera. This way, you can see your path from all angles as well as the final result.

(You will probably need to reduce the Magnification to 50% for each view to fit everything in. If you still have trouble seeing all the layers, turn the page and read *Using the Camera Tools*.)

5 Select **Under** again to reveal its motion path. Drag the motion path handles in the Left view while watching the result in the other views. Try to arrange a straighter entry into the second keyframe, while keeping the swooping-in motion you had originally. This will require some back-and-forth editing to get it the way you want. Press **0** to RAM Preview, and the Active Camera view will play back your results. After you're happy, click on the word Position for **Pressure** to highlight its motion path, and adjust it.

Feel free to get more creative with the move, such as starting the words completely offscreen. Our version is in **Comps_Finished > 03-3D Animation _final**. Of course, yours does not have to look like ours – just as long as you feel you have a better grasp of editing motion paths in 3D space. Save your project before moving on.

After you have set up your animation, select a layer and choose Layer > Transform > Auto-Orient. Choose the Orient Along Path option and click OK. The layer will now bank and turn as it zooms down into position. We used this trick in our **03-3D Animation_final2** comp.

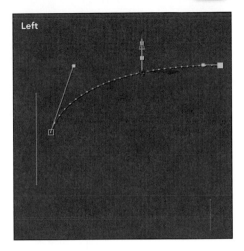

4 When you view your motion path from the Left view, you may find it doesn't arc into its final position quite as you had planned. This is the danger of editing paths only in the Active Camera view.

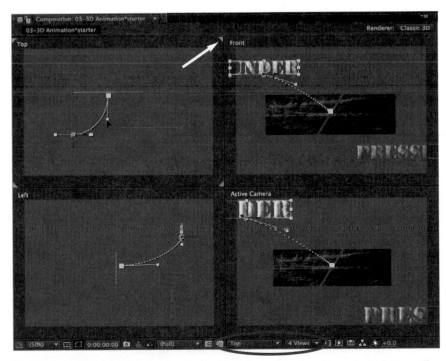

5 Edit in one view while watching the result in the other views (the selected view will have yellow triangles in its corners). It will take a bit of compromise to get a path you're happy with. Remember, what really counts is the result in the Active Camera view!

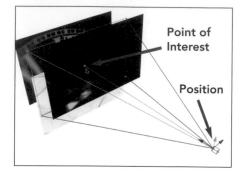

Point of
Interest

Position

The Position value for a camera defines
where its body is located. It may optionally
have a second value known as the Point
of Interest, which helps aim the camera.
Its field of view is illustrated by the lines
radiating out from the camera's body.

The 3D Camera

Moving layers in 3D space is very useful, but the real fun happens when you
move a camera through that space. Once you know how to animate a 3D layer,
you have mastered most of what you need to animate a camera. The main
differences are:

- There is a different set of tools used to move and view the cameara. They are
explained in *Using the Camera Tools* on the next page.

- It has Angle of View and Zoom parameters (the two are linked), which affect
how much of the composition is visible, as well as relative perspective.

- It optionally has an "anchor point" that is called its Point of Interest. Rather
than a center point, this is where the camera is being aimed.

Adding a Camera

1 Close all previous comps by selecting Close All from the
Comp panel's dropdown menu.

Return to the Project panel and open **Comps > 04-Basic
Camera*starter** – it contains an expanded version of the logo
from the previous exercise. The layers that make up the logo
have already been arranged in 3D space for you. Rather than
animate these layers, this time you're going to animate a
camera around them. They should have their Position values
exposed; we've arrayed them around Z = 0.0, as this will be
the center of our 3D world

2 Select Layer > New > Camera; the Camera Settings dialog
will open. Set the Type popup in the upper left to Two-Node
Camera, which will expose its Point of Interest.

The Preset popup near the top simulates a number of
common lenses. Higher numbers are telephoto lenses, which
means the camera will have a large Zoom value and reduced
perspective distortion; smaller numbers are wide-angle lenses,
which translates to a small Zoom value and exaggerated
perspective distortion. The 50mm preset matches the comp's
invisible default camera, so pick it for now. Disable the Enable
Depth of Field option, then click OK.

3 Make sure your new **Camera** layer is selected. Press **P** to
reveal its Position, then **Shift A** to reveal its Point of Interest.
Note that the Point of Interest's Z value is 0.0, which places it
in the center of our logo layers.

2 Select New > Layer > Camera, set Type to Two-Node
Camera, and select the 50mm preset.

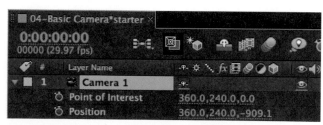

3 Initially, the X and Y values for the camera's Position and
Point of Interest are the middle of the comp. Position's Z
equals the Zoom value, while Point of Interest's Z is set to 0.0.

▼ Using the Camera Tools

After Effects provides a set of Camera tools for moving the 3D camera as well as panning and zooming around the alternate 3D views. They are selected from the Tools panel; you can also press **C** to toggle between them.

△ The Camera tools are used for moving the camera in Active Camera view, as well as for editing the layout of the other views.

Moving the Camera

To use these tools for manipulating the camera, you need to be in a Camera view (such as Active Camera or Camera 1) and have a camera layer selected.

Orbit Camera tool: Use this tool to rotate how the camera views the scene. If the camera's Auto-Orientation is set to Orient Towards Point of Interest (the default), you will be moving the body of the camera (its Position), and it will pivot about its Point of Interest. If the camera's Auto-Orientation is Off (see page 220), you will be editing the Orientation values for the camera.

Track XY Camera tool: This tool pans around a scene by moving the camera up, down, left, and right. It edits the X and Y Position and Point of Interest values.

Track Z Camera tool: Use this tool to push the camera in on a scene or to pull it back. Normally it edits just the camera's Z Position. If you click, then press **⌘** (*Ctrl*), *then* drag, it will edit both the Z Position and Point of Interest values together.

The biggest "gotcha" comes when you create one keyframe for the camera's Position, go to another point in time, and move the camera using the Orbit Camera tool to create a second Position keyframe. Although you may have seen a nice arc while you were moving the camera in the Comp view, the resulting motion path will be a straight line between keyframes. Edit their Bezier handles to create a rounded arc.

Navigating the Views

If you are in any of the Orthographic (Front, Left, Top, Back, Right, Bottom) or Custom views, these tools do not edit the camera's values. Instead, they zoom and pan around these views strictly for preview purposes.

Orbit Camera tool: Use this tool to re-pose these temporary views on your 3D scene. It does not work in the Orthographic views.

Track XY Camera tool: This replaces the Hand tool and pans around your view.

Track Z Camera tool: This acts as a continuous zoom tool, allowing you to smoothly zoom in and out on your desired view *without the camera icon changing its size.*

Unified Camera Tool

If you have a three-button mouse, try using the Unified Camera tool. The three buttons switch between Orbit, Track XY, and Track Z modes. Make sure you assign the action Middle Click to your middle mouse button.

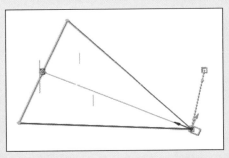
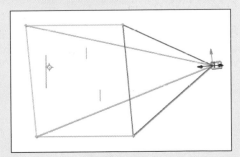

△ The Orbit Camera tool affects the Position of a default 2-point camera (left) or the Orientation of a 1-point camera (right).

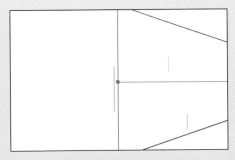
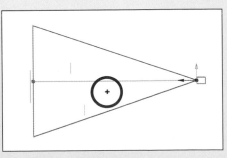

△ If you find yourself zoomed in too close in a view (left), use the Track Z Camera tool to zoom out and the Track XY Camera tool to recenter your view (right).

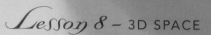
▼ The Camera Settings Dialog

This initially daunting dialog is really just asking you two things: how wide or narrow is the camera's field of view, and how much it should blur out-of-focus layers.

If you are familiar with cameras and lenses, this dialog gives you a number of ways to precisely define your camera, including by Angle of View (a common 3D program parameter), or by Focal Length and Film Size (the camera sensor size). You can also define your depth of field by aperture or f-stop.

If you are a camera newbie, the parameter you are most interested in is Zoom. Set Units to Pixels: When the camera is the Zoom value's distance from a layer, the scale of the layer will not be altered in 3D space. All other layers will appear larger or smaller depending on how close to or far away they are from the camera. The smaller the Zoom value, the more exaggerated this effect will be.

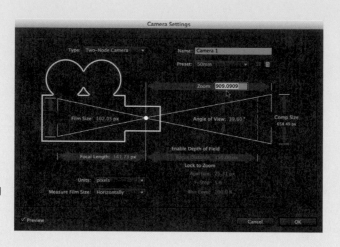

4 Set up 2 Views in the Comp panel: Active Camera (upper) and Top (lower). Use the Camera Track tools to zoom out and pan the Top view until you can see the camera and the layers. Background courtesy Artbeats/ Liquid Abstracts.

4 In the Comp panel, select 2 Views – Vertical. Set the upper view to Active Camera, and the lower view to Top. You will probably need to set the Magnification for both to 50%.

Is the Top view zoomed in too close to see the camera as well as the layers? Hover the cursor over the Comp panel and press **C** until the cursor changes into a two-way arrow (the Track Z tool). In the lower view, drag down or to the left until the camera's field of view outline is about half the width of the viewer. Press **C** three times to change the cursor to a four-way arrow (the Track XY tool) and drag upward until the layers and the camera are centered in this view. (These tools are discussed in *Using the Camera Tools*, page 215.)

Moving the Camera

5 As with any 3D layer, you could scrub the camera's values in the Timeline panel or drag it directly in the Comp panel (the same rules for axis constraints apply).

For a more interactive experience, select the Orbit Camera tool: With the cursor over the Comp panel, press **C** until it changes into a ball with an arrow curving around it. Drag around in the Active Camera view (the upper one) and watch how the camera moves in the Top view below. You can also watch the Position values change in the Timeline panel.

Press **V** to switch back to the Selection tool. In the Top view, drag the boxy camera icon (this is its Position); notice how moving it changes the perspective in Active Camera view.

6 Make sure the lower view is selected – there will be yellow triangles in its corners. Set the 3D View popup for it to Front.

In the Front view, carefully click on the crosshair: This is the camera's Point of Interest, which determines what is centered in its sights. Drag it while watching the result in the Active Camera above to get a feel for how it works. Also try dragging it in other views, such as Custom View 3.

7 Time for the payoff: setting up a camera move!

• Press **Home** to make sure you are at 00:00.

• Click on the stopwatches for **Camera**'s Point of Interest and Position to enable keyframing.

• Use whatever combination of tools and views you prefer to set up a camera pose you like.

• Press **End** to move to the end of this comp and set up a new camera pose.

RAM Preview and observe your camera move. Even though you set up the start and end poses, you might not be happy with how it looks in the middle. Rather than adding a third keyframe, try adjusting the motion paths for the camera's Position and Point of Interest. These are common Bezier paths, just like those you edited for 3D layers in the previous exercise. You can switch Select View Layout to 4 Views to get a better picture of your path, or pick one view at a time to work in.

Our version is **Comps_Finished > 04-Basic Camera_final**. We decided to leave the Point of Interest focused on the middle of the logo, and instead created a series of alternating fast and slow Position moves to generate surprise and excitement. We enabled motion blur for the logo layers to further enhance the impression of speed.

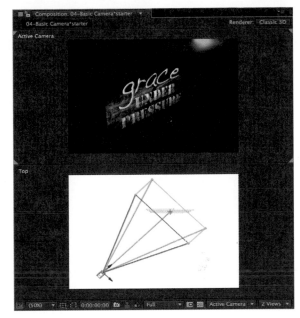

5 Use the Orbit Camera tool to pose the camera off-axis to the logo.

6 Use the Selection tool to move the Point of Interest, changing what is centered in the camera.

Motion blur enhances the effect of fast 3D camera moves – but there is a render penalty involved.

3 For best results, make sure the Camera's Point of Interest is located at the point you wish to orbit around.

4 With an orbit camera rig, the camera is parented to a null object with its Point of Interest equaling the null's Position.

Camera Rigs

It can be challenging to move a camera precisely the way you want using just the Camera tools and Bezier paths. Some advanced animators build *camera rigs* in which the camera is attached to one or more null objects using parenting (Lesson 6). This allows you to break down complex animations into simpler components, with each null dedicated to a specific movement such as rotation.

As mentioned back in *Using the Camera Tools* (page 215), orbiting – when the camera circles around an object or point in space – is one of the harder moves to perfect using conventional tools. However, an orbit camera rig is one of the easiest to build – especially since Adobe added a menu command for it in After Effects CS5.5.

1 Return to the Project panel and open **Comps > 04b-Camera Rig*starter**. It contains a scene similar to the previous exercise, where all the layers are arranged around a Position of 360, 240, 0. Make sure the Parent column is exposed in the Timeline panel; if it isn't, press **Shift F4**.

2 Add a Layer > New > Camera. Make sure Type is set to Two-Node Camera, select the 35mm preset, and click OK. Note how the layers separate more in space: Their Position values didn't change; the 3D perspective has been exaggerated by using a "shorter" lens with a wider Angle of View (the default camera was 50mm).

3 Press **P** and then **Shift A** to reveal the camera's Position and Point of Interest (POI). Note that the Point of Interest is also at 360, 240, 0: For the orbit rig to work as expected, the POI must be located at the point you wish to orbit around; life will also be easier if the Camera's X and Y Position values are the same as its POI before you build the rig.

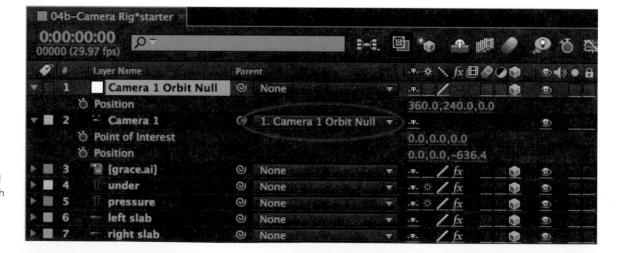

4 With **Camera 1** still selected, choose Layer > Camera > Create Orbit Null (CS5 users, see note below). A new layer named **Camera 1 Orbit Null** will be added to the comp, and the camera will be parented to it. Press **P** to reveal the new null's Position. Note that the camera's original Point of Interest value has been copied to **Camera 1 Orbit Null**'s Position. The camera's Point of Interest has been zeroed out, and its Position reflects just its offset from its parent.

*(Note: If you are using CS5, create a Layer > New > Null Object, enable its 3D Layer switch, and make sure the null has the same Position as your camera's POI. Then parent **Camera 1** to this new null.)*

5 Change the Select View Layout popup to 2 Views – Horizontal. If needed, set the left side view to Top and use the Camera tools to zoom back until you can see the logo layers in the middle and camera at the bottom of the view. Press **V** to return to the Selection tool.

6 Select **Camera 1 Orbit Null** and press **Shift R** to reveal its Rotation and Orientation values in the timeline. With the current time set to 00:00, enable keyframing for Y Rotation. Then locate to 3:00 in time and scrub the Y Rotation value: The camera will be swung around the null as if on the end of a pole.

Set Y Rotation to 1x+0° (precisely one rotation). Press **Page Up** to go back one frame to 02:29 and press **N** to end the Work Area here. RAM Preview; you will now have a perfectly looping orbit animation.

7 Scrub the camera's Z Position value. Because it is parented to **Camera 1 Orbit Null**, this value now controls how far away the camera is from the center of the orbit. Keyframe the camera's Z Position to create a push in or pull back during the orbit.

> ▼ **Rendering Breaks**

Be careful of how 2D and 3D layers are arranged in your timeline. Only those 3D layers that are adjacent to each other in the timeline stack will render as a group inside the 3D renderer. When they are part of the same group, they can intersect and cast shadows on each other.

You can easily break this inter-action by placing certain types of layers between the 3D layers. These layers include: 2D layers (with the exception of null objects); any adjustment layer other than lights (even if its 3D switch is enabled); and any layer that has a layer style applied to it. If needed, rearrange the layers in the timeline.

8 Scrub **Camera 1 Orbit Null**'s Y Position. This simulates an "elevator" move with a camera crane, moving up and down relative to the objects in your world. Keyframe this parameter as well. RAM Preview, and imagine how hard it would have been to create the same move using a Bezier motion path!

Our result is in **Comps _Finished > 04b-Camera Rig_final**. Don't forget that you can stagger the timing of the individual property movements, as well as use the Graph Editor (Lesson 2) to add speed changes.

8 Camera rigs make it possible to create complex, precise movements out of a series of very simple animations such as Y Rotation or Z Position.

Cameras and Auto-Orientation

Both 2D and 3D layers can be set to automatically orient themselves along their motion paths. 3D cameras bring a couple of additional twists to this idea…

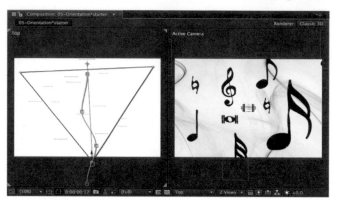

2 In the layout 2 Views – Horizontal, with the **Camera** layer selected, you can see an overview of the camera path from the Top view (left) and the result in Active Camera view (right). Initially, the camera always points toward its Point of Interest; a graphical line connects the camera's body to this point. Background courtesy Artbeats/Dreamlight.

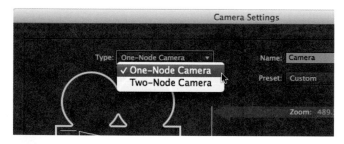

3 The Camera Type setting determines whether it has a Point of Interest (Two-Node) or not (One-Node).

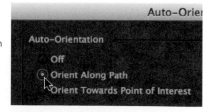

4 The Auto-Orientation dialog provides an alternative way to determine where the camera is pointed.

1 In the Project panel's **Comps** folder, double-click **05-Orientation*starter** to open it. This composition contains a number of music symbols hanging in 3D space, a 3D camera, and a 2D background plus soundtrack. RAM Preview; the camera gently weaves through the notes.

2 Set Select View Layout to 2 Views – Horizontal. Verify that the left view is set to Top and the right view is set to Active Camera.

Select the camera and study its path: We have set its Point of Interest to focus on the last symbol and animated its Position (the camera's body). As the camera body moves left and right, it turns to always face its Point of Interest.

Alternate Orientations

Let's say we want a more exciting animation. The Two-Node Camera type we originally chose can be a bit tricky to animate for complex flight paths, as you would have two motion paths to worry about – so let's try some alternatives.

3 Select the Camera layer and press **P** followed by **Shift A** to reveal its Position and Point of Interest. Then double-click it to open its Camera Settings dialog. Change the Type to One-Node Camera and click OK. The Point of Interest parameter, as well as the line that connects it to the camera in the Comp views, will disappear, leaving just the Position value for the camera's body. Scrub the current time indicator, and note how the camera always points straight ahead.

If the camera were a car or airplane, it would turn to follow its motion path rather than always face the same direction. You can animate the rotation of the camera to simulate this turning. Or, you can let After Effects do the work for you!

4 With the camera still selected, open Layer > Transform > Auto-Orient. Off is the same as a One-Node Camera. Select the option Orient Along Path and click OK.

As you drag the current time indicator through the time-line, in the Top view you will see the camera automatically turn to follow its path. In the Active Camera view, the result will be a much more obvious movement as the camera swoops around. This makes it easy to create thrill-ride-style 3D camera animations.

However, be aware that using the Orient Along Path option will often require more work on your part! Make sure there is always something interesting to look at as the camera swings around. You may also need to smooth out kinks in your motion path that will cause sudden camera movements. This is where mastery of the Graph Editor and use of the roving keyframes option (both discussed in Lesson 2) come in handy.

Orient Towards Camera

RAM Preview or scrub the current time indicator through time. As the camera swings along its path, it occasionally looks at some of the musical symbols from quite a skewed angle. The resulting perspective distortion can often look interesting. Other times, it distorts objects such as client logos a bit too much for their taste, and can break the illusion of 3D space as you view layers from their sides. Therefore, there's one more auto-orientation trick you should know about:

5 Click on layer 2 (**repeat**), then **Shift**+click on layer 14 (**demisemiquaver**) to select all of the music symbols. Study the Comp panel for a moment, in particular how the axis arrows for the symbols are all pointing in the same direction.

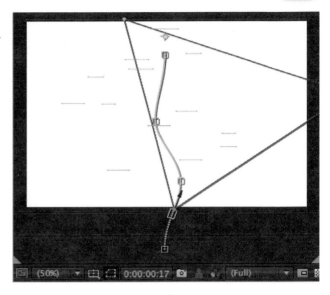

4 Setting the camera to Orient Along Path means it will automatically steer along its motion path, creating more obvious movements during its flight. (However, it does not "bank" the camera to lean into its turns the way an airplane or bike rider might. To simulate this, you will need to manually keyframe the Z Rotation for the camera.)

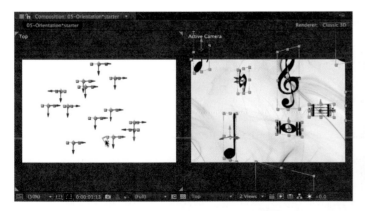 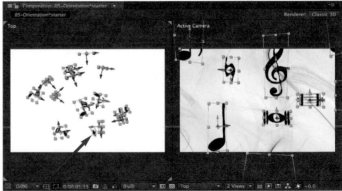

Open Layer > Transform > Auto-Orient again – this time for the 3D layers, rather than the camera. Select the option Orient Towards Camera, and click OK. Watch what happens in the Comp panel: All of the symbols swivel to face directly toward the camera. You can really see this behavior when you scrub the current time indicator. (If you are uncertain whether you followed our directions correctly, compare your result with our **Comps_Finished > 05-Orientation_final**.)

5 Normally, layers point where they're told by their Orientation and Rotation parameter (left). However, 3D layers can be set to automatically orient toward the 3D camera as it moves around (right). (The red arrow is pointed at the camera.)

Camera Depth of Field Blur

An important visual cue is focusing sharply on a point in space and blurring other layers that are either closer or farther away. After Effects has long supported this *depth of field* blur; its quality and speed were both vastly improved in After Effects CS5.5. Let's work through an example of enabling Depth of Field and employing it to focus on a specific layer:

1 Open **Comps > 05b-Depth of Field*starter**. It contains a variation of the scene you worked with in the previous exercise, employing a Two-Node camera. Initially, all of the musical symbol layers (as well as the 2D background) are perfectly sharp. If you haven't already, select View Layout to Two Views – Horizontal, with the left view set to Top and the right view set to Active Camera.

2 Double-click the **Camera** layer to open its Camera Settings dialog. To better simulate a real camera's measurements, change the Units popup in the lower left to millimeters. Note that the Film Size parameter defaults to 36mm, which matches the width of traditional 35mm still image film. This also matches the sensor size of the Canon 5D camera, which is popular for shooting video and some movies.

▽ tip

Lock to Zoom

The camera's Zoom parameter defines at what distance layers are scaled 100% by 3D perspective. You can optionally enable Lock to Zoom in the Camera Settings dialog so the focal plane for depth of field blur matches the 100% zoom plane.

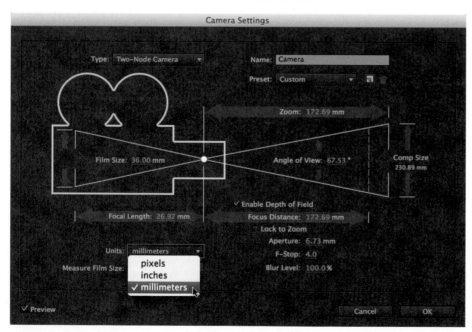

3 The bottom half of the Camera Settings Dialog helps you simulate real cameras.

3 Check the Enable Depth of Field switch in the lower right portion of this dialog. This enables a set of parameters underneath, including the interrelated Aperture size and F-Stop. Make sure Lock to Zoom is disabled (you will be setting the Focus Distance in the next few steps) and set F-Stop to 4, which is a common setting for a fairly shallow Depth of Field effect. Click OK when done.

4 With **Camera** still selected, type **A A** (two As in quick succession) to open its Camera Options in the Timeline panel. These parameters are near identical to the ones you saw in the Camera Settings dialog, with the ability to keyframe them.

Move the current time indicator to 01:14. Scrub the Focus Distance parameter while watching your two Comp panel views. In the Top view, you will notice an additional line moving perpendicular to the Point of Interest line. This is the focal plane: Layers that are along this line will be perfectly in focus. You can visually confirm this by glancing at the Active Camera view. Layers will get progressively blurrier the farther away they are from this line. If this blur is hard to see, you can magnify its effect by increasing the Blur Level.

5 After Effects can help set the Focus Distance parameter. Set the current time to 04:27 or later, which is the end pose. Select the **repeat** layer (#2) and *Shift*+click the **Camera** layer. Then choose Layer > Camera > Set Focus Distance to Layer (in After Effects CS5, you will have to manually scrub Focus Distance until the focal plane aligns with the final hero layer). The **repeat** layer will become sharp. Scrub the current time indicator; notice how the various layers fall into and out of focus as the focal plane passes through them during the animation.

6 Say you want to "pull focus" so the **repeat** layer is always sharp. With **Camera** and **repeat** still selected, choose Layer > Camera > Link Focus Distance to Layer. After Effects will create an expression that dynamically adjusts the Focus Distance parameter to keep the chosen layer on the focal plane. (Note that this works only with Two-Node cameras and in After Effects CS5.5 and later.) Return to 1 View and RAM Preview; you can also open our **Comps_Finished > 05b-Depth of Field_final**.

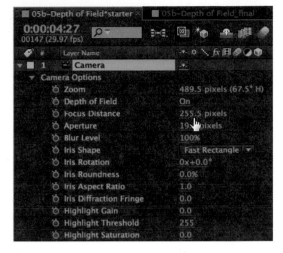

4 Most of the camera's parameters may also be edited (and animated!) directly in the Timeline panel.

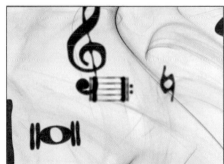
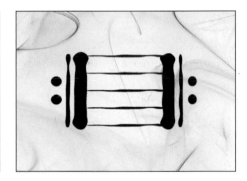

5 Selective use of depth of field blur can help guide the user's focus during an animation.

In After Effects CS5.5 and later, you also have a number of Iris and Highlight parameters you can adjust to tweak the visual qualities of the blur – such as changing the Iris Shape from Fast Rectangle to the more realistic Hexagon. These parameters have been duplicated in the Blur & Sharpen > Camera Lens Blur effect, which may be applied to 2D footage. Experiment with the effect settings in **Comps_Finished > 05c-Camera Lens Blur_final** for a taste of its creative possibilities.

◁ The Iris parameters (both in the 3D camera and the 2D Camera Lens Blur effect) can create beautiful looks with bright highlights. Footage courtesy Artbeats/Timelapse Cityscapes.

1 If no lights are present, 3D layers are evenly lit. Footage courtesy Artbeats/Time & Money.

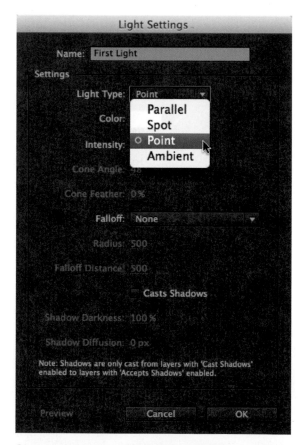

3 You can edit the Light Settings when you make a new light, or any time later during a project. These settings can also be edited in the Timeline panel.

3D Lights

If you don't add a light to a scene, After Effects will automatically illuminate all 3D layers equally so that they are just as bright as they were as 2D layers. However, adding a 3D light can considerably enhance the mood of a scene.

1 Save your project. Select Close All from the Comp panel's drop-down menu to close all previous comps. Then open **Comps > 06-Basic Lights*starter**. It contains a single 2D video layer.

2 To see the results of 3D lights, you need at least one 3D layer.

• Enable the 3D layer switch (the cube icon) for **Clock.mov**.

• Then enable the Lock switch for the layer so you don't accidentally move it while playing with your light.

3 Select the menu item Layer > New > Light. The Light Settings dialog will open. Let's go over some of its parameters:

• *Light Type* decides how the light rays are cast. *Ambient* illuminates everything evenly; *Parallel* casts straight rays as if from a distant source. More useful are Spot and Point. *Point* is akin to a bulb hanging in space. *Spot* is the most versatile, as you can control how narrow a cone it casts. Choose Point for now.

• *Intensity* is the brightness of the light. It can be cranked over 100% to blow out a scene or reduced below 0% to create pools of darkness in a complex scene. Set it to 100% for now.

• *Cone Angle* and *Cone Feather* are available only with the Spot light type (and are disabled with a Point light). They control how wide an area of light is cast and how soft its edges are.

• *Color* is – ta da! – the color of the light. Start with a white light. You can later change it to a pale blue to cool down a scene, or a pale orange to warm it up.

• We'll deal with falloff and shadows in the next two exercises, so leave them off for now.

• Give your light a useful name such as **"First Light"** and click OK. (If you get a warning dialog, you missed step 2.)

4 The corners of **Clock.mov** will darken a bit as the light falls away, creating a subtle vignette. **First Light** will be selected; press **P** to reveal its Position, then **Shift T** to reveal its Intensity.

4 Point lights can be used to create simple vignettes and hot spots by playing with their position and increasing their intensity.

- Scrub the Z Position parameter for **First Light**. As the light moves closer to the layer, the illuminated area will become smaller and more focused; back it away, and the layer will be illuminated more broadly and evenly.

- You can also scrub the X and Y Position values or place your light interactively by dragging it around the Comp viewer. The same rules apply as for any other 3D layer: If you click on one of the axis arrows or otherwise see an axis character next to your cursor, your dragging will be constrained to that dimension.

- Scrub Intensity: It controls how brightly the layer is lit. (Return it to somewhere between 100% and 150% for now; don't be shy about editing it later.)

5 Double-click your light layer (**First Light**) to reopen its Light Settings. Set Light Type to Spot, Cone Angle to 60, Cone Feather to 0, and click OK. Now you will have a sharply defined pool of light, rather than a soft vignette. (If the pool is very small, set the light's Z Position to –400 to back it away from the layer.)

A longer list of parameters should twirl open in the Timeline panel. You will see that Spot lights are similar to normal 3D cameras in that they have both a Position and a Point of Interest. Just like a camera, the Point of Interest helps you aim the light. If the light is selected, you will see both the light's body and its anchor-point-like Point of Interest in the Comp panel. Practice dragging these around to develop a feel for how they work.

Now experiment with scrubbing its Cone Angle and Cone Feather parameters. You can quickly achieve a variety of cool looks – especially when you also manipulate its Position and Point of Interest to control the angle the light is cast! In **Comps_Finished > 06-Basic Lights_final** we had fun animating the light's parameters. Play with your own light and save your project before moving on.

▽ tip

Light Settings

To edit a light's settings, double-click it, or select the layer and type **A A** to reveal its parameters in the Timeline panel.

▽ tip

Flickering Lights

Try adding a wiggle expression (Lesson 7) to a light's Intensity to make it flicker. Cone Angle and Cone Feather are fair game as well. Apply wiggle to a Spot light's Point of Interest to create an automatic searchlight.

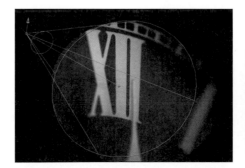

5 You can achieve a variety of interesting looks with Spot lights.

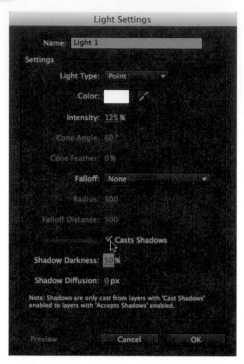

2 Create a new light and make sure you enable Casts Shadows.

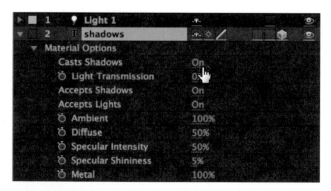

3 Type **A A** (two **A**s in quick succession) to reveal a layer's Material Options, including Casts Shadows.

Casting Shadows

Lights in After Effects also have the ability to cast shadows. For shadows to happen, you need three things:

- A light enabled to cast shadows.

- A 3D layer to cast the shadows.

- A 3D layer to receive shadows, that is also farther away from the light than the layer casting the shadows.

In this exercise, you will become familiar with setting up shadows, plus how lights, layers, and shadows interact.

1 Return to the Project panel and double-click **Comps > 07-Shadows*starter**. It contains two layers that are already enabled for 3D and spread out in Z space: Layer 1 (**shadows**) is a text layer, and layer 2 (**shadow catcher**) is a still image.

2 Select Layer > New > Light. In the Light Settings dialog, set the Light Type to Point and Intensity to 125%. Enable the Casts Shadows option, and for now set Shadow Darkness to 50% and Shadow Diffusion to 0 pixels. Click OK, and a new **Light** layer will be added to your comp. The illumination of the layers will change, but no shadows will be visible yet…

By default, 3D layers can receive shadows, but do not cast them. This is because shadows require a lot of computing power, and After Effects does not want to slow you down if you didn't want them. In this case, we do want them:

3 Select the layer **shadows** and type **A A** to reveal its Material Options. The very first parameter is Casts Shadows; as we hinted, it defaults to Off. Click on Off to toggle it to On; the shortcut to toggle shadows on and off for selected layers is **⌥ Shift C** (**Alt Shift C**). Now you will see some rather large shadows cast from the text!

3 *continued* Casts Shadows can be toggled between Off (A), On (B), and Only (C). Background courtesty Artbeats/Exteriors.

While you're here, let's quickly explore two other useful options:

• Click on the Casts Shadows value one more time, and it will toggle to Only. Now you will see only the shadow, not the original layer.

• Toggle Casts Shadows back to On, then scrub the Light Transmission parameter. At 0%, the shadow is black; at 100%, it is the color of the layer casting the shadow. (By the way, this also applies to multicolored layers, including video…) Set it back to 0% for now. Then press **P** to reveal this layer's Position again, just to remember where it resides in 3D space.

• Select **shadow catcher** and type **A A** to reveal its Material Options. Click its Accepts Shadows parameter to toggle through its options. After Effects CS6 added an Only option (which we'll put to use in Lesson 9). Return it to On when done.

4 Select the **Light** layer to see its axes in the Comp panel and press **P** to reveal its Position. Move the light either by scrubbing its Position values or interactively dragging it in the Comp panel. As you do so, the size and position of the shadow changes. Note that as the light gets closer to the layer casting the shadow, the shadow gets wider. Back the light away in Z space (high negative values), and the shadow will get smaller.

5 Scrub the Z Position values for **shadows** and **shadow catcher**. The closer these two layers are to each other, the tighter the shadow. Return them to their original positions when done (**shadows** at 360, 278, 0; **shadow catcher** at 340, 42, 250).

6 Select **shadow catcher** and press **R** to reveal its Orientation and Rotation properties. Scrub its X or Y Rotation values to tilt it in relation to the layer casting the shadow: The shadow will be angled too. (If you rotate it too far, you will see the edge of this layer; there will be numerous occasions where you need to enlarge layers to avoid this embarrassment during 3D animations!)

7 Select **Light** again, and type **A A** (two **A**s in quick succession) to reveal its Light Options. Scrub the Shadow Diffusion parameter: This controls how soft the shadow is at the cost of longer render times. Then scrub Shadow Darkness: It controls how dark ("dense") the shadow is.

Now that you have an idea of how shadows interact, go ahead and put your newfound skills to work by setting up an animation for the light and perhaps the 3D layers.

▽ **tip**

Shadow Only

The Shadow Only option added in CS6 is useful for creating "shadow catcher" layers; these can simulate 3D shadows falling on 2D layers. More on this technique in Lesson 9.

▼ **The Comp Viewer**

An initially disconcerting feature of working with the 3D views other than Active Camera is that a portion of the Comp panel will render your layers, while the rest (the pasteboard) will not. The size of this area has no effect on your final render; it merely reflects your current zoom level. This is why we suggest keeping Magnification set to Fit up to 100%, and using the Camera tools to zoom and pan around your views.

6–7 You can quickly create interesting looks by altering the position and rotation of the 3D layers and the light. Increasing the light's Shadow Diffusion parameter creates soft shadows – at the price of longer render times.

Light Falloff

So far, the lights you've created have gone on forever to illuminate all layers in a composition. This is not realistic; the strength of real light falls off over distance. After Effects CS5.5 and later has a Light Falloff feature:

1 Open **Comps > 08-Light Falloff*starter**. It contains a set of layers arranged at varying distances from the camera. You can confirm this numerically by selecting all the layers and pressing **P** to reveal their Position values or visually by setting Select View Layout to 2 Views – Horizontal and setting the left view to Top.

2 Add a Layer > New > Light. Set Light Type to Point, Color to white, Intensity to 125%, and disable Casts Shadows. Click on the Falloff popup to reveal options: None, Smooth, and Inverse Square Clamped. The last one is a more accurate representation of reality, where light gets weaker over distance; so choose Inverse Square Clamped for now. Set Radius to 500 and click OK.

3 You should notice the illumination varying across your layers. With your light selected, press **P** to reveal its Position, set Z Position to –500, and move the light to the right so it's in front of the right-hand speaker.

4 Type **A A** to reveal the Light Options in the Timeline panel. The Radius determines how large your light is; the Intensity of the light starts falling off from this distance outward. At its initial value of 500, it just touches the middle

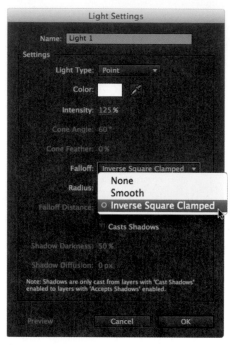

2 The Falloff parameters help simulate real lights.

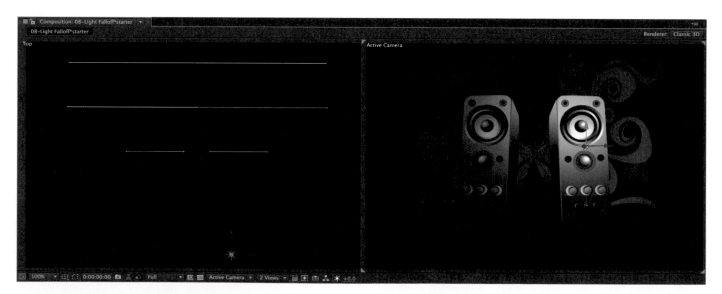

3–4 With Falloff set to Inverse Square Clamped, layers that are within the Radius value are fully illuminated, while layers farther away are lit more dimly. Illustration courtesy iStockphoto, exdez, Image #2066496.

layer (**flourishes**). Scrub the Radius value to get a feel for how this size interacts with the illumination of the various layers. For example, a value of 350 means the outer edge of full illumination just touches the surface of the right speaker and falls off across the rest of its face as well as the other layers in the scene.

5 Change Falloff to Smooth. This makes light falloff easier to control: Radius still sets the size of the light, while Falloff Distance determines how far away from the Radius the light stops completely.

6 Set Falloff Distance to 10 and scrub Radius. Now you can use the light to "reveal" the layers as the light expands to touch and encompass more of their surface. You can use one of the Custom Views to get a better idea of what the light is doing to the layers that are farther back.

7 Experiment with balancing the Falloff Distance, Radius, and light's Position against each other to control which portions of the layers are revealed. We've created an animation demonstrating some of the possibilities in **Comps_Finished > 08-Light Falloff_final**.

6 A Falloff type of Smooth gives you control over how far a light reaches into a scene.

▼ Material Options

In addition to a light's settings, the Material Options for each 3D layer control how that layer reacts to lights. For example, *Diffuse* determines how strongly a layer receives illumination from most lights; *Ambient* sets how strong it is illuminated only by lights with a Light Type of Ambient. If you have trouble illuminating a specific layer strongly enough, increase these values. A light's Color affects the Diffuse and Ambient illumination of the layers.

Specular Intensity determines the strength of the specular highlight (the "hot spot") that is added to the layer's Diffuse value, while *Specular Shininess* determines how small ("tight") that highlight is. To create more dramatic lighting effects, increase both of these values above their defaults. (High values work well with the Classic 3D Renderer; a little goes a long way with the Ray-traced 3D Renderer.)

Metal determines the color of the specular highlight. Its default of 100% means the

Ö Ambient	100%
Ö Diffuse	50%
Ö Specular Intensity	50%
Ö Specular Shininess	5%
Ö Metal	100%

layer's underlying color is used for the highlight; a value of 0% means the light's color is used instead. We usually leave this at 100%, unless we're having trouble illuminating dark layers (which means the highlight would also be dark) – then we decrease Metal to see more of the light's color in the specular highlight.

▽ tip

Animation and Extrusion

You can use any of the text animation tricks you learned back in Lesson 5 along with extruded and ray-traced text; the new 3D geometry will be rendered for each frame on the fly.

▽ tip

Draft Mode

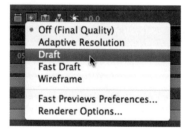

If you find your computer is too slow to work through these exercises, click on the Fast Previews button at the bottom of the Comp panel and select Draft mode. This reduces the quality of the ray tracer, speeding it up in exchange. We will discuss Fast Previews as well as ray-tracing quality later in this lesson.

Ray-traced 3D Renderer

For years, "3D" layers in After Effects did not have any depth, which became readily apparent when viewing layers on-edge. The underlying rendering engine was previously referred to as the Advanced 3D Renderer; as of CS6 it is now known as the Classic 3D Renderer.

After Effects CS6 introduced a new ray-traced 3D rendering engine that allows vector-based text and shape layers (Lesson 11) to be extruded and beveled, giving them thickness. Pixel-based layers such as movies or photographs may not be extruded as of CS6, but they can be bent, which can still add dimension to a scene. Additional features offered by the Ray-traced 3D Renderer are the ability for 3D layers to be transparent as well as reflective, plus the ability to wrap a layer around a composition as an *environment map*.

Using the new Ray-traced 3D Renderer does come at a cost:

• It is more computationally intensive than the Classic 3D Renderer – significantly so. Once you introduce features such as transparency or reflections, your render times will skyrocket. As of CS6, the cure for this is to use a computer with an Adobe-approved NVIDIA video card or chip ("GPU") that supports its CUDA programming language. A list of these supported cards may be found at *www.adobe.com/products/aftereffects/tech-specs.html*; check it before purchasing a new computer or video card as the list will expand over time. Note that many Mac laptops do not have an NVIDIA CUDA-compatible chip, which severely handicaps their usability with this feature.

• As of CS6, it does not support many 2D-related compositing features, such as effects, masks, mattes, stencils, and blending modes. Other 2D layers inside the same composition may use these features, just not 3D layers while the Ray-traced 3D Renderer is selected.

The Ray-traced 3D Renderer introduced in After Effects CS6 enables a number of new looks.

Each composition may use either the Classic 3D Renderer or Ray-traced 3D Renderer, but not both. You will find yourself choosing between these rendering engines depending on which features you need (for example, blending modes versus extrusion) as well as speed. For the next several exercises, we will explore features unique to the Ray-traced 3D Renderer.

Extrusion and Beveling

If you have After Effects CS6 or later, open project
file **Lesson_08_RT** and dive in:

1 Open **Comps > RT1-Bevel & Extrude*starter**.
It contains a text layer with its 3D Layer switch
enabled, plus a camera positioned at an angle to
the text. Even from this shallow angle, you can tell
the text layer has no thickness. Twirl open the layer
extrude in the Timeline panel; you will see the parameter categories Text, Transform, and Material Options.

2 This widescreen composition was created using the Classic 3D
Renderer; you can confirm this by glancing at the upper right corner
of the Composition panel, which includes a new Renderer button.
This currently says Classic 3D. To change the rendering engine, click
this button which opens the Advanced tab of Composition Settings.
Change the Render popup to Ray-traced 3D and click OK.

  If this is the first time you've selected the Ray-traced 3D Renderer
since launching After Effects, you will see an Alert dialog about what
you will gain and lose. Read this dialog to remind you of the consequences of your choice, then click OK again. A new parameter category
named Geometry Options will appear in the Timeline panel for **extrude**.

3 Twirl open **extrude** > Geometry Options and slowly scrub Extrusion
Depth while watching the Comp panel: The text will get thicker.
However, this is hard to see, as the sides of the text have the exact
same color as the face. To shade them differently, you need to add
at least one light.

4 Add a Layer > New > Light.
Change its name to "**Light 1 – Key**,"
set Light Type to Point, Color to
white, Intensity to 200% (ray-traced
scenes tend to need more light),
and Falloff to None; enable Casts
Shadows and set Shadow Darkness
to around 60%. Click OK: Now the
sides and faces are more clearly
defined. Drag this light toward the
upper right of the Composition
panel so you can see the sides of
your text more clearly.

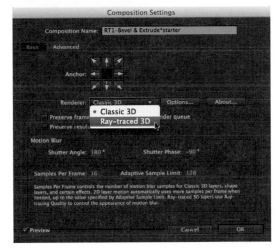

1 This composition
initially uses the
Classic 3D Renderer
(displayed in the
upper right corner
of the Composition
panel), meaning the
characters can't
have thickness.

2 When you change the Renderer to Ray-traced
3D in the Composition Settings > Advanced dialog,
you may see an alert of the features that will be
enabled and disabled by this choice.

3–4 When you initially extrude your text, it can be hard to tell the difference between the
faces and the sides of the characters (left). You will need to add at least one light so these
surfaces are shaded differently, revealing the layer's true dimension (right).

Angular

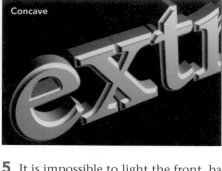

Concave

Convex

6–7 After Effects CS6 provides three basic bevel styles (aside from None): Angular, Concave, and Convex.

 tip

Bevels and Fonts

Be aware that bevels increase the size of each character, to the point where they might start touching each other. You may need to use a lighter font weight than you otherwise might expect, increase the tracking of the entire word or line, or increase the kerning between problematic pairs of characters. Some of these concepts are discussed in Lesson 5.

5 It is impossible to light the front, back, and all sides of an extruded layer with a single ordinary light. You will need to add at least one other Point, Parallel, or Spot light on the opposite side to illuminate the dark areas, or use an Ambient light as it illuminates all parts of all layers equally. Add Layer > New > Light; set Light Type to Ambient and Intensity to a low value such as 15%. Change the name to "**Light 2 – Ambient Fill**" and click OK. (Note that ambient lights have no Position value.)

6 To add some style to your text – as well as enhance the way it catches light – change **extrude** > Geometry Options > Bevel Style to Angular, which will add a flat chisel-style bevel to your extruded type. Scrub the Bevel Depth to get a look you like.

7 Try the other Bevel Style options. Convex produces a rounded bevel, which is good for softer looks. Concave produces a scooped-out bevel, which creates more opportunities to catch light and produce shadows in interesting ways; use Concave for the following steps.

9 For a classy look, try lower Bevel Depth and Extrusion Depth values, and increase the Specular values under Material Options. Also enable Cast Shadows for the text layer.

8 Increase Bevel Depth to 10. Notice how the insides of the "e" and "d" characters are starting to swell shut? Reduce Geometry Options > Hole Bevel Depth: This parameter scales back the Bevel Depth value just for these closed shapes, known in typography as *counters*. (Feel free to reduce Bevel Depth to something that looks less bloated.)

9 To make the lighting effect more dramatic, take advantage of the Material Options (discussed in the sidebar on page 229): Twirl open this parameter section for extrude, increase Specular Intensity to 100%, and slightly increase Specular Shininess until the specular hot spots look more like small glints. Also set Cast Shadows to On, as characters can cast shadows onto themselves and each other with the Ray-traced 3D Renderer. Drag **Light 1 – Key** around the composition and note how the light plays off the various surfaces.

Bending Layers

Although you cannot extrude video or still image layers in After Effects CS6, you can still bend them:

1 Open **Comps > RT2-Bend Layers*starter**. It contains a still image sequence that already has its 3D Layer switch enabled. We've also increased its Specular Intensity, Specular Shininess, and Metal Material Options to provide an obvious specular "glare" from the golden light already in this composition. Feel free to move the light around to see how the specular highlight moves in response, then Undo to return it to its original location.

▽ factoid

Live Photoshop 3D

The Live Photoshop 3D layers demonstrated in the second edition of this book are no longer supported in After Effects CS6.

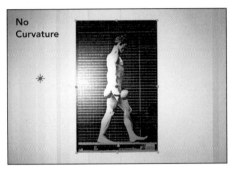

No Curvature

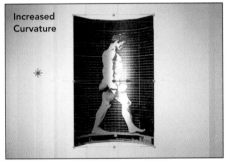

Increased Curvature

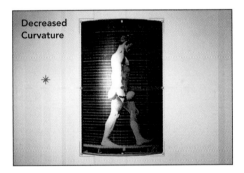

Decreased Curvature

2 Twirl open the **Muybridge_[01-10].tif** layer to reveal its Geometry Options. Scrub Geometry Options > Curvature, and note how the layer bends toward you and away from you. At maximum curvature, the layer forms a half-cylinder, pushed forward or back from its original surface. (To make this more obvious, you may enable the Video switch for the **Camera 1** layer.)

The specular highlight also appears to travel across the layer as you do this, even though the light, camera, and layer are not changing position. This is a result of the varying angle between the light, surface of the layer, and camera. Indeed, a common 3D trick is to add a slight curvature to otherwise flat layers so that animating the light, camera, or layer will result in more interesting movement of the resulting lighting patterns.

3 You may have noticed that the layer folds in obvious segments as you increase the Curvature value; set Curvature to 100% to make this more apparent. To create a more smoothly rounded surface, increase the Geometry Options > Segments value. A value around 20 cures most problems with bending.

4 With **Muybridge_[01-10].tif** still selected, press 🆁 to reveal its Rotation and Orientation values. Have fun posing and animating the layer in various ways. Note that layers are curved only around the Y axis; to curve around a different axis, you will need to first pose the layer in a precomp (Lesson 6), then curve and reorient the layer in your final comp; see our example in **Comps_Finished**.

2 Flat layers tend to have broad specular highlights). As you increase or decrease the Curvature, the highlight moves and becomes thinner as it illuminates a reduced area of the curved surface. Muybridge sequence courtesy Dover; background courtesy Artbeats/Digital Web.

3 At maximum curvature, the layer takes on the appearance of a series of folded panels (A). Increase its Segments parameter to smooth it out (B).

The goal in **RT3-Transparency** is to make this text translucent but still readable.

3 Set Transparency to 50% then compare this look to the snapshot you took earlier with Opacity set to 50%.

Transparency

Another advantage of the Ray-traced 3D Renderer over Classic 3D is its support for true transparency, compared with simple opacity.

1 Close your previous comps, then open **RT3-Transparency*starter**. It contains an already-extruded 3D text layer in front of what is currently a 2D background. Note the broad diffuse lighting of this text layer, plus the specular hot spots in the bevels as well as the dot of the i.

2 Select the **Cairns** text layer and press **T** to reveal its Opacity. Scrub its value to get a feel for how it affects each surface of the extruded text, allowing you to see the back surfaces. Note how the specular highlights also fade with the Opacity value. Set Opacity to 50% and click the Take Snapshot button (the camera icon) along the bottom of the Composition panel to take a snapshot of this look; the shortcut is **Shift**+**F5**.

3 Return Opacity to 100%, and with **Cairns** still selected, type **A A** to reveal its Material Options. Slowly scrub the Transparency parameter and note that the specular hot spots keep their original brightness as the diffuse lighting on the text fades away. Set Transparency to 50% and press the Show Snapshot button (the head-and-shoulders icon; the shortcut is **F5**) to compare your previous snapshot with this new look.

4 Set Transparency to 100%. Now you will see only the specular highlights, as if your text was made of a polished, perfectly transparent material. To add more definition to the layer, increase Transparency Rolloff: This parameter reduces the transparency of surfaces that are at an angle to the camera. At 100%, the sides of the text (which are edge-on to the camera) reappear.

4 When Transparency for an extruded layer is set to 100% (left), its diffuse lighting disappears, and only the specular highlights remain. To add definition, increase Transparency Rolloff, which makes surfaces at angles more opaque (right).

5 In the real world, light rays are deflected at angles when they hit the transition between two different materials such as air and glass. To simulate this, After Effects has an Index of Refraction parameter. Slowly increase it, and note how the back bevels appear to move closer as their light rays are bent by the front of the text.

6 2D layers are visible through transparent 3D layers, but they otherwise do not interact. To get a more dramatic look, enable the 3D Layer switch for **Whimsical.jpg**. Portions of the background image will now be offset as it is viewed through your transparent, refractive text. When Index of Refraction is at 1.00 for the **Cairns** layer, there is no change; slowly increase this value to see the effect more clearly. *(Note: The effects of refraction are exaggerated in the initial release of After Effects CS6 shown here; refractions should become more subtle and realistic in a later release. Be aware of this if you open an early project in a later version.)*

7 The farther apart layers are, the more obvious the effects of refraction. Select **Whimsical.jpg** and press **P** to reveal its Position. Scrub its Z Position to the right to push it farther away from the camera and note how it is distorted through your transparent text. Set its Z Position to 1400, then slowly scrub Index of Refraction for **Cairns** to see how much more quickly the background 3D image is offset inside the faces of your transparent text.

Although text made out of blocks of glass or acrylic is cool, it can be hard to read. Fortunately, After Effects gives you a way to set different colors and Material Options for each set of surfaces of an extruded object:

8 Twirl up the **Cairns** layer and twirl it back down again until you see the Text category subhead in the Timeline panel. On the same line as the subhead Text is an Animate button – you may remember this from Lesson 5 when you worked with Text Animators. Click Animate, and select Bevel > Transparency. This will create a new Animator and Range Selector in the timeline, with Bevel Transparency defaulting to 0%. This makes the bevels opaque, providing a good outline for your otherwise transparent extruded text. Use the Add button on the same line as Animator 1 to add other properties or treat other surfaces.

7 Index of Refraction bends light rays as they travel through transparent objects. This distortion is more pronounced if the layers are farther apart. (We temporarily set Specular Intensity to 0% so you could see through the text more easily.)

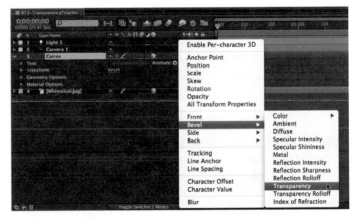

8 You can target the color and Material Options of individual groups of surfaces by using the Animate and Add buttons text layers (above). Here we made the bevels opaque to add definition to the text (below).

Since ray-traced layers in After Effects CS6 don't support texture maps, you may want to use reflections to add more interest to the faces of otherwise boring text or shapes.

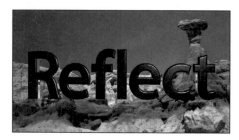

2 Reflections in After Effects are "energy conserving" – as you increase Reflection Intensity, diffuse and ambient lighting is reduced. If there's nothing to reflect, your layer will go black. However, you can see reflections in the extruded sides of the text.

▽ tip

Ray-tracing Quality

If you notice any unpleasant artifacts, they can be addressed by increasing the Ray-tracing Quality (covered on page 239).

4 To see reflections with the default Material Options settings, the reflection source must not be between the camera and the layer you are viewing. It must also be illuminated to bounce light rays back toward your hero layer.

Reflections

An alternative to seeing through a layer to another behind, is seeing the reflections of other layers that may be in front or off to the sides of the layer you're working on:

1 Open **Comps > RT4-Reflections*starter**. We've already set up some beveled and extruded text as well as a large still image behind. The only layers currently in front of the text are a camera (with a short lens length, to exaggerate the perspective distortion so that we can see the sides of the extruded text) and a Point light (with a slight orange tint to help warm up the color of the text).

2 Select the **Reflect** layer and type **A A** to reveal its Material Options. Slowly increase the Reflection Intensity to 100%; the text will go black! What's going on?

After Effects employs an *energy conserving shader*. This means that as Reflection Intensity is increased – which would normally add illumination to a layer – the effects of diffuse and ambient lights as well as transparency are reduced to help avoid over-illuminating a scene. (Note that the specular highlights keep their intensity; they're affected by Reflection Rolloff, which we'll keep at 0% for this exercise.) As there is no other layer in front of your text, there is nothing to reflect. Combined with the attenuation of the lighting, this means the layer appears darker.

However, look at the extruded sides of the text: You *will* see some reflections there, based on light rays bouncing from the layer behind off the sides and toward the camera. That's nice, but clearly what we need is a layer in front of our text for it to reflect.

3 Choose a view layout of 2 Views – Vertical, with the lower view set to Top.

4 Select the layer **Toadstool Rock.jpg** and press **P** to reveal its Position. Scrub its Z Position to the left to pull the layer forward. Initially, the layer will be between the camera and the text, blocking your view; hold **Shift** while scrubbing to move the layer faster. Once it is behind the camera, you can see the text again, but you may not see a reflection yet; you need to illuminate the reflection source for it to bounce light rays back toward the text. Keep scrubbing until **Toadstool Rock.jpg** is behind the light as well.

5 Here are a couple of tricks to sidestep these obscuration and illumination issues: With **Toadstool Rock.jpg** still selected, type **A A** to reveal its Material Options. Toggle Appears in Reflections to Only; that solves the camera obscuration problem. Then toggle Accepts Lights to Off: That returns the layer to its original color values regardless of your scene's lighting.

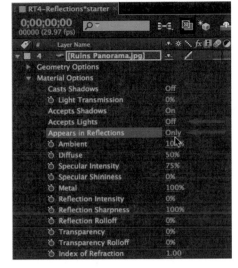

5 To make the position of the reflection source less critical, set Appears in Reflections to Only and Accepts Lights to Off.

6 With **Toadstool Rock.jpg** still selected, press **P** to reveal its Position again and scrub its values, or move it in your 3D views. Its placement relative to the **Reflect** layer – including rotation – determines the size and framing of the reflections.

7 Reflections are not always mirror-sharp in the real world; quite often they are softened by imperfections on the surface of an object. For the **Reflect** text layer, slowly decrease Reflection Sharpness; the reflections will become blurry. This parameter interacts with the distance to the layer being reflected: If

the reflection source is close, its reflections will appear sharper. If you are having trouble getting your reflections as soft as you like, move the reflection source farther away and optionally scale it to get the reflection pattern you desire.

7 Decrease Reflection Sharpness to create blurry reflections.

You may have noticed that soft reflections look noisy. This is from not having enough rays active in the Ray-traced 3D Renderer. We'll deal with image quality issues like this in a moment. But first, we want to show you one more trick with reflections.

▽ tip

Optimal Environment

The best candidate for an environment layer is a 360° panorama that also covers 180° from above to below. It should have a 2:1 aspect ratio and be very large: at least 6k for standard def video and as high as 18k for high def. You can build an environment map out of multiple images in a precomp.

▼ Math for Maps

To calculate how much of the environment layer is visible, take the Camera's Angle of View, divide it by 360°, and multiply it by the width in pixels of your image. In the case of **Ruins Panorama.jpg** (which is 6000 pixels wide) and **Camera 1 – 28mm** (which has a 65.5° Angle of View), the calculation is 65.5 ÷ 360 x 6000 = 1092 pixels visible at once: plenty for this 872 pixel–wide composition, but not enough to stretch across a 1920 pixel–wide high-definition video frame without degradation.

Disable the Video switch for **Camera 1 – 28mm** to use the comp's default 50mm camera which has a 39.6° angle of view. In this case only 660 pixels are visible; notice it now looks a bit soft. Turn **Camera 1** back on when done.

Environment Layers

Another way to simplify the placement of a reflective source (or a background image) is to wrap a layer completely around your world:

1 Open **Comps > RT5-Environment Map*starter**.

2 The still image **Ruins Panorama.jpg** is special: It contains a seamless panorama. Select it and choose the menu item Layer > Environment Layer. Now you will see only a small portion of the image, as it has been stretched to wrap 360° around your 3D world.

2 Setting Layer > Environment Layer takes a selected panoramic image and wraps it completely around your 3D world. Ruins courtesy iStockphoto, bischy, Image #1350819.

3 Select the **enviro** text layer and type **A A** to reveal its Material Options. Increase its Reflection Intensity; the portion of the environment layer behind the camera will be reflected.

4 Twirl open **Ruin Panorama.jpg**, and you will see that its normal Transforms and Material Options sections have been replaced with a minimal set of Options. Scrub Y Rotation: The background image will pan in one direction, and the reflection will pan in the other.

5 Toggle the Appears in Reflections parameter for **Ruin Panorama.jpg**. This allows you to choose if the environment layer is used only as a backdrop (Off), only as a source for reflections (Only), or both (On, the default).

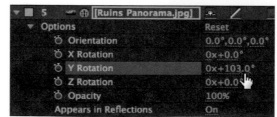

5 Use an environment layer's Options (left) to orient it as desired for both the background and reflections (above).

Ray-tracer Image Quality

You can adjust the quality produced by the Ray-traced 3D Renderer. As increasing quality drastically increases render times, this is a step best left for last, just before you render your final output.

1 Open **Comps > RT6-Ray-tracer Quality*starter**. It includes some highly reflective text. Although the reflected image is sharp, if you look closely you may notice the edges look a bit noisy or aliased; this is the first clue that you may need to increase the quality settings.

2 Select the text layer **rays** and type **A A** to reveal its Material Options. Decrease Reflection Sharpness to around 50%. The reflections will become blurrier – as well as noisier.

3 Click on the Ray-traced 3D button in the upper right corner of the Comp panel, or open Composition > Composition Settings and click on the Advanced tab. On the same line as the Renderer popup menu is a button labeled Options – click it. A Ray-traced Renderer Options dialog will open.

Ray-tracing Quality determines how many light rays are calculated per pixel. Its effect is more obvious in soft reflections and motion blur, as well as extruded edges. A setting of 3 means a box of 3×3 rays – 9 total – will be used.

The Anti-aliasing Filter affects how these rays overlap between adjacent pixels. Box is the default; higher settings (Tent, then Cubic) blur them together more, which smoothes out aliased edges at the price of slightly softening the final image. Subjectively, the Ray-tracing Quality setting has a far larger impact on the image quality, the Anti-aliasing Filter sets the final bit of polish and can often be left at Box.

4 Increase the Ray-tracing Quality to 10 (which is 100 rays per pixel) and click OK but do not close the Composition Settings dialog – the Comp panel will update in the background (assuming that the Preview switch is enabled). After a pause, the image will improve considerably. Tweak Ray-tracing Quality to find the lowest value that produces acceptable results, then click OK in the Composition Settings dialog.

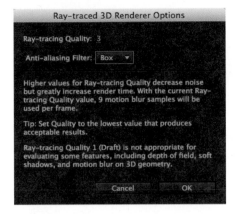

3 Composition > Composition Settings > Advanced > Options opens the Ray-traced 3D Renderer Options, which controls its image quality.

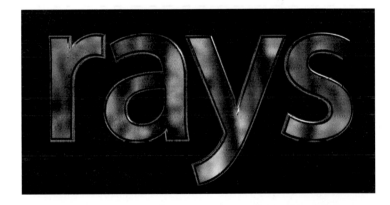

4 The default setting of 3 for Ray-tracing Quality often produces visual noise in soft reflections as well as around the edges (above); higher settings such as 9 or 10 provide acceptable results for most scenes (below).

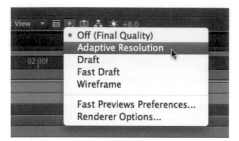

The Fast Previews mode is set along the bottom of the Composition panel. Rendering always takes place at the final quality, regardless of the Fast Previews setting. The preferred workflow is to use Fast Previews as necessary while building your project, then tweak the Ray-traced Renderer Options right before rendering.

Fast Previews

Ray-traced rendering looks beautiful, but it is computationally intensive. Even with an Adobe-approved CUDA-enabled NVIDIA GPU, it's easy to start bogging down your computer – and without one, CPU-based rendering is many times slower. This can make After Effects frustrating to use when you're trying to craft a ray-traced scene or animation. Therefore, After Effects CS6 implemented a new set of Fast Preview modes that allow you to trade off quality versus interactivity while working. Let's get a feel for what those trade-offs are.

1 Still in the **Lesson_08_RT.aep** project, open **Comps > RT7-Fast Previews*starter**. It makes use of several features specific to the Ray-traced 3D Renderer, including soft reflections, transparency, and an environment layer, as well as 3D shadows. The Fast Previews mode is currently set to Off, which means After Effects is always rendering at its final image quality.

2 Click on the Camera icon in the Tools panel along the top of the application window. If you have a three-button mouse, select the Unified Camera tool; otherwise select Orbit Camera tool. (Using the Camera tools was covered back on page 215.)

3 Click in the Comp panel and drag to orbit around your view. Unless you have an exceptionally high-end graphics card, updates will be sluggish with Fast Previews set to Off (Final Quality).

4 Release the mouse and click on the Fast Previews button along the bottom-right of the Comp panel; a menu of choices will appear. Select Adaptive Resolution: This mode reduces the resolution of your image on the fly while you're dragging a layer or scrubbing a parameter; once you

3–5 Fast Previews modes of Off (Final Quality), Adaptive Resolution during dragging (at 1/4 resolution), and Draft.

release the mouse, After Effects will rerender the scene at final quality. Click and drag around the Comp panel; After Effects will be a lot more interactive – with the trade-off that the image may look a bit crunchy while you're dragging. Note that the Fast Previews icon turns yellow while adaptive resolution is engaged.

You can set the minimum resolution for this mode by clicking Fast Previews and selecting Fast Previews Preferences: This will open the Preferences > Previews dialog. If you find the default setting of 1/8 to be too crunchy, you can set Adaptive Resolution Limit to 1/4; for large frames sizes, you might want to go 1/16 to make this mode even more interactive.

5 Click on Fast Previews and set it to Draft. This choice still uses the Ray-traced 3D Renderer, but sets Ray-tracer Quality down to one ray per pixel. You still have extrusions, reflections, and transparency, but the reflected or transparent images will look very noisy. However, After Effects will be far more responsive than with Fast Previews set to Off, and the image quality will not change while dragging. Note that the Fast Previews icon is always yellow now, indicating that you are seeing a preview rather than the final render quality.

The three previous Fast Previews modes take advantage of approved NVIDIA CUDA GPUs to accelerate them; After Effects will still be sluggish if you're relying on CPU-based rendering. The next two modes are accelerated by any modern OpenGL GPU, regardless of the manufacturer.

6 Set Fast Previews to Fast Draft. This mode dispenses with reflections, transparency, shadows, and environment layers, keeping just extrusions, color, and basic lighting. As basic as this is, it's still enough to arrange your scene and design an animation move, and it might be the only responsive option for those who do not have an approved NVIDIA CUDA GPU.

7 Finally, set Fast Previews to Wireframe. Here you get only outlined boxes representing your layers. But it sure is fast, isn't it?

There are shortcut keys for quickly switching between the Fast Previews modes: Hold ⌘ ⌥ (**Ctrl** **Alt**) and press **1** for Off, **2** for Adaptive Resolution, **3** for Draft, **4** for Fast Draft, and **5** for Wireframe.

Fast Previews Before CS6

If you are still using After Effects CS4, CS5, or CS5.5 (which came before the Ray-traced 3D Renderer was introduced), Fast Previews had a very different set of choices. We demonstrated these options as part of our video series for *After Effects Apprentice 2nd Edition*. You can find this movie in the **Lesson 08 > 08-Video Bonus** folder. If you want to follow along as you watch it, open **Lesson_08.aep**, and use the **08-Light Falloff*starter** composition.

▽ tip

Share View Options

Fast Previews is normally set for the currently active view; if you have multiple 3D views open and want them all to switch to the same setting at once, open the Select View Layout menu and select Share View Options to enable it.

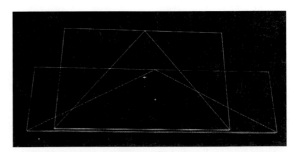

6–7 Fast Draft mode (left) dispenses with many of ray tracing's niceties but is very responsive. Wireframe mode (right) should be reserved for only the most complex scenes and slowest computers.

▽ tip

Draft 3D Button

If you find your computer is particularly slow while working in 3D and setting Fast Previews doesn't help enough, toggle Draft 3D along the top of the Timeline panel: This switch disables lights and camera depth of field. If your shadows disappear, make sure you didn't accidentally turn this switch on!

Quizzler

Earlier in this lesson in comp **RT2-Bend Layers**, you learned how to bend flat artwork such as image scans. For your challenge, use project file **Lesson_08_RT.aep** and open the composition **Quizzler > Butterfly*starter**. It contains a scanned butterfly illustration which we've already arranged in 3D space for you, including setting up a light and a camera, and setting Material Options > Light Transmission for **Butterfly_2.psd** to 100% so that the light shines through the butterfly.

Your job is to make the butterfly flap its wings and float across the top of the tulips in the scene, maintaining a somewhat even height. Watch the movie **Quizzler > Butterfly.mov** for reference. For an additional challenge, think about how you could make it appear to fly behind some of the flower petals; we'll show you an advanced solution to this problem in Lesson 10.

Butterfly courtesy Dover; footage courtesy Artbeats/CrackerClips CC-FH101-74.

Idea Corner

Here are a few ideas for how to take what you've learned in this lesson to the next level. The first idea can be tried in After Effects CS5 through CS6; the rest require the Ray-traced 3D Renderer introduced in After Effects CS6.

With Lesson_08.aep:

The source file has many more buildings for you to play with to create your city scene. Duplicate layers to create even more.

• To keep the **02-Multiplaning** exercise simple, we did not use all of the buildings in Russell Tate's original illustration. In the Project panel, twirl open the **Sources > illustrations** folder; the **Cityscape_full** comp has over twice as many elements for you to play with. In addition to arranging them in a horizontal line, you can also try arranging them as a street to travel down in Z space, akin to the music symbol flythrough in **05-Orientation**. Also try using Depth of Field blur to focus on buildings in the middle, while buildings closer or farther away are progressively blurrier.

With Lesson_08_RT.aep (CS6):

• Twirl open the Idea Corner folder and then open the **Camera Rig_RT** comp. Extend the camera rig exercise (pages 218–219) by using real extrusion and bevels instead of faking it with 2D effects so the layers have actual thickness when you view them on-edge. Indeed, since the Ray-traced 3D renderer does not allow you to apply effects to 3D layers, you will need to do a little work to colorize the **grace** layer. Remember that you cannot extrude flat artwork like the rock texture, but you can bend it.

▽ tip

Multiple Cameras

You may create multiple cameras in a comp. The top camera in the layer stack is the active camera. You can trim camera layers to edit between the various cameras.

As of After Effects CS6, you no longer need to use 2D effects to fake depth and dimension in 3D scenes.

Our version is in **Idea Corner > Camera Rig_RT**. We cheated a little by selecting the original Illustrator layer for **grace** and using another new feature in After Effects CS6: Layer > Create Shapes from Vector Layer. (Shape layers are covered in Lesson 11.)

• You learned while working through **RT2-Bend Layers** that you can bend a single layer by 180° into a half cylinder. Try forming a full cylinder by pairing two layers together. Once you have that, parent them together (Lesson 6) and animate them as a single object.

We have an example of this concept in **Idea Corner > RT2-Bend & Spin Layers**. The trick is making a portion of your cylinder transparent so you can see through to the other side. You learned several techniques for creating transparency in Lesson 4; in our example here we used Effect > Channel > Set Matte to convert the luminance of the grayscale Muybridge scans into the layer's own alpha channel. Once you've done that, try placing or animating objects, such as a ribbon of type, through the center of your cylinder.

• You can combine text animation with 3D text. Try creating a line of text; extrude and bevel it using what you've learned in this lesson, then apply a text animation preset (or even better, create your own text animation using what you learned in Lesson 5). Experiment with shadows, transparency, and reflections to get some interaction between the characters as they animate into place.

After Effects CS6 does not support the creation of "primitive" shapes such as cylinders and cubes, but you can re-create many of these shapes by arranging individual 3D layers. Here a pair of flat layers are bent and parented together to form a rotating cylinder.

Track and Key

Tackling several essential skills for creating special effects.

▽ In This Lesson

244   tracking overview

246   Warp Stabilizer *(new in CS5.5)*

249   point-based tracking and stabilization

250   creating track points

252   applying stabilization

253   fixing bad tracks

254   2D motion tracking

255   applying a motion track

256   tracking interlaced footage

256   Radio Waves effect

257   applying tracks to effect points

259   planar tracking with mocha AE

262   pasting the mocha track into After Effects

263   Bezier Warp effect

264   3D Camera Tracker *(new in CS6)*

265   defining the plane; moving the target

266   creating a Track Null; parenting

268   adding 3D text and a shadow catcher

270   stabilizing position, rotation, and scale

273   keying using the Keylight effect

275   creating garbage mattes

276   Rolling Shutter Repair *(new in CS6)*

▽ Getting Started

Make sure you have copied the **Lesson 09-Track and Key** folder from this book's disc onto your hard drive, and make note of where it is; it contains the project file and sources you need to execute this lesson.

Life is easy when you can capture everything exactly the way you want it. But reality often intervenes: Maybe the camera shook too much. Or maybe it wasn't possible to have the actors perform in front of the exact background or computer screen required. And you might not get permission to shoot arcs of electricity across a canyon, or hang a banner from a skyscraper.

Therefore, if you are interested in a career creating visual effects, you need to learn how to *stabilize* footage, *motion track* objects in footage, and *key* (create an alpha channel for) footage shot against a blue or green background so that you can place it over a new background. In this lesson, you will get a chance to practice all three.

Tracking Overview

The basic concept behind Motion Tracking and Stabilization ("tracking" for short) is to follow specific features in a shot as those features move around from frame to frame. Once that is done, you can perform some nice tricks:

• Stabilize the footage: If you know a feature was supposed to be in the same place from frame to frame, but it actually moves (maybe because the camera was held by hand rather than mounted on a tripod), After Effects can track that movement, then warp or animate the layer in the opposite direction so the shot appears to be steady.

• Make one object follow another: If you know how a feature is moving through a scene, you can make another layer follow the exact same path. For example, you can replace one computer screen, license plate, or poster with another, or have words follow a person around. Effect control points may also be animated to follow a feature throughout a shot.

• Reconstruct where the camera was: After Effects CS6 introduced a 3D Camera Tracker that automatically identifies hundreds of features and analyzes their movements. It uses their relative movement to reverse-engineer where the camera originally was and how it moved through a scene, and how far away various surfaces such as walls were from the camera.

After Effects offers a variety of tracking tools with their own strengths, weaknesses, and methods of working. Two of the newer tools – the Warp Stabilizer and 3D Camera Tracker – are highly automated, choosing the features to track for you. By contrast, the legacy "point" tracker in After Effects requires you to identify one or more features in the footage for it to then track. Similar but different, the third-party "planar" tracker mocha AE (from Imagineer Systems) requires you to identify a flat surface for it to follow throughout a shot.

After Effects CS6 includes two trackers and two stabilizers: the 3D Camera Tracker introduced in CS6 (A), the Warp Stabilizer introduced in CS5.5 (B), and the legacy point-based motion tracker (C) and stabilizer (D). The first two are used in the Composition panel; the second two must be used in the Layer panel.

In all cases, the best features to track have clearly defined shapes with distinct edges that don't change their underlying shape over time (although perspective may change, as long as those changes are not too drastic). These features should also have contrasting color or brightness compared with the pixels around them. Once After Effects (or mocha AE) has this initial idea of what to look for, it searches for the same feature in the next frame of footage. Once it finds the same feature, it updates its understanding of where the feature is and what it looks like now, and looks for it in the next frame.

The remaining options in the Tracker panel apply to the legacy tracker and stabilizer. (Note: This dialog is slightly different in earlier versions.)

Tracking one feature is often enough. However, sometimes it is useful to track multiple features. If you track two points, After Effects can calculate the angle and distance between them, allowing you to rotate and scale the layer being attached or stabilized. And if you track four points (such as the four corners of a poster) or an entire plane, then After Effects or mocha AE can take perspective distortion into account and "corner pin" a new object over the object you are tracking. And as alluded to above, the Warp Stabilizer and 3D Camera Tracker track hundreds of points. This is so Warp Stabilizer can construct a mesh to warp the moving image into the desired shape, or the 3D Camera Tracker can reconstruct the original 3D world these features occupied.

The third-party planar tracker mocha AE from Imagineer Systems is also bundled with After Effects; in CS6 it is accessed from the Animation menu (previously, it was a standalone application).

In this lesson, we will explore each of these tracking and stabilization tools, suggesting which ones to use for specific tasks. At the end, we'll combine this knowledge with keying to replace the background in a greenscreen shot. We'll also introduce the Rolling Shutter Repair effect, which can remove image distortion from certain footage.

Warp Stabilizer

As cameras keep getting smaller, more of them are being carried by hand or attached to unusual places such as the side of a car or handlebars of a bike. Although many cameras have some form of image stabilization built in, the often-shaky result may still be distracting. After Effects CS5.5 introduced a highly automated tool known as the Warp Stabilizer that can smooth out the camera shake in many (but not all!) shots.

1 Open this lesson's project file: **Lesson_09.aep**. In the Project panel, the **Comps** folder should be twirled open (if not, do so now). In this folder, locate and double-click **WS-Warp Stabilizer*starter** to open it.

2 This comp contains one layer: **Elephant.mov**. Press **0** on the numeric keypad to RAM Preview the clip and watch it closely: Despite the camera operator's best efforts to create a smooth pan, there are wobbles in the motion – particularly near the end of the clip when the camera stops panning.

3 Open the Tracker panel and apply the Warp Stabilizer (top). After Effects will analyze (A) then stabilize (B) the clip automatically. Footage courtesy Artbeats/ASC113.

▽ factoid

Multitasking

Analyzing and stabilizing a clip can take Warp Stabilizer some time – especially on larger or longer clips. Therefore, After Effects will allow you to continue to work on other compositions while these computations take place in the background.

3 Select **Elephant.mov** and press **Home** to return to its start. Open Window > Tracker. In After Effects CS6, click Warp Stabilizer; in CS5.5, click Stabilize Motion. (This feature was not offered prior to CS5.5.)

When you do so, the Effect Controls panel will open showing the Warp Stabilizer effect applied to your clip. Initially, a blue banner will be displayed over the Composition panel – this indicates Warp Stabilizer is analyzing the clip frame by frame; progress will be updated in the Effect Controls. Next, an orange banner will appear as After Effects stabilizes the clip.

4 When the analysis and stabilization are complete, the clip will appear to be scaled up slightly. RAM Preview again: The panning movement will be smoother, especially at the end of the clip.

Underneath the hood, After Effects has tracked multiple features of the shot, determined what areas contained the dominant movement (usually the background) and what areas had opposing movement (usually the foreground, such as the elephant), figured out the motion path for the background, and then smoothed that movement. It then panned and scaled up the clip to make sure it always covered the entire viewing frame; the amount of scaling is displayed in Warp Stabilizer > Borders > Auto-scale.

After viewing the resulting dreamlike motion, you may be tempted to say "That's great; I'm done!" – but you can tweak the shot further if you desire.

5 In the Effect Controls panel, increase Warp Stabilizer > Stabilization > Smoothness from its default of 50% to 200%. After Effects will restabilize the clip (requiring it to be scaled up slightly more); RAM Preview again. The panning movement will be even more constant and sedate. Tweak this parameter to taste.

6 Stabilization > Method controls how After Effects rearranges the pixels to create smooth motion. The default of Subspace Warp has the ability to warp the background differently than the foreground to correct parallax errors between the two. If the result has a noticeably rubbery look, try less sophisticated methods: Perspective warps the entire frame as a unit; the other two choices perform no warping and merely offset transform properties (scale, rotation, and position) for the layer. Choose the option that is least distracting to watch.

7 Borders > Framing determines how After Effects will then treat the stabilized image to make it more presentable:

• *Stabilize, Crop, Auto-scale* (the default) performs the minimum amount of scaling required to make sure the entire frame is covered by a portion of the original image.

• *Stabilize, Crop* keeps scale at 100% (maximizing image quality) at the expense of not covering the entire frame. Instead, it performs the minimum amount of cropping required to keep the edges stable.

• *Stabilize Only* leaves it to you to deal with the edges that are exposed by the stabilization process (note the pink background color in the figures below).

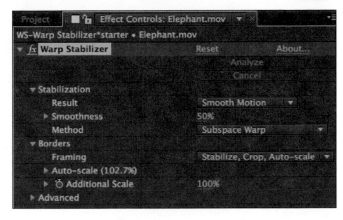

4 The Warp Stabilizer effect contains a number of parameters you can tweak to improve the final stabilized shot.

7 The default framing method of Stabilize, Crop, Auto-scale (above) fills the frame by balancing off smoothed movement with automatic scaling (A). Stabilize, Crop doesn't scale the result, but crops the edges so they remain consistent for the duration of the shot (B). Stabilize Only leaves any scaling, cropping, or reframing up to you (C).

8 The Framing option of Stabilize, Synthesize Edges (above) copies pixels from adjacent frames in time to fill in the edges as well as possible without scaling (right).

8 Set Borders > Framing to *Stabilize, Synthesize Edges*. This mode turns off Auto-scale and deals with edge issues by looking for visual information in adjacent frames that it can copy and paste to the current frame to cover the missing areas. At the start of this clip, there is no additional information for the left edge of the frame – but by the time you get to 00:22, it has found enough pixels elsewhere in time to cover the gap. To see how much area Synthesize Edges is synthesizing, toggle Framing between Stabilize Only and Stabilize, Synthesize Edges.

When Synthesize Edges cannot find enough material to cover the entire frame, there are three parameters you can balance off each other to help make up the difference:

• Decrease Smoothness. This decreases how much After Effects has to offset the original image to compensate for undesired movements.

• Increase Borders > Additional Scale until the edges are covered.

• Twirl down the Advanced section and increase the Synthesis Input Range. This allows Warp Stabilizer to search earlier and later in time to find replacement pixels. For this clip, set both Smoothness and Additional Scale to 100% and locate to 04:00 in time: There is a small gap along the top of the frame. Increase Advanced > Synthesis Input Range, and more of the gap will be filled in.

Sometimes your original clip will have artifacts around the edges that you don't want used to fill in missing pixels.

▼ Locked Down Camera

Most traditional motion stabilizers remove all camera motion in a shot, compared with Warp Stabilizer's attempts to merely smooth out this motion. However, Warp Stabilizer can also remove all motion. To do this:

• Set Stabilization > Result to No Motion.

• Ignoring the edges for now, choose the Stabilization > Method that produces the fewest visual artifacts.

• Set Borders > Framing to the desired method for dealing with missing edge information. Since Warp Stabilizer is no longer allowed to pan the image to help recenter it, more severe cropping or scaling will be required.

For example, with **WS-Warp Stabilizer*starter**, a Framing method of Stabilize, Crop, Auto-Scale requires us to twirl open the Borders > Auto Scale section and increase Maximum Scale to 239%. This is a case where Synthesize Edges can really help – as long as you have lots of additional source material earlier and later in time (often called "handle") for After Effects to use.

You can crop out these undesired pixels using the Advanced > Synthesis Edge Cropping section. Advanced > Synthesis Edge Feather determines how softly the new edges are blending into the existing frame.

There are two additional Advanced parameters that are not required by this example, but are still good to be aware of:

• Detailed Analysis tracks even more elements in the original clip, at the expense of calculation time and larger file size (all of Warp Stabilizer's internal data are stored with the effect in the project file).

• Rolling Shutter Ripple attempts to remove the "jello-cam" artifacts caused by the type of image sensor used in cell phones, DSLRs, and some other cameras. If some of this wobble is still visible after stabilization, try setting it to Enhanced Reduction.

If Warp Stabilizer produces unexpected results, the usual culprit is that After Effects is trying to stabilize a part of the image it should be ignoring – such as a person walking by. This can often be fixed by temporarily masking out the undesired elements in a precomp, analyzing the precomp with Warp Stabilizer, then removing the mask.

Point Tracker and Stabilizer

There are many occasions when you want to explicitly decide which features in a shot to track, and what to do with the resulting information. This is where the legacy point-based motion tracker and stabilizer are useful. Both require similar workflows to perform the initial track. After you learn the basic setup, we'll show how to apply this track to stabilize a clip, followed by having additional layers and effects follow a feature in the clip.

1 Open **Comps > 01-Stabilization*starter**.

2 This comp contains a single layer to stabilize. RAM Preview and watch the Comp panel closely: The image bobs up and down slightly. If this movement isn't obvious, place your cursor near the ground; you will see the ground shift as the clip plays.

While previewing the footage, look for features that might make good features to base your stabilization off of: something that has good contrast, that keeps roughly the same shape and position throughout the shot, and that isn't obscured by another object.

3 In the upper right corner of the application window, click on the Workspace popup and select Motion Tracking. This will open the Tracker panel. Setting up the point-based tracker and stabilizer needs to take place in the Layer panel; double-click **Wildebeests.mov** to open its Layer panel.

▽ tip

Docked Layer Panel

In some of the earlier lessons, we had you undock the Layer panel to make it easier to position alongside the Comp panel. In this lesson, it is fine to have the Layer panel docked into the same frame as the Comp panel; you can simply switch between the two as needed.

▽ tip

Panning and Zooming

To zoom into and out of a display such as the Layer panel, you can use the ⌘ on Mac (**Ctrl** on Windows) and the ➕ and ➖ keys above the normal keyboard, or the scroll wheel on a mouse. Press and hold **Z** to temporarily switch to the Zoom tool, then click to zoom in. To pan around the display, hold either the spacebar or **H**, then click and drag inside the display.

2 Double-click the **Wildebeests.mov** layer to open it in the Layer panel. Features that have good contrast are good candidates for the tracker to follow. Footage courtesy Artbeats/Animal Safari.

4 Click Stabilize Motion in the Tracker panel (above, right). A track point will be created (above).

Search Region
Feature Region

5 When you see a cursor with four arrows at its tail, you can then move the track point as a group (left). While you're dragging the track point, it turns into a magnifier (right).

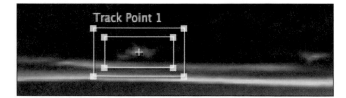

6 Drag the inner feature region large enough to just enclose your feature; drag the search region a little larger than the feature region. Note that dragging a corner of the feature or search regions will move all corners symmetrically around its center. To move just one corner, press ⌘ (Ctrl) while dragging.

Track Points

4 Click the Stabilize Motion button in the Tracker panel. (In CS5.5, click Track Motion and set Track Type to Stabilize.) This will create a *track point*, which consists of two boxes and a crosshair:

• The inner box is the *feature region*, which you will use to enclose the feature you wish to follow.

• The outer box is the *search region*, which tells After Effects how far to search in the next frame for a group of pixels that matches what was in the feature region in the previous frame.

• The crosshair in the middle of these boxes is the *attach point*. It is the center for any stabilization that takes place. When tracking, it defines where the Anchor Point for the new layer will be placed.

5 You need to set up your track point at the time you plan to start the track; press Home to return to 00:00. Hover over the track point until the cursor changes to a black pointer with four arrows at its tail, which indicates you can move the entire track point as a unit.

Drag the track point to a feature you identified in step 2. The bright cloud fragments make good candidates; we're going to pick the one on the left. Center the track point over your desired feature. While you're dragging, you'll notice that the track point turns into a magnifier, making this easier.

6 The feature we chose to track is larger than the default size of the feature region. Drag the feature region's corners until it encloses the entire cloud fragment plus a small fringe around it. Also make sure the search region is big enough to take into account how much the feature moves from frame to frame. Zoom into the Comp panel if you need to.

Performing the Track

7 In the Tracker, click on Options. Incorrect options will result in a bad track!

• The most important section is Channel. Set this based on how your feature stands out from the pixels around it. In this case, the clouds are all the same basic hue, but the bright bits have considerably different luminance than their surroundings – so check Luminance.

• You can usually leave Process Before Match disabled; use it only if you have trouble tracking. If the footage is out of focus, enable it and try Enhance; if it is noisy, try Blur.

• You always want to leave Subpixel Positioning on, and most of the time you want to leave Track Fields off (see the sidebar *When Tracks Go Wrong* on page 253). Enable Adapt Feature On Every Frame only if your feature constantly changes shape or size every frame. We often set the popup below to Adapt Feature and leave Confidence at 80% – this tells After Effects to keep looking for the same feature unless it thinks it has changed too much.

Click OK when you're done.

8 Click on the Analyze Forward button in the Tracker. After Effects will search each frame for the feature you've defined.

When it is finished, you will see a motion path created for Track Point 1. In this case, its individual points will be all bunched together, as the feature doesn't move that much. Press **U**, and in the Timeline panel you will see a large number of keyframes applied to Track Point 1.

It's a good idea to save your project right after performing a successful track so that you can revert back to it if something goes wrong afterward. After that, the next step is taking these keyframes and doing something useful with them!

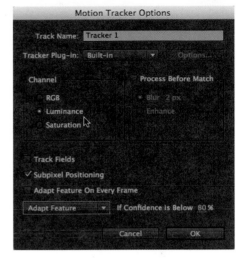

7 Always check the tracker's Options before performing a track. Most important is to set Channel based on what's unique about your selected feature.

▽ tip

Motion Blur Baked In

Stabilizing a clip will not remove motion blur already in the original shot. Shots with a lot of motion blur can even look strange if they're rock-steady, but blurred.

8 Click Analyze Forward (left). After Effects will then chase your feature around the shot from frame to frame. When done, you will see a motion path for your track point in the Layer panel (below, left) and a large number of keyframes in the Timeline panel (below).

9 Verify the Tracker settings, click Apply (above), and keep the default of applying to both X and Y dimensions (right). Keyframes will then be created for the layer's Anchor Point to stabilize the clip (below).

Applying Stabilization

9 In the Tracker, make sure Track Type is set to Stabilize and Motion Target is set to **Wildebeests.mov** (if it isn't, click on Edit Target). Then click Apply. A Motion Tracker Apply Options dialog will open; set Apply Dimensions to X and Y Dimensions and click OK.

After Effects will bring the Comp panel forward; press **Shift A** to reveal the new Anchor Point keyframes in the Timeline panel. These keyframes offset the movement detected for your feature region, causing the footage to be stabilized.

To verify that your stabilization worked, RAM Preview. You might want to place your cursor over a feature in the Comp viewer to verify that the footage is no longer bobbing as much as before. It may still wander very slightly; it is hard to get a perfect track – especially on your first try!

Congratulations: You now have the basic skills required to perform most motion tracking and stabilization chores.

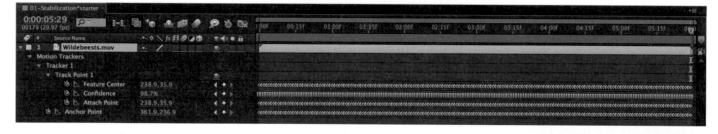

Cleaning Up

Now for the bad news: Scrub the current time indicator along the timeline and watch the top edge of the Comp viewer. That pink area you see is the comp's background color peeking through (we made it an obnoxious color to make it more noticeable). As a result of the layer being moved to make it appear stable, it is no longer centered, and therefore doesn't cover the entire frame.

Let's try a few ways to compensate for this. The best solution will vary from job to job, depending on how much the layer moves and what looks best.

▽ tip

Matching Blur

To create a more realistic composite, it is a good idea to enable Motion Blur for a new layer that tracks a feature in a clip – especially if the tracked object is moving fast.

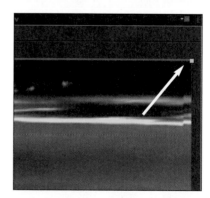

After stabilizing, you may see some of the background color (pink, in this case) around the edges of the Comp viewer.

10 Select **Wildebeests.mov** and press **S** to reveal its Scale. Scale up the footage slightly until it covers the entire frame throughout the entire timeline. The cost of this is a slight softening of the image as you scale over 100%. If the unwanted gaps are biased toward a particular side, shift the Position of the clip slightly in that direction to reduce the amount of additional Scale needed. (This is where the Warp Stabilizer demonstrated earlier shines, as it automatically scales and recenters the stabilized shot.)

10 One solution is to scale up the footage until it covers the entire frame.

11 Return the layer's Scale to 100%, and press ❜ (the apostrophe key) to reveal the Action and Title Safe grids. If the offending area is well outside the Action Safe area, you may be able to rely on the television's bezel cutting it off. However, you should fill these areas with *something*, just in case. Here are a couple of ideas:

• Cover the background with a solid. Select Layer > New > Solid. Click on the Make Comp Size button, and eyedropper a color from around the edges of the footage. Click OK and drag this new solid down the layer stack to sit behind your tracked footage. This creates a solid color border to fill the revealed areas.

• Select **Wildebeests.mov** and type ⌘ **D** on Mac (**Ctrl** **D** on Windows) to duplicate it. Select the copy on the bottom (layer 2), press **Home**, then press **A** to reveal its Anchor Point; its value should read 360,243 (its initial location at the center of the comp). Click on Anchor Point's stopwatch to delete the keyframes created by applying the stabilization. You will now have an echo of the footage in the revealed areas. This is the approach we took in our version, **Comps_Finished > 01-Stabilization_final**.

• If drastic correction is needed, consider cropping the stabilized clip in a precomp, then creating a frame around it for a "picture in picture" effect.

▼ When Tracks Go Wrong

Not all footage can be tracked accurately; be prepared for some disappointment and compromise. If you notice the track point wandering away from the targeted feature during the Analyze step, press any key to stop, then try these corrective actions:

• Scrub the time marker in the Layer panel back until the track point looks correct, then click Analyze Forward again.

• If that doesn't work, return to the start and modify your track point, try different Options, or try tracking a different feature.

• If the feature grows larger over time, you might need to delete this track, press **End**, set up your track points there, then click Analyze Backward instead of Forward.

• If there is no one good feature to track over the entire shot, track one feature until After Effects loses its way, hold down ⌥ **Shift** (**Alt** **Shift**), and drag the track point to a new feature while leaving the attach point where it was (otherwise, the resulting track will jump suddenly at this point).

• If the feature you want to track goes off screen, you may need to create an offscreen keyframe manually and let After Effects interpolate between this and the last good tracker keyframe.

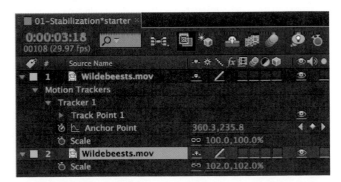

11 You can also clean up the edges by using a carefully colored solid or a copy of the original footage.

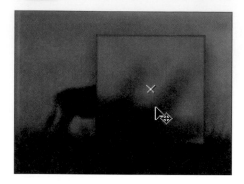

2 As you drag the track point, it will magnify what's inside the feature region. Center this region over the horns of the smaller wildebeest.

2D Motion Tracking

Now that you know your way around the legacy point tracker, let's put your newfound skills to work with a typical motion tracking exercise.

1 Close all previous comps by selecting Close All from the Comp panel's dropdown menu. In the Project panel, double-click **Comps > 02-Tracking Objects*starter** to open it. It contains three layers: the wildebeest footage from the previous exercise, a text layer, and a small pointer. The plan is to make the text and pointer follow the head of one of the wildebeests, as if we could read its thoughts.

2 After making sure the Tracker panel is visible, press **Home**. Select the **Wildebeests.mov** layer, then click Track Motion in the Tracker panel. This will open your clip in its Layer panel and create a track point.

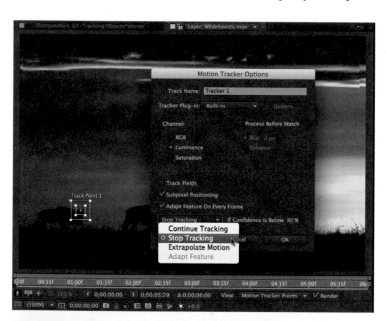

Click inside the track point somewhere that you see the black cursor with the four-arrow tail, and drag the track point until it is centered over the horns of the wildebeest at the left. As it so happens, the default size of the feature region encloses the horns nicely, so there's no need to resize the Track Point boxes.

3 Click on the Options button in the Tracker and position the Motion Tracker Options dialog where you can still see the wildebeest.

First is setting Channel. What sort of contrast is there between the wildebeest's horns and the sky behind? Luminance – so select that option.

Next comes the Adapt Feature settings. The feature you want to track – the horns – changes over the course of the shot as the wildebeest turns his head back and forth. In this case, enable the Adapt Feature on Every Frame option. Set the popup below to Stop Tracking so it will be obvious if After Effects can't follow this feature any longer. Then click OK.

Press **Home** and click the Analyze Forward button in the Tracker. After it is finished, After Effects will display the track path in the Layer panel.

3 Since the horns change during the shot, enable Adapt Feature on Every Frame (top left). To know if After Effects loses the scent, set the popup below to Stop Tracking. Click Analyze Forward; when done, you will see the track's motion path (left).

Applying the Track

Time to apply the results of your motion tracking. There's a quick and dirty way to do this, and a more clever way…

4 To decide which layer will receive your motion track, click the Edit Target button in the Tracker panel. In the Motion Target dialog that opens, there will be a popup for Layer. Hmm…two layers want to get the track, and you can select only one. You could apply the track twice, or you could use a trick you picked up back in Lesson 6: using parenting and null objects.

5 Click Cancel in the Motion Target dialog. Instead, create a dummy layer to receive the track to which you can later attach as many other layers as you want.

Select Layer > New > Null Object; it will appear in the Timeline panel. It's initial position is unimportant. Back in the Tracker panel, click on Edit Target again, and this time select your null. Click OK and verify that the name of the null appears next to Motion Target.

Click on Apply and click OK in the Motion Tracker Apply Options dialog that appears. The Comp panel will come forward. Select your null object, and you will see its new motion path in the Comp panel.

Type **F2** to deselect all and clean up the display. Scrub the current time indicator and note how the upper left corner of the null follows the head of the wildebeest.

6 Time to parent your other layers to this null:

• Select the text layer **I have no idea where**, then **Shift**+click the **pointer** layer to select it as well. Drag them into your desired position in relation to the second wildebeest's head.

• Press **Shift** **F4** to reveal the Parent panel (if it's not already visible). With your two layers still selected, click on the Parent popup for either one of them and choose your null. (You can turn off the eyeball for the null; it will still work as a parent.)

RAM Preview: The text and pointer will follow the wildebeest across the comp. Our version is in **Comps_Finished > 02-Tracking Objects_final** – we added a second line of text to make the shot more interesting. And don't forget to save your project…

5 Create a new null and choose it in the Tracker's Motion Target dialog (above). Click Apply and the null will now follow the head of the second wildebeest (below).

6 Use parenting to attach your additional graphical layers to the null (above); now they will all follow the wildebeest's travels (top).

In this exercise, you will track a mountain peak as we fly past it and apply an effect that will make it seem like radio signals are being broadcast from it. Footage courtesy Artbeats/Mountain Peaks 2.

▼ Tracking Interlaced Footage

Usually, you want to separate fields (enabling Preserve Edges) plus remove pulldown, if present. Then you can disable Track Fields in the Motion Tracker Options for most footage. However, if there are sudden changes in the movement of the tracked feature where one field is very different from another, you may need to enable Track Fields to more accurately follow this motion. Conversely, if you are having trouble locking onto a feature to track and there is very little motion in this feature, try turning off field separation just while you are tracking.

2 The Radio Waves effect (inset) creates a series of shapes that appear to be "born" from a moveable Producer Point (right). These shapes can change size and opacity over time.

Tracking for Effects

In addition to making a layer follow an object in another layer, you can also use motion tracking to have effects follow a feature around a layer by assigning the tracked motion to an effect point. In this exercise, you will track a mountain peak and use results to send out radio waves from that peak.

1 In the Project panel, double-click **Comps > 03-Effect Track*starter** to open it. It contains one layer, which is an aerial pullback over a range of mountain peaks. RAM Preview it, thinking about which peaks might be candidates for tracking.

2 Select **Mountain Peaks 2.mov**. Then apply Effect > Generate > Radio Waves. (If needed, dock the Effect Controls panel into the Project frame.) RAM Preview. The mountain footage will be replaced by a series of concentric blue circles emanating from the center. Press **End** for now, so you can see several waves on screen and become familiar with the Radio Waves controls:

• In the Effect Controls panel, make sure the Wave Motion section is twirled down, and increase Frequency to increase the number of waves (we used 2.00). Alternatively, you can reduce the Expansion value to slow down how fast the waves fly off screen. Then try decreasing the Lifespan (we tried 2.000): You will notice that the waves start to die away as they get older.

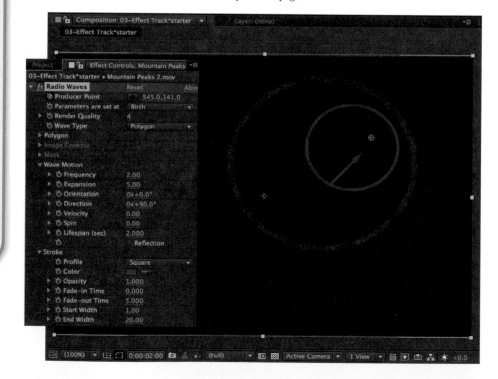

• If needed, twirl open the Stroke section. Decrease the Start Width and increase the End Width (we used 1.00 and 20.00, but set these to taste); you will now see the waves start skinny and grow thicker with age.

• Press **Home** and click on the stopwatch next to Producer Point (near the top of the Effect Controls) to enable keyframing. Move the time indicator a few seconds later, click on the crosshair icon next to Producer Point, then click somewhere in the Comp viewer. Do this a couple more times until you reach the end of the comp. RAM Preview: You will notice that the waves remember where they were born, creating an interesting trail over time.

3 Verify that the Tracker panel is visible; if not, select the Motion Tracking Workspace or open Window > Tracker. Make sure **Mountain Peaks 2.mov** is still selected, then click Track Motion in the Tracker panel.

The Layer panel will open. The original footage should now be visible again, even though the Radio Waves effect is still applied. This is controlled by the View popup along the bottom of the Layer panel: Switch it to Radio Waves (the motion path for Producer Point will be visible), then back to Motion Tracker Points.

4 Press **Home** to make sure you are at the start of the clip. Hover the cursor over the track point until the now-familiar black pointer with the four-arrow tail appears. Click and drag the track point over one of the peaks. We chose the pointy peak near the middle of the frame, as it remains visible for the entire shot and keeps good contrast with its background during the shot. Be sure to enlarge the track and search regions to enclose a good part of the peak.

5 Click on Options in the Tracker. The foreground peaks are about the same brightness as the mountains behind but are a different color; therefore, set Channel to RGB. The mountain peaks only change shape a little during the shot, so go ahead and disable Adapt Feature on Every Frame, and instead set the popup below to Adapt Feature (meaning it will adjust its search only when the feature has changed quite a bit). Finally, give your track point a name at the top of the dialog, such as "**middle peak.**" Click OK.

3–4 Click on the Track Motion button in the Tracker panel, and select Motion Tracker Points from the Layer panel's View popup. Place the track point over one of the peaks, looking for an area with clean edges and good contrast.

5 In the Motion Tracker Options, set Channel to RGB, disable Adapt Feature On Every Frame, and set the bottom popup to Adapt Feature.

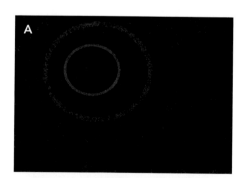

6 After the track is finished, verify that the Motion Target is the effect's Producer Point before trying to apply the track.

▽ tip

Storing Multiple Tracks

If you have a track or stabilization that you think might work, but want to try another, click on Track Motion or Stabilize Motion again. Your previous and new tracks will be saved as keyframes for the same layer, and you can apply either one later. Rename tracks in the Options dialog to keep straight which track is which.

7 After you apply the track, the Radio Waves will animate across the screen (A). To composite the waves over the mountains, duplicate the layer, delete the effect from the copy underneath, and use a blending mode on the top layer to mix (B, and right).

6 Click Analyze Forward in the Tracker. If the track stops before the end of the clip, press Analyze Forward again – this will refresh and continue the track. When finished, click Edit Target to open the Motion Target dialog. Make sure that Effect Point Control option is selected, and that Radio Waves/Producer Point is selected in the adjacent popup. Click OK.

Back in the Tracker click Apply, set Apply Dimensions to X and Y, then click OK. This will replace your trial animation in step 2 with the motion tracker's data.

7 RAM Preview, and Radio Waves will create a nice set of moving circles for you. But where are the mountains? Radio Waves does not have any "composite" options that allow you to see it and the underlying layer. No problem – just duplicate the layer and use that:

• Twirl up the open parameters in the Timeline panel to reduce the clutter. Select **Mountain Peaks 2.mov** and use Edit > Duplicate.

• Select the bottom copy of **Mountain Peaks 2.mov** and select Effect > Remove All.

Tweak the Radio Waves effect on the top layer to taste. Press **F4** to reveal the Modes column and try compositing the waves with modes such as Add or Overlay. Our version is saved in **Comps_Finished > 03-Effect Track_final**.

Make sure you save your project. In an Idea Corner at the end of this lesson, we'll also challenge you to continue working with this composition and track a second peak, applying the results to an effect with two effect points.

Applying tracks to effect points is a skill that is useful in both motion graphics and visual effects. For example, you can apply the track to the center of a radial blur effect to create an interesting selective focus look. It is also quite common to track light sources in real scenes or 3D renders and apply them to lens flare centers.

Next, you'll move up to a more challenging task that involves planar tracking and the corner pin effect.

Planar Tracking with mocha AE

A common tracking task is to follow a computer screen or mobile device display, a poster on a vehicle or wall, or other rectangular image, and replace it with a new image. To perform this with the legacy point tracker in After Effects, you need to track the four corners of the source rectangle – which means four times the chance for error. A far better tool is mocha AE, which has been bundled with After Effects since CS4. mocha tracks the entire shape of the target rectangle (or other plane) rather than individual corners, often producing superior results. However, its user interface is very different from After Effects'. Let's work through an exercise so you can gain some familiarity with mocha.

mocha is a powerful tracking and stabilization system that is optimized for tracking planar surfaces. Footage courtesy Artbeats/Medical Montage.

Tracking in mocha

1 Close any previous comps and open **04-mocha AE*starter**. It contains two video layers: **MRI Computer.mov**, which you will be tracking, and **Heart Monitor.mov**, which is your replacement screen. We've initially disabled **Heart Monitor.mov**'s Video switch so it won't obscure **MRI Computer.mov**.

2 In After Effects CS6, select **MRI Computer.mov** and choose the menu item Animation > Track in mocha AE. A New Project dialog will open that points to this clip, already loaded with its duration, frame rate, pixel aspect ratio, and other data. If you had trimmed the clip, this would also be reflected inside mocha.

(In After Effects CS4 through CS5.5, mocha AE is a separate application placed in the After Effects folder. Launch it, start a File > New Project, click the Choose button for Import Clip, and navigate to **Lesson 09-Track and Key > 09_Sources > movies > MRI Computer.mov**. By the way, the user interface changed between CS5 and CS5.5.)

Click OK to open the clip in mocha. Use the View menu to either scale the clip by 100% or to fit the available display space. To pan the image's framing, hold X while dragging.

2 A mocha project is based on the clip you wish to track or stabilize. Therefore, the New Project dialog contains detailed information about the source clip.

▽ tip

mocha Resources

To access the mocha AE documentation, press **F1** while inside mocha. The Tracking Basics section is a particularly worthwhile read for a new user. And mocha's product page *www.imagineersystems.com/products/ mochaAE* is a good jumping-off place for additional tips and tutorials.

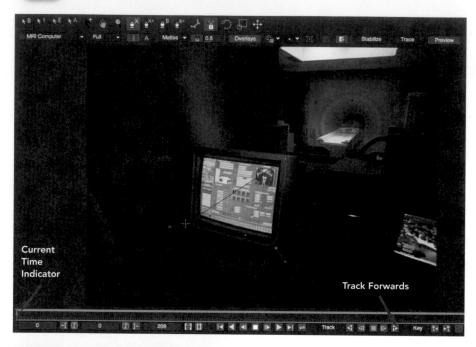

Current Time Indicator

Track Forwards

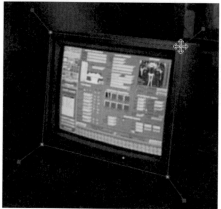

3 Select the Create X-Spline Layer tool and click around the outer edges of the monitor (top). Adjust the tension and position of your four corners (above).

Show Planar Surface

Stabilize

Show Planar Grid

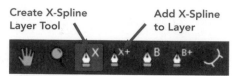

Create X-Spline Layer Tool

Add X-Spline to Layer

3 You define the plane to track by drawing a shape around it. mocha has tools for Bezier masking (akin to that used by After Effects) and for X-Splines. To get some practice with the latter, select the Create X-Spline Layer tool.

• Place the current time indicator (the white bar) at the start of the clip and click around the four corners of the face of the monitor. You can be some-what loose, but be careful not to enclose too much of a separate plane such as the bulletin board on the left. Click on the first point to close your shape.

• X-Splines create rounded corners by default, which are helpful for organic shapes. To square off the corners, pull out the blue handles extending from each point to change the "tension" of the shape through that corner.

• Clean up the location of your corners by clicking and dragging them. A magnified version will be displayed along the left side of your image.

Part of mocha's power is that you can draw additional shapes to define more areas to track by using the Add X-Spline to Layer tool (see figure above). This is particularly handy when you have only a few identifiable features to track on the same plane that are spread out. Overlaps between shapes are excluded from the track; it is useful to exclude reflections, shadows, and people moving in front of your plane. You can define and animate shapes to remove these so-called obscurations. Fortunately, this clip is easy for mocha to track.

4 Click the Track Forwards button along the bottom right side of mocha's time-line. After mocha has finished analyzing the shot, scrub its current time indicator and check how well the shape you drew stuck to the face of the monitor.

5 Next is defining the surface you wish to paste a new graphic onto. Enable Show Planar Surface (see figure to the left); a blue rectangle will be overlaid on top of your clip. Move the four corners of this rectangle to the corresponding corners of the image on the monitor. Place the corners just beyond the bright blue of the image, as you want your new graphic to completely cover this image. (We'll deal with distortions in the monitor's face back in After Effects.)

6 To better visualize whether you have a solid track, enable Show Planar Grid: A pink grid will be attached to your planar surface, extending well beyond its boundaries. The current grid spacing may not be optimal for viewing your scene; open View > Viewer Preferences and adjust the size of the grid dividers. Unlike After Effects, you don't scrub these values left and right; click and move the mouse in a circular direction to change their values, or enter values directly. Values of 18,16 worked well for us.

Scrub the current time indicator or press the spacebar for realtime playback, and observe how solid the track is. If the track wanders, there are a couple of ways to correct it (short of performing a new track from scratch):

• You can nudge the location of the Planar Surface; mocha will automatically keyframe and interpolate changes for you.

• mocha has a dedicated Adjust Track panel along the bottom of the display with tools to help your fine-tuning. Using this advanced feature is covered in mocha's online documentation (press **F1** to access).

7 It's time to export your track. Select the Track tab along the bottom left of the mocha display and click Export Tracking Data, or use File > Export Tracking Data. Select the middle Format choice of After Effects Corner Pin [supports motion blur]. Click Save for a text file to be saved to your drive for archiving. If you are ready to return to After Effects right now (which we are), open Export Tracking Data again and click Copy to Clipboard.

You can quit mocha now if you like. You will be asked if you would like to save your project; mocha has already been auto-saving your intermediate results inside the **09_Sources > Results** folder (alongside the source clip mocha was using).

5–6 Set up the Planar Surface to correspond to the existing display (left and inset) and view the Planar Grid to make sure that the perspective is correct and the track is solid (above).

7 You can export your tracking data to a text file, or directly to the clipboard to then paste onto a layer in After Effects.

Pasting the Track into After Effects

If you did not have success performing the track in mocha (or were just feeling lazy today), we've saved both our mocha project and our results. To see how we set up our project, open mocha, then open **Lesson 09-Track and Key > 09_Sources > Results > MRI Computer_prebuilt.mocha** (you'll be prompted to relink to the original movie in the Sources folder). If you want to use our exported track, open **Results > mocha screen track.txt** in a text editor, select all, and copy.

8 Bring After Effects forward again. Since pasted keyframes start at the current time indicator, select **MRI Computer.mov** and press **I** to locate to its in point.

Select **Heart Monitor.mov** (your replacement display), enable its Video switch, and paste. Press **U** to reveal its keyframes, and you will see that the Corner Pin effect has been applied to this layer, with each of the four corners keyframed. The Transform properties Position, Scale, and Rotation have also been keyframed. By choosing the "supports motion blur" export option, mocha calculated where the center of the tracked surface was and how it moved over time. This allows you to enable motion blur for the new layer (although it's not necessary on this slow-moving shot).

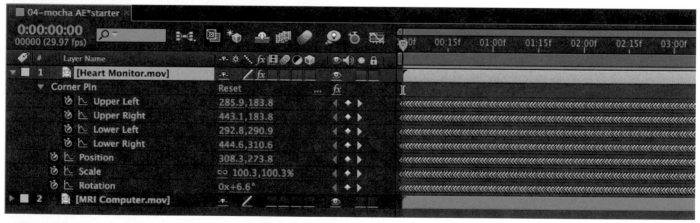

8 Paste the track data onto the new display layer. It will be pasted over the original display (top), with both Corner Pin and normal Transform properties keyframed to match the movements of the underlying layer (above). Data display courtesy Artbeats/Control Panels 1.

9 If there are mismatches between layer and comp sizes, the new graphic will not initially align with the underlying clip. Press **A** to reveal **Heart Monitor.mov**'s Anchor Point, hold ⌘ (**Ctrl**), and slowly scrub its values until the new screen better aligns with the old monitor – in our case, we had to nudge Y to 246.0. Just worry about aligning the corners for now; we'll deal with the bulging of the original screen in just a moment.

Improvements

RAM Preview your current composition: You should have
a pretty solid track. However, there is still the issue of the blue
of the old display peeking out around the corners of your new
display graphic, even though you were careful in defining the
Planar Surface. You are seeing the results of the monitor's old-
style glass tube being bowed out. Therefore, this composite
will require a little more work to make the result convincing:

10 Select **Heart Monitor.mov** and choose Effect > Distort >
Bezier Warp. Look at the Comp panel: After applying this
effect, your new display went flying off into space! This was
caused by the order in which the effects are being applied.
In the Effect Controls panel, drag Corner Pin to below Bezier
Warp; now it will look correct.

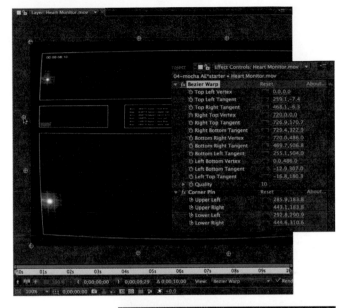

11 Bezier Warp allows you to use the familiar Bezier handles
(from mask shapes and motion paths) to gently warp a layer.
We find it best to edit in the Layer panel while watching the
results in the Comp panel. Select View > New Viewer, then
double-click **Heart Monitor.mov** to open its Layer panel in
the unlocked view. You can also drag out the Layer panel so
you can see it and the Comp panel at the same time.

In the Layer panel, set the View popup to Bezier Warp.
You will notice a series of 12 crosshairs around its outline.
Leave the ones in the corners – the warp vertices – alone.
Slowly drag the handles ("tangents") along the left outward,
watching the result in the Comp panel. Move them just
enough until the blue fringe has been covered up in the
final composite and a proper bowed perspective has been
added to your new display graphic.

11 Apply
Bezier Warp
before Corner
Pin and tug its
tangent handles
outward (above)
to bow your new
screen to match
the distortions of
the original CRT
monitor (right).

When you're happy with the warp, close the locked
Comp view (or otherwise reset your workspace), bring the
Comp panel forward, and RAM Preview. Our version is
Comps_Finished > 04-mocha AE_final; we added the
"filmic glow" trick you learned back in Lesson 3 to help unify
and add production value to the look of the final composite.
And if you're curious, **Comps_Finished > 04L-Corner
Pin_final** is the same composite executed with the legacy
point tracker with Track Type set to Perspective Corner Pin
(which required a lot more work to get acceptable tracks
for each corner).

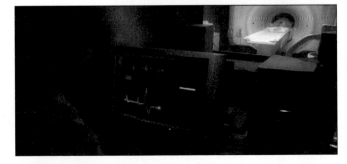

The final composite, with some additional processing to unify
and enhance the composite.

3D Camera Tracker can be used to add other images or text to already-shot footage. Clip courtesy Artbeats/C032v1; photo courtesy iStockphoto/Kativ/image #20039696.

▽ tip

Reasons for Failure

If the 3D Camera Tracker fails when trying to solve the camera's location, the most likely culprit is a wrong default camera definition. Change the Shot Type popup to Variable Zoom or enter its fixed angle of view (if known) and analyze again. If it still fails, try the different Advanced > Solve Method choices. For more accurate tracks, remove lens distortion in a precomp using the Distort > Optics Compensation effect.

3D Camera Tracker

The 3D Camera Tracker (introduced in After Effects CS6) is fundamentally different from the other trackers you've used so far in this lesson: Instead of providing access to the movements of individual features in a piece of footage, it calculates how the original camera moved through a scene and creates a 3D camera to replicate these movements. Additionally, it provides the stationary 3D coordinates of various points in the original footage. By placing new 3D layers at these coordinates, they will appear to move with the same perspective as in the original shot. This makes it possible to add new signs to walls, float text in the middle of these worlds, and perform other tricks.

To get some practice using the 3D Camera Tracker, we'll use aerial footage of downtown Los Angeles as a starting point to develop some promotional ideas for the LA Philharmonic.

Hanging a Poster

Our first idea is hanging a large poster or banner on one of the buildings. In this exercise we will cover the fundamentals of using the 3D Camera Tracker; we'll assume you've worked through this composition before tackling the next exercise.

1 Close any previous comps and open **Comps > CT_1-Poster*starter**. It contains our aerial footage, plus a precomp that holds a mockup of the poster. For now, we've turned off the Video switch for **LA Phil Poster**.

2 Make sure Window > Tracker is open. Select **Los Angeles Aerial.mov** and click Track Camera. (Again: This feature was not available prior to CS6.)

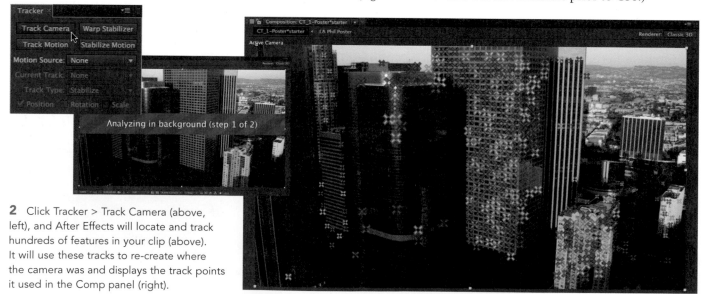

2 Click Tracker > Track Camera (above, left), and After Effects will locate and track hundreds of features in your clip (above). It will use these tracks to re-create where the camera was and displays the track points it used in the Comp panel (right).

The Effect Controls panel will open with the 3D Camera Tracker effect applied to your clip. Similar to the Warp Stabilizer demonstrated earlier, you will see a pair of banners informing you of the progress in analyzing this shot. This process can take some time; you can work on other compositions (or make a nice cup of tea) while the 3D Camera Tracker works in the background.

When After Effects has finished calculations, you will see a number of colored crosses overlaid on your clip. These crosses indicate points After Effects tracked throughout the shot. They are visible only when the 3D Camera Tracker effect is selected in the Effect Controls or Timeline panels. Their sizes indicate their relative distance from the camera; notice that the crosses on the background buildings are smaller. If the crosses are too big or too small for your taste, you can adjust 3D Camera Tracker > Track Point Size.

Scrub the timeline; track points appear and disappear as After Effects uses and discards them. If you notice any track points sliding along a surface, they are in error; select and delete these bogus points to improve the quality of calculations.

3 Press **End** to where you can see the right side of the central building more clearly. To place a new layer at a location in 3D space that matches the orientation of this (or any) wall, you must choose at least three points to define your target plane. There are three ways to do that:

• With the Track Points visible, hover your cursor over the Comp panel (but not directly on a point). After Effects will triangulate three nearby points and display a red target in the center. Click, and those three points will be selected to use.

• Click and drag to "lasso" (surround) a cluster of points. After Effects will average them together to define the target plane. If the points are close together, you'll need to reduce the Track Point Size to see the resulting target sitting behind them.

• Click on the first desired point, then **Shift**+click additional points. Again, After Effects will average them together to define the target plane.

We tend to use a combination of the second and third techniques. For more accuracy, choose points that are far apart, making sure they are on the desired wall. Then add more points around the center to get a better average. The target's orientation will give you a clue as to whether you are picking good points; if you see it skewed at an angle that does not match your plane, deselect your most recent points and try others.

4 Hover the cursor over the center of the target until you see a four-headed arrow appear at the base of the cursor. This means you can move the target, which will be the center of the new layer you are about to create. Drag the target to where you would like to locate your poster. While you see this cursor, you may also press **⌥** (**Alt**) and scrub to resize the target as desired.

3 You can define the plane you are about to create a layer on by hovering the cursor and having After Effects pick three points for you (A), lasso a group of points (B), or hand-select points by **Shift**+clicking them (C). To make it easier to see what we're doing, we decreased the Track Point Size to 50% and increased the Target Size to 150%.

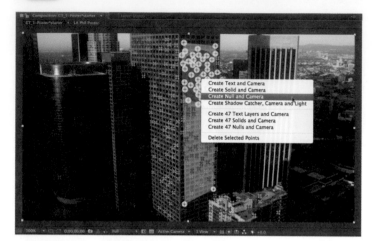

5 After choosing a set of points to define the desired plane and relocating the target to the desired location on that plane, right-click and choose the new layers you would like After Effects to create with this information.

6 Enable Video and 3D Layer for the poster precomp and hold **Shift** while parenting it to the Track Null created by the 3D Camera Tracker (top). The poster will appear where your target was located (above), although it's a bit askew!

5 After locating the target, *right-click* anywhere on the ghosted white shape between your chosen points (be careful not to click normally or you will lose your selection!). You will be presented with a list of choices of whether you want to create a text, solid, or null object layer, as well as whether you want to create one layer at the center of the target or one for each point you selected. As 3D Camera Tracker has not yet created a camera that corresponds to the camera position it solved for this clip, each choice will also contain the option "and Camera." Choose Create Null and Camera.

6 Enable the Video and 3D Layer switches for the **LA Phil Poster** precomp layer. Press **Shift**+**F4** to reveal the Parent column. Click on the Parent popup for **LA Phil Poster**; to the right you will see a note appear that you can hold the Shift key to move this prospective child directly to the location of the null (compared with the normal behavior of keeping any offset that currently exists between the two). Since we'd like to move the child, add **Shift** and select **Track Null 1**. After you release the mouse, the poster will appear on the side of the building.

7 The poster will initially appear askew. The 3D Camera Tracker has no concept of where the ground is, so the Z orientation of the layers it creates can be off. Select **Track Null 1** and press **R** to reveal its Orientation and Rotation and set Z Orientation to 0°.

• Select **LA Phil Poster** and drag it beneath **Track Null 1** to visually group the layers in the Timeline. Press **S** to reveal its Scale. Scrub it larger to make the poster cover most or all of the width of that side of the building. Don't worry about scaling past 100%, as the layer is being scaled down by its placement in 3D space. We edited Scale for the poster instead of the null because we prefer to leave the null at 100% in the event we parent different-sized layers to it later.

• If the poster still looks a bit askew, hold ⌘ (*Ctrl*) and slowly scrub the X and Y Rotation values for **Track Null 1** (not the poster) by small amounts until the poster looks nicely squared-up compared with the windows and sides of the wall. Here, we're perfecting the null's location in case we parent other layers to it later.

• With **Track Null 1** still selected, drag its X or Y axis arrows in the Comp panel to slide the poster into its desired location on the wall. Editing in the Comp panel rather than the Timeline panel takes the orientation of the null into account, so dragging an axis arrow slides the poster along the building rather than through the world's coordinate system.

8 RAM Preview. The poster should appear to stick to the side of the building. If you notice some slight sliding of Position, that's due to errors in the track. You could try tweaking the null's Z Position until you get better results, creating another null using different track points. Or, deleting your current null and camera, enable 3D Camera Tracker > Advanced > Detailed Analysis and try again. Life lesson: Automated tracking is rarely perfect; you look for acceptable compromises and hand-tweak the results if necessary.

9 Back to the fun stuff: It's unrealistic to have our poster blot out the building completely. These banners often have a grid of holes in them to allow people inside the building to look out, as well as to reduce catching the wind.

To improve a composite like this, you can use blending modes. Press **F4** to reveal the Modes panel, and try modes such as Overlay, Soft Light, and Hard Light for the **LA Phil Poster** layer. The advantage of using modes is that the reflections traveling across the building's windows during the shot will still be visible in the final composite, adding to its realism. Soft Light got the closest to our personal vision; to beef it up we duplicated the **LA Phil Poster** layer, set its mode to Normal, and reduced its Opacity until we got our desired look.

Note that in After Effects CS6, only the Classic 3D Renderer supports blending modes for 3D layers. If you had set Composition Settings > Advanced > Renderer to Ray-traced 3D, modes (as well as masks, mattes, effects, and other processing) would be disabled. Which rendering engine you use with the 3D Camera Tracker depends on the final look you're going for.

7 To make the poster appear less skewed, zero out the null's Z Orientation and carefully tweak its X and Y Rotation (above) (in this situation, we find Rotation operates in a more intuitive fashion than Orientation). Drag the null's X and Y 3D axis arrows in the Comp panel to slide it into position along the building's face (below).

9 Blending modes help composite your new layer on top of the original footage. We also added the Channel Blur effect and blurred just the alpha channel to soften the edges.

4–5 Use the 3D Camera Tracker to create a new text layer (above) and edit it to taste (below).

7 Align the shadow catcher's outlines to the edge of the building.

Text and Shadows

Next we're going to extend our use of the 3D Camera Tracker by adding text, letting it float in space in front of the building, and adding a "shadow catcher" so the 2D footage will appear to receive a shadow from the 3D text with the proper perspective. You can continue with the composition you were using in the previous exercise or open **Comps > CT2-Text*starter**.

1 We're going to add text to the face rather than side of the central building, so press (Home) to locate to 00:00 where this face is most visible.

2 Select the 3D Camera Tracker effect applied to **Los Angeles Aerial.mov**. You can do this in the Timeline panel (press **E** to reveal effects) or Effect Controls panel (press **F3** to bring forward). The Track Points will reappear in the Comp panel (if you can't see them easily, increase the Track Point Size).

3 Select a set of track points on the face of the building. We used the lasso method to grab a large set of points to average together. Drag the target to where you think you'd like to center your text.

4 Right-click on the target and choose Create Text. (If you are using our **CT2-text*starter** comp, or had closed and reopened your project, you will also see "and Camera" appended onto your choice, as 3D Camera Tracker doesn't realize it already created a camera earlier. That's okay; just delete the duplicate camera.) Select the **Text** layer, press **R**, and enter 0° for its Z Orientation.

5 Double-click the **Text** layer to select the text, type in your preferred wording such as "**new season**" and press (Enter). Then choose Window > Workspace > Text to open the Character and Paragraph panels. In the Paragraph panel, click on the Center Text option. In the Character panel, set the Font Family and Style, Font Size, Leading, and Fill and Stroke Color to taste. We chose Myriad Pro to match the poster and eyedroppered colors from the surrounding buildings. Press **V** to return to the Selection tool when you're done.

6 Choose the 3D Camera Tracker effect again, lasso a number of points on the face of the building as you did in Step 3, and move the target a little lower than the center of the text (where its shadow would fall). Right-click, and this time choose Create Shadow Catcher and Light. The 3D Camera Tracker effect will create a light with Casts Shadows enabled, as well as a shadow catcher layer with its Material Options set to only receive shadows and otherwise be invisible.

7 Select **Shadow Catcher 1**, press **R**, and set its Z Orientation to 0°. Then press **S** and scrub its Scale until the outline of the shadow catcher aligns with the right edge of the face of the building.

8 Select your text layer and drag its Z axis arrow (the blue one) to the left until the text separates away from the front of the building. You will see a shadow appear on the building itself.

9 The text will probably be under-lit, and the direction of the shadow may not match the rest of the scene. Take advantage of the alternate 3D Views (Lesson 8) to move the light into a more advantageous position. You can also adjust the Intensity and Shadow Darkness of **Light 1** (and, optionally, the other Material Options for the text layer) to get your desired look. You can return to the normal single Active Camera view when you're done.

10 You have a nice shadow on the front of the building – but not the side. No problem; repeat Steps 6 and 7, this time creating a Shadow Catcher for the right side of the building. Carefully scale and reposition the shadow catcher so it just covers the right side and is underneath where the shadow falls. If necessary, tug on the handles for the shadow catcher layers to scale them taller to catch all of the shadow. (If you can't see a shadow on the side of the building, you may need to move **Light 1** in the positive X direction to bring it around to the corner of the building.)

11 You might have noticed that the poster is no longer illuminated. This is because the light is not hitting it directly. The easiest way to make it visible again is to select your poster layer(s), press **A A** to reveal its Material Options, and set Accepts Lights to Off to restore its 2D color values. If you're curious, our final version is **Comps_Finished > CT2-Text_final**.

8 Pull the text away from the building using its Z axis arrow.

9 Take advantage of additional 3D views to tweak the placement of the light to get good illumination plus interesting shadows.

11 Our final version, after tweaking the position of the light as well as other details such as text tracking and position.

The source shot was provided by the Pixel Corps (*www.pixelcorps.com*) and is from the production of its film *Europa*. Pixel Corps shot most of the action on a greenscreen stage with the intention of later placing the actors in a 3D environment.

1 Since the HD frame is so large, set the Comp panel to 50% Magnification (or smaller, if needed) and Auto Resolution.

2 Select the movie, click Stabilize Motion in the Tracker, then enable Position, Rotation, and Scale.

Background Replacement

In this final exercise, you will take a hand-held shot of a pair of actors on a green-screen stage, stabilize the shot, remove ("key out") the green, and place the result over a new background to make it appear the shot originally took place outdoors.

For an added challenge, this composition is created at the high-definition resolution of 1920×1080 pixels. Since this frame is larger than most monitors, change the panel magnification as needed. Note that we have saved this source footage using the common HDV frame size of 1440×1080 pixels. These pixels are "anamorphic" in that they are supposed to be displayed wider, yielding the same result as a normal HD 1920×1080 frame. It will look normal in the Comp panel; in the Layer or Footage panels, you will see the original, squeezed image.

Stabilizing Position, Rotation, and Scale

This will be your most challenging track in this lesson, as you will need to stabilize not just position but also rotation and scale. The good news is the greenscreen stage already has nice tracking dots placed on it. The bad news is one of the actors walks in front of the dots you need…

1 Close your previous comps. In the Project panel, double-click **Comps > 05-Keying*starter** to open it. If you can, arrange your panels so you can view the Comp panel at 50% Magnification; if not, set Magnification to 33%. Set Resolution to Auto and it will optimize the number of pixels calculated.

RAM Preview this shot, paying particular attention to the tracking dots. Any dots that go off screen during the shot are of less use. Note that the camera moves in closer during the shot and rotates a bit. The new background you will be placing this action over does not move. Therefore, you will need to stabilize position, rotation, *and* scale!

2 Select **PXC_Europa.mov** and press (Home). With Window > Tracker visible click Stabilize Motion (in CS5.5, click Track Motion and set Track Type to Stabilize). The movie will open in the Layer panel with a default track point.

In the Tracker panel, enable the checkboxes for Rotation and Scale in addition to the default Position. This will create a second track point. To stabilize rotation and scale, After Effects needs to measure distance between two points over time, as well as the angle between them.

3 Still at 00:00, start with Track Point 1 on the left. Drag Track Point 1 over the upper left tracking dot, because it remains visible throughout the entire shot. Drag a corner of its feature region (the inner box) to make it just larger than the green square on the background. In the process, bump the search region (the outer box) to be about twice the size of the feature region.

For Track Point 2, think for a moment about which dot to track. It should be as far away from Track Point 1 as possible: The greater the distance between track points, the more accurate the scale and rotation tracks. It would hopefully remain visible throughout the shot as well. The second actor walks in front of all of the dots on the right; the middle dot in the upper row is obscured the least – so place Track Point 2 over it.

Resize Track Point 2. Again, do not make the track point larger than necessary; if you do, it will slow down the track, and After Effects will have more trouble when the actor walks in front of the dot.

4 In the Tracker panel, click on Options. The dots are the same color as the background but lighter, so pick Luminance for Channel. Further down, Adapt Feature On Every Frame should be off. Click on the popup underneath; since we know one of the features we will be tracking will be obscured during part of the track, select the option to Extrapolate Motion. This tells After Effects that if it cannot find the feature it's tracking, keep going in the same direction and hope it reappears. Click OK.

5 Time for some trial and error. Click Analyze Forward and keep your eye on Track Point 2, especially when the actor walks in front of its dot:

• If you set up a good track point, it will wander temporarily when the actor walks in front, but will find its dot again a few frames after he passes.

• If the track point follows or appears to "bounce off" the actor when he passes in front of the dot, the track point was too large. First Undo to remove the old track, tighten up the feature region, and analyze again.

• If the track point finds the dot after the actor passes but then loses the dot again later, the search region is too small. Undo, increase the outer rectangle very slightly, and try again.

*If you tried several times and still can't get a good track, open **Comps > 05-Keying*starter2** and continue with this comp instead. Double-click layer 1 to open its Layer panel and set View to Motion Tracker Points.*

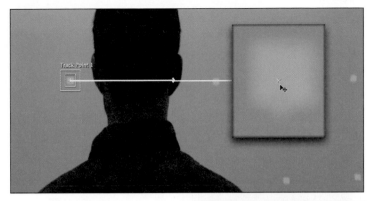

3 Enlarge the track points just enough to fit around the bright square dots. Place them over a pair of dots that are far apart but aren't too obscured during the course of the shot (above). For best results, make sure Track Point 2 in particular is a fairly tight fit around the dot (right).

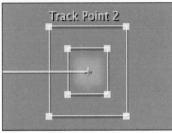

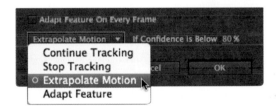

4 In the Motion Stabilization Options, set the Confidence popup to Extrapolate Motion. This tells After Effects what to do when the actor walks in front of one of the dots we're tracking.

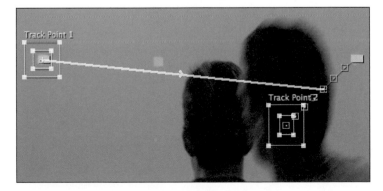

5 If Track Point 2's search region (the outer rectangle) is too large, it will follow the actor rather than re-find its dot.

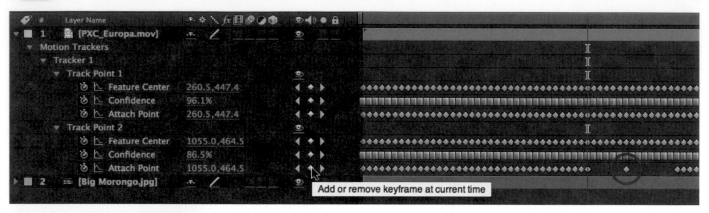

	#	Layer Name					
▼	1	🎞 [PXC_Europa.mov]					
▼		Motion Trackers					
▼		Tracker 1					
▼		Track Point 1					
		⏱ ⌐ Feature Center	260.5,447.4	◄ ◆ ►			
		⏱ ⌐ Confidence	96.1%	◄ ◆ ►			
		⏱ ⌐ Attach Point	260.5,447.4	◄ ◆ ►			
▼		Track Point 2					
		⏱ ⌐ Feature Center	1055.0,464.5	◄ ◆ ►			
		⏱ ⌐ Confidence	86.5%	◄ ◆ ►			
		⏱ ⌐ Attach Point	1055.0,464.5	◄ ◆ ►			
▶	2	⬚ [Big Morongo.jpg]					

Add or remove keyframe at current time

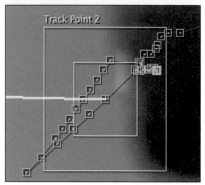

Track Point 2

6 When the attach point at the Center of Track Point 2 begins to wander (above), that's a bad keyframe. Delete it (top) and any other rogue keyframes (the lonely keyframe in the middle of the gap is probably the only other bad one).

7 After stabilization, the layer will be smaller at the end of the comp, as After Effects had to reduce its scale to remove the camera move. Disable keyframing for Position and move the layer so it touches the bottom of the screen.

6 With **PXC_Europa.mov** selected, type **U** to see all of the tracker's keyframes. There will be a noticeable gap in Track Point 2's Attach Point keyframes when the actor passed in front of the dot. Let's make sure After Effects interpolated the motion correctly through that area.

Slowly scrub the current time indicator in the Timeline panel while watching the Layer panel. When the actor's chin crosses into Track Point 2 at 01:11, you will see it snap away from the dot it was tracking. Stop at this frame, and delete the corresponding Attach Point keyframe.

Scrub later in time until you see Track Point 2 snap back into its correct position over the dot – that's a good keyframe. Delete any keyframes between this one and the keyframe you deleted above (there's probably just one, in the middle of the gap). Now as you scrub through this area, Track Point 2's boxes will still wander, but the attach point (at the end of the line connecting Track Point 1 and 2) will stay on course. Save your project.

7 Depending on your skill or luck, that was probably tedious. Now enjoy the payoff and some final tweaks before moving onto the greenscreen:

• Make sure Motion Target is still set to **PXC_Europa.mov** and click Apply, then OK. After Effects will bring the Comp panel forward.

• RAM Preview; the actors will now be stable. However, their layer will get smaller as After Effects compensates for the camera movement, leaving a gap at the bottom of the composition. Press **End**, where the gap is at its largest.

• Press **F2** to Deselect All and twirl up the Motion Trackers section in the Timeline panel to save space. Still at time 03:23, disable keyframing for Position, then reposition **PXC_Europa.mov** to where it just sits on the bottom of the composition (around Y = 482).

Your next task is to "key out" the green in the **PXC_Europa.mov** layer so you can see a new background layer behind it. The term *keying* is short for keyhole: creating a cutout so you can see through one object to view another.

Keylight

Continue to use the comp you built in the prior section, or start with our version **05-Keying*starter3**.

8 Select the layer **PXC_Europa.mov**, press `Home` and apply Effect > Keying > Keylight, a high-end keying plug-in that comes bundled with After Effects. Then follow these steps to perfect your key. This is an interactive process, so have patience and be prepared to repeat some of these steps to balance the desired results:

• In the Effect Controls panel, click on the eyedropper for Screen Colour and click in a green area near the actor. This is your initial key. Not bad! However, if you look at the right side of the actor's neck, it's partially transparent and the background layer is showing through. For now, turn off layer 2 so you can concentrate on your key. If not already enabled, toggle on the Transparency Grid to better check the transparency of your key.

• Back in the Effect Controls panel, change the View popup to Status. This produces an exaggerated display of the key's transparency.

• Twirl down the Screen Matte section. Slowly increase Clip Black until most of the gray outside the actor disappears. Press ⌘ (`Ctrl`) to scrub in finer increments. You may leave the gray squares in the background (otherwise you'll start cutting into his head).

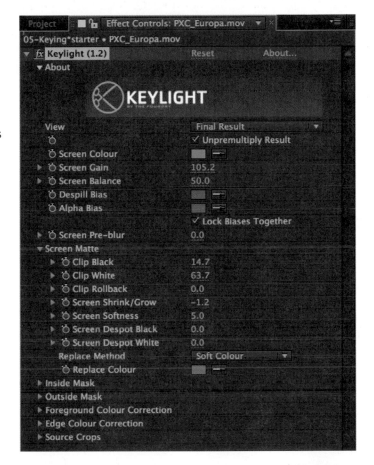

8 Eyedropper the green area near the first actor to get an initial key (A). Change Keylight's View popup to Status (B). Carefully increase Clip Black and Screen Gain until the area outside the actor turns black (C). Decrease Clip White to maintain the solid areas in the actor, keeping a gray fringe in the semitransparent areas (D). Our initial set of numbers is shown (top); there is more than one valid combination.

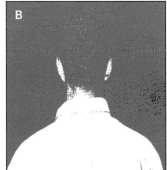
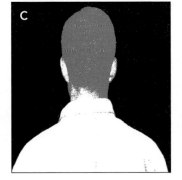
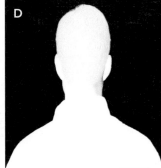

• Slowly increase Screen Gain until the rest of the gray just barely disappears. Balance these two values against each other until you've made the smallest total increase while eliminating the gray.

• Slowly decrease Clip White until the gray in the actor's head turns white or light green. Don't push this too far; you want to keep some gray (which denotes transparency) around his hair's edge, as well as in the motion blurred areas as he moves.

• Scrub the current time indicator through the timeline, checking that the black areas stay black and the light areas stay light.

• Change Keylight's View back to Final Result and preview your work. If the edges around the actors are too hard-edged, increase Clip White slightly.

9 Turn on the Video switch for layer 2 again so you can see your key in the context of its new background. Not too bad! But there are a couple of areas where it could be improved:

• Move to around 02:18. See the dark fringe on the first actor's arm? That's the result of decreasing Clip White too much. However, if you increase Clip White, you may start to see the background through the second actor's head. Tweak this parameter to reach a compromise.

• The edges around the actors are a little hard, especially when they are moving fast. Slightly increase Screen Softness to blend them better into the scene. If too much fringe starts to appear, you can balance this by decreasing Screen Shrink/Grow. (These two adjustments will also help the dark fringe problem.)

9 The composite looks pretty good (A). However, decreasing Clip White too much can result in hard edges, such as the black fringe on the actor's arm while moving (B). Increasing Screen Softness and decreasing Screen Shrink/Grow can help this problem, as well as the overall composite (C).

▽ tip

Keylight Documentation

For more documentation on Keylight, go to www.thefoundry.co.uk and select Plug-ins > for After Effects > Keylight. Look for the header Support & Training; under it will be links for the Keylight user guide, plus some example files you can practice with.

10 The final step consists of a bit of color correction to better match the actors to their new environments. While still at frame 02:18 (where you can see the actor's skin), click on the eyedropper for Despill Bias, then click on a pinkish skin area such as the left actor's forehead. This will remove some of the green cast or "spill" caused by shooting on a greenscreen stage.

It would be customary at this point to then spend time color correcting the foreground and/or background to better match each other, to help sell the illusion that the actors really were in this new room when the footage was shot. At a minimum, try using Levels to adjust the gamma and Hue/Saturation to adjust the hue. For more advanced color correction work, learn Synthetic Aperture's Color Finesse, which comes bundled with After Effects.

RAM Preview; not bad, eh? This might be a good time to save your project.

Our version is in **Comps_Finished > 05_Keying_final**. In it, we also keyframed Screen Softness to start out sharp when the actor is closest and getting softer later in the shot. Of course, you can spend a lot more time further finessing this shot – and those who do are the ones who earn the big bucks!

These basic keying instructions can be applied to most shots. The overall goal is to do the least amount of damage to the outlines of the objects you want to keep. This comes with practice as well as compromise. If you have a series of shots taken with the same actors, lighting, and set, you may be able to reuse your keying settings, but most of the time you will have to approach each shot fresh.

It takes a lot of patience and attention to detail to be a good visual effects artist, so it's not for everybody – but films are relying on visual effects work more and more, so it's a good skill to have.

10 The original footage has a green cast (A). Using the Despill Bias eyedropper on their flesh tones helps remove this (B). In our final version, we brightened the actors using Levels and tweaked their color using Hue/Saturation (C).

▽ tip

Finer Control

Hold down ⌘ (*Ctrl*) as you scrub values such as Clip Black, Clip White, and Screen Gain for finer control.

▼ **Masking to Help Keying**

When working with greenscreen footage, there may be extraneous objects that you don't wish to see in the final composite such as mic booms, light stands, props, the edge of the stage, and so on. If they're not also painted green, you will need to create a *garbage matte* to mask them out.

Another reason to create a garbage matte is simply to reduce the area you need to key. For example, perhaps the corners of the frame are not as well lit as the center where your foreground is, making your keying job more difficult.

A garbage matte could be as simple as creating a loose rectangular mask shape around your foreground; the mask does not need to follow the edges closely as the key will take care of that. If necessary, animate the mask throughout the clip by setting keyframes for the mask path.

For more intricate shapes, create a loose mask with the Pen tool (masking and animated masks were covered in Lesson 4). When there are multiple actors involved, you could even create one mask for each actor.

△ Creating an animated "garbage matte" (the yellow outline) that loosely encloses the actors will remove extraneous details and reduce the area you need to key.

There will be times when you cannot get a satisfacory key with just one application of Keylight. On tricky shots, you may need to divide the frame into sections – for example masking out the head and keying that with one setting, then keying the body separately.

▼ Rolling Shutter Repair

Digital cameras with CMOS sensors – including cameras ranging from cell phones to video-capable DSLRs to the RED ONE – typically have what is commonly known as a "rolling" shutter, which captures a frame of video one scan line at a time. Due to time lag between scan lines, not all parts of the image are recorded at exactly the same time, causing motion to ripple down the frame. If the camera or the subject is moving, the rolling shutter can cause distortions, such as leaning buildings and other skewed images. Dealing with this footage can cause headaches – especially when you're attempting to composite the footage with nondistorted images, such as 3D layers and text.

After Effects CS6 introduced a Rolling Shutter Repair effect that contains a pair of user-selectable algorithms to help fix problematic footage such as hand-held shots and tripod pans. To see it at work, open **Comps > RS-Wobbly Building*starter**. It contains a brief clip of a building that we intentionally shot with a lot of camera movement, using a Canon 5D Mark II. Press the *Page Down* key to step through the clip a frame at a time, and note how the building seems to compress and stretch as the camera moves up and down. Pick a pair of adjacent frames where this distortion is particularly obvious, such as 00:09 and 00:10.

Select **Wobbly Building.mov** and apply Effect > Distort > Rolling Shutter Repair. Use *Page Up* and *Page Down* to step between the problematic adjacent frames; some of the distortion has been removed, but not all. In the Effect Controls panel, increase the Rolling Shutter Rate value and step through the problematic frames again; now the building will become more solid (but the cameraman should still be fired!). This value will need to be tweaked depending on how each clip was shot.

Change the Advanced > Method popup to Pixel Motion: Whereas the default Warp setting merely distorts the existing image, Pixel Motion reconstructs new pixels based on their motion. With this shot, these new pixels actually look a touch sharper, and the building is even more solid – at the expense of slower render times. The Advanced options of Detailed Analysis (Method = Warp) and Pixel Motion Detail (Method = Pixel Motion) help if you have objects in the frame moving in separate directions.

Rolling Shutter Repair can't fix every shot – for example, it has problems if the camera is "locked off" (not moving) and there is strong motion in the scene – but it can improve the production value of a number of clips.

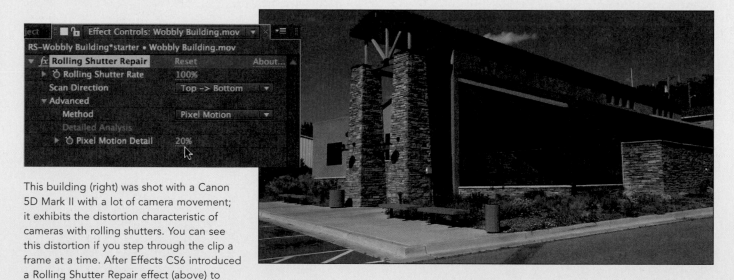

This building (right) was shot with a Canon 5D Mark II with a lot of camera movement; it exhibits the distortion characteristic of cameras with rolling shutters. You can see this distortion if you step through the clip a frame at a time. After Effects CS6 introduced a Rolling Shutter Repair effect (above) to help fix such problematic shots.

Idea Corner

• If you have access to a camera, shoot your own footage of people walking across campus or down the street. Then practice tracking them and placing text or other objects over their heads and the like. Then use the 3D Camera Tracker to place new signs on the sides of the buildings in the shot.

• Open the **Lightning_starter** comp in the **Idea Corner** folder and track another mountain peak, but this time from the mountain range in the background. Then apply Effect > Generate > Advanced Lightning, apply your tracks to Lightning's two effect points, and set Lightning Type to Strike. Our version is the **Lightning-final** comp. Alternately, add a soundtrack to your project and use Generate > Audio Spectrum or > Audio Waveform in place of Lightning.

• For the 3D Camera Tracker exercise, use the Ray-traced 3D Renderer (Lesson 8) so that you can extrude and bevel the text, and make it partially transparent. The downside is you won't be able to use blending modes for the poster.

Quizzler

• In the **Quizzler > Quizzler 1** folder, open the **Mask problem*starter** comp and RAM Preview. The wildebeests footage has an added rectangular mask. However, even though the footage has been stabilized, the mask is wobbling. Your mission is to make the stabilized animals play inside a static mask so it looks like **Mask_fixed.mov** in the same folder. Give it your best shot, then check it against the solution in **Quizzler Solutions > Quizzler 1**.

• In the second exercise, you learned how to stabilize the **Wildebeests.mov** shot; in the third exercise, you learned how to track it and make other layers follow one of the animals. How would you stabilize *and* track this shot? Use the comp **Quizzler 2 > Stable+Track*starter** as a starting point. A movie of the final shot is in the same **Quizzler 2** folder; one potential answer is in **Quizzler Solutions** – but don't peek until you try to solve it first.

• In the final exercise, you stabilized the greenscreen shot to match the new background, which didn't move. The result is a locked-down shot, which can lack the energy of a hand-held shot. So, rather than stabilize the foreground shot **PXC_Europa.mov**, how would you make the new background take on the same camera movement as was in the foreground? Again, we've provided a movie of the result for you to study in the **Quizzler 3** folder and a starter comp. One potential solution is in the **Quizzler 3_solution** folder.

Track two peaks in the Mountain Peaks 2 shot and use this to make the Generate > Advanced Lightning effect jump from peak to peak.

The more realistic Ray-traced 3D Renderer looks good combined with the results of the 3D Camera Tracker.

How do you both track *and* stabilize the same shot, and still get the new layers to match the resulting motion? Try to find a solution with Quizzler 2.

Paint, Roto, and Puppet

Exploring Paint, Roto Brush, and the Puppet tools.

▽ In This Lesson

279   basic painting
281   erasing strokes
281   Paint Channels
282   Paint blending modes
282   brush duration bar
283   animating strokes
284   revealing a layer
285   creating organic textures
286   tablet settings
287   cloning
288   transforming strokes
289   basic Roto Brush
292   Roto Brush workflow; the base frame
294   propagating strokes
296   corrective strokes
298   refining the matte
300   Puppet Pin tool
301   animating Puppet pins
302   Puppet Overlap tool
303   recording puppet animation
303   Puppet Starch tool
304   multiple shapes

▽ Getting Started

Copy the **Lesson 10-Paint, Roto, and Puppet** folder from this book's disc onto your hard drive, and make note of where it is; it contains the project files and sources you need for this lesson.

This lesson will focus on advanced techniques for manipulating and enhancing layers: Paint, Roto Brush, and the Puppet tools.

After Effects Paint is based on a simplified version of Adobe Photoshop's paint tool, with the added element of time. It allows you to paint nondestructively onto a layer, and to reveal or erase parts of an underlying image; Paint can also clone from one area of an image to another, as well as from a different frame. Paint only works in the Layer panel, but every single stroke is exposed in the Timeline panel, allowing you to retime, edit, and animate the brush settings and location of the stroke after the fact.

Roto Brush is an intelligent paint tool that helps automate the time-consuming process of separating a foreground object (such as an actor) from its background, allowing new imagery to be placed behind it. To accomplish this, you draw simple strokes that define the foreground and background, and After Effects determines the boundary between the two.

The **Puppet** tool provides an alternate way to warp layers. Imagine your image being printed on a sheet of rubber, which is automatically trimmed to the outline of your layer. Then imagine pushing pins through areas of that layer, such as where feet and hands are. Then imagine dragging some of those pins around…

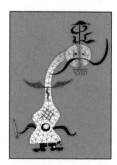

Paint Basics

We'll start by becoming familiar with After Effects Paint. It contains three tools: Brush, Clone Stamp, and Erase. In this exercise, we will practice using all three.

1 Open the project file **Lesson_10.aep**. In the Project panel, make sure the **Comps** folder is twirled down, then double-click the comp **01-Paint Basics*starter** to open it. This comp consists of a still image of a fanciful mask that has an alpha channel.

2 Select Window > Workspace > Paint. This will open the Paint and Brushes panels which allow you to control and customize the Paint tools. It will also

There are three main Paint tools: Brush, Clone Stamp, and Erase.

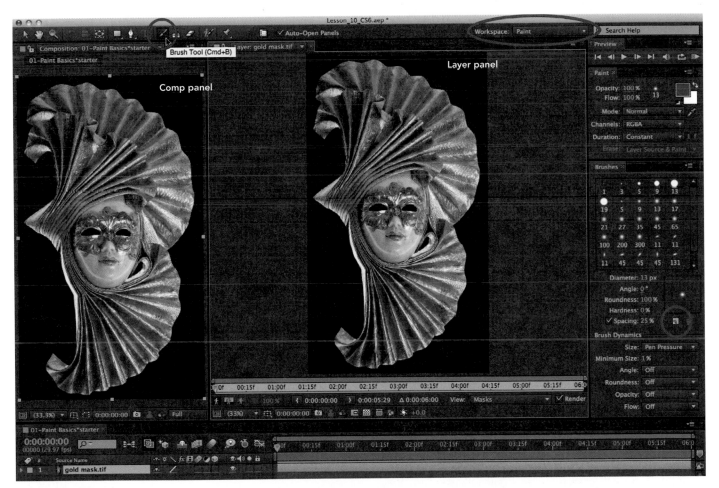

2 Open or create a Workspace that includes the Paint and Brushes panels. These are essential for working with After Effects Paint. You can choose to Save Current Settings as New Brush by clicking the icon circled in red. Note that the Paint tools must be used in the Layer panel.

▽ tip

Quick Size

To interactively resize the brush tip for either After Effects or Roto Brush, press ⌘ on Mac (**Ctrl** on Windows) and drag to set the diameter; release the modifier key and continue to drag to set the feather amount (Hardness).

rearrange your viewers so that the Comp panel takes the place of your Project panel and the Layer panel takes center focus. This is because After Effects Paint must be used in the Layer panel. If you use this layout, be sure to select Window > Project and dock the Project panel into the left side with the Comp; this will make it easy to open other comps when instructed. Of course, you can also make your own custom workspace that includes the Paint, Brushes, and Layer panels.

3 Double-click **gold mask.tif** to open it in the Layer panel. Then select the Brush tool. The shortcut is ⌘ **B** on Mac (**Ctrl** **B** on Windows); this will toggle through the three Paint tools. Note that the Paint panel will be grayed out unless one of the three paint tools is selected.

Each tool has its own set of Paint panel settings. When you change the brush size for the Brush tool, for example, this does not affect the size of the Eraser. The Erase popup is active only when the Eraser tool is selected. The Clone Options in the lower half of the Paint panel will be grayed out unless the Clone Stamp tool is selected.

If this is the first time you are using Paint, the defaults are fine for now. Feel free to pick a foreground color other than bright red plus a different brush size. However, make sure that the Paint panel's Mode popup is set to Normal, Channels is set to RGBA, and Duration to Constant. Opacity should also be set to 100%.

4 Check the bottom of the Layer panel: The Render switch should be enabled. Then draw a few strokes on the gold mask image in the Layer panel to get the hang of things. Try a few different Brush Tip sizes and foreground colors.

Key concept: Changing the settings in the Paint panel affects new strokes only, not existing strokes. But every stroke you draw will appear in the Timeline panel, where you can edit and even animate them. Press **P P** to reveal the Paint parameters in the Timeline panel.

Paint is an "effect" as far as After Effects is concerned. However, if you open the Effect Controls panel, the only option is Paint on Transparent, which is also available in the Timeline. The View popup in the Layer panel confirms that Paint renders after Masks in the rendering order.

4 In the Layer panel, once you make a stroke with the Brush tool, the View popup will change to Paint. Try different brushes and paint colors. Mask courtesy iStockphoto, JLGutiérrez, image #1914878.

▼ Erasing Strokes

If you made a mistake while painting, you might be inclined to reach for the Eraser tool. Be aware that this tool also creates vector-based Eraser strokes in the Timeline panel, resulting in more items for you to manage.

However, if you set the Erase popup in the Paint panel to Last Stroke Only and pick a small brush tip, you can erase portions of the last brush stroke *without* creating a new Eraser stroke. Try out both methods so you can compare the results.

You can invoke the Erase Last Stroke Only mode *while the Brush tool is selected* by pressing ⌘ Shift (Ctrl Shift) and then erasing. Note that when you do this, the Brush Tip size used for erasing is defined by the Eraser tool's last brush size, *not* the Brush tool's current size! If you want to use this handy shortcut, we recommend you *first* set the Eraser to a smaller brush size with a similar Hardness value as the Brush tool *before* starting to paint. Then you'll be able to quickly switch modes and erase pixels as you paint.

△ The Last Stroke Only option in the Erase menu allows you to erase portions of the last stroke without creating Eraser strokes in the Timeline.

Painting the Eyes

Now that you've had time to play, let's work through some exercises and explore the various options available. To quickly delete all your practice strokes, use the menu command Effect > Remove All. Press Home to ensure the current time indicator is at 00:00. Set the Layer panel's Magnification to 100% (or higher) to better see what you are doing; remember you can hold down the spacebar and drag the image in the Layer panel to reposition it.

5 Let's start by adding some eye shadow to the eyelids of our mask. Make sure the Brush tool is selected. Select any color you like in the Paint panel. In the Brushes panel, pick a soft brush around 20 to 30 pixels in size.

Paint around the eyelid on the left side, making sure you slightly overlap the empty eye socket. Notice how the paint draws inside the eye socket? This is because the Channels popup in the Paint panel defaults to RGBA: the RGB color channels, plus the Alpha transparency channel. As a result, your paint stroke's alpha channel is *added* to the underlying layer's alpha.

Undo to remove the first stroke, change the Channels popup in the Paint panel to RGB, and paint the left eyelid again. Now the stroke is confined to the RGB channels only.

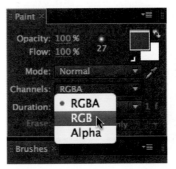

5 Painting with Channels set to RGBA results in your strokes going outside a layer's original alpha channel (left).

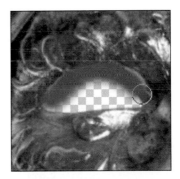

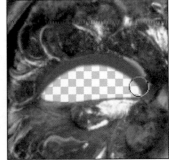

5 *continued* Set Channels to RGB (left), and your strokes will be confined to draw inside the underlying layer's alpha (right).

6–7 Set the Brush's mode to Overlay, and your stroke will be blended into the underlying image (above). Many of the Paint and Brush Tip parameters for each brush stroke appear in the Timeline panel for later editing and animation (right).

▼ Brush Duration Bar

Because the Duration popup in the Paint panel was set to Constant, both Brush strokes will appear for the entire duration of the layer. However, you can drag these gray duration bars to move them earlier or later in time, and trim them – just as you can with ordinary layer bars. By animating the Opacity parameter in Stroke Options, you can also make individual strokes fade up and down.

▽ tip

Painting Order

Because Paint is an effect, you can apply multiple instances of Paint to the same layer and combine it with other effects. You can determine the order in which the effects render by dragging them up and down in the Effect Controls or Timeline panels.

6 Press **P P** to reveal Brush 1 in the Timeline panel. To the right of Brush 1 is a Blending Mode popup for the individual stroke (not to be confused with the Mode popup for the entire layer). To better blend the stroke with the underlying image, select Overlay or Color mode, or another one that suits your fancy. By selecting the Brush, you will also see a thin line appear in the Layer panel that illustrates the middle of your stroke.

While you're here, twirl down Brush 1 > Stroke Options. Notice that you can change the size, color, opacity, and much more of any stroke *after* you've created it! (You can even change the Channels – you don't have to redo the stroke!)

7 Before painting the right eyelid, set the Mode popup in the Paint panel to the same mode as you just chose for Brush 1. Channels should still be set to RGB.

Important! *Press* **F2** *to deselect Brush 1* – otherwise, you will replace it with your new stroke! Now paint over the right eyelid; your new settings will be used. When you're done, Brush 2 will appear in the timeline with its Mode already set.

Painting the Lips

8 In the Paint panel, pick a nice red color for the lips and set the Mode popup to Color. In the Brushes panel, again select a smallish brush (we used the Soft Round 21 pixels brush).

Press **Home** to make sure you are at 00:00. Check that no existing Brush strokes are selected (press **F2** if so). Using one continuous stroke, paint the top lip and continue around painting the bottom lip until the lips are completely covered. When you release the mouse, Brush 3 will be added to the Timeline panel.

9 As you are finished creating paint strokes for now, press **V** to return to the Selection tool; it's best not to edit with the Brush tool active as it's too easy to replace a selected stroke.

• In the Timeline panel, twirl down Brush 3 > Stroke Options.

• Scrub the Stroke Options > Start parameter: Your stroke will wipe off as the value increases. Return Start to 0%.

• Now scrub the Stroke Options > End parameter; reducing the value wipes the stroke off in reverse.

• Set End to 0% and enable its animation stopwatch to set the first keyframe at 00:00.

• Move later in time to 01:00 and set End to 100%.

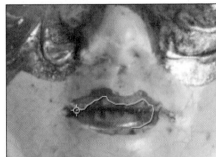

Press **0** on the numeric keypad to RAM Preview: The "lipstick" will now animate on over one second, following the same path you used to paint it. Note that if the Timeline panel is selected, the preview will play in the Comp panel; to preview in the Layer panel, make sure it's selected before you press **0**.

9 As you scrub either Start or End under a Brush's Stroke Options (above), your brush stroke will write on (left).

10 Feel free to also animate Brush 1 and 2 to draw on the eye shadow over time. Your strokes are already done; all that's left is to animate the End parameter:

• Click on the word End for Brush 3 to select both keyframes and Edit > Copy.

• Press **Home** (as keyframes are pasted starting at the current time).

• Select Brush 1, then **Shift**+click Brush 2 to select it as well.

• Paste, and both of these brushes will also get your End keyframes.

RAM Preview, and all three brush strokes will animate in sync. To offset them in time, simply drag the stroke bars in the timeline so that they are staggered in time. A handy shortcut is to move the current time indicator to where you want the stroke to start. Start dragging the stroke bar, then press **Shift** as you get close; it will snap to this time.

10 After you twirl up a Brush in the Timeline panel, dots along its bar will indicate where its underlying keyframes are located. Note that in our final version, we animated the Start parameter for Brush 1 to reverse the animation. We've also moved Brush 3's duration bar so that it starts later in time. To name a stroke, select it, press **Return**, enter a new name, then press **Return** again.

The goal in this exercise is to use Paint to reveal a series of shapes during this colorful animation.

2 To quickly view just the alpha channel, ⌥+click (*Alt*+click) in the Show Channel switch along the bottom of a viewer. The alpha of our bird shows the rough paper texture used.

Painting to Reveal

Quite often, you will not use Paint to directly create visible strokes; instead, you will use Paint to reveal other layers you've already created. This can give the impression that you are "painting on" more complex imagery. This trick will be the focus of our next exercise.

1 Close all previous comps by selecting Close All from the Comp panel's drop-down menu. Type ⌘ **O** (*Ctrl* **O**) to reopen the Project panel. (If the Project panel is taking up valuable space, you can always dock the Project panel into the Comp panel's frame.) Double-click **Comps > 02-Write On*starter** to open it and RAM Preview. (It's large and therefore may take a little while to render.)

Select any layer in this gritty but colorful composition and press **U** to see its keyframes; also feel free to solo layers to see them in isolation. The individual layers were created by hand (see the sidebar *Creating Textures*, opposite page), then combined using techniques you've learned in earlier lessons including blending modes, track mattes, frame blending, and wiggle expressions.

To add even more interest to this composition, you're going to "paint on" the first few layers using animated paint strokes. If you want to see where you're heading before diving in, play **Finished Movies > 02-Write On.mov**.

2 To reveal an image, its layer has to start off invisible, then gradually be revealed over time. Painting on an invisible layer isn't very easy, though – so you'll make the layer transparent in a later step. You'll start by painting in its new alpha channel:

• Double-click layer 1 – **auto-bird.tif** – to open it in its Layer panel. Make sure your comp is at Full Resolution by pressing ⌘ **J** (*Ctrl* **J**).

• ⌥+click (*Alt*+click) on the Show Channel icon along the bottom of the Layer panel to view just the Alpha. You will see a textured white shape against a black background.

• Select the Brush tool. In the Paint panel, check that Opacity and Flow are both set to 100%. Set the Mode popup to Normal.

• Select Alpha from the Channels popup. The colors change to black and white; click on the double-arrow icon to toggle the colors so that the Foreground color is white. It's important to paint these strokes *only* in the layer's alpha channel; painting in the RGB channels will obliterate the original color of the layer.

• Set the Duration popup to Write On. The Write On option will automatically set the keyframes for the stroke's End parameter (based on how fast you paint).

• In the Brushes panel, select a round brush with a diameter of around 50 pixels. Change its Hardness value to around 80%.

▼ Creating Textures

For this exercise, we created a variety of fun sources using inexpensive art supplies. After they dried, we scanned them into the computer. They are contained in the **Sources > Crish Design** folder. Here is how some of them were made:

- **ink texture** was created by smearing printing ink on paper with a putty knife.

- **waxpaper matte** was created by rolling printing ink on wax paper then pressing it onto paper.

- The four sources beginning with the word **"auto"** were created with India ink and a calligraphy tool known as an automatic pen. They were all scribbled in one pass in just a few seconds – it's best not to think too hard to get this look! Once scanned, we created a Photoshop action to invert these black-and-white images and move them to an alpha channel so their backgrounds would be transparent in After Effects.

- The **"rough"** icons were created loading India ink into a folded pen – another calligraphy tool. Drawing on rough water-color paper gives the edge texture, which is more organic than the otherwise beloved Stylize > Roughen Edges plug-in.

- **sunprint sequence** contains a series of ten images cropped out of a blurred abstract watercolor. This sequence was slowed down and looped in its Interpret Footage settings, then Frame Blended in the comp to create crossfades.

- We also created some of our own stamps by heating special foam and pressing found objects into them.

Have fun creating some of your own textures and marks. Check out your local library and the web for more ideas on creating textures from the fine arts and crafts world. *Automatic, folded,* and *ruling pens* all make great marks; a web search will show instructions for how to make a folded pen from a soda can!

- Press **Home** to make sure you are starting at 00:00. In the Layer panel, paint from the bottom up in one continuous stroke over the course of a few seconds, moving your brush as necessary to eventually cover the entire bird.

When you release the mouse, the paint stroke will disappear. This is because Write On automatically created keyframes for End, starting at End = 0%. Press **U** to see these keyframes in the Timeline panel, then scrub the time indicator to see the stroke animate. If you're not happy with the stroke, Undo and try again.

(Note: If you took longer than 10 seconds to draw your stroke, the second End keyframe may not be visible. In the Timeline panel, drag the Brush 1 bar to the left until you can see the second keyframe, and move it earlier in time. Then return the Brush 1 bar to start at 00:00.)

◁ Feel free to drag the top of the Brushes panel to cover the Clone Options.

2 *continued* Configure a roughly 50-pixel brush to paint on just the Alpha channel, using Write On for its Duration, and paint over the image from the bottom up.

A

B

C

3 When the RGB channels are viewed, you'll initially see paint blobs plus your bird (A). Toggle the Paint on Transparent option On, and you'll see just your strokes (B). Apply Effect > Channel > Set Matte, and the bird's original alpha channel will cut through your strokes, yielding the desired effect (C).

3 Press **V** to return to the Selection tool. Return the Layer panel Channels popup to RGB mode and scrub the timeline. Hmm…a black blob on a black bird – not our intention. Time to finish the illusion:

• With **auto-bird** still selected, press **F3** to open its Effect Controls panel, which will show the Paint effect. Toggle Paint on Transparent option to On. Now the layer will start off transparent.

• The remaining problem is that the original alpha has been replaced with the paint stroke. To retrieve it, apply Effect > Channels > Set Matte. The default options reapply the alpha from the layer's source.

RAM Preview and adjust the timing of the Stroke Options > End keyframe to taste. Bring the Comp panel forward and preview your reveal in the context of the other layers.

Our version is in **Comps_finished > 02-Write On_final** if you'd like to check it out.

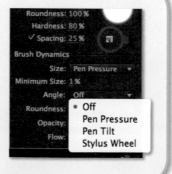

▼ Tablet Settings

A pressure sensitive tablet such as a Wacom is a great companion for Paint. The Brush Dynamics section at the bottom of the Brushes panel allows you to set how the pen's pressure, tilt, or stylus wheel affects the brush as you paint. Click on the Save Current Settings as New Brush button to remember your favorite configurations.

Don't stop here! Repeat the above steps with the **rough-triangle** layer (you may need to keyframe the brush diameter for this one as it starts skinny in the center and gets thicker as it unwinds), the **stairs** layer (adjust Brush Tip Roundness to create a flatter brush to get more of a wiping effect), and the **zigzag** layer (experiment with adjusting the Brush Tip Angle parameter).

Our version is in **Comps_finished > 02-Write On_final**, where we've also staggered the timing of the layers, scaled and rotated **rough-triangle**, and added some wiggle expressions to heighten the craziness.

Using the Clone Stamp Tool

If you are familiar with cloning in Photoshop, the Clone Stamp tool in After Effects works in a similar fashion: It samples pixels from one part of a layer and copies them to another part. But in After Effects, you can also animate the timing of clone strokes as well as transform them.

1 Close all previous comps and open **Comps > 03-Cloning*starter**. For this exercise, we suggest you continue using Workspace > Paint so you can view the Comp and Layer panels side by side.

The background is a series of frame blended still images; focus on the **misc splats.tif** layer. A variety of "ink splats" are scattered around this footage. You'll use the Clone Stamp tool to add a few more, then transform them.

2 Just like the other Paint tools, you can use the Clone Stamp tool only in the Layer panel. Press **Home** to return to 00:00, then double-click **misc splats.tif** to open its Layer panel. Verify that the Channels popup at the bottom of the Layer panel has been set back to RGB.

3 Select the Clone Stamp tool. The Paint panel will update to show the last settings used for this tool. Opacity and Flow should be at 100%; set Mode to Normal, Channels to RGBA, and Duration to Constant.

• Verify that the Clone Options are visible at the bottom of the Paint panel. The Aligned switch should be disabled; this will allow you to clone multiple copies without having to reset the origin point.

• Set your Brush size to a largish Diameter such as 80 so you can clone the splats easily. Increase the Hardness value to reduce the possibility of picking up stray pixels.

4 Finally, you are ready to start cloning:

• Press the ⌥ (*Alt*) key; the cursor will change to a crosshair icon (left). Click on the first splat you want to copy. The Source Position will update in the Paint panel.

• Release the ⌥ (*Alt*) key. Then paint where you'd like to drop a new splat. Because the Aligned switch is off, you can click again in a new location to repeat the same item elsewhere on the layer.

• As soon as you create one stroke, the Paint effect is applied. (If the Effect Controls panel comes forward, dock it with the Comp panel and bring the Layer panel forward again.)

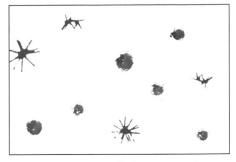

In this exercise, you will clone some of these ink splats to create a busier layer, and animate them to appear at different times.

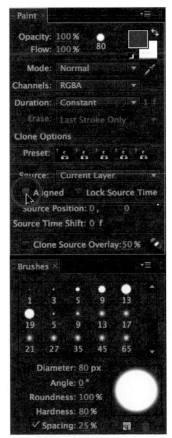

3 Select the Clone Stamp tool (top left). The Clone Options will become active in the Paint panel (above). Use the above settings for Paint and Brushes. For this exercise, Aligned should be disabled (circled).

▽ tip

What's in a Stroke

In After Effects, Mask Paths and Brush Paths are both vector based, and you can copy and paste between them. You can also copy paths from Illustrator. Before you paste, though, be sure to click on the existing property name (such as Brush 1 > Path) to "target" it. You can also use expressions to link all paths that have been created with the Pen tool.

▽ gotcha

Replacing Strokes

Be warned that if a Brush stroke is already selected in the Timeline panel, and you draw a new stroke, the selected stroke will be replaced. Press **F2** to deselect all strokes before drawing new strokes.

Have fun cloning other spots until your layer is nicely populated with splotches (see figure, right), which you can then practice animating:

5 Press **P P** to reveal the Paint effect in the Timeline panel; you may need to resize its frame to see all of your individual Clone stroke bars. You can then edit parameters of the individual strokes:

• Press **V** to return to the Selection tool. To move a cloned object after the fact, select one of your Clone strokes in the Timeline panel, and its Anchor Point (plus the center line of any "brushing" you did) will appear in the Layer panel. Drag it to a new position; when you release the mouse, the Comp panel will update to show its new location in context.

• To create variations on the cloned originals, twirl down one of your Clone strokes in the Timeline panel, then twirl down its Transform settings. Scrub the Rotation and Scale settings while watching the Comp panel. Go ahead and keyframe these parameters to animate the clone.

• Try offsetting some of the Clone strokes in the Timeline panel so that they start at different points in time. That way, they will appear to "pop" on. To fade them on, animate their Stroke Options > Opacity parameter.

• To remove a cloned stroke, select it (in the Layer panel or the Timeline panel) and press **Delete**.

• To remove a splat on the original layer, use the Eraser tool: Set the Channels to RGB and the background color to white, then you can erase without creating a "hole." The render order of the strokes goes from bottom to top in the Timeline panel, so make sure After Effects gets a chance to render the clone before you erase its source!

• You can also clone a clone, just like you can in Photoshop. And if you clone an animated Clone stroke, the second clone will also animate!

Continue cloning, erasing, and transforming until you have a nice balance and arrangement of ink splats. If you want to compare results, open Window > Project (it's near the bottom of the list) and view our version **Comps_Finished > 03_Cloning_final**.

5 In the Timeline panel, you can slide the Clone stroke bars in time and transform how each stroke is drawn. Transform properties can also be animated.

Roto Brush

Roto Brush is an intelligent paint tool that helps automate the process of creating an alpha channel for an object (the *foreground*) to separate it from the rest of the image around it (the *background*). To accomplish this, you draw simple strokes that define the foreground and optionally the background, and After Effects determines the boundary between the two. After Effects then uses motion estimation to track how this boundary changes over time, with help from you in the form of corrective brush strokes. It's not perfect, but it's often better than trying to paint or mask every frame by hand.

We'll start with a simple task so you can gain familiarity with Roto Brush's basic tools. We'll move on to a more challenging exercise, guiding you through the preferred workflow for achieving optimal results. Mastering this workflow will provide you with a far more rewarding experience than simply applying Roto Brush at its default settings.

Instant Gratification

1 Close any previous compositions and open **Comps > RB1-Butterfly*starter**. RAM Preview; a butterfly wafts over a tulip garden. The problem is that the butterfly looks unnatural flying in front of all the flowers – from this camera angle it should be behind the foreground tulips. To make this happen you need to cut out the foreground flowers and paste a copy of them in front of the butterfly.

2 Select **Tulips.mov** and press ⌘ D (*Ctrl* D) to duplicate it. Press *Return* to highlight the duplicate layer's name and change it to "**Tulips – Foreground**." Press *Return* again to accept the new name.

3 Using Roto Brush can be time consuming and tedious, so you don't want to use it on more frames than necessary. Scrub the current time indicator until you reach the frame where the butterfly's wing first touches a tulip petal. With **Tulips – Foreground** selected, press ⌥ [(*Alt* [) to trim the layer's in point. Then scrub the time indicator to the last frame where the butterfly touches a petal and press ⌥] (*Alt*]) to trim the layer's out point.

Roto Brush Tool. Drag over foreground; Option-drag over background. (Option+W)
RB1–Butterfly*starter

The Roto Brush tool is to the right of the Paint tools. Like the Paint tools, it must be used while in the Layer panel.

▽ factoid

Rotoscoping

The term *rotoscoping* was originally used to describe the process in which the movement of live actors was traced to create an animation. It is now commonly used to describe the process of cutting out a foreground object (such as an actor) from its background.

1 The goal is to make the butterfly fly behind the foreground flowers without having to paint or mask every single frame. Tulips courtesy Artbeats/CrackerClips CC-FH101-74; butterfly illustration courtesy Dover.

4 In the Timeline panel, drag **Tulips – Foreground** above **Butterfly Flight.mov**. Place the current time indicator at 01:10; the foreground clip currently obscures the butterfly.

4 Trim a duplicate of the background to cover the time span you wish the flowers to be in front of the **Butterfly Flight** layer.

7–8 Drag the Roto Brush Foreground tool inside of the area you wish to keep. Add as many strokes as necessary to fully define your desired foreground (above). After Effects will draw a pink Segmentation Boundary between what it believes to be the foreground and the background (below).

9 The short yellow bar is your Base Frame (right) where you initially drew strokes to define the foreground and the background. The Roto Brush Span indicates how many frames before and after the Base Frame this information will be propagated. The thin green bar indicates which frames Roto Brush has calculated; it must calculate them in sequential order.

5 Make sure the Comp panel's Resolution is set to Full; this is required to work accurately with the Roto Brush tool. Then double-click **Tulips – Foreground** to open it in the Layer panel: As with Paint, Roto Brush must be used in this panel so you have an unaltered view of your source layer.

6 Select the Roto Brush tool (it's the icon of a little man being tickled by a big paint brush!). Move the cursor over the Layer panel; a green circle with a + symbol in the middle will appear. As with the Paint tools, you can resize this brush by pressing ⌘ (*Ctrl*), then clicking and dragging. Set it to be roughly twice the width of the foreground tulip stems.

7 Click near the top of the middle petal of the foreground tulip and drag downward toward the base of the petals. You don't need to be precise, but it's essential that your brush touches only the flower petals (the foreground) and not the sky (the background). Release the mouse and a pink *Segmentation Boundary* will be drawn around this flower's petals. The Effect Controls panel will also open with a Roto Brush effect applied to this layer.

8 Remember that the butterfly's wings touched more than one flower. Click and drag through the petals of the second foreground flower to the right; a Segmentation Boundary will also surround it.

9 Turn your attention to the Layer panel's timeline. You will see a short yellow bar at its time marker. This indicates a *Base Frame*, which contains the foreground and background definitions Roto Brush will use to guess motion in the rest of the clip. Now look for the gray bar with arrows pointing away from the Base Frame: This defines the *Roto Brush Span*, which is how far before and after the Base Frame After Effects will try to "propagate" your strokes. Note that it does not completely cover the trimmed segment for this layer.

Just as with the Paint tools, the **1** and **2** keys may be used to step backward and forward in the Layer panel when the Roto Brush tool is active. Press **2** to step forward: After a pause, a green bar will extend from the Base Frame to the time marker's location. This indicates After Effects has calculated any movement between frames and has updated the Segmentation Boundary to match. Refining this propagation is the secret to achieving good results with Roto Brush; we'll discuss this at length in the next exercise.

10 Click the Composition panel's tab to bring it forward. The butterfly is behind the flower petal – hurray! But before you get too excited, RAM Preview: After a pause for Roto Brush to calculate each frame, the butterfly disappears briefly starting around 02:00. This is because your Roto Brush Span did not last for the duration of this layer.

11 Click the Layer panel's tab to bring it forward again and locate its time marker just after the Roto Brush Span

ends. The Segmentation Boundary will surround the entire frame. Since Roto Brush seemed to be working fine up until this point, you can drag the right end of the Roto Brush Span to the right until it covers the entire trimmed segment for this layer. Bring the Comp panel forward again and RAM Preview; the butterfly will now fly behind the foreground flowers as desired.

11 If necessary, trim the Roto Brush Span to extend it for the desired number of frames.

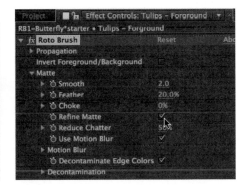

12 Move the current time indicator to 01:12 and closely observe the edge between the petal and wing: A faint black "matte line" is visible. To improve this, enable Refine Matte for Roto Brush in the Effect Controls panel. This engages the second half of the Roto Brush effect that deals with color "contamination" plus calculates motion blur. As a final touch, slightly reduce the Opacity for **Tulips – Foreground** to make the petal translucent.

Trust us, using Roto Brush is rarely this easy – but now you have a taste for what is possible and why it's worth learning this tool. So let's move on to a more typical, challenging example.

12 Initially, Roto Brush may create hard edges around your foreground shapes such as the flower petal here (A). Enable its Refine Matte section (center) to improve this. In **Comps_Finished > RB1-Butterfly_final**, we also reduced the layer's opacity to make the petal translucent (B).

We want to replace the original word processor screen with a far sexier data control screen (above). To do so, you'll need to cut out the hands and arm so they reappear in front of the monitor (below). Screen courtesy Artbeats/Control Panels 2; footage Artbeats F129-02.

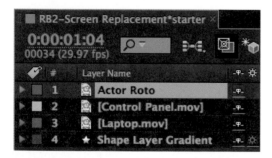

2 Duplicate the main footage (**Laptop.mov**), rename it (**Actor Roto**), and drag it above the layer it is supposed to appear in front of (**Control Panel.mov**).

Screen Replacement Roto

This next exercise is based on replacing the screen graphics on a computer. The screen replacement part is relatively easy; we've already done it for you using mocha (introduced in Lesson 9). The challenge is that the actor obscures part of the screen – and that just won't do.

Workflow

Although the details will vary with each job, there is a general workflow to follow with Roto Brush to achieve optimal results:

• Identify the foreground you wish to separate from its background.

• Choose a representative Base Frame where the maximum amount of the foreground is visible.

• Define the Base Frame using a collection of Foreground and Background Roto Brush strokes.

• Move a few frames away from the Base and tweak the Propagation parameters to optimize Roto Brush's tracking of the shot.

• Return to the Base frame, then step away from it one frame at a time, adding Foreground and Background Strokes as needed.

• Tweak the Matte parameters to refine the resulting alpha channel.

Creating a Base Frame

1 Open **Comps > RB2-Screen Replacement*starter**. This comp contains three layers: the already tracked replacement screen (**Control Panel.mov**), the original shot (**Laptop.mov**), and **Shape Layer Gradient** to control the blur across the screen. Scrub the current time indicator through the shot, noting which parts of the actor are obscured by the new screen: his hands as well as portions of his right wrist and upper arm.

2 Your goal is to create a version of the original shot that contains just the obscured sections to paste in front of the new screen. Duplicate **Laptop.mov**, rename it "**Actor Roto**," and drag it above **Control Panel.mov** in the Timeline panel.

3 Double-click **Actor Roto** to open it in the Layer panel. Scrub the Layer panel's time marker through the clip to become familiar with it.

An optimal Base Frame is where the foreground is most clearly revealed. Roto Brush finds it easier to propagate its Segmentation Boundary when details disappear (for example, when gaps between individual fingers close), compared with the sudden appearance of new details (such as separated fingers).

You may create multiple Base Frames during the course of a shot. In this case – where there are multiple instances when the gaps between fingers open then close again – we'll pick one instance to work on for now. The frame at 01:04 is a good candidate, as there is a gap between the index and middle finger of the left hand and we can still see most of the little finger on the right hand.

4 Select the Roto Brush tool. Move the cursor over the Layer panel, press ⌘ (*Ctrl*), then drag to resize the brush to be just smaller than the right wrist.

Our focus is to create a good matte (alpha channel) for the hands and right sleeve, as they actually move in front of the screen. Since we're going to grab part of the sleeve, we need to go ahead and select the entire shirt as our foreground element; otherwise, the resulting matte edge may cause visual artifacts if just part of the shirt is grafted back on top of the original shot. Fortunately, we don't need to be as critical in cutting out the rest of the shirt as we have to be with the hands.

3 The frame at 01:04 should make a good Base Frame, as we can see most of the hands plus gaps between individual fingers.

5 Click near the top of the actor's middle three fingers and drag a continuous stroke along the arm and up across the shoulders. The green color indicates you are drawing a Foreground stroke. When you release the mouse, a pink Segmentation Boundary will loosely surround the actor where Roto Brush detected edges between foreground and background.

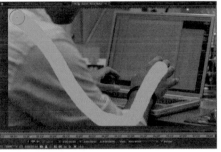 

5 Drag a broad green Foreground stroke along the arm and shirt (left). The Segmentation Boundary will loosely enclose the actor, and a Base Frame plus Roto Brush Span will be created in the Layer panel's timeline (right).

6 Roto Brush initially defined too much of the clip as the foreground; you need to teach it which areas are actually part of the background. Resize the brush smaller, then hold ⌥ (*Alt*): The brush will turn red with a – sign in the middle, indicating you're about to draw a Background stroke. Starting in the background area, drag through areas that are supposed to also be in the background (not included in the cutout), including the laptop's frame and keyboard. Chances are some of the foreground will now be selected as background. The next step is fine-tuning this distinction.

6 Hold ⌥ (*Alt*) and drag a red Background stroke to remove the laptop from the Segmentation Boundary; notice that the stroke starts in the background area when extending the background.

7 Use Foreground strokes to include the fingers inside the Segmentation Boundary (A); notice that our new stroke overlaps the existing foreground area. Use Background strokes to exclude areas between fingers and other undesired details (B). Spend some time carefully defining the boundary around the hands; beyond the screen, we're just interested in a consistent edge between differing colors (C).

7 Zoom in to 200% or 400% to see details; hold the spacebar and drag to pan around the screen. Work on correcting the fingers: If they're outside the Segmentation Boundary, drag Foreground (green) strokes through them. If gaps between the fingers are also enclosed by the Segmentation Boundary, resize the brush smaller, hold ⌥ (*Alt*), and carefully drag Background (red) strokes between the fingers. If you touch the fingers accidentally while doing so, Undo and try again.

Draw additional Foreground and Background strokes as needed to create a really good Base Frame, paying special attention to the fingers. Don't be too distracted by small imperfections in the Segmentation Boundary; it is just a rough centerline between the foreground and background – as long as it's within a pixel or so of the desired edge, you're good.

Propagation

Now that you've taught Roto Brush the difference between the foreground and background, your next step is to refine how Roto Brush propagates this information across adjacent frames.

8 Return to 100% zoom so you can see the entire image. Press **1** or **2** to move a few frames earlier or later than the Base Frame and check how well Roto Brush is propagating your initial input. Depending on how you defined that Base Frame, you might see some problems crop up such as a gap reappearing between the fingers on the left hand.

9 In the Effect Controls panel, twirl down the Propagation section of the Roto Brush effect. Enable View Search Region, and the image will be converted to grayscale, with yellow zones showing you where Roto Brush is looking for the boundary between foreground and background. There are three parameters that control the Search Region:

• *Search Radius* controls how far Roto Brush searches for movement from frame to frame. If the Segmentation Boundary appears to be left behind as your foreground moves, increase Search Radius. If your foreground is moving slowly but the Segmentation Boundary reaches out and grabs an area it shouldn't, decrease

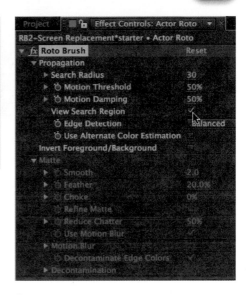

it. At 01:00 in our version, the region missed the tip of the right little finger; increasing Search Radius to 33 cured it.

• *Motion Threshold* affects how Roto Brush determines if an edge is moving. In our version, at 01:07 this yellow zone disappears around the left edge of the right hand, suggesting Roto Brush might be missing slow movement along this edge. This indicates that Motion Threshold may be set too high, so reduce it slowly until yellow is visible all around the edge – about 35% worked for us.

• *Motion Damping* controls how tight Roto Brush makes the Search Region for edges that are moving slowly. Noisy footage may fool Roto Brush into thinking an edge is moving when it isn't; in that case, increase Motion Damping. If the Segmentation Boundary is failing to pick up slight movements, decrease Motion Damping. The default is fine for this shot.

When you're done tweaking these parameters, disable View Search Region.

10 Now let's deal with how the actual Segmentation Boundary is calculated to see if we can improve the problem with the gap in the left hand:

• *Edge Detection* sets how Roto Brush determines the Segmentation Boundary between foreground and background. The Favor Predicted Edges option estimates where the edge should be based on the location of those edges in adjacent frames, and works best in this case. The Favor Current Edges option puts an emphasis on edges found just in the current frame, which can work better with rapidly changing imagery (but not on this shot). The Balanced option considers both equally.

• *Use Alternate Color Estimation* alters the internal algorithm used to determine what is foreground and what is background. In this shot, enabling it fixed some problems and created others; we left it off.

9 Enable Roto Brush > View Search Region (above) to see where Roto Brush is looking for movements in the segmentation before foreground and background.

A fast-moving finger sticking outside the yellow outline (A) may mean the Search Radius needs to be larger.

A gap in the yellow outline (B) indicates we need to decrease Motion Threshold to pick up slight movement.

10 Setting Edge Detection to Balanced or Favor Current Edges causes problems with the gap in the left hand (A). Setting it to Favor Predicted Edges works much better (B).

Making Corrections Over Time

You've done what you can to aid Roto Brush's automated process of propagating your Base Frame across adjacent frames. From here on you'll have to perform some manual labor to correct Roto Brush when it goes astray.

All corrections are propagated from the Base Frame outward along the Roto Brush Span. Therefore, it's important to catch and correct errors as close to the Base Frame as possible to reduce the number of corrections you'll have to perform later (or earlier) in time.

11 Return the Layer panel's time marker to where you created the Base Frame (01:04). Press **1** to step earlier in time. Carefully scan the Segmentation Boundary, looking for places where it deviates from the outline of the hands. For example, at 01:03 we noticed that the gap between the fingers on the left hand could be better defined. So zoom in close, resize the Roto Brush small enough to fit into the remaining gap, hold **⌥** (*Alt*) and draw a Background stroke into this gap.

When you make small corrective strokes into areas with sharp angles – such as between these fingers – you may be disappointed to see the Segmentation Boundary did not outline the space you thought you defined. Part of the reason is this boundary is displaying the approximate centerline for what may later be a softly defined semitransparent area. Another is that the smoothing for the boundary may be too high.

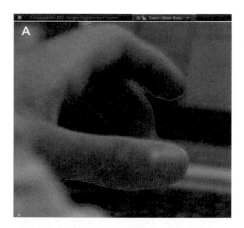

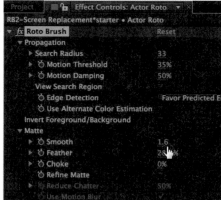

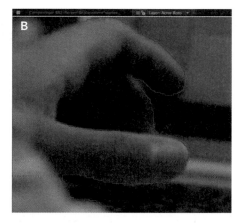

11–12 Getting the Segmentation Boundary to properly outline tight spaces with sharp angles requires a combination of small Roto Brush strokes (A) and judicious reduction of Matte > Smooth (center, B).

12 Make sure Roto Brush > Matte is twirled open in the Effect Controls panel and slowly decrease Matte > Smooth while watching the Segmentation Boundary. The goal is to allow the boundary to travel as far into this narrow space as needed, without causing a jagged outline for the rest of the boundary between foreground and background. You can tweak the Matte parameters later as needed; for now, setting it around 1.6 should give you a more satisfying outline.

13 Continue stepping earlier in time, carefully scanning the Segmentation Boundary on each frame for irregularities. In this clip, the bracelet, fingertips, and spaces between fingers are the most susceptible to problems – in particular, watch for a gap opening and closing in the left hand before 01:00. Correct any problems with additional Foreground and Background strokes. Focus most on the hands, but make sure you don't suddenly lose track of the shirt or keyboard.

Your corrective strokes will be propagated to subsequent frames in the direction that the Roto Brush Span arrows are pointing (away from the Base Frame). If you notice a new problem crop up that you didn't spot before, back up a frame or two and verify it didn't actually appear on a previous frame (that's closer to the base frame). Again, the sooner you can catch and fix problems, the less work you'll have to do later.

14 Every time you add a corrective stroke, the Roto Brush Span is extended in the direction indicated by its embedded arrows. If you are fortunate enough to step 20 frames in a row without correction, you will go beyond the end of the span and the Segmentation Boundary will surround the entire frame. No problem; either step back a frame and make a new corrective stroke, or drag the end of the Roto Brush Span to cover additional frames.

15 Once you're satisfied that you've created a good Segmentation Boundary for the first portion of this clip, return the time marker to the Base Frame at 01:04 and repeat this process stepping forward a frame at a time. Remember to scan around the entire Segmentation Boundary and to make corrections as early as possible.

Create a good Segmentation Boundary out to 01:27 and press **N** to end the work area here. After this frame, the left hand starts to rise again, creating new gaps between the fingers. On a real production job, it would be a good idea to create a new Base Frame later in time (perhaps around 02:09) and start a second Roto Brush Span to cover this new set of movements. Roto Brush will seamlessly join together spans that touch each other in the Layer panel's timeline.

13–14 Corrective strokes will be propagated earlier or later in time in the direction the Roto Brush Span arrows are pointing (away from the yellow Base Frame). If the Segmentation Boundary outlines the entire frame (above), drag the Roto Brush Span longer to cover additional frames as required (right).

15 When the fingers on the left hand start to rise again at 02:09, it might be a good idea to stop working on your original Roto Brush Span and start another.

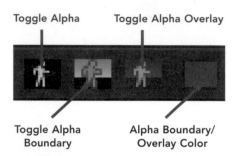

Toggle Alpha   Toggle Alpha Overlay

Toggle Alpha   Alpha Boundary/
Boundary   Overlay Color

Refining the Matte

You've done the tedious work; now it's time to have Roto Brush clean up the edges. (If you gave up during the earlier steps, open **Comps_finished > RB2-Screen Replacement-Step 16** to pick up from this point in the exercise.)

16 Return to your original Base Frame at 01:04, set the Magnification to 200%, and center the hands in the Layer panel. Click the Toggle Alpha Boundary button along the bottom left of the Layer panel to disable viewing of the Segmentation Boundary and observe your cut-out hands. At this point you're viewing the raw results of Roto Brush's matte.

16–17 Click Toggle Alpha Boundary (above) to turn off the Segmentation Boundary and see your raw matte (A). Enable Roto Brush > Matte > Refine Matte to allow the Roto Brush effect to perform automatic cleanups (B).

17 In the Effect Controls panel, enable Refine Matte. Now partial transparency, motion blur, and color *decontamination* (removing the background color from the semitransparent areas of the foreground) are enabled.

18 Click on the tab for the Composition panel to view your composited image. Earlier we suggested you reduce Matte > Smooth to allow the Segmentation Boundary to cut further into the gaps between fingers; the result is a slightly rough matte outline. Now that you've finished defining the boundary, balance Smooth, Feather, and Choke off of each other to create a smooth, antialiased (slightly soft) edge without uninvited colors becoming visible around the edges.

Check different points in time to make sure the parameters you choose look good everywhere. For example, we found a value for Smooth of 2.0 looked okay at 01:03, but looked terrible around 00:15. We settled on Smooth = 4.0 to get rid of unsightly aliasing, Feather = 50% to create a softer edge, and Choke = 20% to compensate for this wider feather revealing a bit of the background – but your results may vary depending on the Segmentation Boundary you created. Also remember that you can keyframe these values over time, depending on what a shot requires. This comes in handy if focus changes during the shot.

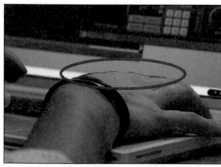

18 A low Smooth setting may look good on some frames, but can cause unsightly edges to appear on other frames (circled above). Always check your edits across multiple points in time.

If your foreground isn't moving, but the matte around its edges is changing from frame to frame anyway, increase Roto Brush > Matte > Reduce Chatter. By contrast, if Roto Brush seems to be ignoring slight movements or if it erodes fast-moving edges, try decreasing Reduce Chatter.

19 Move to around 00:26 where the right hand is moving quickly and note the partially transparent motion blur along the top of the hand. Twirl down the Matte > Motion Blur section; this is where you can further tweak its look. For this shot, we found enabling Higher Quality yielded a slightly more natural look around the right fingertips.

20 Twirl down Matte > Decontamination and enable View Decontamination. The white band is where Roto Brush is performing color correction. This area changes size depending on how much motion blur or other partial transparency exists. If visible color spill extends beyond this area, use Increase Decontamination Radius to correct a wider zone.

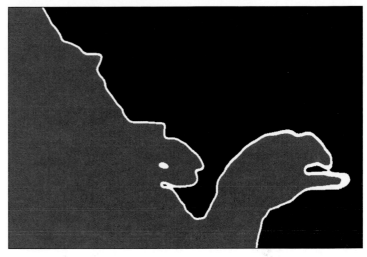

Disable View Decontamination and tweak these settings as required by each individual shot to increase or reduce the amount of decontamination Roto Brush performs. For this shot, we also found enabling Extend Where Smoothed made tiny improvements in small areas such as where fingers came together.

20 When Roto Brush > Matte > Decontamination > View Decontamination is enabled, the white area shows you where Roto Brush will be performing smoothing and color correction. Disable this option and examine these areas in the final composite for potential problems such as colored outlines.

21 RAM Preview and observe how your composite is working at normal speed. Stubborn artifacts that are apparent on still frames may be less noticeable when the scene is moving. On the other hand, you may find some areas where you didn't get the Segmentation Boundary quite right, or otherwise need to tweak your settings.

The two biggest mistakes users make with Roto Brush are assuming it is fully automatic after you create your initial Foreground strokes, and assuming the results will be perfect. Neither is true; some shots will require a lot of work on your part, including using the Paint tools to fix edges in the alpha channel that Roto Brush just can't get right. Some may require you to simply start over (we performed this roto four times before we were happy) or to break the shot into smaller sections. But in the end, Roto Brush can still save a lot of time compared with having to paint or mask every detail of every frame by hand.

21 The final composite looks clean and natural. It took some work to get here, but less than the alternatives.

Three Puppet tools give you new possibilities in warping layers.

The Puppet Tool

After Effects contains a set of three distortion tools collectively known as the Puppet tool. These provide an alternate way to warp layers. As you might guess from the name, they are particularly well suited for character animation, although they can also be used for entertaining effects on other types of layers.

The core element of the Puppet tool is the idea of a *pin*. Pins serve two purposes:

• They stabilize elements that you *don't* want to move, such as feet that are supposed to stay on the ground.

• They act as handles to drag elements that you *do* want to move, such as a hand reaching or waving.

After the pins are placed, the Puppet tool then warps the layer between the stationary pins and the moving handles. It also includes other useful options, such as a Starch tool that reduces how much an area warps, and an Overlap tool that ensures that the part of the layer you are dragging will cross over in front or behind another part of the same layer.

Puppet Pin Tool

1 Close All previous compositions. If you were previously using the Paint workspace, reset the Workspace popup to Standard (and if the layout still looks odd, select Workspace > Reset "Standard"). In the Project panel, locate and open **Comps > 04-Puppet*starter**. Select **MiroMan.psd**: a fanciful character with a few appendages to play with.

2 Select the Puppet Pin tool in the Tools panel; a set of options will appear to the right in the Tools panel. Enable the Mesh: Show switch, leave Expansion at 3, and set the Triangles value to 500 or so.

Press **Home** to make sure you are at 00:00 – this is important because unlike most other parameters inside After Effects, the Puppet tool enables animation and creates a keyframe as soon as you create a pin.

3 Click on one of MiroMan's ankles to pin it in place. A yellow pin will appear where you clicked. **MiroMan.psd** will also be overlaid with a mesh of triangles, which indicate how the layer has been divided for warping. Click on the other ankle to pin both into place.

2–3 Select the Puppet Pin tool and enable Mesh: Show (circled). Clicking on the layer with this tool places a yellow pin (where the arrow is pointing), plus reveals the mesh of triangles the Puppet tool will use to break up and warp your layer.

Credit: We drew this character in Adobe Illustrator while referring to an image in the Dover book of public domain art *Treasury of Fantastic and Mythological Creatures*. He is based on a character in the Joan Miró painting *The Harlequin's Carnival (Le Carnaval d'Arlequin)* 1924/25.

4 Click on the arm on the left, at the point where it meets the pencil. This is a handle we want to move.

Now for the fun bit: Click on the yellow dot for the pin you just created (the cursor will turn white, with a four-way arrow at its tail) and drag it around the Comp panel. **MiroMan** will warp to follow your dragging, with the ankles remaining pinned in place.

Notice how the feet beyond the ankles counter-rotate slightly as you drag, helping give the impression of the character stretching on his tippy-toes. If you don't want the toes to move, undo to a prestretched pose, pin the toes as well, then get back to dragging and stretching the arm with the pencil.

5 Click on the top of the pencil to add another pin. Hover the cursor over this new pin; it will change to the four arrow pointer. Drag this new pin, and the pencil will bend.

Animating Pins

6 Now let's animate your arm and pencil:

• Hold **Shift** and press **Page Down** to move forward 10 frames. Move the tip of the pencil into a new position.

• Press **End** to move to the end of the comp. Select the pins for both the pencil tip and where the arm meets the pencil. You can drag a marquee around them, or **Shift**+click them. Drag this pair together into a new position.

Press **0** on the numeric keypad to RAM Preview and watch your simple animation. Remember, After Effects enabled keyframing for you automatically to save you from having to dive into the Timeline panel chasing after every single pin. With the layer selected, press **U** and you will see your keyframes.

We've animated a few more pins in our version **Comps_Finished > 04-Puppet_final**; select **MiroMan > Puppet** in the Timeline panel to see these pins.

4 Dragging the pin on the arm warps the entire character, pivoting around the pins (at the ankles) that you're not moving.

6 After Effects automatically enables every Puppet Pin for keyframing.

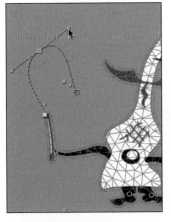

◁ When you select an individual pin, its motion path is displayed in the Comp panel; drag handles to edit it.

△ You can give each pin a descriptive name in the Timeline panel: Simply select it, press **Return**, type a new name, and press **Return** to accept.

▼ Puppet Part Stacking Order

You have control over which layer pieces will pass in front of or behind other layer pieces. Using the Puppet Overlap tool, click on specific sections of the body, then increase or decrease the Extent value to include more or less of the area. (Increase the Mesh Triangles value for finer increments.) Once the Overlap regions are set, the In Front values for each pin determines the stacking priority for a pin's area.

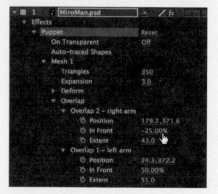

△ In **Comps_finished > 05-Puppet-overlap_final**, the left arm moves in front of the body, but the right arm goes behind due to a negative In Front value.

Puppet Overlap Tool

An important feature of the Puppet tool is the ability to control how your character behaves when you drag one piece to overlap another.

1 Open **Comps > 05-Puppet-overlap*starter**. This is the same character you've been working with.

2 Select **MiroMan.psd**. If Puppet isn't visible in the Timeline panel, press **E** to reveal effects. Select the word Puppet in the Timeline panel, and you will see three yellow circles in the Comp panel that show where we've already placed pins for you: on the two ankles and on the wrist on the left (the one holding the pencil).

3 Select the Puppet Pin tool and disable the mesh to make it easier to see what's going on. Drag the pin on the wrist so that it moves across his left hip: The warped element will go *behind* the body. Now drag the pin up and over this shoulder: The pencil will move in *front of* the body. You can control what element passes in front of or behind another:

• Undo to return to normal. Select the Puppet Overlap tool. A gray outline of the unwarped body will appear. Inside this gray outline, click on what would be the middle of the pencil. A blue dot will appear, and its outline will be shaded in white, following the size of the mesh triangles. The size of the shaded area is determined by the Extent parameter in the Tools panel. The default is 15; increase Extent value until the entire left arm is filled in.

• Press **V** to return to the Selection tool. Drag the pin on the wrist over the character's hip – now the arm and pencil will pass in front of his body! (Note that setting the In Front parameter to a negative value will move it behind.)

This is a fairly simple animation. For more complex moves, you may need to set Overlap pins on the body as well. The In Front parameter controls which part is in front of another; you can even keyframe it if needed.

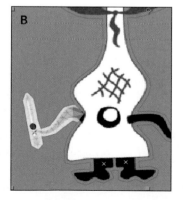

3 Normally, the arm will pass behind the body when you drag it behind his hips (A).

Place an Overlap Pin on the pencil, and set the Extent value (see above) to cover the pencil and arm (B); now it will pass in front of the body (C).

Recording Puppet Animation

The Puppet tool has a version of Motion Sketch (discussed in Lesson 2) to make it easier to animate pins. To practice this, open **Comps > 06-Puppet-sketch*starter**:

4 Select **MiroMan.psd**. If Puppet isn't visible in the Timeline panel, press **U** to reveal it; we've already placed pins on the ankles and the left arm. Select the left arm pin, and press the **⌘** (**Ctrl**) key and hover the cursor over the yellow pin on the left arm: The cursor will look like a stopwatch.

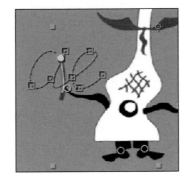

While still holding **⌘** (**Ctrl**), click on this pin and start dragging it around. After Effects will start recording your animation as you drag. It will stop either when you release the mouse or time runs out in the comp.

In the Comp panel, you will see a motion path for the pin you dragged as well as keyframes in the timeline. Press **0** on the numeric keypad to RAM Preview.

If you don't like the results, you can always undo and try again, edit the motion path, or refine your animation using the Graph Editor (Lesson 2). You can also use the Smoother keyframe assistant (Lesson 2) to simplify the path, making it easier to edit. If you have trouble drawing a path you like in real time, select the Puppet tool and click on the Record Options in the Tools panel. This will allow you to record at a different speed than it will play back at, as well as to control the display and how much automatic smoothing will take place.

Puppet Starch Tool

Sometimes, portions of your layer may be more flexible than you wish, or other kinks may appear. One solution is to increase the number of triangles for a layer. Another is to use the Puppet Starch tool.

1 Open **Comps > 07-Puppet-starch*starter**. Make sure the Puppet Pin tool is selected, then select the layer **MiroMan.psd**. In the Comp viewer, look for the yellow circles: We've added pins to his feet, plus three for his big red tie.

2 Click on one of the pins at the ends of his tie and drag it around. As you move to more extreme positions, you might notice some strange kinks in the neck.

3 To fix these kinks, select the Puppet Starch tool. A gray outline will illustrate the shape of the original unwarped layer. Click in this gray area in the middle of the neck where the tie would cross it – this will add a red starch pin to your layer. Wait a second while After Effects calculates; the neck will straighten out. Return to the Selection tool and try dragging the tips of the tie again to compare.

◁ **4** Hold **⌘** (**Ctrl**) while dragging a pin, and its animation will be recorded automatically (left).

▽ In our comp, **04b-Puppet_final** (below), we animated the wrist and pencil, then copied the keyframes for Pin 4 (the pencil tip). These keyframes were pasted to the Brush Position of the Write On effect on a solid layer. A little tweaking, and our MiroMan is "write on"!

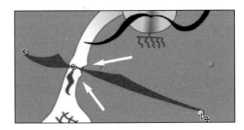

3 When warping a layer, kinks may appear, such as in the neck here (above). Clicking in the problem area with the Puppet Starch tool selected will "stiffen" the neck (below), helping to straighten out the kinks.

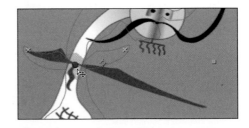

Deforming Multiple Shapes

Quite often, the alpha channel for a layer defines a single enclosed shape. When you apply a Puppet Pin to this shape, you get a single mesh to distort. However, some layers have complex alpha channels that define multiple discrete shapes. A perfect example is text: Each character forms its own shape; the letters "i" and "j" contain multiple shapes. With these layers, you can use Puppet to deform each shape independently or have it deform the entire layer as a single shape. We'll play with both of these techniques, plus learn a bit about rendering order and effects.

1 Close any previous comps and open **Comps > 08-Multiple Shapes*starter**. It contains a text layer with a Ramp effect filling the text with a linear gradient from top to bottom, followed by a Bevel Alpha effect to stylize the edges.

2 Select the Puppet Pin tool. Make sure Mesh: Show is enabled in the Tools panel; the default settings of Expansion = 3 and Triangles = 350 are otherwise fine.

3 Placing a Puppet Pin inside one character of a text layer creates a mesh for just that character (A). Add multiple pins and you can deform that character independent of the others (B).

3 Click near the bottom of the "r" to place your first pin. The r – but no other characters – will be filled with a mesh. Add pins to its top left and right, and have fun dragging these pins to deform the character. Leave it in a deformed state.

4 Open Window > Effect Controls (shortcut: **F3**). In addition to the aforementioned Ramp and Bevel Alpha effects, you will see the Puppet effect that performs the deformations. Deselect all effects (shortcut: **F2**) and look at the Comp panel: Despite your deformations, the blue-to-white gradient still reaches from the top to the bottom of the character. This is because Ramp and Bevel Alpha are being calculated before Puppet. Press the Take Snapshot button (the camera icon) to take a snapshot of this state.

5 Drag the Puppet effect before (above) Ramp and Bevel Alpha, and again deselect all effects. Now the gradient and bevel are rendered *after* the deformations. Note how the gradient in the r starts and stops in the

Effects > Puppet

4–5 Effect rendering order is very important – particularly when using Puppet. If Puppet follows other effects (above), the deformations happen after the image treatments; if the Puppet effect is first, the image is treated after deformation (right). Study the gradients and edges in these two images to understand this impact.

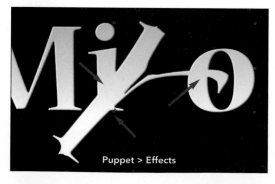

Puppet > Effects

same place as the other characters, despite its deformation. Press the Show Snapshot button to recall the snapshot and compare this look with the original arrangement. Which look is better depends on the requirements of each job. For this, we prefer the original arrangement as it helps the r stand out when its shape overlaps adjacent characters.

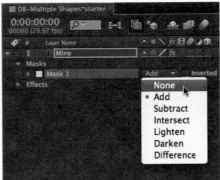

6 Add a Puppet pin to the dot on top of the i and note that it receives a mesh – but not the stem of the i. After Effects does not know these two shapes are part of the same character, so they will get separate meshes. This makes it more difficult to animate the whole character as a unit.

7 Delete the Puppet effect to return to your starting point.

• With the layer still selected, choose the Rectangle tool. Drag a generous rectangular mask around the i, being careful not to touch the adjacent characters.

• Characters outside the mask shape will disappear. To make them visible again, reveal **Miro** > Masks > Mask 1 in the Timeline panel and change its Mask Modes popup from Add to None. This disables the masking operation while keeping the mask shape. (Remember the location of the mask outline in the Comp panel, as it's possible to get After Effects into a state where you won't see this outline for the next step.)

8 Select the Puppet Pin tool again. Carefully click inside the mask outline, but not on the i itself. After Effects will fill the entire mask shape with a mesh. Add another pin at the opposite end of the mesh, and now you can deform the i as a whole.

9 Delete Mask 1 as well as the Puppet effect. Now draw a mask around the entire word. Add a Puppet Pin inside one of the corners of the mask to define the mesh. Then add more pins and move their positions: The entire word will deform as if on a single sheet of rubber, regardless of the shapes defined by the alpha channels for each individual character. Hopefully these examples will open your mind to additional creative possibilities with the Puppet tools.

7–8 Mask just the i (left), set its Mask Mode to None (center) to not have the mask create transparency, and then click inside the mask shape but not on the i itself (above). Puppet will then use the mask shape to define the mesh (above).

9 Mask as many characters as you want, and add pins inside the mask shape: Now the entire layer can be warped as a unit, rather than as individual characters. Increase the number of Mesh Triangles or use the Starch tool to smooth out kinks in the final deformation.

Shape Layers

Creating, animating, and extruding vector-based shapes.

▽ In This Lesson

306 creating a shape layer
307 Stroke and Fill settings, editing shapes
308 multiple shapes
309 Even-Odd Fill
310 shape effects
311 creating buttons
312 Shape Repeater
314 compound shapes; Merge Paths
316 gradients
317 shape pen paths
318 Wiggle Transforms
320 advanced strokes; dashes and gaps
322 animating a stroke
323 create shapes from vector layers *(new in CS6)*
324 extruding shape layers *(new in CS6)*

▽ Getting Started

Make sure you have copied the **Lesson 11-Shape Layers** folder from this book's disc onto your hard drive, and make note of where it is; it contains the project file and sources you need to execute this lesson.

As previously noted in Lesson 4, the Shape and Pen tools are context sensitive:

• If any layer other than a shape layer is selected, After Effects assumes you want to draw a mask on the selected layer.

• If no layer is selected, After Effects assumes you want to create a new shape layer.

• If a shape layer is selected, you can choose between drawing a new shape or a mask.

One of the most versatile features in After Effects is *shape layers.* You can draw free-form shapes or a number of standardized parametric shapes, each with its own Stroke and Fill. You can also apply shape operators (effects) to modify and animate the shapes.

Shapes can be used to create anything from simple abstract objects to entire cartoons. Our focus here will be on graphical elements. We'll start by leading you through a grand tour of what you can do with the basic tools. We'll then show you how to create a few useful objects, as well as perform common tasks ranging from creating abstract imagery to animating a path along a map.

Make a Shape

1 Open this lesson's project file **Lesson_11.aep.** In the Project panel, locate and double-click **Comps > 01-Shape Play*starter** to open it. It is currently empty.

2 Click on the Shape tool in the Tools panel along the top of the application window and press the mouse button until a menu pops open. Select the Rounded Rectangle option. When you select this tool, Fill, Stroke, and Stroke Width options will appear in the Tools panel to the right. You can use these to change the color of your shapes before or after you create them.

• Click on the word Fill (not the color swatch) to open the Fill Options dialog. Here you may select between fill mode buttons: None, Solid, Linear Gradient, and Radial Gradient. You can also set the Blending Mode popup and Opacity for the fill. Choose Solid Color and Normal mode. Set Opacity to 50% and click OK.

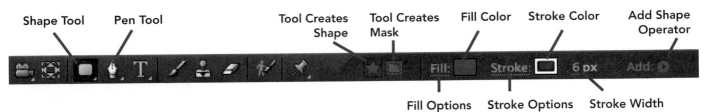

Shape Tool   Pen Tool   Tool Creates Shape   Tool Creates Mask   Fill Color   Stroke Color   Add Shape Operator

Fill Options   Stroke Options   Stroke Width

2 When you select a Shape tool, Fill and Stroke options will appear along the right of the Tools panel (above). To create a full-frame shape, select the shape you want, and double-click the Shape tool.

Clicking on Fill or Stroke will open an options dialog (left) where you can set the desired type, opacity, and mode. Click on the swatches to select a color.

▽ tip

Reshape as You Draw

You can use the up/down arrow keys or mouse scroll wheel while you drag a shape to change the roundness of its corners (Rounded Rectangle) or the number of points it has (Polygon or Star). These are the same as for mask paths; see Lesson 4 for more details.

• To the right of Fill is its color swatch. Click on it to select your color (choose what you like; we'll use red). You can also ⌥+click on Mac (**Alt**+click on Windows) this button to toggle between the fill modes.

• Next is Stroke Options; it has the same choices as Fill Options. Choose a Solid Color fill with the Blending Mode set to Normal and Opacity = 100%.

• Next is Stroke Color, which has the same choices as Fill Color. Choose whatever color you like; we'll go with white.

• The last option is Stroke Width, with a scrubbable value. Start with 6 pixels.

3 Click and drag in the Comp panel, and your shape will appear. An object called **Shape Layer 1** will also be added to the Timeline panel, already twirled open to reveal your first shape group: Rectangle 1 in this case.

Edit a Shape

4 Twirl down Rectangle 1 to reveal what makes up your initial shape group: Path, Stroke, Fill, and Transform.

Temporarily twirl down Stroke 1 and Fill 1 – you will see the same parameters as in the Tools panel, and more. We'll experiment with them later; twirl them up for now.

The default arrangement is Stroke over Fill. Click on Fill 1 in the Timeline panel and drag it just above Stroke 1 until a black line appears above it. When you release the mouse, the fill will now be over the stroke (you will see some of the stroke's line because you set the Fill to 50% in step 2). Undo to get back to stroke over fill.

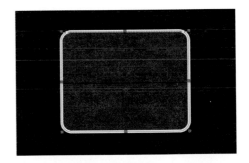

3 Click and drag directly in the Comp panel to create a new Shape.

4 Twirl down Rectangle 1.

▼ Shape Positions

There are three different types of Position values (and for that matter, Transform properties) in a shape layer, each of which may be edited and animated:

• Each shape path – such as Rectangle Path 1 – has its own Position inside its shape group.

• Each shape group – such as Rectangle 1 – has its own Transform > Position. Its initial value is based on where you drew the first shape path and is shown as an offset from the center of the overall layer. To center a new shape in its layer and the composition, set this to 0,0.

• An overall shape layer (including all of its groups) also has a normal Transform section, which includes Position.

5 Twirl down Rectangle Path 1 and explore its parameters:

• Size is akin to a shape path's scale. Scrub its values, trying it with the Constrain Proportions switch (the chain link) turned on, then off. Set it to 200, 200 when you're done.

• Position offsets this path (Rectangle Path 1) inside its group (Rectangle 1). Leave it at 0,0.

• Roundness controls how rounded your rectangle is, ranging from square-edged to a circle. Set to taste.

Unless you were very careful with how you dragged your shape, it is probably not centered in the Comp panel – even though the shape's Position value is 0,0. This is where the shape group's Transform properties come in:

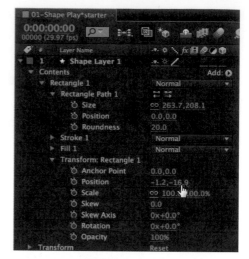

5–6 Each shape path has its own Size and Position, plus parameters (such as Roundness) that control the shape. In addition, a shape group has its own set of Transform properties.

6 Twirl down Transform: Rectangle 1. These parameters are for an entire shape group. Currently, you have only one shape in your group, but these come in really handy as you create more complex composite shapes.

Play with these parameters to become familiar with them. Then set Transform: Rectangle 1 > Position to 0,0 to center your rectangle in the Comp panel.

Multiple Shapes

A shape layer can contain more than one shape path.

7 Click and hold on the Rounded Rectangle tool until its popup menu appears, then select the Ellipse tool. Tweak the Fill and Stroke settings if you like.

Make sure **Shape Layer 1** is still selected (otherwise, you'll create a new layer!). Drag out your new shape in the Comp panel.

7 With **Shape Layer 1** selected, click and drag a new shape in the Comp panel (right). A new shape group will be added in the Timeline panel (above). Delete Ellipse 1 when done.

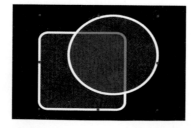

When you release the mouse, a new shape group called Ellipse 1 will be added to **Shape Layer 1** in the Timeline panel. Twirl Ellipse 1 down, and you will see it has its own Path, Stroke, Fill, and Transform. You can play with these parameters if you like.

When done, select Ellipse 1 and delete it.

8 Instead of creating a new shape group, you can add a new shape path to the group you're already working on. To do this, select the group's name (i.e., Rectangle 1) in the Timeline, or a member of its group (such as Rectangle Path 1). Then click on the Add button either in the Timeline panel (to the right of Contents) or in the Tools panel (to the right of Stroke Width). Just for something different, select Polystar. It will share the same Fill and Stroke settings as Rectangle Path 1, as they belong to the same shape group.

9 Twirl down Polystar Path 1 and experiment with its parameters. This is one of the most versatile shape paths: It has a popup to turn it into a Star or a Polygon, plus you have a lot of control over how many points or sides it has and how rounded its corners are.

To create interesting looping shapes, try setting Inner and Outer Roundness to very large positive or negative values. After you've had some fun playing, set up a shape where the Polystar's outline forms interwoven or overlapping lines, either within the Polystar's own shape or intersecting the Rectangle.

10 Twirl down Fill 1. Set its Fill Rule popup to Even-Odd. Now alternating sections of the overlapping shapes, rather than the entire shape, will be filled.

There is a lot more that can be done with combining shapes, which we'll explore in later exercises. For now, either delete Polystar Path 1 or twirl it up and click on the eyeball next to it to turn it off.

Save your project before continuing. You can also open **Comps_Finished > 01-Shape Play_final1** to pick up this exercise at this step so you can jump into playing with shape operators (also known as shape effects).

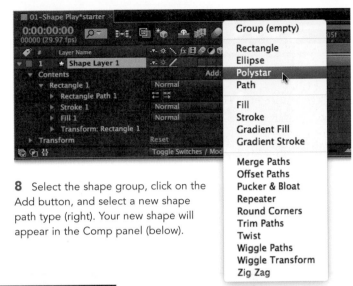

8 Select the shape group, click on the Add button, and select a new shape path type (right). Your new shape will appear in the Comp panel (below).

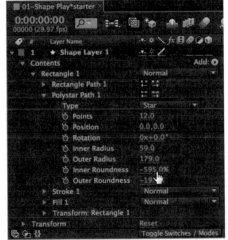

9–10 The Polystar is one of the most versatile shape paths (left). Adjust it until it partially overlaps the rectangle underneath (A), then change Fill > Fill Rule to Even-Odd to create a pattern of filled areas and holes (B).

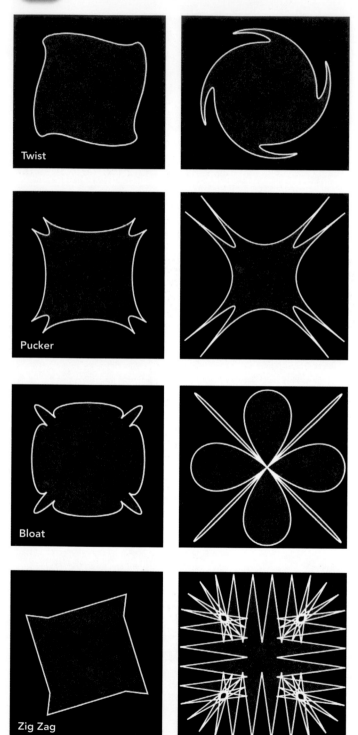

Shape Effects

In addition to creating shape paths, there is a wide variety of shape operators that can be employed to modify those shapes. Continuing with the comp you've been working with, let's have fun exploring a handful of them:

11 Click on Add (above), then select Trim Paths from the popup menu. Twirl down Trim Paths in the Timeline panel and scrub Start and End while watching the Comp panel: Only a portion of your shape will be drawn. Set one or

Trim Paths

both to a value between 0 and 100%, then scrub Offset: The shape will appear to rotate or chase itself. This attribute is particularly useful when you don't have a fill, as it allows you to create animated stroke effects. When you're done, twirl up Trim Paths and turn off its eyeball to disable it.

12 Select Add > Twist, twirl it open, and scrub its Angle parameter: This adds a nice, organic distortion to stiff shapes. Twirl it up and disable it when done.

13 Select Add > Pucker & Bloat; your rectangle will take on an overstuffed appearance. This attribute bends the path segments between the shape path vertices: In this case, the lines between the corners and the rounded corners themselves. Twirl down Pucker & Bloat and scrub its Amount (try positive and negative values): You can create some really wild shapes this way. When you're done, twirl it up and turn off its eyeball.

14 Select Add > Zig Zag. This can be thought of as a spiky version of Pucker & Bloat. Twirl it down and scrub its Size and Ridges parameters: You can quickly create anything from mad scrawls to cool, angular, geometric figures. Change the Points popup from Corner to Smooth to create a more freehand-drawn look. When you're done, twirl it up and turn off its eyeball.

15 Select Add > Wiggle Paths. Initially, it will look like static has been added to your shape's path! Twirl it down and experiment initially with its Size and Detail parameters, along with the Points popup.

This effect is special in that it self-animates: Press **0** on the numeric keypad to RAM Preview, and your shape will dance for you! Play with Wiggles/Second and Correlation to change the dance speed and pattern. When you're done, twirl it up and turn off its eyeball.

16 Select Add > Wiggle Transform. Initially, nothing happens; Wiggle Transform defaults to having no effect. Twirl down Wiggle Transform 1, then the Transform section underneath it. Scrub the two Position parameters; your shape will be offset in the Comp viewer. Like Wiggle Paths, Wiggle Transform auto-animates: RAM Preview, and your shape will now wander about the composition. Scrub Wiggle Transform 1 > Wiggles/Second to alter how fast it moves (RAM Preview again to see the result of your changes). Experiment with the other Wiggle Transform 1 > Transform parameters such as Scale and Rotation.

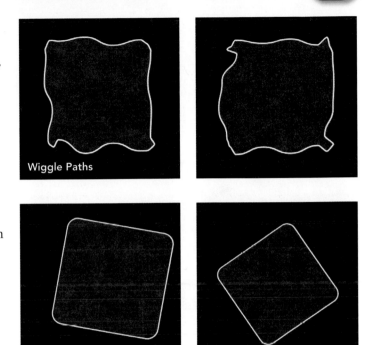

Wiggle Paths

Wiggle Transform

Wiggle Transform really comes into its own when combined with the Repeater, which is what we'll play with in the next exercise. Save your project.

▼ Building Better Buttons

The combination of shape layers plus layer styles (Lesson 3) will help you create far more interesting buttons, text bars, and other graphical elements. Here are a few ideas worth exploring:

• A slight amount of Pucker & Bloat can add interest to shapes, such as a slight "bow" to rectangular buttons. Same for Twist and Zig Zag. These work better on simple shapes, such as rectangles.

• Inside a Shape group's Transform properties is a Skew property that can cause a button or bar to "lean."

• Gradient Fill with Type set to Radial can be used to simulate a change in lighting from the center to the outer edges of a button; set Type to Linear to get color changes across bars.

• Layer > Layer Styles have far more interesting bevels and drop shadows than normal effects. These give your buttons and bars apparent thickness and perspective.

• Explore other layer styles. For example, Layer Styles > Inner Shadow can add interesting coloration and gradations to buttons: Change the Color, try different Blending Modes, and experiment with Angle and Distance. Also experiment with Bevel and Emboss > Altitude: Increasing its value can add stronger specular highlights to a shape.

△ The bar on top is a simple rectangular shape with a gradient. The two underneath add Pucker & Bloat, Skew, Bevel and Emboss, Inner Shadow, and Drop Shadow to create more dimensional looks.

The Repeater makes it easy to convert single shapes (left) into more complex arrangements (below).

▽ tip

More Shapely

After Effects ships with dozens of animation presets for shape layers. You can find lots more at *tinyurl.com/ShapeTextPresets*

The Repeater

One of the most useful shape effects is the Repeater. It takes the contents of a shape group and replicates it, with each replication having an altered position, scale, and/or rotation.

1 Return to the Project panel and double-click **Comps > 02-Repeater*starter**. It contains a shape layer that looks a bit like a flower petal or a flame. Twirl down **Shape Layer 1** > Contents > Group 1 in the Timeline panel: This layer contains a freeform Path created using the Pen tool, and it employs a Gradient Fill (don't worry; you'll learn about both in later exercises).

2 Select **Shape Layer 1** and choose Add > Repeater. Twirl down Repeater 1 and increase the value for Copies to 5 to create more petals.

3 Twirl up Group 1 to save space in the Timeline panel, and twirl down Repeater 1 > Transform: Repeater 1. These parameters control how each repeat varies from the original. The values accumulate for each copy. The Position value defaults to X = 100 and Y = 0, which means each copy is offset to the right by 100 pixels. Reduce the X value to fit all five petals onscreen.

Slowly scrub the value for Offset. As you set it to negative values, petals will appear to the left of the original, in the negative X direction. "Negative copies" get the opposite treatment of positive copies.

Hold down the ⌘ (*Ctrl*) key and scrub Offset. This modifier allows you to scrub in finer increments than whole numbers. The copies will seem to "animate through" the original petal's position.

When you're done experimenting, set Copies to –2. You should now have five petals centered around the original.

4 Slightly increase the value for Transform: Repeater 1 > Scale. The copies before the original will be smaller; the copies after the original will be larger. Scrub Transform: Repeater 1 > Rotation and again observe how copies before and after the original behave.

5 Set Transform: Repeater 1 > Position to 0,0 and > Scale to 100%. The petals will now be stacked on top of each other. Next, set Transform: Repeater 1 > Rotation to some small value such as 30°, and note how they pivot in an array around the original shape's Anchor Point.

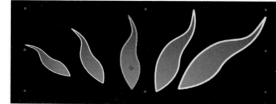

4 "Positive" copies of the original shape (to the right of center) receive successive applications of the Repeater's Scale and Rotation values, growing larger and rotating more (above and right). "Negative" copies receive the opposite treatment, in this case growing smaller and rotating in the opposite direction.

6 Scrub Transform: Repeater 1 > Anchor Point's values, and observe how the petals move through this central point. What the Repeater is doing is offsetting the Anchor Point (the object's center) for each individual copy of the original layer.

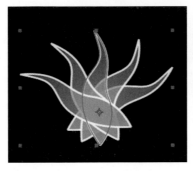

7 The shape you feed into the Repeater affects the replicated result. Twirl down Group 1 > Transform: Group 1. If you scrub the Scale or Rotation values in the group's Transform, the entire result will rotate or scale, as you are affecting the original shape that is getting

7 With no positional offset, repeated and rotated shapes stack on top of each other (above left). Offsetting the original shape group's Anchor Point (right) helps array them in a circle (above right).

repeated. Return these values to their starting point. Also reset Transform: Repeater 1 > Anchor Point to 0,0.

Now set Transform: Group 1 > Anchor Point to X = 0 and Y = 100: The petals will spread out in an arc. This is because the original shape is now offset from the center of the shape group, and the Repeater is rotating copies of that offset shape around the group's center. Go back to the Repeater and have fun playing with its Copies and Rotation values until you create a sunflower, adjusting the group's Anchor Point value to taste.

8 The order of shape effects in relation to the Repeater has a big impact on the final result. With **Shape Layer 1** selected, choose Add > Wiggle Transform; it should appear above the Repeater in the Timeline panel. Twirl down Wiggle Transform 1 > Transform and scrub its Position or Scale values: All of the petals will be moved or scaled by the same amount. This is because the original petal is being transformed, and then that one petal is being replicated. RAM Preview to see how all the petals pulse in unison.

Now drag Repeater 1 above Wiggle Transform 1: All the petals will be transformed individually. This is because the original petal is being replicated, and *then* all of those replicated petals are being wiggled individually. RAM Preview and note how they pulse independently of each other. The Wiggle Transform 1 > Correlation parameter controls how unified or disparate the pulsing is. Our version is **Comps_Finished > 02-Repeater_final**.

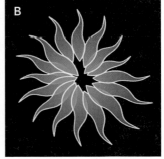

8 When Wiggle Transform is added before the Repeater, all petals are transformed equally (A). When Wiggle Transform is placed after the Repeater, each repeated petal gets a different transformation (B).

▼ Compound Shapes

One of the more useful shape effects is Merge Paths. This effect helps you make "compound" shapes – for example, the cutout in the middle of letters like O. We'll employ them in this exercise to create a gear.

1 Click on the Comp panel's view menu and select Close All to close your previous comps. In the Project panel, double-click **Comps > 03-Gear*starter** to open it. It is currently blank.

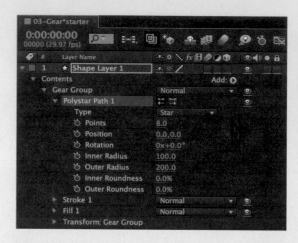

2 We'll start by making the teeth of the gear:

• **Q** is the shortcut key to toggle through the Shape tools. Type **Q** until you see a star shape in the Tools panel.

• Click on the word Fill in the Tools panel, make sure Solid Color is selected, set Opacity to 100%, and click OK.

• Click on the word Stroke. Set it to Solid Color and 100% Opacity.

• Set Fill Color, Stroke Color, and Stroke Width to taste.

• Click in the middle of the Comp panel and drag outward to create roughly the size of gear you want; add the **Shift** key while dragging to prevent the shape from rotating. Release the mouse and a new **Shape Layer** containing the shape group Polystar 1 will be created in the Timeline panel.

• Since you'll be adding shapes to this group, let's rename it: Select Polystar 1, press **Return**, type "**Gear Group**" and press **Return** again.

3 Next, let's tweak the default Star into something that more resembles a gear:

• First, center the shape in the comp. Twirl down Gear Group in the Timeline, then twirl

down Transform: Gear Group. Set Position to 0,0 and twirl up Transform: Gear Group.

• Twirl down Polystar Path 1. Set Points to the number of teeth you want in your gear.

• Tweak Inner and Outer Radius to set up what will be the angle of your gear teeth. We find that making Outer Radius about twice the value of Inner Radius works well for gears.

• Zero out the Roundness values; we want sharp teeth for our gear. Twirl up Polystar Path 1 when done.

4 Next, trim off the spikes on your teeth:

• Make sure Gear Group is selected (not just the entire **Shape Layer**), click the Add button, and select Ellipse.

• Twirl down Ellipse Path 1. Scrub Size until the ellipse is just inside the star's outer points.

5 At this point, the ellipse is being filled and stroked as well, when you really want to use it just to chop off the star's points. Time to combine them into a compound path:

• Make sure Gear Group is selected. Select Add > Merge Paths.

• Twirl down Merge Paths 1 and set its Mode popup to Intersect. (Feel free to try out the other options, of course.)

3 Tweak Polystar Path's parameters to set up the number, size, and slope of your gear teeth.

4 Add an Ellipse shape path.

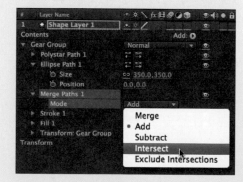

5 Add Merge Paths, and set it to Intersect.

5 *continued*:

• Further tweak Ellipse Path 1's Size to taste. Then twirl up Ellipse Path 1 plus Merge Paths 1 when done.

6 Now, let's fill in the bottom of your teeth. Making sure Gear Group is selected (so that you don't accidentally start a new group):

• Select Add > Ellipse again. Drag Ellipse Path 2 underneath Merge Paths 1.

• Twirl Ellipse Path 2 down, increase its Size to fill in the bottom of the teeth, and twirl it up. This new ellipse will also be stroked; Merge Paths can fix that as well.

• Select Add > Merge Paths again. Drag Merge Paths 2 below Ellipse Path 2.

• Twirl down Merge Paths 2 and verify that its Mode is set to Add. The ellipse will be added to the result of the first Merge Paths attribute to make one shape.

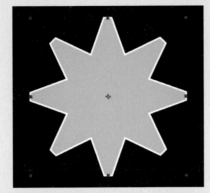

5 *continued* When you set Merge Paths to Intersect, the ellipse chops off the star's points.

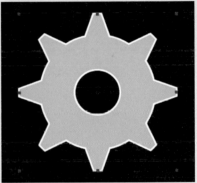

7 The last step is adding a third Ellipse Path and Merge Paths pair to cut the hole out of the middle (above).

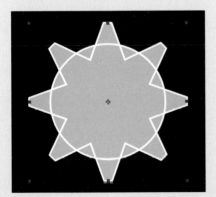

6 Add a second Ellipse path after the initial Merge Paths to fill in the bottom of the gear teeth (above).

6 *continued* Add a second Merge Paths and drag it after your new Ellipse (above right). Now the stroke will follow the result of the compound path, instead of the individual shapes (right).

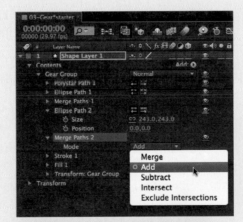

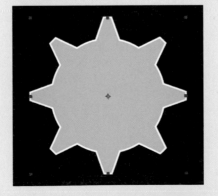

7 The last step is the hole in the middle:

• Make sure Gear Group is still selected. Then select Add > Ellipse and drag Ellipse Path 3 underneath Merge Paths 2. Tweak its Size to taste and twirl it up.

• Select Add > Merge Paths. Drag Merge Paths 3 below Ellipse Path 3.

• Twirl down Merge Paths 3 and set its Mode to Subtract to have the final ellipse cut out from the composite shape.

If you got lost along the way, feel free to explore our versions. In **Comps_Finished > 03-Gear_final2**, we used polygons instead of ellipses to file down and fill in the gear teeth to get a chunkier look.

We created a crosshair with shapes in
Comps_Finished > 04-Display_final,
then used it to track a subject in
Display_final2. Footage courtesy
Artbeats/Business on the Go.

▽ try it

Crosshair Shape

The Rounded Rectangle is the basis of our
crosshair shape; it can be easily made into
a square, circle, or shapes in-between.
In this exercise, twirl down Rectangle 1 >
Rectangle Path 1 and play with Roundness.

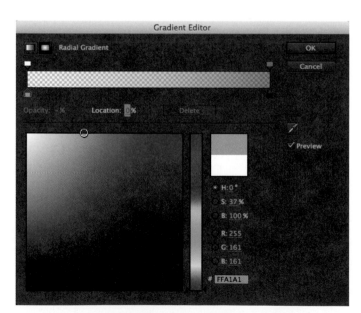

2 The Gradient Editor allows you to set the
color and transparency of your gradient.

Crosshairs

Dials, crosshairs, and other objects that can help you build faux informational
displays are often useful. While building a sample crosshair, we'll employ a few
additional shape layer tricks: gradients, pen paths, and groups.

Gradient Editor

1 Open **Comps > 04-Display*starter**. Since this is an element to be used in
a later composite, we made this comp a smaller square rather than full-frame
video size. We also set the background color to a grayish tint, which helps us
better see what's happening with our transparency and colors.

We've also made a starter rounded rectangle for you. Rectangle 1 should be
twirled open in the Timeline panel; if it isn't, twirl down **Shape Layer 1**, then
Contents, then Rectangle 1.

2 Rather than use solid colors, let's fill the center of our crosshair with a
partially transparent gradient:

• Select **Shape Layer 1** (the highest level of the layer).

• Hold down the ⬛ (**Alt**) key and click on the Fill Color swatch in the Tools
panel. It should change from a solid to a gradient.

> • Release ⬛ (**Alt**) and click on the Fill Color swatch
> again. The Gradient Editor will open. Position it so that you
> can also see the Comp panel while editing your gradient.
>
> • Select Radial Gradient mode by clicking on the second
> of the two icons in the upper left corner.
>
> • Click on the pointer at the upper left corner of the
> gradient bar: This Opacity Stop sets the opacity of the
> center of the gradient. We want to see through the center
> of our crosshair, so set its Opacity to something low, such
> as 15% or less.
>
> • Click on the Opacity Stop along the right; this is for the
> outer edge of the gradient. We want to keep some trans-
> parency in the corners, so set it roughly around 50%.
>
> • Click on the pointer in the lower right corner of the
> gradient bar: This is the Color Stop for the outer edge of
> the gradient. Set it to black.
>
> • Finally, click on the Color Stop to the left: This is the
> center color. Pick a color to taste, and note how it tints
> the center of the gradient in the Comp viewer. Click OK
> when finished.

• Press **V** to make sure the Selection tool is active and verify that Gradient Fill 1 is selected for your shape layer in the Timeline panel. In the Comp panel, you should see a pair of solid dots with a line between them: These define where the gradient starts and ends. Drag the outer dot until you are happy with the way the gradient "falls off" in your display.

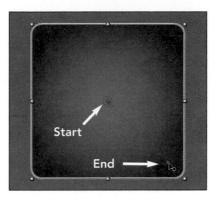

Pen Tool

Using the Pen tool to create shape paths is very similar to creating mask paths (Lesson 4). We'll use the Pen tool to create our crosshairs:

3 To help precisely draw our lines, make sure the Window > Info panel is open and visible. Also make sure **Shape Layer 1** (not Rectangle 1) is selected.

4 Press **G** to select the Pen tool. In the Tools panel, make sure Tool Creates Shape is enabled.

We want to draw a vertical line centered in our 400-pixel-wide comp, so move the cursor over the Comp panel until Info says X = 200 and Y = 20, then click. Move the cursor downward to X = 200 and Y = 380, and click again: Your line will appear.

5 In the Timeline panel, a new group called Shape 1 will appear. Twirl it down; it will contain your new Path, plus its own Stroke, Gradient Fill, and Transform.

You still need to create the horizontal crosshair; best to place it in the same group as the vertical one. Select Shape 1, then Add > Path. Path 2 will appear.

In the Comp panel, with the Pen tool still selected, place the cursor at X = 20 and Y = 200, and click to start your new path. Then place the cursor at X = 380 and Y = 200, and click again to finish your horizontal crosshair. Press **V** to return to the Selection tool.

6 The advantage of having a separate group for the crosshairs is that you can make them a different color and width. Twirl down Shape 1 > Stroke 1 (under Path 2) and change the Color, Opacity, Stroke Width, and Line Cap to taste. You now have your crosshair!

Our crosshair shape is in **Comps_Finished > 04-Display_final**; we then used it to track a "person of interest" in **04-Display_final2**.

Using the Pen Tool

For a more in-depth look at how to draw pen-based shapes, watch **Lesson 11 > Video Bonus > Drawing Pen Shapes.mov**, excerpted from our *After Effects Apprentice* video series.

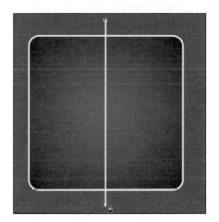

4 Select the Pen tool and enable Tool Creates Shape (left). With the help of the Info panel, create a vertical line (above).

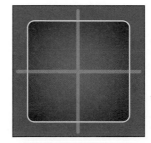

6 By placing the crosshair paths in their own group, they can also have their own Stroke settings (above and left).

Our goal in this exercise is to take a single shape (above) and turn it into a swarm of objects animating left and right (below).

2 Add > Wiggle Transform, then drag it below Stroke 1 and Fill 1.

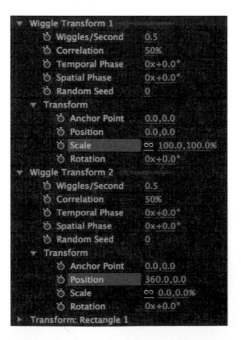

Abstract Imagery

A combination of simple shapes, Wiggle Transform, and the Repeater can be used to create random, self-animating textures. Apply a few effects or layer styles, and suddenly you have a complex graphical element that otherwise might have taken hours to create.

1 Select Close All from the Comp panel's dropdown menu to close all previous comps. Open **Comps > 05-Abstract*starter**. It contains a simple rounded rectangle. We like using Rounded Rectangles because it is so easy to change them from lines to circles to squares by simply adjusting their Size and Roundness parameters.

2 Twirl down **Shape Layer 1** > Contents. Select Rectangle 1, and choose Add > Wiggle Transform. The Wiggle Transform shape effect will appear below Rectangle Path 1 but above Stroke 1. We often find it better to wiggle and repeat an already-colored shape path so that the copies of the original shape can interact with each other. Otherwise, you'll be applying a single fill and stroke to the composite image. Therefore, drag Wiggle Transform below Fill 1 in the shape attributes stack.

3 Twirl down Wiggle Transform 1, then the Transform section inside this effect (not the shape group's nor layer's Transform). This composition is 720 pixels wide, so set Wiggle Transform's Position value to X = 360 to have the shape move across the entire width of the comp. It would also be fun to have the shape change in size as it moves, so increase Wiggle Transform's Scale to 100%. Finally, we want a slower, more mysterious movement, so lower the Wiggles/Second speed to around 0.5.

4 Press **O** on the numeric keypad to RAM Preview, and observe the result: The shape does indeed "wiggle" around in a random manner. However, as the shape moves to the left, it always gets smaller, and as it moves to the right, it always gets bigger. Unfortunately, Wiggle Transform's properties wiggle in unison: They move in a positive direction together, and in a negative direction together. Fortunately, you can apply more than one copy of Wiggle Transform to a shape layer, and each copy will animate independently of the others.

5 Select Wiggle Transform 1 and press **⌘ D** (**Ctrl D**) to duplicate it. In Wiggle Transform 1, set its Position value to 0,0 while keeping its 100% Scale. Then twirl down Wiggle Transform 2 > Transform and set its Scale to 0% while keeping its Position value of X = 360, Y = 0.

5 To wiggle more than one transform property independently of each other (such as Scale and Position), you will need to add one Wiggle Transform shape effect per transform property. Here we duplicated Wiggle Transform 1.

RAM Preview again, and now you will observe that the object's changes in size are no longer linked to its changes in position.

6 Now it's time to create that swarm we promised: Twirl up Wiggle Transform 1 and 2, select Rectangle 1, and choose Add > Repeater. It will initially appear below Wiggle Transform 2.

Twirl down Repeater 1 > Transform: Repeater 1, and set its Position value to X = 0, Y = 0; Wiggle Transform 2 will be providing the position offsets.

Wait a second: There's only one shape in the Comp panel, even though the Repeater defaults to Copies = 3. What's going on? Right now, the repeats are happening after the wiggles. To have each copy wiggle independently, drag Repeater 1 above Wiggle Transform 1 so that the repeats happen before the wiggles. Now you will see three copies.

Increase the number of Repeater 1 > Copies until you have a nice swarm; we used a value of 20. RAM Preview and enjoy the mayhem.

7 Now that you have the basic motion happening, you can make several modifications to enhance the end result:

• Set the Blending Mode popups for Stroke 1 and Fill 1 to something more interesting, such as Color Dodge, Pin Light, or Vivid Light. This will cause the colors in the duplicated shapes to interact with each other.

• Add a blur effect, such as Effect > Blur & Sharpen > Box Blur, and increase the Blur Radius. At Box Blur's default of Iterations = 1, the result is a "squinting" effect; increase Iterations to get a smoother blur. At higher Iterations values, the result is a floating haze. Or, reduce Iterations to 1 or 2, and add Layer > Layer Styles > Outer Glow. Twirl down Outer Glow, and experiment with its parameters, such as Size and Color.

• Feel free to modify the original shape, either by altering Rectangle Path 1's parameters, or adding other shape effects such as Pucker & Bloat.

Our result is saved in **Comps_Finished > 05-Abstract_final**.

5 *continued* Employing independent Wiggle Transforms for Scale and Position gives us the randomness we're after.

6 Add > Repeater and place it above the Wiggle Transform effects (below). Increase the number of Copies and enjoy the resulting swarm (above).

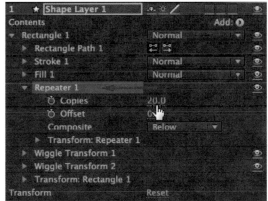

7 The addition of Box Blur plus a few shape effects create a hazy, amorphous result.

▽ factoid

The Hidden Path

The Toggle Mask and Shape Path Visibility button along the bottom left of the Comp panel controls whether a shape's outline is drawn when selected. It must be on to edit a pen path or a gradient; otherwise, you can turn it off.

2 Select the Pen tool, enable RotoBezier mode, set Fill to None, and set the Stroke to taste (you can always edit its color and width later).

▽ try it

Fill and Stroke Are Live

When a shape is selected, the Fill and Stroke parameters in the Tools panel are still "live" – edit them, and your shape will update.

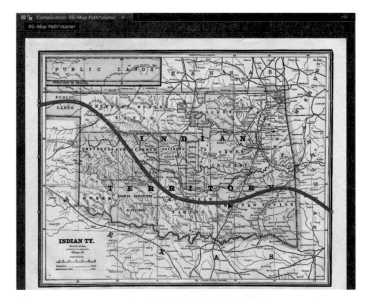

3 Click several points to define a path across the map.

Stroked Paths

We'll finish our exploration of shape layers by tackling another common task: Drawing a path on a map or underscoring other elements in a composition, then stroking that path. Shape layers are particularly well suited to this job as you can design interesting dashed patterns to stroke your path.

1 Save your project and close your previous comps. Then open **Comps > 06-Map Path*starter**.

This large comp contains a scan of a map of Indian Territories in the 1890s. Try to resize your Comp panel's frame to view it at 50% Magnification.

2 We locked the **Indian Territory.jpg** layer so you can't draw a mask on it by accident, when you actually want to create a new shape layer. Press **G** to select the Pen tool, then enter the following settings using the Tools panel:

• Enable the RotoBezier option to make it easy to create a fluid path.

• Since you're drawing a line, your shape will not need to be filled. Press **⌥** (**Alt**) and click on the Fill Color swatch until it is a gray box with a red line through it, which means "no fill."

• Click on Stroke, make sure it is in Solid Color mode, and set its Opacity to 100%. Click OK.

• Set the Stroke Color to taste, thinking of what might provide a good complement to the map's colors. We choose a dark turquoise green.

• You want a thick stroke to outline your path, so increase the Stroke Width to around 16 pixels.

3 Visualize a path you want to create across this map, perhaps telling a story of an expedition from east to west. Click on the dark line along the right edge of the map to start your path. Then click several additional points across the map until you reach the left-hand border. There is no need to click and drag; RotoBezier automatically calculates the curve between the points you create. To edit your path, click and drag your existing points. [Before CS6, hold **⌘** (**Ctrl**) then click.]

Press **V** to switch back to the Selection tool when done. A line indicating the stroke's path will be drawn down the middle of your stroke. (If you like, toggle off Mask and Shape Path Visibility to see your stroke more clearly.)

3 *continued* You can click on Toggle Mask and Shape Path Visibility at the bottom of the Comp panel to hide the yellow path.

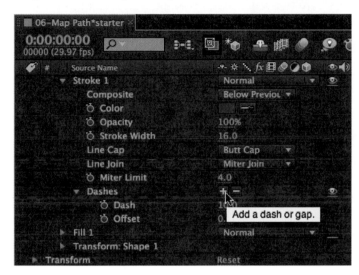

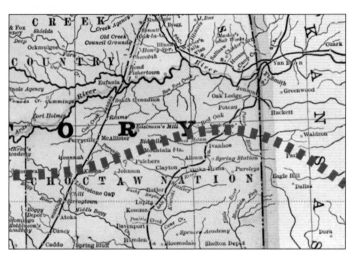

4 The default stroke is a solid line, but it's possible to design your own pattern along the stroke. In the Timeline panel, twirl down **Shape Layer 1** > Contents, then Shape 1, then Stroke 1 to reveal the Stroke's parameters.

The last Stroke parameter is Dashes. Twirl it down; it does not contain any segments yet. Click on the + button; the stroke will now be a dashed line.

4 Click on the + switch next to Stroke 1 > Dashes to convert the line from solid to dashed.

5 Let's get a better look at that stroke. Increase the Comp panel's Magnification to 100%. While pressing the space-bar, click and drag in the Comp panel to recenter the display so that you can see the starting point of your stroke.

The default stroke has squared-off edges. Click on the popup for Stroke 1 > Line Cap and set it to Round Cap. Then scrub the Dash value for Stroke 1 > Dashes to spread out the segments.

As you increase Dash, you might have noticed that the length of the dashes and the space between them grow at the same time. If you want independent control over these, click on the + button again. A new parameter called Gap will appear. Tweak Dash and Gap to get a segment/space pattern you like.

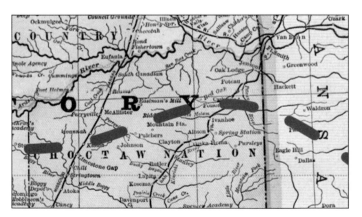

5 To create more elegant dashes, set Stroke 1's Line Cap popup to Round Cap. Tweak the Dash and Gap values to taste.

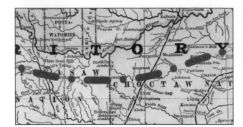

6 Add two pairs of Dash and Gap values to your stroke to alternate line segments with dots.

Ö Stroke Width	16.0
Line Cap	Round
Line Join	Miter J
Ö Miter Limit	4.0
▼ Dashes	+ −
Ö Dash	45.0
Ö Gap	35.0
Ö Dash	0.0
Ö Gap	35.0
Ö Offset	0.

6 Say you want alternating dots and dashes. Click on + twice more to add another Dash and Gap. Set the value of the second Dash to 0 to create dots between segments. Set the two Gap values the same to have even spaces on either side of the dots.

7 Type **Shift** **/** to see the entire map in the Comp panel again. Scrub Dashes > Offset and watch your stroke travel along its path. (Think of the uses you would have for animating this…) Tweak the Dashes settings – and the other parameters in Stroke 1 – until you are happy with your line, then twirl up Stroke 1.

Animating the Stroke

A line tells you what to look at; an animated line tells you a story. Think back to the first shape exercise, where you took a whirlwind tour of some of the available shape attributes: Which one trimmed a shape's path? That's right: Trim Paths.

8 Select Shape 1, then Add > Trim Paths. Twirl down Trim Paths 1 and scrub the End parameter: The path will shorten and lengthen as you do so.

• Press **Home** to make sure you are at 00:00, set End to 0%, and click on its stopwatch to enable keyframing for it.

• Press **End** and set Trim Paths 1 > End to 100%.

• This is a big map to load into RAM for a preview, and you are probably already looking at it at 50% Magnification or smaller – so why render more pixels than you're seeing? Click on the Resolution popup along the bottom of the Comp panel (it should say Full) and select Auto. Then press **0** on the numeric keypad to RAM Preview your animation or press **Shift** **0** to preview every other frame.

9 The flat dashed line can be a little hard to read against the flat map. Since shape layers are indeed their own layers, you can apply layer styles or effects to help them stand out from the other layers in your comp:

Make sure **Shape Layer 1** is still selected, then apply Layer > Layer Styles > Drop Shadow. Twirl it down in the Timeline panel, and increase the Distance and Size parameters until the line starts to "lift off" of the map.

If you had any trouble following this exercise, go ahead and peruse our version, **Comps_Finished > 06-Map Path_final**. We added one more touch: Layer > Layer Styles > Bevel and Emboss, which adds further dimension.

▼ The Public Domain

This map of Indian Territories was scanned from *Cram's Unrivaled Family Atlas of the World*, printed in the 1890s. It is old enough that its copyright has expired, and therefore it is in the public domain.

Many people misunderstand what really is and isn't in the public domain (call it wishful thinking). We recommend reading *The Public Domain* from Nolo Press: It contains sound legal advice on what can and can't be used, as well as numerous sources for public domain materials.

9 Our final map, with animated dash illustrating our journey. Shown with Bevel Alpha and Drop Shadow layer styles added.

Create Shapes from Vector Layer

A nice feature added in After Effects CS6 is the ability to convert a vector-based layer – such as artwork from Adobe Illustrator – into a shape layer. Once you do this, you can change its color and edit its shape paths while staying inside After Effects, plus add shape effects and otherwise animate it.

1 Save your project and close your previous comps. Then open **Comps > 07-Vectors to Shapes*starter**. It contains an Illustrator file that has been imported into After Effects as Footage (Merged Layers).

2 Select **Quarry Studios logo.ai** and choose Layer > Create Shapes from Vector Layer. (This command is not available in versions prior to CS6.) The Video switch for this layer will be turned off, and a new layer named **Quarry Studios logo Outlines** will appear. The image in the Comp panel will be unchanged, as After Effects has accurately converted this Illustrator vector artwork into a shape layer. Not all attempts will be this successful; for example, Illustrator gradients will be converted to a solid color, and some compound paths may have issues.

3 Twirl open **Quarry Studios logo Outlines** > Contents; you will see that 18 shape groups have been created: one for each letter, plus one for each colored shape and black stroke. Make sure Shape Path Visibility is enabled; as you select a shape group, it will be outlined in the Comp panel, and its Fill or Stroke color will be displayed above in the Tools panel. Remember that you can rename shape groups to something more descriptive.

4 Select Group 18, which is the large purple shape. Click Add and choose Pucker & Bloat: It will now become a rounded shape. Feel free to try other shape effects such as Wiggle Paths or Wiggle Transforms to animate the letters or pieces.

 Comps_Finished > 07-Vectors to Shapes_final contains our version, where we added gradients, wiggled paths, blending modes, and transformations. We also used Add > Group and dragged all the characters into this new shape group to make them easier to manage.

2 After using Layer > Create Shapes from Vector Layer, the original layer remains with its Video switch (the eyeball) turned off, and a new shape layer will be created above it.

4 After conversion, you can apply shape effects to the resulting shape groups. Here, the purple shape has had Pucker & Bloat applied, rounding it compared with the other untouched colored shapes.

Once vector layers have been converted into shapes, they can be animated and otherwise altered inside After Effects (as in our final comp).

1 Your starting shape in its 3D world. Your goal is to extrude it as well as make it translucent and reflective. Note that the Ray-traced 3D Renderer has been selected. Panoramic environment courtesy iStockphoto, bischy, Image #1350819.

2–5 Use the Geometry Options (above) to extrude and bevel the shape (below).

Extruding Shape Layers

In Lesson 8 on 3D Space, we demonstrated the use of the new Ray-traced 3D Renderer with text layers. Shape layers also work wonderfully with this rendering engine, including support for extrusion, beveling, transparency, and reflections. If you are new to the Ray-traced 3D Renderer, we suggest you first work through the "RT" exercises in Lesson 8 (including the section covering the various Fast Preview options), before playing with this next exercise.

1 Close your previous compositions and from **Lesson_11.aep** open **Comps > 08-Extruding Shapes*starter**. We've already set up an initial scene, including a star-like shape layer with its 3D Layer switch enabled, a pair of lights (one with a Type of Spot, and the other Ambient), and an Environment Layer (**Ruins Panorama.jpg**) wrapped around our world. The Renderer button in the upper right corner of the Composition panel indicates we've already set this comp to use the Ray-traced 3D Renderer (edited by clicking this button). If you don't see this button, or if the shape layer appears to be intersecting the background image, the Classic 3D Renderer is selected – remember, the following features are not supported in versions prior to CS6.

2 Twirl down Shape Layer 1 > Geometry Options. Scrub Extrusion Depth; the shape will get thicker.

3 Set Bevel Style to Angular, and a bevel will appear between the face and sides of the shape. Try out the different styles: Convex gives a soft rounding to the shape; Concave creates a scooped bevel.

4 Increase Bevel Depth to 5 or greater. Bevels add to the bulk of shapes; you may find you need to decrease the size of your shape – or at least the Extrusion Depth – to get back down to the overall size you intended.

5 The original shape parameters remain live. For example, click on the Fill swatch in the Tools panel and use the eyedropper to select the sky for your shape's color.

6 Twirl down **Shape Layer 1** > Material Options and increase the Transparency value. The Fill color of the shape will become translucent although its specular highlights will remain visible. Set it to a value around 90% so you can still make out the shape (see figure to the right). If you want to add more definition, increase the Transparency Rolloff value: This alters the transparency of surfaces that are at more severe angles to the camera, such as the sides.

7 The real magic of transparent objects comes when you increase the Index of Refraction parameter. At its default value of 1.00, your object is just a ghost in thin air, not actually altering the light rays going through it. But as soon as you increase it, the light rays of 3D layers are deflected at angles as they travel through transparent objects, causing visual distortions.

8 Increase Reflection Intensity: Now the sky plus other scenery on the other side of the environment layer's world will be reflected, tinted by the Fill color of the shape.

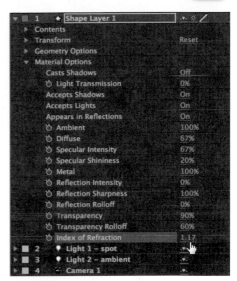

6–7 Transparent objects are ghost-like. The Index of Refraction (right) makes them appear more glass-like (above).

9 By default, the Material Options affect every surface of your shape. However, you can target the front, back, sides, and bevels individually. Let's create a chrome frame for the star shape.

• Set Reflection Intensity back to 0%. Twirl down Contents and select the shape group Polystar 1 to target it. Click on the Add button you used for shape effects earlier in this lesson and choose Bevel > Reflection Intensity. An operator called Material Options: Polystar 1 will be added below this shape group's Transform section. Increase Bevel Reflection Intensity to 100%.

• If you want to remove the blue tint coming from the Fill color, choose Add > Bevel > Color and set the Bevel Color to white.

8 Increase Reflection Intensity to see other 3D layers in your ray-traced object.

10 You can add (and animate!) normal shape effects as well. For example: With Polystar 1 still selected, choose Add > Twist to create a more interesting shape. In **Comps_Finished > 08-Extruding Shapes_final** we had additional fun changing the Roundness settings for the Polystar to create looped shapes at the points of the star, then used Offset Paths set to a negative value to detach the loop shapes to create little droplets.

9–10 You can add shape effects as well as animate the parameters of extruded shape layers.

Final Project

Creating a show opening, from draft to completion.

▽ In This Lesson

326   delivery specifications

327   music considerations; creating the main comp

328   spotting music

329   mocking up the 3D world; Label colors

330   3D view layouts

331   initial camera move; Separate Dimensions

334   placing the 3D background

335   3D Camera Tracker

336   time stretch; frame blending

337   typesetting the title

338   applying text animation presets

339   timing animation to music

340   using shapes to create a video frame

342   creating a reusable element

343   crafting an efficient composition hierarchy

344   replacing placeholders; ETLAT

345   filling out the background

346   creating animated lines

348   using expressions to animate to music

350   enabling Motion Blur; rendering a proof

351   delivering a broadcast package

352   ideas for enhancing the final project

▽ Getting Started

The project file and sources are contained in the **Lesson 12-Final Project** folder on this book's disc; copy this folder to your hard drive. This project file contains numerous intermediate comps for you to check your work against.

It's time to pull together a variety of skills you've learned in the previous lessons and put them to work. Your assignment is to create the opening for a show about surviving heart attacks. We'll start by creating a mock-up of a 3D world, testing the camera move, then replacing each placeholder with the final elements.

We're going to assume you already have some experience using After Effects (or can refer back to earlier lessons as needed), so our instructions will be a bit sparser than normal. Our focus here will be on design considerations, as well as how to plan out a project – including recovering when that plan doesn't work.

Before You Begin (Any Job!)

Before you start any motion graphics job, it's important to learn the client's parameters: what format your final render should be delivered in, as well as their budget to shoot or otherwise acquire visual elements. In this case, we've been

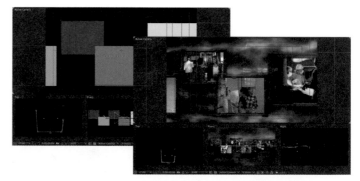

In this final project, you will follow a typical real-world workflow, proceeding from a proof-of-concept mock-up (left) to the finished piece (right). Videos courtesy Artbeats and iStockphoto.

told final delivery is to be a 1920×1080 pixel high-definition video file, 20 to 30 seconds in duration, at 23.976 frames per second – the video equivalent of the traditional film frame rate. (Since we don't want to overtax your computer, we're building this project at half that size – 960×540 – and have scaled down the source material accordingly.) Although it is to be delivered with a 16:9 widescreen image aspect ratio, we have been told to "protect" for 4:3 center-cut, where a standard definition version is cropped out of the middle of a scaled-down version of the final image. We've also been told the budget is tight, so we're going to use high-definition footage only for the "hero" shot, and employ lower-cost standard definition video for additional elements. We'll also be creating elements from scratch.

The next task is to nail down the music. We like to use the soundtrack as a timing grid for our animation – so the sooner we can specify at least the tempo of the music, the better. We researched typical heart rates and found they fall in the range of 60 to 100 beats per minute (bpm), with 72 being common for men. We then looked at our chart of "Magic Tempos" for animation (included in the **Lesson 12-Final Project > 12-Bonus Content** folder) and found that for 23.976 video, a musical tempo of 71.93 bpm produces a nice, clean animation rate of 20 frames per beat (fpb). We instructed the composer to use this tempo for the soundtrack, and he handed us back a piece of music just under 25 seconds in length – perfect. Now we're ready to start without fear of having to throw out and redo a lot of our work if we learned these details later.

Part 1: Outlining the Main Composition

Before we go too far down the road creating elements, it is wise to first mock up a rough version of our composition, spot the music (Lesson 5), and test the timing of the 3D camera move (Lesson 8) to make sure our general idea is going to work.

Creating the Main Comp

1 Open the project file **Lesson_12.aep**, set the Workspace to Standard, then Reset it. If you want to peek and get an idea of where you're going, open the **Finished Movies** folder, open the **Final Comp.mov** in the Footage panel, and RAM Preview. (Remember that pressing the spacebar will initiate a Standard preview without audio.)

2 Select the **Comps** folder in the Project panel; this is where you'll keep the compositions you create. Then choose Composition > New Composition. Name it " **Final Comp**" (we add a leading space so it will sort to the top of

▼ Previsualization Aids

It's not unusual to be asked to supply a series of *style frames* before starting a motion graphics projects. These are often still images that show the look and feel of the overall design, including the type choices and the color palette. The frames could also show the progression from start to finish, including notes on how transitions might occur. We prefer to use After Effects rather than Photoshop to create these style frames, since we have access to all the tools we'll be using for the real animation. By trying out various plug-in settings, you can save research time when the design is eventually approved. You can also help the client better visualize your ideas by creating mini-animations to show how type or effects will animate or transitions will occur.

You might also be asked to supply an *animatic* (an animated storyboard), which is what you will be creating in Part 1 of this lesson. These block out the major sections and transitions in a more complex animation or commercial, and they test the progression of scenes before live action is shot. This helps avoid spending time animating or shooting a scene that later ends up on the cutting room floor, or finding out that a crucial part of the story is missing. Animatics can be a series of stills with captions, or simple 2D or 3D animations with voiceovers, depending on the time constraints and budget of each job.

Corporate video projects often include a *script*. Go through the script with the producer, highlighting the sections you will need to create motion graphics for, and coordinate with the video editor to make sure all graphics are accounted for.

the **Comps** folder); based on our client specs and music enter a Width of 960, Height of 540, Square Pixels, Frame Rate of 23.976, Start Timecode of 0:00, and Duration of at least 25:00. Set the Background Color to black, then click on the Advanced tab and set the Renderer to Classic 3D (called Advanced 3D prior to After Effects CS6). Click OK.

Spotting the Music

3 Back in the Project panel, twirl down **Sources > music**. Select **Final Beat.wav** and type ⌘ / on Mac (**Ctrl** / on Windows) to add it to **Final Comp**.

4 With **Final Beat.wav** selected, type **L** **L** (two **L**s in quick succession) to reveal its audio waveform. A series of tall, evenly spaced spikes are easy to see in the waveform. Press **.** (the decimal key on the numeric keypad – MacBook users may alternately press **Ctrl** **.**) to preview just the audio and note how the heartbeats as well as drums correspond to these spikes.

5 Move to 00:05 where the stronger (taller) of the two beats in the first heartbeat occurs. With **Final Beat.wav** selected, press **✳** (asterisk on the numeric keypad; MacBook Pro users may press **Ctrl** **8**) to place a Layer Marker.

Now let's see if the composer did what we asked: Press **Shift** **Page Down** twice to jump ahead 20 frames to 00:25. Lo and behold – there's another beat there, just as we planned! Press **✳** to place another marker, and continue to do so throughout the soundtrack.

2 Create your final composition based on the client's delivery specifications plus the duration of the music. It's not a bad idea to make your final comp longer than you think you'll need; it's easier to shorten a comp than extend it after you've done a lot of work.

5–6 For the most part, tall spikes in the waveform correspond to an audible beat every 20 frames. Our final spotted soundtrack contains markers for the main beats as well as comments where the music changes.

6 Now that you have the major beats marked out, go back and preview the music again, listening for major events or sectional changes such as the start and end of the main body of the music, as well as prominent details such as cymbal rolls or the last piano note. Double-click these markers to open their Layer Marker dialogs and enter short Comments to note these events. Then twirl up the **Final Beat.wav** layer. Our version is in **Intermediate Comps > 01_Spotted Music**; save your own project so you don't lose your work.

Mocking Up the 3D World

Our budget allows us to use a full-frame high-definition footage for the final "hero" shot, but we have to use smaller standard-definition footage for the other video clips. Scaling up standard-def video to fill a high-def frame can look ugly. A common design workaround is to place an assortment of smaller videos in 3D space, perhaps adding a stylized frame to make them more interesting.

We joke that working in 3D takes three times as long. As tempting as it may be to create a visually beautiful world right from the start, the prudent approach is to first mock up your world and test your camera move to make sure your design works before spending too much time implementing it.

An effective way to use small standard definition or even web videos in a high-definition project is to arrange them in a 3D world, adding frames to make them more interesting.

7 Let's start with the hero. As mentioned earlier, we're working at half size, so we need to create a stand-in layer that is at least 960×540 pixels for the high-def hero. Then we need to leave space for its frame. As a starting point, let's leave roughly 25% of its height (an additional 140 pixels) all around for the frame.

Choose Layer > New > Solid, enter a Width of 1100 and Height of 680, and set the color to yellow. Name it "**Hero Shot**" and click OK. It will automatically be centered in the composition, which is the planned final placement. Then in the Timeline panel, click on the color swatch in the Label column at the far left and choose Yellow.

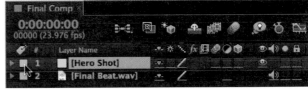

7 Set the Label color (where the cursor is pointing) the same as your solid's color. By doing so, it will be easy to correspond what you see in the Comp and Timeline panels.

8 Our smaller videos are 320×240 pixels (roughly half the square-pixel size of standard def NTSC video). Again, we want to leave about another 25% of the height (60 pixels) for the frame. Choose Layer > New > Solid and set Width to 380 and Height to 300. Set the color to red, name it "**Extra 1**" and click OK. Then change its Label color to Red to match.

9 Duplicate **Extra 1**. With the duplicate selected, choose Layer > Solid Settings; After Effects will automatically change its name to **Extra 2**. Change its color to green, click OK, then change its Label color to Green. Repeat this twice more for **Extra 3** and **4**, coloring them blue and orange respectively.

10 Next let's arrange the layers horizontally. Type ⌘ — (Ctrl —) to scale down the Comp panel to 25% Magnification, or until **Hero Shot** is less than a third as wide as the Comp panel. Press the spacebar to temporarily engage the Hand tool, and drag the visible portion of the comp to the right, leaving an empty pasteboard to the left.

▽ tip

The Magic Tempos

Specific music tempos correspond to simple integer numbers of frames between musical beats. A chart of these tempos at various frame rates – plus the reasoning behind them – is included on the book's DVD-ROM in **Lesson 12-Final Project > 12-Bonus Content**.

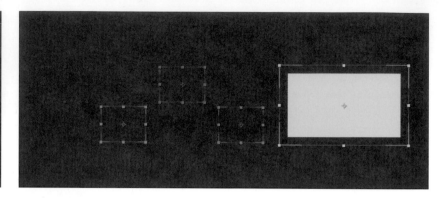

10 Arrange the **Extra** layers on the pasteboard as a "gallery wall" of images for the camera to pan across (right). If you want to space them uniformly, use the Align panel, or check their Position values (above). *(Note: Align works with 2D layers, but not 3D layers, so use this tool before you enable the 3D Layer switches in Step 11.)*

Drag the **Extra** layers to the left and arrange them in a pleasing pattern. Press **P** to reveal the Position of selected layers to numerically verify their arrangement. We personally chose to spread the **Extra** layers 500 pixels apart in X and staggered ±170 pixels in Y compared with the centerline of **Hero Shot**; you can align their top and bottom edges or make a freestyle arrangement. Just make sure **Extra 4** does not overlap **Hero Shot**, as you need to see it unobstructed at the end.

11 Our mock-up has our video layers arranged as a gallery wall, spaced evenly in X and staggered in both Y and Z. Our version is in **Intermediate Comps > 02_3D Mockup**.

11 Select all of the layers except **Final Beat.wav** and enable their 3D Layer switches. Set the View Layout option to 4 Views – Bottom and verify the view ports are set to Active Camera, Top, Front, and Right. Remember you can use the Camera tools (page 215) to optimize these views; the quickie solution is to select each of the bottom view ports. Then choose View > Look at All Layers.

Arrange layers **Extra 1** through **4** in Z space to create multiplaning (explained on page 210) when the camera pans by them. We chose to stagger them ±150 pixels in Z compared with **Hero Shot**, but again you have some freedom here. Leave **Hero Shot** at its original Z Position; this will make it easier to craft the camera move in the next section.

Creating the Camera Move

We communicated with the musician that our idea was to have a camera move that slowly pans past a bunch of videos, settling on the hero shot and title. With that information, plus the title of the show, he crafted a piece where the music starts mysteriously with just a heartbeat; a cymbal roll leads from this into the piano melody. The melody then ends with another cymbal roll leading into a large crash, returning to the original heartbeat.

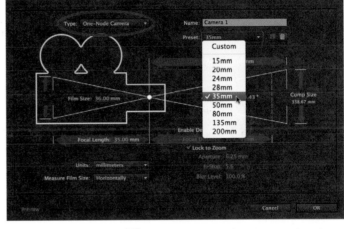

The animation can now be synced in time with these musical accents: We'll start looking at just an abstracted background (which we'll build later), pulling back during the first cymbal roll to reveal the video screens when the melody starts. We'll pan past the videos during the melody and zoom in during the second cymbal roll to end on our hero video – and show title – at the crash. The remaining duration will give the viewer time to read the main title (and for the editor to fade to black or crossfade into the first scene of the show).

12 Create a Layer > New > Camera. For simple pans, pull-backs, and push-ins, a one-node camera (with no Point of Interest) is easier to use. Select this option from the Type popup, then chose a Preset of 35mm (a "short" lens) to exaggerate the perspective distortion during the moves. Disable Depth of Field and click OK. When you create a new camera, it defaults to showing any layer that has its Z value at 0 at its original size, which is perfect for framing **Hero Shot**.

12 Create a one-node camera with a short lens length. This will make it easier to control for simple panning moves and exaggerate the perspective distortion in 3D so we get more impact from relatively simple moves.

13 Quite often, a good strategy for creating an animation move is to start where you'll end – in this case, centered on **Hero Shot** at the time of the crash. Locate the current time indicator ("CTI" for short) to 16:21 where you've marked the crash in the soundtrack. With **Camera 1** selected, press **P** to reveal its Position. Right-click on the word Position and choose Separate Dimensions, then enable keyframing for the X, Y, and Z Position parameters. This will make it easier to keyframe the pull out and push in (Z Position) separately from the pan (X Position).

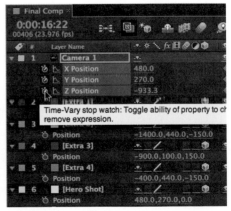

13 Enable Separate Dimensions (left) to make it easier to keyframe each component of the camera move. Then enable keyframing for X, Y, and Z Position (right). Note how the X and Y Position of the newly created camera match the default position of **Hero Shot** – that was by plan, not by accident.

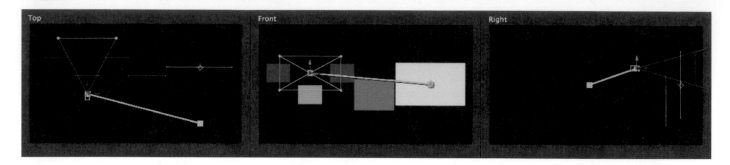

14 We've keyframed our beginning and ending poses. Next is creating the camera move in-between.

14 We've chosen to start our move centered between **Extra 1** and **Extra 3** and above **Extra 2** so when we pull back we'll see three of our video frames. (You may have a different arrangement in space than us; modify our instructions as needed to match your world.)

• Move to 01:01 – the heartbeat where the cymbal roll starts. In our arrangement, **Extra 2** (green) is centered in X between the red and blue solids, so take its X Position value and enter it for **Camera 1**'s X Position.

• Next take the Y Position of **Extra 1** and **3** and enter it for **Camera 1**'s Y Position.

• Finally, scrub Camera 1's Z Position to zoom into the scene until the **Extra** layers disappear off the edges of the Active Camera view. In the process, keyframes for all three values will be set.

15 Press **K** until the CTI (current time indicator) jumps to the marker where the piano melody begins (03:13); if you go too far, press **J** to jump back in time.

• To pan across the center of the screens, set **Camera 1**'s Y Position back to 270.

• With the Active Camera view selected press **'** (apostrophe) to toggle on the Title/Action Safe Grids and scrub **Camera 1**'s Z Position until all the visible **Extra** screens sit inside at least the upper and lower Action Safe grid. Remembering that the client asked us to protect for the inner 4:3 center-cut area, we backed up in Z even farther to –1800 to make sure all viewers saw multiple screens at once. Don't touch the X Position; we want to continue a smooth horizontal pan.

16 We noticed there are three beat markers between the two "pull back" keyframes we just set. To keep the same pacing for the final push in, move to 14:09 (three beats before the ending crash), click once on **Camera 1**'s earlier Z Position keyframe at 3:13 and copy it, then paste it to the current time.

17 **Camera 1**'s Z Position should still be selected. Press **Shift** and click the words X Position in the Timeline panel to select all of the Position keyframes, and press **F9** to apply Animation > Keyframe Assistant > Easy Ease to them. Press **0** on the numeric keypad (MacBook users may press **Ctrl** plus the normal **0** key) to RAM Preview your animation.

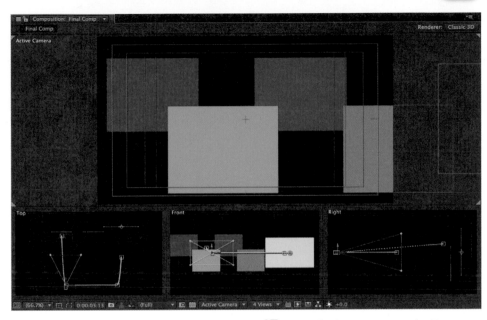

Feel free to tweak the position of the layers and camera until you have a move you like. In our case, we decided we wanted the **Extra** layers to overlap when we panned past them; we also thought the **Extra** layers were looking a bit small compared with the **Hero Shot**. To solve both problems, we scaled up the **Extra** layers by 165%, as they were still far enough back in 3D space that we wouldn't be blowing up their pixels. This in turn required us to push in further for our initial keyframe (at 01:01) to make sure the **Extra** layers didn't encroach on our view.

Marking the Camera's Timing

Our version to this point is in **Intermediate Comps > 03_Camera Move**; note the addition of Composition Markers (pages 145–146). Once we settled on the camera move, we thought it would be useful to note when the various video layers come into and go out of view. This will help us if we want to time an action in these videos to when they are on screen, or if the clips aren't long enough to last the entire composition. To add these to your own composition:

18 Locate the CTI to the first camera keyframe at 01:01 when the video layers are all out of view. Then press (Page Down) to step forward a frame at a time until you reach the first frame when the **Extra** layers come into view. Press (F2) to deselect all layers. Hold (⌥) (Alt) and press (*) on the numeric keypad to open the Composition Marker dialog. Enter a brief Comment about which layers appear and click OK. Repeat this procedure as each new layer enters the camera's view.

19 Keep stepping forward until the first layer disappears from view. Press (Page Up) to back up one frame, and press (⌥ *) ((Alt *)) to create a new Comp Marker. Enter the name of the layer that is about to leave and click OK. Repeat this for each of the remaining Extra layers as they leave the camera's view.

17 In our final camera move, the **Extra** layers overlap after being scaled up 165%. We made sure we pulled back enough in Z to fit multiple screens inside the safe areas.

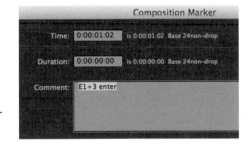

18–19 You can add helpful Comments to both Composition and Layer Markers (above). Create Comp Markers (below) noting when each layer enters and leaves the camera's view. This will come in handy later when you need to trim or otherwise edit the timing of these layers.

▽ factoid

Shoot Your Own

Yes, the client brief was we had to save money on stock footage – but we created this background ourselves! Look inside **Lesson 12-Final Project > 12-Bonus Content** for an article we wrote for Artbeats on creating backgrounds like these.

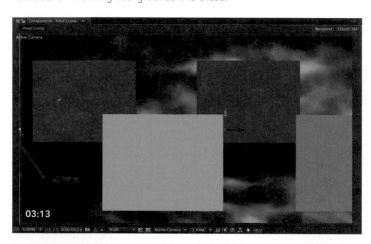

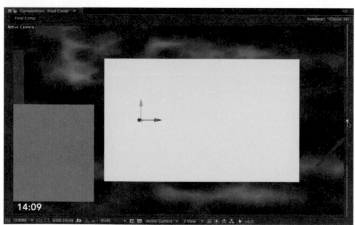

2 Push the background layer far away in Z, then scale it up and position it so that its edges (indicated in both figures by the red arrows) remain out of view at the extremes of the camera's movement. If you tweak the camera move later, remember to come back and recheck this to make sure no gaps reappear. Background courtesy Artbeats/Liquid Abstracts.

Part 2: Background and Hero Layers

Now that we have our 3D world and camera move mocked up, we can start to insert the real layers. We'll start by placing the background (because it's quick and easy, and sometimes it's nice to feel like you're making progress), then focusing on the real hero shot plus our show's title. Before diving in, save your project, then use File > Increment and Save to start a new version number.

If you're just joining us, our version to this point is **Intermediate Comps > 03_Camera Move**.

Placing the Background

1 Back in the Project panel, twirl down **Sources > movies**. Select **Liquid Abstract.mov** and drag into **Final Comp**, placing it below the **Extra** and **Hero** layers.

You can often get away with a soft, full-frame 2D layer as a background for a 3D world. But it doesn't take much work to place it in 3D, where you can enjoy the benefits of multiplaning.

2 Enable the 3D Layer switch for **Liquid Abstract.mov** and press **P** to reveal its Position. Push it far back in Z so it appears to be far away and doesn't move as much as the foreground layers. We used a value of Z = 5000.

Then press **Shift S** to reveal its Scale, and scrub it larger until it fills the frame (add **Shift** to scrub in larger increments). Check the second and third camera keyframes – where it has the widest view of your world – to make sure the background layer remains in view for the entire composition. To minimize how much you have to scale up this layer, try sliding it in X so that its left edge is just out of view at the second keyframe, and its right edge is just out of view at the third camera keyframe.

With our camera move, we found that a Scale value of just over 900% was enough (as seen in **Intermediate Comps > 04_Background**). This means the layer will still be viewed at more than 100% of its original 2D size, but since it's intended to be an out-of-focus background anyway, we're less concerned than we would be if it was a foreground layer.

Tracking the Hero Camera

Next, we want to track the original camera movement in our hero footage so our title will appear to move as if it existed in the original scene. To do this, we're going to use the 3D Camera Tracker introduced in After Effects CS6 (Lesson 9). Our hero footage is not an ideal shot to track – there are too many people moving in the scene, and too few stationary features to track – but as we're not performing a critical composite, just capturing the spirit of the move is good enough.

3 Select the **Comps** folder in the Project panel and create a Composition > New Composition. Set its size to 960×540, Square Pixels, Frame Rate to 23.976, and Duration to 25:00 to match **Final Comp**. Enter the name "**Hero + Title**" and click OK. You can set the View Layout back to 1 View for now.

4 Twirl open the **Sources > movies** folder and drag **Surgery.mov** into your new comp. With **Surgery.mov** still selected, if you're using CS6, choose Animation > Track Camera. You will see a blue Analyzing banner followed by an orange Solving banner.

5 We want to place the title in front of the foreground surgeon. Drag the CTI through the duration of the clip, looking for a Track Point that appears stuck to his body that is preferably near the center of the frame where our title will go. Select this point, then right-click it and choose the option Create Null and Camera. An animated **3D Tracker Camera** layer plus a stationary **Track Null 1** layer will be added to the timeline.

If you have After Effects CS5.5 or earlier, you can copy our **3D Camera Tracker** and **Track Null 1** layers from **Intermediate Comps > 05_Tracked Hero** and paste them into your composition. Or, you can try to approximate the move yourself by creating a Layer > New > Camera and keyframing it. Note the 3D Camera Tracker solved this scene as having a small Angle of View; use a value of 5 to 10° to match the perspective in the shot.

5 Select a stable Track Point on the foreground surgeon, right-click, and create a null object as well as a camera (above). These will be added to the timeline (below). (CS5 and 5.5 users can copy our null and camera layers.) Footage courtesy iStockphoto, evandrorigon, image #17590052.

▽ factoid

Previewing Frame Blending

To RAM Preview with frame blending, don't forget to enable the master Frame Blending switch in the Timeline panel for both **Hero + Title** and in **Final Comp**. Disable it to speed up previews of **Final Comp**. To ensure you render with Frame Blending, open the Render Settings and make sure Time Sampling > Frame Blending is set to On For Checked Layers (the default in most templates).

Time Stretching the Hero

We have a problem: Our hero footage is only 09:07 in duration, but we need it on screen considerably longer than that. We can either try to find a longer suitable clip, or slow down our existing clip. As the music has a dreamy quality, let's go with the latter approach.

6 Click on the Timeline panel tab for **Final Comp** and double-click the Comp Marker for when **Hero Clip** first entered the camera's view. Note its Time; in our version, it's 05:20.

7 Return to the **Hero + Title** comp. Click the time display in the upper left corner of the Timeline panel and enter the time you noted in the previous step. Select the **3D Camera Tracker** and **Surgery.mov** layers, and press **[** (left bracket) to start both layers at this time. Press **B** to start your work area here as well.

8 Press **End** so the Comp panel is displaying the last frame of the composition. With both **3D Camera Tracker** and **Surgery.mov** still selected (so that you'll slow them both down together), use the following shortcut to stretch their out points to the current time: **⌘ ⌥ ,** (comma) (**Ctrl Alt ,**). To check the amount of time stretch applied, right-click on one of the timeline's column headers and choose Stretch.

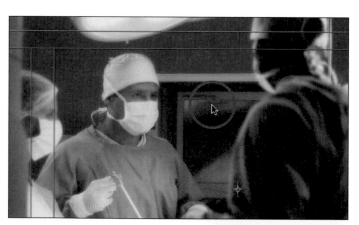

9 Stretch the footage and camera move as needed to cover the length of time this shot will be visible in **Final Comp**. Then enable Pixel Motion mode for **Surgery.mov** (right, circled) plus Frame Blending preview for the composition. Some artifacts may appear (above), but we think they're minor enough to live with.

9 RAM Preview. The hero footage is slower, but appears to stutter a bit. To cure this, make sure the Switches column is visible in the Timeline panel (press **F4** if it isn't) and click twice inside the Frame Blending switch for **Surgery.mov** to enable Pixel Motion for this layer (Lesson 7). Then enable the master Frame Blending switch along the top of the Timeline panel. RAM Preview again, watching closely for any artifacts in the Comp panel such as portions of the image appearing to melt. If this is bothersome, you may need to set **Surgery.mov** to Frame Mix rather than Pixel Motion frame blending mode. Our result is in **Intermediate Comps > 06_Stretched Hero**.

Creating the Title Text

The client has told us the name of this show is *Surviving a Heart Attack*.
We've decided to put the emphasis on the words "Heart Attack" to grab
the viewer's attention.

10 As the camera is constantly pushing into our hero shot, and
the title will be tied to this camera move, press **End** to jump to the
last frame of **Hero + Title** where objects are at their largest. Make
sure the Title/Action Safe grids are visible; press **'** if they aren't.

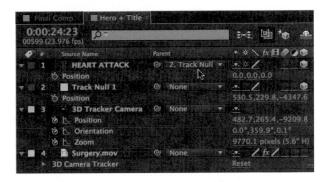

11 Double-click the Text tool – this will create an empty text
layer centered in the comp. The Character and Paragraph panels
should open automatically. Type "**HEART**" and press **Return** to
start a new line. Then type "**ATTACK**" and press **Enter** (not **Return**)
to accept your text. If the two words are not centered, bring the
Paragraph panel forward and click the Center Text button.

12 Enable the 3D Layer switch for **HEART ATTACK**, then press **Shift F4** to
open the Parent panel. Click on the Parent popup for **HEART ATTACK**, then
add the **Shift** key: Adding **Shift** will place the child at exactly the same position
as the parent with no offset (including in Z space). Select **Track Null 1** from the
popup, and **HEART ATTACK** will jump forward to this location.

12 Hold the **Shift** key while parenting
HEART ATTACK to **Track Null 1** so that
the text layer initially has no offset from
the null's position. This is particularly
important to maintain the null's Z Position
as the camera moves through the world.

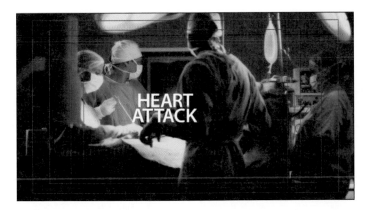

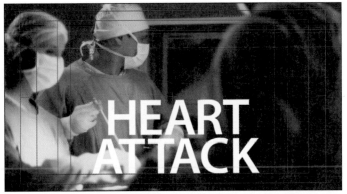

13 With **HEART ATTACK** still selected, bring the Character panel back
forward, set the text color to white, and style the text as you feel appropriate.
As we're restricted by the fonts that shipped with After Effects, we chose Myriad
Pro Semibold for its strong, serious look; feel free to choose something different.

Press **P** to reveal the text layer's Position, and offset it from the null in X
and Y to place it roughly centered horizontally, sitting on top of the Title Safe
grid near the bottom of the frame. Scrub the CTI to verify that the text moves
as if it was in the operating room at the time this footage was shot.

13 Set the text to taste, working with
Font Size, Leading, and Kerning. We
tightened up some spaces and aligned
the vertical bars of the T and K. Make
sure the text stays inside the Title Safe
grid throughout the camera move.

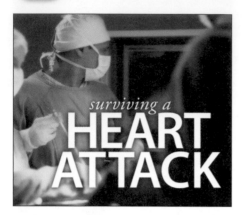

14–15 We set the subtitle in a contrasting font on its own layer, making it easier to animate separately. A broad drop shadow applied to both text layers helps separate them from the underlying footage.

▽ factoid

Guide Layers

Guide layers (used in Step 16) are handy for scratch audio tracks, grid overlays, or FPO (For Position Only) template layers. You can optionally render them in Render Settings.

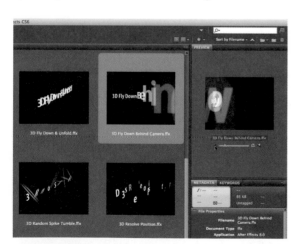

18 Preview the numerous text animation presets provided in Adobe Bridge. Double-click one to apply it to your selected layer back in After Effects.

14 You can mix and match fonts and sizes inside the same text layer, but it's usually better to break words and lines up into their own layers. Repeat Steps 11 through 13 to create a second text layer, this time typing "**surviving a**" with no return in-between. Set it smaller, and position it on top of the word HEART. We went with Adobe Garamond Pro Italic (a lighter serif font that is also bundled with After Effects) for contrast with the main words.

15 We're having a little trouble with readability; the white text doesn't have enough contrast with the brighter areas in **Surgery.mov**. Adding a stroke is one solution; we prefer adding Effect > Perspective > Drop Shadow. We set Distance to 0 to center the shadow, increased Opacity to 100%, then increased the size until we had a nice dark glow around the words.

Save your project; our version is in **Intermediate Comps > 07_Title Set**.

Applying Text Animation Presets

It's nice that the title is following the camera move in our hero, but we think we can add even more drama by having it animate on in time with the music. To save time, we're going to use a pair of text animation presets, but feel free to apply what you've learned in Lesson 5 and create your own animation!

16 Bring **Final Comp** forward again, and select the already-spotted soundtrack layer **Final Beat.wav**. Copy it, bring **Hero + Title** back forward, and paste. To make sure this copy of the soundtrack plays only in this precomp and not in **Final Comp** as well, enable Layer > Guide Layer for **Final Beat.wav**.

17 In **Final Comp**, we started our final camera push in at the beat between the last piano note and the second cymbal roll; that's a good first guess as to where to start the title animation as well. Locate the CTI to this marker (at 14:09), as keyframes for animation presets are applied starting at the current time.

18 Select **HEART ATTACK**, then click on the Options menu in the upper right corner of the Effects and Presets panel and choose Browse Presets. This will launch Adobe Bridge, opened to the **Presets** folder.

Double-click the **Text** folder to open it. As our title is already in 3D space, we went to the **3D Text** folder first. Explore the different presets to choose a suitable animation; selecting a preset causes an animated preview to play. As the subject matter is rather weighty, we gravitated toward simpler moves such as 3D Fly Down Behind Camera.ffx. Double-click the preset you chose; After Effects will come forward, with this preset applied to **HEART ATTACK**, starting at the current time. Press **U** to see the keyframes that the preset has added to the text layer and RAM Preview.

19 Locate back to 14:09, select the **surviving a** layer, and return to Adobe Bridge. To keep the focus on the words HEART ATTACK, you might want to choose an even simpler preset for this subtitle; we went with Text > Animate In > Fade Up Characters.ffx. Double-click the preset you chose to apply it to **surviving a**.

20 RAM Preview: The text animations finish prematurely, before the crash cymbal hits. Select **surviving a** plus **HEART ATTACK** and press **U** to reveal their keyframes (if you haven't already). Slide their ending keyframes to align with the CRASH marker at 16:21. We see the second keyframe of the preset we chose for **HEART ATTACK** has an Easy Ease icon; to make the animation land harder, hold **⌘** (*Ctrl*) and click it to convert it to a linear keyframe.

RAM Preview again. For us, the animation appears too languid now, so we moved the first keyframes later to align with the cymbal marker at 15:05.

Finally, locate to the first keyframes for the text layers, and with both layers selected press **⌥** (*Alt*) to trim their in points to the current time. Now After Effects won't spend time calculating the text until they start their animation.

21 Time for a payoff: In the Project panel, select the precomp you've been building, **Hero + Title**. Then click on the Timeline panel tab for **Final Comp** and select the placeholder layer **Hero Shot**. Press **⌘⌥/** (*Ctrl Alt /*), and your precomp will be swapped in for your placeholder. RAM Preview; don't you just love it when a plan comes together? Save your project, then File > Increment and Save to start a new version number.

Our versions are **Intermediate Comps > 08a_Title Animated** and **08b_Hero Precomp Placed**.

20 Time the text animation keyframes to match the soundtrack. (Instead of moving the keyframes later in time, another option would have been converting them to Easy Ease keyframes to match the camera's interpolation back in **Final Comp**.)

21 Back in **Final Comp**, replace the placeholder solid **Hero Shot** with your precomp **Hero + Title**. This is finally starting to look like something…

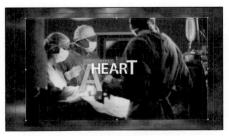

Using the Pen Tool

For a more in-depth look at how to draw pen-based shapes, watch **Lesson 11 > Video Bonus > Drawing Pen Shapes.mov**, excerpted from our *After Effects Apprentice* video series.

2 Use colors present in **Surgery.mov** to set up a radial gradient for your shape layer.

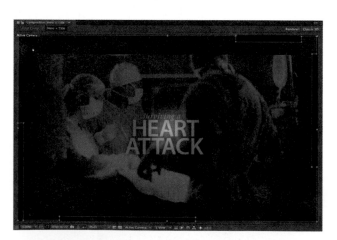

3 Create an interesting, notched frame shape just inside the comp's boundaries. Hold **Shift** as you create new points to help constrain the angle of your edges.

Part 3: Framing the Videos

Now that the main title is done (whew!), you can turn your attention to making the other elements look nice. In this Part we'll create the frames for the **Hero** and **Extra** videos, and swap the **Extra** precomps into **Final Comp**.

Framing the Hero Video

1 Bring the **Hero + Title** comp forward. We originally created it at the size of the hero video, but now we need some extra space to add the frame. Open the Composition Settings, and increase Width to 1100 and Height to 680 to match your original mock-up. Click OK; additional space will be visible around **Surgery.mov**. Then turn off the Action/Title Safe Grids to tidy up the display.

2 Rather than create a simple rectangular frame, let's take advantage of shape layers (Lesson 11) to create a higher-tech look.

• Make sure no layer is selected, choose the Pen tool, and disable the RotoBezier option. Hold **⌥** (*Alt*) and click on the color swatch to the right of the word Stroke in the Tools panel until it is set to None (look for the red slash).

• Click on the word Fill, choose the Radial Gradient option, set the Opacity around 70% to create a semitranslucent frame, and click OK.

• Move to around 15:00 (where you can see the entire scene), click the color swatch to the right of Fill to open the Gradient Editor (page 316). Select the left Color Stop, click the eyedropper, and choose the green from the surgeon's cap. Drag the circle in the Color Picker down and to the right to make it darker and more saturated. Then select the right Color Stop, and eyedropper the dark blue blanket covering the patient. Remove any other color stops, set the Opacity Stops to 100%, and click OK.

3 Click in the upper left corner of the Comp panel to create your first point; a Shape Layer will be created starting at the beginning of the comp. Hold the **Shift** key down to constrain the angle of your lines, then move your cursor to the right and click most but not all of the way across the top of the panel. Still holding **Shift**, move the cursor down slightly until the Pen icon reappears, then click again to create a notch in your frame. Continue this way around the visible portion of your composition. You can be as conservative or crazy as you like! (We know this description is vague; look at the accompanying figures to get our intention.) When you close your path, use the cursor keys to nudge the first point as needed to create clean, straight lines before and after. (Note that we'll round the corners in Step 6.)

4 Repeat this procedure, this time creating what will become the inner edge of your frame (see figure below). Create lines outside the edge of **Surgery.mov** to produce a floating frame effect; add the occasional notch or tab that overlaps the video to suggest physical supports. Press **V** to choose the Selection tool when you're done.

5 After Effects took your actions to mean you wanted two shape groups inside the same shape layer, when in reality you wanted both paths to be in the same group to create a compound shape. In the Timeline panel, twirl open Contents > Shape 2 and drag its Path 1 down into Contents > Shape 1 just below the other path. Delete the group Shape 2 when you're done and reselect Shape 1.

6 Click on the arrow to the right of the Add button for **Shape Layer 1** and choose Merge Paths; it will be added below Path 2 (if necessary, drag it into place). Twirl it open and set its Mode to Subtract: Now **Surgery.mov** will be clearly visible in the center of your frame.

Click the Toggle Mask and Shape Path Visibility button along the bottom left of the Comp panel to hide the path. Click Add again and choose Round Corners; twirl it open and slowly scrub its Radius to set how smooth the corners are. Set to taste.

7 Select Contents > Shape 1 and look for the blue dots in the center of the Comp panel that represent the start and end points of your radial gradient. Drag the end point (the one to the right) outward until you get a nice transition from green to blue for your frame. To add a final bit of dimensionality, add Layer > Layer Styles > Bevel and Emboss and tweak to taste.

Save! Our version is saved as **Intermediate Comps > 09_Hero Frame**.

5 After creating your inner and outer frame edges (left), drag the path from your second shape group into the first group (above). You can then delete the second group.

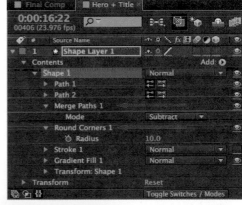

△ **6** Use the shape operator Merge Paths to cut the inner path out of the outer path, then Round Corners to soften the edges of your compound path.

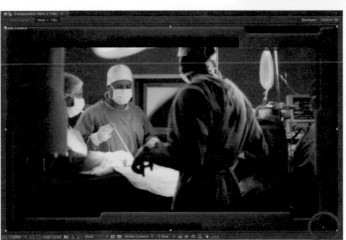

◁ **7** Finish off your frame by dragging out the gradient handle (circled in red), and add the Bevel and Emboss layer style.

Interpret Footage: Joggin

Main Options Color Management

Alpha

Ignore   Inver

Straight – Unmatted

Premultiplied – Matted With Color:

Guess

Frame Rate

Use frame rate from file: (29.970 fps)

Conform to frame rate: 23.976 frames per se

Non-Drop Frame ▾ Δ 0:00:12:21

9 Conform the frame rate of this extra video clip to 23.976 fps so no frames will be skipped when it plays back inside **Final Comp**. This has the side effects of slowing it down and increasing its duration, both of which are desirable in this case.

10 Using the Pen tool, draw the inner and outer frame paths, as you did earlier for the hero frame. If you have trouble seeing your shape path, change the shape layer's Label color to something brighter. If you accidentally created a mask path on the movie layer, cut the mask path and paste it to a shape layer's Path property.

Framing the Extra Videos

Now that you've framed the hero video, you just have to repeat that procedure four times for the extra videos…or repeat it just once and be clever about reusing that frame.

8 Back in the Project panel, select the **Comps** folder and type ⌘ N (*Ctrl* N) to create a new composition. Set a Size of 380×300 (matching the placeholder solids you made earlier), Square Pixels, with a Frame Rate of 23.976 fps and a Duration of 25:00. Leave the background color black, name it "**Extra Video 1**" and click OK.

9 Select **Sources > movies > Jogging.mov**; its details will appear at the top of the Project panel. We see its duration (10:09) is a bit short, and its frame rate is 29.97. To reinforce our dreamlike mood (and to extend its running time), click the Interpret Footage button at the bottom left of the Project panel (page 3), conform its frame rate to 23.976 fps, and click OK. Then type ⌘ / (*Ctrl* /) to add it to your new composition. As the video itself is just 320×240 pixels, there already is some room around it for a frame.

10 Press *F2* to deselect the video layer and choose the Pen tool. Its settings – radial gradient fill, no stroke, RotoBezier off – should be the same as when you last used them in Step 2. Since this is a smaller comp, feel free to zoom in 200%. Click in the upper left corner of the composition view to start your frame outline, then hold *Shift* and click around near the edges of the Comp viewer, occasionally zigging and zagging to create notches as you did in Step 3 for the hero frame. Then repeat to create a second path, tracing just outside the video's outline but occasionally overlapping it to imply structural supports. Press *V* to return to the Selection tool when you're done.

11 The drill is the same as it was for the hero video frame:

• Twirl open **Shape Layer 1** > Contents > Shape 2, select Path 1, and drag it just below Path 1 for Contents > Shape 1.

• Delete Shape 2 and reselect Shape 1.

• Add > Merge Paths, making sure it appears just below Paths 1 and 2. Twirl it open and set its Mode to Subtract.

• Add > Round Corners and tweak its Radius to taste.

• In the Comp panel, drag the Gradient Fill End Point outward until you see the gradient colorize the frame.

◁ **11** Merge the inner and outer frame paths using Subtract mode and add Round Corners, then adjust the Gradient Fill End Point. You now have your prototype frame. Footage courtesy Artbeats/FTN110.

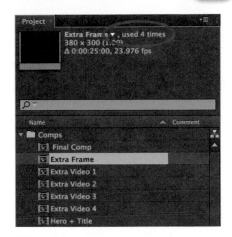

13 After creating the comp **Extra Video 1** – which uses **Extra Frame** as a precomp – duplicate **Extra Video 1** three times so each video will have its own precomp, all referring to the same frame.

▽ factoid

Add > Path

Rather than make two separate Shape Paths, you could start to create your inside path by clicking Add > Path to Shape 1. However, due to a "boog" this doesn't work in the initial release of After Effects CS6.

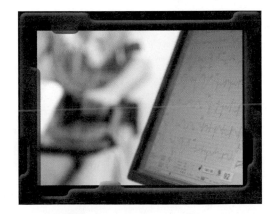

14–15 In the **Extra Video 2** precomps, create a variation on your single frame by rotating it, then replace the video layer with **Stress Test.mov**. Footage courtesy iStockphoto/mvmkr/file #19041492.

If you can't see these points, make sure the Selection tool is active, not the Pen tool. (You can also twirl open Gradient Fill in the Timeline panel and scrub its End Point value there.)

12 Once you have a frame design you like, right-click its layer and choose Pre-compose. After Effects will default to Move All Attributes (Shape Layers have no "source" so the Leave All Attributes option is grayed out). Disable Open New Composition, rename it "**Extra Frame**" and click OK. **Shape Layer 1** will be replaced with the precomp **Extra Frame**. Apply Layer > Layer Styles > Bevel and Emboss to this layer, and tweak to taste.

13 In the Project panel, select Comps > **Extra Video 1** and press ⌘ D (Ctrl D) to duplicate it three times. After Effects will automatically name these comps **Extra Video 2**, **Extra Video 3**, and **Extra Video 4**. The precomp **Extra Frame** will be used by all of these **Extra Video** comps.

14 Double-click **Extra Video 2** to open it. Select the **Extra Frame** layer, press R to reveal its Rotation, and set Rotation to 180°. This is the intelligent cheater's way to create a "new" frame. As layer styles are calculated after transformations including Rotation and Scale, the light direction on the bevel stays the same.

15 Select **Jogging.mov**. Then in the Project panel, select **Sources > movies > Stress Test.mov**. We see its frame rate is 25 fps; open Interpret Footage and conform it to 23.976 fps. Then type ⌘ / (Ctrl /) to replace **Jogging.mov** with this new source.

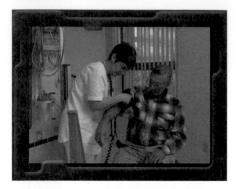

16–17 In the **Extra Video 3** (above) and **Extra Video 4** (below) precomps, create variations on your single frame by scaling it, and replace the video in each. Footage courtesy Artbeats/Healthcare.

16 Open **Extra Video 3**. Select **Extra Frame** and press **S** to reveal Scale. Disable its Constrain Proportions switch (the chain link icon) and set its Y Scale to –100%, creating another variation on your original frame. Then select **Jogging.mov** and replace it with **Sources > movies > Physical Therapy.mov**. It will take on the shorter duration of **Jogging.mov**; click and drag the end of its layer bar to extend it to its full duration.

17 Finally, open **Extra Video 4**. Select **Extra Frame** and press **S** to reveal Scale. Disable Constrain Proportions, and this time set its X Scale to –100%. Then select **Jogging.mov** and replace it with **Sources > movies > Blood Pressure.mov**. Again, click and drag the end of its layer bar to extend it to its full duration.

18 Open your **Final Comp** again. Select the placeholder layer **Extra 1**. Then in the Project panel select **Comps > Extra Video 1** and press **⌘ /** (**Ctrl /**) to replace the solid with your new precomp. Repeat this procedure for **Extra 2**, **3**, and **4**. Scrub the CTI through **Final Comp** or RAM Preview it; if you like, slide the layer bars for **Extra Video 1**, **2**, **3**, or **4** to alter their timing relative to the overall camera move.

19 We just noticed a detail about our **Extra Frame** that we don't like: There is an extended gap down one side. No problem! ETLAT (Edit This, Look at That) to the rescue. Click the Lock icon along the top of the Comp panel for **Final Comp** (see figure). Open a View > New Viewer, then double-click **Comps > Extra Frame** to open it into this viewer. Enable the Toggle Mask and Shape Paths Visibility switch along the bottom of its Comp panel, then twirl down **Shape Layer 1** > Contents. Select Shape 1, and the points for its shape paths will appear. With the Selection tool (**V**) active, select the offending points and use the cursor keys to nudge them to their desired position. As you tweak your frame, all four frames will update in the **Final Comp**. When you're done, close the Comp panel for **Extra Frame**, then disable the Lock for **Final Comp**'s viewer. Bring **Final Comp** forward again if necessary.

19 By reusing the same frame in all the **Extra Video** comps, edits to the shape in **Extra Frame** will automatically ripple through all **Extra Video** comps into the **Final Comp**.

RAM Preview; well done for finishing the core of this project. Our version of the project at this point is saved in **Intermediate Comps > 10_Videos In Place**. Save, then Increment and Save before adding some final details.

Part 4: Filling Out the Background

Now that the most important elements are done, we can spend time dressing up the background. We'll employ "text as texture" to add interest, then animate a set of faux vital signs displays to reinforce the medical vibe.

Background Text

1 A motivated intern transcribed the results of a blood test into a layered Photoshop document for us. Select the **Sources > stills** folder in the Project panel, type ⌘ **I** (**Ctrl I**), navigate to **Lesson 12-Final Project > 12_Sources > stills**, and double-click **Lab Results.psd**. In the dialog that opens, set Import Kind to Composition and click OK. A composition named **Lab Results** – as well as a folder containing the original layers – will be added to the **stills** folder.

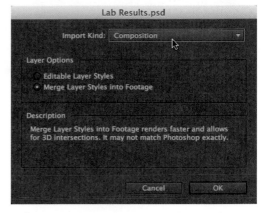

1 Import the layered Photoshop file as a Composition. This will allow you to access the source layers individually.

2 Open the **Lab Results** comp. Nothing will be visible initially; this is because the intern created black text, and the comp's Background Color is also black. (Toggle the Transparency Grid to see the black text.) Assuming the intern didn't rasterize the Photoshop text into pixels, you can edit these layers in After Effects.

Type ⌘ **A** (**Ctrl A**) to Select All and choose Layer > Convert to Editable Text. In the Character panel, click on the Set To White swatch to change the Fill Color for the selected text; you can also change their Font Style (weight) to make them bolder or thinner. Then press **F2** to Deselect All. Solo the individual layers to inspect them; turn off all Solo switches when you're done.

2 Use the Layer menu to convert the four Photoshop layers into editable After Effects text layers, noted by the "T" layer icons in the Timeline panel (below). Solo the individual layers and choose a "hero" to feature at the start of the camera move.

3 Now you can start adding these layers into your **Final Comp**.

• Select **Results 1** and copy it. Bring **Final Comp** forward, press **?** to enable the Title/Action Safe Grid, and set the View Layout back to 4 Views – Bottom. Press **Home** to see the camera's initial pose, and paste.

• Enable the 3D Layer switch for **Results 1** and press **P** to reveal its Position. Slide it to the left in X until it is visible in the camera's view, then push it back in Z space behind the **Extra Video** layers until the size feels good (you can change its Scale as well). Make sure it is inside the center-cut Title Safe grid so the viewer will have something to look at before the camera starts moving. Scrub the CTI to test the camera move; the text should multiplane nicely behind the **Extra Video** layers as the camera pans left to right.

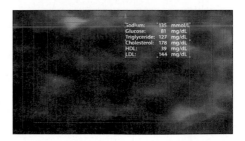

3 Before the camera starts moving, place at least one of the lab results layers within the center-cut Title Safe area.

4 Array the lab result layers throughout your 3D world so they peek in and out behind the video layers during the camera move. Remember that this "text as texture" is supposed to act as wallpaper rather than as focal points; in our version we reduced their Opacity to 30%, added a slight blur, and used Add mode to help them melt into the background.

▽ tip

Quick Access

If you have points in time you want to keep referring back to often – such as our camera keyframes at 03:13 and 14:09 – locate the CTI to the desired time and press **Shift** plus **0**–**9** along the top of the alphanumeric keyboard (not the numeric keypad). This will set a numbered Comp Marker. Then simply press that number in the future to jump back to that point in time.

4 Copy and paste the other three layers into **Final Comp** and scatter them around the 3D world so they peek out from behind the video layers at various points during the camera's move. To reduce the visual importance of these layers, we blurred them slightly, reduced their Opacity, and used the Add blending mode (our version is saved as **Intermediate Comps > 11_Wallpaper**).

Vital Signs

Next we want to create a series of "vital signs" traces akin to EKG lines traveling throughout our world. We know they need to be big to extend across the entire camera move, but we don't yet know how big – so we'll use Shape Layers, which render sharp no matter how much we scale them up.

5 Select the **Comps** folder and type ⌘ **N** (**Ctrl N**) to create a new comp to test our ideas in. Give it a Width of 2000, Height of 200, Frame Rate of 23.976, and Duration of 25:00. Name it "**Vital Signs Test**" and click OK. Give the Comp panel as much room as you can, and set the View Layout back to 1 View.

6 Select the Pen tool. +click (**Alt**+click) on the swatch to the right of Fill until you see the red "no" slash. Then +click (**Alt**+click) on Stroke's swatch until you see a solid color. Click on the Stroke swatch normally to open its color picker, set it to white, and click OK. Then set Stroke Thickness (the number to the right of the swatch) to 2 px.

7 Click once at the far left of the visible area of the Comp panel, centered vertically. A new shape layer will appear in the timeline. Then hold **Shift** and click at the far right of the Comp panel; a line will appear. Return to the Selection tool.

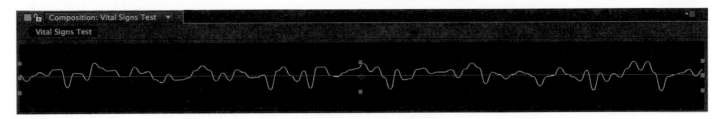

8 Twirl open **Shape Layer 1** > Contents and select Shape 1. Then click on the arrow to the right of Add and select Wiggle Paths (it will be added after Path 1). Twirl open Wiggle Paths 1, increase Detail to 100 (the maximum), and increase Size until around 100 as well. The initial line is very jagged; as we've already gone with a softer rounded look for the video frames, set the Points popup to Smooth. Press the spacebar; the path will automatically animate. Although this "wiggly worm" look is interesting, it's not how vital signs monitors usually work, so set Wiggles/Second down to 0 to freeze it in place.

9 Select Add > Trim Paths. Twirl it open and scrub its End parameter to around 5%. This is how you can reveal just a small segment of your path. Then scrub Offset: This is how you make the reveal travel along your path, which is closer to what we envisioned. (Note that the Idea Corner at the end of this lesson shows how to create more accurate EKG patterns.)

• Press (Home) and enable keyframing for Trim Paths 1 > Offset. Right-click on the word Offset and select Reset from the menu to return its value to 0°.

• Then press (End) and set Offset to 4x+0.0°. RAM Preview; tweak the second Offset keyframe to control the speed of the trace.

• Temporarily disable the Trim Paths shape operator (just click its eyeball switch; don't delete it) so you can see the entire path again for the next step.

10 Now let's place this graphic into our **Final Comp**:

• Select **Shape Layer 1**, press (Return) to highlight its name, and rename it "**Vital Signs 1**." Press (Return) again to accept this name, and Copy the layer.

• Then switch to **Final Comp**, Paste, and enable its 3D Layer switch (if necessary, press (F4) to toggle the Switches column forward).

• Press (P) to reveal its Position and press (Shift) (S) to also reveal its Scale. Push it back in Z space to around the area where you placed the **Results** layers, and initially center it in your world according to your Top or Front views. Now balance off its X Position and its Scale so it remains visible for the entire camera move. Our "worst case" camera keyframes (where we see the left and right edges of our world) are at 03:13 and 14:09, so we kept checking those. Then slide **Vital Signs 1** in Y until you have a compelling placement, such as traveling behind the center line of one of your **Extra Video** layers.

8 Use the Wiggle Paths operator to turn your straight line into a random waveform.

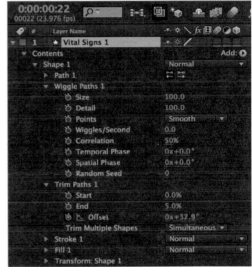

9 Use the Trim Paths operator (above) to isolate a portion of it and use Offset to animate this reveal (below).

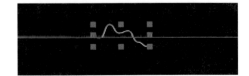

▽ tip

Cleaning Up

If you no longer need to see a column in the Timeline panel (such as Stretch or Parent), right-click on its header and choose Hide This. This will reduce clutter in the timeline.

11 We want the viewer to have something interesting to look at from the very first frame of the final video, so press (Home). Twirl open **Vital Signs 1** > Contents > Shape 1 and re-enable Trim Paths 1. Twirl down its parameters and increase its Offset value until the pulse is visible just inside the center-cut Action Safe grid on this initial frame.

12 We used five copies of the **Vital Signs** animation, each running at a different speed.

12 Duplicate **Vital Signs 1** a few times and arrange these additional pulses vertically in your world to help fill in the dead areas. If you push a copy further away in Z, remember to increase its Scale to compensate. Fortunately, Wiggle Paths randomizes its pattern for every layer, so each one will look different. Still, add some variation by editing Wiggle Paths > Detail or Trim Paths > End and > Offset so the pulses have different shapes and travel at different speeds. Our version is saved in **Intermediate Comps > 12_Vital Signs**; remember to save your version as well.

Blur to the Music

The vital signs traces are fun, but they have no connection to the music. They're also a bit stark, drawing our attention away from the foreground videos. Let's solve both problems at once by blurring them in time with the music.

13 With **Final Comp** forward, set the Comp view to 1 View. Choose the menu option Animation > Keyframe Assistant > Convert Audio to Keyframes. A layer named **Audio Amplitude** will be created; select it and press (U) to reveal its keyframes: These reflect the loudness of the soundtrack at each frame.

14 We know we want to blur the traces, but we don't know by how much. To make it easier to tweak this amount later, apply Effect > Expression Controls > Slider Control to the **Audio Amplitude** layer. Press (Return) and rename this slider "**Maximum Blur**." Also twirl down Maximum Blur in the Timeline panel to reveal its slider; you need to reveal parameters before you can tie expressions to them.

15 Press **Home** where you should be able to see **Vital Signs 1**.

• Select **Vital Signs 1** and apply Effect > Blur & Sharpen > Box Blur. Set Blur Dimensions to Vertical; this will make the waveform easier to "read" while still effecting it.

• Then press **⌥** (**Alt**) and click on the stopwatch for its Blur Radius parameter. This parameter will appear in the Timeline, ready to accept an expression. You're going to use the linear interpolation expression you learned back in Lesson 7 (pages 188–189) to translate from audio amplitude to blur amount:

• Type "`linear(`".

• Drag the expression pick whip to **Audio Amplitude** > Effects > Both Channels > Slider – this is the parameter you're following.

• Type "`, 0, 100, 0,`" – this sets the input range (0–100) and sets the lower limit of the output range to 0.

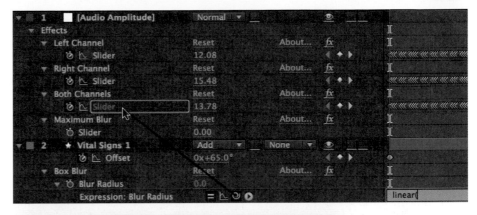

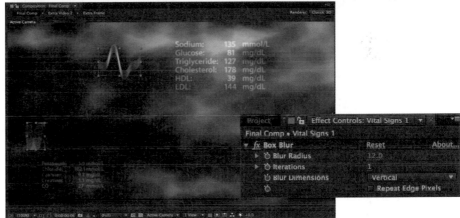

• For the upper limit of the output range, drag the pick whip to Maximum Blur's slider. Then type "`)`" and press **Enter** to finish the expression.

• Scrub Maximum Blur until **Vital Signs 1** has a nicely stylized look. Step through time or RAM Preview and tweak Maximum Blur to taste (you might want to solo the layer to speed up previews). Remember you can also keyframe this parameter in the event you want to reduce the amount of blur when the music gets louder at 03:13.

• Once you're happy with your blur animation for **Vital Signs 1**, copy its Box Blur effect – this copies its expression (and any keyframes) as well. Press **Home** and paste it to the other **Vital Signs** copies, and all of them will now blur in time with the music. You can still adjust Maximum Blur after you do this, as all the copies are pointing to the same slider.

• Finally, to unify the look of the background, set all the **Vital Signs** layers to the same Opacity and blending mode as you used for the **Results** text layers.

Our version is in **Intermediate Comps > 13_Musical Blur**. Remember to save, then Increment and Save – you're about to render!

15 Use a combination of typing and the pick whip (top) to create a linear interpolation expression linking Audio Amplitude to Blur Radius. When you're done, the vital signs traces will get larger and blurred on every heart beat or drum hit (above).

Rendering Center-Cut

A movie from our *After Effects Apprentice* video training series demonstrating one way to render a center-cut version from a widescreen comp is included in **Lesson 12-Final Project > 12-Bonus Content** folder.

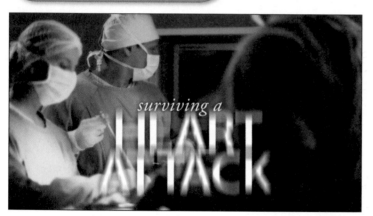

Blurring the main title in time with the ending heart beats adds tension to the final result.

Our final proof, ready to render and send to the client. Note that we've set up the Render Queue in this project to create widescreen and center-cut versions of our finished composition; our render is in **Finished Movies**.

Part 5: Finalizing the Proof

RAM Preview **Final Comp** and look for anything that could use refinement before you send this proof to the client. We've spotted a handful of things we'd like to tweak:

• The **Hero** and **Extra** video screens would benefit from a drop shadow to help separate them from the background and each other. You could set up a 3D light with shadows, or simply apply a Drop Shadow effect. We chose the latter; we set Distance to 0 and Softness to 50 to create a dark glow, and increased Opacity to 75% to make them more apparent.

• Motion Blur (page 57) will help obscure how close we are to the **Extra** layers during the initial pull back, plus it will smooth out the pan. Select all the layers, enable the Motion Blur switch for one, and enable the Timeline panel's master Motion Blur switch. While you're at it, also enable Motion Blur for the **surviving a** and **HEART ATTACK** layers back in the **Hero + Title** precomp.

• The animated blur on the **Vital Signs** layers is cool; it probably would look cool on the main title as well. Copy the **Audio Amplitude** layer from **Final Comp** and paste it into **Hero + Title**. Then copy the Box Blur effect applied to one of the **Vital Signs** layers and paste it to the **HEART ATTACK** layer in Hero + Title. Adjust or keyframe the Maximum Blur slider applied to **Audio Amplitude** to taste, perhaps introducing this blur only after the text has finished its animation.

When you're done tweaking, bring **Final Comp** forward and choose Composition > Add to Render Queue. We discuss the process of rendering in detail in the *Appendix* following this lesson. The most important tip we can share is the one we started this lesson with: First, ask your clients what they need. Editors may have a timeline built around a specific codec, such as Apple's ProRes. They may want to use their camera's native codec, such as DVCPRO HD or XDCAM. And don't forget to enable Audio in the Output Module as well.

▼ Creating a Package

A common request when you're creating a title for a show – broadcast or corporate – is to deliver a "package" of related elements. We've included these additional compositions inside the **Comps_Finished > Package** folder; their renders are in the **Finished Movies** folder.

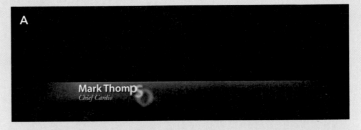

Lower Third Design

This is a simple template for the client to create lower thirds to place over people being introduced in the video (A). It is common in corporate work, but is also used occasionally to establish location or time in some dramas. You need to pick and style the fonts, as well as design a bar to help make the text readable over the video underneath. Ask the client (or check the script) for how many lines of text they'll need; it's not unusual to deliver two-, three-, and four-line versions with different bar heights. These will ultimately be rendered with an alpha channel to be placed over the appropriate footage by the editor.

We created an animated lower third that resolves into a still image for the editor to extend as long as necessary. In our comp we have sample footage inserted in the background and tagged as a Guide Layer so it won't appear in the render; we also observed the 4:3 center-cut areas.

Looping Background

The editors may need to cut tables of text, picture-in-picture shots, and other non-full-screen imagery into their program. You can help them by providing background textures (B) related to the opening title that loop, so they can place them end to end for as long as they need. We provided a few different versions with varying levels of complexity.

Bumpers, Sweepers, and Chapter Heads

Other common elements include a "bumper" (C) to come out of a commercial and go back into the program, a "sweeper" to bridge two parts of a program together, or a "chapter head" to mark a new section in a corporate video when there are no commercials to provide breaks. These short pieces of video can either be crossfaded into the following clip, or have an alpha channel and provide a "reveal" transition into a clip underneath. In our package, we're asking the client to process the first clip of each new section through our **Bumper** comp in After Effects so we can bring it out of our 3D world.

Project Files

It is becoming more common to deliver project files along with a job. Before you start, ask the client ahead of time what version of After Effects and any third-party effects they own, and make sure you restrict yourself to those. When you're done, clean up your comp naming and project folders, add comments and layers markers wherever appropriate (the better job you do, the more likely they'll hire you for the next job), and use File > Collect Files to make sure you gather all the sources into one folder before sending the finished bundle off to the client.

Idea Corner

You've accomplished a lot in this lesson – but if time and budget allows, there are always ways to further raise the production value of a job. Here are a few embellishments we applied to the comps in the **Idea Corner** folder:

• To make the background more interesting, we precomposed it and added a grid of "O"s. We did this by creating one small O in the middle of the precomp using a Shape Layer, then used a Repeater (page 312) to duplicate it horizontally, and another Repeater to duplicate this line vertically. We then added the Block Dissolve transition and applied the wiggle expression (page 192) to its Transition Completion parameter to make the Os blink on and off. (We used this same trick in **Package > Looping Background**.)

• One of the principles of art is "repetition, with variation." In **Idea Corner > Final Comp IC** (see figure to the left), we created variation in the **Vital Signs 2** trace layer by deleting Trim Paths to leave its entire length visible. We then tweaked its Wiggle Paths settings to make it self-animate, plus have less detail than the other more-animated traces. Solo this layer and RAM Preview to better see the result.

• For the lab results "wallpaper" layers, we deleted the static numbers and replaced them with copies of the Text > Numbers effect, set to randomize a range of values. We placed these in precomps (**Lab Results 1** through **4**) and enabled Composition Settings > Advanced > Preserve Frame Rate When Nested Or In Render Queue to lock in a slower rate for the comp.

• The videos looked a bit hard-edged inside their soft, rounded frames, so we added a rounded rectangle mask to them, feathered the edges 2 pixels, and set Mask Expansion to –1 to stop the layer edges from cropping the feather. We also faded out the mask and frame in **Hero +Title IC** after it arrives in its final position.

• Speaking of those videos, they came from different sources, and all have different color tones. We did some simple color correction to better unify them. On the **Extra Video IC** comps, we just used Effect > Color Correction > Photo Filter and choose warm or cool presets as needed for our starting points. For the **Hero** video, we applied Color Correction > Selective Color, set the Color popup to Neutrals (the supposed mid-grays), and reduced the amount of Yellow present.

▽ tip

Higher Fidelity

For high-definition video, use the Best Settings template for Render Settings. Then click "Best Settings" to open the Render Settings dialog and set Color Depth to 16 bits per channel to avoid banding in color gradients.

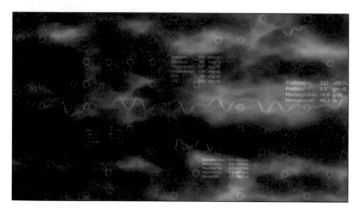

△ Our improved background, with animating circular elements plus a constant **Vital Signs** trace that provides some variation from the others.

◁ We rounded and blurred the edges of the videos, and did some minor color correction to help unify them.

• To focus the viewer on the center of the frame, we applied a 3D spot light to the scene. We parented it to the camera so it would always be centered where the camera was looking; the increased angle of the light rays toward the edges created a vignette effect. We tweaked Light Falloff (introduced in After Effects CS5.5) to slightly darken the background layers as well. Toggle **Light 1** on and off in **Final Comp IC** to see its effect.

We played around a bit with also having the light cast 3D shadows, but frankly it was difficult to get the balance we wanted to achieve; we stuck with our cheat of just using Drop Shadow effects to help separate the layers, although we did increase the shadow Opacity to compensate for the increased lighting in the middle of the frame.

• Here is the extra points bonus for you to try: Using Wiggle Paths created a quick stylized line for our **Vital Signs** layers, but real EKG traces don't look like that! In the **Sources > stills** folder, we included a high-resolution scan of a real EKG chart. Use the Pen tool to trace these lines; you can still use Trim Paths to animate a reveal across their length. Seem like a lot of work? Here's our cheat: Draw only one cycle of each line, then use the Repeater (after Trim Paths) to duplicate the path across the width of the chart. Tweak the start and end points of your single cycle to make sure they match up. Just to prove we wouldn't ask you to do anything we wouldn't do ourselves, our version is in comp **Idea Corner > EKG Chart**.

That was a good challenge! We packed in a lot of tips and advice; we hope you find them useful in your own work.

△ On the left the scene has no additional lighting; on the right we've added a light to focus the viewer's attention on the center foreground of our composition. Explore our settings in **Final Comp IC** (below).

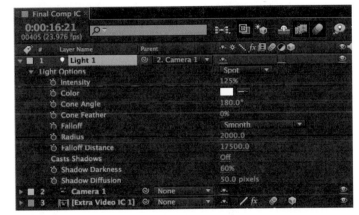

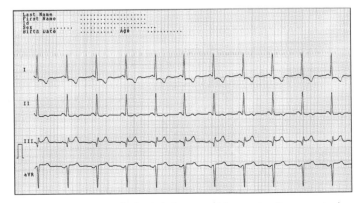

△ To create more realistic vital signs graphics, try tracing an actual EKG chart. Image courtesy iStockphoto, muratseyit, file #7820336.

Appendix - Rendering

Unleashing your creations on the world.

▽ In This Lesson

354   The Render Queue (movie)
354   rendering: under the hood
355   Render Settings Templates
355   Output Module Templates
356   rendering movies
356   rendering sequences
357   issues that affect image quality
359   field flicker (movie)
361   3:2 Pulldown

▽ tip

Online Help

More information on rendering and file formats is contained in the Adobe Help Center: Press **F1** from inside After Effects and use the Search function.

Render Queue Guided Tour

We have shared a QuickTime movie that will give you a tour of the parameters in both the Render Settings and Output Module. It is in the **Appendix > Appendix-Video Bonus** folder on this book's DVD.

After you finish creating your masterpiece in After Effects, you need to render it out to a file so it can be edited into a film or video, or posted to a website. We covered basic rendering at the end of Lesson 1; here we will give you additional advice for other situations that commonly arise. You can also press **F1** to open the After Effects Help file and scroll to the bottom of that introductory page to see a number of render-related topics.

Whenever possible, you should determine your output format *before* starting a project. Then you can build your compositions – or at least, your final composition – with this size and frame rate in mind. This will ultimately lead to fewer headaches than if you later try to conform your work to a different format.

Rendering: Under the Hood

When you are ready to render a composition, make sure that it is open with its Comp or Timeline panel selected, or select it in the Project panel. Then choose Composition > Add to Render Queue (previously called Make Movie); the shortcut is **Ctrl ⌘ M** on Mac (**Ctrl M** on Windows). The comp will be added to the Window > Render Queue panel: This is where you manage your renders. You can then edit the parameters used to render a comp in the Render Queue's Render Settings and Output Module dialogs.

When After Effects renders a composition, two distinct steps take place in order:

• A frame is first rendered based on the Render Settings and is temporarily stored in RAM.

• This frame is then saved to disk using the Output Module settings.

This system means you can have multiple Output Modules per composition, saving the same render to different files during a single render pass – a great time saver.

0:00:00:00 (1)	0:00:05:08 (159U)	0:00:09:29 (300)

▼ Current Render **Renderi...inal Comp"** **Elapsed: 4 Seconds** | Stop | Pause | Render |

Rendering
Composition:
Layer:
Stage: Preparing Output

Frame Times
Last: 0 Seconds
Difference: +0 Seconds
Average: 0 Seconds

File Name	File Size	Est. Final File Size	Free Disk Space	Over-flows	Current Disk
Final Comp_anamorphic.mov	18.9 MB	35.8 MB	486 GB	0	12–Core Work

Render	🏷	#	Comp Name	Comment	Status	Started
▼	☐	1	Final Comp	audio only – full length	Rendering	6/13/12...4

▼ Render Settings: ▼ **DV Settings** **Log:** Errors Only ▼
None

Quality: Best
Resolution: Full
Size: 872 x 486
Proxy Use: Use No Proxies
Effects: Current Settings
Disk Cache: Read Only
Color Depth: Current Settings

Frame Blending: On for Checked Layers
Field Render: Lower Field First
Pulldown: Off
Motion Blur: On for Checked Layers

Solos: Current Settings

Time Span: Work Area
Start: 0:00:00:00
End: 0:00:09:29
Duration: 0:00:10:00
Frame Rate: 29.97 (comp)
Guide Layers: All Off

Skip Existing Files: Off

▼ Output Module: **Custom: QuickTime** + – **Output To:** ▼ Final Comp_anamorphic.mov
/Volumes/12-Core Work/ Final Comp_anamorphic.mov

Format: QuickTime
Output Info: DV25 NTSC

Channels: RGB
Depth: Millions of Colors
Color: Premultiplied
Resize: 720 x 486 (High Qual)
Crop: T:4, L:0, B:2, R:0
Final Size: 720 x 480
Profile: –
Embed Profile:

Include: –
Output Audio: 48.000 kHz / 16 bit / Stereo

Post-Render Action: None ▼

Message: Renderi...RAM: 3% used of 24.0 ...**Renders Started:** 6/13/12, 9:44:2...**Total Time Elapsed:** 4 Secon..**Most Recent Error:** None

The Render Queue panel, with the Render Progress, Render Settings, and Output Module sections all twirled down. To edit the Render Settings and Output Module parameters, click on the template name to the right of the words Render Settings and Output Module; to change the name of the rendered file and the location where it will be saved, click on the file name to the right of Output To.

Templates

The parameters that make up Render Settings and the Output Module can be saved as templates, making it easy to render other compositions using the same parameters. These templates can be selected from popups in the Render Queue; they may also be accessed under the Edit > Templates menu. Default templates may be assigned in that menu or by holding ⌘ (*Ctrl*) as you select a template in the Render Queue.

▽ tip

Big Windows

The Render Queue panel normally opens in the same frame as the Timeline panel, which can be a bit cramped. With the Render Queue panel selected, press to temporarily expand it to take up the entire application window. This trick works with any panel, too!

▽ tip

Trillions of Colors

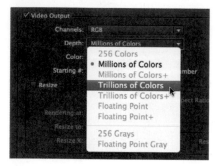

To verify if a codec or file format will support 16 bpc color depth, set Color Depth in Render Settings to 16 bits per channel, then see if Trillions is offered as a choice for Depth in the Video Output section of the Output Module.

▽ factoid

Scaling Interlaced Renders

If you have enabled Field Rendering in the Render Settings, be careful when using the Stretch section in the Output Module: Stretching the Height will destroy your fields. Altering the Width is okay.

Image sequences are a common alternative to movie files. The image number is inserted into the [####] at the end of the file's name when it is saved to disk.

Which Format Should I Render To?

This is one of the most common questions among After Effects users. There is no simple answer, but we can give you some guidelines.

Your first choice is always to give the clients what they want. Ask what format they would prefer; chances are good that After Effects supports it. This may include a QuickTime or AVI movie, or an image sequence.

Movies

QuickTime and AVI come with a set of standard *codecs* (compressor/decompressors or coder/decoders). Many cameras compress their captures to a specific codec, such as HDV or H.264; editors will often want your output in the same format so they can easily intercut it with other footage. If you or your client will be using a specific video card, it most likely requires its own codec. The software that comes with the card (or worst case, the Support section of the manufacturer's website) will include an installer for the necessary codec.

If instead you are rendering an element that will be reused inside an After Effects project or composited with other footage (or if you want to future-proof your archives), you will want to save it using the highest quality format available. A common solution is QuickTime using the Animation codec with its Quality set to 100. This combination is *lossless* (in other words, it won't change any pixels), is mildly space-efficient, and can support an alpha channel (set to Millions of Colors+), with the shortcoming that it supports only 8 bits per channel of color resolution; high-end work is better off with 16 bits per channel. If you can accept some image compression and don't need an alpha channel, a good alternative is H.264: Open its Format Settings, and verify its Profile is set to High and the Bitrate values are set to 6 Mbps (Megabits per second) or higher.

Sequences

QuickTime or AVI movies are handy because they wrap up all of the individual frames of a movie into a single file. However, there are occasions when an image sequence is the better choice. Some 3D software packages and high-end video systems (such as the Autodesk Flame) prefer sequences. Several options – such as TIFF, SGI, or PNG sequences – are lossless, contain data compression to reduce the file size, offer alpha channels, and support more bits per color channel.

To render a sequence, select the desired file type from the Format popup at the top of the Output Settings dialog; the word "Sequence" will follow the file type's name. Each frame will get its own number; how many digits used is determined by number of # symbols.

Issues That Affect Image Quality

For a motion graphics designer, delivering a high-quality render to your client is of the utmost concern. If you are new to After Effects, however, you may have concerns about why pixels appear less than perfect. Here is an assortment of potential problems and solutions:

• The image in the Comp panel looks "crunchy." Solution: Check if the Comp panel's Magnification is set to less than 100%; numbers that are not clean divisions of 100% look particularly bad. A workaround is to set Preferences > Previews > Viewer Quality to More Accurate. And remember: Magnification affects viewing the comp panel only while working, not rendering.

• The Comp panel is at 100%, but images appear "blocky." Solution: Check that the composition's Resolution is set to Auto or Full. When you render, make sure the Resolution popup in Render Settings is also set to Full.

• Layers are not moving smoothly, or they look aliased when rotated or scaled. Solution: Check that the layer's Quality switch is set to Best (the default), which makes layers move smoothly and antialiases them when they are transformed or distorted. When you render, make sure the Quality popup in Render Settings is also set to Best.

• The layer is set to Best Quality, but you've applied a blur or distortion effect and it doesn't render smoothly. Solution: Check if the effect offers different levels of antialiasing in the Effect Controls panel, and if so, set the Antialiasing popup to High. (Note that it will also take longer to render.)

• Ray-traced 3D images look "noisy" – especially in areas of reflection or transparency. Solution: Open Composition Settings > Advanced > Renderer > Options and increase the Ray-tracing Quality setting until these areas look smooth. The Anti-aliasing Filter popup in this same section can also have an incremental effect on edges of ray-traced 3D objects.

When Magnification does not equal a clean value such as 100%, the image in the Comp panel can look crunchy (above). This will not affect your final render. But if you want higher quality previews, either resize the Comp panel so Magnification is a clean value such as 50% or 100%, or set the Previews > View Quality preference to More Accurate (below), which antialiases these viewers at any Magnification. Background courtesy Artbeats/Light Alchemy.

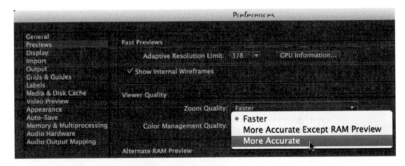

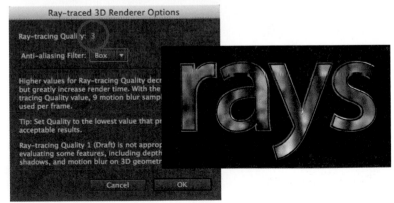

The default Ray-traced 3D Renderer Options setting of 3 rays (left) often produces visual noise in soft reflections as well as around the edges (right); higher settings such as 9 or 10 provide acceptable results for most scenes.

If banding is noticeable in the image (A), increase Project Settings > Color Settings > Depth to 16 bpc (B). Footage courtesy Artbeats/Establishments: Urban.

▽ tip

Adobe Media Encoder

For advanced rendering – including compressing for the web, and having After Effects compositions render while you work – check out Adobe Media Encoder (AME), which is included with the Production Premium and Master Collection suites. A set of resources on AME may be found at *tinyurl.com/UsingAME*.

If alternating horizontal lines appear offset from each other (above), you need to separate the fields in your source footage (Lesson 5). The images will still appear a little crunchy (right), but this is far better than combining pixels from two different points in time. Footage courtesy Artbeats/Penguins.

• There is visible "banding" in an image where what are supposed to be smooth color gradients instead appear as bands of distinct color. Solution: Click on the "8 bpc" indicator at the bottom of the Project panel to open the Project Settings, and change Color Settings > Depth to 16 bits per channel (bpc); also make sure you are rendering to a higher bit depth (discussed earlier). Alternatively, you may need to add a small amount of noise to the image to break up this pattern. The After Effects Help file also contains some useful pointers; search for "color basics."

• The image looks fine in the Comp panel, but looks pixelated in the final render, exhibits banding, and otherwise looks yucky. Solution: The render is being compressed too heavily. If you have control over the final output, increase the quality or bit rate setting for the codec used. Otherwise, someone downstream from you may be compressing it too heavily; some of the advice above on reducing banding may help.

• Imported still images look a little softer in After Effects than they do in Photoshop or Illustrator. Solution: Create artwork in other programs where the width and height are an even number of pixels. See *Resampling in Action* on page 360.

• Images in the Comp panel look fatter or skinnier than they should, and circular objects look like eggs. Solution: D1/DV pixels are not square, so this could be correct behavior if you have placed a square pixel image into a D1/DV NTSC or PAL comp. See the *Non-Square Pixel* sidebar in Lesson 3. Another potential issue is you're viewing a widescreen anamorphic composition or footage; if this bothers you, enable the Toggle Pixel Aspect Ratio Correction button that resides along the bottom of the viewer.

• There are alternating horizontal lines akin to comb teeth running through a movie in the Comp panel. Solution: The movie is interlaced, and you need to separate the fields in the Interpret Footage dialog. See the section *Separating Fields* in the *Wiggling Text* exercise in Lesson 5 (page 140). If you need to output a progressive frame (no fields), then consider using a third-party effect such as Fields Kit from RE:Vision Effects.

• Movies in the Comp panel are alternating between sharp and soft. Solution: The source movie is interlaced and separated, but the source movie's frame rate may not be in sync with the Comp's frame rate. Select the source in the Project panel and open File > Interpret Footage > Main. Then conform the source's frame rate to the correct rate – 29.97 frames per second (fps) for NTSC video, 25 fps for PAL, and so on. Even if "frame rate from file" says the movie is 29.97 already, some content is fixed by conforming its Frame Rate to 29.97. Yes, sometimes it's just voodoo...

• You play back a rendered movie on a television monitor, and some parts are "flickering" slightly. Solution: You may need to selectively blur these high-contrast areas.

• You play back a field-rendered movie on a video monitor, and the flicker is really, really bad. Solution: The field order of the movie may not match the hardware chain and the fields therefore may be reversed. See the *Rendering with Fields* sidebar in Lesson 5 (page 143).

• You render a movie with an alpha channel, and when you composite it in your editing program, it has a black "fringe." Solution: Render with a straight alpha channel, not the default premultiplied alpha. Or, see if your editing program can unmultiply the render.

• You render with an alpha channel and the movie looks really ugly when viewed in QuickTime Player. Solution: Congratulations! You successfully rendered a straight alpha channel, but QuickTime Player is showing you only the RGB channels with the extra "bleed." Import this movie into your editing program – and relax! (This is also discussed in the *Rendering with an Alpha Channel* exercise in Lesson 5, page 142.)

Subpixel Positioning

When a layer is set to Best Quality (the default), it will use subpixel positioning; this allows a layer to be positioned using less than one pixel for smoother motion. How much less? After Effects resolves to 16 bits of subpixel resolution, so each pixel is divided into 65,536 parts width and height. With that kind of resolution, there are more than 4 billion subpixels. Technically speaking, that's known as "a lot."

To see the numerical results of this precision, park the current time indicator between two interpolating Position keyframes, select the layer, and press ⌘ Shift P (Ctrl Shift P) to open the Position dialog. The dialog will show values for the X and Y axes for 2D layers: Numbers to the left of the decimal point are the integer values used by Draft Quality, while the fractional numbers indicate the subpixels used by Best Quality.

Field Flicker

A few years ago we created video training courses: *Understanding Fields & Interlacing* and *Working with 3:2 Pulldown*. The **Appendix-Video Bonus** folder contains a movie on dealing with flicker problems with interlaced video from the *Fields & Interlacing* course.

If you view your straight-alpha render in a QuickTime viewer, you will see just the RGB color channels, which includes pixels that extend beyond the alpha (above). View it in the After Effects Footage panel which factors in the alpha channel, and you will see that it is actually clean (below).

When Position is interpolating between keyframes, check out the current value – the subpixel numbers to the right of the decimal point are used when the layer is set to Best Quality (the default).

When a layer is set to Draft Quality, movement is calculated using whole pixels only. While this lets you set up keyframes and preview them more quickly, you might find the results a little bumpy.

In addition to smoother motion, Best Quality also ensures that effects and transformations are rendered with full antialiasing. Draft Quality renders without antialiasing (this is particularly noticeable with vector artwork such as text, shape, and solid layers, or Illustrator sources).

Resampling in Action

A benefit of Best Quality and subpixel positioning is that layers are antialiased (or resampled) when they are transformed. While good antialiasing is desirable (especially with distortion effects), the softness that resampling adds can be unwanted when you're just placing, say, a non-moving image or title created in Illustrator or Photoshop in your comp at 100%.

To avoid this unwanted resampling, we need to understand why and when it kicks in. As it happens, After Effects resamples a layer whenever it uses subpixel positioning, and that means whenever the difference between the Anchor Point value and Position value is not a whole number. Check out the following example comps in **Appendix.aep**:

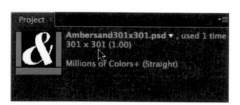

The Anchor Point of a layer defaults to its center. When the layer is an odd number of pixels tall or wide (above), this results in a half pixel being used for the Anchor Point (below), which can unnecessarily soften the image under some circumstances.

- **Resample_1**: Your layer is even sized, 300 pixels wide by 300 high, which places the Anchor Point in the center at 150,150. You place this image in an even-sized 640×480 pixel comp and Position it in the center (320,240). The difference between 150,150 and 320,240 is a whole number, so the layer does not get resampled. Toggle the layer between Draft and Best Quality, and you'll see that there is no change.

- **Resample_2**: Toggle the layer between Draft and Best, and see the image shift and soften slightly. This is because this layer is odd sized, 301 pixels wide by 301 high, which places the Anchor Point at 150.5,150.5. When it's positioned in the middle of this even-sized 640×480 pixel comp, the difference between 150.5,150.5 and 320,240 is not a whole number, so the layer will be resampled.

As you can see, you can avoid resampling for non-moving images by creating sources with even sizes in Photoshop or Illustrator. If all else fails, you may be able to avoid unnecessary resampling by changing the Position of the layer by a half pixel up or down, left or right, until the image pops into sharpness.

This resampling issue is completely separate from the previewing, antialiasing, and ray-tracing quality issues that may arise with 3D layers. We covered those in the Ray-tracer Image Quality and Fast Previews sections in Lesson 8.

▼ Artboard Gotcha

Recent versions of Illustrator added a series of Video and Film profiles (templates) for standard sizes. One of the benefits of these templates is that they include a second artboard (Artboard 2) that is much larger than the template size; any layers that spill onto the pasteboard are not cropped off when you import the file into After Effects as a composition. Unfortunately, because Artboard 2 is centered on a half pixel (for some unknown reason), all objects on Artboard 1 render softly in AE. If you don't need to bleed objects onto the pasteboard, we recommend you delete Artboard 2.

▼ 3:2 Pulldown

3:2 Pulldown is a process originally used to convert between film – which normally runs at 24 fps (frames per second) – and NTSC video, which runs at 29.97 fps. Today, it is more common to find video cameras use this to convert a filmic capture rate of 23.976 fps to the 29.97 fps that must be recorded on tape.

To make this conversion work, film was slowed down from 24 to 23.976 fps: the same ratio as between 30 and 29.97. Frames of film were then repeated for either two or three successive video fields (there are two fields per video frame) in a pattern that eventually led to four frames of film – or images captured by the camera's sensor – being spread across five frames of video.

There are several different patterns in use; After Effects supports two on input: classic 3:2 Pulldown and 24Pa ("advanced" pulldown). Each version can then have several different "phases" – namely, where you started in the pattern.

In the Interpret Footage dialog, there is a Guess button for each that helps determine the correct phase. After Effects often guesses right, but not always; verify its guess by double-clicking the footage item to open it in its Footage panel, then step through the resulting frames using **Page Up** and **Page Down** (or the Previous Frame and Next Frame buttons in the Preview panel). If you see the "comb teeth" pattern of interlacing on any frame, After Effects guessed wrong; use the Remove Pulldown popup in the Interpret Footage panel and manually try different phases until all signs of interlacing disappear.

When it comes time to render, you can reintroduce the classic 3:2 Pulldown pattern by following these steps:

• Build your final composition at 23.976 fps.

• In Render Settings, set Field Render to the choice required by your output format (for example, Lower Field First for DV; Upper Field First for high def).

• Below Field Render, pick a phase in the 3:2 Pulldown popup. If this render is going to video or DVD, any phase will do. You need to worry about phase only if your render is part of an offline film edit; if so, then make sure the clip lines up with the comp's start point and use the same phase for rendering as you used in the clip's Interpret Footage dialog.

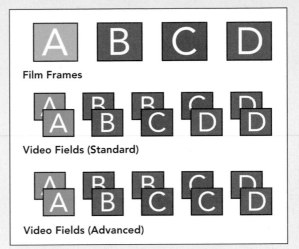

Film Frames

Video Fields (Standard)

Video Fields (Advanced)

Pulldown is a technique used to spread four frames of film across ten fields (five frames) of video.

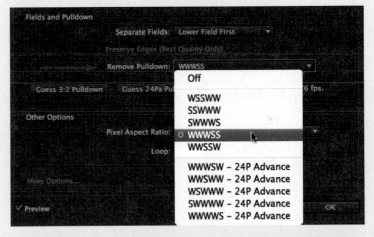

If your sources have Pulldown, remove it in the Interpret Footage dialog (above). Create your comps at 23.976 fps, which is more efficient. Then when you render, reintroduce Pulldown in the Render Settings (below).

Resources

Some of our favorites places to learn more about motion graphics and After Effects.

- Our own website crishdesign.com will let you know what we're up to. Key pages to visit include:

  articles.crishdesign.com
  books.crishdesign.com
  onlinetraining.crishdesign.com

- We create training videos for lynda.com. Sign up for a free 7-day trial at:

  lynda.com/go/chrisandtrish

- ProVideo Coalition "brings together the industry's best writers, bloggers and video gurus under one URL." Check out our PVC blog at:

  provideocoalition.com

- These are some of our favorite forums, websites, and blogs when we need to find information about After Effects:

  blogs.adobe.com/toddkopriva
  adobe.com/support/aftereffects
  AE Portal by Rich Young at provideocoalition.com
  subscribe to the AE-LIST at media-motion.tv/ae-list.html

- When you need to feed the other side of your brain, also visit:

  motionographer.com
  artofthetitle.com
  motiongraphics.nu

- Here are good sources for scripts and plug-ins (including freebies):

  motionscript.com
  aenhancers.com
  toolfarm.com
  redgiantsoftware.com

Credits

Production Credits

Cover & Interior Design
Trish Meyer

Cover Calligraphy
Denis Brown (*QuillSkill.com*)

Page Layout
Trish Meyer

Copy Editor
Mandy Erickson

Proofreader
Sam Molineaux-Graham

Indexer
Ken DellaPenta

Media Credits

We'd like to thank Julie Hill and Trish McClesky of Artbeats, who provided the majority of the footage used in this book. Additional still images and video were provided by iStockphoto, 12 Inch Design, Pixel Corps, and Crish Design. All music provided by Crish Design. For usage rights, please read the various license agreements on this book's DVD.

Index

Numerics

3:2 pulldown, 361
3D Camera Tracker, 245, 264–69, 335
3D Layer switch, 206, 207
3D space. *See also* 3D Views
  axis arrows, 207–9
  cameras in, 214–17
  continuous rasterization in, 207
  enabling layers in, 206, 207
  extrusion in, 231–32, 324–25
  intersecting layers in, 209, 219
  layer order in, 208
  lights in, 224–27
  motion paths, 212–13
  moving cameras in, 214–17
  moving layers in, 208
  multiplaning and, 210–11
  perspective, 206, 210–11, 214, 217, 221
  rendering breaks, 219
  rotation and orientation, 137–38, 208–9
  scale and, 207
  text animation, 136–39
  thickness of layers in, 209, 230
  working in, 329–30
3D Views
  Active Camera, 210, 213
  Custom, 210
  menu, 5, 210
  multiple, 213
  navigating, 215
  orthographic views, 210–11
  shortcuts, 210
  switching between, 210

A

action safe area, 133, 337
Active Camera, 210, 213
Adaptive Resolution, 240–41
Add blend mode, 74–75
Add mask mode, 104
Add Vertex tool, 100, 111
Adjust Exposure, 5
adjustment layers
  animating, 91
  applying effects to, 86–87, 121, 180
  blending modes and, 87
  creating, 86
  filmic glow technique, 87
  icon, 86
  scaling, 86, 91
Adobe Audition. *See* Audition
Adobe Bridge. *See* Bridge
Adobe Illustrator. *See* Illustrator
Adobe Media Encoder (AME), 358
Adobe Photoshop. *See* Photoshop
Align panel, 29, 159, 330
alpha channels
  defined, 15, 18
  masks and, 112
  mattes and, 112
  premultiplied, 18
  rendering with, 142–43
  stencils and, 112
  straight, 18
  transparency, 35
  viewing, 35, 142–43
alpha mattes. *See* track mattes

Always Preview This View, 5, 7
ambient lights, 225, 229
anchor points
  animation, 26, 39, 42–43
  defined, 40
  image quality and, 360
  motion control, 42–43
  moving, 40–41
  offset, 138–39
  Per-Character 3D, 138–39
  precomps and, 169
  rotating around, 138–39
  shortcut, 21
  in text animation, 131
Anchor Point tool, 3, 41
Angle Control effect, 193
Angle of View, 214, 216
animatics, 327
animation. *See also* animation presets; keyframes; text animators
  3D, 212–13
  anchor point, 26, 39, 42–43
  character, 153, 300–303
  effect point, 77–78
  Hold keyframes, 60

animation (*continued*)
  motion control, 42–43
  multiple layers, 28–29
  opacity, 26–27
  overshooting, 63
  position, 21–22
  Puppet tools, 300–303
  rotation, 26–27
  scale, 26–27
  "slam down" style, 60–61
  strokes, 283, 322
  syncing, to audio, 144–46, 195, 328, 331, 339, 348–49
  text, 122–23, 125, 136–39
  track mattes, 117
animation presets
  3D text, 139
  Adobe-supplied, 82–83, 148
  applying, 81–83, 148
  Behaviors, 83
  Brainstorm and, 88–89
  creating, 79–80
  editing, 149
  expressions in, 188, 192
  organizing, 81–82
  saving, 80–81, 150

Video Bonus Index

The following is a summary of the QuickTime tutorial movies included on this book's DVD:

Pre-Roll
  UI Overview
  Manipulating the UI

Lesson 3 – Layer Control
  Effect & Presets Panel

Lesson 4 – Transparency
  Mask Interpolation

Lesson 5 – Type & Music
  Creating Text
  Creating a Text Animator
  Using Audition – Simple and More Advanced

Lesson 6 – Nesting
  Edit This Look At That (ETLAT)

Lesson 8 – 3D Space
  OpenGL Before CS6

Lesson 11 – Shape Layers
  Drawing Pen Shapes

Lesson 12 – Final Project
  Center-Cut Rendering

Appendix
  Field Flicker
  Rendering

animation presets (*continued*)
searching for, 81, 148
for shape layers, 312
text, 139, 148–50, 338–39
visibility of, 82
video bonus, DVD (Lesson 3)
animation stopwatch, 6
animator. *See* text animators
antialiasing, 66, 357, 360
application window, 2
aspect ratio
pixel, 90, 185, 358
scaling layer, 20
attach point, 250
audio
adding, to comps, 144
basics of, 144
bit depth, 144
distortion, 146, 147
importing, 144
mixing, 146–47
music tempos, 328, 329
previewing, 144
sample rate, 144
syncing to, 144–46, 195,
328, 331, 339, 348–49
turning on/off, 144
volume controls, 8, 146–47
waveforms, 145
Audio panel, 8, 146, 147
Audio Spectrum effect, 107
Audio Waveform effect, 107
Audition, 147
Auto Bezier keyframe, 25, 48, 58
Auto Color effect, 30–31
Auto-Keyframe Properties, 6
auto-orientation, 56, 220–21
Auto Save, 16
A/V Features column, 6
axis arrows in 3D, 207–9

B

backgrounds
color setting, 20, 35
creating, 334
looping, 351
stencils and, 119–20
textures for, 285
banding, 358

Base Frame, 290, 292–94
baseline shift, 123
Behavior presets, 83
Bevel Alpha effect, 31
Bevel and Emboss style, 85, 311
bevels (3D)
Bevel Style, 232
Bevel Depth, 232
Bezier handles, 24, 25, 39, 52
Bezier masking, 100–101
Bezier Warp effect, 263
bit depth, 144, 356, 358
blending modes
for 3D layers, 267
defined, 74
effects and, 76–78
lighting effects, 161
overview, 74–75
Paint, 282
text, inter-character, 149
Block Dissolve transition, 352
blurs
Box Blur effect, 319
Camera Lens Blur effect, 223
depth of field, 222–23
Directional Blur effect, 204
Fast Blur effect, 86–87
motion, 56–57, 127, 251,
252, 350
Radial Blur effect, 79–80
for reflections, 237
for text, 127, 134
Boris Beat Reactor, 195
Box Blur effect, 319
Brainstorm, 6, 88–89
Bridge, 4, 12–13, 148, 338
Bring Comp Panel Forward, 6, 7
Bring Timeline Forward, 5
Brush Duration Bar, 282
Brushes panel, 9, 279
Brush strokes. *See* strokes
Brush tool, 3, 279, 280–82
bumpers, 351
buttons, creating, 311

C

caches, 34
calligraphy tools, creating
textures with, 285
Camera Lens Blur effect, 223

cameras
3D Camera Tracker, 245,
264–69, 277, 335
Active Camera view, 210, 213
adding, 214
Angle of View, 214, 216
auto-orientation, 220–21
depth of field, 214, 216,
222–23
field of view, 214, 216
f-stop, 216
moving, 214–17, 331–33
multiple, 213, 243
one-node, 220, 331
Orbit Camera tools, 215
Orbit Camera Null, 219
Point of Interest, 214
Position, 214
rigs, 218–19, 243
settings, 214, 216, 222
shake, 246
tools, 3, 215
Track Camera tools, 215
two-node, 218, 220
Unified Camera tool, 215
View options, 210
Zoom value, 214, 216, 222
Camera Type setting, 220
Cartoon effect, 88–89
Casts Shadows option, 226–27
CC Grid Wipe effect, 120
CC Twister effect, 120
center-cut versions, 327, 332,
350
chain link icon, 20, 134, 308
Channel Blur effect, 267
channels. *See* alpha channels
chapter heads, 351
character animation, 153,
300–303
Character panel, 9, 123–25
children. *See* parenting
Classic 3D Renderer, 17, 136,
208, 230, 267, 332
Clone Stamp tool, 3, 279,
287–88
cloning, 287–88
codecs
defined, 356
missing, 356

Collapse Transformations, 178–79
Color Control, 194
color correction, 352
color decontamination, 298, 299
color depth, setting, 356
Color Dodge mode, 76–77
Color mode, in Paint, 282
Color Picker, 20, 76
colors
background, 20, 35
Info panel and, 8
selecting, 20
"comb teeth" artifacts, 140, 358,
361
comments, 145, 333
Comp Flowchart View, 5
Comp Marker Bin, 6
comp markers, 146, 333, 346
Composite on Original option,
107
Composition Flowchart, 5, 6, 162
Composition (Comp) panel
3D views and, 227
adding layers in, 23
basics of, 5
degraded image in, 5, 357,
359
managing, 18
multiple, 4
navigating composition
hierarchies, 162
Options menu, 5
switches in, 5
zooming in, 5, 18
compositions. *See also*
Composition panel; nesting
compositions; precomps
audio, adding to, 144
basics of, 14–15
building, 19–23
closing, 79
creating, 17, 327–28
duplicating, 164, 343
footage, adding to, 1, 14, 19,
22, 23, 40
guides, 158
importing layered files as,
36–37, 345
length of, 328
looping, 205

compositions (*continued*)
multiple cameras in, 243
multiple views of, 4, 213
naming, 17
navigating hierarchies of, 162
render order issues, 173
rulers, 158
safe areas, 133, 337
settings, 17
in the Timeline panel, 6
compound effects, 179–80
comps. *See* compositions
Continuous Bezier keyframe, 25
continuous rasterization, 60, 123,
176–77, 207
contrast
Levels effect for, 75
luma mattes and, 116
Convert Audio to Keyframes,
195, 348
Convert Vertex Point tool, 48,
100, 111
copying and pasting
effects, 30–31
keyframes, 61
Corner Pin effect, 262–63
Create Orbit Null, 219
Create Shapes from Vector Layer,
323
crossfades, 68–70, 197, 285
crosshairs, 316–17
Current Time, 5, 7
Current Time Indicator, 6

D

D1
frame dimensions, 90
pixel aspect ratio, 90, 358
Darken mask mode, 104
Delete Vertex tool, 100, 111
delivery specifications, client's,
326–27, 328, 350
depth of field, 214, 216, 222–23
Detailed Analysis, 249, 276
Difference mask mode, 105
Diffuse, 229
Directional Blur effect, 204
Disk Cache, 34
dissolves, 69
Draft 3D switch, 6, 242

Drop Frame timecode, 62
Drop Shadow effect, 31, 97, 98,
115, 121, 185, 311, 338, 350
Duration, 17
DV
frame dimensions, 90
pixel aspect ratio, 90, 358
timecode system, 62

E

Easy Ease assistant, 27, 47, 48
Edge Detection, 295
Edit This/Look At That (ETLAT)
technique, 167, 344
Effect Controls panel, 9, 79–80,
167
effect points, 76, 77–78, 256
effects
adjustment layers, 86–87, 121,
180
Angle Control, 193
applying, 30–31, 76–78,
79 80
Audio Spectrum, 107
Audio Waveform, 107
Auto Color, 30–31
Bevel Alpha, 31
Bezier Warp, 263
blending modes and, 76–78
Box Blur, 319
Camera Lens Blur, 223
Cartoon, 88–89
CC Grid Wipe, 120
CC Twister, 120
Channel Blur, 267
Color Control, 194
compound, 179–80
copying and pasting, 30–31
Corner Pin, 262–63
Directional Blur, 204
Drop Shadow, 31, 97, 98, 115,
121, 185, 311, 338, 350
Effect Controls panel, 9
Expression Controls, 193–94
Fast Blur, 86–87
Fill, 107
Keylight, 273–75
Lens Flare, 76–78, 204
Levels, 75
Lightning, 205, 277

effects (*continued*)
Linear Wipe, 120, 151
masks and, 97, 101, 103, 121
mattes and, 115, 121
Optics Compensation, 264
Paint, 279–88
parenting and, 153, 155
Photo Filter, 352
Puppet, 302
Radial Blur, 79–80
Radial Wipe, 188
Radio Waves, 256–58
render order of, 174, 263, 302
Rolling Shutter Repair, 245,
276
Roto Brush, 278, 289–99
Roughen Edges, 285
Scribble, 103, 107
searching for, 79
Selective Color, 352
Shape, 310–13
Slider Control, 193
stencils and, 118–19, 121
Stereo Mixer, 146, 147
Stroke, 107
Timewarp, 197
Tint, 80, 81, 101, 121
tracking and, 256–58
Transform, 181
Tritone, 75, 87
Turbulent Displace, 117, 119,
120
Vegas, 107
Venetian Blinds, 120
viewing parameters, 9
Warp, 169, 181
Warp Stabilizer, 245, 246–49
Effects & Presets panel, 9, 79, 81
video bonus, DVD (Lesson 3)
Ellipse tool, 94, 99
Enable Frame Blending, 6,
196–97, 336
Enable Motion Blur, 6, 56–57, 127
environment layers, 238
Eraser tool, 3, 279, 281
ETLAT (Edit This/Look At That)
technique, 167, 344
Expression Controls, 193–94
expressions
advantages of, 153

expressions (*continued*)
in animation presets, 188, 192
copying and pasting, 190
creating, with pick whip, 182,
184–85
defined, 153, 182
deleting, 191
disabling, 191
editing, 191
finishing, 190
language menu, 189
linear, 187–89
looping, 190–91
parenting vs., 184
resources on, 205
and simple math, 185–86
wiggle, 192, 204
extrusion, 231–32, 324–25
third-party options, 136
eyeball icon, 44, 46

F

fades, cross-, 68–70, 197, 285
Falloff, 228–29
Fast Blur effect, 86–87
Fast Previews, 5, 230, 240–41
feathering masks, 97, 108–11
feature regions, 250
fields
defined, 140
flicker, 359
rendering with, 143, 356, 361
separating, 140, 358
file format support, 15
files. *See* footage
Fill effect, 107
film frame rates, 62, 327
filmic glow technique, 87, 263
First Vertex Point, 102
flicker, 225, 359
Flowchart, 5, 162
FLV format, 1
folders
creating new, 4, 16
favorite, in Bridge, 13
importing, 18
renaming, 16
footage
adding, to composition, 1, 14,
19, 22, 23, 40

footage (*continued*)
  alpha channels, 18
  in Bridge, 13
  defined, 1, 14
  high-definition, 270, 329, 352
  importing, 4, 13, 17–18, 36–37
  interlaced, 140, 143, 256
  looping, 71
  pointers to, 1
  selecting, in Project panel, 3–4
  stabilizing, 244–49, 252–53, 270–72
  trimming, 66–67, 70
Footage panel, 67, 359
frame blending, 196–97, 336
frame rates
  common (including film, NTSC, and PAL), 62
  conforming, 73, 359
  Preserve Frame Rate, 198–99
  pulldown, 361
  stop motion, 198
frames. *See also* panels
  defined, 2
  options arrow, 10
  resizing, 9, 10
Free Transform Points, 96, 98
freeze frames, 200
f-stop, 216

G

garbage mattes, 275
gradients, 316–17, 340
Graph Editor
  display, 6, 45
  editing graphs, 39, 47–49
  opening, 6, 44, 203
  panning and zooming time, 46
  Separate Dimensions in, 50–53
  Speed Graphs, 46, 48, 58–59
  Value Graphs, 45, 46, 51, 52
greenscreen, 270–75
grids, viewing, 5, 7
grouping. *See* expressions; nesting compositions; parenting; precomps
Grouping Alignment parameter, 133
guide layers, 338
guides, 5, 7, 29, 158

H

H.264, 356
Hand tool, 3, 18
HDV, 270
Help page, 1, 354
hicon (high contrast) mattes, 116
Hide Shy Layers, 6
high-definition footage, 270, 329, 352
Hold keyframes, 60–61, 63

I

Illustrator
  artboards in, 360
  importing from, 36–37
  layers in, 36–37
  masks and, 116
  stencils and, 119
  text in, 37
image quality, 239, 357–60
Import As popup menu, 36
Import File dialog, 71, 72
importing
  audio, 144
  as composition, 36–37, 345
  folders, 18
  footage files, 4, 13, 17–18
  Illustrator files, 36–37
  image sequences, 72
  Photoshop files, 36–37, 84–85, 345
Index of Refraction, 235, 325
Info panel, 8
Inner Shadow style, 311
in points, 66
"Instant Sex" technique. *See* filmic glow
Inter-Character Blending, 149
interlacing, 140, 143, 256
interpolation
  animated mask shapes, 107
  between keyframes, 38
Interpret Footage dialog, 3, 18, 62, 71, 73, 90, 361
intersecting, in 3D, 209, 219
Intersect mask mode, 105

J

JavaScript. *See* expressions

K

kerning, 123
keyboard shortcuts
  3D Views, 210
  Add to Render Queue, 354
  After Effects Help, 1, 354
  Anchor Point property, 21
  audio waveform, 145
  auto-orientation, 56
  Brush tool, 280
  comp markers, 145, 346
  compositions, creating new, 17, 165
  compositions, duplicating, 164
  Deselect All, 16
  Easy Ease keyframe assistant, 27, 47, 48
  Effect Controls panel, 9, 167
  Fast Previews modes, 241
  footage, importing, 18
  frame, maximize size, 9
  Free Transform Points, 96, 98
  Graph Editor, 203
  Hold keyframe, 60
  Import File dialog, 71, 72
  layer markers, 145
  layers, selecting all, 44
  layers, trimming, 66
  Look at Layers, 218
  mask, 93, 94
  nudging scale, 42
  Opacity property, 21
  Pan Behind tool, 41
  panning, 249
  Pen tool, 78, 93, 106, 111
  Position property, 21
  project, saving, 16
  properties, revealing, 39
  Rotate tool, 20, 21
  ruler, 158
  Scale property, 21
  Selection tool, 20
  solids, 30
  Timeline panel, 9
  Time Stretch, 336
  transformations, 21

keyboard shortcuts (*continued*)
  Undo, 23
  work area, 33
  zooming, 18, 249
keyframe assistants
  accessing, 49
  Convert Audio to Keyframes, 195, 348
  Easy Ease, 27, 47–48
  Motion Sketch, 54–55, 91
  Sequence Layers, 69–70
  Smoother, 55
  Time-Reverse, 59
Keyframe Interpolation dialog, 59
keyframes. *See also* motion paths
  adding, 22
  animation, 21
  Auto Bezier, 25, 48, 107
  basics of, 15, 21–22, 38–39
  Bezier handles, 24, 25, 39, 52
  changing position, 22
  changing timing, 22
  changing type, 48, 58
  Continuous Bezier, 25
  coordinating, 49
  copying and pasting, 61
  deleting, 22
  editing multiple, 47–48
  enabling, 21
  Hold, 60–61, 63
  influence of, 38
  interpolation between, 38
  Linear, 25, 48
  looping, 190–91
  masks and, 99, 107
  navigation arrows, 22
  nudging, 26
  roving, 58–59
  Separate Dimensions, 50–53
  smoothing, 27
  spatial, 25, 39
  speed curves, 58–59
  stretching/compressing, in time, 57, 73
  temporal, 39, 107
  time-reversing, 59
  velocity of, 38
keying, 93, 244, 272–75
Keylight effect, 273–75

L

Label colors, 329
layer markers, 145–46
Layer panel
    anchor points, 40–41
    basics of, 7
    display modes, 298
    docking, 249
    masking in, 96–97
    opening, 7
    Render checkbox in, 7
    tracking in, 249
    trimming layers in, 67
    View popup in, 7
layers. *See also* adjustment layers
    2D, 207
    3D, 206, 207–9
    adding, to comps, 1, 22–23
    bending, 233, 243
    constraining movement of, 16
    continuously rasterized,
        176–77, 207
    defined, 1, 14
    environment, 238
    guide layers, 338
    in Illustrator, 36–37
    in points, 66
    in the Layer panel, 7
    luminance, 121
    in mattes, 121
    moving, in time, 23, 65–66
    multiple, arranging and
        replacing, 28–29
    nudging, 26
    order of, 14, 23, 64–65, 208
    out points, 66
    parenting, 152–53
    in Photoshop, 36–37, 151
    precomposing, 168–69, 170–71
    reflecting, 236–38
    revealing, with Paint, 284–86
    scaling, 20
    selecting all, 44
    sequencing, 69–70
    size of, 15
    sliding, 66
    slipping, 68
    snapping, 19

layers (*continued*)
    solid, 4
    soloing, 70
    splitting, 66
    Transform properties, 20
    trimming, 66–67, 70
layer styles
    applying, 85
    Bevel and Emboss, 85, 311
    importing Photoshop files
        with, 36–37, 84–85
    Inner Shadow, 115, 311
    Outer Glow, 85, 319
    uses for, 84, 311
leading, 123
Leave All Attributes option, 170,
    174, 175
Lens Flare effect, 76–78, 204
Levels effect, 75
Lighten mask mode, 104
Lightning effect, 205, 277
lights (3D)
    adding, 224–25
    animating, 224–25
    default settings, 229
    editing settings for, 224
    falloff, 228–29, 353
    flickering, 225
    shadows and, 226–27
    types of, 224–25
Light Transmission, 227
Linear Dodge mode, 77
Linear keyframe, 25, 48
Linear Wipe effect, 120, 151
Live Photoshop 3D, 233
Live Update, 6
Local Axis Mode, 3
Lock and Snap to Guides,
    158
Lock switch, 163, 164, 224
Lock to Zoom, 222
looping
    backgrounds, 351
    compositions, 205
    footage, 71
    keyframes, 190–91
Loop options, 8
lower third design, 351
luminance (luma) mattes. *See*
    track mattes

M

Magnification, 5, 7, 18, 357
markers, 145–46
masks (masking)
    adding points, 100, 107
    alpha channel and, 112
    animating, 98
    Bezier, 100–101
    closed, 101
    creating, 95, 96–97
    defined, 92–93
    deleting points, 100, 107
    editing, 96, 101
    effects and, 97, 101, 103, 121
    Expansion, 99, 108–9
    Feather, 97, 108–11
    First Vertex Point, 102
    Free Transform Points, 96, 98
    greenscreen and, 275
    interpolating between, 102
    keyframes and, 99
    in Layer panel, 96–97
    Mask Path parameter, 98, 99
    modes, 104–5
    multiple, 104–5
    opacity, 99, 104–5
    with Pen tool, 100–101
    render order, 172–73
    RotoBezier, 106–7
    Scribble effect and, 103
    selecting all points on, 100
    shapes vs., 95, 306
    shortcuts, 93, 111
    softening edges of, 97
    tools for, 94–95, 99, 100
    tracing outlines of, 100–101
    turning off/hiding, 105, 106
    variable mask feathering,
        108–111
    vignettes with, 99
Mask Feather tool, 108–111
Material Options, 229
mattes. *See* track mattes
Merge Paths, 314–15, 341
Mesh, Puppet, 300, 304–5
Metal, 229
Mini-Flowchart, 6, 162
mocha AE, 245, 259–63
modes. *See* blending modes

motion blur
    applying, 56–57
    enabling, 53, 56, 57, 127, 350
    Render Settings, 57
    Shutter Angle, 56, 57
    tracking and, 251, 252
motion control, 42–43
Motion Damping, 295
motion paths
    creating, 24–25
    defined, 21
    editing, 22
    for effect point, 77–78
    moving, 43
    smoothing, 55
    tracing, with mouse, 54–55
Motion Sketch keyframe
    assistant, 54–55
Motion Threshold, 295
motion tracking. *See* tracking
Move All Attributes option,
    168, 174
movies
    codecs, 356
    image sequences, 72–73
    looping, 71
    rendering, 32, 356
    trimming clips, 66–67
multiplaning, 210–11
Multiply mode, 74, 75
music. *See* audio
Mute Audio, 8
Muybridge, Eadweard, 91

N

nesting compositions. *See also*
    precomps
    advantages of, 115, 153, 158,
        163
    with common source, 163–67,
        344
    described, 153, 158–60
    render order and, 174–75
    track mattes, 114–15
New Comp, 3
New Folder, 3
Non-Drop Frame timecode, 62
NTSC video
    frame dimensions, 90
    frame rates, 62

null objects
changing size of, 156
defined, 156
for camera rig, 219
for master controllers, 194
for 3D Camera Tracker, 266
parenting with, 156–57

O

opacity. *See also* alpha channels
animating, 26–27
Mask Opacity, 99, 104–5
shortcut, 21
Open New Composition option, 174
Optics Compensation effect, 264
Options menu, 3, 6, 7, 10
orbit camera rig, 218–9
Orbit Camera tool, 215
orthographic views, 210–11
Outer Glow, 85, 319
out points, 66
Output Module Settings, 142,
354–55
video bonus, DVD (Appendix)
Overlay Edit, 67
Overlay mode, 75
overshooting, 63

P

packages, creating, 351
padlock icon, 167
Paint. *See also* strokes
basics of, 278, 279–83
blending modes, 282
Channels, 281
erasing, 281
order of strokes, 282
panel, 9, 279
revealing layers with, 284–86
tablet settings, 286
PAL
frame dimensions, 90
frame rates, 62
Pan Behind tool, 3, 68
panels. *See also individual panels*
defined, 2
docking, 11
dragging, 10, 11
locking, 167
maximizing, 9, 355

panels (*continued*)
types of, 2–9
undocking, 10
panning
in 3D, 210–11, 332–333
in the Graph Editor, 46
Pan Behind Tool, 3, 41, 68
panoramas, 238
PAR. *See* pixel aspect ratios
Paragraph panel, 9, 123, 124, 125
paragraph text, 123
parenting
chains, 153, 156–57
character animation, 153
defined, 152–53
effects and, 153, 155
expressions vs., 184
with nulls, 156–57
opacity and, 155
scaling and, 157
setting up, 154–55
Pen tool, 3, 78, 93, 94, 100–101,
111, 307, 317, 340
Per-character 3D animation,
136–39
perspective, 206, 210–11, 214,
217, 221
Photo Filter, 352
Photoshop
importing from, 36–37, 84–85,
345
Layer styles in, 84–85
Text Layers, 37, 151
pick whip tool
expressions, 182, 184–85
parenting, 154
pixel aspect ratios, 90, 185, 358
Pixel Motion, 197, 276, 336
Play/Pause, 8
Point lights, 224, 225
Point of Interest, 214
point text, 123
Polygon tool, 94
Polystar, 309
Position property
anchor point and, 42–43
animating, 21–22
editing, 20
nudging, 26
in shape layers, 308

Position property (*continued*)
shortcut, 21
stabilizing, 270–72
precomps
advantages of, 153, 170
anchor points and, 169
defined, 153, 160
editing, 160
of groups of layers, 168–69
Leave All Attributes option,
170, 174, 175
Move All Attributes option,
168, 174
navigating heirarchies of, 162
opening, 7, 160
Open New Composition
option, 174
render order and, 174–75
of single layers, 170–71, 343
size of, 165
Preserve Frame Rate, 198–99
previewing
audio only, 144
Fast Previews, 5, 230, 240–41
individual layers, 70
RAM Preview, 8, 21, 22
Preview panel, 8
previsualization aids, 327
Project Flowchart View, 3
Project panel, 3–4, 19
projects
creating, 16, 44
files, delivering to clients, 351
footage in, 1, 4
moving, 1
organizing, 4
saving, 16
Project Settings, 3, 62
public domain, 322
Pucker & Bloat, 310, 311
pulldown, 361
Puppet tool
basics of, 278, 300
deforming multiple shapes,
304–5
Mesh, 300, 304–5
Puppet Overlap, 302
Puppet Pin, 3, 300–301, 304–5
Puppet Starch, 303
recording animation, 303

Q

Quality (Best/Draft), 66, 357,
359–60
QuickSearch box, 6, 9
QuickTime, 356, 359

R

Radial Blur effect, 79–80
Radial Gradient, 340
Radial Wipe effect, 188
Radio Waves effect, 256–58
RAM Preview
caches and memory, 33, 34
with frame blending, 336
initiating, 21, 33
options, 8, 33
reducing time for, 33
rendering to disk, 33
work area, 34
Randomize Order, 129
Ray-traced 3D Renderer
3D Camera Tracker and, 267,
277
bending layers, 233, 243
beveling, 232
Classic 3D Renderer vs., 208,
230, 267, 332
environment layers, 238
extrusion, 231–32, 324–25
Fast Previews, 240–41
image quality, 239, 357
reflections, 236–38
shape layers and, 324–25
transparency, 234–35
Rectangle tool, 94, 95
Refine Matte, 291, 298–99
Reflection Intensity, 325
reflections, 236–38
refraction. *See* Index of Refraction
Region of Interest, 5, 7
Render checkbox, 7
rendering. *See also* render order;
Render Settings
3:2 pulldown, 361
with alpha channel, 142–43
basics of, 32, 354
breaks, 219
center-cut and widescreen
versions, 350

Rendering (continued)
fields, 143, 356
format for, 356
image sequences, 356
movies, 32, 356
path for rendered file, 32
templates, 355
video bonus, DVD (Appendix)
render order
2D vs. 3D, 219
default, 172–73
of effects, 174
exceptions, 176–80
precomps and, 174–75
solving issues of, 173–75
Render Queue panel, 6, 32, 142,
355, 361
Render Settings
3:2 pulldown options, 361
color depth, 356
default, 32
motion blur options, 57
templates, 355
video bonus, DVD (Appendix)
Repeater, 312–13, 319, 352
resampling, 360
Reset Exposure, 5
Reset workspace, 10
Resolution, 5
Ripple Edit, 67
Rolling Shutter Repair effect,
245, 276
Rolling Shutter Ripple, 249
rotation
3D, 137–38, 209
animating, 26–27, 41
auto-orientation, 56
editing, 20
Graph Editor, 47
nudging, 26
Rotate tool, 3, 20
shortcut, 21
stabilizing, 270–72
RotoBezier masks, 106–7
Roto Brush
Base Frame, 290, 292–94
basics of, 278, 289–91
common mistakes with, 299
corrections, 296–97
propagation, 290, 294–95

Roto Brush (continued)
Refine Matte, 291, 298–99
Span, 290, 291
strokes, 293, 294, 296, 297
workflow for, 292
rotoscoping, 68, 289
Roughen Edges effect, 285
Rounded Rectangle tool, 95
rulers, 29, 158

S

safe areas, 133, 337
sample rate, 144
scale
3D layer, 207
above 100%, 60, 123, 157,
177, 207, 332
animating, 26–27, 41
aspect ratio and, 20
continuous rasterization and,
60, 123, 177, 207
editing, 20
nudging, 26, 42
parenting and, 157
scrubbing, 26
shortcut, 21
stabilizing, 270–72
Screen mode, 74
Scribble effect, 103, 107
scripts, 327
scrubbing
controlling amounts, 26
defined, 20
Search Radius, 294–95
search regions, 250
Segmentation Boundary, 290–99
Selection tool, 3, 20
Selective Color, 352
Select View Layout menu, 5
Separate Dimensions, 39, 50–53,
331
Sequence Layers assistant, 69–70
shadow catcher, 268–69
Shadow Darkness, 227
Shadow Diffusion, 227
Shadow Only option, 227
shadows
3D lights and, 226–27
Drop Shadow effect, 31, 97,
98, 115, 121, 185, 338, 350

shadows (continued)
Inner Shadow style, 115
shape layers
animation presets for, 312
creating, 94, 306–7
editing, 307–8
extruding, 324–25
framing video with, 340–44
Gradient Editor, 316–17
masks vs., 95, 306
multiple paths, 308–9
reshaping, while drawing, 307
shape effects (operators), 310–13
Stroke and Fill settings,
306–7, 309
stroked paths, 320–22
from vector layers, 323
Shape tools, 3, 94, 306–7
Share View Options, 241
Shininess. See specular shininess
shortcut keys. See keyboard
shortcuts
Show Channel and Color
Management Settings, 5, 7
Show Last Snapshot, 5, 7
Show Planar Grid, 261
Show Reference Graph, 44
Shutter Angle, 56, 57
Silhouette Alpha mode, 119
Silhouette Luma mode, 118
Skew, 311
"slam down" technique, 60–61
Slider Control effect, 193
slip editing, 68
slow motion, 200
Smoother keyframe assistant, 55
SMPTE timecode, 62
solids
applying effects to, 76–78
black, uses of, 76
changing size of, 78
creating, 4, 30, 35
defined, 4, 30
reusing, 35
shortcuts, 30
Solo switch, 70
sound. See audio
Source Text, 150
speaker icon, 144
Specular Intensity, 229

Specular Shininess, 229
Speed Graphs, 46, 48, 58–59
Spot lights, 224, 225
stabilization
point-based (legacy), 245, 249,
252–53, 270–72
Warp Stabilizer, 245, 246–49
Star tool, 94
Stencil Alpha mode, 119
Stencil Luma mode, 118
stencils
alpha, 119
alpha channel and, 112
backgrounds and, 119–20
creating, 118–19
defined, 93
effects and, 118–19, 121
luma, 118
track mattes vs., 93, 118
Stereo Mixer effect, 146, 147
still images
bending layers, 233
sequences of, 72–73, 356
stop motion tricks, 198–99
Stroke effect, 107
strokes. See also Paint; Roto Brush
animating, 283, 322
duration of, 282
erasing, 281
naming, 283
paths, 320–22
replacing, 288
transforming, 288
style frames, 327
subpixel positioning, 251, 359–60
Subtract mask mode, 104
sweepers, 351
Switches/Modes columns, 74
Synthesize Edges, 248

T

tablet settings, 286
Take Snapshot, 5, 7
templates. See rendering
text
3D, 136–39, 231–32, 268–69
animating, 122–23, 125,
136–39 (see also text
animators)
bars, 311

text (*continued*)
baseline shift, 123
basics of, 123–24
beveling, 232
blurred, 127, 134
cascading, 129–31
creating, 123–24
on a curve, 135
deforming, 304–5
editing mode, 124
extruding, 231–32
fading, 131
horizontal/vertical, 124
kerning, 123
layer mode, 124
leading, 123
overlapping, 149
paragraph, 123
on a path, 135
Per-character 3D, 136–39
Photoshop integration, 37, 151
point, 123
selecting, 122–23, 126
as texture, 345–46
title safe area, 133, 337
tracking, 123, 134
transparent, 234–35
typesetting tips, 125
wiggling, 140–41
video bonus, DVD (Lesson 5)
text animation presets. *See*
animation presets
text animators
adding more properties, 127–28
Anchor Points and, 131
based on words, 132–33
creating, 127
motion blur for, 127
overview, 125
Randomize Order, 129
Range Selectors, 126
setting text for, 125
Wiggly Selector, 140–41
video bonus, DVD (Lesson 5)
time
current, 5, 6, 7
display modes, 62
panning and zooming, in
Graph Editor, 46
reordering, 203

Time Display, 6
Timeline panel
adding layers in, 23
basics of, 6
hiding columns in, 347
layers in, 65
reordering columns in, 6, 19
trimming layers in, 66, 70
time remapping, 200–203
Time-Reverse assistant, 59
Time Stretch, 73, 196, 336
Timewarp effect, 197
Tint effect, 80, 81, 101, 121
titles. *See* text
title safe area, 133, 337
Toggle Alpha Boundary, 298
Toggle Hold Keyframes, 60, 61
Toggle Mask and Shape Path
Visibility, 5, 320
Toggle Pixel Aspect Ratio
Correction, 5, 7, 90, 185, 358
Toggle Transparency Grid, 5, 7,
35, 142
Toggle Viewer Lock, 5, 7, 9
Tools panel (toolbar), 3
Track Camera tools, 215
Tracker panel, 245, 246, 250
Track Fields, 256
tracking (motion). *See also*
stabilization
3D Camera Tracker, 245,
264–69, 277, 335
basics of, 244–45
channels for, 257
for effects, 256–58
fixing bad, 253
interlaced footage, 256
multiple features, 245
multiple tracks, 258
planar, with mocha AE, 245,
259–63
point-based (legacy), 245,
249–53, 254–55
tracking (text), 123, 134
track mattes
alpha, 93, 112–13
animating, 117
combining masks and, 112
creating, 112–13, 116
defined, 93

track mattes (*continued*)
effects and, 115, 121
hicon (high contrast), 116
luminance (luma), 93, 116, 121
nesting with, 114–15
stencils vs., 93, 118
uses for, 112
track points
creating, 250
positioning, 254
size, 265
Transform effect, 181
Transform properties
editing, 20
resetting, 39
shortcuts, 21
transparency, 234–35. *See also*
alpha channels; keying; masks;
opacity; stencils; track mattes
Transparency Grid. *See* Toggle
Transparency Grid
Trapcode Sound Keys, 195
trimming layers, 66–67, 70
Trim Paths, 310, 347, 348, 352,
353
Tritone effect, 75, 87
Turbulent Displace effect, 117,
119, 120
"twirling down/up," 6, 20
Twist, 310, 311
Twixtor effect, 197
Type tool, 3, 122

U
Undo, 22, 23
Use Alternate Color Estimation,
295
user interface, 2–11
video bonus, DVD (Pre-Roll)

V
Value Graphs, 45, 46, 51, 52
variable mask feathering, 108–11
vector layers, creating shapes
from, 323
Vegas effect, 107
Venetian Blinds effect, 120
video. *See also* footage
bending layers, 233
frame rates, 62

video (*continued*)
framing with shapes, 340–44
interlaced, 140, 143, 256
pixel aspect ratio, 90
safe areas, 133, 337
Video switch, 82, 83
View Axis Mode, 3
Viewer dropdown menu, 7, 9
View Modes, 7
View popup, 7
vignettes, 99, 225
Vivid Light mode, 161
volume controls, 8, 146–47

W
Wacom tablet, 286
Warp effect, 169, 181
Warp Stabilizer, 245, 246–49
waveforms, 145
wiggle expression, 192, 204
Wiggle Paths, 311, 347, 348,
352, 353
Wigglerama behavior, 83
Wiggle Transform, 311, 313,
318–19
Wiggly Selector, 140–41
work area, 33
workspaces
defined, 2
managing, 10–11
naming, 11
preset, 10
resetting, 11, 16
Standard, 10–11
video bonus, DVD (Pre-Roll)
World Axis Mode, 3

X
X-Splines, 260

Z
Zig Zag, 310, 311
zooming
cameras and, 214, 216, 222
in Comp panel, 5, 18
in the Graph Editor, 46
shortcuts, 18, 249
in Timeline Panel, 6
Zoom tool, 3